Colombia Handbook

Charlie Devereux

66 99

Hallucinatory – that's just the way everyday life is in Colombia. All the time, you say to yourself, did I just see that?

Barbet Schroeder, director of Our Lady of the Assassins

Footprint story

It was 1921

Ireland had just been partitioned, the British miners were striking for more pay and the federation of British industry had an idea. Exports were booming in South America – how about a handbook for businessmen trading in that far away continent? The Anglo-South American Handbook was born that year, written by W Koebel, the most prolific writer on Latin America of his day.

1924

Two editions later the book was 'privatized' and in 1924, in the hands of Royal Mail, the steamship company for South America, it became The South American Handbook, subtitled 'South America in a nutshell'. This annual publication became the 'bible' for generations of travellers to South America and remains so to this day. In the early days travel was by sea and the Handbook gave all the details needed for the long voyage from Europe: what to wear for dinner; how to arrange a cricket match with the Cable & Wireless staff on the Cape Verde Islands and a full account of the journey from Liverpool up the Amazon to Manaus; 5898 miles without changing cabin!

1939

As the continent opened up, the South American Handbook reported the new Pan Am flying boat services, and the fortnightly airship service from Rio to Europe on the Graf Zeppelin. For reasons still unclear but with extraordinary determination, the annual editions continued through the Second World War.

1970s

Many more people discovered South America and the backpacking trail started to develop. All the while the Handbook was gathering fans, including literary vagabonds such as Paul Theroux and Graham Greene (who once sent some updates addressed to "The publishers of the best travel guide in the world, Bath, England").

1990s

During the 1990s the company set about developing a new travel guide series using this legendary title as the flagship. By 1997 there were over a dozen guides in the series and the Footprint imprint was launched.

2000s

The series grew quickly and there were soon Footprint travel guides covering more than 150 countries. In 2004, Footprint launched its first thematic guide: Surfing Europe, packed with colour photographs, maps and charts. This was followed by further thematic guides such as Diving the World, Snowboarding the World, Body and Soul escapes, Travel with Kids and European City Breaks.

2008

Today we continue the traditions of the last 87 years that have served legions of travellers so well. We believe that these help to make Footprint guides different. Our policy is to use authors who are genuine experts who write for independent travellers; people possessing a spirit of adventure, looking to get off the beaten track.

Title page: The dome of San Pedro Claver, built in 1603. **Above:** Festivities in Mompós.

Colombia is a land of superlatives. It has the third largest barrier reef, the fourth highest number of endemic species, more bird species – and possibly more festivals and carnivals – than anywhere else in the world. No other South American country has a greater variety of music and no country in the world has a people as disarmingly generous, hopelessly romantic and bafflingly optimistic. From glacier fields atop Andean peaks and Amazon rainforest to tropical coastlines and deserts, almost every type of scenery can be found here.

Its people are no less diverse. The majority *mestizo* population, Afro-Latinos on the coast and 60 indigenous groups all contribute to the cultural mix that has produced world-renowned artists such as Gabriel García Márquez and Fernando Botero.

Forget guerrilla conflicts and kidnappings. While these still exist, their stranglehold has considerably diminished. There are still no-go areas but the beaten track has enough barely trodden paths to satisfy anyone's quest for the authentic and the magical.

⬡ 7 Planning your trip

8 Where to go
11 Itineraries
12 Colombia highlights and
   itineraries map
14 Six of the best national parks
16 Six of the best festivals
18 When to go
19 Rainfall and climate charts
20 Sport and activities

22 How big is your footprint?
24 Colombia on screen and page

⬡ 25 Essentials

26 Getting there
27 Getting around
31 Sleeping
33 Eating and drinking
37 Festivals and events
40 Essentials A-Z

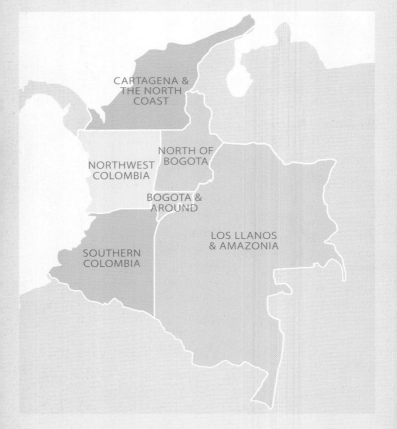

CARTAGENA &
THE NORTH
COAST

NORTH OF
BOGOTA

NORTHWEST
COLOMBIA

BOGOTA &
AROUND

LOS LLANOS
& AMAZONIA

SOUTHERN
COLOMBIA

Contents

↘ **53 Bogotá and around**
62 Sights
90 Around Bogotá

↘ **95 North of Bogotá**
98 Boyacá Department
117 Santander Department
130 Norte de Santander Department

↘ **139 Cartagena and the North Coast**
142 Cartagena
161 Around Cartagena
174 Barranquilla
179 Santa Marta and around
195 East to Venezuela
203 San Andrés and Providencia

↘ **213 Northwest Colombia**
216 Medellín
238 Around Medellín
249 Chocó
253 La Zona Cafetera

↘ **281 Southern Colombia**
284 The Cauca Valley
301 Popayán and Tierradentro
314 San Agustín and around
320 The far south

↘ **331 Los Llanos and Amazonia**
334 Los Llanos
338 Amazonia

↘ **347 Background**
348 History
353 Modern Colombia
356 Economy
358 Government
358 Education
359 Culture
370 People
371 Land and environment

↘ **897 Footnotes**
384 Basic Spanish for travellers
389 Index
395 Advertisers' index
396 Complete title listing
398 About the author
399 Acknowledgements
408 Credits

↘ **8**
Where to go

↘ **11**
Itineraries

↘ **12**
Colombia highlights and
itineraries map

↘ **14**
Six of the best national parks

↘ **16**
Six of the best festivals

↘ **18**
When to go

↘ **19**
Rainfall and climate charts

↘ **20**
Sport and activities

↘ **22**
How big is your footprint?

↘ **24**
Colombia on screen and page

Planning your trip

MIKE HARDING/SOUTHAMERICANPICTURES

Bahía Taganga, set in a semi-
circular bay, is surrounded by
scorched hills dotted with
tree cacti.

Where to go

A country as large and varied as Colombia has a great deal of sights worth visiting. A comprehensive look at the country will require a good deal of time and planning. If you have limited time and want to see as much as possible, you could consider air travel. If you have more time, there are good Pullman and minibuses.

You will almost certainly arrive in the country via Bogotá or Cartagena, so a look at these two cities is a good place to start.

Bogotá

Like most capital cities, at least in Latin America, Bogotá is crowded, noisy, polluted and disorganized. Yet it is a proud, cosmopolitan city with impressive modern buildings and services. The historical centre, La Candelaria, has a wealth of fine colonial churches and buildings. For a great view of the city, take the cable car to the top of Monserrate. A visit to the Gold Museum, with its dazzling collection of pre-Columbian art, is a mind-boggling experience. There

is excellent accommodation in all categories. Bogotá is the best place for information on the whole country and has comprehensive transport links. Places to visit nearby include Guatavita, Zipaquirá, the many towns down to the west towards the Río Magdalena, and the parks of Chicaque, Chingaza and Sumapaz (check for security). You may decide to spend the night in one of these places and there is plenty of good accommodation on offer. Midweek stays can be particularly good value.

Cartagena

Cartagena is more relaxed than Bogotá, though it is not without the problems of a big modern city. It is colonial Spain's finest legacy in the Americas, impressive in every respect. Spend several days here as there is so much to see. It is also the best base for visits to the Caribbean coast and the islands: check out the beaches and the watersports available. Beaches along the coast and on the offshore islands can be visited, as can

Above: Local bus, Cartagena.
Opposite page: Supreme Court, cathedral and Archbishop's Palace, Plaza Bolívar, Bogotá.

the strange mud volcanoes nearby.
To the northeast, Barranquilla has its
own attractions, including a spectacular
carnival, perhaps the finest in Latin America
after Rio de Janeiro. Mompós is a superb
colonial town that can be visited from
either Barranquilla or Cartagena, but you
will have to stay overnight. Cartagena is
also the gateway to San Andrés, a popular
island resort, and to the charming
neighbouring island of Providencia.

Medellín

Medellín, with its recent history of over-
industrialization and violent drug cartels
behind it, is now a modern, vibrant city with
many new buildings that complement
the old, restored architecture. There is plenty
of modern art to see, fascinating places to
visit in the surrounding Department of
Antioquia and friendly, outgoing people to
meet. The *paisas* (as the locals are known)
leave the city at the weekends and head for
the countryside; tourists should follow their
lead. Santa Fe de Antioquia, a remarkable,
preserved colonial town, is an easy day trip
but you will almost certainly want to stay
the night. The journey to Rionegro takes you
through some beautiful countryside, and to
the west of Medellín, El Peñol, the towering
black rock overlooking Guatapé and its huge
lake, should not be missed. There are many
delightful places with lakes and waterfalls
in this region. To the southwest of Medellín
is Jericó and particularly recommended
for a visit is Jardín, truly a garden village.
Medellín is also the jumping-off point for
Quibdó, the Chocó and the northern part
of Colombia's Pacific coast.

Cali

The 'capital' of the south, Cali is about the
same size as Medellín and has a similar
unhappy past. However, it is now
reinvigorated and has an attractive, lively
atmosphere, which springs from its
interesting mix of inhabitants. The locals
have combined to make this the finest
popular music centre of the continent and
this is well illustrated by their passion for salsa.

The Farallones National Park is a few
kilometers to the west. To the north is
Darién; with its Calima museum and lake
it is a recommended trip. Buenaventura is
accessible from Cali, as is the central section
of the Pacific coast and the island of Gorgona.

Above: Salt cathedral, Zipaquirá. This architectural and artistic feat is carved inside a working salt mine.
Opposite page: Tayrona National Park, Magdalena Department, has golden-sand beaches in small, secluded bays that are excellent for swimming and sunbathing.

The rest of Colombia

A quarter of the population live in the four cities listed above, but to find the heart of Colombia you must look elsewhere. The country is strongly regionalized and this stems from the rugged terrain and its early history, when many different indigenous groups lived separately. All roads do not lead to Bogotá; hence the importance today of the *departamentos* and their capitals. In the 19th century some were independent countries for a short time (eg Antioquia) and these were often Spanish settlements. The fierce pride of the later inhabitants ensured the preservation of their heritage and virtually all are worth a visit, but of particular interest are Popayán, Tunja, Pereira, Neiva and Bucaramanga.

Smaller places that express even better the feel of colonial Colombia are spread around the western part of the country. They include Villa de Leiva, Santa Fe de Antioquia, Mompós, Monguí and Barichara. If you are looking for fine scenery, it is all here: from deserts (La Guajira and Tatacoa) to the wettest area of the Americas (Chocó); from one of the hottest places in South America (Norte de Santander) to the snows of the Nevados.

For beach lovers, Colombia has two long coastlines that give access to plenty of palm-fringed tropical paradises. Thanks to increased security, the Darién's Caribbean coastline has opened up to visitors and isolated villages such as Capurganá and Sapzurro are rewarding destinations for the intrepid traveller, as are the villages of Bahía Solano and Nuquí on the Pacific coast. Offshore are many coral islands. Further afield, the island of Providencia is full of culture and laid-back charm, and its Seaflower Bioreserve barrier reef offers some of the best and most extensive diving in the Caribbean. There are deep river gorges (Chicamocha), high mountain chains (Cocuy and Sierra de Santa Marta) and many areas of fine *páramo* for walking and trekking. Colombia also has its own stretch of Amazon, and Leticia is recommended as a good, well-organized place to experience the jungle. In addition to all this, there are 55 national parks spread throughout the country.

Some particularly outstanding attractions that it would be a pity to miss are: the archaeological sites of Ciudad Perdida, San Agustín and Tierradentro; the wax palms above Salento; the flamingos near Riohacha; the mud volcanoes near Arboletes; the wonderful rich green countryside of the Zona Cafetera; the Gold Museum in Bogotá; the walled city in Cartagena; El Peñol rock; Parque Botero in Medellín; Las Lajas sanctuary; and the Zipaquirá salt cathedral.

Itineraries

Two weeks

The fast northern loop

To see as much as possible in such a short space of time will require air travel and some pre-planning. Most visitors to Colombia make a beeline for its sparkling Caribbean coast. Start by flying from Bogotá to Santa Marta and the beaches of Tayrona National Park. After a few days unwinding it's a short hop along the coast to Cartagena. Spend a couple of days exploring the city's labyrinthine walled city before relaxing on Playa Blanca or the coral island of the Islas del Rosario (depending on your budget). The colonial town of Mompós is a worthwhile (though travel-heavy) stopover on the way to Medellín. After taking in the Antioquian capital's culture and nightlife, spend a few days sampling the department's beautiful traditional villages, such as Santa Fe de Antioquia or Guatapé, before catching a plane back to Bogotá.

Three weeks

The more leisurely northern loop

An extra week allows for more bus travel and a chance to see Colombia's interior up close. Start by exploring Bogotá and its colonial sector, La Candelaria. A visit to the Gold Museum is a must. It's then a short bus ride to Villa de Leiva, with the magnificent Zipaquirá salt cathedral a convenient stopover. Soak up Villa de Leiva's colonial atmosphere over a couple of days and explore its many surrounding attractions before heading up to San Gil for some rafting, kayaking and hiking. The neighbouring village of Barichara will provide more colonial architecture. From San Gil, make your way up to Santa Marta and follow the same loop as above as far as Medellín and on to Bogotá, stopping off at the Río Claro Nature Reserve en route.

Four weeks or more

The figure of eight

A month or more will give you the opportunity to see a good chunk of the country – though you will have to travel fast. Start by following the northern loop described above and then from Bogotá, take a bus due south stopping off at the Tatacoa desert for a night under the stars. From nearby Neiva it's a hard day's slog (but a worthwhile one) to Tierradentro. Spend a couple of days exploring the extraordinary tombs in the surrounding hills before heading down to San Agustín for a well-earned rest in one of the town's many comfortable country *hostales* and for some horse riding in its stunning countryside. From San Agustín it's a spectacular drive to the dazzling white city of Popayán, which has several attractions in its environs such as the market at Silvia. From here, head to the salsa-mad city of Cali, but try and be there for the weekend. Next, venture into the 'coffee zone' for a stay on a coffee *finca*. The village of Salento and the Valle de Cocora are a must if you find yourself in this region, as are the snowy peaks of Los Nevados. From here it's an nine-hour bus journey or a short flight back to Bogotá.

RM/SHUTTERSTOCK

Colombia highlights & itineraries

See colour maps in centre of book

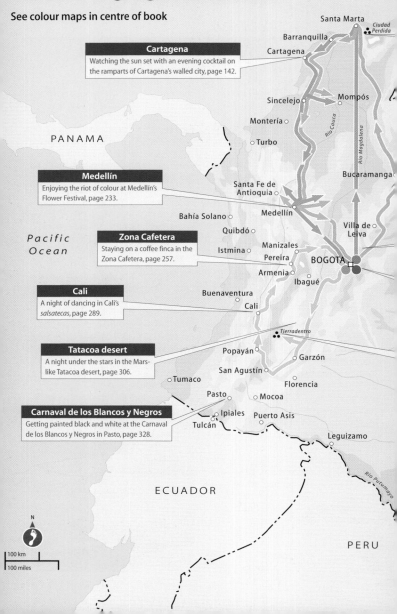

Cartagena
Watching the sun set with an evening cocktail on the ramparts of Cartagena's walled city, page 142.

Medellín
Enjoying the riot of colour at Medellín's Flower Festival, page 233.

Zona Cafetera
Staying on a coffee finca in the Zona Cafetera, page 257.

Cali
A night of dancing in Cali's *salsatecas*, page 289.

Tatacoa desert
A night under the stars in the Mars-like Tatacoa desert, page 306.

Carnaval de los Blancos y Negros
Getting painted black and white at the Carnaval de los Blancos y Negros in Pasto, page 328.

PANAMA

Pacific Ocean

ECUADOR

PERU

Santa Marta
Ciudad Perdida
Barranquilla
Cartagena
Sincelejo
Mompós
Montería
Turbo
Bucaramanga
Santa Fe de Antioquia
Medellín
Villa de Leiva
Bahía Solano
Quibdó
Istmina
Manizales
Pereira
BOGOTÁ
Armenia
Ibagué
Buenaventura
Cali
Tierradentro
Popayán
Garzón
San Agustín
Tumaco
Florencia
Pasto
Mocoa
Ipiales
Puerto Asis
Tulcán
Leguizamo

Río Cauca
Río Magdalena
Río Putumayo

N

100 km
100 miles

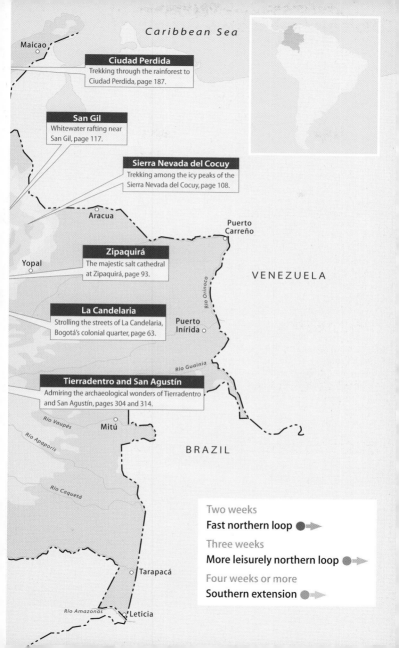

Caribbean Sea

Maicao

Ciudad Perdida
Trekking through the rainforest to
Ciudad Perdida, page 187.

San Gil
Whitewater rafting near
San Gil, page 117.

Sierra Nevada del Cocuy
Trekking among the icy peaks of the
Sierra Nevada del Cocuy, page 108.

Aracua

Puerto
Carreño

Zipaquirá
The majestic salt cathedral
at Zipaquirá, page 93.

Yopal

VENEZUELA

Río Orinoco

La Candelaria
Strolling the streets of La Candelaria,
Bogotá's colonial quarter, page 63.

Puerto
Inírida

Río Guainía

Tierradentro and San Agustín
Admiring the archaeological wonders of Tierradentro
and San Agustín, pages 304 and 314.

Río Vaupés

Mitú

Río Apaporis

BRAZIL

Río Caquetá

Tarapacá

Río Amazonas

Leticia

Two weeks
Fast northern loop ●➤

Three weeks
More leisurely northern loop ●➤

Four weeks or more
Southern extension ●➤

National parks

Los Nevados

The snow-capped peaks of Los Nevados rise sharply from the lush green fields of Colombia's coffee heartland to form a 58,300-ha park of cloudforest, glaciers, hot springs, volcanic lakes and moorland dotted with 12-m-high *frailejón* shrubs.

The park is home to three volcanoes, the highest of which is Nevado del Ruiz, which last erupted in 1985, burying the village of Aremero under a mudslide. Nevado de Tolima and Nevado de Santa Rosa reach comparable heights and all three are popular climbing destinations. Los Nevados is one of the last sanctuaries for the Andean condor, and is also home to the golden eagle and various species of hummingbird.

El Cocuy

The Sierra Nevada del Cocuy is one of Colombia and South America's premier climbing and hiking destinations. This seldom-visited mountain range in the northeast of the country is a place of savage beauty. It has over 22 snow-capped, jagged peaks rising up to 5322 m.

The largest South American expanse of glaciers north of the equator, El Cocuy is a mecca for professional climbers but also offers plenty of interest for nature lovers thanks to its biodiversity. Among the plants that can be seen are *frailejón*, *cojín* and *cardoon* cactus, while animals include the spectacled bear, wild boar, puma and several types of monkey.

Puracé

Covering a massive 86,600 ha, most of which lies over 3000 m above sea level, Puracé is home to a wide range of plants and animals, as well as several indigenous communities. The indigenous Páez and Guambiano still live by traditional means within the park. Rare animal species such as the mountain tapir, the Andean spectacled bear and many varieties of orchid, moss and lichen can be seen.

Volcán Puracé, from which the park takes its name, is a popular climb but for those who don't wish to attempt the 4760-m peak there are also many waterfalls, lakes, trails and multi-coloured, sulphurous pools to visit around the base.

TONY MORRISON/SOUTH AMERICAN PICTURES

Opposite page: Sierra Nevada de Santa Marta.
Above: Toco toucan; Colombia has the widest variety of toucans in the world, with 21 species.

Titi leoncito, the world's smallest monkey.

Old Providence

Spanning some 32 km, Old Providence has the third-longest barrier reef in the world and forms part of the UNESCO Seaflower Biosphere Reserve that also incorporates the neighbouring island of San Andrés. Famed for the colours of its waters, a spectrum of blues and greens, the coral reefs submerged off the Caribbean island of Providencia, along with onshore mangrove swamps and tropical forest, it has been identified as a biodiversity 'hotspot'.

The archipelago offers divers and snorkellers the opportunity to see a range of marine life, such as parrotfish, triggerfish, surgeonfish, the masked hamlet and several species of coral. On land, the well-preserved tropical forest plays host to rare species such as the silver snake and the *Leptodactylus insularis*, an endemic toad, while Tres Hermanos caye is a haven for several species of bird.

Amacayacú

About 60 km from Leticia and surrounded by several rivers feeding the Amazon and Putumayo rivers, within the 293,500 ha of Parque Nacional Natural Amacayacú, live over 500 species of bird and around 150 species of mammal, including pink dolphin, danta, *manatí* and *Titi leoncito*, the world's smallest monkey, as well as giant *Victoria regia* water lilies, which can measure up to 2 m across.

Large sections of the park are flooded for part of the year, which accounts for the incredible diversity of aquatic life, and during this time visitors can explore the area in dug-out canoes. Communities of Tikuna, who live within two to four hours of the park office, can also be visited.

Macuira

At the northeast tip of the remote La Guajira peninsula, Parque Natural Nacional Macuira is an oasis of tropical forest in the middle of a semi-desert. Almost all the moisture that makes it possible for a cloudforest to survive in such conditions comes from morning dew. This is generated by the series of 500-m-high hills that rise directly from the barren wasteland.

Named after the Makui people (ancestors of the indigenous Wayúu) who almost exclusively inhabit the peninsula, Macuira is located in one of the most remote yet fascinating parts of Colombia. The park boasts over 140 species of bird, 17 of which are endemic, as well as a large number of insects, iguanas, toads and frogs.

Festivals

Semana Santa in Mompós

Almost every town in Colombia has a Holy Week celebration and almost all hold elaborate ceremonies. The most impressive are those at Popayán and Pamplona, while the sombre processions in Mompós have their own magic.

This beautiful colonial town was declared a UNESCO World Heritage Site in 1995 for its glorious architecture. Cut off from the world by two branches of the Magdalena river, with little road access, the town has scarcely changed in the last 100 years, and neither has its Easter festival, first documented in 1643.

Hundreds of local young men dressed as Nazarenes take enormous pride in carrying heavy floats depicting the 14 stages of the cross to each of the town's seven churches. A brass band sets the tempo and the slow shuffle through the town's streets can take up to 10 hours.

Barranquilla Carnival, with parades, floats, street dancing, beauty contests and general mayhem.

The Barranquilla Carnival

As Colombia's main port, Barranquilla has attracted a mix of cultures from around the world and this diversity is reflected in its famous carnival. Declared a 'Masterpiece of the Oral and Intangible Heritage of Humanity' by UNESCO in 2003, Barranquilla's carnival is widely considered second only to Rio.

Colombia's largest party, this is one of the best advertisements of the country's rich cultural heritage, with some of its most traditional forms of music on show. Dances such as the *cumbia* and the *fandango* are performed by families who have been participating for generations. There are also spectacular float processions, parades and beauty queens.

Celebrations really get going four days before Ash Wednesday when an edict is read out that everyone must party. The official carnival begins on the following Saturday with the *Batalla de las Flores*, is followed by Sunday's *Gran Parada*, and culminates on Tuesday with the funeral of Joselito Carnaval.

Medellín's Flower Festival

In late July/early August each year, thousands descend upon Medellín to see the city given over to a four-day homage to one of Colombia's biggest exports – the flower.

Concerts, street parties, antique car parades and a *Paso Fino* horse parade, take place during the week.

But the throngs really come to see the *Desfile de Silleteros* in which flower-growers file through the city streets carrying their elaborate displays mounted on wooden 'chairs'. More than 400 families from the village of Santa Elena compete to see who can grow the finest flowers and create the most fantastic designs, which are then judged in the Anastasio Girardot Stadium at the end of the three-hour parade.

An annual event since 1957, the Flower Festival has been one of the main catalysts for transforming Medellín's image from a centre for drug-trafficking and gun crime into the capital of flower power.

Festival de la Leyenda Vallenato

Vallenato has surpassed the country's other forms of traditional music to become Colombia's most popular genre. Colombians, especially those from the Atlantic coast, have a seemingly insatiable appetite for this accordion-led folk music and nowhere is this more evident than at Vallenato Legend Festival in Valledupar, which takes place every April.

A four-day binge of raucous festivities, featuring all-night *parrandas*, or house parties, and street concerts, as well as panel discussions and traditional storytelling, the festival concludes with the selection of the best artists by the judges. Winning this accolade can send a musician's record sales through the roof.

Carnaval de Blancos y Negros

One of the oldest carnivals in the Americas, the Carnival of Blacks and Whites takes place in Pasto over the New Year. Festivities begin with a city-wide water fight on 28 December followed by parades to commemorate the *Llegada de la Familia Castañeda*, a peasant family from El Encano whose arrival in Pasto in 1928 is recreated with all their travel gear in tow – kitchen crockery, mattresses and all.

The most important events are the Día de los Negros on 5 January and the Día de los Blancos the following day. On 'black day' people smear each other's faces with black grease while on 'white day' they throw talc or flour at each other. The significance of the carnival is unclear but historians believe it references a slave rebellion in Antioquia in the 17th century and that plastering each other in black and white is meant to commemorate the black slaves' emancipation. Whatever the history, it has developed into a riot of dancing, parades and dressing up in colourful costumes.

Medellín's flower festival involves parades, music and equestrian shows.

Corraleja de Sincelejo

The capital of the Atlantic coast's cattle industry, each January Sincelejo hosts a running of the bulls that makes Pamplona's *Fiesta de San Fermín* seem sanitized by comparison.

Up to 40 bulls are released into a large wooden ring full of *manteros* (bullfighters). Anyone can take part but it's mainly young adolescents, eager to show their bravura to watching girlfriends, who are foolish enough to consider it. Some wield capes with which to draw the bulls, whilst others just do their best to avoid a goring and try to exhibit sufficient machismo to be able to hold their heads high at the parties that follow. The most daring are rewarded with money and bottles of rum thrown into the arena by the crowd.

This is not an event for the faint-hearted. Injuries, even deaths, are common but this has done nothing to deter the people of Sincelejo from staging the annual free-for-all.

When to go

The climate varies little in Colombia and other than the Chocó (northwest Colombia) where it rains almost daily, you will see plenty of sun year-round. There are no seasons to speak of and temperatures are dictated mainly by altitude. However, travellers should take note that between March and September is the rainy season in the eastern departments, which can make travel difficult because of landslides and flooding. See page 375 for more detailed information on climate.

The best time for a visit is December to February, on average the driest months. It's worth remembering, though, that this is holiday season for many Colombians and prices rise significantly in the most popular places, and transport, including internal airlines, can be busy. During this period, a number of major annual fiestas are held, for example in January in the south (Popayán and Pasto) and in February, at the opposite end of the country, Barranquilla Carnival. These events bring the locals out in force and it is a fun time to visit. Equally, Easter is a local holiday time and almost every town has superb celebrations. In July and August, accommodation prices tend to rise because of school holidays.

Above: An indigenous Tayrona village near the Lost City. **Opposite page:** Bahía Taganga.

Colombia

Activity	J	F	M	A	M	J	J	A	S	O	N	D
Witness Mompós' austere Holy Week processions		★	★									
Kick back on the glorious beaches of Tayrona National Park	★	★	★	★	★	★	★	★	★	★	★	★
Watch humpback whales congregate off the beaches of the Pacific coastline							★	★	★	★		
Stroll along the streets of Cartagena's stunning walled city	★	★	★	★	★	★	★	★	★	★	★	★
Enjoy the many parades at Medellín's world-famous flower festival							★	★				
Dance beyond dawn in Bogotá's cosmopolitan nightclubs	★	★	★	★	★	★	★	★	★	★	★	★
Party with the throngs at Barranquilla's enormous carnival	★	★										

Rainfall and climate charts

Bogotá

Month	Average temperature in °C max-min	Average rainfall in mm
Jan	19 - 09	58
Feb	20 - 09	66
Mar	19 - 10	102
Apr	19 - 11	147
May	19 - 11	114
Jun	18 - 11	61
Jul	18 - 10	51
Aug	18 - 10	56
Sep	19 - 09	61
Oct	19 - 10	160
Nov	19 - 10	119
Dec	19 - 09	66

Tunja

Month	Average temperature in °C max-min	Average rainfall in mm
Jan	20 - 06	206
Feb	20 - 07	33
Mar	20 - 08	473
Apr	20 - 09	674
May	19 - 09	72
Jun	18 - 09	383
Jul	18 - 08	343
Aug	18 - 08	300
Sep	19 - 08	464
Oct	19 - 08	903
Nov	19 - 08	608
Dec	19 - 07	38

Cúcuta

Month	Average temperature in °C max-min	Average rainfall in mm
Jan	31 - 21	37
Feb	31 - 22	33
Mar	32 - 22	57
Apr	32 - 22	106
May	33 - 23	85
Jun	33 - 23	37
Jul	33 - 23	32
Aug	34 - 23	33
Sep	34 - 23	72
Oct	33 - 23	140
Nov	32 - 22	117
Dec	31 - 21	69

Cartagena

Month	Average temperature in °C max-min	Average rainfall in mm
Jan	31 - 23	08
Feb	31 - 23	01
Mar	31 - 24	01
Apr	32 - 25	31
May	32 - 25	92
Jun	32 - 25	115
Jul	32 - 25	94
Aug	32 - 25	124
Sep	32 - 25	144
Oct	31 - 25	244
Nov	31 - 25	132
Dec	31 - 24	37

Medellín

Month	Average temperature in °C max-min	Average rainfall in mm
Jan	22 - 12	70
Feb	22 - 13	75
Mar	22 - 13	130
Apr	22 - 13	168
May	22 - 13	204
Jun	22 - 13	153
Jul	22 - 12	155
Aug	22 - 12	130
Sep	22 - 13	141
Oct	22 - 13	172
Nov	21 - 13	146
Dec	21 - 13	131

Armenia

Month	Average temperature in °C max-min	Average rainfall in mm
Jan	30 - 19	295
Feb	30 - 19	299
Mar	30 - 20	436
Apr	29 - 20	587
May	29 - 19	484
Jun	29 - 19	251
Jul	30 - 19	129
Aug	30 - 19	17
Sep	30 - 19	425
Oct	29 - 19	52
Nov	28 - 19	604
Dec	29 - 19	361

Cali

Month	Average temperature in °C max-min	Average rainfall in mm
Jan	30 - 19	295
Feb	30 - 19	299
Mar	30 - 20	436
Apr	29 - 20	587
May	29 - 19	484
Jun	29 - 19	251
Jul	30 - 19	129
Aug	30 - 19	17
Sep	30 - 19	425
Oct	29 - 19	52
Nov	28 - 19	604
Dec	29 - 19	361

Popayán

Month	Average temperature in °C max-min	Average rainfall in mm
Jan	30 - 19	295
Feb	30 - 19	299
Mar	30 - 20	436
Apr	29 - 20	587
May	29 - 19	484
Jun	29 - 19	251
Jul	30 - 19	129
Aug	30 - 19	17
Sep	19 - 06	425
Oct	22 - 07	52
Nov	26 - 09	604
Dec	28 - 11	361

Leticia

Month	Average temperature in °C max-min	Average rainfall in mm
Jan	32 - 22	209
Feb	32 - 22	181
Mar	32 - 22	205
Apr	32 - 22	200
May	31 - 22	219
Jun	31 - 22	137
Jul	31 - 21	101
Aug	32 - 21	116
Sep	32 - 22	120
Oct	32 - 22	156
Nov	32 - 22	167
Dec	32 - 22	164

Sport and activities

Hiking

ⓘ Several walking clubs such as **Sal Si Puedes** (T1-2833765) and **Corporación Clorofila Urbana** (T1-6168711, www.clorofilaurbana.org), organize walks in the countryside just outside Bogotá and further afield.

Colombia's varied topography offers a wealth of options for the hiking enthusiast. Everything from jungle treks and scampers over glacier fields to leisurely strolls through Arcadian landscapes can be enjoyed here. In Los Nevados and El Cocuy, Colombia has a couple of mountain ranges to rival any along the Andean chain. Other national parks such as Puracé offer countless waterfalls, lakes and trails to explore. To get up close and personal with tropical wildlife the Colombian Amazon is the place to go. **Reserva Natural Palmarí** (actually in Brazil but best accessed from Leticia), offers guided jungle walks ranging from one to 72 hours.

Diving

ⓘ Operators are listed in the relevant places throughout the book.

With two extensive coastlines it's not surprising that Colombia offers myriad diving opportunities. Top of the list for aquatic aficionados must be the San Andrés and Providencia archipelago, which boasts the third-largest barrier reef in the world. The several dive shops dotted around the two islands offer huge choice for exploring this underwater wonderland. The Caribbean coast is known for its large brain coral and the fishing village of Taganga has established itself as a dive centre. There are coral islands off Cartagena and Tolú while

Above: Canoing and kayaking in the Chocó.
Opposite page left: Taganga Bay, a fishing village near Santa Marta. **Opposite page right**: Anemone, brain coral and other colourful creatures on a reef in the Caribbean sea.

Capurganá on the Darién coast has some excellent dive sites. On the Pacific coast, Bahía Solano offers the chance to explore a scuttled navy vessel. Further south the ex-prison island of Gorgona has countless exotic fish and turtles, while the remote island of Malpelo is heaven for hammerhead shark fans.

Parapenting

ⓘ Operators are listed in the relevant places throughout the book.

Squeezed between the Andean mountain ranges of the Central and Eastern cordilleras that create a very effective wind tunnel, the Mesa de Ruitoque near Bucaramanga is the perfect place for parapenting. With two very professional schools, one of which even has its own hostel, this is the perfect place to learn how to glide the sky. Nearby San Gil has two excellent locations for

paragliding, one of which involves a flight over the spectacular Chicamocha canyon.

Rafting and kayaking

ⓘ Operators are listed in the relevant places throughout the book. See page 128 for San Gil operators.

The town of San Gil has become the unofficial capital of the Colombian adventure sports scene. Three whitewater rivers flow through or near it, offering a range of difficulty levels to satisfy everyone from the timid beginner to the seasoned adrenalin junkie. There are many companies offering professional and safety-conscious guidance and equipment, as well as new thrills such as hydrospeed, best described as whitewater boogie boarding. In southern Colombia, the village of San Agustín catches the Magdalena river at its wildest, while Cubarral on the Ariari River near Villavicencio is another popular rafting destination.

How big is your footprint?

The benefits of international travel are self evident for both hosts and travellers: employment, understanding of different cultures and business and leisure opportunities. At the same time there is clearly a downside to the industry. Where visitor pressure is high and/or poorly regulated, there can be adverse impacts to society and the natural environment. Paradoxically, this is as true in undeveloped and pristine areas (where culture and the natural environment are less 'prepared' for even small numbers of visitors) as in major resorts.

The travel industry is growing rapidly and increasingly its impact is becoming apparent. These impacts can seem remote and unrelated to an individual trip or holiday,

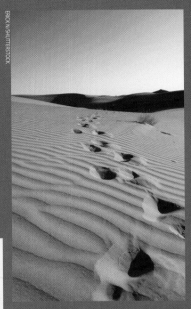
ERICK N/SHUTTERSTOCK

but individual choice and awareness can make a difference in many instances and, collectively, travellers are having a significant effect in shaping a more responsible and sustainable industry.

Of course travel can have beneficial impacts and this is something to which every traveller can contribute. Many national parks are part funded by receipts from visitors. Similarly, travellers can promote patronage and protection of important archaeological sites and heritage through their interest and contributions via entrance and performance fees. They can also support small-scale enterprises by staying in locally run hotels and hostels, eating in local restaurants and by purchasing local goods, supplies and arts and crafts.

Vulnerable places in Colombia

Leticia The Amazon's vast array of species are under threat from hunting and tourism. Seek out tour guides with sound environmental practice and do not buy any animal products as souvenirs.

San Agustín Unsurprisingly, this town has become increasingly popular thanks to its mysterious sculptures and majestic countryside. Unfortunately, with mass tourism comes litter and damage. Be sure to take your rubbish home and do not climb on the stones.

Islas del Rosario The coral reefs of the Caribbean coast are already showing signs of damage from global warming. Snorkellers and divers can avoid contributing further by not stepping on the coral and ensuring that boats drop anchor on sand rather than coral.

Travelling light

The point of a holiday is, of course, to have a good time, but if it's relatively guilt-free as well, that's even better. Perfect ecotourism would ensure a good living for local inhabitants, while not detracting from their traditional lifestyles, encroaching on their customs or spoiling their environment. Perfect ecotourism probably doesn't exist, but everyone can play their part. Here are a few points worth bearing in mind:

▶▶ Think about where your money goes and be fair and realistic about how cheaply you travel. Try to put money into local people's hands; drink local beer or fruit juice rather than imported brands and stay in locally owned accommodation wherever possible.

▶▶ Haggle with humour and appropriately. Remember that you want a fair price, not the lowest one.

▶▶ Think about what happens to your rubbish. Take biodegradable products and a water bottle filter. Be sensitive to limited resources like water, fuel and electricity.

▶▶ Help preserve local wildlife and habitats by respecting rules and regulations, such as sticking to footpaths, not standing on coral and not buying products made from endangered plants or animals.

▶▶ Don't treat people as part of the landscape; they may not want their picture taken. Ask first and respect their wishes.

▶▶ Learn the local language and be mindful of customs and norms. It can enhance your travel experience and you'll earn respect and be more readily welcomed by local people.

▶▶ And finally, use your guidebook as a starting point, not the only source of information. Talk to local people, then discover your own adventure.

Tourists admiring *Victoria regia* water lilies in Leticia.

Colombia on screen and page

Books to read

No Colombian author has had a greater influence on the country's literature than Gabriel García Márquez. The publication of *One Hundred Years of Solitude* in 1967 popularized the magic realism genre, while *Love in the Time of Cholera* and *Chronicle of a Death Foretold* offer fascinating glimpses into life on the Caribbean coast.

Jorge Isaacs' *María* is considered one of the most important novels in 19th-century Latin American literature. It is the tragic love story of María and her cousin Efraín.

Colombia's history has inspired a number of fine journalistic works; try *The Making of Modern Colombia: A Nation In Spite Of Itself*, by David Bushnell. Alma Guillermoprieto is probably the finest journalist currently writing on Latin America and her chapters in *The Heart That Bleeds: Latin America Now* and *Looking For History: Dispatches From Latin America* are balanced accounts of the 1990s political scene.

Drugs and guerrillas have shaped much of the literature on Colombia, and *Killing Pablo: The Hunt For The World's Greatest Outlaw*, by Mark Bowden, is a gripping tale of how drug baron Pablo Escobar was captured and killed.

Films to watch

Years of conflict stymied the Colombian film industry, but with increased security, a number of films have emerged in the past few years. Mike Newell's adaptation of Gabriel García Márquez's *Love in the Time of Cholera* was critically panned but nonetheless has some sumptuous photography that will put you in the mood for visiting Cartagena. A better effort was the 1987 production of *Chronicle of a Death Foretold*, featuring a young Rupert Everett and filmed in Mompós.

Most films about Colombia chart some aspect of its violent history. *María Full of Grace* is a beautifully crafted story about a poor factory worker tempted into becoming a drugs 'mule'. French director Barbet Schroeder's adaptation of Fernando Vallejo's novel, *Our Lady of the Assassins*, recreates life in a Medellín slum and was a commercial hit, while Víctor Gaviria's *Rodrigo D – No Futuro* (1989) was the first Colombian film to feature at the Cannes Film Festival. Rodrigo Triana's comedy *Soñar No Cuesta Nada* was another commercial hit, based on the true story of an army platoon that found US$40 million buried at a guerrilla camp.

Contents

26 Getting there
  26 Air
  27 River
  27 Road
  27 Sea

27 Getting around
  27 Air
  28 Rail
  28 Road
  31 Maps

31 Sleeping

33 Eating and drinking
  34 Regional specialities
  35 Restaurants
  36 Drinks

37 Festivals and events

40 Essentials A-Z

Footprint features

30 Driving in Colombia
32 Sleeping price codes
34 Eating price codes
38 Bizarre festivals
44 Colombian Spanish

Essentials

Getting there

Air

International flights arrive principally at Bogotá and Cartagena, but there are also direct flights to Medellín, Cali, Pereira, Barranquilla and San Andrés. Fares are significantly lower in the low season, outside the peaks times of Easter, July, August and December.

From Europe
There are direct flights to Bogotá from Paris with **Air France** (www.airfrance.com), and from Madrid with **Avianca** (www.avianca.com), **Iberia** (www.iberia.com) and **Comet** (www.aircomet.com). Flights from London go via Europe or the USA.

From North America
Continental (www.continental.com) has direct flights from New York, Cleveland and Houston. **American Airlines** (www.aa.com) flies direct from Miami to Bogotá. The main hub for **Delta** (www.delta.com) is Atlanta. **Spirit Air** (www.spiritair.com) has direct flights to Cartagena via Miami. **Air Canada** (www.aircanada.com) flies direct to Bogotá from Toronto.

From Australia and New Zealand
LAN (www.lan.com) has connections with Sydney and Auckland via Santiago in Chile.

From Latin America
Avianca (www.avianca.com) has direct connections with Bogotá from Buenos Aires, Caracas, Lima, Mexico City, Panama City, Quito, Santiago and San José. **TACA** (www.taca.com) flies direct to Bogotá from Lima, Montevideo and San José and from Lima to Medellín. **Copa** (www.copa air.com) has direct flights from Panama City. **Aerolíneas Argentinas** (www.aerolineas.com.ar) has two flights a week between Buenos Aires and Bogotá. **LAN** has direct connections from Santiago.

Discount travel agents

In the UK
Dial A Flight, T0870-3662186, www.dial aflight.com. Discount flight specialists.
Exito Latin American Travel Specialists, T1800-655 4053,www.exito-travel.com.
STA Travel, T0870-160 0599, www.statravel. co.uk. Specialists in low-cost student/youth flights and tours, student IDs and insurance.
Trailfinders,T020-7938 3939, www.trailfinders.com.
Travel CUTS, T1-866-246 9762, www.travel cuts.com. Specialist in student discount fares, IDs and other travel services.
Trips Worldwide,T0117-311 4400, www.tripsworldwide.co.uk.

World Gate Travel Tours, T020-7278 29999, www.worldgatetraveltours.com. Specialists in Latin American travel.

In North America
Air Brokers International, T01-800-883 3273, www.airbrokers.com. Consolidator and specialists in Round the World and Circle Pacific tickets.
Discount Airfares Worldwide On-Line, www.etn.nl/discount.htm. A hub of consolidator and discount agent links.
STA Travel, www.statravel.com. Branches in Los Angeles, New York, San Diego, Boston, Chicago, Seattle and Washington DC.

In Australia and New Zealand
Contours Travel, T03-9670 6900,
www.contourstravel.com.au.
Flight Centre, in Australia, T133133,
www.flightcentre.com.au; in New Zealand,
T0800-243 544, www.flightcentre.co.nz.

STATravel, in Australia, T1300-360960,
www.statravel.com.au; in New Zealand,
T04-385 0561, www.statravel.co.nz.
Trailfinders, T1300-780212,
www.trailfinders.com.au.
Travel.com.au, T02-9249 6000, outside
Sydney: T1300-130482, www.travel.com.au.

River

Colombia shares borders with Brazil and Peru at Leticia on the Amazon. It is possible to cross from these countries by ferry, but the going is slow and difficult. **Amazon Cruises and Adventures** ① www.amazoncruiseonline.com, operates between Iquitos and Leticia.

Road

The main Colombia–Venezuela crossings are at Cúcuta–San Antonio (page 133) and Maicao–Paraguachón for Maracaibo (page 199). The border with Ecuador is crossed at Ipiales–Rumichaca (page 325). ▸▸ *See Visas and immigration, page 50.*

Foot

If travelling independently on foot, there are many more places for entering or leaving Colombia. These include from Ecuador via Puerto Asís, from Panama via the Darién Gap and from Venezuela across the Río Orinoco, none of which are advised at the moment under current security circumstances.

Sea

Colombia can be reached from Ecuador entering via Tumaco. There are various ways to reach Colombia from Panama by sea but only the Capurganá route is currently considered safe.

Getting around

Air

Colombia has a well-established national airline network with several competing airlines. Although internal flights are not cheap, if you have little time it may prove a worthwhile option. **Avianca, Aires, Satena** and **AeroRepública** are the four main airlines. **Easyfly** is a relatively new budget airline with flights to more obscure locations near popular tourist destinations. There are also several localized airlines such as **Aerolíneas de Antioquia**, which serve smaller destinations.

A useful search engine for sourcing cheap flights is www.despegar.com. It may be worth using a travel agent to look for flights as they often have discount arrangements with certain airlines. **Doble Vía** ① *T211 2754,* and **Vivir Volando** ① *T601 4676, www.vivirvolando.com,* in Bogotá, and **Destino Colombia** ① *www.destinocolombia.com,* in Medellín, are recommended.

Domestic airlines

AeroRepública, Cra 10, No 27-51, Loc 165, Bogotá, T3209090, www.aerorepublica.com. Colombia's second largest airline after it was bought out by Panamanian carrier Copa. Flies to most of the main destinations.
Aires, T2940300 (Bogotá), T01 800 052 4737 (rest of the country), www.aires.aero. Smaller airline with services to some of the remoter destinations as well as the main ones.
Avianca, Av El Dorado No 92-30, Bogotá, T457862, www.avianca.com. Offices in every major city in Colombia. The country's national airline, Avianca flies to most destinations. The drawback is that all connections must go via Bogotá.
Easyfly, www.easyfly.com.co. New budget airline with cheap flights to obscure destinations near popular tourist cities.
Satena, Av Eldorado 103-08, Entrada 1, interior 11, Bogotá, T1-605 2222), T4-3614056 (Medellín), T01 900 331 7100 (rest of the country), www.satena.com.co. Government-owned airline with flights to most destinations.

Rail

Colombia used to have an extensive railway system but due to lack of funding most of the lines have fallen into disrepair or are used purely for cargo. There are two exceptions. On weekends, a tourist train runs north from La Sabana station in downtown Bogotá, stopping at Usaquén and continuing to the salt cathedral at Zipaquirá and Cajicá. See www.turistren.com.co for more information.

The Tren Turístico Café y Azúcar, another tourist train, operates only at weekends and public holidays between Cali, Buga and La Tebaida. Another line leaves Cali for La Cumbre, on the way to Buenaventura. See www.trenturisticocafeyazucar.com for more information. Sadly, an attempt to resuscitate a third railway line between Santa Marta and Gabriel García Márquez's hometown of Aracataca appears to have stuttered to a halt. Dubbed 'The Yellow Train of Macondo', the line was opened in 2007 to a great fanfare with 'Gabo' himself aboard for its maiden voyage but a regular service has so far failed to materialize.

Road

While there are few motorways, the main roads in Colombia are mostly in good condition and journeys are generally comfortable. From Bogotá two roads run north towards the coast. To the northeast, a road heads high over the mountains of Boyacá and up to

Bucaramanga before straightening up as it makes towards the Sierra Nevada de Santa Marta. Another road climbs northeast from here toward Cúcuta and the Venezuelan border.

A second road leaves Bogotá to the northwest and joins the Magdalena River Valley at Honda. It follows the river until it reaches a fork at Puerto Triunfo. The eastern artery cuts back toward Bucaramanga. The western branch leads to Medellín.

Medellín is on the course of the Pan-American Highway, the single, continuous road that links most of the countries in the Americas, beginning in Canada and ending in Chile (interrupted only at the border between Panama and Colombia). In Colombia, after Darién, it begins again at Turbo and runs due south, passing through Medellín, the Zona Cafetera, Cali, Popayán, Pasto and reaches Ecuador via Ipiales.

There are two further main roads exiting Bogotá. One runs southeast over (and under) high mountain passes towards Villavicencio and the Llanos. The other heads south towards Neiva. It eventually joins up with the Pan-American Highway at Pasto but not before tackling some treacherous terrain around Mocoa.

Bus

On the main routes, the bus network is comprehensive and buses are generally comfortable and efficient. Arriving at one of the large bus stations, the choice of carriers can be daunting, but it also has its advantages as there are frequent services and competition between different companies allows for a bit of haggling.

On main routes there is usually a choice of operators with varying degrees of quality and speed. The cheapest, *corrientes*, are essentially local buses, stopping frequently, uncomfortable and slow but offering plenty of local colour. *Pullman* or *servicio de lujo* (luxury) are long-distance buses, usually with air conditioning, toilets and DVDs (almost always violent pirate films dubbed in Spanish or music videos). *Colectivos*, also known as *vans* or *busetas*, are usually 12-20 seat vehicles but also seven-seater cars, pick-up trucks or taxis, rather cramped but fast, saving several hours on long journeys. The latter are also known as *por puestos* (pay-by-the-seat) and will not leave until all the places have been filled. The cost of tickets is relatively high by Latin American standards. Fares shown in the text are middle of the range but should be treated as no more than a guide.

Car

With a good road network, self-driving is becoming an increasingly popular way of seeing Colombia. It's an especially good way of exploring rural areas such as the Zona Cafetera where public transport will only take you between the main cities. The kind of motoring

Driving in Colombia

If there is one rule that is always adhered to on Colombian roads it is that 'might is right'. Colombians may have impeccable manners in personal exchanges but when they step into a car, like Jekyll and Hyde, their character transforms. Overtaking around blind corners, ignoring traffic lights – anything goes. The worst culprits are truck drivers who seem to treat their job as a permanent rally. They are closely followed by bus drivers, with the rest not far behind. In cities, especially Bogotá, pedestrians have few rights. So mind how you go, look both ways twice when crossing the road, sit tight on the bus or in a taxi, and pray.

you do will depend on the car you set out with. While a normal car will reach most places of interest, high ground clearance is useful for badly surfaced or unsurfaced roads and for fording rivers. Four-wheel drive vehicles are recommended for flexibility in mountain and jungle territory. Wherever you travel you should expect from time to time to find roads that are badly maintained, damaged or closed during the wet season; expect delays because of floods and landslides. There is also the possibility of hold-ups from major roadworks. Do not plan your schedules too tightly. There are *peajes* (toll stations) every 60-100 km or so on major roads: tolls are around US$1.80. Motorcycles and bicycles don't have to pay.

Safety Before taking a long journey, ask locally about the state of the road and check if there are any safety issues. Roads are not always signposted. Avoid night journeys; the roads may not be in good condition, lorry and bus drivers tend to be reckless, and animals often stray onto the roads. Police and military checks can be frequent in troubled areas, keep your documents handy. In town, try to leave your car in an attended *parqueadero* (car park), especially at night. Only park in the street if there is someone on guard, tip US$0.20.

Spare no ingenuity in making your car impenetrable. Your model should be like an armoured van: anything less secure can be broken into by the determined and skilled thief. Avoid leaving your car unattended except in a locked garage or guarded parking space. Adult minders or street children will generally protect your car fiercely in exchange for a tip. Be sure to note down key numbers and carry spares of the most important ones (but don't keep all spares inside the vehicle).

Documents National driving licences may be used by foreigners in Colombia, but should be accompanied by an official translation if in a language other than Spanish. International drivers licences are also accepted. Carry driving documents with you at all times.

When you cross the border into Colombia, make sure you keep any papers you are given; you will be asked to produce them when you leave. Bringing a car in by sea or air is much more complicated: you will usually be required to hire an agent to clear it through customs, which can be a slow and expensive process. To bring a car into Colombia, you must have documents proving ownership of the vehicle, and a tourist card/transit visa. These are normally valid for 90 days and must be applied for at the Colombian consulate in the country that you will be leaving for Colombia. A *carnet de passages* is recommended when entering with a European registered vehicle.

Insurance for the vehicle against accident, damage or theft is best arranged in the country of origin, but it is getting increasingly difficult to find agencies who offer this service. In Latin American countries it is very expensive to insure against accident and theft.

Fuel prices are around US$5 per gallon for standard petrol, US$6 per gallon for super and US$3.50 per gallon for diesel. Prices are likely to fluctuate in the current economic climate.

Car hire Car hire, though relatively expensive especially, if you are going to the remoter areas and need 4WD or specialist vehicles, is convenient for touring, and the better hotels all have safe parking. The main international car rental companies are represented at principal airports but may be closed on Saturday afternoons and Sundays. There are also local firms in most of the departmental capitals. In addition to passport and driver's licence, a credit card may be asked for as additional proof of identity (Visa, MasterCard, American Express), and to secure a returnable deposit to cover any liability not covered by the insurance. Check the insurance carefully; it may not cover you beyond a certain figure, nor for 'natural' damage such as flooding. Ask if extra cover is available. You should be given a diagram showing any scratches and other damage on the car before you hired it.

Maps

A decent map can be difficult to find but sound out the nearest tourist office and they should be able to provide at least a map of the town.

There are few road maps but the *Guía Rutas de Colombia*, available at all toll booths, provides a relatively decent map. Try also major bookstores such as **Pan-Americana**.

The **Instituto Geográfico Agustín Codazzi** ① *www.igac.gov.co*, produces general and specialist maps of the country. Unfortunately, this institution is receiving increasingly less funding from the government and many maps may be out of date.

Sleeping

In Colombia there are a number of quite exceptional hotels that are well worth seeking out. They are usually in colonial towns and not necessarily very expensive. There is a small network of youth hostels, of varying quality and used extensively by Colombian groups, but international members are welcome.

There are many names in Colombia for hotels including *posada, pensión, residencia, hostal, hostería, hospedaje, hospedería, mesón* and *hotelito*. Ignore them all and simply look at the price range for what to expect. *Motels* are almost always pay-by-the-hour 'love hotels' (see page 269) for use by illicit lovers and prostitutes and their clients. Most of the time, especially with the more expensive drive-in ones on the outskirts of town, the names will provide an obvious enough clue (eg 'Passion Motel'), but this is not always the case. Some *residencias* also double up as *acostaderos*, or love hotels. It's best to avoid these.

The more expensive hotels add on 16% IVA (value-added tax) to bills. Strictly speaking foreigners should be exempt from this but there seems to be some confusion about the application of this law. Raise the matter with your hotel and you may well get a discount. Some hotels add a small insurance charge.

From 15 December to 30 April, and 15 June to 31 August, some hotels in main holiday centres may increase prices by 20-30%. In some hotels outside the main cities you can only stay (very cheaply) at *en pensión* rates, but no allowance is made for missing a meal.

The Colombian hotel federation, **COTELCO** ① *www.cotelco.org*, has lists of authorized prices for all member hotels, which can be consulted at tourist offices. In theory, new laws require all hotels to be registered, but to date this is incomplete particularly with

Sleeping price codes

LL	Over US$200	**L**	US$151-200	**AL**	US$101-150
A	US$66-100	**B**	US$46-65	**C**	US$31-45
D	US$21-30	**E**	US$12-20	**F**	US$7-11
G	US$6 and under				

Price of a double room in high season, including taxes.

regard to cheaper hotels. Most hotels in Colombia charge US$1 to US$6 for extra beds for children, up to a maximum (usually) of four beds per room. Prices are normally displayed at reception, but in quiet periods it is always worth negotiating and ask to see the room before committing.

When booking a hotel from an airport or bus station, try to speak to the hotel yourself; most will understand at least simple English and possibly French, German or Italian. If you use an official tourist agent, you will probably pay a little more as a booking fee. If you accept help from anyone else, you could be putting yourself at risk.

In cheaper hotels, beware of electric shower heaters, which can be dangerous through faulty wiring. Hotels are sometimes checked by the police for drugs. Make sure they do not remove any of your belongings. You do not need to show them any money. Cooperate but be firm about your rights.

Toilets may suffer from inadequate water supplies. In all cases, however, do not flush paper down the pan but use the receptacle provided. Carry toilet paper with you as cheaper establishments as well as restaurants, bars, etc may not provide it.

Camping

Local tourist authorities have lists of official campsites, but they are seldom signposted on main roads, so can be hard to find. Permission to camp with tent, campervan or car may be granted by landowners in less populated areas. Many *haciendas* have armed guards protecting their property, which can add to your safety. Do not camp on private land without permission. Those in campervans can camp by the roadside, but it is not particularly safe and can be difficult to find a secluded spot. If you have a vehicle, it is possible to camp at truck drivers' restaurants or sometimes at police or army

posts. Check very carefully before deciding to camp: you may be exposing yourself to significant danger.

Youth hostels

La Federación Colombiana de Albergues Juveniles ① *www.fcaj.org.co*, is affiliated to the International Youth Hostel Federation (IYHF) and has 11 hostels around the country centred on Bogotá, where there are 105 beds in Candelaria, T2803041, in the old centre of the city at Carrera 7, No 6-10. The other hostels are in Armenia, Barichara, Cartagena, Medellín, Paipa, Providencia, San Agustín, Santa Marta, Taganga and Villavicencio. Hostels are often full at holiday periods, December to January and June to mid-July; it's best to telephone in advance during these times. Otherwise, it's usually possible to arrive without a reservation. Membership can be taken out in Colombia: Hostelling International Cards are recognized and qualify for discounts. See also the **Colombian Hostel Association** ① *www.colombianhostels.com*, which has hostels in Bogotá, Bucaramanga, Cartagena, Cali, Manizales, Medellín, San Gil, Salento, San Agustín, Taganga and Ville de Leiva. **Hostel Trail Latin America** ① *Cra 11, No 4-16, Popayán, T0131-208 0007 (UK), www.hosteltrail.com*, is an online network of hostels and tour companies in South America providing information on locally run businesses for backpackers and independent travellers.

Homestays

In many places, it is possible to stay with a local family; check with the local tourist office to see what is available. This is a good option for those interested in learning Spanish informally in a family environment. However, if you take formal classes, you should have a student visa (see Visas and immigration, page 51). See also the Staying on a coffee *finca* box, page 257.

Eating and drinking

Like many Latin American countries, cuisine is not one of Colombia's main draws. But the food is better than in most countries and there are some delicious regional specialities, which you will surely wish to try. Colombia's food used to vary greatly from one area to the next. Now, however you will find regional food available in all the major cities, though local variations do creep in.

Some of the standard items on the menu are: *sancocho*, a meat stock (may be fish on the coast) with potato, corn (on the cob), yucca, sweet potato and plantain. *Arroz con pollo* (chicken and rice), one of the standard Latin American dishes, is excellent in Colombia. *Carne asada* (grilled beefsteak), usually an inexpensive cut, is served with *papas fritas* (chips) or rice and you can ask for a vegetable of the day. *Sobrebarriga* (belly of beef) is served with varieties of potato in a tomato and onion sauce. *Huevos pericos,* eggs scrambled with onions and tomatoes, are a popular, cheap and nourishing snack available almost anywhere, especially favoured for breakfast. *Tamales* are meat pies made by folding a maize dough round chopped pork mixed with potato, rice, peas, onions and eggs wrapped in banana leaves (which you don't eat) and steamed. Other ingredients may be added such as olives garlic, cloves and paprika. Colombians eat *tamales* for breakfast with hot chocolate. *Empanadas* are another popular snack; these are made with chicken or various other meats, or vegetarian filling, inside a maize dough and cooked in a light oil. *Patacones* are cakes of mashed and baked *platano* (large green

Eating price codes

🍴🍴🍴 Over US$12   🍴🍴 US$6-12   🍴 Under US$6

Prices for a two-course meal for one person, excluding drinks or service charge.

banana). *Arepas* are standard throughout Colombia; these are flat maize griddle cakes often served instead of bread or as an alternative. *Pan de bono* is cheese flavoured bread. *Almojábanas*, a kind of sour milk/cheese bread roll, great for breakfast when freshly made. *Buñuelos* are 4-6 cm balls of wheat flour and eggs mixed and deep-fried, also best when still warm. *Arequipe* is a sugar-based brown syrup used with desserts and in confectionary, universally savoured by Colombians. *Brevas* (figs) with *arequipe* are one of the most popular items to take home with you.

Regional specialities

Bogotá and Cundinamarca *Ajiaco de pollo* (or *ajiaco santafereño*) is a delicious chicken stew with maize, manioc (yuca), three types of potato, herbs (including *guascas*) and sometimes other vegetables, served with cream and capers, and pieces of avocado. It is a Bogotá speciality. *Chunchullo* (tripe), and *morcilla* (blood sausage) are popular dishes. *Cuajada con melado* is a dessert of fresh cheese served with cane syrup, or *natas* (based on the skin of boiled milk).

Boyacá *Mazamorra* is a meat and vegetable soup with broad and black beans, peas, varieties of potato and cornflour. *Care* (or *mazamorro* in Antioquia and elsewhere) is a milk and maize drink, which, to confuse matters further is known as *peto* in Cundinamarca. *Puchero* is a stew based on chicken with potatoes, yuca, cabbage, turnips, corn (on the cob) and herbs. *Cuchuco*, another soup with pork and sweet potato. *Masato* is a slightly fermented rice beverage. *Longaniza* (long pork sausage) is also very popular.

Santander and Norte de Santander *Mute* is a traditional soup of various cereals including corn. Goat, often served with *pepitoria* (its innards) and pigeon appear in several local dishes. *Hormigas culonas* (large-bottomed black ants) is the most famous culinary delight of this area, served toasted, and particularly popular in Bucaramanga at Easter time. Locals claim they have aphrodisiacal powers. *Bocadillo veleño* is similar to quince jelly but made from guava. It takes its name from Vélez, but can be found elsewhere in Colombia. *Rampuchada* is a north Santander stew based of the fish of the Zulia river which flows into Venezuela. *Hallacas* are cornmeal turnovers with different meats and whatever else is to hand inside, typical of neighbouring Venezuela, like an oversized *tamal*. Dishes featuring chickpeas and goat's milk are popular in this part of Colombia. *Carne oreada* is salted dried meat marinated in a *panela* and pineapple sauce and has the consistency of beef jerky.

Cartagena and the north coast Fish is naturally a speciality the coastal regions. In *Arroz con coco*, rice here is often prepared with coconut. *Cazuela de mariscos*, a soup/stew of shellfish and white fish, maybe including octopus and squid, is especially good. *Sancocho de pescado* is a fish stew with vegetables, usually simpler and cheaper than *cazuela*. *Chipichipi*, a small clam found along the coast in Barranquilla and Santa Marta, is a standard local dish served with rice. *Empanada* (or *arepa*) *de huevo*, which is deep fried with eggs in the middle and is a good light meal. *Canasta de coco* is a good local sweet: pastry containing coconut custard flavoured with wine and surmounted by meringue.

Tolima *Lechona*, suckling pig with herbs is a speciality of Ibagué. *Viudo de pescado* is a dish based on small shellfish from the Opía (a local) river. *Achira* is a kind of hot biscuit.

Antioquia *Bandeja paisa* consists of various types of gut-busting grilled meats, *chorizo* (sausage), *chicharrón* (pork crackling), sometimes an egg, served with rice, beans, potato, manioc and a green salad; this has now been adopted in other parts of the country. *Natilla*, a sponge cake made from cornflour and *salpicón*, a tropical fruit salad.

Cali and south Colombia In contrast to most of Colombia, menus tend not to include potato (in its many forms). Instead, emphasis is on corn, plantain, rice and avocado with the usual pork and chicken dishes. *Manjar blanco*, made from milk and sugar or molasses, served with biscuit is a favourite dessert. *Cuy*, *curí* or *conejillo de Indias* (guinea pig), is typical of the southern department of Nariño. *Mazorcas* (baked corn-on-the-cob) are typical of roadside stalls in southern Colombia.

Restaurants

In the main cities (Bogotá, Cartagena, Medellín and Cali) you will find a limitless choice of menu and price. The other departmental capitals have a good range of specialist restaurants and all the usual fast food outlets. Only in the smaller towns and villages, not catering for tourists, will you find a modest selection of places to eat. Watch out for times of opening in the evenings, some city areas may tend to close around 1800 (eg La Candelaria in Bogotá), and times may be different at weekends. On Sundays it can be particularly difficult to eat in a restaurant and even hotel restaurants may be closed.

The basic Colombian meal of the day is at lunchtime, the *almuerzo* or *comida corriente*, with soup, main course and fruit juice or *gaseosa* (soft drink). If you are economizing, ask for the *plato del día*, *bandeja* or *plato corriente* (just the main dish). This can be found everywhere, many restaurants will display the menu and cost in the window.

The cheapest food available is in markets (when they are functioning) and from street stalls in most downtown areas and transport terminals. The problem is whether it is safe and also if it will agree with you. The general rules apply: keep away from uncooked food and salads, and eat fruit you have peeled yourself. Watch what the locals are eating as a guide to the best choice. Wash it down with something out of a sealed bottle. Having said that, take it easy with dishes that are unfamiliar especially if you have arrived from a different climate or altitude. On the other hand, you may find that fresh fruit drinks, wherever prepared, are irresistible in which case you will have to take your chance!
➤➤ *See Health, page 41.*

Restaurants are more difficult to evaluate than hotels because, as everywhere, they come, change and go. We try to give you a tested choice at all available price levels. Food is generally good, occasionally very good. Note that more expensive restaurants may add a discretionary 16% IVA tax to the bill.

Most of the bigger cities have specific vegetarian restaurants and you will find them listed in the text. The **Govinda** chain is widely represented. Be warned that they are normally open only for lunch. In towns and villages you will have to ask for special food to be prepared.

Drinks

Colombian coffee is always mild. *Tinto*, the national small cup of black coffee, is taken at all hours. If you want it strong, ask for *café cargado*; a *tinto doble* is a large cup of black coffee. Coffee with milk is called *café perico*; *café con leche* is a mug of milk with coffee added. If you want a coffee with less milk, order *tinto y leche aparte* and they will bring the milk separately.

Tea is popular but herbal rather than Indian or Chinese: ask for *(bebida) aromática*, flavours include *limonaria*, *orquídea* and *manzanilla*. If you want Indian tea, *té Lipton en agua* should do the trick. *Té de menta* (mint tea) is another of many varieties available but you may have to go to an upmarket café or *casa de té*, which can be found in all of the bigger cities. Chocolate is also drunk: *chocolate Santafereño* is often taken during the afternoon in Bogotá with snacks and cheese. *Agua de panela* (hot water with unrefined sugar) is a common beverage, also made with limes, milk, or cheese.

Soft bottled drinks are universal and standard, commonly called *gaseosas*. If you want non-carbonated, ask for *sin gas*. Again you will find that many of the special fruits are used for bottled drinks. Water comes in bottles, cartons and small plastic packets: all safer than out of the tap.

Many acceptable brands of beer are produced, until recently almost all produced by the Bavaria group. Each region has a preference for different brands. The most popular are **Aguila**, **Club Colombia**, **Costeño** and **Poker**. **Club Colombia** won the prestigious Monde Selection 'Grand Gold Medal with Palm Leaves' in 2008, marking it out as one of the best beers in the world. The **Bogota Beer Company** has its own small brewery in Chapinero and has several bars around the city serving delicious draught beer modelled on British and German ales.

A traditional drink in Colombia is *chicha*. It is corn-based but sugar and/or *panela* are added and it is boiled. It is served as a non-alcoholic beverage, but if allowed to ferment over several days, and especially if kept in the fridge for a while, it becomes very potent.

The local rum is good and cheap; ask for *ron*, not *aguardiente*. One of the best rums is **Ron Viejo de Caldas**, another (dark) is **Ron Medellín**. Try *canelazo* cold or hot rum with water, sugar, lime and cinnamon. As common as rum is *aguardiente* (literally 'fire water'), a white spirit distilled from sugar cane. There are two types, with *anis* (aniseed) or without. Local table wines include **Isabella**; none is very good. Wine is very expensive, as much as US$15 in restaurants for an acceptable bottle of Chilean or Argentine wine, more for European and other wines.

Warning Care should be exercised when buying imported spirits in some bars and small shops. It has been reported that bottles bearing well-known labels have been 'recycled' and contain a cheap and poor imitation of the original contents and can be dangerous. You are probably safe purchasing in supermarkets. Also note that ice may not be made from drinking water.

Fruit and juices

Colombia has an exceptional range and quality of fruit – another aspect of the diversity of altitude and climate. Fruits familiar in northern and Mediterranean climates are here, though with some differences, including: *manzanas* (apples); *bananos* (bananas); *uvas* (grapes); *limones* (limes; lemons, the larger yellow variety, are rarely seen); *mangos* (mangoes); *melones* (melons); *naranjas* (orange; usually green or yellow in Colombia); *duraznos* (peaches); and *peras* (pears).

Then there are the local fruits: *chirimoyas* (a green fruit, white inside with pips); *curuba* (banana passion fruit); *feijoa* (a green fruit with white flesh, high in vitamin C); *guayaba* (guava); *guanábana* (soursop); *lulo* (a small orange fruit); *maracuyá* (passion fruit); *mora* (literally 'black berry' but dark red more like a loganberry); *papaya*; the delicious *pitahaya* (taken either as an appetizer or dessert); *sandía* (watermelon); *tomate de árbol* (tree tomato, several varieties normally used as a fruit); and many more.

All of these fruits can be served as juices, either with milk (hopefully fresh) or water (hopefully bottled or sterilized). Most hotels and restaurants are careful about this and you can watch the drinks being prepared on street stalls. You will be surprised how delicious these drinks are and the adventurous can experiment to find their favourite. Fruit yoghurts are nourishing and cheap; **Alpina** brand is good; *crema* style is best. Also, **Kumis** is a type of liquid yoghurt. Another drink you must try is *champús*, a corn base, with fruit and lemon.

Festivals and events

There are more festivals, parties and carnivals in Colombia than days in the year. Every city, town and village has at least three or four annual events in which local products and traditions are celebrated with music, dancing and raucous revelry (these are listed throughout the book). Below are some of the most significant. ►► *See also Background, page 368.*

January
2-3 Jan Feria de Manizales Festivities include horse parades, beauty pageants, bullfighting and a general celebration of all things coffee in Manizales.

5-6 Jan Carnaval de los Blancos y Negros The city of Pasto celebrates one of Latin America's oldest carnivals in which everyone daubs each other in black grease and white flour to commemorate the emancipation of black slaves. Celebrations begin late Dec with communal water fights and floats. There is dancing, parades and lots of costumes.

5-10 Jan Carnaval del Diablo The town of Ríosucio in Caldas has celebrated this homage to the devil every 2 years since 1915. The whole town effectively becomes a masked ball as locals dress up as devils and other characters in a festival in which Hispanic, black and indigenous traditions collide.

20 Jan Corraleja de Sincelejo Jan is bullfighting season in Colombia and many towns hold events. Most famous of these is the Corraleja at Sincelejo, a sometimes brutal show in which the town's youth display their bravura against 40 bulls released into a ring. Injuries – even deaths – are frequent.

February
2 Feb Fiesta de Nuestra Señora de la Candelaria Celebrated in towns, including Cartagena and Medellín, this religious cult festival was inherited from the Canary Islands, where 2 goatherds witnessed the apparition of the Virgin Mary holding a green candle.

February-March
Barranquilla Carnival (moveable) Beginning 4 days before Ash Wednesday, this is one of the best carnivals in South America. 4 days of partying are compulsory by law and involve parades and plenty of dancing.

March-April
Semana Santa (movable) Celebrated almost everywhere in Colombia, but the processions in Popayán (the 2nd largest in the world after Sevilla, Spain), Mompós and Pamplona are particularly revered.

Bizarre festivals

García Márquez once said, "five Colombians in a room invariably turns into a party". It could also be said that a couple of hundred Colombians in a village invariably turns into a festival. Colombians will use almost anything as a pretext for a celebration. Below are some of the most bizarre.

Festival del Burro, San Antero, Córdoba
The people of the Caribbean coastal town of San Antero love their donkeys. So much so that they have a festival dedicated to them. Each year around Easter time the town's donkeys are paraded through the streets – in drag. Some wear lipstick and mascara, feather boas and pearl necklaces, while others sport jeans or bikinis, and the best get-up wins a prize. They have even built a Burrodome, a special stadium where man and beast can hang out drinking beer and listen to *vallenato*.

Yipao, Armenia, Quindío, October
Willys jeeps first arrived in Colombia in 1946 for the United States and they have become the most popular vehicles in the Zona Cafetera's hilly countryside thanks to their robust handling and capacity to carry weights far beyond their size. Colombians demonstrate their admiration for these Second World War army jeeps by holding *yipao*s – competitions in which Willys' owners must try and load as much produce as is physically possible onto their vehicles and parade down the street, often performing wheelies as they go. The most popular of the *yipao*s is held in Armenia each October as part of the city's annual fiesta but the largest is in Calaracá in July, which in 2006 set a Guinness World Record for the largest jeep parade with over 370 Willys jeeps taking part.

Tomatina, Sutamarchán, Boyacá
The premise of this festival is very simple: dump a bunch of tomatoes in a field and get several thousand people to throw them at each other. In 2008, the local authorities estimated that 10 tons of tomatoes were thrown, squashed and pulped during this messy fight, which takes place each June. This festival probably took its cue from the Tomatína in Buñol, near Valencia in Spain, which claims to be the world's largest vegetable fight.

April

26-30 Apr Festival de la Leyenda Vallenata One of the most important music festivals in Colombia, 4 days of hard partying in Valledupar culminate in the selection of the best *vallenato* musician.

June-July

22 Jun-2 Jul Festival Folклórico y Reinado Nacional del Bambuco The city of Neiva hosts *Bambuco* dancing competitions and various parades in which bikini-clad beauty queens float downriver on boats while up to 5000 (often) drunken women ride horseback through Neiva's streets. It culminates in the crowning of a *Bambuco* queen.

28 Jun-2 Jul Torneo Internacional del Joropo The city of Villavicencio gives itself over to a celebration of *llanero* culture with more than 3000 couples dressed in traditional outfits dance *Joropo* in the streets, a large horse parade, a beauty contest and *coleo* (a type of rodeo) making up the events.

August

1-10 Aug Feria de la Flores Concerts, street parties, antique car parades, a *Paso Fino* horse parade and the *Desfile de Silleteros*, in which flower-growers file through the city streets carrying their elaborate displays mounted on wooden 'chairs', have made this festival in Medellín a world-renowned event.

Most windy weekend in Aug **Festival del Viento y de Cometas** Villa de Leiva's enormous cobbled plaza fills with hundreds of kite-fliers displaying models of all shapes and sizes. Competition is fierce.

September

13-14 Sep **Jazz al Parque** Bogotá's parks resonate to the sound of pianos, saxophones and trumpets during this festival that has grown exponentially since it first began in 1996. Musicians from all over the world converge on Colombia's capital for a weekend.

20 Sep-9 Oct **Fiestas de San Pacho** For 20 days in late Sep/early Oct, the streets of Quibdó in El Chocó convert themselves into a big party venue to commemorate the death of Saint Francis of Assisi. Religious processions, parades and *sancocho* cookouts all combine in this fusion of Catholicism and African customs.

October

Encuentro Mundial del Coleo More than 40,000 people descend on Villvicencio each year to watch mounted cowboys display their skills at *coleo*, a sport not dissimilar to rodeo that involves upending bulls by grabbing them by the tail and twisting until they fall over.
Concurso Mundial de la Mujer Vaquera The female population of the Llanos proves why they have better cowboy skills than men.

November

Late Nov **El Pirarucú de Oro** This music festival in Leticia reflects the Colombian Amazon capital's position on the edge of 2 frontiers. With influences from Brazil and Peru, the festival hosts a competition that celebrates music from the region.
First 2 weeks of Nov **Independence of Cartagena and Concurso Nacional de la**

Belleza Cartagena celebrates being the first department to win independence from the Spanish each 11 Nov with parades and traditional dancing in the streets. This has been somewhat supplanted by the National Beauty Pageant in which the winner will go on to represent Colombia at Miss Universe.

December

7-8 Dec **Festival de Luces** The skies above Villa de Leiva are lit by one of the best pyrotechnic shows in Colombia while the streets of this colonial town are illuminated by hundreds of candles in this most picturesque of festivals.

25-30 Dec **Feria de Cali** What started as a bullfighting festival involving the best Spanish and South American matadors is now a city-wide party where Cali's self-imposed title of 'capital of salsa' is reaffirmed every year. The festival is opened by an impressive *Paso Fino* horse parade.

Public holidays

1 Jan Circumcision of our Lord
6 Jan Epiphany*
19 Mar St Joseph*
Easter Maundy Thursday; Good Friday
1 May Labour Day
1 May Ascension Day*
22 May Corpus Christi*
29 Jun Saint Peter and Saint Paul*
30 Jun Sacred Heart*
20 Jul Independence Day
7 Aug Battle of Boyacá
15 Aug Assumption*
12 Oct Columbus' arrival in America*
1 Nov All Saints' day*
11 Nov Independence of Cartagena*
8 Dec Immaculate Conception
25 Dec Christmas Day
* When these do not fall on a Mon, the public holiday will be on the following Mon. Public holidays are known as *puentes* (bridges).

Essentials A-Z

Accident and emergency

Contact the relevant emergency service and your embassy in Bogotá. Make sure you obtain police/medical reports in order to file insurance claims.

Emergency services
Police: T112; **Ambulance**: T125 or 132; **Fire**: T119; **Red Cross ambulance**: T127; **CAI Police**: T156.

   If you have problems with theft or other forms of crime, contact a **Centro de Atención Inmediata (CAI)** office for assistance. Only at a CAI police office is it possible to report a theft and get the relevant paperwork, not at other police stations. In Bogotá the CAI office is: downtown, C 60 y Cra 9, T2177472, La Candelaria, Cra 7 y C6.

Children

Travel with children can bring you into closer contact with Colombian families and, generally, presents no special problems – in fact the path may even be smoother for family groups. Officials are sometimes more amenable where children are concerned and they are pleased if your child knows a little Spanish. For more detailed advice on travelling with children, see Footprint's *Travel with Kids*.

Bus travel
Remember that a lot of time can be spent waiting for and riding buses, which are sometimes crowded and uncomfortable. You should take reading material as it is difficult to find and expensive. Local comic strips are a good way for older children to learn a bit of Spanish. But reading on the bus itself, especially on winding mountain roads, may make children (and adults) nauseous.

Fares
On long-distance buses you pay for each seat, and there are no half-price fares. For shorter trips it is cheaper, if less comfortable, to seat small children on your knee. Sometimes there are spare seats that children can occupy after tickets have been collected.

Food
This can be a problem if the children are not adaptable. It is easier to take food with you on longer trips than to rely on meal stops where the food may not be to taste. It's best stick to simple things like bread and fruit while you are on the road. Biscuits, packaged junk food and bottled drinks abound. In restaurants, you may be able to buy a *media porción* (half portion), or divide a full-size helping between 2 children.

Customs

On arrival
Customs checks take place at airports and frontiers for both arriving and leaving travellers (see Visas and immigration, page 50). Do not carry drugs or firearms of any kind and take care that no-one tampers with your baggage.

Disabled travellers

Provision for the disabled is limited in Colombia. Wheelchairs and assistance are available at major airports but inconsistent. Modern and public buildings are being provided with ramps and relevant lifts, and some streets have sidewalk breaks mainly for vendor trollies and bikes, but are usually adequate for wheelchairs. As yet, serious concern for the disabled is not evident in the country.

But, of course, only a minority of disabled people are wheelchair-bound and it is now widely acknowledged that disabilities do not stop you from enjoying a great holiday. Some travel companies are beginning to specialize in exciting holidays, tailor-made for individuals depending on their level of ability.

For general information, consult the **Global Access – Disabled Travel Network**, www.globalaccessnews.com.

Drugs

As is all too well known, Colombia is part of a major drug producing and smuggling route and still produces roughly 80% of the world's cocaine. Police and customs activities have greatly intensified and smugglers increasingly try to use innocent carriers. Do not carry packages for other people without checking the contents (indeed taking suspicious packages or gift-wrapped presents of your own through customs could give problems). Be very polite if approached by policemen, or if your hotel room is raided by police looking for drugs. Colombians who offer you drugs may well be setting you up for the police, who are very active on the north coast and San Andrés island, and other tourist resorts. There are established penalties, which include prison, fines and deportation of any foreigner caught using any drug.

Electricity

110 Volts AC, alternating at 60 cycles per second. A voltage converter may be required if your device does not run on 110 Volts. Most sockets accept both continental European (round) and North American (flat) 2-pin plugs.

Embassies and consulates

Visit www.cancilleria.gov.co for a full list of addresses.

Gay and lesbian travellers

Colombia has some of the most progressive laws in favour of homosexuality in Latin America. While same-sex marriages and civil unions are yet to be legalized, common-law marriage property and inheritance rights for same-sex couples were approved by the Constitutional Court in May 2007. Most of the big cities have gay neighbourhoods. Bogotá in particular has large and thriving gay scene. But outside of the big cities homosexuality has little acceptance. It is therefore prudent to respect local sensibilities.

Health

See your GP or travel clinic at least 6 weeks before departure for general advice on travel risks and vaccinations. Try phoning a specialist travel clinic if your own doctor is unfamiliar with health conditions in Colombia. Make sure you have sufficient medical travel insurance, get a dental check, know your own blood group and if you suffer a long-term condition such as diabetes or epilepsy, obtain a Medic Alert bracelet/necklace (www.medicalert.co.uk). If you wear glasses, take a copy of your prescription.

Vaccinations
It is advisable to vaccinate against polio, tetanus, typhoid, hepatitis A, and rabies if going to more remote areas. If visiting the Amazon you will most likely be asked to produce a yellow fever certificate at the airport in Leticia and may well be turned away if you can't. Malaria is a danger in the Amazon and other tropical areas such as the Darién and El Chocó. Specialist advice should be taken on the best anti-malarials to use.

Health risks
The most common cause of travellers' **diarrhoea** is from eating food contaminated food. In Colombia, drinking water is rarely the culprit, although it's best to be cautious

(see below). Swimming in sea or river water that has been contaminated by sewage can also be a cause; ask locally if it is safe. Diarrhoea may be also caused by viruses, bacteria (such as E-coli), protozoal (such as giardia), salmonella and cholera. It may be accompanied by vomiting or by severe abdominal pain. Any kind of diarrhoea responds well to the replacement of water and salts. Sachets of rehydration salts can be bought in most chemists and can be dissolved in boiled water. If the symptoms persist, consult a doctor. Tap water in the major cities is in theory safe to drink but it may be advisable to err on the side of caution and drink only bottled or boiled water. Avoid having ice in drinks unless you trust that it is from a reliable source.

Travelling in high altitudes can bring on **altitude sickness**. On reaching heights above 3000 m, the heart may start pounding and the traveller may experience shortness of breath. Smokers and those with underlying heart or lung disease are often hardest hit. Take it easy for the first few days, rest and drink plenty of water, you will feel better soon. It is essential to get acclimatized before undertaking long treks or arduous activities.

Mosquitoes are more of a nuisance than a serious hazard but some, of course, are carriers of serious diseases such as **malaria**, so it is sensible to avoid being bitten as much as possible. Sleep off the ground and use a mosquito net and some kind of insecticide. Mosquito coils release insecticide as they burn and are available in many shops, as are tablets of insecticide, which are placed on a heated mat plugged into a wall socket.

If you get sick

Contact your embassy or consulate for a list of doctors and dentists who speak your language, or at least some English. Doctors and health facilities in major cities are also listed in the Directory sections of this book. Good-quality healthcare is available in the larger centres of Colombia but it can be expensive, especially hospitalization. Make sure you have adequate insurance (see below).

Useful websites

www.btha.org British Travel Health Association.

www.cdc.gov US government site that gives excellent advice on travel health and details of disease outbreaks.

www.fco.gov.uk British Foreign and Commonwealth Office travel site has useful information on each country, people, climate and a list of UK embassies/consulates.

www.fitfortravel.scot.nhs.uk A-Z of vaccine/health advice for each country.

www.numberonehealth.co.uk Travel screening services, vaccine and travel health advice, email/SMS text vaccine reminders and screens returned travellers for tropical diseases.

Insurance

Travel insurance is a must for all visitors to Colombia. Always take out insurance that covers both medical expenses and baggage loss, and read the small print carefully before you set off. Check that all the activities you may end up doing are covered. Mountaineering, for example, is excluded from many policies; also make sure that coverage is not excluded at high altitude. Check if medical coverage includes air ambulance and emergency flights back home. Be aware of the payment protocol: in Colombia you will have to have to pay out of your own pocket and later request reimbursement from the insurance company. Before paying for any medical services, insist on getting a fully itemized invoice. In case of baggage loss, have the receipts for expensive personal effects like cameras and laptops on file, take photos of these items, note the serial numbers and be sure to leave unnecessary valuables at home. Keep the insurance company's telephone number with you and get a police report for any lost or stolen items.

Internet

Public internet access is available in many but not all areas of Colombia; small towns and villages may not have connectivity. As elsewhere, however, the internet has completely replaced postal and telephone services for most travellers. Cyber cafés are frequented not only by tourists, but also by many locals, and sometimes get crowded and noisy. Keep an eye on your belongings.

Both the cost and speed of access vary, with the best service generally available in the largest cities. Hourly rates are usually US$1-4. Many hotels now have Wi-Fi available, as do some public spaces such as parks.

Language

The official language of Colombia is Spanish and it is spoken by the majority of the population. However, there are also some 60 aboriginal languages spoken by the indigenous communities. A form of creole English is spoken on the islands of San Andrés and Providencia. English, or any other foreign language, is absolutely useless off the beaten track. With even a little knowledge of Spanish you will be able to befriend Colombians, and to exchange ideas and insights. So it's well worth learning the basics before you arrive – or take a course at the start of your trip (see below). Note that if you are intending to do any formal studies, you must obtain a student visa (see Visas and Immigration, page 51), which can be obtained once in the country. See the box on page 44 for some useful Spanish phrases.

Colombian Spanish

Colombians display a sometimes excessive inclination for politeness.

Nowhere is this more evident than in their language. Colombian Spanish is characterized by a punctilious, sometimes archaic, courteousness. Step inside any shop or taxi in the interior (the coast has its own rules, separate from the rest of the country) and you are likely to be bombarded by forms of address such as *'a la orden'* (at your service), *'que esté bien'* (may you be well), *'con mucho gusto'* (with pleasure); in departments such as Boyacá, you may even be addressed as *'su merced'* (your mercy).

And politeness isn't only for strangers. They even use the third person, formal *usted* (you) with their children.

Colombians speak little English, or any other foreign language, and it's up to the traveller to make the effort to learn some Spanish. Without any language skills, you will feel like someone peering through the keyhole at the country. But Colombians are so gregarious that with just a modest knowledge of the language they will talk at you for hours and the Colombian accent is one of the easiest to understand.

When first arriving in Colombia, it's a good idea to start your trip with some lessons at a language school. With that in mind, see the relevant sections through-out the book for listings of language schools.

Amerispan, 1334 Walnut St, 6th floor, Philadelphia, PA 19107, USA, T215-7511100/T1-800-879 6640, www.amerispan.com, offers Spanish immersion and volunteer programmes throughout Latin America, including in Bogotá, Cartagena and Medellín.

Media

Magazines

Magazines are partisan, best is probably *Semana*, www.semana.com and *Cambio*, www.cambio.com.co, owned by *El Tiempo* newspaper (see below). Bogotá has a couple of excellent English-language magazines, *El Mono* and *The City Paper*, www.thecity paperbogota.com, both distributed in hotels, hostels and bars around town.

Newspapers

Most of the major cities have a paper, usually with a regional bias.

Bogotá: *El Tiempo*, www.eltiempo.com.co, *El Espectador*, www.elespectador.com.co, *La República*, www.larepublica.com.co.
Cartagena: *El Heraldo*, www.elheraldo.com.co.
Cali: *El País*, www.elpais.com.co, *Nuevo Diario Occidente*, www.diariooccidente.com.co, *El Pueblo*.
Medellín: *El Mundo*, www.elmundo.com, *El Colombiano*, www.elcolombiano.com.

Radio

Colombia has a wealth of radio stations. Try **W Radio**, www.wradio.com.co, for up-to-the-minute news. You may be able to pick up the *BBC World Service* or *Voice of America* with a long-wave radio.

Television

The 2 principal television stations are **RCN** (state owned) and **Caracol** (private). Colombian TV is well known for its 'soaps' (*telenovelas*), which are exported to other Spanish-speaking countries. Satellite television with access to *CNN* and *CNN en Español* is available in even the cheapest hotels.

Money → US$1 = 2334.50 pesos (Nov 2008)

While this book was being researched, the exchange rate was US$1=1800 Colombian pesos, but by the time it went to press the rate had significantly changed (see above). To check the latest exchange rate see www.xe.com.

Colombia's currency is the *peso*. The following denominations of banknotes circulate: 50,000, 20,000, 10,000, 5000, 2000 and 1000, as well as coins worth 500, 200, 100 and 50. Large bills may be hard to use in small town so carry plenty of notes in small dominations (10,000 and below). Watch out for forged notes. The 50,000-peso note should smudge colour if it is real, if not, refuse to accept it.

There is a variety of ways for visitors to bring their funds to Colombia. You are strongly advised to combine 2 or more of these, so as not to be stuck if there are problems Always carry some US$ cash; they will work when and where all else fails.

ATMs and credit cards

As it is unwise to carry large quantities of cash in Colombia, credit cards are widely used, especially MasterCard and Visa; Diners Club is also accepted. American Express (Amex) is only accepted in expensive places in Bogotá. Many banks accept Visa (Visaplus and ATH logos) and Cirrus/MasterCard (Maestro and Multicolor logos) to advance pesos against the card, or through ATMs. There are ATMs for Visa and MasterCard everywhere but you may have to try several machines before you find one that works. All **Carulla** supermarkets have ATMs.

The ATM system is different to banks in Europe; the machine does not retain your card during the withdrawal. Insert your card for scanning and withdraw immediately, then proceed as normal. If your card is not immediately given back, do not proceed with the transaction and do not type in your pin number. Money has been stolen from accounts when cards have been retained.

ATMs dispense a frustratingly small amount of cash at a time. The maximum withdrawal is often 300,000 pesos (about US$160), which can accrue heavy bank charges over a period of time. For larger amounts try: **Davivienda** (500,000 per visit) and **Bancolombia** (400,000 per visit).

If planning to use credit and debit cards be sure to warn your bank back at home in advance as they think it has been stolen and block your card. Find out how much your bank charges for foreign withdrawals. It may be worthwhile opening an account with a bank that does not charge such as **Nationwide** in the UK.

Credit card loss or theft: Visa call collect to T+44 20-7937 8091 or F+44 17-3350 3670; MasterCard T0800-912 1303.

Note Only use ATMs in supermarkets, malls or where a security guard is present. Don't ask a taxi driver to wait while you use an ATM. Be particularly vigilant around Christmas time when thieves may be on the prowl.

Exchange

Cash (preferably US$ or euros) and TCs can, in theory, be exchanged in any bank, except the **Banco de la República**. In smaller places it's best to go early; take your passport. It can be difficult to buy and sell large amounts of sterling, even in Bogotá.

In most sizeable towns there are *casas de cambio* (exchange shops), which are quicker to use than banks but sometimes charge higher commission. US$ and euros are readily accepted but other international currencies are all but impossible to negotiate.

Hotels may give very poor rates of exchange, especially if you are paying in dollars. It is dangerous to change money on the streets and you may well be given counterfeit pesos. Also in circulation are counterfeit US$ bills. You must present your passport when changing money (a photocopy is not normally accepted).

When leaving Colombia, try to sell your pesos before or at the border, as it may be difficult to change them in other countries.

Traveller's cheques
When changing TCs, you will need to show your passport and you may be asked for a photocopy (take a supply of photocopies with you). The procedure is always slow, sometimes involving finger printing and photographs. The best currency to take is US$; preferably in small denominations. Sterling TCs are practically impossible to change. To change Amex TCs, use major banks; you may have to provide proof of purchase. Obtaining reimbursement for lost Amex TCs can be straightforward if you have the numbers recorded. You may be asked for proof of purchase, as well as a *diligencia de queja* (police certificate) explaining the circumstances of loss; apply to their offices in Bogotá at C 85, No 20-32, T593 4949, Mon-Fri 0800-1800, Sat 0900-1200. Banks may be unwilling to change TCs in remote areas, so always have some local currency (and US$ for emergencies). TCs are not normally accepted in hotels, restaurants or shops.

Cost of living
Prices are generally lower than Europe and North America for services and locally produced items, but more expensive for imported and luxury goods. Modest, basic accommodation will cost about US$10-12 per person per night in Bogotá, Cartagena, Santa Marta and colonial cities like Villa de Leiva, Popayán or Santa Fe de Antioquia, but a few dollars less elsewhere. A *comida corriente* (set lunch) costs about US$1.50-2 and breakfast US$1-1.75. A la carte meals are usually good value and fierce competition for transport keeps prices relatively low. Internet cafés charge US$1-4 per hr.

Opening hours
Business hours are generally Mon-Fri 0800-1200, 1400-1700, Sat 0900-1200. A longer siesta may be taken in small towns and tropical areas. Banks in larger cities do not close for lunch. Most businesses such as banks and airline offices close for official holidays while supermarkets and street markets may stay open. This depends a lot on where you are, so enquire locally.

Police and the law

You are required to carry your passport at all times, although this is seldom asked for outside border areas. In the event of a vehicle accident in which anyone is injured, all drivers involved are usually detained until blame has been established, which may take several weeks. Never offer to bribe a police officer. If an official suggests that a bribe must be paid before you can proceed on your way, be patient and they may relent.

In general, however, there are few hassles and most police are helpful to travellers.

Post and courier

There are 2 parallel services; **Deprisa**, operated by the national airline **Avianca**, and **4-72**, previously known as Correos de Colombia or Adpostal. Both have offices in major cities but only **4-72** can be found in small towns and rural areas. Both will take parcels for overseas. Prices are usually similar but not always identical for overseas mail. Anything important should be registered.

Servinetrega, **DHL** and **Fedex** also handle overseas parcels.

Safety

Travellers confirm that the vast majority of Colombians are polite, honest and will go out of their way to help visitors and make them feel welcome. In general, anti-gringo sentiments are rare.

Drugs and scams

Visitors should keep in mind that Colombia is part of a major cocaine-smuggling route and avoid any involvement. See Drugs, page 41, for further details.

There have been reports of travellers being victims of *burundanga*, a drug obtained from a white flower, native to Colombia. At present, the use of this drug appears to be confined to major cities. It is very nasty, almost impossible to see or smell. It leaves the victim helpless and at the will of the culprit. Usually, the victim is taken to ATMs to draw out money. Be wary of accepting cigarettes, food and drink from strangers at sports events or on buses. In bars watch your drinks very carefully.

Other Colombian scams may involve fake police and taxicabs and there are variations in most major cities.

Theft

Pickpockets, bag snatchers and bag slashers are always a hazard for tourists, especially in crowded areas such as markets or the downtown cores of major cities. There have been reports of assaults in the Candelaria area of Bogotá, especially at night. Keep alert and avoid swarms of people. You should likewise avoid deserted areas, such as parks or plazas after hours. Be especially careful arriving at or leaving from bus stations. As a rule these are often the most dangerous areas of most towns and are obvious places to catch people carrying a lot of important belongings.

Leave unnecessary documents and valuables at home. Those you bring should be carried in a money-belt or pouch, including your passport, airline tickets, credit and debit cards. Hide your main cash supply in several different places. If one stash is lost or stolen, you will still have the others to fall back on. Never carry valuables in an ordinary pocket, purse or day-pack. Keep cameras in bags or day-packs and generally out of sight. Do not wear expensive wrist watches or jewellery. If you are wearing a shoulder-bag or day-pack in a crowd, carry it in front of you.

Hotel security

The cheapest hotels are usually found near markets and bus stations but these are also the least safe areas of most Colombian towns. Look for something a little better if you can afford it, and if you must stay in a suspect area, try to return to your hotel before dark. If you trust your hotel, then you can leave any valuables you don't need in their safe-deposit box, but always keep an inventory of what you have deposited. If you don't trust the hotel, change to one you feel safe in. An alternative to leaving valuables with the hotel administration is to lock everything in your pack and secure that in your room; a light bicycle chain or cable and a small padlock will provide at least a psychological deterrent for would-be thieves. Even in an apparently safe hotel, never leave valuable objects strewn about your room.

Guerrillas

The government has had considerable success in its fight against left-wing guerrillas such as the **FARC**, but the internal armed conflict in Colombia is almost impossible to predict and the security situation changes from day to day. For this reason, it is essential to consult regularly with locals for up-to-date information. Taxi and bus drivers, local journalists, soldiers at checkpoints, hotel owners and Colombians who actually travel around their country are usually good sources of reliable information. Since 2002, incidents of kidnapping and homicide rates in major cities have been declining. Travelling overland between towns, especially during the holiday season and bank holiday weekends, has in general become much safer due to increased military and police presence along main roads. However, the government has launched a major offensive against the guerrillas (especially in the south) and in some areas fighting between the armed forces and guerrilla groups has intensified.

Women travellers

Unaccompanied foreign women may be objects of much curiosity. Don't be unduly scared – or flattered. Avoid arriving anywhere after dark. Remember that for a single woman a taxi at night can be as dangerous as wandering around alone. If you accept a social invitation, make sure that someone knows the address and the time you left. Ask if you can bring a friend (even if you do not). As elsewhere, watch your alcohol intake at parties with locals, especially if you are on your own. A good general rule is always look confident and pretend you know where you are going, even if you do not. Don't tell strangers where you are staying.

Student travellers

If you are in full-time education you are entitled to an **International Student Identity Card (ISIC)**, which is sold by student travel offices and agencies in 70 countries. The ISIC may give you special prices on transport and access to a variety of other concessions and services, although these are relatively uncommon in Colombia. Teachers are entitled to an **International Teacher Identity Card (ITIC)**. Both are available from www.isic.org. If undertaking any form of study in Colombia, you will need a student visa (see Visas and immigration, page 51).

Tax

Departure tax Departure tax is US$33, and is not included in any airline tickets. Visitors who stay longer than 2 months pay a reduced fee of US$23. International Airport Tax and the Revenue stamp can be paid in Colombian pesos, at the equivalent current exchange rate for IATA dollars for the day.

VAT/IVA 16%. Ask for an official receipt if you want it documented. Some hotels and restaurants add IVA onto bills, but foreigners do not officially have to pay (see Sleeping, page 31).

Telephone → *Country code +57.*

National and international calls can be made from the many public phone offices found throughout all major cities and even in rural towns. You are assigned a cabin, place your calls, and pay on the way out. There is usually a screen that tells you how much you are spending. Prices vary considerably. You can also make calls from street vendors who hire out their mobile phones (usually signposted '*minutos*').

It is relatively inexpensive to buy a pay-as-you go SIM card for your mobile phone. Calls are on the whole cheap but there is a complicated system for making calls from mobiles. For calling landlines, 03 must be affixed before the area code and number. For calling mobile numbers, the 0 is dropped.

Time

GMT -6 all year round.

Tipping

A voluntary charge is added to most bills but you can ask to have this taken off if you are not happy with the service.

Tourist information

Contact details for tourist offices and other information resources are given in the relevant sections throughout the text. The Colombian government is making a big push to promote tourism and most *alcaldías* (municipalities) have some sort of tourist office, whose staff are invariably very helpful but the qualifications of staff, resources available and standards of service vary enormously in smaller towns. Keep your expectations modest and you may be pleasantly surprised.

Websites

www.colombianhostels.com Network of Colombian backpackers' hostels.
www.clubhaciendasdelcafe.com Extensive list of coffee *fincas* in the Zona Cafetera.
www.conexcol.com Colombian search engine covering many topics.
www.despegar.com Cheap flights website for travel within Latin America.
www.gobiernoenlinea.gov.co Government website with information on new laws and citizen rights, in Spanish and English.
www.hosteltrail.com/colombia Reviews of hostels, tour agencies and destinations.
www.ideam.gov.co Weather and climate information.
www.igac.gov.co Instituto Geográfico Agustín Codazzi Official maps of Colombia.
www.invias.gov.co Instituto Nacional de Vias, (National Road Institute). Current details on the state of the roads with maps etc.
www.lab.org.uk Latin American Bureau site, based in the UK. Publishes books and holds talks on Latin American issues.
www.poorbuthappy.com/colombia Reliable information on travel, jobs and safety, in English.
www.posadasturisticas.com.co Information on places to stay in Colombia, including the Chocó.
www.presidencia.gov.co The government website.
www.quehubo.com Listings site.

Tour operators

In the UK
4starSouth America, T0800-011-2959 www.southamerica.travel.
Colombia57 Tours, Travel and Logistics, T0800 789157 (UK free phone), www.colombia57.com.
Condor Journeys and Adventures, T01700-841 318, www.condorjourneys-adventures.com.
Dragoman, T01728-861 133, www.dragoman.co.uk.

Exodus Travels, Grange Mills, T0845-863 9600, www.exodus.co.uk.
Exploratory Overland Expeditions, T01564-829 242, www.eoe.org.uk.
Explore, T0845-013 1537, www.explore.co.uk.
Intrepid Travel, T0203-147 7777, www.intrepidtravel.com.
Journey Latin America, T020-8747 8315/ T0161-832 1441, www.journeylatin america.co.uk.
LATA (Latin American Travel Association), info@lata.org, www.lata.org. Useful country information and listing of UK operators specializing in Latin America.
Trips Worldwide, T0117-311 4400, www.tripsworldwide.co.uk.

In North America
4starSouth America, T1800-747 4540, www.southamerica.travel.
GAP Adventures, T1800-708 7761, www.gapadventures.com.

In South America
Surtrek, Av Amazonas 897 y Wilson, Quito, Ecuador, T593-2250 0530, www.surtrek.com. Offers customized private group and individual adventure tours throughout South America.

Visas and immigration

When entering the country, you will be given a copy of your DIAN (customs) luggage declaration. Keep it safe; you may be asked for it when you leave. If you receive an entry card when flying in and lose it while in Colombia, apply to any **DAS** office (see Visa extensions, below) who should issue one and re-stamp your passport for free. Normally, passports are scanned by a computer and no landing card is issued, but passports still must be stamped on entry. Note that to leave Colombia you must get an exit stamp from the **DAS**. They often do not have offices at the small border towns, so try to get your stamp in a main city.

It is highly recommended that you photocopy your passport details, including entry stamps which, for added insurance, you can have witnessed by a notary. Always carry a photocopy of your passport with you, as you may be asked for identification. This is a valid substitute for most purposes though not, for example, for cashing TCs or drawing cash across a bank counter. Generally acceptable for identification (eg to enter government buildings) is a driving licence, provided it is plastic, of credit card size and has a photograph. For more information, check with your consulate.

Tourist visas
Tourists are normally given 90 days permission to stay on entry, though this is not automatic. If you intend to stay more than 30 days, make sure you ask for longer.

Nationals of the Republic of Ireland, countries of former Eastern Europe (except Romania) and the Middle East (except Israel), Asian countries (except Japan, South Korea, Malaysia, Phillipines, Indonesia and Singapore), Haiti, Nicaragua, and all African countries need a visa to visit Colombia. At the time of writing, visa restrictions for nationals of the Republic of Ireland had been lifted, but in this and any other cases of doubt, check regulations before leaving your home country. Visas are issued only by Colombian consulates. When a visa is required you must present a valid passport, 3 photographs, the application form (in duplicate), US$48 or equivalent (price varies according to nationality), onward tickets, and a photocopy of all the documents (allow 2 weeks maximum).

Visa extensions
If not granted at the border, an extension (*salvoconducto*) can be applied for at the DAS (security police) office in any major city. The *salvoconducto* is only issued once for a period of 30 days and is usually processed within 24 hrs. It is best to apply 2-3 days

before your visa expires. Bring 2 recent photos and copies of your passport. If you overstay on any type of visa, you will be charged a fine, minimum US$55 up to US$800. The DAS office in Bogotá is C 100, No 11B-27, T601 7200, www.das.gov.co (see page 88). Arrive early in the morning, expect long queues and a painfully slow bureaucratic process. DAS does not accept cash payments; these are made at the appropriate bank with special payments slips.

Alternatively, if you have good reason to stay longer (eg for medical treatment), apply at the embassy in your home country before leaving. If you wish to stay between 7-10 days longer on a tourist visa, go to a DAS office with your onward ticket and they will usually grant you a free extension on the spot. An onward ticket may be asked for at land borders or Bogotá international airport. You may be asked to prove that you have sufficient funds for your stay.

Student and business visas
If you are going to take a Spanish course, you must have a student visa. You may not study on a tourist visa. A student visa can be obtained while in Colombia on a tourist visa. Proof of sufficient funds is necessary (US$400-600 for a 6-month stay is usually deemed sufficient). You must be first enrolled in a course from a bona fide university to apply for a student visa.

Various business and other temporary visas are needed for foreigners who have to reside in Colombia for a length of time. The Ministerio de Relaciones Exteriores (not DAS), Cra 13, No 93-68, of 203, T6400974/T6408576, Mon-Fri 0730-1200, processes student and some work visas. In general, Colombian work visas can only be obtained outside Colombia at the appropriate consulate and or embassy.

You must register work and student visas at a DAS office within 15 days of obtaining them, otherwise you will be liable to pay a hefty fine. Visas must be used within 3 months. Supporting documentary requirements for visas change frequently. Check with the appropriate consulate in good time before your trip.

Weights and measures

Colombia uses the metric system.

Wildlife and national parks

National parks
See also Background, page 380.
National parks are administered by Unidad Administrativa Especial del Sistema de Parques Nacionales Naturales (UAESPNN). The main office is at the Ministerio del Medio Ambiente, Oficina de Ecoturismo, 4th floor, Banco Agrario building, Carrera 10, No 20-30, Bogotá, T243 3004, www.parques nacionales.gov.co, 0800-1745. Staff can provide information about facilities and accommodation, and have maps. If you intend to visit the parks, this is a good place to start and ask for up-to-date details and to obtain a permit (see below). The *National Parks Guide* is attractive and informative, US$50, providing lavishly illustrated scientific information. There is a library and research unit (*Centro de Documentación*) for more information. Permits are obtainable here and at the many offices near the parks themselves.

Permits are required to visit the parks (usually free) and admissions is charged at park entrances. Some prices vary according to high and low seasons. High season includes: weekends, Jun-Jul, Dec-Jan, public holidays and Semana Santa.

Other useful address include: Asosiación Red Colombiana de Reservas Naturales de la Sociedad Civil, C 2 A, No 26-103, San Fernando, Cali, T2558 5046, a network of privately-owned nature reserves that work with local people to build a sustainable model of environmentally friendly tourism. Instituto Colombiano de Antropología e

Historia, Calle 12, No 2-41, T1286002,
Mon-Fri 0800-1700, also has
useful information.

Volunteering

Volunteers can apply to work as park rangers
at some national parks; details are available
from the UAESPNN office in Bogotá (see
above). There are 20 or so parks participating
in the scheme (minimum 30 days);
Corales del Rosario National Park has been
particularly recommended. If you have a
specific or professional scientific interest
and would like to study in one of the parks,
bring a letter from an educational or
research institution from your home
country indicating your subject of interest.

Websites

www.minambiente,gov.co Colombia
Ministry of the Environment. Environmental
legislation and general information.

www.humboldt.org.co Site of Institute
Von Humboldt, probably the most important
environment research organization in
Colombia. An excellent site with descriptions
of the different ecosystems in the country
and projects with ethnic communities.
www.conservation.org Conservation
International site. Click on the 'Andean
Programme' for details about projects
in Colombia.
www.iucn.org International Union for
the Conservation of Nature. One of the
best sites for information on biodiversity
protection worldwide with links to South
America/Colombia including projects
in protected areas and national parks.
www.coama.org.co Details of conservation
projects in the Amazon and Orinoco regions.
www.natura.org.co Fundación Natura
for scientific information on several
national parks where they have projects.
www.survival-international.org
Information on indigenous communities
in Colombia.

Contents

56 Ins and outs
61 Background

62 Sights
62 La Candelaria
71 Monserrate
72 Downtown Bogotá
75 North of the centre
76 Listings

90 Around Bogotá
90 Southwest to Parque
Natural Chicaque
90 Bogotá to Honda
91 Guatavita
92 Zipaquirá
93 Listings

Footprint features

54 Don't miss ...
69 Anantas Mockus
70 Emeralds
73 Cementerio Central
92 The legend of El Dorado
93 The salt cathedral
of Zipaquirá

Bogotá & around

At a glance

🚌 **Getting around** TransMilenio
or taxi in Bogotá. Bus to outlying
areas.

🕐 **Time required** 3-4 days to
explore city highlights, 1-2 weeks
for excursions.

☀ **Weather** Cool and rainy most of
year in Bogotá, warmer in low-lying
regions around.

✘ **When not to go** Good all year.

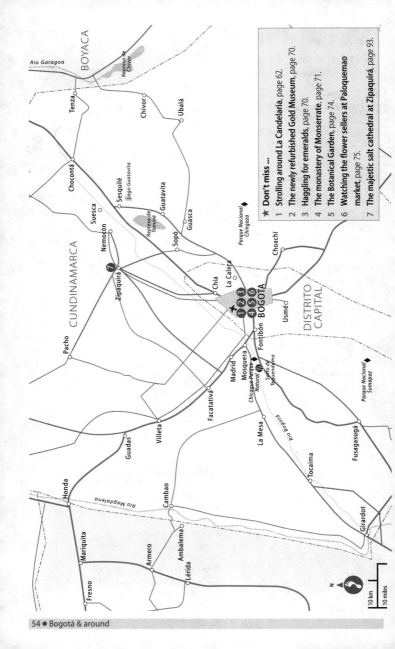

BOYACA

Río Garagoa

Represa de Chivor

Tenza

Chivor

Ubalá

Chocontá

CUNDINAMARCA

Suesca

Sesquilé
(Lago Guatavita)

Guatavita

Guasca

Nemocón

Represa de Tomine

Sopó

Pacho

Zipaquirá

Chía

La Calera

Parque Nacional Chingaza

Choachí

Fontibón

BOGOTA

Usmé

DISTRITO CAPITAL

Madrid

Mosquera

Chicaque Parque Natural

Salto de Tequendama

Facatativá

Villeta

La Mesa

Río Bogotá

Tocaima

Parque Nacional Sumapaz

Fusagasugá

Guadas

Honda

Río Magdalena

Cambao

Girardot

Mariquita

Armero

Ambalema

Lérida

Fresno

N

10 km
10 miles

Don't miss ...

1 Strolling around La Candelaria, page 62.
2 The newly refurbished Gold Museum, page 70.
3 Haggling for emeralds, page 70.
4 The monastery of Monserrate, page 71.
5 The Botanical Garden, page 74.
6 Watching the flower sellers at Paloquemao market, page 93.
7 The majestic salt cathedral at Zipaquirá, page 93.

Colombia's capital is a vast, sprawling, traffic-choked metropolis set high in a valley surrounded by the mountains of the Cordillera Oriental. Thanks to some enterprising local governance, Bogotá has undergone something of a renaissance in the past 15 years and has become one of the most exciting capitals in Latin America, its nightlife, dining, fashion and culture equal to anything that Buenos Aires or Rio de Janeiro can offer. However, it's a city that still suffers from shocking extremes of wealth and poverty, a city where air-conditioned, tinted-windowed cars stand bumper to bumper with rubbish-collecting horse and carts and where the conspicuous consumption on show in the enormous, flashy shopping centres and the gated communities of the north of the city stand in stark contrast to the depressing shanty towns to the south and east.

To the north is effectively a new city, characterized by the opulent restaurants, bars and nightclubs of the Zona G, Zona T and Parque 93.

The old centre is La Candelaria, a rabbit warren of colonial buildings, narrow, cobbled streets, theatres, universities and countless cafés buzzing with intellectual debate. La Candelaria is home to one of Latin America's most impressive cultural attractions, the Gold Museum, a dazzling display of pre-Columbian treasures. Outside the noisy, polluted centre there are numerous attractions and pretty towns to visit, perfect for day or weekend excursions, most impressive of which is the extraordinary salt cathedral at Zipaquirá.

Getting there → *Phone code: 1. Population: 8,500,000. Altitude 2650 m. Average temperature 14°C.*

Air The International airport has two terminals, **El Dorado** and the **Puente Aéreo**, the latter 1 km before the main terminal. Both are on Avenida El Dorado. Most international flights arrive at El Dorado; however some **Avianca** flights from the USA come into the Puente Aéreo. The arrival procedure is much the same at both terminals. If you are changing planes in Bogotá, there is complimentary transport between terminals.

El Dorado ① *T4251000*, has comfortable departure areas where the usual duty-free shops are of a high standard. There are many snack bars and restaurants on first floor, with Wi-Fi points throughout. International calls can be made from **Telecom** on the first floor, which is open until 2100, and accepts credit cards. There is a post office in main arrivals lounge and two tourist offices run by the city tourist authority, one on the right near the international arrivals exit and the other in a similar position near the domestic arrivals exit. They are open daily during normal hours. Hotel and general information is available. Exchange rates are marginally less favourable than in the city, but pesos cannot be changed back into dollars at the airport without receipts. The **Banco Popular** by the barrier changes traveller's cheques (they may request copy of purchase receipt) and there is a *casa de cambios* alongside, which changes cash only. They may not be open at holiday times. When closed, ask airport police where to change money. Car hire counters are opposite the *casa de cambios*. Allow at least two hours for checking in and going through the comprehensive security. There is no baggage deposit. You must reconfirm all flights around 48 hours before flight time. Use only uniformed porters.

Puente Aéreo has ATMs which accept international credit cards. There is a **Presto** fast-food restaurant, **Telecom** with international call facilities but no exchange service and an internet cafe. Otherwise, services are similar to those at El Dorado.

The taxi fare from airport to city is a fixed charge, US$10, more at night and early morning. Make sure you get a registered taxi, normally yellow, found to your right as you leave the main terminal. You can also go left to the far end of the main terminal to domestic arrivals where you can get a ticket, from the booth just inside the building, which will fix the price of your journey – recommended. There is a separate taxi rank outside. You will be expected to tip if you are helped with any luggage. Unofficial taxis are not advisable. Use only uniformed porters. There are *colectivos* (US$1 plus luggage per person) to the centre. In the city centre take buses and black and red *colectivos* marked 'Aeropuerto' to the airport. Watch belongings inside and outside airport, especially at night. ›› *See Getting around, below and Transport page 85, for full details.*

Bus The long-distance bus terminal is **Terminal de Transportes** ① *near Av Boyacá at C 33B, No 69-59, there is also access from Cra 68.* To get into town take buses marked 'Centro' or 'Germania'. The 'Germania' bus goes up through the centre and La Candelaria. Taxi fares from the terminal to the city are about US$5, depending on the destination, with a surcharge at night and on public holidays. Go to the appropriate exit and obtain a slip from a vending booth, which shows the exact fare to your destination. Do not take unofficial taxis, which are normally touting for particular hotels.

Getting around
Visitors should not be too active for the first 24 hours. Some people get dizzy at Bogotá's altitude. Be careful with food and alcohol for a day or two. Walking in the downtown area

and in Candelaria is recommended, as distances are short and the traffic is heavy. North Bogotá is more spacious and buses and taxis are more convenient. Between the two and elsewhere, transport is necessary.

TransMilenio This is Bogotá's highly successful new traffic-busting transport system, inaugurated in 2001, consisting of articulated buses on dedicated lanes. It can be a little baffling to work out at first but is a quick, cheap way to get around once you get the hang of it. It runs north to south along Autopista Norte and Avenida Caracas with branches to various destinations in the west of the city. There is a spur along Calle 80 and a link to La Candelaria (Parque de Los Periodistas on Avenida Jiménez de Quesada with a stop at the Gold Museum). *Corriente* services stop at all principal road intersections while *expresos* have limited stops. The journey from the centre to the north takes less than 30 minutes. Journey cost US$0.65. Using the TransMilenio is a good, quick way of getting around the city but it tends to be crowded. See www.transmilenio.gov.co for more details.

Local bus Bus fares are from US$0.55 up, depending on length of route and time of day. Most buses have day/night tariff advertised in the window. *Busetas* charge a little more. There are some red and white *ejecutivo* routes with plush(!) seats, at US$0.40. Fares are a bit higher at night and on holidays. Urban buses are not good for sightseeing because you will most likely be standing.

Car rental Whilst not cheap, if you are in the city for several days this could be a good option. ▸▸ *See details in Transport, page 85.*

Taxi Taxis are the best way to get between sectors of the city, and at night are recommended for all journeys. All taxis have meters: insist that they are used. The starting charge is US$2 and an average fare from North Bogotá to the centre US$8. ▸▸ *See details in Transport, page 85.*

Orientation

The Calles (abbreviated 'C', or 'Cll') run at right angles across the Carreras ('Cra' or 'K'). It is easy enough to find a place once the address system, which is used throughout Colombia, is understood. The address C 13, No 12-45 would be the building on Calle 13 between Carrera 12 and 13 at 45 paces from Carrera 12; however *transversales* (Tra) and *diagonales* (Diag) can complicate the system. The Avenidas (Av), broad and important streets, may be either Calles (like 26) or Carreras (like 14) or both (like 19 which is Calle in the Centre and Carrera in the North). Avenida Jiménez de Quesada, one of Bogotá's most well known streets, owes its lack of straightness to having been built over a river-bed (which, incidentally was opened up again in 2000). The Calles in the south of the city are marked 'Sur' or 'S'; this is an integral part of the address and must be quoted.

The mountains of the eastern cordillera lie east, a useful landmark for getting your bearings. Most of the interesting parts of the city follow the line of the cordillera in a north-south line. La Candelaria, full of character, occupies the area bounded by Avenida Jiménez de Quesada, Calle 6, Carrera 3 and Carrera 10. There is some modern infill but many of the houses are well preserved in colonial style, of one or two storeys with tiled roofs, projecting eaves, wrought ironwork and carved balconies. The main colonial churches, palaces and museums are concentrated around and above the Plaza Bolívar. Some hotels are found in this part, more along the margins, eg Avenida Jiménez de

Quesada. Downtown Bogotá runs in a band northeast along Carrera 7 from Avenida Jiménez de Quesada to Calle26. It is a thorough mix of styles including modern towers and run-down colonial and later buildings, together with a few notable exceptions. The

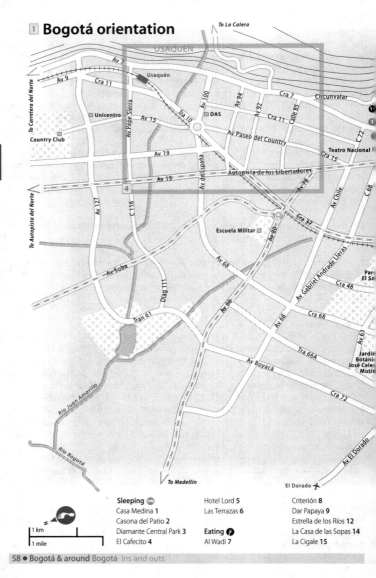

1 Bogotá orientation

To La Calera

USAQUÉN

Av 7

Av 9   Cra 11

Usaquén

Cra 7   Circunvalar

Av 100   Av 94   Av 92   Cra 11   Calle 85

Unicentro   Av 15   Tra 10   DAS

Country Club

Av Paseo del Country

Teatro Nacional

Av 19   Cra 15   C 72

Av del España

Av 13   Autopista de los Libertadores

Av 127   C 116   Av 78   Av Chile   C 68

Escuela Militar   Cra 37

Av 80

Av Suba   Av 68   Av Gabriel Andrade Lleras   Cra 48   Parc El Sa

Diag 111   Cra 68   Av 63

Tran 61   Av 80   Av 58   Jardí Botáni José Cele Mutis

Tra 66A

Av Boyacá   Cra 72

Río Juan Amarillo

Río Bogotá

To Medellín

El Dorado   Av El Dorado

To Carretera del Norte

To Autopista del Norte

Av Pepe Sierra

1 km
1 mile

Sleeping 🛏
Casa Medina **1**
Casona del Patio **2**
Diamante Central Park **3**
El Cafecito **4**

Hotel Lord **5**
Las Terrazas **6**

Eating 🍴
Al Wadi **7**

Criterión **8**
Dar Papaya **9**
Estrella de los Ríos **12**
La Casa de las Sopas **14**
La Cigale **15**

streets are full of life and can be paralysed by traffic at busy times. The pavements can be congested too, particularly Carrera 7 and Avenida 19. From Calle 50 to Calle 68 is El Chapinero, once the outskirts of the city and now a commercial district with a sprinkling

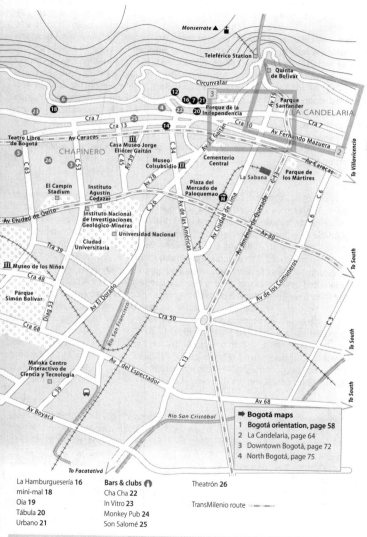

Bogotá maps
1 Bogotá orientation, page 58
2 La Candelaria, page 64
3 Downtown Bogotá, page 72
4 North Bogotá, page 75

La Hamburguesería 16	**Bars & clubs**	Theatrón 26
mini-mal 18	Cha Cha 22	
Oia 19	In Vitro 23	TransMilenio route
Tábula 20	Monkey Pub 24	
Urbano 21	Son Salomé 25	

of old, large, middle-class mansions. It also doubles up as the epicentre of Bogotá's thriving gay scene, with many bars and clubs. Next to the National Park, along La Séptima is La Merced, a cluster of English country-style houses. A few blocks further south, along Carrera 4 between Calle 25 and Calle 27, is the Bohemian area of La Macarena, formerly inhabited by struggling artists but now becoming increasingly fashionable with many good restaurants and bars. Beyond Calle 60, the main city continues north to a comparatively new district, North Bogotá, which is split into various points of interest. Most of the best hotels, restaurants and embassies are in this area, which is regarded as the safest in Bogotá. Between Carrera 4 and Carrera 5 and Calle 68 and Calle 71 is what is known as the Zona G (for 'gourmet'), home to some of Bogotá best (and most expensive) restaurants. The T-shaped pedestrianized area made up by Calle 83 and Carrera 13 is Bogotá's Zona Rosa (also known as the Zona T) with many fashionable bars, clubs and restaurants. Further north the streets around Parque 93 have some of the most expensive bars and restaurants in the city, while at the very limits of the city, off Carrera 7 between Calle 117 and Calle119, is Usaquen, formerly a satellite town of Bogotá with a pleasant plaza, and a popular evening and weekend excursion for *rolos* (as *bogotanos* are sometimes called), looking to get a break from the metropolis.

Safety
As in any city of this size, take care not to tempt thieves by careless display of money or valuables. Also, anyone approaching you with questions, offering to sell something or making demands, may well be a thief or a con-artist. Beware, they may be well-dressed and plausible, may pose as plain-clothes officials, and often work in pairs. Read the Safety section in Essentials carefully and the comments in the various paragraphs below. Especially recommended is to take taxis, preferably radio taxis, if travelling in the city at night. Also, do not forget to watch where you are going, especially in the wet. Potholes in both roads and pavements can be very deep. La Candelaria district is relatively safe by day, but there have been several reports of muggings and robberies by night. You may be hassled by beggars. If returning to your hotel at night, take a taxi and keep the doors locked. Watch out for con-men in and near the Plaza de Bolívar. Best to ignore anyone who approaches – a wave of the hand is sufficient.

If you have problems with theft or other forms of crime, contact a **Centro de Atención Inmediata (CAI)** ① *downtown C 60 y Cra 9, T217 7472, La Candelaria, Cra 7 y C6, there are many offices throughout the city, or T156, for assistance.* Only at a CAI police office is it possible to report a theft and get the relevant paperwork, not at other police stations.

Tourist information
There are several tourist-information kiosks dotted around the city. **La Candelaria** ① *Plaza Bolívar, Cra 8, No 9-83, T3274916, ext 173, daily 0800-1800.* Also has internet connection with first 15 minutes free for tourists. Good local guide books and maps. **El Dorado airport** ① *International terminal T4139053, daily 0900-2100. National terminal T4138732, daily 0900-2100.* **Bus station** ① *Módulo 5, local 127, T2954460, 0700-1700.* **Centro Internacional** ① *Cra 13, No 26-62, T3374413, 0700-1700.* **Unicentro shopping centre** ① *Entrada 8, 1st floor, T6121967, daily 0900-2100.* There is also the **Colombia Tourist Board – Proexport** ① *C 28, No13A-15, piso 35, T5600100, www.visitcolombia.com.*

The National Parks office ⓘ *Cra 10, No 20-30, T2433004, www.parques nacionales.gov.co*, though for accommodation in many of them you must contact Aviatur who hold concessions in the most popular locations, www.concesionesparquesnat urales.com. Full details are given on page 51.

Best time to visit
Bogotá is an all-year-round-city. Holiday times such as Easter and Christmas are quiet, but attractions are closed, as many are on Monday if they have been open over the weekend.

Climate Bogotá has a temperate climate; hot in the middle of the day but normally much cooler at night, when a light sweater or even a coat may be required. Theoretically there is a wet season from April to November but there is not much rain in the middle of the year and there can be showers at any time.

Background
The city of Santa Fe de Bogotá (also written Santafé and with or without accent) was founded by Gonzalo Jiménez de Quesada on 6 August 1538 in territory inhabited by the indigenous Muisca. The name of the king, Bacatá, was adopted for the new city. In 1575, Philip II of Spain confirmed the city's title as the 'very noble and very loyal city of Santafé de Bogotá', adopting the name of Jiménez de Quesada's birthplace of Santa Fe in Andalucía. It was the capital of the Viceroyalty of Nueva Granada in 1740. After independance in 1819, Bogotá became the

capital of Gran Colombia, a confederation of what is today Venezuela, Ecuador, Panama and Colombia and remained capital of Colombia as the other republics separated.

For much of the 19th century, Bogotá suffered from isolation in economic terms mainly due to distance and lack of good transport. Population in 1850 was no more than 50,000. By 1900, however, a tram system unified the city and railways connected it to the Río Magdalena. Migrants from the Colombian countryside flocked to the city and by 1950, the population was 500,000, and the move to develop the north of the city accelerated. Since then it has re-emphasised its position as the dominant city in Colombia.

The official name of the city is now simply Bogotá, the urban area of the metropolis is known as the Distrito Capital (DC), and it is also the capital of the surrounding Department of Cundinamarca.

Sights

La Candelaria

The Plaza de Bolívar, marked out by the city's founders (as Plaza Mayor), is at the heart of the city. Around the Plaza are the narrow streets and mansions of the **Barrio La Candelaria**, the historical and cultural heart of the city occupying the area of some 70 city blocks to the south of Avenida Jiménez de Quesada, north of Calle 6 and east of Carrera 10 (see map). Because the main commercial and residential focus of the city moved down the hill and to the north early on, much of the original colonial town remains. It is one of the best-preserved major historical centres in Latin America, and as such has attracted artists, writers and academics to fill the sector with theatres, libraries and universities, for which Colombia has a very high reputation in the Spanish-speaking world. There are some delightful sights, especially the colonial houses with their barred windows, carved doorways, red-tiled roofs and sheltering eaves. The local authorities are helping to preserve and renovate properties and the cobbled streets, a feature of Candelaria. Many of the best of Bogotá's churches and colonial buildings are in this district. Some hotels are found in this part, more along the margins, for example Avenida Jiménez de Quesada. The streets are relatively uncrowded and safe, although care should be exercised after dark. West of Carrera 10 and south of Calle 6 is seedier and not recommended for pedestrians. **Note** Most museums and tourist attraction are open Tuesday to Sunday around 0900-1700, but may be closed for a period in the middle of the day. Times are frequently changed. Entry is often free but may be a modest US$1 or so. Very little is open on Mondays. The best time to visit the churches is before or after Mass (not during). Mass times are 0700, 1200 and 1800.

Plaza Bolívar and around

Plaza de Bolívar is the central square of Bogotá, with a statue of the Liberator at its centre. The cathedral stands on the northeast corner of the square. The first was completed in 1553 to replace a small chapel where Fray Domingo de las Casas said the first mass in Bogotá. The present building was constructed between 1807 and 1823. It has a fine, spacious interior, redecorated (1998) in cream and gold with high ceilings across three naves. There are lateral chapels in classical style, a notable choir loft of carved walnut, wrought silver on the altar of the Chapel of El Topo and elaborate candelabras. Treasures and relics include paintings attributed to Ribera and the banner brought by Jiménez de Quesada to Bogotá in the sacristy, which also houses portraits of past Archbishops. There are monuments to Jiménez and to Antonio Nariño inside the cathedral. In one of the chapels near the altar is buried **Gregorio Vázquez de Arce y Ceballos** (1638-1711), the most notable painter in colonial Colombia. A number of his paintings can be seen in the Cathedral, which is open most days from 0900-1200. Next to it is the **Capilla del Sagrario** ① *Cra 7, No 10-40, T2436626*, built at the end of the 17th century. There are two aisles with wooden balconies above and a fine red/gilt ceiling and screen. The inside of the dome was painted by Ricardo Acevedo Bernal. There are several paintings by Gregorio Vázquez de Arce y Ceballos. Mass is celebrated at 0800 and 1700 during the week. Next door is the **Palacio Arzobispal** ① *Cra 7, No 10-20*, with splendid bronze doors, and opposite, at the bottom of Calle 10, is **Colegio de San Bartolomé** ① *Cra 7, No 9-96*, originally Bogotá's oldest university, founded in 1573, and where many notable Colombians of the past were educated, including Antonio Nariño, Antonio Ricaurte and General Santander. The imposing early-20th-century classical building, now an important secondary school, fits appropriately into the corner of Plaza Bolívar.

On the south side of the Plaza de Bolívar is the Capitolio Nacional, originally the site of the Viceroy's Palace. In 1846, Thomas Reed, born in Tenerife and educated in England, was commissioned to build the Capitolio, but it was fraught with difficulties from the start. Construction was suspended in 1851, to be recommenced in 1880 by Pietro Cantini, who finished the façade to the original design in 1911. The rest was finally 'finished' in 1927 by Alberto Manrique Martín. Many other architects and engineers were involved at various times. In fact it is still being restored, now by the Instituto Nacional de Vías (National Road Institute), which has a department that specializes in maintaining national monuments. The Capitolio houses several Ministries, the Supreme Court, Consejo de Estado and Congress. On the corner of Carrera 8/Calle 10 is the **Casa de Los Comuneros** ① *Cra 8 No 9-83, can be visited during normal business hours.* The building dates from the 17th century when it housed commercial premises with living quarters above and typical wrought-iron balconies. There are also preserved examples of later modifications to the building from the 19th and 20th centuries. It now belongs to the **Instituto Distrital de Cultura y Turismo** and includes the main tourist office of the city.

The **Alcaldía** ① *Cra 8, No 10-65*, Bogotá's city hall, is on the west side of the Plaza. It is known as the Lievano Building, and is in the French style of the early 20th century. Until 1960, the ground floor galleries were business premises. On the north side of the Plaza you will see the **Palacio de Justicia**. The former building was badly damaged when the Army recaptured it from the M19 guerrillas who attacked and took it over in 1985. Eventually it was pulled down and a new one was completed in April 1999.

On the northeast corner of Calle 11/Carrera 7 is the Museo 20 de Julio, also known as the **Casa del Florero** ① *Calle 11, No 6-94, T2826647, Tue-Fri, 0900-1700, Sat and Sun 1000-1600, US$1.70, reduction for ISIC cards,* in a colonial house, which houses the famous flower vase that featured in the 1810 revolution. The owner of the vase, the Spaniard José González Llorente refused to lend the vase for the decoration of the main table at an event in honour of Antonio Villavicencio, a prominent 'Creole'. This snub was used as a pretext by the Creoles for the rebellion against the Spaniards which led to the independence nine years later of Nueva Granada. A copy of the Declaration of Independence is on display. The museum has collections of the Independence War period, including documents and engravings and some fine portraits of Simón Bolívar. Two doors above the museum (Calle 11 No 6-42) is an attractive inner courtyard, now a restaurant, which is worth a look.

Just off the plaza is **Iglesia de San Ignacio** ① *C 10 No 6-35*, built by the Jesuits between 1605 and 1635 with plans from Rome. Over the choir and the galleries is a rich ceiling in Moorish style and emeralds from Muzo in Boyacá were used in the monstrance. Paintings by Gregorio Vázquez de Arce y Ceballos are in the nave. Opposite is the **Plazuela de Rufino Cuervo**, one of the few original squares in Candelaria, a garden of trees and flowers with balconied buildings around and the dome of the Capilla del Sagrario visible above. The Palacio Arzobispal (Cardinal's Palace) is to the left. To the right of the square is The **Museo de Trajes Regionales** ① *C 10, No 6-36, T2826531, Mon-Fri 0930-1630, Sat 1000-1600*, with a display of present and past regional dress, and a collection of hand-woven textiles showing pre-Columbian techniques. This is the house where Manuela Sáenz, Bolívar's mistress, lived. At the back of the square is **La Imprenta**, where Antonio Nariño's translation of Thomas Paine's 'Rights of Man' was published in 1794. This had a

2 La Candelaria

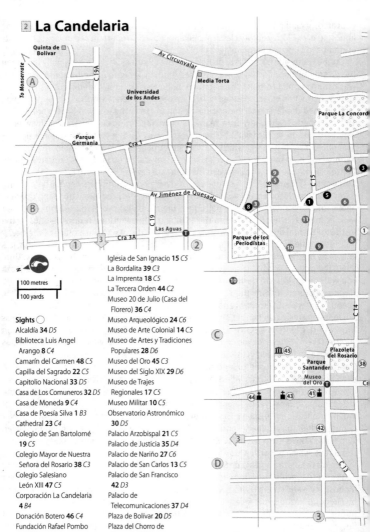

Sights ○

Alcaldía **34** D5
Biblioteca Luis Angel
  Arango **8** C4
Camarín del Carmen **48** C5
Capilla del Sagrado **22** C5
Capitolio Nacional **33** D5
Casa de Los Comuneros **32** D5
Casa de Moneda **9** C4
Casa de Poesía Silva **1** B3
Cathedral **23** C4
Colegio de San Bartolomé
  19 C5
Colegio Mayor de Nuestra
  Señora del Rosario **38** C3
Colegio Salesiano
  León XIII **47** C5
Corporación La Candelaria
  4 B4
Donación Botero **46** C4
Fundación Rafael Pombo
  11 C5
Iglesia de La Candelaria **7** B4
Iglesia de la Veracruz **43** C3
Iglesia de Nuestra Señora
  María del Carmen **25** C5
Iglesia de San Agustín **26** C6
Iglesia de San Francisco **41** C3

Iglesia de San Ignacio **15** C5
La Bordalita **39** C3
La Imprenta **18** C5
La Tercera Orden **44** C2
Museo 20 de Julio (Casa del
  Florero) **36** C4
Museo Arqueológico **24** C6
Museo de Arte Colonial **14** C5
Museo de Artes y Tradiciones
  Populares **28** D6
Museo del Oro **45** C3
Museo del Siglo XIX **29** D6
Museo de Trajes
  Regionales **17** C5
Museo Militar **10** C5
Observatorio Astronómico
  30 D5
Palacio Arzobispal **21** C5
Palacio de Justicia **35** D4
Palacio de Nariño **27** C6
Palacio de San Carlos **13** C5
Palacio de San Francisco
  42 D3
Palacio de
  Telecomunicaciones **37** D4
Plaza de Bolívar **20** D5
Plaza del Chorro de
  Quevedo **2** B4
Plazuela de Rufino Cuervo
  16 C5
Santa Clara **31** D5
Teatro Colón **12** C5
Teatro Libre de Bogotá **3** B4

Sleeping ⬤

Abadia Colonial **1** B4
Ambala **2** C3
Casa Platypus **3** B2
de la Opera **7** C5
Fátima **4** B3
Hostal Sue **5** B3

Hostal Sue Candelaria **6** B3
Oceania **8** B3
Platypus **9** B3
San Sebastián **10** B3
The Cranky Croc **11** B3

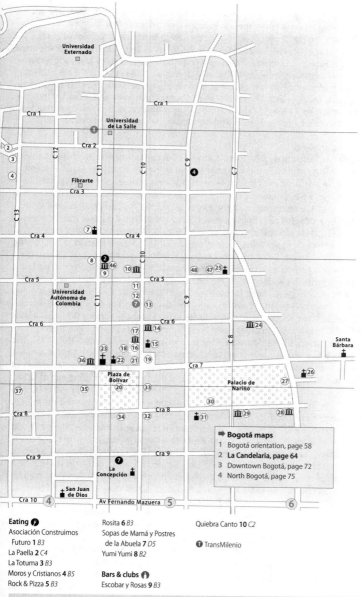

Universidad
Externado

Cra 1

Universidad
de La Salle

Cra 1

Cra 2

C12

C11

C10

C9

C7

Fibrarte
Cra 3

C13

Cra 4

Cra 4

Cra 5

Universidad
Autónoma de
Colombia

Cra 5

Cra 6

Cra 6

C8

Santa
Bárbara

Cra 7

Plaza de
Bolívar

Palacio de
Nariño

Cra 8

Cra 8

Cra 9

Cra 9

La
Concepción

San Juan
de Dios

Cra 10

Av Fernando Mazuera

➡ **Bogotá maps**

1   Bogotá orientation, page 58
2   La Candelaria, page 64
3   Downtown Bogotá, page 72
4   North Bogotá, page 75

Eating 🍴

Asociación Construimos
 Futuro **1** *B3*
La Paella **2** *C4*
La Totuma **3** *B3*
Moros y Cristianos **4** *B5*
Rock & Pizza **5** *B3*

Rosita **6** *B3*
Sopas de Mamá y Postres
 de la Abuela **7** *D5*
Yumi Yumi **8** *B2*

Bars & clubs 🍸

Escobar y Rosas **9** *B3*

Quiebra Canto **10** *C2*

🚍 TransMilenio

profound influence on the growing demand for independence from Spain (see above). You can read an extract from the text in Spanish on the wall of the building.

Opposite, on the corner of Calle 10/Carrera 6 is the **Museo de Arte Colonial**① *Cra 6, No 9-77, T2841373/2866768, Tue-Fri 0900-1700, Sat-Sun 1000-1600, US$1.10*, one of the finest colonial buildings in Colombia. It belonged originally to the Society of Jesus, and was once the seat of the oldest University in Colombia and of the National Library. It has a splendid collection of colonial art and paintings, including a whole room of works by Gregorio Vázquez de Arce y Ceballos, all kinds of silver, furniture, glassware and utensils of the time. Particularly impressive is the collection of portable writing cabinets with inlay marquetry in one of the upstairs rooms. There is a private chapel and two charming patios.

East of Carrera 6

Further up Calle 10, at No 5-51, is the **Palacio de San Carlos**, where Bolívar lived for a time. He is said to have planted the now huge walnut tree in the courtyard. On 25 September 1828, there was an attempt on his life and his mistress, Manuela Sáenz, thrust him out of the window (a plaque facing Calle 10 marks the event) and he was able to hide for two hours under the stone arches of the bridge across the Río San Agustín, now Calle 7. Santander, suspected of complicity, was arrested and banished. Later, it was the home of the Presidents of Colombia at various times until 1980. At present it houses the Ministry of Foreign Affairs. Opposite is the **Teatro Colón**① *C 10, No 5-32*. It opened in 1892 on the fourth anniversary of Columbus' discovery of America. It presents operas, ballets, plays and concerts and is the home of the Colombian Symphony Orchestra which performs there regularly. The auditorium is late 19th century, lavishly decorated and seats 1200. Guided tours can be arranged Mondays-Fridays 0900-1700 or ask if you can have a look around when the theatre is not in use. Next door is the **Fundación Rafael Pombo**① *C 10/Cra 5*, named after the writer of children's books, who lived here. The foundation is dedicated to services to children, including a library, workshops and a film studio.

Across Carrera 5 is the **Museo Militar**① *C 10 No 4-92, Tue-Sun 0900-1630, US$1*. The building was originally constructed to house part of the National University but is now a museum devoted to the Colombian armed forces and has a interesting collection of weapons. There is also a detailed presentation of the independence campaign of 1819.

One block north is the **Casa de Moneda** (The Mint)① *C 11, No 4-93, Mon-Fri 1000-2000, Sun 1000-1600, closed Tue, free*. The mint was established on this site in 1620 and the present building dates from 1753, constructed with traditional materials including stone and adobe. Note the courtyard and thick walled arcades. The exhibition traces the history of currency from the earliest trading in gold, salt and tumbago to the present day. There is good commentary (much also in English) with interactive exhibits. The hoard of 1630 coins, known as the *Tesoro del Mesuno*, which was found in 1936 on a small island in the Río Magdalena, is displayed. There is a coin and banknote exhibition upstairs and occasional extra art shows. Next door, a permanent display of Fernando Botero's work was opened in 2000 as **Donación Botero**① *Wed-Mon 1000-1700, free*, with three salons of his sculptures and paintings as well as an impressive collection of works by Picasso, Matisse, Lucian Freud, Henry Moore, Dalí and Giacometti, among others. Well worth a visit.

Opposite and running the full block between Carrera 4 and Carrera 5 is the **Biblioteca Luis Angel Arango**① *C 11, No 4-14, free internet service available for 30 mins but in great demand*, a facility of the Banco de la República, and one of the best-endowed libraries in Latin America. There are research rooms, art galleries and three reading rooms. The cafeteria on the sixth floor has a good view and reasonable food. They also have premises on the other side of Calle 11. There is a splendid concert hall, where public concerts are usually cheap or free. The library is very popular with students, who will be found queuing an hour before it opens at 0800 to secure a study place in the reading room. On the corner of Calle 11/Carrera 4 is **Iglesia de La Candelaria**, part of an Augustinian friary originally established in 1560. This is an 18th-century three-nave colonial church with some fine carving and a gilded reredos. The structure is in poor shape and desperate steps have been taken to buttress the southwest corner.

A few blocks north of here is **Casa de Poesía Silva** ① *C 14, No 3-41, T2865710, www.casadepoesiasilva.com, Mon-Fri 0900-1300, 1500-1800, free*. The poet José Asunción Silva lived here until his death in 1895. This is a good introduction to the restored colonial house, with a peaceful garden patio. There is a museum, bookshop and a fine audio and book library with taped readings of almost every Spanish-speaking author. CDs can be bought in the bookshop. There are also lectures and poetry readings.

Up from the Casa de Poesía to Calle 14/Carrera 2, turn right up a delightful narrow way (Callejón del Embudo) to the **Plaza del Chorro de Quevedo**, which is believed to be the centre of the Muisca village of Teusaquillo (or Tibsaquillo) and was certainly where Jiménez de Quesada took possession of the territory in the name of King Charles of Spain to form the kingdom of New Granada on 6 August 1538. The centre of the city later moved down to flatter ground (around what is now the Parque Santander), but a commemorative chapel (now a cultural centre) was built on the corner of this plaza and many other houses were built around and below. The name dates from about 1800 when Father Francisco Quevedo provided a *chorro* (well) for the local people. From time to time during the day you will see many students here taking a break from their studies at the several universities nearby, adding to the activity (and the safety) of the area until around 2000 in the evening.

Down Calle 13 is the first home of the **Teatro Libre de Bogotá** ① *C 13, No 2-44, T2814834*. It still houses a professional acting school with occasional public performances. The main home of this company is now in Calle 62, Chapinero, (see under Entertainment). Also on this street is the **Corporación La Candelaria** ① *C 13, No 2-58, T336-0888*, part of the government of the Barrio and an information point. Look in at the attractive colonial patio, with its trees and lawns. At present, under the guidance of the Corporacíon, efforts are being made to reinstate the 'cobbled' streets with modern techniques but with very successful results. They have another office across the street which also has information and sells T-shirts, etc.

South of Plaza Bolívar

One block south of the plaza is the museum of **Santa Clara** ① *Cra 8, No 8-91, T3376762, Mon-Fri 0900-1700, Sat and Sun 1000-1600*, formerly the church of the convent of Clarissa nuns, built between 1619 and 1630 and preserved very much as it was in the 17th century. There is a comprehensive collection of religious art including paintings by Gregorio Vázquez de Arce y Ceballos, and some fine interior decoration with coffered ceilings and lattice screens and windows behind which the nuns attended Mass concealed from the public. Note the extensive remains of the original wall paintings. Though discreet signs on the walls tell you what to look for, a guide is a great help, ask at the entrance. Concerts are occasionally staged here.

Opposite is the **Observatorio Astronómico**, built in 1802, one of the first in Latin America, while further south, at Carrera 8/Calle 8 is the **Museo del Siglo XIX** ① *Cra 8, No*

7-93, T2817362, Mon-Fri 0830-1730, Sat-Sun 0900-1300, formerly a private house, renovated in the republican style around 1880. It was acquired by Bancafé in 1977 and now has a collection of 19th-century paintings, clothes and furniture. The *Botica de los pobres* is a fascinating recreation of a 'poor man's chemist' shop of the period. Note the decoration of the rooms on the second floor and the staircase woodwork. A 19th-century-style coffee shop was opened in 2000, which has good coffee to order, mini sandwiches and snacks, it is not cheap but is very pleasant. There are newspapers and books to read.

Another block south, past the front of the Palacio de Nariño to Calle 7/Carrera 8, is the **Museo de Artes y Tradiciones Populares** ① *Cra 8, No 7-21, T3421266, Mon-Fri 0830-1730, Sat 0930-1300, 1400-1700*, in the old 16th-century monastery of San Agustín, with an interesting collection of traditional arts and crafts, particularly ceramics, wood and textiles. It has a colourful shop, a reasonably priced bar and a good restaurant serving Colombian food accompanied by regional music. The entrance to the **Palacio** (or **Casa**) **de Nariño**, the presidential palace, is on Calle 7. It has a spectacular interior with a fine collection of contemporary Colombian paintings. Enquire if there are guided tours. The ceremonial guard is normally changed daily at 1730.

Opposite is the **Iglesia de San Agustín**, built between 1637 and 1668, the tower being a later addition. It is strongly ornamented with an interesting coffered ceiling in the crypt. Note the ceilings in the nave and also the chandeliers. It was restored in 1988 and inside has a bright, cheerful appearance. There are several paintings by Gregorio Vázquez de Arce y Ceballos. The Image of Jesus was proclaimed Generalissimo of the army in 1812.

East of here is the **Museo Arqueológico** ① *Cra 6, No 7-43, Tue-Fri 0830-1700, Sat 0930-1700, Sun 1000-1600, US$1.65*, which is sponsored by the Banco Popular. This is the restored mansion of the Marqués de San Jorge, which is itself a beautiful example of 17th-century Spanish colonial architecture. The museum is arranged in themes rather than periods and is not well labelled. However it is an impressive and comprehensive collection of decorated ceramics from all the early cultures of Colombia. The restored murals of the original house are also interesting.

A block further east is the **Iglesia de Nuestra Señora María del Carmen** ① *Cra 5, No 8-36, T3420972*, the most striking church in Bogotá. The architecture is bright and interesting with a graceful western tower and fine cupola over the transept, all in red and white, brick/stone construction. It has recently been repainted to brighten this corner of Candelaria. Inside the red/white motif continues with elegant arches and an impressive altar. The stained glass windows, unusually illustrating fruit and flowers, are slanted to give maximum light to the congregation and the windows in the apse are particularly fine. The overall impression of freshness and light is emphasised by the detail in the rose windows of the clerestory and the intricate ornamentation inside and outside the building. Time your visit to see inside; masses are normally at 0700, 1200 and 1800. Next to the church along Carrera 5 is the **Colegio Salesiano Leon XIII**, a boys college. Inside, a cobbled 'street' leads upwards with three courtyards and the buildings of the former Carmelite community on the left, all in the same style as the church, now serving the school. On the corner of Carrera 5/Calle 9 is the former Carmelite chapel with its bell tower above and a rounded balcony on Calle 9 housing the altar of the chapel. This building, known as the **Camarín del Carmen** was faithfully restored as a colonial building in 1957 and is now used as a theatre. The entrance is Calle 9, No 4-77.

Anantas Mockus

In the early 1990s, Bogota had a reputation as a world capital of anarchic disorder. It was choked with traffic and pollution, and kidnappings, murders and car bombings were rife, while much of the population suffered abject poverty.

Enter 'anti-politician' Antanas Mockus, the son of Lithuanian immigrants and a former mathematics professor at the Universidad Nacional de Colombia who served as Mayor of Bogota for two terms (1995-1996 and 2001-2003) and oversaw the city's transformation into a place where citizens felt safe to walk the streets.

Mockus first came to public attention when he dropped his pants and mooned a class of students in order to get their attention. His time in office would be full of equally confrontational initiatives.

Many felt that it would take a superhero to restore a sense of moral fibre to a society apparently falling apart at the seams and Mockus took them at their word, often dressing up in spandex and a cape and taking on the character of 'Supercitizen'.

To combat *bogotanos'* disregard for the highway code he employed 420 mime artists to mock and shame motorists into heeding stoplights and pedestrian crossings, believing that Colombians were more afraid of ridicule than being fined. When there was a water shortage in the city he starred in an ad on TV in which he was shown turning off the water while he soaped in the shower.

To tackle gun crime he offered an amnesty on guns in exchange for food and had the melted metal from the weapons recast as spoons for babies. He also encouraged a 'Ladies' Night' in which men were asked to stay at home while their wives went out on the town.

While many mocked Mockus, labelling him little more than a clown, many of his initiatives were effective. Homicide rates fell from 80 per 100,000 to 23 per 100,000 during his tenure, while traffic accidents decreased 50% and water usage by 40%. His government managed to provide a sewage system that reached 100% of the population, up from 78%. He even managed to leave a US$700 million surplus to his successor, partly aided by his success in persuading 63,000 people to pay a voluntary extra 10% tax.

North of Plaza Bolívar

From Plaza Bolívar, Carrera 7, which was the first important street of Bogotá, runs four blocks to Avenida Jiménez de Quesada, connecting the administrative centre of the city with Parque Santander, the first residential area and now the commercial hub of the capital. This street is locally known as the Calle Real del Comercio. On the corner of Carrera 7/Calle 12A is the **Palacio de Telecomunicaciones**, the headquarters of the country's postal services on the site of the colonial church of Santo Domingo. In the building there is the **Museo Postal**. Up Calle 13 and left at Carrera 6 there are two universities: **La Gran Colombia**, and **38 Colegio Mayor de Nuestra Señora del Rosario** near the corner at Calle 14, No 6-25. The latter school is the second oldest in Bogotá, was founded by Father Cristóbal de Torres of the order of Santo Domingo in the 16th century and is a typical cloistered school of the period. **José Celestino Mutis**, the botanist, taught natural sciences and medicine here. You can buy a good cheap lunch at the cafeteria and great crêpes. Alongside is the chapel of the Order – **La Bordalita**. Inside is an embroidered Virgin made by Queen Isabel de Borbón for Father Cristóbal on his appointment as Archbishop of Santa Fe de Bogotá. The elegant façade has some fine stone carvings above the entrance.

Emeralds

Thinking about buying a diamond? Think again. A fine emerald is a much rarer gemstone, and the finest emeralds in the world hail from Colombia. Like diamonds, emeralds are evaluated according to the four 'C's – Color, Clarity, Cut and Carat weight – although color, not clarity, is considered the most important attribute. A dark green emerald is considered the most precious variety, although they range in color. Unlike other gemstones all emeralds have flaws or 'inclusions'.

However, rather than detracting from their value, inclusions are said to give an emerald its personality.

If you are in the market for a stone, go to Avenida Jiménez in Bogotá, which is the heart of Colombia's unofficial emerald exchange. The emeralds sold here come from Colombia's three most prolific mines – Muzo, Coscuez and Chivor – all located in the cloudforests of Boyacá, just a few hours to the north. These mines have a long history that dates back to AD1000, long before the Spanish invasion. To catch a glimpse of some exquisite examples of emerald jewellry from pre-Hispanic times, check out the Museo del Oro in Bogotá, see below.

Although not strictly in the Barrio de Candelaria, the cluster of interesting buildings around the **Parque Santander** are appropriately part of Old Bogotá, with three of the finest churches in Colombia. After crossing Jiménez de Quesada, the **Iglesia de San Francisco** is immediately to your left. It is an interesting mid-16th-century church with paintings of famous Franciscans, choir stalls, a famous ornate gold high altar (AD1622), and a fine Lady Chapel with blue and gold ornamentation. The remarkable ceiling is in Spanish-*Mudéjar* (Moorish) style. Try to see this church when fully illuminated. Behind it along Avenida Jiménez de Quesada is the **Palacio de San Francisco** ⓘ *Av Jiménez No 7-50*, built between 1918 and 1933 for the Gobernación de Cundinamarca, on the site of the Franciscan friary. Designed in the republican style, it has a fine façade and competed to some degree with the Capitolio Nacional. It is now part of the Rosario University. Next to the San Francisco church and overlooking Parque Santander is the **Iglesia de la Veracruz**, first built eight years after the founding of Bogotá, rebuilt in 1731, and again in 1904. In 1910 it became the Panteón Nacional e Iglesia de la República. José de Caldas, the famous scientist, was buried under the church along with many other patriots victims of the Spanish 'Reign of Terror' around 1815. It has a bright white and red interior and a fine decorated ceiling. Fashionable weddings are held here. Across Calle 16 is the third major church **La Tercera Orden**, a colonial church famous for its carved woodwork along the nave and a high balcony, massive wooden altar reredos, and confessionals. It was built by the Third Franciscan Order in the 17th century, hence the name.

Museo del Oro On the northeast corner of the Parque de Santander is the **Museo del Oro** (the Gold Museum) ⓘ *Cra 6, No 15-82, T3421111*, in the splendid premises of the Banco de la República. This collection is a 'must', and is perhaps the finest museum in all of South America. There are more than 35,000 pieces of pre-Columbian gold work in the total collection, most of which is held here. The rest is divided between other regional Museos de Oro (all of which are worth a visit), sponsored by the Banco de la República throughout Colombia. Many thousands of pieces are displayed.

On two upper floors, a full display is made of the dozen or so pre-Spanish indigenous groups that have been identified in Colombian territory, and how they found and worked gold and other metals. It is a fascinating story, illustrated by many examples of their work. They used techniques, some might say, unsurpassed by goldsmiths of today.

The first display floor sets the scene, each culture set in its geographical and historical environment, explaining the characteristics of their art. There are illustrative models including one of Ciudad Perdida as it would have looked when inhabited. In each section there are helpful portable boards with explanatory notes in English. The second floor has many more examples of the extraordinary goldwork of these pre-Columbian peoples. The centrepiece of the exhibition is the Salón Dorado, a glittering display of 8000 pieces inside an inner vault – an unforgettable experience.

On the ground floor there is a souvenir/bookshop, and exhibition rooms. Audio guides can be hired at the ticket office. On the first floor, 20-minute films are shown throughout the day, times and languages are displayed. The museum was closed for refurbishment in 2008 but is due to reopen at the end of the year. There is a temporary exhibition on show at the Biblioteca Luis Angel Arango.

Monserrate

ⓘ *T284 5700 (answer service also in English), fare to Monserrate US$5 adult and child return. The funicular runs Mon-Sat 0740-1140; the cable car runs Mon-Sat 1200-2400 every 20 mins; both Sun and holidays 0530-1730. Times change frequently.*

There is a very good view of the city from the top of Monserrate (3210 m), the lower of the two peaks rising sharply to the east. It is reached by a funicular railway and a cable car. The new convent at the top is a popular shrine and pilgrimage site. At the summit, near the church, a platform gives a bird's-eye view of the city's tiled roofs and of the plains beyond stretching to the rim of the Sabana. Sunrise and sunset can be spectacular. The **Calle del Candelero**, a reconstruction of a Bogotá street of 1887, has plenty of street stalls and snack bars. Behind the church are popular picnic grounds. There are two upmarket touristy restaurants at the top, both overpriced and closed Sunday. If you wish to walk up, possibly the safest time is at the weekend about 0500, before the crowds arrive but when there are people about. At this time you will catch the sunrise. The path is dressed stone and comfortably graded all the way up with refreshment stalls at weekends every few metres. It takes about one and a quarter hours up (if you don't stop).

Safety It is best not to walk to the top of Monserrate alone; and do not display cameras openly. On no account walk down in the dark. On weekdays it is not recommended to walk up and especially not down. You should also take a bus or taxi to the foot of the hill Monday to Friday and, at all times, from the bottom station into town. There are usually taxis waiting by the footbridge across the road. In 2007, there were reports of tourists being mugged at the summit and the bottom, even during the day. The walk up to Guadalupe, the higher peak opposite Monserrate, is not recommended.

Quinta de Bolívar

ⓘ *C 20, No 2-91 Este, T336 6419, Tue-Fri 0900-1700, Sat-Sun 1000-1500, US$1.30, reductions for students and children, guided tours.*

At the foot of Monserrate is the Quinta de Bolívar, a fine colonial mansion with splendid gardens and lawns. There are several cannons captured at the battle of Boyacá. The elegant house, once Bolívar's home, is now a museum showing some of his personal possessions and paintings of events in his career. Opposite the Quinta is the attractive campus of the prestigious private university, Los Andes.

Downtown Bogotá

Downtown Bogotá, the old commercial centre with shops, offices and banks, runs in a band northwards from Avenida Jiménez de Quesada. It is very patchy, with a thorough mix of architectural styles, including modern towers and colonial buildings in various states of repair. This commercial hub narrows to a thin band of secondary shops extending between Carrera 7 and Avenida Caracas to around Calle 60. The streets are full of life; they are also paralyzed by traffic and choked with fumes much of the time. The pavements can be very congested too, particularly Carrera 7 and Avenida (Calle)19. Many of the budget hotels and some of the better ones are found in this area, which is not considered very safe.

The commercial centre of Bogotá has been weakened in recent years by the migration north of company headquarters and offices, yet the area seems busier than ever. For the visitor there are plenty of attractions. For the immediate area of Parque de Santander, see La Candelaria, page 62.

Iglesia de San Diego ① *Cra 7, No 26-37*, was built about 1606 by the Franciscans and a chapel to the Virgin was added in 1629. There is a fine statue of Our Lady in the chapel dedicated to the countryside (which surrounded it when it was built). The monastery was built about 1560, and the fine Moorish ceiling can still be seen. Local craft items are sold in part of the old San Diego monastery adjacent to the church.

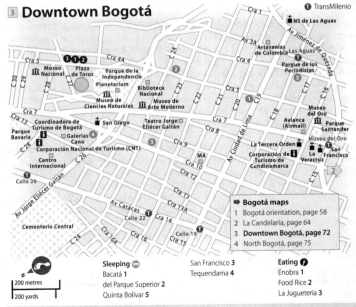

3 Downtown Bogotá

➜ Bogotá maps
1 Bogotá orientation, page 58
2 La Candelaria, page 64
3 **Downtown Bogotá, page 72**
4 North Bogotá, page 75

200 metres
200 yards

Sleeping 🛏
Bacatá **1**
del Parque Superior **2**
Quinta Bolívar **5**
San Francisco **3**
Tequendama **4**

Eating 🍴
Enobra **1**
Food Rice **2**
La Juguetería **3**

Cementerio Central

The tomb of Leo S Kopp in Bogotá's Cementerio Central has something of a cult following. Kopp was a German migrant who founded Bavaria Beer, Colombia's largest brewer. Famously generous, he was known to find employment for anyone who came and asked him.

It appears that his capacity for giving continues after his death. On any given day it's not uncommon to see the poor and the unemployed laying flowers at his grave or kissing the magnificent bronze statue that guards it. Hearsay has it that the statue retains its radiance thanks to a civil servant who, having prayed at the feet of Kopp's statute, was rewarded with a job and now shows his gratitude by secretly cleaning and shining the effigy.

Iglesia de Nuestra Señora de las Aguas ① *Cra 3, No 18-66*. This charming 17th-century church has a wide façade with seven bells overlooking a small park and Avenida Jiménez de Quesada. The name refers to the San Francisco river, which now flows under the avenida. It has a single nave and a baroque altar, with a wood carving of tropical fruits at its base. The convent next door has been inhabited by Dominicans for over a century. It has served as a hospital and a school since then, now it is occupied by **Artesanías de Colombia**, one of the best places to buy local crafts.

Teatro Jorge Eliécer Gaitán ① *Cra 7, No 22-47, T3346800, www.teatrojorge eliecer.gov.co*, built in art-deco style around 1945 as a movie house, it is now one of the biggest theatres in the country, holding an audience of over 1500 for shows, concerts and theatre productions.

Museo Nacional ① *Cra 7, No 28-66, T3348366, www.museonacional.gov.com, Tue-Sat 1000-1800, Sun 1000-1700, US$1.65 (pensioners free), guided tours in English every Wed at 1600*; founded by Santander in 1823 and later moved to this building, a former prison built around 1900, designed by Thomas Reed (see Capitolio Nacional). It houses a well-displayed archaeological collection, one of the best in the country. Even if you are short of time, try to see this display. There is a collection of gold items in the vault. The top floor has a fine art section, comprising 20th-century national paintings and sculptures. Expensive but good café and tasty cakes. There are also salads and desserts named after exhibits.

Museo de Arte Moderno ① *C 24, No 6-00, www.mambogota.com, Tue-Sat 1000-1800, Sun 1200-1700, US$1.80, half price for students*, has an appropriately modern building, inaugurated in 1953. It has an interesting, well-displayed collection of modern Colombian artists, with sculptures, graphic arts and so on represented. Good café and bookshop. If you want to photograph in the museum you must obtain permission from the office.

Museo de Ciencias Naturales ① *C 26/Cra 7, T3344571*, has a comprehensive collection of the country's flora and fauna. In 2000 it is in the process of transferring to the new Maloka Science and Technology Centre in the west of the city (see below).

Parque de la Independencia

Parque de la Independencia is popular at weekends though not recommended for visits during the week. In the park is the **Planetarium** ① *C 26/Cra 7, T3344548, Tue-Sun 1100, 1430 and 1630*, offering lectures, courses, seminars, and a public astronomical show. There are occasional *son et lumière* (light and sound) shows, and there's also a good **internet café** ⓘ *US$1 per hr.* Beside the park is the **Plaza de Toros** (bull ring) ⓘ *9 Parque de los Mártires (Park of the Martyrs), Cra 14 (Av Caracas)/C10-11*, with a monument, on the site of the Plaza in which the Spanish shot many patriots during the struggle for independence.

Chapinero and around

The centre of Bogotá comes to a natural end where Cras 7 to 13 come together beyond the Centro Internacional, a large complex that includes the **Tequendama Hotel**. In the link between Central and North Bogotá, there are a number of places of interest.

Casa Museo Jorge Eliécer Gaitán ⓘ *C 42, No 15-52*, is the former residence of the populist leader whose assassination in April 1948 triggered the infamous 'Bogotazo', at the outset of La Violencia. The museum is dedicated to this period of Colombia's history.

Instituto Nacional de Investigaciones Geológico-Mineras (INGEOMINAS) ⓘ *Diagonal 53, No 34-53*, has a library and pleasant museum. It is in the corner of the Universidad National campus, close to other Earth Science institutions including the Instituto Geográfico Agustín Codazzi.

Museo de los Niños ⓘ *Cra 48, No 63-97, T2257587, www.museodelosninos.org.co, US$6.50, Tue-Fri 0900-1330, 1415-1500, Sat, Sun and holidays 0930-1500, guided tours*, natural sciences explained for children.

Museo Colsubsidio ⓘ *C 26, No 25-42, T3431899*, has exhibitions of contemporary artists, and other special events.

The Universidad Nacional is housed in the Ciudad Universitaria, and with about 13,000 students is much the largest in the country. Unlike the older centres of learning in Candelaria, it has plenty of space, and is still expanding.

Teatro Nacional ⓘ *C 71, No 10-25, T2174577, www.teatronacional.com.co*. Traditional presentations by national and international artists with important facilities for training young people. They have other premises in North Bogotá.

Teatro Libre de Bogotá ⓘ *C 62, No 9A-65, T2171988, www.teatrolibre.com*. Frequent presentations, formerly in Candelaria where they still have a base.

Jardín Botánico-José Celestino Mutis ⓘ *Av 57, No 61-13, T4377060, www.jbb.gov.co, Mon-Fri 0800-1700, Sat, Sun and hols 0900-1700*. These interesting and well-organized botanical gardens have a collection of over 5000 native orchids, plus roses, gladioli and trees from all over the country. If you can't get to the national parks, you can at least see many of the local species here. It has a fine documentation centre with resident experts.

Maloka Centro Interactivo de Ciencia y Tecnología ⓘ *Cra 68D, No 40A-51, T4272707, www.maloka.org, Mon-Thu 0800-1700, Fri 0800-1800, Sat 1000-1900, Sun and hols 1100-1900, US$9.50, including cinema*. A complex of science exhibits and instructive entertainment for all ages. There are over 200 exhibits in nine halls, a 135° large-screen cinema, internet rooms, restaurants and other facilities. A full visit takes about three hours.

Along Calle 26 with Carrera 16 is the **Cementerio Central**, an oval-shaped construction full of large mausoleums and pine trees. This is Bogotá's principal cemetery, built between 1830 and 1929 and many of Colombian history's most influential figures are buried here, including Luis Carlos Galán, whose assassination while campaigning for president sparked the beginning of La Violencia, and leader of the M19 guerrilla group Carlos Pizarro, also murdered. Round the corner from the inner ellipse is the grave of Leo S Kopp, founder of Bavaria, Colombia's largest beer company. Presided over by an impressive bronze statue, the site has something of a cult following (see box, page 73).

Nearby is the **Plaza del Mercado de Paloquemao** ① *Av 19 with Cra 22*, an enormous covered market with over 1800 stalls selling fruit and vegetables, meats, herbs and flowers as well as some handicrafts. To catch the flower market in full flow, visit between 0500 and 1000.

North of the centre ◉❼ ▸▸ pp76-89.

Beyond Calle 60, the main city continues north to a comparatively new area, North Bogotá, where there has been great commercial expansion with the development of wealthy suburbs around. Most of the best hotels and restaurants are in this area, which is regarded as relatively safe. The T-shaped area made up by Calle 83 and Carrera 13 is the **Zona Rosa**, also known as the Zona T. Many bars, clubs and restaurants are here. Small towns, such as Chapinero, **Chicó** and Usaquén have been absorbed, and the city now extends north to around Calle 200. Many commercial and financial companies have moved here but most government offices and many businesses remain downtown. North of Calle 68 is an band of wealthy suburbs, business centres, shopping malls and classy restaurants. The best hotels are scattered through this area, which is regarded as reasonably safe.

North Bogotá is noted for its huge, lavish shopping malls, which have sprung up in the last few years. They are worth a visit even if the prices don't grab you. The Hacienda Santa

4 **North Bogotá**

➡ **Bogotá maps**
1 Bogotá orientation, page 58
2 La Candelaria, page 64
3 Downtown Bogotá, page 72
4 **North Bogotá, page 75**

❶ TransMilenio

500 metres
500 yards

Sleeping ⬤
Andino Royal 1
Morrison Hotel 2
Viaggio Suites 3
Windsor House 4

Eating ❼
80 Sillas 5
El Corral 6
H Sasson 7
Kathmandu 8
K-Listo 9
La Hamburguesería 11

Salto del Angel 12
Wok 13

Bars & clubs ❻
Alma 14
Gótica 15

Bárbara has been constructed within a large country mansion, and parts of the colonial architecture, arches, and stone floors have been incorporated. Even some of the old gardens have been retained.

Museo Mercedes de Pérez ① *Cra 7, No 94-17, Mon-Fri 1000-1700, Sat 0800-1200, guided tours US$1.40*, formerly the Hacienda de El Chicó, is a fine example of colonial architecture. It contains a world-wide collection of mostly 18th-century porcelain, furniture and paintings.

Usaquén
Usaquén was once one of the more important towns and is now absorbed by the growing metropolis of Bogotá. The small plaza in the centre has become an attractive shopping and restaurant area, popular in the evenings. The railway station can be used for the tourist train to Zipaquirá at weekends (see Transport, page 85, for more details). **World Trade Center** ① *C 100, No 8A-49, T2183484*, is a large convention and exhibition centre with all the usual services. The **Bogotá Royal Hotel** is alongside.

⊚ Bogotá listings → *Phone code: 1.*

Hotel and guesthouse prices
LL over US$200	L US$151-200	AL US$101-150
A US$66-100	B US$46-65	C US$31-45
D US$21-30	E US$12-20	F US$7-11
G US$6 and under		

Restaurant prices
₸₸₸ over US$12   ₸₸ US$6-12   ₸ under US$6

⊚ Sleeping
Accommodation is plentiful in Bogotá. All 3 sections of the city have top-class and middle-range hotels but budget travellers will find more choice in the Downtown and La Candelaria areas. If possible, book hotels in advance, even if only from the airport or bus terminal. For hostel organizations, see page 33.

Taxi drivers at the airport or bus station occasionally say that the hotel you have chosen is 'closed', 'not known', etc, especially the cheaper ones listed in Candelaria. Insist they take you to the right address.

La Candelaria *p62, map p64*
L Hotel de la Opera, C 10, No 5-72, T3362066, www.hotelopera.com.co. This privately owned hotel was previously the residency of Simón Bolívar's personal guard. Spread out over 2 buildings; 1 colonial,

1 Republican, now joined together, this is Colombian opulence at its best, with period pieces adorning its exquisite rooms. It has 2 rooftop restaurants with superb views as well as a sauna, gym and pool. The junior suites have original bathtubs.
AL Abadia Colonial, C 11, No 2-32, T3411884, abadiacolonial@gmail.com, www.abadiacolonial.com. Fine colonial building in the heart of the Candelaria. Comfortable rooms if a little small. Best to ask for a street-facing room as otherwise they have no windows. Has Wi-Fi, cable TV, safe and a restaurant serving Italian food. Recommended.
A Casa Platypus, Cra 3, No 16-78, T2811801, www.platypusbogota.com. From the owner of the Platypus, this hotel is aimed at 'the parents of backpackers' or anyone with a larger budget. In a beautiful colonial building overlooking the Parque de los Periodistas, it has excellent rooms with extra large beds and duvets, a kitchen and a fine roof terrace with views of Monserrate. Recommended.
C San Sebastián, Av Jiménez, No 3-97, T2438937. The lobby of this hotel has some amusing Picasso imitation murals and it was plainly a fashionable location in its time but those days are long gone. The rooms are a

little dated but it's functional and has hot water, internet, Wi-Fi and good writing desks as well as good views of Monserrate.

D Ambala, Cra 5, No 13-46, T3426384, www.hotelambala.net. In a pretty colonial building, Ambala's rooms are clean but a little small and with dated decor.

D The Cranky Croc, C 15, No 3-46, T3422438, www.crankycroc.com. Brand new for 2008, this Aussie-run hostel is located in a beautiful 300-year-old building, carefully restored to retain many of the original features. Excellent facilities include Wi-Fi and internet, free luggage storage and a lounge with a fireplace. Has several private rooms with bathrooms and dorms with bunks (**F**).

D Hostal Fátima, C 14, No 2-24, T2816389, www.hostalfatima.com. Fátima is a maze of brightly coloured rooms and sunny patios with lots of stained-glass windows and potted plants. It has lots of added bonuses such as a sauna and jacuzzi, a TV room and even a dance studio teaching contemporary and jazz dance, yoga and pilates. Has several private rooms with bathrooms as well as dorms with bunks (**F**).

D Hostal Sue, C 16, No 2-55 and **Hostal Sue Candelaria**, Cra 3, No 14-18, T3348894 and T3412647, www.hostalsue.com. A new Sue (pronounced 'Su-ay') seems to spring up every year, so popular have these hostals become. A 3rd has just opened up (enquire at first 2 for details). All have excellent facilities, including Wi-Fi, internet, kitchen, free lockers, laundry service and places to relax in

hammocks. Candelaria has a ping-pong table too. The difference between them is that they attract different crowds: the 1st is for a younger crowd, keener on partying, the 2nd two for those seeking a quieter atmosphere. Dorms with bunks (**F**) available.

D Oceanía, C 14, No 4-48, T3420560. An element of faded grandeur pervades this large building, with peeling paint and a large forecourt. The rooms are relatively clean and have private bathrooms, while its restaurant serves a *menú ejecutivo* for US$4.

D Platypus, C 16, No 2-43, T3520127, www.platypushotel.com. As the first backpacker's hostel to open in Colombia, the Platypus has built a reputation for having all the facilities you would expect, such as internet access and Wi-Fi, a book exchange and a kitchen. A string of other hostels have since opened up in the Candelaria offering similar services but what still makes the Platypus stand out is owner Germán Escobar's encyclopaedic knowledge of Colombia. Has 12 private rooms with bathrooms and several dorms with bunks (**F**).

Downtown Bogotá *p72, map p72*
The downtown area of Bogotá suffers from petty crime and muggings by night.
LL Tequendama, Cra 10, No 26-21, T3820300, www.cptequendama.com.co. 1 of Bogotá's traditional grand hotels, the Tequendama has been witness to some of Colombia's most important political events since its inauguration in 1953. With 2

HostelTrail.com
latin american hostel network

Info on all the best hostels and tours in Colombia & Latin America

restaurants, a spa, Wi-Fi throughout and large rooms it is well equipped for the conferences it invariably hosts.

AL Bacata, C 19, No 5-20, T2838300, www.hotelbacata.com.co. Another traditional Bogotá hotel, Bacata has large rooms with minibar, cable TV and Wi-Fi, as well as a spa, gym and pizzeria.

A Hotel del Parque Superior, Cra 5, No 23-34, T3363600, www.hoteldelparque superior.com. In the heart of the Centro Internacional, this 1980s hotel has had little work done on it since it was built but it does have a pool, sauna, Wi-Fi and breakfast included.

A San Francisco, Cra 10, No 23-63, T2861677, www.sfcol.com. This modern hotel has good-sized rooms, a restaurant, Wi-Fi, free breakfasts and free transfer to and from the airport.

B Quinta Bolívar, Cra 4, No 17-59, T3376500, www.hotelquintabolivar.com. Located on the edge of the Candelaria, this Republican-era building has cosy rooms and breakfast is included.

Chapinero and around p74, map p58
LL Casa Medina, Cra 7, No 69A-22, T3120299, www.hotelescharleston.com. Built in 1945 by Santiago Medina, with its stone columns and carved wooden doors this hotel is Bogotá at its most refined. It has a gym, Wi-Fi, iPod docks, a gym and a fine restaurant in a wooden panelled room.

A Casona del Patio, Cra 8, No 69-24, T2128805, casona@telecom.com.co, www.lacasonadelpatio.com. With 14 immaculate rooms set around a sunny patio and well situated near the Zona G, this is one of the best mid range options in Bogotá, Has cable TV and Wi-Fi. Recommended.

B Las Terrazas, C 54, No 3-12, T2555777. Well-placed in a quiet area of Chapinero Alto, this hotel is popular with foreigners. The building is an interesting shape, a kind of half pyramid, meaning that each room has a large balcony with excellent views of the city. Has Wi-Fi and cable TV. First 2 floors are student residences.

B-E El Cafecito, Cra 6, No 34-70, T2858308, bogota@cafecito.net, www.cafecito.net. From the owners of the popular hostals in Ecuador, El Cafecito offers an excellent alternative to staying in La Candelaria. Well located in the English architecture neighbourhood of La Merced and near the restaurants of La Macarena and the clubs of Carrera 7, the building has an interesting history, having once been an asphalt factory belonging to mayoral candidate Moreno de Caro. It has a a an excellent Wi-Fi-enabled café serving crêpes and cocktails and several rooms with and without private bathrooms, as well as bunks in dorms. Recommended.

C Diamante Central Park, C 53, No 10-78, T2102463, www.hoteldiamantecentral park.com. In the heart of El Chapinero, this hotel is a bit of an ugly block but is nonetheless pretty good value. Has Wi-Fi, cable TV and safes in each room.

C Hotel Lord, C 63, No 14-62, T2111880, hotel_lord@yahoo.com.ar. Popular with Colombian businessmen, some of the rooms are a little small and have only windows onto corridors but the street-facing ones are good value with cable TV and good light. Has an internet room and a restaurant.

North of the centre p75, map p75
LL Andino Royal, C 85, No 12-28, T6513092, www.hotelesroyal.com. Well placed between Parque 93 and the Zona Rosa, this modern hotel has all the conveniences you would expect including a gym, Wi-Fi and cable TV. The rooms are light and airy with large windows.

LL Morrison Hotel, C 84 Bis, No 13-54, T2566513, www.morrisonhotel.com. Conveniently located near the Zona T, this hotel, with a contemporary British design, has large rooms with Wi-Fi, LCD TVs and thermo-acoustic windows. It looks out onto the beautiful parque León de Greiff.

L Windsor House, C 95, No 9-97, T6343630, www.ghlhoteles.com. English-style luxury hotel with large rooms. Some have jacuzzis, all have a safe, minibar and use of a gym and Turkish bath.

A Viaggio Suites, Cra 18, No 86A-36, Edificio Virrey, T6222525, www.viaggiosuites.com. Excellent value short- and medium-term apartments. Spacious, modern and clean with fitted kitchens, daily house keeper and breakfast included. All apartments have Wi-Fi and laundry service. Prices drop for longer stays. Recommended.

❷ Eating

Restaurants are spread throughout the city. The more exotic and fashionable places to eat are in North Bogotá but Candelaria has its bistros and good value, typical Colombian food. Take local advice if you want to eat really cheaply in markets or from street stalls. Take note that few restaurants in La Candelaria are open in the evening.

La Candelaria *p62, map p64*
♔♔ **La Paella**, C 11, No 5-13. Opposite the Centro Cultural García Márquez, this restaurant serves Spanish food and specializes in paellas.
♔♔ **Rosita**, C 13A, No 1A-26. On the lovely Plazoleta Chorro de Quevedo, this is an excellent little lunchtime spot. Sells cookbooks.
♔ **Asociación Construimos Futuro**, C 15A, No 2-21. Good breakfasts served up by a neighbourhood co-operative. Has Wi-Fi.
♔ **La Totuma**, Cra 2, No 13A-58. On the hip Callejón del Embudo, this restaurant serves economic sushi and the excellent lunchtime deal of a bowl of teppanyaki for just US$3. Colourful surroundings.
♔ **Moros y Cristianos**, C 9, N0 3-11. Cuban food served in a sunny, glass-covered patio. Open till midnight on Fri, otherwise lunchtime only.
♔ **Rock and Pizza**, Cra 2, No 13A-56. Great pizzas at reasonable prices. Upstairs is a chicha bar.

♔ **Sopas de Mamá y Postres de la Abuela**, Cra 9, No 10-59. A real *rolo* institution, this restaurant serves traditional Colombian broths such as *ajiaco* and *sancocho* in a beautiful 2nd-floor gallery with stained-glass windows and large panelled wooden doors. Its other speciality is puddings, which include a secret formula for fried ice cream!
♔ **Yumi Yumi**, Cra 3, No 16-40. Tiny hole-in-the-wall restaurant serving sandwiches, crêpes, fruit juices and cocktails. Open late most nights and offers free tickets to clubs in the Zona Rosa.

Chapinero and around *p74, map p58*
Bogotá has several gastronomic zones. The Zona 'G' ('G' stands for gourmet) is much talked about but La Macarena, comprising several blocks along Carrera 4 has several very good restaurants at a fraction of the cost. Formerly an area frequented by artists, it is now becoming increasingly hip.
♔♔♔ **Criterión**, C 69A, No 5-75, T3102810. This restaurant has minimalist decor and a French-influenced menu of dishes such as *foie gras*, goat's cheese salad, shellfish and various types of steak as well as a large wine list.
♔♔♔ **Estrella de los Ríos**, C 26B, No 4-50, T3374037, www.estrelladelosrios.com. Costeña Estrella calls her small place an 'anti-restaurant'. Her idea is that your dining experience should feel much like she is cooking for you at home. Hence, you must book 24-hours in advance and she reserves the right to turn you away if she doesn't like you! Estrella, the author of several cookbooks, conjures up *costeño* and Cuban food in her intimate kitchen for US$35 for 5 courses, excluding alcohol. Highly recommended.
♔♔ **Dar Papaya**, C 69A, No 4-78, T5415013. *Dar papaya* is a popular Colombian expression which roughly translated means 'to expose yourself'. The owners of this smart restaurant attempt to expose a fusion of Asian and Latin American cuisine, with some success. Dishes include ceviches, wraps, salads and soups.

El Patio Caffe, Cra 4A, No 27-80, T2826121. French bistro in Gallic surroundings serving dishes such as chicken in tarragon sauce.

Enobra, Cra 4, No 26-37. Fashionable, chic restaurant with sparse decor serving tapas and various cuts of steak.

La Cigale, C 69A, No 4-93, T2496839. This French restaurant does all the Gallic specialities you would expect, including terrines and magret de canard.

La Juguetería, C 27, No 4-03, www.restaurantelajugueteria.com. A bit of an Andrés Carne de Res but in town, La Juguetería cooks up excellent steaks in a frankly slightly disturbing atmosphere: the restaurant's decoration theme is dolls and they hang everywhere. Some of the tables are even made out of dolls' heads.

mini-mal, Cra 4A, No 57-52, T3475464, www.mini-mal.org. As the name suggests, the focus of this restaurant/bar/design shop is on minimalism. The menu is contemporary Colombian cuisine with alternative takes on Pacific, Caribbean, Andean and Amazonian recipes.

Oia, C 70A, No 5-67, T8117846. This popular restaurant serves up a mixture of food and tapas from the Mediterranean – French, Greek, Italian and Spanish – in lovely surroundings with a pleasant outdoor patio. It also has a bistro section which serves quiches, paninis and juices.

Tábula, C 29 bis, No 5-90. Gourmet international menu in stylish surroundings a couple of blocks from La Macarena.

Urbano, Cra 4, No 27-09. Urbano serves excellent chicken, steaks and fish in interesting sauces. It has some quirky touches, including antique oil dispensers to hold your cutlery and bizarre revolving menus.

Al Wadi, C 27, No 4-14. Healthy Lebanese food, including kebabs, falafel and various types of rice.

El Cafecito, Cra 6, No 34-70. Café belonging to the hostel of the same name, El Cafecito has an excellent varied menu that includes rosti, pancakes, salads, sandwiches, world coffees and herbal teas as well as cocktails.

All of this is served in the fine surroundings of an English-style mansion in La Merced.

Food Rice, Cra 4, No 26-13. This restaurant has a simple but effective formula: it only does rices, but rice dishes from around the world, everything from Chinese to Malaysian to Indian. There are some good vegetarian options. Does home delivery.

La Casa de las Sopas, C 34, No 13-20. Excellent lunchtime venue serving traditional Colombian soups and broths, including ajiaco, mondongo and sancocho.

La Hamburguesería, Cra 4A, No 27-27, www.lahamburgueseria.com This fast-food chain is becoming increasingly popular in Bogotá for the quality of its hamburgers and hotdogs. There are several more outlets spread around town. Does home delivery.

North of the centre p75, map p75

North of C 76 there are 3 popular areas for eating and drinking. The Zona T, also known as the Zona Rosa is a T-shaped pedestrianized area, comprising C 83 and Cra 13, and has some of Bogotá's best restaurants and bars. Further north is Parque 93, for many years the most exclusive address in Bogotá, although some of Colombia's chain restaurants are now beginning to encroach upon its territory. Beyond, on C 117 with Cra 7 is Usaquén, formerly a town in its own right but now a part of the big metropolis, and a popular venue for evening and weekend dining.

H Sasson, C 83, No 12-49. Harry Sasson is one of Colombia's best known chefs and owns a number of Bogotá's most popular restaurants. H Sasson does contemporary Asian food such as crispy duck and curries in stylish surroundings.

Salto del ángel, Cra 13, No 93A-45, T6226427. This enormous restaurant on Parque 93 has a large varied menu of steaks, ceviches and picking food as well as some international options which include fish and chips. At weekends, after dinner, the tables are cleared and it becomes a popular upmarket disco.

Wok, Cra 13, No 82-74. Fashionable Asian cuisine restaurant. R La Esquina de la Mona, C 82, No 14-32. Cheap but good fast food, including parrillas, pinchos, ribs and burgers.

El Corral, C 93A, No 14-30. This popular Colombian burger chain is a cut and some more above McDonald's. It serves mainly large hamburgers as well as onion rings and other side orders.

K-Listo, C 83, No 12A-36. Fast-food chain serving stuffed *arepas* and *empanadas*.

Usaquén *p76, map p75*

Kathmandu, Cra 6, No 117-26, T2133276. This restaurant serves Asian, Chinese and Arabic food in a series of rooms brimming with gilt-edged Buddha statues and other Asian decorations.

80 Sillas, C 118, No 6-05, T6192471. All kinds of ceviches and other seafood served in wooden elevated patios with encroaching ferns.

La Hamburguesería, C 118, No 7-40, T2141943. This hamburger diner, part of a popular Bogotá franchise, has very good burgers as well as salads, club sandwiches and soups. It often has live music at the weekends.

🎵 Bars and clubs

La Candelaria *p62, map p64*

This area has little to offer in the way of nightlife but **Escobar y Rosas**, Cra 4, No 15-01, in a converted old chemist is packed on Fri-Sat nights with a student crowd.

QuiebraCanto, Cra 5, No 17-76, in a colonial house, plays world music, funk and salsa to a friendly crowd and is best on Wed and Thu nights.

North of the centre *p75, map p75*

Most bars and clubs are concentrated in the Cra 11-13, C 80-86 region, known as the Zona Rosa – a lively, upmarket area where many restaurants open late. Some of these have live entertainment. Further south along Cra 7,

from C 32 up to C 59 draws an edgier crowd of filmmakers, artists and students.

Alma Bar, C 85, No 12-51, T6228289, open Wed-Sat 1900-0300, entry US$11-27, is a relatively new bar/club playing crossover Colombian/Western music.

Cha Cha, Cra 7, No 32-26, www.elcha cha.com In what used to be the old Hilton hotel, this 42nd-floor club, with spectacular views of the city, is currently Bogotá's most fashionable venue, attracting the city's richest and most beautiful. European DJs playing electronic music are the norm.

Gótica, Cra 14, No 82-50, T2180727, open Wed-Sat 1000-0400, entry US$8, plays a mixture of hip hop, electronica and crossover.

In Vitro, C 59, No 6-38. What started as a weekly meeting of friends to show their short films and documentaries has developed into one of Bogotá's hippest clubs. Shows short films during the week while the weekends are reserved for an eclectic mix of salsa, rock'n'roll and indie music. Tue and Wed night are especially popular as entrance is free. Frequented by filmmakers, artists and students.

The Monkey Pub, Cra 5, No 71-45, Edificio La Strada, piso 2. English pub serving draught beers and the occasional Guinness.

Son Salomé, Cra 7, No 40-31, Piso 2. Popular salsa venue.

Theatron, C 58, No 10-32, www.theatronde pelicula.com. In an old cinema theatre, this spectacular gay venue, spread out over 4 floors and with a capacity of 4000 has to be seen to be believed. It includes a rooftop garden and several different rooms playing everything from *vallenato* to electronic music. It accepts straight couples but beyond a certain point within the building it's men only.

🎭 Entertainment

Bogotá *p56, maps p58, p64, p72 and p75*
Guía del Ocio (known as GO) has listings on restaurants and clubs, as does *Plan B*, formerly a newspaper, now only online

(www.planb.com.co) and Vive.in
(www.vive.in).

Cinema

Consult *El Espectador*, *El Tiempo* or *PlanB*
magazine for listings; there are frequent
programme changes.
Cine Bar Lumière, Cra 14, No 85-59,
T6360485. US$5 weekends and holidays,
cheaper mid-week, comfortable airplane-
style seats, food and drink.
Cine Bar Paraíso, Cra 6, No 119B-56,
T2155361, (Usaquén).
Cinemanía, Cra 14, No 93A-85, mainstream
and foreign art films.
Museo de Arte Moderno (see page 73) shows
Colombian and foreign films every day, all day.
In Vitro, C 59, No 6-38, is a popular nightclub
that also shows Colombian and international
arthouse films during the week.

There are cinema complexes in the
principal shopping centres (see below).
The best are **Centro Comercial Andino**,
Unicentro, and **Atlantis**. Most have
discounted rates on Tue. For programme
times call **CineColombia**, T4042463.

Foreign films are shown on weekend
mornings in some commercial cinemas and
there are many small screening rooms
running features. Admission US$2-4. There is
an international film festival in Oct (*Festival de
Cine de Bogotá*) and a European film festival.

⊛ Festivals and events

Bogotá *p56, maps p58, p64, p72 and p75*
There are many local religious festivals and
parades at Easter and Christmas. One of the
best is the Fiesta de Reyes Magos (Three Kings)
in Jan in the suburb of Egipto (up the hill to the
east of Candelaria) with traditional processions.
Mar Iberoamerican Theatre Festival,
www.festivaldeteatro.com.co, a biennial
event (next 2010) hosted by Bogotá.
Apr-May Feria Internacional del Libro (book
fair) is held in Corferias, Cra 40, No 22C-67,
www.corferias.com.

May, Jun and Sep Temporada de Opera
y Zarzuela is held in the Teatro Colón in
with international artists.
Aug Opera season.
Sep Candelaria Festival, with street theatre,
music and dance events. Also the **Festival
Internacional de Jazz** takes place.
Oct Rock al Parque, biggest annual rock festival
in Latin America (www.rockalparque.gov.co).
Dec Expoartesanía fair, at Corferias. An
excellent selection of arts and crafts and
regional food from across Colombia.
Highly recommended.

○ Shopping

Bogotá *p56, maps p58, p64, p72 and p75*
There is a 16% value-added tax on all
purchases. Heavy duty plastic for covering
rucksacks etc, is available at several shops
around C 16 and Av Caracas; some have
heat-sealing machines to make bags to size.
In **Barrio Gaitán**, Cr 30 y C 65, are rows of
leather shops. This is an excellent area to buy
made-to-measure leather jackets, good value;
not safe at night, go during the day. Designer
labels are cheaper in Colombia than in Europe.

Bookshops

Books in Colombia are generally expensive.
Ateneo, C 82, No 13-19, in the north of the
city. Good selection of Colombian titles,
knowledgeable staff.
Authors, C 70, No 5-23, T2177788,
www.authors.com.co. Run by American
owner, sells English-language books.
Exopotamia, C 70, No 4-47. Good selection
of books and Latin music, also branch in
Biblioteca Luis Angel Arango in Candelaria.
Forum, C 93, No 13A-49, just off Parque 93.
Foreign magazines, CDs, pleasant atmosphere.
Librería Central, C 94, No 13-92. Some
English- and German-language books.
Librería Nacional bookstores across town
eg Unicentro and Santa Bárbara shopping
centres. Good Colombian history and current
affairs section and some foreign press.

Panamericana, Cra 7, No 14-09. Disorganized, but has some guidebooks and maps. Other branches in the city.

Taschen, C 26, No 10-18, next to Hotel Tequendama. Art books, small selection of English books and foreign magazines. Also at Museum of Modern Art.

Tower Records in Andino shopping centre, C 82, Cra 3, sells foreign press.

Villegas Editores, Av 82, No 11-50, int 3. Great coffee-table books on Colombia.

Newspapers

US and European newspapers can be bought at Librería Oma, at Tacos de la 19, near the corner of Cra 7/C (Av) 19, or at Papeles La Candelaria, C 11, No 3-89, open daily, also has internet, fax and sells Latin-American cultural magazines, US, European and other papers 2 days after publication.

There are several excellent English-language newspapers. The *City Paper*, for good travel stories on Colombia. *El Mono* for humorous pieces on life in Colombia. Both are available at many hotels, hostals, embassies and popular bars such as the **Bogota Beer Company**.

Camping equipment

Monodedo, Cra 16, No 82-22, T6163467. Good selection of camping and climbing equipment. Enquire here for information about climbing in Colombia.

Computer repair

Tempo's System, C 79, No 16-22, Local 4, piso 2, T6919707, temposystem@gmail.com. Ask for Ever Rodriguez, an excellent, trustworthy technician. Also try nearby **Unilago** shopping centre.

Handicrafts

Artesanías de Colombia, Claustro de Las Aguas, next to the Iglesia de las Aguas, Cra 3A, No 18-60; Cra 11 No 84-12 by CC Andino; and in Plaza de los Artesanos, Tr 48, No 63A-52. Beautiful but expensive designer crafts.

Tienda Fibrarte, Cra 3, No 11-24. *Artesanías* from around Colombia and Latin America. Good fique products, coca tea. Credit cards accepted.

Galerías Cano, Ed Bavaria, Cra 13, No 27-98 (Torre B, Int 1-19B), also at Unicentro, and Loc 218, Airport. Sell textiles, pottery, and gold and gold-plated replicas of some of the jewellery on display in the Gold Museum.

Markets

Mercado de Pulgas (flea market), Cra 7/C 24, in car park beside Museo de Arte Moderno, on Sun afternoons and holidays. A better flea market can be found at the Usaquén market around the plaza on Sun, also a good arts and crafts market at the top of the hill in Usaquén.

Pasaje Rivas, C10 y Cra10. Persian-style bazaar. Hammocks, ceramics, cheap. A small arts and crafts market is open on most days opposite Hotel Tequendama in the centre.

Paloquemao food market, Cra 27, entre C19 y 22. Bogotá's huge central market, good to visit just to see the sheer abundance of Colombia's tropical fruits and flowers. Cheap stalls serving *comida corriente*. Safe. Flower section best between 0500 and 1000.

San Andresito, Cra 38 y C12. Popular contraband market, cheap alcohol, designer sports labels, electrical goods, football shirts. Relatively safe.

Jewellery

The pavements and cafés along Av Jiménez, below Cra 7, and on Plazoleta del Rosario are used on weekdays (especially Fri) by emerald dealers. Rows of jewellers and emerald shops also along C 12 with Cra 6. Great expertise is needed in buying: there are bargains, but synthetics and forgeries abound.

Emerald Trade Centre, Av Jiménez, No 5-43, p 1. German/English spoken.

GMC Galería Minas de Colombia, C20, No 0-86, T281 6523, at foot of Monserrate diagonal from Quinta de Bolívar. Good selection of jewellery at reasonable prices.

La Casa de la Esmeralda, C 30, No 16-18. Wide range of stones.

Photography

Poder Fotográfico, Cra 5, No 20-60, T3429678, for good developing in 2-3 hrs, used by professionals, also camera repairs. Other photo shops nearby. **Foto Japón,** branches all over the city, gives free film, branch at Cra 7, No 14-32.

Shopping malls

Unicentro, a large shopping centre on Cra 15, No 127, www.unicentrobogota.com.co (take 'Unicentro' bus from centre, going north on Cra 10 takes about 1 hr). **Centro Granahorrar,** Av Chile (Calle 72), No 10-34, is another good shopping centre; **Hacienda Santa Bárbara,** Cra 7 Nº 115 – 60, www.haciendasantabarbara.com.co; **Bulevar Niza,** Cra 58, No 125A-59, www.centrocomercialniza.com; **Centro Comercial Andino,** Cra 11, No 82-71, www.centroandino.com.co.; Centro Comercial Unilago, Cra 15, No 78-33, www.unilago.com. For computers, gadgets and repairs. **Exito, Pomona** and **Carulla** chains are probably the best supermarket groups in Bogotá. Some stores have pay by weight salad bars.

▲ Activities and tours

Bogotá *p56, maps p58, p64, p72 and p75*
Bullfighting
There are *corridas* on Sat and Sun during the season (Jan and sometimes Feb), and occasionally for the rest of the year, at the municipally owned **Plaza de Santamaría,** near Parque Independencia. The brick bull ring was built in 1927 and has a capacity of 16,000. In season, the bulls weigh over 335 kg; out of season they are comparatively small. (Local bullfight museum at bullring, door No 6.) The **Corporación Taurina de Bogotá,** C 70A, No 6-24, T3341628, www.ctaurina.com, holds a summer festival every year in early Aug. Boxing matches are held here, too.

Football

Tickets for matches at El Campín stadium can be bought in advance at **Federación Colombiana de Fútbol**, Av 32, No 15-42, www.colfutbol.org. It is not normally necessary to book in advance, except for the local Santa Fe–Millonarios derby, and of course, internationals.

Hiking

Sal Si Puedes hiking group arranges walks every weekend and sometimes midweek on trails in Cundinamarca, and further afield at national holiday periods eg Semana Santa; very friendly, welcomes visitors. Hikes are graded for every ability, from 6 km to 4-day excursions of 70 km and more, camping overnight. The groups are often big (30-60), but after the preliminary warm-up exercises, and the Sal Si Puedes hymn, the regime relaxes and it is possible to stray from the main group. Reservations can be made and paid for a week or so in advance at Cra 7, No 17-01, office 739, T2833765, open 0800-1200 and 1400-1800. This is a very good way to see the National Park areas in the Cordillera Oriental near Bogotá, eg Chingaza and Sumapaz. They also occasionally go at holiday times to the major tourist attractions of Colombia eg Tayrona, San Agustín, Leticia and Gorgona. **Corporación Clorofila Urbana,** Cra 33, No 96-13, T6168711, www.clorofila urbana.org, offers similar walking opportunities with an emphasis on environmental awareness. **Confraternidad de Senderismo Ecológico El Respiro,** Transversal 48, No 96-48, T2530884/ T6178857, is another group offering walks.

There are several other groups, good information on Fri in *El Tiempo* newspaper, *Eskape* section and in the monthly *Go Guía del Ocio* guide (has a small section in English and French).

Caminar por Colombia, Cra 7, No 22-31, of 226 B, T286 7487, caminarcolombia@ hotmail.com, is a recommended operator offering walks around the capital every Sun, US$10 for small groups, includes transport and guide.

Horse riding
Cabalgatas Carpasos, Km 7 Vía La Calera, T3687242, www.carpasos.com. About US$27 pp for leisurely ride outside Bogotá for groups of 4-5. Horse riding at night too.
Cabalgatas San Francisco, C 51A, No 76A-15, T2957715. Daily rides around coffee farms, in the mountains, by rivers and lakes, US$10 per hr.

Rafting and kayaking
Fundación Al Verde Vivo, Calle 95 N° 32-40 of 203, T2183048, www.alverdevivo.org, organizes adventure water sports while trying to minimize environmental impact.
Natura Vive, T311-809 4207, www.natura vive.com. Speciaists in various locations.

Rock climbing
La Gran Pared, Cra 7, No 49, T2850903, www.granpared.com. Artificial rock-climbing wall in the centre of Bogotá. US$6.50 per hr including equipment.

Skydiving
Club de Paracaidismo Saint Michel, C 68 with Cra 68, T2498923, www.skydivecolom bia.com. 2-day courses with 3 jumps from US$267.

Tour operators
Colombia Quest, Av 15 No 122-71, of 1-511, T7043936/T(281)383-9615 (in USA), www.colombiaquest.com. Specializes in trips around Bogotá, especially around La Candelaria and Zipaquirá. Also shopping and clubbing tours. Very knowledgeable guides. English, French, German and Japanese spoken. Recommended.
De Una Colombia Tours, Cra 26a, No 40-18, Apto 202, T3681915, www.deuna colombia.com. Dutch-run tour agency with tailor-made trips throughout Colombia and an emphasis on introducing tourists to the country's people as well as its landscapes. Particularly experienced in Los Nevados and Sierra Nevada del Cocuy.
Ecoguías, Cra 3, No 55-10, of 501, T3475736. Colombian-British team specializing in eco-tourism, trekking, adventure sports and stays on *fincas*. Efficient and well organized.

Travel agents
Local travel agents can often prove more economical for buying flights than dealing with the airlines direct.
Doble Vía, Carrera 11, No 77-20, T2112754. National and international flights. Best for fights to Leticia with **AeroRepública**.
Vivir Volando, Cra 16, No 96-64, T6014676, www.vivirvolando.com. Flights and packages to Pacific, Amazon and Caribbean coast. Strong links with **Satena**.

Transport

Bogotá *p56, maps p58, p64, p72 and p75*
Air
Since international and domestic flights use both the main **El Dorado** airport, T4251000,

Original
Sophisticated
Tailor made ■

COLOMBIA QUEST

info@colombiaquest.com   +57 (1) 7043936   www.colombiaquest.com

and the **Puente Aéreo**, you must check which terminal your flight will use.

To **Cartagena** hourly flights with Avianca and AeroRepública. To **Medellín** with Avianca, Satena and AeroRepública. To **Cali** with Avianca, AeroRepública and Satena. To **Bucaramanga** with Avianca and AeroRepública. To **Barranquilla** with Avianca and AeroRepública. To **Armenia** with Avianca, Easyfly and Aires.

Local airline offices AeroRepública, Cra 10, No 27-51, Local 165, T342722, Reservations T3209090. Aires, Aeropuerto El Dorado, T0190033199440, or at Cra 11, No 76–11, Local 103, T3213649. Avianca, Av 19, No 4-37, Local 2, T2849860, airport T4139862. Satena, Cra 10, No 26-21, of 210, T4238500, military airline, not the best for comfort and delays.

International airline offices Air France, Cra 9A, No 99-07, Torre 1, T6506000. American, C 71A, No 5-90, Local 101, T4398022. British Airways, T018009156641 (toll free). Continental, Cra 7, No 71–21, Torre A, Oficina 2, T3425279 or Cra 10, No 26-35, local 7, T018009440219. Iberia, Cra 19, No 85-11, T6166111, airport, T4138715. Lufthansa, C 100, No 8A-49, Torre B, piso 8 T6180300. Mexicana, Av 15, No 114-36, Oficina 108. Qantas, C 116, No 9-35, piso 1, T2132062. TACA, C 113, No 7-21, Local 124, T018009518222 (toll free). Varig, Cra 7A, No 33-24, T6507100. Most airlines, local and international, have offices in both central and North Bogotá. Many international airline offices are closed on Sat and Sun.

Bus
Local Buses stop (in theory) by 'Paradero' boards but there are very few left and normally passengers flag buses down near street corners. Bus fares are from US$0.55 up, depending on length of route and time of day. Most buses have day/night tariff advertised in the window. *Busetas* (small and green) charge a little more and can be dirty. There are some *ejecutivo* (red and white)

routes with more comfortable seats, at US$0.70. *Colectivos* are small vans, cramped but faster, US$0.80. To go north, pick one up at C 19/Cra 3, or any bus marked 'Unicentro'; they follow Cra 7. Fares are a bit higher at night and on holidays. The network is complicated and confusing. However, people waiting for the buses are more than happy to help you to find the correct one.

Long-distance The long-distance bus terminal, **Terminal de Transportes**, is near Av Boyacá (Cra 72) between El Dorado (Av 26) and Av Centenario (C 13). There is also access from Cra 68. The exact address is C 33B, No 69-59, T2951100, www.terminaldetransporte. gov.co. The terminal is divided into modules serving the 4 points of the compass; each module has several bus companies serving similar destinations. If possible, buy tickets at the respective ticket office before travelling. It is possible to bargain with the various bus companies and reduce the price of a ticket. To get to the terminal take a bus marked 'Terminal terrestre' from the centre or a *buseta* on Cra 10. A taxi costs around US$4.40 from the centre, with a surcharge at night. As with the airports there is an effective system to stop drivers overcharging. Give your desired address at a kiosk, which will print out a slip with the address and price. Fares and journey times are given under destinations below. If you are travelling north, you can significantly cut down on the journey time by taking the *Transmilenio* to Portal del Norte, thus avoiding an arduous journey through Bogotá's traffic. Velotax *busetas* are slightly quicker and more expensive than ordinary buses, as are *colectivos*, which go to several long-distance destinations. The terminal is well organized and comfortable, but, as usual, watch out for thieves who are also well organized – the number of reports of baggage thefts there are increasing. Free self-service luggage trolleys are provided. There are shops, restaurants and ATMs. There are also showers at the terminal (between Nos 3 and 4).

Modulo 4 also has a clinic giving vaccinations, open 0700 to 1900, US$24 for non-nationals.

International If going to Venezuela, it is better not to buy a through ticket to Caracas with **Berlinas de Fonce** as this does not guarantee a seat and is only valid for 2 Venezuelan companies; moreover no refunds are given in Cúcuta. Ideally, if you have time, make the journey to Cúcuta in 2 stages to enjoy the scenery to the full. Bus connections from San Antonio de Táchira in Venezuela to Caracas are good. There are buses from Lima (Peru) to Caracas (Venezuela) that travel through Ecuador run by **Transportes Ormeño**. This weekly service is not recommended mainly because of the several days it takes and the unreliability of the timetable. The cost to **Lima** is about US$166, to **Quito**, US$83, to **Caracas**, US$155. Much better (and cheaper) is to do the trip in stages and enjoy the countries you are travelling through.

Car rental
Dollar Rent-a-Car, Av El Dorado, No 98-50, T413 5599 and at airport, one of the cheapest. **Hertz**, at airport, T2882636, and at Av Caracas, No 27-17, T3276700.
Colombia Rent a Car, Av Boyacá, No 63-12, T47135032.

Taxi
If you are short of time, have luggage or valuables, or at night, take a taxi. They are relatively cheap, there are many of them about and the service is generally good. If you take one on the street, try to pick one that looks in good condition. It should also be yellow and the driver's official ID card with photo should be visible; non official taxis are not recommended. At busy times, empty taxis flagged down on the street may refuse to take you to less popular destinations.

All official taxis are metered. The *taxímetro* (meter) registers units starting at 25 then calculates the time and distance travelled.

The driver converts the total into pesos using a green fare table. If the conversion card is not displayed, the driver should show it to you. Check before taking your first taxi if there are any additional charges above what the meter/conversion card states eg: night charge or other surcharge; a list of legal charges should be posted in the taxi.

Radio taxis are recommended for safety and reliability. When you call, the dispatcher gives you a cab number, write it down and confirm this when it arrives. There is a small charge but it is safer. Try these numbers: T2111111, T3111111, T4111111 and T2233333. Tipping is not customary, but is appreciated. If you are going to an address out of the city centre, it is helpful to know the area you are going to as well as the address, eg Chicó, Chapinero (ask at your hotel).

Train
Long-distance services were suspended in 1992. There are no passenger services at present from Bogotá **La Sabana** station at C 13 y Cra 19, except a tourist steam train, which runs on Sat, Sun and holidays at 0830 calling at **Usaquén**, C 110, **Transversal 10**, in the north of the city at 0920, going north to **Zipaquirá**, 1130, and **Cajicá**, 1230, returning at 1515 and back in Bogotá Usaquén at 1640 and La Sabana at 1740. Adult US$15, child 2-10, US$9.40. Information, Turistrén Ltda, C 13, No 18-24, T3750557, www.turistren.com.co.

Directory

Bogotá *p56, maps p58, p64, p72 and p75*
Banks
Banks are everywhere in Bogotá where there is commercial activity. Some head offices are grouped around the **Avianca** building at the corner of Plaza San Francisco, others have moved to North Bogotá on or near C 72.

The best way to obtain pesos in Bogotá is to use ATMs. Any other method will require your passport and, often, queues. Since it will probably require at least 2 or 3 attempts, either go downtown or in the north, where there are many banks. Unfortunately, there are no rules; there are countless ATMs accepting MasterCard, Visa and other cards; but machines may be down or out of cash, or just don't accept the cards stated. ATMs also tend to give out a frustratingly small amount of cash at a time (though you can go back several times a day), resulting in much money lost in transaction fees. Most banks have a paltry COP300 (US$167) maximum, though **Davivienda** (COP500/US$278) and **Bancolombia** (COP400/US$222) are more generous. Those in more affluent areas tend to dispense more.

Exchange **Emerald Trade Center**, Av Jiménez, Cra 5-43, Local 128, T2866181, open 0800-1800, accepts Thomas Cook TCs. **Titan**, Cra 7, No 18-42, Local 116, T3413875. **Cambios Country**, Cra 11, No 71-40, Of 201, and at El Dorado airport, T413 8979. Several other city offices, good rates, speedy service. **Orotur**, Cra 10, No 26-05 (below Hotel Tequendama in pedestrian subway) is quick and efficient, cash only, including sterling. **Cambios New York Money**, in CC Unicentro, Av 15, No 123-30, loc 1-118, accepts sterling, efficient. Other *cambios* on Av Jiménez de Quesada, between Cras 6 and 11, and in the north of the city. On Sun exchange is virtually impossible except at the airport. CC Hacienda Santa Bárbara has several *cambios* but buying sterling can be difficult. To replace lost Amex TCs, **American Express**, Expreso Viajes y Turismo, C 85, No 20-32, T593 4949 (has other branches), open 0800-1900, Sat 0900-1400, with full details, a police report of the loss and preferably proof of purchase. They first authorize cash advance on Amex cards and then direct you to the appropriate bank (**Banco Unión Colombia**).

Cultural centres

British Council, Cra 9, No 76-49, Piso 5, T3259090, www.britishcouncil.org/colombia. New modern centre, open Mon-Fri 0900-1700, good TEFL library, British newspapers. **Centro Colombo Americano**, C 19, No 2-49, T3347640 or C 110, No 15-36, T2755052, www.colombobogota.edu.co. English and Spanish courses, recommended. Also in Medellín. **Alianza Colombo-Francesa**, Cra 3, No 18-45, T3411348 and Cra 7, No 84-72, T2368605, www.alianza francesa.org.co. Films in French, newspapers, library monthly bulletin, etc. Other branches in major cities across Colombia. **Goethe Institut**, Cra 7, No 81-57, T2551843, www.goethe.de/ins/co/bog/deindex.htm.

Embassies and consulates

Austria, T3263680 (emergencies) **Australia**, Cra 18, No 90-38, T6365247. **Belgium**, Apto 3564, C 26, No 4A-45, 7th floor, T3800380, bogota@diplobel.org. **Brazil**, C 93, No 14-20, piso 8, T2180800. **Canada**, Cra 7, No 114-33, piso 14, T6579951, www.dfait-maeci.gc.ca **Cuba**, Cra 9, No 92-54, T6217054. **Ecuador**, C 89, No 13-07, T6350322, www.embajada ecuacol.net. **France**, Cra 11, No 93-12, T6381400, www.ambafrance-co.org. **Germany**, Cra 69, No 25B-44, Piso 7, T4232600, www.bogota.diplo.de. **Italy**, C 93B, No 9-92, T2186680, www.ambbogota. esteri.it. **Israel**, C 35, No 7-25, Piso 14, T3277500. **Japan**, Cra 7, No 71-21, Torre B, piso 11, T3175001. **Netherlands**, Cra 13, No 93-40, piso 5, T6384200. **Mexico**, C 82, No 9-25, T6104070. Panama, C 92, No 7-70, T2575067. **Spain**, C 92, No 12-68, T6220090. **Sweden**, C 72 Bis, No 5-83, piso 9, Edif Av Chile, T3256180, www.swedenabroad.com. **Switzerland**, Cra 9, No 74-08, Of 101, T3497230. **United Kingdom**, Cra 9, No 76-49, 9th floor, T3268300. **USA**, C 22D Bis, No 47-51, T3150811. **Venezuela**, Cra 11, No 87-51, piso 5, T6401213 (610 6622 visa information), 0830-1200. Visas can be collected the following day 1200-1630. Enquire by telephone before you go.

Immigration

DAS head office, Cra 28, No 17A-00, T208 6060, www.das.gov.co. Open 0730-1530, or T153. Cundinamarca office, C 58, No 10-55,

T5701077. Dirección de Extranjería (for extending entry permits): C 100, No 11B-27, T6017200, open Mon-Thu 0730-1600, Fri 0730-1530. DAS will not authorize photocopies of passports; look in Yellow Pages for notaries, who will.

Internet

Most hotels and hostels and some restaurants are now Wi-Fi-enabled and provide several computers for surfing the net. There are many internet cafés, charging US$1-2 per hr.

Listelnet Communications, Cra 3, No 15-47. Skype and heaphones. International calls. **Café Xanaledra**, Cra 4, No 12-78 Esquina. Skype and headphones as well as coffee, tea and cake. **Café del Cubo**, Cr 4, No 13-57, Mon-Sat 0900-2200. The tourist kiosk on Plaza Bolívar, Cra 8, No 9-83, has 3 computers. First 15 mins free. **Coffeemail**, CC Santa Bárbara. Mon-Sat 1030-2000, Sun 1400- 1800. Helpful staff. US$1-2 per hr. **Foto and Internet Café**, Tequendama Hotel/Centro Internacional complex (2nd floor), loc 164, helpful, good service, Mon-Fri 0700-2000, Sat 0900-1600, US$0.90 per hr. **Web Café**, Diag 27, No 6-81, Mon-Fri 0900-2000, Sat 1000-1800.

Language courses

You need a student visa, not a tourist visa, to study. Some of the best Spanish courses are in the **Universidad Nacional**, T316 5000, www.unal.edu.co, about US$180 for 2 months, 8 hrs per week, or **Universidad de los Andes**, T3394949, www.uniandes.edu.co, US$300, 6 weeks, and **Pontificia Universidad Javeriana**, T320 8320 ext 4620, www.javer iana.edu.co. Good-value Spanish courses at the **Universidad Pedagógica**, C 72, No 11-86, T594 1894. Good reports, around US$90 for 40 hrs, 2 hrs per day, one of the cheapest on offer. Language exchanges with students wishing to learn English are also popular. Enquire at Platypus hostel. **Carmen Trujillo**, T3158741325 (mob)/T70439636, carmen. trujillo@ colombiaquest.com is recommended. English, French and Italian spoken.

Medical services

Cruz Roja Nacional, Av 68, No 66-31, T428 0111. Open 0830-1800, consultations/ inoculations US$12.50. **Fundación Santa Fe de Bogotá**, C 119, No 9-33, T6293066, and **El Bosque**, C 134, No 12-55, T274 0577, are both modern, private hospitals, with good service. For vaccinations, try **Clínica Marly**, C 50, No 7 -72, T2454729. **Doctor** Dr Paul Vaillancourt, Cra 11, No 94A-25, Of 401, T6356312. English-speaking. Dr Brigitte Scholz, C 183, No 76-65, T6704982. **Dentist** Hyung Kuk Kim, Diagonal 86A, No 32-43, T6161151, tmask10@hotmail.com. English-speaking. **Chemists** Farmacity, is a chain of new, well-stocked chemists open 24 hrs across the city. For 24-hr home deliveries in Bogotá, T5300000, C 93A, No-13-41, off Parque de la 93, Cra 13, No 63A-67, among others.

Post office

Main **Avianca** ticket office and **Deprisa** airmail office in basement of Ed Avianca, Cra 7, No 16-36, open 0730-1900 Mon to Fri, 0800-1500 Sat, closed Sun and holidays (poste restante 0730-1800, Mon-Sat, letters kept for 1 month, US$1 per letter). Parcels by air are sent from here too. Also Cra 7 y C 26-27, near Planetarium; C 140 between Cra 19 y Autopista. Parcels by air, contact **Avianca**. Adpostal, Cra 7, No 27-54, handles international parcels. **Couriers** Servientrega, C 64, No 89A-83, T5437300 (international), T7700410 (national). Deprisa, C 64A, No 94-69, T5405300, Ext 46. DHL, C 19, No 4-29. **Fedex**, Cra 7, N 16-50, T2433315.

Telephone

Emergency Fire T119, Ambulance T125, Red Cross T132, Red Cross ambulance T127. CAI Police T156 or 112. **International** Calls can be made from several **Telecom** offices in centre of Bogotá (eg in the **Tequendama Hotel** complex, Cra 13, No 26-45, Mon-Sat 0800-1900); all close within ½ an hour of 2000 and may be closed on holidays. Purchase of phone cards is recommended if you are using call boxes.

Around Bogotá

The buzz of Bogotá can sometimes be tempered by its chilly nights and frequent drizzle. But just a few hours away in most directions it can be pleasingly sunny and hot. Exiting northwest from the city, the road swiftly descends towards the Magdalena River valley and a string of pretty towns such as Guaduas and Honda. To the southwest, on the edge of the Sabana de Bogotá, lies the cloud-forested Chicaque Parque Natural, a private nature reserve popular with hikers and horse riders. Just before the road reaches the hot plains of the Magdalena River that lead to Neiva is Girardot, a popular weekend retreat for bogotanos nicknamed the 'swimming pool city'. Driving due north of Bogotá in the direction of Boyacá are two of the country's most impressive cultural trophies. The Laguna de Guatavita was a lake prized by the Muisca and is believed to be the source of the legend of El Dorado. A few kilometres beyond is the salt cathedral at Zipaquirá, a truly awe-inspiring monument to religious devotion. ▸▸ *For listings, see pages 93-94.*

Southwest to Parque Natural Chicaque

The Simón Bolívar Highway runs from Bogotá to Girardot, the former main riverport for Bogotá, now a popular second-home venue thanks to its climate. Only small boats can go upriver from here and it is known for the volume of swimming pools built by weekending *bogoteños*. This 132-km stretch is extremely picturesque, running down the mountains. About 20 km along this road from the centre of Bogotá is **Soacha**, now the end of the built-up area of the city. A right fork here leads along a poor road to the Indumil plant, 3 km after which there is a large sign for the **Parque Natural Chicaque** ① *daily 0800-1600, US$9.* Take a bus to Soacha and ask for onward transport. The entry booth is 300 m down a track.

The park is a privately owned 300-ha estate of principally cloudforest between 2100 m and 2700 m on the edge of *La Sabana de Bogotá*. The property, which has never been developed, now has some 10 km of trails down and around 500 m of cliffs, with a supplementary peak and an 80 m waterfall. It is a popular spot for walkers and riders at weekends with good facilities for day visitors and a new Swiss-style *refugio* at the bottom level, about one hour down the trail from the entrance. This provides meals and accommodation for 70 or so costing US$20-25 a day including meals and other facilities for day visitors. There is an abundance of birds, butterflies and a great natural diversity of forest cover. The owner also reports frequent sightings of UFOs.

Bogotá to Honda ⊜⊘▲⊜ ▸▸ *pp93-94.*

La Sabana de Bogotá is dotted with white farms and groves of eucalyptus. The road to Honda passes through two small towns; Fontibón and Madrid. **Facatativá** is 40 km from Bogotá. Some 3 km from Facatativá, on the road to the west, is the park of **Piedras de Tunja**, a natural rock amphitheatre with enormous stones, numerous indigenous pictographs and an artificial lake. Some 71 km from Facatativá on the road to Honda, **Villeta** is a popular weekend resort for Bogotanos. It is a busy town at the centre of the *panela* (unrefined sugar cane) industry and is in a cattle-raising area. Not far away are the waterfalls of **Quebrada Cune** ① *open 0800-1200, 1400-1800.* They are helpful and have a good map of the town. The annual **National Panela Festival** is for three days in January and there is a Band Festival in mid-August. Look out for *Piedra de Bolívar* (Bolívar stone), on which is marked all the occasions when Bolívar passed through the town.

Midway between Villeta and Honda is **Guaduas**. In the towns of the *tierra caliente* northwest of the capital, Guaduas preserves its colonial charm more than the others. Founded three times between 1572 and 1644, it was a stopover on the *camino real* between Bogotá and the river at Honda. Policarpa Salavarrieta, heroine of the independence movement, was born here on 26 January 1796. There is a statue of her in the plaza and the **Casa de La Pola** where she lived is one block from the plaza and now an interesting museum (free). **Calle Real** is the best-preserved colonial street. The oldest house in town is the Alcaldía on Avenida José Antonio Galán. Simón Bolívar slept in the room on the second floor before leaving by river for Santa Marta. About 10 km outside the town is the Salto de Versalles, a lovely 45 m waterfall, now a National Monument. There is a public swimming pool in Guaduas and a Sunday market. The best local dish is *quesillos*.

Honda

Four hours from Bogotá, on the west bank of the Magdalena, is Honda, a pleasant old town surrounded by hills and with a picturesque colonial section of steep, narrow cobbled streets and brightly coloured houses. It was founded in 1539 and in its pomp it was an important trading port for goods coming down the Magdalena from the Atlantic coast to Bogotá. With an average temperature of 33°C, Honda is a hot place. The former President of Colombia, Alfonso López, was born here and there is a **Casa Cultural** ① *C 13/ Cra 11, open Tues to Sat 0830-1200 and 1400-1800, Sun and public holidays 0830-1300, US$0.50,* dedicated to him, with some interesting photographs from the period. To reach the colonial part of town, cross any of the three bridges that span the Gualí river, a tributary of the Magdalena. **El Salto de Honda** (the rapids which separate the Lower from the Upper Magdalena) are just below the town. In February the Magdalena rises and fishing is unusually good. People come from all over the region for the fishing and the festival of the Subienda, as the season is called.

The town has an interesting covered market, selling mostly fruit and vegetables but some *artesanías* too, in a grand old building next to the river. At the top of the town, up some steep cobbled streets, is the parque principal with a fine stone church, **El Alto Rosario**, and a statue dedicated to David Hughes Williams, an Englishman who became a popular town mayor.

Guatavita ▶▶ *Colour map 2, C5.*

About 75 km from Bogotá, overlooking the lake is the small, modern town of Guatavita Nueva, which was built in colonial style when the old town of Guatavita was submerged by the reservoir. The original inhabitants were unwilling to stay in the new town, so it is now a weekend haunt for *bogoteños* and tourists. There is a cathedral, artisan workshops and two small museums; one devoted to the indigenous Muisca and the other to relics of the old Guatavita church, including a delightful Debain harmonium. The Sunday market is best in the morning, before *bogoteños* arrive. To get there, catch a bus from Bogotá.

Laguna de Guatavita (also called **Lago de Amor** by locals), is where the legend of El Dorado originated. The lake is a quiet, beautiful place. You can walk right round it close to the water level in 1½ hours, or climb to the rim of the crater in several places. Opinions differ on whether the crater is volcanic or a meteorite impact, but from the rim at 3100 m there are extensive views over the varied countryside. Access to the park is only permissible with a permit obtained from the **Corporación Autónoma Regional de Cundinamarca (CAR)** ① *Cra 7, No 36-45/11, T3209000, www.car.gov.co, US$6.50.*

The legend of El Dorado

The Spanish came to South America with an insatiable obsession for gold. Nowhere was this more exemplified than in their search for El Dorado, a fruitless quest that drove them to explore the wildest regions of the continent and was responsible for the deaths of thousands of indigenous locals and Spanish alike.

The basis for the legend is established fact. It tells of an annual custom in which the Chibcha king was coated with gold dust and set adrift on a ceremonial raft.

He would dive into the lake and emerge cleansed of the gold. It was said that the lake also had precious offerings thrown in.

The lake was eventually identified as Guatavita, just north of Bogotá, and the story verified by the discovery of a miniature raft made from gold wire that now holds pride of place in Bogotá's Museo de Oro.

Several attempts have been made to drain Lake Guatavita and many items recovered but never on the scale the Spanish imagined.

Getting there

Flota Aguila, at the bus terminal, US$3, two to three hours, several departures during the morning; last return bus at 1730. You can walk (two to three hours) or ride (US$7 per horse) from Guatavita Nueva to the lake. An easier approach is from a point on the Sesquilé–Guatavita Nueva road (the bus driver will let you off) where there is a sign 'via Lago Guatavita'. There is a good campsite and places to eat nearby. From the main road to the lakeside the road is paved as far as a school, about half way. Follow the signs. This road and subsequent track can be driven in a good car to within 300 m of the lake, where there is a car park and good restaurant. Taxi tour from Bogotá costs around US$60 for a full day.

Zipaquirá ◐ ▸▸ pp93-94. Colour map 2, C5.

ⓘ *Entry to the new cathedral is US$8, including 1¼ hrs guided tour and film showing history of salt mining, car park US$2, daily 0900-1800, Sun Mass at 1300, admission by ticket. The entrance to the cave is in hills about 20 mins' walk west of the town. There is an information centre and a museum at the site.*

A further 13 km beyond is Zipaquirá (commonly called Zipa), centre of a rich cattle-farming district, and famous for its rock salt mine (which has been exploited for centuries) and fabulous salt cathedral. This should not be missed. The sight of this remarkable architectural and artistic achievement is enough to leave even the most cynical atheist genuflecting in awed appreciation. Salt has been mined here since the 15th century, long before the Spaniards came and established the town in 1606. Many kilometres of tunnels have been excavated since then. There was a shrine in the cave carved by the miners into the salt many years before the original cathedral started to take shape in 1950. It was dedicated in 1954 to Nuestra Señora del Rosario (patron saint of miners). Continuing deterioration made the cave unsafe and it was closed in 1990. A new salt cathedral was begun in 1991 and opened on 16 December 1995 by President Samper. It is 500 m from, and 58 m below, the old cathedral. There is a short section before the 14 stations of the cross. Each station has been sculptured by a different artist; at their centre is a cross 4 m high, subtly lit and imaginatively executed. This is followed by sections representing the choir, narthex, baptistry (with a natural water source) and sacristy. Finally, at the lowest

The salt cathedral of Zipaquirá

There are few sights in Latin America as likely to convert even the staunchest of non-believers as the monumental salt cathedral of Zipaquirá. This fantastic architectural and artistic feat, carved inside a working salt mine, is a true measure of Colombians' religious devotion.

The site on which the cathedral is built has been a working mine since the time of the Muiscas. There was a shrine in a cave carved by miners for many years before anyone had the idea of building a cathedral. Gradually it was elaborated upon, and over the years it began to take shape. In 1954 it was dedicated to Nuestra Señora del Rosario, the patron saint of miners, and became a popular pilgrimage site, but was closed in 1990 due to structural problems.

A new cathedral, constructed half a kilometer from the site of the original, was begun in 1991 and opened on 16 December 1995 by President Samper. Visitors enter through a mineshaft and descend through twisting tunnels punctuated by 14 small chapels representing the stages of the cross, each of which has been designed by a celebrated Colombian artist.

At the lowest point of the cave, 180 m below the surface, a large nave has been carved out of the rock, supported by enormous columns that would not look out of place in Tolkien novel.

point in the cave, 180 m below the surface, are the nave and the north and south aisles with huge pillars growing out of the salt and dominated by the central cross, 16 m high. All is discreetly illuminated and gives a modern and austere impression.

The church in the attractive central plaza is also worth a visit for its stonework (despite its external appearance, it has a modern interior). The market on Tuesday is good for fruit and vegetables.

Nemocón → *Colour map 2, C5.*

Around 15 km northeast of Zipaquirá, at Nemocón, there are salt mines and a church, but the mines are now not operating and closed to visitors. However, there is a small but interesting **Museo de Sal** on the plaza, which includes local history and the beginnings of the salt industry in the time of the Muisca people. The main salt mine is four blocks above the museum, with some bizarre lampposts on the approach road.

◉ Around Bogotá listings → *Phone code: 1.*

For Sleeping and Eating price codes and other relevant information, see pages 31-36.

● Sleeping

Honda *p91*

All accommodation is across the Gualí river in the newer part of Honda.

C-D Hotel Calle Real, Cra 11, No 14-40, T2517737. Relatively new and possibly the best option in town. The rooms are clean and there is a small swimming pool on the roof. Prices vary according to whether you want a/c or a fan. Parking available.

D Riviera Plaza, C 14, No 12-09, T3128937520. The French Riviera it is not but nonetheless it has modern, clean rooms around a large swimming pool. If you get the rooms at the end there are good views over the river Gualí and the colonial part of town.

D Asturias Plaza, Cra 11, No 16-38, T2513326. Large, rambling hotel near the bus terminal with swimming pool, private bathrooms and cable TV. The rooms are a little dusty but otherwise ok.

Zipaquirá p92
C Cacique Real, Cra 6, No 2-12, T8510209, www.caciquereal.com. Recently declared a Patrimonio Cultural, this fine little hotel has a lovely courtyard with hanging baskets and good rooms with cable TV and hot water. There's Wi-Fi in the lobby and a car park.
D Casa Virrey, C 3, No 6-21, T8523720, casavirreyorani@hotmail.com. New building with 36 clean, comfortable rooms and private bathrooms. Laundry service available.
E Torre Real, C 8, No 5-92, T8511901. Light and airy rooms with large beds. Laundry service available.

🍴 Eating

Honda p91
There are several places to eat in the old town, along the river.

Zipaquirá p92
🍴 **Funzipa**, C 1, No 9-99. Enormous ranch with beautiful garden and original ovens for cooking salt. Serves *parrillas* and *bandejas*.
🍴 **La Antigua**, Cra 8, No 3-35. Cheap and cheerful *almuerzo ejecutivo* for US$3. There are several more similar options near the plaza.

🅰 Activities and tours

Honda p91
Tours Honda Travel, C 9, No 21-30, T3173093633, offers boat trips up the Magdalena.
A popular walk is up to the Cerro Cacao en Pelota, one of the hills behind Honda. It takes 30 mins and affords good views of the Magdalena. From Puente Navarro, walk up Calle las Trampas up to Puente Quebrada Seca. Keep asking locals for directions, take lots of water and try to avoid the midday sun.

🚌 Transport

Honda p91
Bus
As a junction point between Bogotá and Medellín, Honda is an ideal place to stop if you want to break up the long bus rides to these destinations. From **Bogotá** with Velotax and Rápido. To **Lima**, US$11, 4 hrs. To **Manizales** with Bolivariano, US$11, 4 hrs. **Rápido Tolima** run half-hourly buses to **La Dorada** (1 hr), and beyond, to **Puerto Boyacá** (3 hrs). The new Bogotá–Medellín highway passes around the town.

Zipaquirá p92
Bus
The bus station is 15 mins' walk from the mines and cathedral. There are many buses to/from Bogotá: Cra 30 (Av Ciudad de Quito), marked 'Zipa', **Flota Alianza**, or others from the C 170 terminus of the **TransMilenio** in North Bogotá opposite Exito supermarket, US$2 each way, 1¼ hrs. Zipaquirá can be reached from **Tunja** by taking a Bogotá-bound bus and getting off at La Caro for connection to Zipaquirá, US$2.40. Note when arriving to C170 terminus from Zipaquirá you need to buy a TransMilenio bus ticket to leave the station. To avoid this, ask the driver to drop you off before the bus station.

Train
You can also reach Zipaquirá and some of the surrounding towns via train, see page 87.

Contents

98 Boyacá Department
98 Tunja and around
101 Villa de Leiva
104 Chiquinquirá
105 Ráquira and around
105 Monasterio Desierto de la Calendaria
105 Paipa and around
106 Sogamoso
106 Iza
107 Lago de Tota
108 Monguí
108 Sierra Nevada del Cocuy
110 Listings

117 Santander Department
117 San Gil
119 Barichara
120 Guane
121 Bucaramanga
124 Girón
124 Listings

130 Norte de Santander Department
130 Pamplona
132 Cúcuta
134 Listings

Footprint features

96 Don't miss ...
106 How Lago de Tota was formed
107 Monguí's footballs
131 Simón Bolívar

Border crossing

Colombia–Venezuela
133 Cúcuta–San Antonio

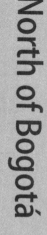

North of Bogotá

At a glance

☺ **Getting around** Walking in town centres; buses, taxis and *colectivos* to explore outlying regions.

● **Time required** 2-3 weeks to explore towns and villages. 1 week for trekking.

☀ **Weather** Variable: cool in mountainous regions around Tunja. Hotter as you head north to Santander.

✖ **When not to go** Good all year.

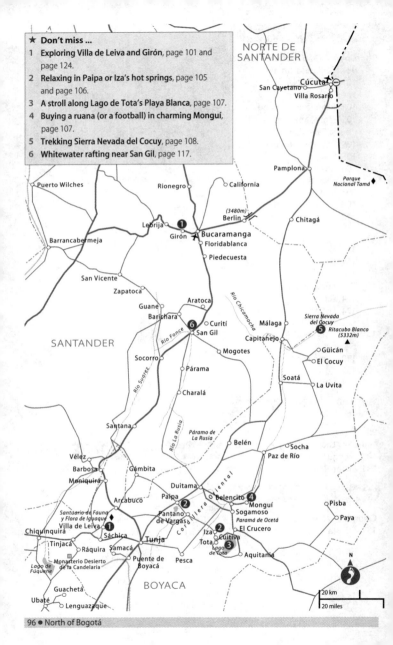

★ **Don't miss ...**

1 Exploring Villa de Leiva and Girón, page 101 and page 124.

2 Relaxing in Paipa or Iza's hot springs, page 105 and page 106.

3 A stroll along Lago de Tota's Playa Blanca, page 107.

4 Buying a ruana (or a football) in charming Monguí, page 107.

5 Trekking Sierra Nevada del Cocuy, page 108.

6 Whitewater rafting near San Gil, page 117.

Heading north from Bogotá towards Venezuela or the Atlantic coast, the road takes you on a historical journey to the heart of Colombia, passing through picturesque valleys, canyons and spectacular high mountain passes. Set on a high plateau is Tunja, capital of the Department of Boyacá. This was the seat of power of the indigenous Muisca and nearby is Laguna Gutavita, believed by many to be the source of the myth of El Dorado. The area also played its part in the liberation of Colombia from the Spanish, particularly at Puente de Boyacá where Simón Bolívar and his troops fought a decisive battle to wrest control of the country from the conquistadors. Boyacá is dotted with dozens of untouched colonial towns and villages, notably Villa de Leiva and Monguí. From the Andean foothills of Boyacá, the road swoops down to the turbulent Río Fonce and the start of the Department of Santander. Here too the Spanish colonial legacy is very much intact, particularly in the charming villages of Barichara, Guane and Girón. In recent years the area's natural resources, with countless tumbling rivers, caves and deep canyons, have made it the capital of Colombia's burgeoning adventure-sports scene, centred around the pretty town of San Gil. From the Department capital of Bucaramanga, a road climbs northeast over moorland for more lessons in independence history around Pamplona and Cúcuta in Norte de Santander. Another road heads north towards the Sierra Nevada de Santa Marta and the Caribbean coast.

Boyacá Department

Boyacá is the cultural and historical heart of Colombia. This department of green valleys and colonial villages was the centre of the Muisca empire, with whom the Spanish fought so vigorously to prize away their gold. The empire's capital was at Tunja, which at the time rivalled Bogotá in size and importance. Today, tourists flock to Villa de Leiva, which with its whitewashed colonial mansions and cobbled streets is becoming a popular weekend retreat for affluent bogotanos. But there are many more undiscovered gems. Villages such as Iza and Paipa with their thermal springs, and Monguí with its rich history and fresh mountain air, are therapy for both body and soul. Best of all, you'll have these places to yourself; many of them are rarely visited. In the northeast of the department is the Sierra Nevada de Cocuy, a mountain range of jagged ice peaks and breathtaking lakes to rival any in South America.

▸▸ *For listings, see pages 110-116.*

Tunja and around ⊖ ⊘ ⊘ ⊛ ⊙ ▲ ⊛ ⊙ ⊙ ▸▸ *pp110-116. Colour map 2, B5.*

→ *Phone code: 8. Population 152,000. Altitude 2780 m.*

Tunja, capital of Boyacá Department, is 137 km from Bogotá, in a cool dry mountainous area, on a platform that slopes down to the north and east to the valley of the Río Chulo. Ugly on the outside but with a soft centre and an interesting history, most travellers shun Tunja, most probably based on impressions gained on arrival at its bus stop. But Tunja is worth a peek, particularly to visit its impressive churches and museums. Moreover, it has very friendly people and good, cheap accommodation. When the Spaniards arrived in what is now Boyacá, Tunja was already an indigenous city, the seat of the Zipa, one of the two Muisca kings. He ruled over the northern part of the Muisca territories, the most populous and well-developed indigenous area of what is now Colombia. It was refounded as a Spanish city by Gonzalo Suárez Rendón in 1539. The city formed an independent Junta in 1811, and Bolívar fought under its aegis during the Magdalena campaign of 1812. Six years later he fought the decisive battle of Boyacá, nearby. The climate is cool, with a mean temperature of 12°C.

Ins and outs

Getting there There are four routes that converge on Tunja, all busy and in good condition. The main road from Bogotá through to Bucaramanga and the Caribbean bears left at the northern outskirts of the town. Straight on leads to Sogamoso, the Lago de Tota and Yopal and to the Sierras of Cocuy. West lies Villa de Leiva and Chiquinquirá. There are good bus services along all these roads; the bus station is near the main highway, which skirts the east side of town. There is no air service to Tunja and the railway no longer takes passengers.

Getting around From the bus station to the main square is a steep walk up, but the centre of the town and the main things to see are readily accessible from the Plaza de Bolívar.

Tourist office In Casa del Fundador, Plaza de Bolívar, helpful staff.

Sights

The **cathedral**, on the Plaza de Bolívar, has a Romanesque façade and right tower, with an unusual balustrade along the roof of the west front. It dates from the end of the 16th century. Inside, it is a mixture of styles, gothic and moorish, with ornamented pillars and colonial paintings. There are several fine side chapels and a mausoleum honouring Gonzalo Suárez Rendón, founder of the city. The **Casa de la Cultura**, opposite the cathedral, also 16th century, contains the **Museo de Museos** in which there are many reproductions of famous, principally European, masterpieces. This is where Simón Bolívar stayed before the battle of Boyacá. Cultural events are held here from time to time. Also on Plaza Bolívar is the **Casa del Fundador Suárez Rendón** ① *Plaza de Bolívar, daily 0800-1200, 1400-1600, US$0.70*, one of the few extant mansions of a Spanish conquistador in Colombia (1539-1543). See the attractive peaceful courtyard with a fine view of the countryside and the unique series of plateresque paintings on the ceilings.

Of the many colonial buildings, the most remarkable is the church of **Santo Domingo**, one block west of the plaza, a masterpiece begun in 1594, with its splendid interior covered with wood most richly carved. There are several chapels in the side aisles, but the Chapel of Our Lady of Rosario, the work of Fray Pedro Bedón, glistens with gold and glass ornamentation and is one of the finest examples of the period in Colombia. Most of the churches, except the San Lázaro chapel, are open for visitors during the day, or at least at Mass times. Two blocks east of the plaza is another fine building, the **Santa Clara La Real chapel** (1580), with some fine wood carving in the Moorish style particularly in the ceiling of the single-nave chapel. There is fine ornamentation everywhere, interesting oil paintings and wall decorations revealed after a recent restoration. This was the chapel to

Sleeping
Alicante **1**
Boyacá Plaza **2**
Casa Colonial **3**
Casa Real **4**
Conquistador de América **5**

Hunza **6**
Imperial **7**
Posada San Agustín **8**
San Ignacio Plaza **9**

Eating
Café Colonial **10**

El Maizal **11**
La Cascada **12**
La Mojarrita **13**
Pizza Nostra **14**
Son y Sabor **15**

the Santa Clara convent, begun in 1574, which was probably the first to be established in Colombia. One of the nuns, Sister Josefa del Castillo y Guevara lived in a cell near the choir for over 50 years and was buried here. Some of her writings are exhibited in the museum into which part of the former convent has been converted. One block from the plaza, on Calle 20, is the house of the writer **Casa Don Juan de Vargas** ① *Tue-Sun 0800-1200, 1400-1800, $1.05 adults, $0.50 children*, built 1590, has been restored as a museum of colonial Tunja, with many interesting exhibits relating to the city. Note the murals, gold candelsticks and particularly the fine ceiling of the upper floor.

One block south, on Calle 19, is the **Casa Juan de Castellanos**, a chronicler and friend of Suárez Rendón, is another notable colonial building, much of it carefully restored and again contains some fine ceiling paintings, both religious and of flora and fauna. **Casa de Capitán Antonio Ruiz Mancipe** is now a bank, on Calle 18, but much of the original has been preserved or restored. Four blocks from the plaza, on Carrera 11, the church of **Santa Bárbara** dates from 1592 and also has much fine ornamentation and a *mudéjar* ceiling. The treasury has many valuable items of gold and silver, part donated by the mother of Charles V of Spain. The chapel of La Epístola is the best of several. In the nearby parish house are some notable religious objects, including silk embroidery from the 18th century.

A short walk further south, in **Parque Bosque de la República**, is the adobe wall against which three martyrs of the Independence were shot in 1816. The wall, and bullet holes, are protected by a glass screen. Ask the tourist police guarding these buildings for information: they are helpful and knowledgeable. The church and convent of **San Francisco** is another 16th-century construction notable for its white colonial façade, sculptures of San Francisco and Mary Magdalen, striated pillars and the gilded arch over the central retable. Also note the Altar de los Pelícanos, believed to have been brought from Quito, which is in the chapel of the Virgin de las Angustias. The church of **San Ignacio** has an interesting embossed façade constructed by the Jesuits in the 17th century. It is now used for cultural presentations. The small **San Lázaro** chapel, dating from 1587, restored during the 18th century, has four semi-circular arches supporting an ornamental ceiling. At 2940 m it overlooks the town and is a fine viewpoint. (Take advice before walking up there).

Excursions

There are two pre-Columbian sites to visit outside the city. The **Cojines del Zaque** (literally the cushions of the Zaque, who was the principal chief of the Muisca government) is a ritual site around a large rock with pillow-like features carved into the rock. It is thought that sacrifices were made here. The **Pozo de Donato**, a short distance northeast out of town on the road to Paipa, was a well or pond also used for Muisca rituals. Legend had it that this included gold offerings. In the early days of the colonisation, a Spaniard by the name of Jeronimo Donato drained the pool looking for gold – which he did not find. The Pozo de Donato is in the grounds of the Universidad Pedagógica, which has done considerable archaeological work in the region. There is a small attractive park now around the pond.

Some 16 km south of Tunja on the main road from Bogotá, is the site of the **Battle of Boyacá** ① *daily 0800-1800, US$1.50 per car*, one of the most significant events in the history of Colombia. Overlooking the bridge at Boyacá is a large monument to Bolívar. Bolívar took Tunja on 6 August 1819, and next day his troops, fortified by a British Legion, the only professional soldiers among them, fought the Spaniards on the banks of the swollen Río Boyacá. With the loss of only 13 killed and 53 wounded they captured 1600 men and 39 officers. Only 50 men escaped back to Bogotá, and when these told their tale, the Viceroy Samao fled in such haste that he left behind him half a million pesos of the royal funds. There are several other monuments, an exhibition hall and restaurant at the site. Bus from Tunja, US$0.60, ask for 'El Puente'.

Villa de Leiva ⬤🔵🔴🟢▲⬤🔵 ➤ pp110-116. Colour map 2, B5.

➔ *Phone code: 8. Population 6800 Altitude 2144 m.*

About 40 km west through the mountains is the colonial town of Villa de Leiva (also spelt Leyva). This is one of Colombia's very special places. It is not on any important through route and there are no significant natural resources nearby to be exploited, so it has been left alone and now is prized by Colombians and visitor alike. The town dates back, like Tunja, to the early days of Spanish rule, but unlike Tunja, it has been declared a National Monument so will not be modernized. It was founded by Hernán Suárez de Villalobos in 1572 by order of the first president of Nueva Granada, Andrés Díaz Venero de Leiva.

It has an enormous, undulating plaza which appears as though it has buckled under the weight of the thousands of feet which have walked across it down the years. At 14,000 sq m it is believed to be the largest cobbled square in South America. Almost the entire village is in pristine condition with whitewashed mansions with terracotta-tiled roofs and streets with cobbles large and uneven enough to twist an ankle.

Villa de Leiva and its surroundings are blessed with a bewildering mixture of topographies and climates. To the west the landscape is semi desert, typified by the reddish clay that is used to make bricks and terracotta tiles and dotted with cacti. Fossils from the Jurassic and Cretacious period are abundant. To the south east, steep hills rise to páramo or moorland, sparse in vegetation. At the nearby Iguaque National Park it is mainly high cloudforest.

Ins and outs

Getting there To reach it from Bogotá, turn left at the Puente de Boyacá monument, and go through the small attractive town of **Samacá** which has a pretty plaza ornamented with bougainvilla arcades. The church has a bright white/yellow interior and a fine gilt retable. Alternatively, go through Tunja and out by the northwest corner of the town. The two roads join and you must turn right at Sáchica for the final 6 km to Villa de Leiva. Most of the public transport goes through Tunja. There is an alternative from Tunja, staying on the main road towards Bucaramanga, and after 34 km, turn left at Arcabuco. This is an unsurfaced road and rough in places but you will see fine scenery as it goes alongside the Iguaque National Sanctuary.

Getting around This is very much a place for walking around. Many of the streets are cobbled and such traffic as there is travels at a snail's pace. If you want to visit the attractions outside Villa de Leiva, there are taxis who will take you.

Tourist information Oficina Municipal de Turismo ① *Cra 9, No 13-04 just off the plaza, open daily 0800-1800*, some local maps, gives advice on cheaper accommodation. **Instituto von Humboldt** ① *Claustro de San Agustín, T7320174*. Excellent research and documentation centre for environmental studies. Publications sold. Call before visiting.

Sights

Two colonial houses are particularly worth a visit. One is the house in which **Antonio Nariño** ① *Cra 9, No 10-39. US$1.70, Fri-Tue 0900-1200, 1400-1600,* lived. He translated the *Rights of Man* into Spanish.

The second is the building known as the **Casa del Primer Congreso** ① *C 13/Cra 9, on the corner of the plaza, free, Tue-Thu 0800-1300, 1400-1700, Sat 0800-1300, 1400-1700,* in which the first Convention of the United Provinces of New Granada was held.

Also worth a visit is the restored birthplace of the independence hero **Antonio Ricaurte** ① *Cra 8/C 15, US$1, Wed-Fri 0900-1200, 1400-1700, Sat, Sun and holidays 0900-1200, 1400-1800, there is a statue of Ricaurte on Plazuela San Agustín.* Ricaurte was born in Villa de Leiva and died in 1814 at San Mateo, Venezuela, in a famous act of courageous self-sacrifice while fighting in Bolívar's army. The house has an attractive courtyard and garden.

On the Plaza Mayor the **Casa-Museo Luis Alberto Acuña** ① *US$1.10, Mon-Sun 0900-1800,* housing fascinating examples of Acuña's work, is well worth a visit.

Villa de Leiva

Sleeping
Candelaria 1
Colombian Highlands 2
Duruelo 3
El Marqués de San Jorge 4
Getsemaní 5
Hostal Sinduly 11

Hostería del Molino
La Mesopotamia 6
Posada de los Angeles 7
Posada Don Blas 8
Plaza Mayor 9
Posada de San Antonio 10

Eating
Casa Blanca 1
Don Quijote 2
La Cocina de la Gata 3
Olivas & Especias 4
Savia 5
Zarina 6

The **Monasterio de las Carmelitas Descalzas** ⓘ *C 14 and Cra 10, US$0.80, Sat-Sun and holidays 1000-1300, 1400-1700*, has one of the best museums of religious art in Colombia. The monastery also includes the **Convento** and the **Iglesia del Carmen** ⓘ *open at mass times: Mon-Fri 0700, Tue 0600, Sat 0700, 0900, 1100, Sun 0600, 0700, 1100*, a simple, dignified church with a large fine Lady Chapel, all worth a visit. The **Iglesia de San Agustín** is now being converted into a museum.

An interesting and well displayed **palaeontological museum** ⓘ *US$1.10, Tue-Sat 0900-1200, 1400-1700, Sun and holidays 0900-1500*, has been opened 15 minutes' walk north of the town on Carrera 9.

Around Villa de Leiva

The wide valley to the west of Villa de Leiva is rich in fossils; 5 km along the road to Santa Sofía you will see the road signs for **El Fósil** ⓘ *daily 0900-1700, US$1.40*. The skeleton displayed is a Plesiosaur group reptile, possibly a small Kronosaurus, found here in 1977, and the museum was built around it. The second exhibit is a baby of the same group, complete with tail, found in 2000 and placed alongside. They were similar to dolphins with flippers and a fine set of teeth. The museum contains a wide selection of other Mesozoic and Cretaceous exhibits.

About 2 km along the road to Monquirá is **La Casa de Terracota**, a house designed and belonging to Colombian architect Octavio Mendoza. This Gaudi-esque construction, built entirely out of ceramic tiles extracted from the local area and worked directly onto the building, claims to be the largest such structure in the world, as well as being cheap, environmentally friendly and earthquake-proof. Almost everything is made from terracotta, including all the furniture, while there are fine examples of mosaics in the showers and clever use of light. Still under construction, Mendoza has not specified as yet what it will be used for when it is finished, though there are rumours he may turn it into a hotel. Entry US$2.70, during construction hours.

About 1 km further along this road, 4 km from Villa de Leiva, is the well-endowed archaeological site of the **Parque Arqueológico de Monquirá** ⓘ *0900-1200, 1400-1700, closed Mon, US$1.80 with guide*, otherwise known as El Infiernito, where there are several huge carved phalluses (which make popular photo opportunties!). This is one of the most important Muisca religious sites in the country and features the only solar observatory in Colombia as well as a *dolmen* burial site. The site was discovered by the Spanish who baulked at the enormous stone penises and proclaimed that the Muisca would be banished to hell, hence the name 'El Infiernito' (hell). Much of it was destroyed and the stone used by local campesinos to build their homes. Some of it still remains and has been studied and maintained since the 1960s by archaeologist Eliecer Silva Célis with the support of the Universidad Pedagógica y Tecnológica de Colombia.

About 1 km beyond El Infiernito is the **Cactus Nursery of Fibas** ⓘ *T3112222399 (mob), www.fibas.org, free, meditation US$5.50 (with free plant), Wed-Sun 0800-1730, Mon and Tue with forewarning*, run by former advertising executive Jaime Rodríguez Roldán. As well as selling many varieties of cactus and other desert plants, the nursery aims to educate visitors in environmentally friendly practices. No fertilizers, even organic ones, are used in nurturing the plants. The centre also features two mazes, based on ancient indigenous designs, in which Jaime holds meditation exercises.

About 6 km beyond the Infiernito turning is a track on the left for the **Monastery of Ecce-Homo** ⓘ *open normal hours, just knock on the door* (founded 1620); note the fossils in the floor at the entrance. The monastery has had a turbulent history. It was built by the Dominicans between 1650 and 1695, but a century later it was taken over by the military and the friars expelled. It was later abandoned until 1920 when it was reclaimed by the Dominicans, and some restoration was done. It has been repeatedly robbed since then, and some of the religious art is now in the Chiquinquirá museum for safe-keeping. What can be seen of the church, chapel and monastery is impressive, but the fabric and roof are in a poor state. There are buses from Villa de Leiva (0800-1615) going to Santa Sofía, US$1.20; it is 30 minutes to the crossing, then a 2 km walk to the monastery. A good day trip is to take the bus to Ecce Homo and walk back to Villa de Leiva via El Fósil and El Infernito. Beyond Santa Sofía is **La Cueva de Hayal**, a cave set in beautiful scenery.

Some 20 km from Villa de Leiva on the road to Arcabuco, there is a right turn for the **Santuario de Fauna y Flora de Iguaque** ① *for non-nationals, children under 12 US$1.90*, a National Park. The entrance to the Park is 3 km from the junction. About 40 minutes' walk up the valley from the entrance is a tourist centre with accommodation for 48 and a restaurant with good food at reasonable prices and a fine view of the surrounding countryside. There are guided paths and a marked trail to Lake Iguaque, a steep walk of 2½ hours. The lake is central to Muisca mythology, for it is from its icy waters that Bachué and a three-year-old boy rose to become the first humans to populate the Earth. The most likely day for a lift is Saturday, market day, but there is a daily bus at 0700 from Villa de Leiva that passes the junction for the Park at Casa de Piedra. It returns at 1300 and 1630. US$11.

The 6750-ha park is mainly high cloudforest of oak, fig and other temperate trees, much covered with epiphytes, lichens and bromeliads. There is a series of high-level lakes, formed in the last Ice Age, at over 3400 m, and the mountains rise to 3800 m. The height creates cloud and there is frequent rain, about 1700 mm a year, giving the park a deep green quality. At the visitors centre, Furachiogua, there is accommodation with seven shared rooms (capacity 48) with bunk beds or single beds, US$15.50 per person. There is also a campsite with showers and toilets and cooking facilities, US$2.70. Colombian Highlands (www.colombianhighlands.com) in Villa de Leiva are recommended for organized tours to the park.

There are a number of expeditions to nearby waterfalls and bathing spots, including Paso del Angel, near Santa Sofía where the narrowest of natural bridges (less than a metre across) links two ridges with the 80-m Guatoque waterfall falling nearby. Some 10 km on the road to Alto de los Migueles is Cascada La Periquera which falls 15 m into the Río La Cebada and is surrounded by lush vegetation. On the road to Monquirá, 2 km from Villa de Leiva, are the Pozos Azules, a series of aquamarine natural pools. On the way to Santa Sofía is Valle Escondido, a verdant valley guarded by imposing mountains. Here there are various lodgings, including El Arca Verde, an eco-friendly *maloka*. It is possible to abseil down some of the valley's many canyons. Colombian Highlands can organize tours to these and other spots.

Chiquinquirá ●❷❸❹❺ ❥❥ *pp110-116. Colour map 2, B5.*

→ *Phone code: 8. Population: 38,000. Altitude: 2550 m.*

On the west side of the valley of the Río Suárez, 134 km from Bogotá and 80 km from Tunja, this is a busy market town for this large coffee and cattle region. In December thousands of pilgrims honour a painting of the Virgin whose fading colours were restored by the prayers of a woman, María Ramos. The picture is housed in the imposing Basílica, but the miracle took place in what is now the Iglesia de la Renovación. In 1816, when the town had enjoyed six years of independence and was besieged by the Royalists, this painting was carried through the streets by Dominican priests from the famous monastery, to rally the people. The town fell, all the same. There are special celebrations at Easter and on 26 December, the anniversary of the miracle. The town is known for making guitars.

Ráquira and around ☺◐◑◑ ▸▸ *pp110-116. Colour map 2, B5.*

In the chibcha language, Ráquira means 'city of pots' and with over 100 *artesanía* shops selling earthenware pottery in a village of just a dozen blocks, Ráquira is rightly considered the capital of Colombian handicrafts. Known for its ceramics, in recent years there has been an influx of cheap products from Ecuador, somewhat diluting its appeal. The village itself has been painted in an array of primary colours and has a picturesque plaza embellished with terracotta statues, including one of a local version of Belgium's Manneken-Pis and another of Jorge Veloza, inventor of the musical genre *carranga*, who was born here.

Monasterio Desierto de la Calendaria ☺ ▸▸ *pp110-116. Colour map 2, B5.*

ⓘ *US$1.10 plus US$0.55 to Hermit's Cave.*

About 7 km from Ráquira is the beautiful 16th-century monastery of La Candelaria. In an otherwise dry area, the monastery is a small oasis, thanks to the water provided by the Río Guachaneco. It has a fine church whose altar displays the painting of the Virgen de la Candelaria by Francisco del Pozo, dating from 1597. The painting was miraculously saved from burning and brought here by Augustinian monks, who founded the monastery in 1604 on the site of a pagan altar. The anniversary of the painting is celebrated each 1 February in addition to 28 August, the saint's day of San Agustín.

The convent has two beautiful cloisters, one featuring a 170-year-old dwarf orange tree, the other virtually untouched since the 17th century. The monastery is an important location for novice Augustinian monks who come here on retreat for one year and are allowed no contact with their family during this time. A guided tour of the monastery includes a visit to the church, the cloisters, which are lined with anonymous 17th century paintings of the life of San Agustín and the catacomb-like Hermit's Cave, originally used by the local indigenous people but appropriated by the monks who built the monastery.

Paipa and around ☺ ▸▸ *pp110-116. Colour map 2, B6.*

ⓘ *daily 0600-2200, US$ 5, children US $3.*

Along the road, 41 km northeast of Tunja is Paipa, noted for the Aguas Termales complex 3 km to the southeast. The baths and the neighbouring Lago Sochagota (boat trips possible) are very popular with Colombians and increasingly so with foreign tourists. From Paipa there is a minibus service, US$0.50, a taxi costs US$1.50, or you can walk in 45 minutes. There are innumerable hotels (**D-F**) and restaurants on the main street of Paipa and on the approach road to the Aguas Termales, though hotels at the springs are more expensive. Paipa is a good place to buy carpets, hammocks and handicrafts.

How Lago de Tota was formed

Many years ago an indigenous family was bequeathed a mysterious vessel of water by the gods. The gift was to be emptied to form a great lake. The husband and wife travelled over many lands looking for a suitable spot to create the lake. Their son and daughter did not understand their parents' obsession and decided to find out what was so special about this jar that they guarded so jealously.

They accidentally spilt the water, causing a disaster. As soon as it hit the ground the water swelled and flooded everything. The landscape changed. The boy, knowing he was the culprit, ran from his parents in fright. The girl ran to her mother and both were turned to stone, forming the two islands that today can be seen opposite Playa Blanca. The father tried to climb up to the moor above the lake but was overcome by the waters and turned into what is today known as the Potrero peninsula.

Sogamoso ●❶❷❸ ➻ pp110-116. Colour map 2, B6.

→ Phone code: 8. Population: 70,000. Altitude: 2569 m.

At Duitama, a town 15 km beyond Paipa known for basket weaving, turn right and follow the valley of the Río Chicamocha for Sogamoso, a large, mainly industrial town. This was an important Chibcha settlement, and a **Parque Arqueológico** ① *Tue-Sun 0900-1300, 1400-1800, US$1.50, US$0.80 children*, has been set up on the original site. A comprehensive museum describes their arts of mummification, statuary, and crafts, including goldworking. Cafetería near the entrance. Camping possible in the grass car park opposite, with permission.

Iza ●❶❷❸ ➻ pp110-116. Colour map 2, B6.

→ Phone code: 8. Population: 2081. Altitude: 2560.

South of Sogamoso the road winds its way through a grassy valley backed by imposing pine-clad hills. After 15 minutes, the road reaches the colonial village of Iza. In Chibcha, Iza means 'place of healing', no doubt a reference to the thermal springs found outside the village. Not much happens in Iza but you could easily spend a week here soaking up its curative atmosphere. It has what could classify as the most beautiful parque principal in Colombia, its four corners guarded by arched yew trees intertwined with bougainvillea bushes. South of the village, lush water meadows, shaded by the drooping fronds of willow trees, run down to the Río Iza. A path runs over a picturesque covered wooden bridge and joins the road leading to the hot springs 1 km away. On Sundays, the plaza is lined with stalls selling all types of sugary puddings.

Iza was founded on 12 February 1780 and today most of its inhabitants make a living from livestock, agriculture and wool spinning. There are several access points to the hot springs. The most popular is Piscina Erika, which has a good-sized concrete pool and a childrens' paddling pool fed by piping hot sulphurous water from the spring just above. Entrance US$3.30 with restaurant, changing rooms and showers. There are also two simple rooms for overnight stays (see Sleeping). Beyond Piscina Erika there is free access to natural pools, popular with locals at weekends. Unfortunately, these marshy pools are not well maintained and have been allowed to clog up with discarded rubbish.

Monguí's footballs

You might not expect it of a tiny village sat high on a mountain in Boyacá but Monguí moonlights as one of the world's principal manufacturers of footballs. As many as 30,000 handmade footballs are exported every month and up to 100,000 during the FIFA World Cup. In 2006, the residents of Monguí made what they claimed was the world's largest ball. Measuring 190 cm tall, 6 m wide and after 37 hours of labour, they submitted it to the Guinness Book of Records. Unfortunately, a football manufacturing firm in Sialkot, Pakistan pipped them to the post with a ball measuring 10.7 m in diameter. For now it will have to settle for second best on record-breaking footballs, but Monguí can still safely stake its claim as probably the most beautiful football-producing village in the world.

There is good hiking around Iza, especially to Cascada El Encanto del Amor, a waterfall in the hills above the village. Ask at the Casa de la Cultura on the plaza or at Posada del Virrey Solis for directions.

Lago de Tota ●● ➤ pp110-116. Colour map 2, B6.

Beyond Iza the road rises sharply through pastures rich in wild flowers, passing through Cuitiva and the indigenous village of Tota. Here, the landscape changes to *páramo* or moorland, the graceful curves of its hills tinged with traces of purple, pink and red, before the road drops down to the steely blue waters of Lago de Tota. At 15 km long and 10 km wide, this is the largest natural lake in Colombia. The indigenous campesinos who populate its edges cultivate tidy patches of onions right up to the water's edge. There are reeds and algae all along the shore and few beaches, the notable exception being Playa Blanca, on the southwest corner of the lake, a beach of white sand with milky green water at its shallows, backed by pine-clad hills. The sight would not look out of place on the Caribbean, but at 3015 m, the water is cold. There is camping and a restaurant serving trout. At weekends Playa Blanca fills up with Colombians but is generally quiet otherwise.

Aquitania, on the eastern shore, is the principal town on the lake. There are plenty of food shops, and restaurants including Luchos, Tunjo de Oro and Pueblito Viejo together on corner of plaza, and a bright, restored church with modern stained glass windows. Above the town is a hill (El Cumbre) with beautiful views. The road eventually does the round of the lake and heads back toward Sogamoso.

Monguí ●● ➤ pp110-116. Colour map 2, B6.

About 12 km northeast of Sogamos is Monguí, once voted 'the most beautiful village in Boyacá'. The department has many contenders for this title but it would be difficult to build a case against this village with its large, cobbled plaza and whitewashed houses with doors and windows painted racing green and embellished with the occasional red. It has a magnificent **Basílica** ① *US$2.20, open only at weekends*, constructed by the Franciscans in the 17th century, which has many oil paintings including the *Virgin de Monguí*, donated by Philip II of Spain. The basilica has a very good museum, which has exhibits that include the convent's original kitchen and dining room with 17th-century reliefs and a mummified cat found in the rafters of the building's ceiling.

Set high in the hills with sweeping views down towards Sogamoso in the valley below, this is a very pleasant place to stroll around, peaceful and quiet. It's not uncommon to see a horse or cow tethered outside the local bar while its owner chews the cud with his neighbour. It has good *artesanía* shops, selling woollen *ruanas* and leather products.

Don't miss the walk down Carrera 3 to the Calycanto Bridge, built by the Spanish out of stone cemented with clay, lime and bull's blood in order to bring large stones across the river to the church. At the top of Calle 4, to the right of the church, is the Plaza de Toros. If you feel energetic, take any path beyond the bull ring to a rock on which stands a shrine to the Virgin and Child, illuminated at night. From here there are tremendous views in all directions. A recommended excursion is east to the Páramo de Ocetá with particularly fine *frailejones* and giant wild lupins, a three-hour walk from Monguí.

Aside from traditional crafts, Monguí is one of the leading manufacturers of footballs. There are many football outlets in town, selling handmade balls. (see box, page 107).

Sierra Nevada del Cocuy ●▲ ⤷ pp110-116.

ⓘ *Entry to the park US$11 for non-Colombians, payable at the park office (on the corner of the main plaza in Cocuy), where you can also obtain a map with the main walking paths.*
The Sierra Nevada del Cocuy is a mecca for hikers and climbers on high altitude in Colombia. This breathtaking mountain area in the national park is located in two departments, Boyacá and Santander and consists of two parallel north-south ranges about 30 km long, offering peaks of rare beauty, many lakes, big cliffs, waterfalls and literally thousands of *frailejone* plants. It is one of the most amazing geographical places in the whole of South America. In an area of about 30 km, there are more than 22 snowy peaks; it meets the biggest mass of snow and ice in South America north of the equatorial line. The snow peaks range from 4900 m to 5322 m of the Ritacuba Blanco, which is the highest one of the park. This park is simply THE place in Colombia for any high-altitude hiker or climber.

The park is accessible in the south from the small town of **El Cocuy** or further north from **Güicán**. Both towns are perfect start or end point for any hiking or climbing activity in the park. On the central square of El Cocuy you will find a miniature model of the mountain area. One of the most spectacular hikes in the park is walking from south to north (or vice versa), during which you will see a great part of what the park has to offer. It might seem to be an easy marked trail but it is highly recommend to go with a guide if you don't know the park as sudden changes in climate means visibility can unexpectedly drop to less than 10 m. You will need to know where to camp and where to get drinking water.

There is no accommodation in the park, so you will need to bring all equipment yourself. Basic food supply can be bought in El Cocuy or Güicán but otherwise you should bring your food from Bogotá. There is no need to bring ice axes or crampons. Temperature can drop below 0°C during the nights as most campsites are around 4000 m. A number of treks and hikes are available. ⤷ *See Activities and tours, page 115, for further information.*

Ins and outs
El Cocuy and Güicán can be reached by direct bus (early morning or late in the evening) from Bogota (10-12 hours) with **Paz del Río**, **Libertadores** and **Concorde** for US$15. Coming from Bucaramanga, switch buses in Capitanejo. Around 0600 milk trucks leave the main plaza of El Cocuy. They can take you to the **Cabañas Guaicany** (the southern entrance of the park), **Finca la Esperanza** (for Laguna Grande de la Sierra) or to **Hacienda**

Ritacuba from where it is about an hour's walk to get to the **Cabañas Kanwarra**. An Expresso (private transport) costs around US$34, which can be arranged at the main plaza in El Cocuy.

When to go
It is best to avoid the peak holiday periods (the last week in December, the first two weeks of January and Easter week) as campsites can get very busy during these times. Dry seasons are December to April and July to August but even in those months it can rain or be very foggy. There has been no problem with safety in recent years.

Sights
La Laguna de La Plaza is probably the most beautiful lake of all those in the Sierra Nevada del Cocuy, surrounded by the snow tops of **Pan de Azúcar** and **Toti** in the west and Pico's **Negro** and **Blanco** on the east. Just below Pan de Azúcar you can see **Cerro El**

Sierra Nevada del Cocuy

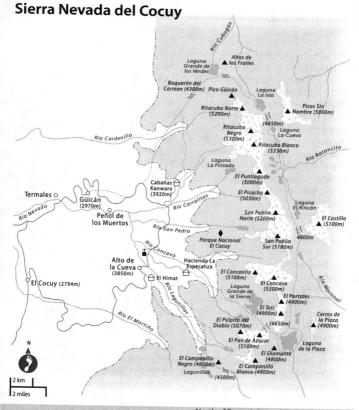

Diamante, a pointy rock that might remind you of a real *diamante*. During sunrise, the color of this rock can change from grey to yellow, gold, red and orange if you are lucky with the weather. **Laguna Grande de la Sierra** is surrounded by the tops of Pan de Azucar, Toti, Portales, Concavo and Concavito and is a perfect spot as base camp to climb up to the summits of (one of) these peaks. **El Púlpito de Diablo** is an enormous, square rock with a shape of an altar at 5000 m. From El Pulpito you can continue to climb up to the top of **Pan de Azúcar** (5100 m) overlooking Laguna de la Plaza on one side and Laguna Grande de la Sierra on the other side. **Valle de los Cojines** is an enormous valley surrounded by snow tops and filled with *cojines* (pillow plants), typical of the region. **Ritacuba Blanco** is the highest mountain of all (5322 m) and is not too difficult to climb. The views at the top over the Valle de Cojines and many other parts of the park is just stunning.

◉ Boyacá Department listings → *Phone code: 8.*

For Sleeping and Eating price codes and other relevant information, see pages 31-36.

● Sleeping

Tunja and around *p98, map p99*
AL Hunza, C 21, No 10-66, T7424111, www.hotelhunza.com. Tunja's grandest hotel, the Hunza has fine views of the Iglesia San Francisco from its lobby. Its modern rooms are spacious, with Wi-Fi throughout, a swimming pool and Turkish bath and a restaurant.
A Boyacá Plaza, C 18, No 11-22, T7401116, hotelboyacaplaza@hotmail.com. This smart, modern hotel has comfortable rooms and includes breakfast and Wi-Fi connection in the price.
B San Ignacio Plaza, C 18, No 10-51, T7437583 hotelsanignacioplaza@hotmail.com. This hotel has a pretty colonial façade, though it's modern on the inside with bright, airy rooms. Also has a restaurant, parking and Wi-Fi.
C Alicante, Cra 8, No 19-15, T7449967, hotelalicante@hotmail.com. With its minimalist design and a sunny patio fringed by varieties of cactus, this hotel is a bargain. The rooms are full of light and have cable TV, while there is Wi-Fi in reception.
C Posada San Agustín, C 23, No 8-63, T7430245. This beautiful colonial building on the Parque Pinzon is a bit of a gem, with comfortable rooms and a gorgeous balustraded courtyard painted olive green.

The hotel is embellished with antiques and photographs of Tunja down the ages, while it also has modern conveniences such as Wi-Fi.
D Casa Colonial, Cra 8, No 20-40, T7422169. This hotel has a nice, sunny patio and rooms with cable TV and en suite bathrooms – though they can be a bit dingy.
D Casa Real, C 19, No 7-65, T7431764, hotelcasareal@yahoo.es. Housed in a beautiful colonial building, this hotel is a real bargain and could easily fetch 3 times the price. The rooms are comfortable and clean with private bathrooms and freshly varnished wooden floorboards. Highly recommended.
D Conquistador de América, C 20, No 8-92, T7423534. The Conquistador has a lovely foyer with a bright skylight, and while the rooms are small they are clean and comfortable with en suite bathrooms and cable TV.
E Imperial, C 19, No 7-43, T7423056. There's nothing outstanding about this small hotel but it does have clean rooms with cable TV and en suite bathrooms.

Villa de Leiva *p101, map p102*
Villa de Leiva is usually quiet on the early days of the week but fills up at weekends.
AL Duruelo, Cra 3, No 12-88, T7320222, www.duruelo.com.co. Villa de Leiva's most exclusive hotel, the building sits on a hill above the town, commanding views across the valley. The rooms are comfortable, though they perhaps could do with refurbishment but its biggest draw is the

4 swimming pools carved into the side of the hill and its spa and massage services. Non-guests can buy a 'Plan Dia', which allows access to the pools, sauna and jacuzzi for US$15.50.

AL La Posada de San Antonio, Cra 8, No 11-61, T7320583, adelgo@hotmail.com. With its thick adobe walls, colourful decor, enormous antique beds and location on the beautiful Parque Nariño, this hotel is a popular choice with weekending *bogotanos*. The hotel also boasts a pool table and Wi-Fi in the lobby.

AL Plaza Mayor, Cra 10, No 12-31, T7320425, www.hotelplazamayor.com.co. Right on the plaza, this worn brick building has a delightful octagonal courtyard with lemon trees and very comfortable rooms, plus Wi-Fi, parking and a good (expensive) restaurant.

A Candelaria, C del Silencio, No 8-12, T7320534, www.hotelcandelaria villadeleyva.com. Located on the delightful cobbled Calle del Silencio, this newly refurbished colonial building has 9 rooms of monastic simplicity with thick, whitewashed walls and wooden beams. It also has a restaurant serving up international cuisine.

A Getsemaní, Av Perimetral, No 10-35, T7320326, www.hotelgetsemani.com. This spa hotel has 25 rooms in 3 styles, all with cable TV and large beds. It also has an indoor pool, Wi-Fi and, of course, the spa with a jacuzzi and various massage treatments.

A Hostería del Molino La Mesopotamia, C del Silencio, T7321832, www.hosteriala mesopotamia.addr.com. This former grain mill dates back to 1568, 4 years before Villa de Leiva was founded, and has retained much of its original lime and mud architecture in the house. It has delightful gardens with running rivulets of water fed by a spring, as well as a superb natural swimming pool. Recommended. Non-guests can use the pool for US$2.80.

B El Marqués de San Jorge, C 14, No 9-20, T7320240, hospederia_elmarquesde sanjorge@yahoo.com. This simple little place has rooms set around a courtyard and offers cable TV, parking and breakfast included.

C Posada de los Angeles, Cra 10, No 13-94, T7320562. This posada has basic, clean rooms in a fine building 2 blocks from the plaza and a restaurant serving American breakfasts and pastas. Be sure to ask for a room overlooking the beautiful Iglesia del Carmen.

D Posada Don Blas, C 12, No 10-61, T7320986. This sweet and simple little place is just 1 block away from the plaza and has small, clean rooms with private bathrooms and cable TV.

D-E Colombian Highlands and Hostal Renacer, Cra 9, No 11-02, T7321379/ T3113083739 (mob), www.colombianhigh lands.com. A 15-min walk from town, this hostel, belonging to English-speaking biologist Oscar Gilède, has some of the most comfortable private rooms you are likely to find in any Colombian backpackers' hostel. This country *finca* has extensive gardens and excellent facilities, including a kitchen, a

Private rooms / bath — Dormitories — Camping
Hammocks — Internet — Kitchen
Hot water 24h — Laundry — Breakfast
Birdwatching — Ecological trail — Spanish classes
COLOMBIAN HIGHLANDS Ecotours & Backpackers
Adventure activities — Ecotourism — Bikes & horses
Tourist information — Links with other hostels

VILLA DE LEYVA
Free taxi when arriving (V. Leyva's bus terminal – hostel)
Free coffee & tea

Carrera 9 No 11- 02 Villa de Leyva, Boyacá - Colombia
Phone: (57) 8 7321379 Cel: 311 3083739 / 310 5529079
info@colombianhighlands.com

www.colombianhighlands.com

wood-fired pizza oven, hammocks, bike hire, internet and dorms with bunk beds. Oscar also runs a tour agency offering a variety of trips including horse rental and adventure sports and has excellent information on the local area. Camping available, US$3.30 with own tent or US$13.80 for a 4-man tent.

D-F Hostal Sinduly, Cra 11, No 11-77, T3143450384, noconadelsol@hotmail.com. Run by Austrian expat Manfred, this 10-bed hostel has 1 private room with bathroom and a couple of dorms in a colonial house 1 block from the plaza. There is use of a kitchen and hot water, and Manfred also arranges trips to a *finca* he owns near the entrance to Iguaque National Park. English and German spoken.

Chiquinquirá *p104*

C El Gran, C 16 No 6-97, T726 3700. This hotel is central, secure and comfortable and includes breakfast, It has a good restaurant, laundry service and parking.

E Sarabita, C 16, 8-12, T726 2068. This business hotel has a pool, sauna (when working) and restaurant, all housed in a building declared a National Monument.

F Moyba, Cra 9, No 17-53, T726 2649, on the plaza. This hotel is a bit dingy, cheaper without private bathroom.

Ráquira and around *p105*

D Hostería Nemqueteba, T7357016. This charming colonial house has a brightly painted patio brimming with bougainvillea as well as a swimming pool.

D Suaya, C del Comercio, T7357029. 1 block from the plaza, this colonial building has brightly painted rooms with en suite bathrooms and hot water.

E La Candelaria, C 5, No 3-24, T7357259. This basic hotel, 1 block from the plaza, has clean rooms with private bathrooms.

Monasterio Desierto de la Calendaria *p105*

Adjoining the monastery is a hotel, often used for spiritual retreats.

A Posada San Agustín, T6210531, www.agustinosrecoletos.com.co. A 16th-century building set around a colourful cloister with flower beds and a water piece, the rooms are simple but comfortable. There are 2 suites with jacuzzis as well as 2 saunas.

Paipa and around *p105*

AL Casona del Salitre, Vía Toca, Km 3, T7851508, www.casonadelsalitre.com. 5 mins' drive from town. A National Monument and a memorable place to stay near the baths and lake in a well-preserved hacienda where Simón Bolívar stayed before the Battle of Boyacá. Hot pools, spa, good restaurant, quiet, fireplace. Highly recommended.

Sogamoso *p106*

E Bochica, C 11, No 14-33, T770 7381. Good value, with comfortable rooms, hot water, TV, tourist info, and a restaurant.

E Valparaíso, C 11A, No 17-56, T771 6935. Near the bus station, this hotel has rooms with private bath and TV. restaurant, sauna, and tourist information.

Iza *p106*

C Piscina Erika, Vereda Agua Caliente, T7790038. Within the thermal springs, the complex has 2 simple but comfortable rooms with en suite bathrooms and access to the pool. Breakfast is included.

D Hotel Santa Isabel, T7790038. Charming colonial building with rooms with beamed ceilings and private bathrooms. It has a restaurant serving *almuerzos* for US$2.70. The owners also run Piscina Erika.

D Posada del Virrey Solis, C 4A, No 4A-75, T7790245. Just off the parque principal on a little plazoleta dominated by an enormous pine tree, this 180-yr-old house, declared a National Monument, has baroque rooms full of religious paintings and iconography, old books and Egyptian statuettes. Breakfast, US$2.20, is served in an eccentric room full of ornate furnishings. The price of the room includes access to the thermal springs at Piscina Erika.

Lago de Tota *p107*

B Pozo Azul, 3 km beyond Camino Real, in a secluded bay on the lake, T619 9524 (Bogotá), also cabins up to 6. With breakfast. Suitable for children, comfortable, watersport facilities, good food.

C Camino Real, Km 20 Vía Sogamoso a Aquitania, T770 0684, on the lake. Pleasant public rooms, colourful gardens, boat slipway, boats for hire, restaurant, sauna, tourist information.

E Residencia Venecia, C 8, No 144, Aquitania. Clean, basic, reasonable.

Camping Playa Blanca, US$2.20 for tent up to 5 people. US$4.40 for over 5.

Monguí *p107*

C El Portón de Ocetá, a beautiful large converted colonial house located near the plaza.

C La Casona, Cra 4, No 3-41, T782498, chopo11110@yahoo.es. This small hostel has clean comfortable rooms with en suite bathrooms behind a restaurant of the same name. It has lovely views down into the valley. Recommended.

D Hostal Calycanto, a pink house next to the bridge with a lovely setting and a restaurant. Best to book in advance.

F La Cabaña, chalet on road beyond river (cross bridge, turn left). Basic but comfortable. Cooks up food if forewarned.

Sierra Nevada del Cocuy *p108, map p109*
El Cocuy

F pp **Cabañas Guaicany**, El Cocuy, at the entrance of Valle de Lagunillas, with shared bathroom. Great views of the Ritacuba Blanco, the peaks of San Pablin Sur and Norte and Concavo. Also possible to camp and to hire horses and/or guide.

F pp **Cabañas Kanwarra**, El Cocuy, located at the foot of Ritacuba Blanc., Cabañas Kanwarra is the perfect starting point to climb Ritacuba Blanco or to walk to Laguna Grande de los Verdes.with shared bathroom.

F pp **Hotel Casa Muñoz**, El Cocuy, on the main square. With private bathroom.

F pp **Hotel Villa Real**, El Cocuywith shared bathroom.

G pp **Finca La Esperanza**, El Cocuy, located at the entrance of Valle de Frailejones. Convenient for the walk to Laguna Grande de la Sierra. Simple rooms with shared bathroom.

🍴 Eating

Tunja and around *p98, map p99*

🍴 **Café Colonial**, Cra 9, No 19-92. This café on the plaza principal has a sunny courtyard dominated by a large magnolia tree and good coffees to boot.

🍴 **El Maizal**, Cra 9, No 20-30, T7425876. This restaurant has a good varied menu of local specialities such as *mondongo* and trout.

🍴 **La Cascada**, Pasaje Vargas, No 10-82, T7445750. This large canteen is a popular lunchtime venue with *almuerzos* at US$2.20.

🍴 **La Mojarrita**, C 18, No 7-43, T7438330. This seafood restaurant is famous in Tunja for its *mojarra* and *sancocho de pescado*.

🍴 **Pizza Nostra**, C 19, No 10-36, T7402040. Pizzas and lasagnes on a pedestrianized street in the centre of town.

🍴 **Son y Sabor**, Pasaje Vargas, No 10-71, T7402970. This typical restaurant has a good, varied menu serving rabbit and trout as well as steaks.

Villa de Leiva *p101, map p102*
Villa de Leiva has dozens of good restaurants with varied international and local menus. Most, but not all, are concentrated in the town's upmarket foodcourts, Casa Quintero (on the plaza) and La Guaca (on the C Caliente).

🍴🍴 **Savia**, Cra 9, No 11-75 (Casa Quintero), T7321778. Savia has an excellent range of organic salads as well as interesting dishes such as chicken in mango sauce.

🍴🍴 **Zarina**, Cra 9, No 11-75 (Casa Quintero). Located in an upmarket foodhall, this small restaurant serves up excellent Lebanese dishes as well as the usual chicken and steak.

Casa Blanca, C 13, No 7-06, T7320821. This popular restaurant has been feeding locals for more than 20 years and serves up regional specialities such as *longaniza*.

Don Quijote, La Guaca, C Caliente (Cra 9), Local No 12. This Spanish restaurant was the winner of Villa de Leiva's gastronomy prize for its enormous leg of lamb cooked in its 400-year-old kitchen. Generous helpings of sangria should help wash it down.

La Cocina de la Gata, Casa Quintero, T7321266. Also in the Casa Quintero is this pleasantly decorated fondue restaurant, which also serves chicken and steak.

Olivas & Especias, Cra 10, No 11-99, T7321261. On the corner of the plaza, this restaurant serves pizzas and pastas in homely surroundings.

Chiquinquirá p104

There are plenty of reasonable places to eat around and near Parque Julio Flores.

Ráquira and around p105

La Raquireñita, Cra 3, No 3-36, T7357025. On the plaza, this lunchtime restaurant is brightly decorated with ceramic masks and other artesanías and serves up a mixture of fish, steak and chicken dishes.

Nemqueteba, C del Comercio, T7357016. This restaurant belonging to the hotel of the same name serves up local trout as well as chicken and steak in pleasant surroundings.

Sogamoso p106

Susacá, Cra 16, No 11-35, T7702587. One of the best restaurants near the centre, its specialities include trout. It has good *comida* with large portions.

Iza p106

There are a couple of restaurants on the parque principal.

M'c Jotas, a little hole-in-the-wall, run by a friendly couple who cook up steaks, chicken and burgers.

❂ Festivals and events

Tunja and around *p98, map p99*
Late May-1st Sun in Jun The main local festival, culminating with the crowning of the 'queen' amid popular and cultural festivities. There is a special ceremony at the chapel of El Topo at this time.
Dec The week before Christmas there is a lively festival with local music, traditional dancing and fireworks.

Villa de Leiva *p101, map p102*
Feb There is an **Astronomical festival** at the beginning of the month, where telescopes are set up in the plaza principal for public use.
13-17 Jul Virgen del Carmen is celebrated each year.
Aug The International Kite Festival is held in the Plaza Mayor.
Nov Judges for the Festival de Gastronomía choose the best individual dish cooked up by the town's restaurant.
7 Dec A festival of light, with impressive firework displays, is held every year from this date.

⊙ Shopping

Tunja and around *p98, map p99*
The market is near the Plaza de Toros on outskirts of town, open every day (good for *ruanas* and blankets). Fri is the main market day.
Tunjartesanal, Cra 9, No 19-56, T7400655. In the **Casa del Fundador**, this shop has an excellent range of high quality regional handicrafts. Open Mon-Sun 0900-1800. Recommended.

Villa de Leiva *p101, map p102*
Shops in the plaza and the adjoining streets have an excellent selection of Colombian handicrafts and offer many bargains.

Arcoiris, C 13, No 7-17, T7321436.
Excellent *artesanías* from all over Colombia.
Market day is Sat, held in the Plaza del
Mercado (not the Plaza Mayor).
Ricardo Luna, C 13, No 7-42, T7320491.
Good leather products.

Chiquinquirá *p104*
Many delightful toys are made locally.
Along the south side of the Basilica are
shops specializing in musical instruments.

▲ Activities and tours

Tunja and around *p98, map p99*
Piri Company, T7431286, www.piri
company.com. Does tours throughout
Boyacá. Very good local knowledge and
can arrange private transport to local
villages. Recommended.

Villa de Leiva *p101, map p102*
Horse riding
Mauricio Cortez, T31180741562. Hires
horses and guides for US$3.30 per hr.

Tour operators
Colombian Highlands, Cra 9, No 11-02,
T7321379, www.colombianhighlands.com.
Biologist Oscar Gilède runs tours of the
local area, as well as trips to local nature
spots such as Iguaque National Park
specifically geared towards botanists,
ornithologists and enthusiasts of adventure
sports such as abseiling and spelunking.
His office on Carrera 9 is also an excellent
source of information on the local area.
Zebra Trips, C Caliente, T3118701749,
www.zebratrips.com. With its zebra-
striped fleet of Land Rovers, this company
provides a fun way to explore the desert
area outside Villa de Leiva.

Sierra Nevada del Cocuy *p108, map p109*
El Cocuy
De Una, based in Bogotá, www.deuna
colombia.com. Dutch-run tour agency with
tailor-made trips throughout Colombia and
an emphasis on introducing tourists to the
country's people as well as its landscapes.
Run a variety of tours in this region, at
different levels of difficulty, such as a 6-day
round-trip trek taking in the Valle de
Lagunillas – Laguna de la Plaza – Laguna del
Pañuelo – Valle de Cojines – Laguna La Isla –
Laguna Grande de los Verdes, and costing
US$260 per person (minimum of 4 people
per group, for smaller group the price
increases). Price includes transport to/from
El Cocuy/Guícán, park fees, camping fees,
cooking equipment and bilingual guide.
A good level of physical fitness is required.

☉ Transport

Tunja and around *p98, map p99*
Bus
The bus station is 400 m steeply down from
city centre. From Bogotá, with **Rápido
Duitama**, **Libertadores**, **Transportes Alianza**
or **Copetran**, 2½-3 hrs, 4½-5 hrs weekends
and holidays, US$5.50. To **Bucaramanga**,
frequent services, 7 hrs, US$19. To **Villa de
Leiva**, frequent services in *colectivo* or mini
bus, US$2.70, 40 mins.

Villa de Leiva *p101, map p102*
Bus
The bus station is on Cra 9 between C 11
and C 12. It is a good idea to book the return
journey on arrival. To **Tunja**, 45 mins, US$2.70
with **Flota Reina**, **Coomultrasvilla**, **Cootax**,
Libertadores or **Trans Alianza**, or microbus
every 15 mins from 0530 to 1830. To **Bogotá**
via Tunja, takes 3-4 hrs, US$10, several
companies, and via Zipaquirá and
Chiquinquirá, US$10. To **Chiquinquirá**, 1 hr,
US$3.30, 6 a day. To **Ráquira** *busetas* at 0730,

0730, 0830, 1230, 1630 US$2.20, 30 mins taxi, US$15. To **Moniquirá**, **1000** connects with bus to **Bucaramanga**, thus avoiding Tunja. To **Iguaque National Park entrance**, 50 mins, US$1.70 at 0915, 1300, 1630.

Chiquinquirá p104
Bus
To **Villa de Leiva**, 1¾ hrs, US$3.30, several daily. To **Tunja**, 3 hrs, US$6. To **Zipaquirá**, US$6. To **Bogotá**, 2½ hrs, US$5.50.

Ráquira and around p105
Bus
Buses leave Villa de Leiva at 0730, 0830, 1230 and 1630, 30 mins, US$2.20. The return journey is more complicated, with only one direct service at 0430; you may have to change at Ramera.

Taxi
Round-trip taxis from Villa de Leiva, US$33.

Sogamoso p106
Bus
Bogotá, 4-4½ hrs, US$11; to **Tunja**, 1-2 hrs, US$5.50.

Iza p106
Bus
From Sogamoso with **Flota Alianzana**, US$2.20. If no buses from terminal in Sogamoso, take a taxi to Puente de Pesca, 5 or 6 blocks away, and catch from there.

Lago de Tota p107
Bus
From Sogamoso, US$2.80, 1½ hr with **Flota Alianzana**. Buses leave every 1½hrs, passing through Iza, Tota and on to **Aquitania**.

Monguí p107
Bus
Buses leave from the plaza. To **Sogamoso**, every 20 mins by buseta, US$1, 45 mins.

❶ Directory

Tunja and around p98, map p99
Banks Several banks in the C 20/Cra 10 area. **Internet** Coffenet, Cra 9, No 19-98, upstairs, US$2 per hour.

Villa de Leiva p101, map p102
Banks Banco Popular and Banco Agrario in the Plaza will give pesos against Visa, limited hours. There is a Visa ATM in the Plaza. **Internet** Redside, Cra 9, No 9-99. Skype, headphones and international calls. **Post office** In Telecom building, C 13, No 8-26.

Iza p106
Telephone There is a Telecom with (pricey) international calls on the Parque Principal.

Santander Department

Tumbling rivers, green valleys and countless immaculately preserved colonial towns and villages – Santander has much to recommend it. Take away the tropical vegetation and you could almost imagine yourself in the mountains of southern Spain. With a burgeoning adventure-sports scene, centred around the town of San Gil, this area of Colombia is becoming an increasingly popular destination for national and foreign visitors alike. What's more, it is also one of the cheapest parts of the country and you will get the chance to sample some of the regional culinary delicacies and stay in delightful colonial hotels without fear of breaking the bank. The village of Barichara was voted the most beautiful in Colombia and was declared a National Monument in 1975, while Girón, just a few kilometres from the industrial capital Bucaramanga, does not lag far behind. Bucaramanga is a modern city with a thriving nightlife and one of the best places for paragliding in the country. ➤➤ *For listings, see pages 124-129.*

San Gil ⊖🄿🄾▲🄑🄒 ➤➤ *pp124-129. Colour map 2, B6.*

→ *Phone code: 7. Population: 28,000. Altitude: 1140 m.*

About 21 km northeast of Socorro, is San Gil, a colonial town with a good climate in the deep valley of the Río Fonce. San Gil is an important centre for adventure sports. The river systems of the Ríos Fonce and Chicamocha run through deep valleys and gorges in this part of Santander, providing the best rafting and canoeing in Colombia (see Activities and tours, page 128). With a broad range of hotels, San Gil is an excellent base from which to explore Santander's string of stunning colonial villages. There is a tourist office here: **Instituto Municipal de Turismo y Cultura** ① *C 15, No 14-66, T7273529.*

Near the centre of the town by the river is the enchanting **Parque El Gallineral** ① *daily, US$2.25, T7240821, there are excellent guides, some English-speaking, be sure to tip generously as they are not paid by the park.* The park, created in 1919, covers 4 ha where the Quebrada Curití runs through a delta to the Río Fonce. It is named after the *chiminango* trees, which make up 80% of the trees in the park. These trees have a natural tendency to lean over and are therefore popular with roosting chickens. There are streams everywhere to create a delightful botanical garden full of butterflies and birds. Notable are the heliconias and the huge *ceiba* near the *playa* where the canoes end their trip down the Río Fonce. Outstanding are the many fine trees covered with moss-like *tillandsia*. There is a restaurant and a superb public natural swimming pool which uses water siphoned off from the Quebrada Curití.

In the centre, the **Parque Principal** has a fountain surrounded by huge *ceiba* and heliconia trees, very attractive when illuminated in the evening. Overlooking it is the **church**, which has interesting octagonal towers. There is a good view of the town from **La Gruta**, the shrine overlooking the town from the north (look for the cross).

Activities

San Gil is increasingly recognized as the centre of Colombia's burgeoning adventure-sports industry. There are a number of activities available in the surrounding countryside. There are many adventure companies in San Gil, some better equipped than others. See Activities and tours, page 128 for recommendations, or speak to Shaun at the Macondo Guesthouse for advice.

Rafting Blessed with three rivers in proximity to each other, San Gil can provide excellent rafting for people of all levels of experience.

The Río Fonce is the main river running through San Gil and is the best one for beginners with Grade II-III rapids. The trip begins 11 km from town and winds up in the centre of San Gil, opposite the Parque Gallineral. A trip costs US$14 with transport and safety equipment. It is best to wear sandals.

The Río Chicamocha has Grade I-IV rapids and travels through the spectacular Chicamocha canyon. The journey starts 1½ hours from San Gil and costs US$84 with a minimum of four people, transport included.

For a more extreme experience, the Río Suárez has Class IV+ rapids. The 20-km trip lasts three hours and costs US$67 per person.

Abseiling Known as rappelling in Colombia, abseiling down Juan Curri, a spectacular three-tier, 180-m waterfall, is a popular activity. A descent down one of the waterfall's 60-m cascades costs US$20 per person.

The Juan Curri waterfall is also a popular hiking destination and has a lovely swimming spot at the base of one of the cascades. You can climb to the second of the three tiers using a number of ladders and ropes. From San Gil, take a bus (US$2) towards Charalá and ask to be dropped off at the waterfall. There are two approaches, passing through private *fincas*. You may have to pay a small fee for access, about US$2. A return taxi fare is US$20.

Paragliding San Gil has two excellent locations for paragliding (known as *parapente*). The most spectacular location is over the Chicamocha canyon and costs US$94, lasting between 30 minutes and one hour. The second is near Curiti and lasts 20-30 minutes, costing US$33.

Kayaking Three-day beginners courses on the Río Fonce, including eskimo roll training in a local swimming pool, cost US$195. More experienced kayakers can make runs on different rivers with experienced guides.

Horse riding Day trips to local swimming spots cost US$14 per person.

Caving On the road to Barichara there are a series of caves known as La Antigua with saloons full of spiders and bats. A guided crawl through small tunnels of mud and water to underground waterfalls costs US$14. Near Paramo is Cueva del Indio, a cave full of stalactites, stalacmites and bats. You have to slide down a zip line into the dark mouth of the cave before wading through waist-level water. Cost is US$14. To get there, take a bus (US$2) from bus station in San Gil or taxi (US$17 return).

Hiking The surrounding countryside has several old indigenous trails, known as the Lenguake or Camino Real, linking many of its beautiful villages. A popular 1½-hour walk is between the historic villages of Barichara and Guane (see under Barichara, below, for more details).

Swimming There are lots of good swimming holes on San Gil's rivers. A local favourite is the Pozo Azul, just outside town, popular on Sundays. The most spectacular option is Pescaderito, just outside Curiti, which has a number of beautiful, clear pools. From the main square in Curiti, walk past the church four blocks and take the road leading out of town.

A bus to Curiti costs US$1.30. Alternatively, Parque Gallineral in San Gil has a spectacular swimming pool fed by water from the Río Fonce.

About 20 km south of San Gil on the road to Duitama, is **Páramo**, (with some accommodation eg Páramo in the Plaza Principal) one of the centres of activity sports (see above). About 30 km further on is **Charalá**, which has a plaza with a statue of **José Antonio Galán**, leader of the 1781 Comunero revolt. It also has an interesting church and Casa de la Cultura. Bus to San Gil, US$2.

Barichara ⊜⊘⊘⊜⊜ ↠ pp124-129. Colour map 2, B6.

→ *Phone code: 7. Population: 10,000 Altitude: 1300 m.*

From San Gil a direct paved road leads in 22 km to Barichara. Often touted as the most beautiful small town in Colombia, it would be difficult to argue against this claim. Barichara is a beautiful colonial town founded in 1741 and designated as a National Monument in 1975. There are several interpretations of this indigenous Guane name, the best is 'the place of rest with flowering trees'. It has a wonderfully peaceful, bohemian atmosphere, with white and green or blue paint everywhere and a lot of fine stonework. The walls of many buildings – whitewashed with doors and zócalos (the lower half of the building) painted

Barichara

Sleeping 🛏
Chia-Ty 1
Corata 2
Hostal Misión Santa Bárbara 3
La Mansión de Virginia 4
La Posada de Pablo 5
Los Tiestesitos 6

Eating 🍴
Color de Hormiga 1
El Compá 2

green, blue or turquoise – are made with a technique called *tapia pisada*, which uses compacted mud mixed with water. The churches are built of the brown stone found all over Santander, and the streets are paved with it throughout. Fortune has been kind to Barichara; it is a prosperous little town, as can be seen by the number of boutique-style *artesanía* and clothes shops. This is very much a place to relax as an increasing number of Colombians find at weekends, mainly from Bucaramanga but also Bogotá. Artists congregate here too, but midweek it is very quiet.

Sights

Among Barichara's places of historical interest, is the house of the former president, **Casa de Aquileo Parra Gómez**. If you wish to visit, ask the lady at the house next door who has the key. The **Casa de Cultura**, on the Parque Principal, has a small exhibition of local historical interest and archeological finds.

The **Catedral de la Inmaculada Concepción** is a fine colonial building, which sets the tone for the town. The façade and twin towers are strikingly illuminated at night. The interior is all in finished sandstone, with fluted columns, a carved wooden ceiling, gallery, cupola and a bright, gold-leaf *reredos*. There are three other interesting churches, **San Antonio** ① *Cra 4/C 5*, with a house for the elderly alongside, **Santa Bárbara** ① *C 6/Cra 11*, at the top of the town, **Jesús Resucitado** ① *C 3/Cra 7*, with the cemetery next to it – all with simple, even stark, interiors. There is a superb wide-ranging view from the *mirador* at the top of Carrera 10 across the Río Suarez to the Cordillera de los Cobardes, the last section of the Cordillera Oriental before the valley of the Magdalena. At the corner of the Carrera 10 and Calle 4, there is a **Piedra de Bolívar**, which shows the number of times the Liberator passed through the village.

You can walk to Barichara from Guane, or vice versa, along a delightful camino real, originally used by the indigenous Guane and later appropriated by the Spanish. The path still retains much of the original paving and most of what fell into disrepair has been restored. You will walk past lush green pastures full of grazing cows and goats and through orchards. It takes about two hours. It is best to leave in the early morning and to carry plenty of water and head protection as the sun can be punishingly hot at midday. There are a couple of *fincas* selling refreshments along the way. From Barichara, walk to the top of the town along Carrera 10 and continue downhill along the stone trail. From Guane, exit the plaza to the left of the church, walk uphill for two blocks and take a left; continue walking and you will eventually hit the path.

There is a more extensive, three day walk to the villages of Barichara, Guane, Villanueva, Los Santos, and the ghost town of Jerico, involving a spectacular descent of the Chicamocha canyon. There are various hostals to stay in on the way, and places to sample local food and drinks. Speak to Shaun at the Macondo Guesthouse in San Gil for more details.

Guane ●●● ›› pp124-129. Colour map 2, B6.

Much like Barichara, the tiny village of Guane, 9 km away by road, is a place seemingly lost in time. That the surrounding valley abounds in fossils only adds to this impression. Former capital of the pre-Columbian Guane culture, it has a beautiful plaza dominated by a **church** of simple but imposing design, with an interesting beamed and ornamented roof, fine wooden doors, a balcony at the west end and an elegant chapel to Santa Lucía to the left of the altar. In the plaza there is a monument, studded with fossils, dedicated to the last Guane chief, Guaneta, and several brilliant-orange acacia trees. Not much happens in Guane: you are as likely to see a donkey parked outside the local shop as a car.

There are many colonial houses and an excellent and surprisingly large **paleontological and architectural museum** ① *daily 0800-1200, 1430-1700, US$1.20*, housed in the Parroquia San Isidro on the plaza. It has an enormous collection of fossils found in the local area (which is constantly being added to), as well as woven Guane textiles and a mummified woman. Ask at the local shop if it is closed. A lady will take you on an informative if rather whirlwind tour.

North to Bucaramanga

North of San Gil on the main road to Bucaramanga is **Curití**, noted for handicrafts in *fique* (agave sisal). Mixed with cotton, it is used to make fabrics, shoes, bags and even building materials. You can see weaving at **Ecofibras** in the village. Near Curití are limestone caves. To visit, see under San Gil, above. About 28 km north of San Gil, a little off the road, is the picturesque village of **Aratoca**, with a colonial church. Near Aratoca you will become aware of the deep valley to the east of the road, the canyon of the **Río Chicamocha**. At one point in the next section, look for the place where the road takes to a narrow ridge with spectacular views on both sides as the river loops round to the southwest. The descent from the heights along the side of a steep cliff into the dry Río Chicamocha canyon, with spectacular rock colours, is one of the most dramatic experiences of the trip to Cúcuta, but, if driving, this is a demanding and dangerous stretch. The deep valley of the river at this point is becoming an interesting place for canoeing and whitewater rafting, especially between Cepitá and Pescadero, which is where the main road crosses the river. There is a grandstand view of this section of the river from near Aratoca. See under San Gil, above, for sporting possibilities in this region. After crossing the river, the road ascends again to the plateau for the remaining few kilometers to Bucaramanga.

Bucaramanga ◎❶❷❸⊛◎▲◎❶ ›› pp124-129. Colour map 2, A6.

→ *Phone code: 7. Population: 539,000. Altitude: 959 m.*

Bucaramanga, 420 km from Bogotá, is the capital of Santander Department. A modern, industrial city with little remaining of its colonial past, it is nonetheless not without charm. It still has a small colonial area, some lovely parks and squares and fine dining and nightlife. It is also an important transport hub, connecting Bogotá with the main border with Venezuela, Cúcuta, and with the Atlantic coast. If you are heading to any of these destinations it is more than likely that you will have to make a stop in Bucaramanga. It stands on an uneven plateau sharply delimited by eroded slopes to the north and west, hills to the east and a ravine to the south. The city's great problem is space for expansion. The metropolitan area has grown rapidly because of the success of coffee, tobacco and staple crops.

The city was founded in 1622 by Paéz de Sotomayor but was little more than a village until the 19th century. Simón Bolívar established his campaign headquarters here in 1813, and lived here for some time in the **Casa de Bolívar** around 1828. Perú de la Croix, a French officer in Bolívar's army wrote his *Bucaramanga Diary* here, an interesting study of his leader. Gold was found in the hills and rivers nearby, hence the Río Oro to the southwest, which were worked until the end of the 19th century.

Ins and outs

Getting there The airport is at Palonegro, on three flattened hilltops on the other side of the ravine, south of the city. There are spectacular views on take-off and landing. Taxi from town US$4; *colectivo*, US$1. Buses are scarce despite the fact that some bus boards say 'Aeropuerto' (direction 'Girón/Lebrija' from Diagonal 15). ►► For flight details, see Transport, page 129.

The **bus terminal** is on the Girón road, with cafés, shops, a bank and showers. Taxi to centre, US$1.50; bus US$0.80. To the Magdalena at Barrancabermeja, 115 km; to Cúcuta, 198 km; to Bogotá, 420 km; to Santa Marta, 550 km, all paved.

Getting around Most taxis have meters; beware of overcharging from bus terminals. The minimum fare is US$1.80 and this should get you to most places within the city centre. When you get in the taxi make sure the driver switches the meter to '42', which is the code for the minimum fare. For longer journeys, taxis usually charge about US$10 per hour. Buses charge US$0.80.

Tourist office On Parque de los Niños, underneath the library, also inside, Instituto Municipal de Cultura, is **Oficina Asesora de Turismo** ① *C 30, No 26-117, T6341132*, maps, etc. **DAS** ① *Cra 11, No 41-13*.

Sights

The city can be divided into three sections, running west to east. The **Parque García Rovira** is the centre of the colonial area where you will find most of the museums and cultural centres.

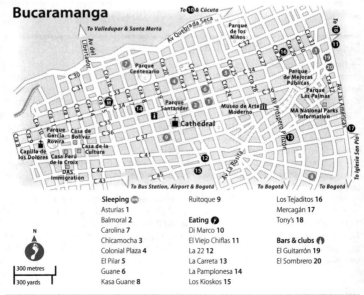

Bucaramanga

Sleeping	Ruitoque 9	Los Tejaditos 16
Asturias 1		Mercagán 17
Balmoral 2	**Eating**	Tony's 18
Carolina 7	Di Marco 10	
Chicamocha 3	El Viejo Chiflas 11	**Bars & clubs**
Colonial Plaza 4	La 22 12	El Guitarrón 19
El Pilar 5	La Carreta 13	El Sombrero 20
Guane 6	La Pamplonesa 14	
Kasa Guane 8	Los Kioskos 15	

N

300 metres
300 yards

The **Parque Santander** is the heart of the modern city and is where most of the budget hotels can be found. Further east is the Zona Rosa, centred around Calle 33 and Carrera 33, where many of the city's better restaurants, bars and clubs are located. Bucaramanga is notable for its green spaces. There are a number of fine parks, including **Parque de Mejoras Públicas** ① *C 36/Cras 29-32*, with an open-air *concha acústica* (concert shell) for public performances, **Parque de los Niños** ① *C 30/Cra 26*, and **Parque Centenario**, from which buses used to leave before the new terminal was built. Other parks worth visiting are **Parue San Pío** ① *C 45, No 33*, with its many trees, and **Parque Las Palmas** ① *C 41, No 30*.

There are several churches of interest. The **Catedral de la Sagrada Familia** ① *C 30/Cra 19*, overlooks the Parque Santander, a clean white Romanesque building with twin towers and statues of the Virgin and San José in between. The church of **San Pío** ① *C 45/Cra 36*, has several paintings by Oscar Rodríguez Naranjo, and the **Capilla de los Dolores** (Chapel of Sorrows) ① *C 35/Cra 10*, was the first chapel to be built in the town and is where the poet Aurelio Martínez Mutis is buried.

Museo de Arte Moderno i *C 37/Cra 26, US$0.50*. Just off Parque García Rovira, is **Casa de Bolívar** ① *Tue-Sat 0900-1200, 1400-1800, US$1, at C 37, No 12-15, T6422542*. This is an interesting ethnographic and historical museum and a centre of research on Bolívar and his period.

Across the street is the **Casa de La Cultura** ① *C 37, Mon-Sat 0900-1800, US$1, No 12-46, T6302046*, in a fine colonial building with exhibitions, film showings and a local *artesanía* display. Also worth a visit is the **Museo Arqueológico Regional Guane** ① *in the Casa de Cultura 'Piedra del Sol', Cra 7, No 4-35, Floridablanca, T6394537*, good collection of Guane culture artefacts and textiles.

Away from the centre, the **Club Campestre** is one of the most beautifully set in Latin America. There is an amusement park, **Parque El Lago**, in the suburb of Lagos, southwest of the city on the way to Floridablanca. On the way out of the city northeast (towards Pamplona) is the **Parque Morrorico**, well maintained with a fine view. There is a sculptured Saviour overlooking the park, a point of pilgrimage on Good Friday.

The suburb of **Floridablanca**, 8 km southwest, has the famous **Jardín Botánico** ① *Tue-Sun 0800-1100 and 1400-1700, US$0.50, take a bus (US$0.80) from Cra 33, Bucaramanga, either Florida Villabel which goes by the botanical gardens, or Florida Autopista (continuation of Cra 33) which goes direct to the square in Florida and you have to walk about 1 km, taxi from the centre, US$3, Eloy Valenzuela* (also known as El Paragüitas gardens), belonging to the national tobacco agency. The Río Frío runs through the gardens, which have been recently reconstructed.

Around Bucaramanga

Lebrija, 17 km to the west, is in an attractive plain, and Rionegro, is a coffee town 20 km to the north with the Laguna de Gálago and waterfalls close by. One fine waterfall is 30 minutes by bus from Rionegro to Los Llanos de Palma followed by a two-hour walk through citrus groves towards Bocas. Complete the walk along an old railway to the Bucaramanga–Rionegro road.

Piedecuesta, 18 km southeast of Bucaramanga, is where you can see cigars being hand-made, furniture carving and jute weaving. Cheap, hand-decorated *fique* rugs can be bought. There are frequent buses to all these towns from the city, or a taxi costs US$6. Corpus Christi processions in these towns in June are interesting. To get there, take bus from Carrera 22, 45 minutes.

The road (paved but narrow) runs east to Berlín, and then northeast, a very scenic ascent through cloudforest to the summit of the Eastern Cordillera and eventually on to Pamplona, about 130 km from Bucaramanga. **Berlín** is an ideal place to appreciate the grandeur of the Eastern Cordillera and the hardiness of the people who live on the *páramo*. The landscape is stark, barren and dramatic, much like the Scottish highlands. The village lies in a valley at 3100 m. The peaks surrounding it rise to 4350 m and the temperature is constantly around 10°C, although on the infrequent sunny days it may seem much warmer. There is a tourist complex with cabins and there are several basic eating places. Camping (challenging but rewarding) is possible with permission. At the highest point on the road between Bucaramanga and Berlín (3400 m) is a café where you can camp on the covered porch.

Girón ◎ ➤ *pp124-129. Colour map 2, A6.*

Girón, a tobacco centre 9 km southwest of Bucaramanga on the Río de Oro, is a little gem of a colonial town. Far from the bustle of industrial Bucaramanga, at weekends it is filled with *bumangueses*, many of whom come for Mass at its beautiful church. In 1963 Girón was declared a National Monument: the buildings are well preserved and the town unspoilt by modernization. By the river are *tejo* courts and popular open-air restaurants with *cumbia* and *salsa* bands. In the square at weekends, sweets and *raspados* (crushed ice delights) are sold, while children buy balloons and are wheeled about in miniature cars. Take the bus from Carrera 15 or 22 in Bucaramanga, US$0.80. A taxi costs US$4.50.

◉ Santander Department listings → *Phone code: 7.*

For Sleeping and Eating price codes and other relevant information, see pages 31-36.

◉ Sleeping

San Gil *p117*
A Bella Isla, north of town, Vía Javel San Pedro, T7242971, www.bellaislaaventura.com. On top of the hill looking out over town, Bella Isla has a beautiful setting in lovely grounds but nonetheless has the feel of a resort hotel that has seen better days. A 1960s building constructed over 4 levels, it does however cater for most needs with large rooms, many with a balcony for hanging a hammock, TV, tennis courts, a swimming pool and Wi-Fi. Breakfast is included in the price.
B Mansión del Parque, C 12, No 8-71 Esquina, T7245622, mansiondelparque@ hotmail.com. Occupying a colonial building on the corner of the parque principal, this is easily the most picturesque hotel in town. The rooms are large with antique furniture and there are internet facilities. Ask for one

of the street-facing rooms, which have balconies for people watching.
C La Posada Familiar, Cra 10, No 8-55, T7248136. Small little place with 6 rooms set around a sunny courtyard with a water piece and hanging plants. Rooms are clean and have TV and private baths. Recommended.
C Mesón de Cuchicute, Km 1 Vía San Gil–Socorro, T7242041. On the western outskirts of town, Mesón de Cuchicute offers either *cabañas* or 2 up, 2 down rooms with balconies looking out onto one of the hotel's 2 enormous pools. With very comfortable beds, all the mod cons (TV, a/c, minibar, room service) and some nice details such as wash basins carved out of local Barichara stone, it represents good value for money.
C Victoria, Cra 11, No 10-40, T7245955. Eccentrically decorated in garish colours which somehow seem to work, the Victoria has some bizarre ornaments, including fake knitted sunflowers in one room. Rooms open onto a long corridor-courtyard with a

fountain. Each room has a/c and even a DVD player but no hot water.

D Abril, C 8, No 10 Esquina, T7248795, hotelabrilsangilss@yahoo.es. Strangely laid out with the reception area essentially in the car park but has clean rooms with antique beds (comfortable), hot water, TV and a minibar.

D Posada del Conde, Cra 10, No 13-17, T7242170, posadadelconde@yahoo.es. Fine old building off the parque principal. Has a restaurant serving breakfasts and the occasional weekend lunch as well as Wi-Fi, though the double rooms have no windows. Prices tend to double during high season.

E Hostal Monkora, C 9, No 8-65, T3154006018 (mob), hostalcasamonkora@hotmail.com. This backpackers' hostel, located in a 150-year-old house 3 blocks from the parque, has 2 private rooms and 2 dorms with bunks, all with shared bathrooms. It also offers a kitchen for use by guests, lots of hammocks, 10 mountain bikes for hire and good information on the local area. A camping zone in the back garden was under construction at the time of writing.

E Santander Alemán, C 12, No 7-63, T7242535, igarnica@hotmail.com. Tiny new place with simple but comfortable rooms. Has an excellent, good-value restaurant serving home-cooked food for US$2.

E San Carlos, Cra 11, No 11-25, T7242542. Sweet little place set round an atrium. Has TV and private bath but some of the rooms have no windows.

E-F Macondo Hostal, C 12, No 7-26, T7244463. With a communal area decked out with hammocks, and an honesty system for drinks and internet, Australian Shaun Clohesy has created more of a home-from-home than a hostel. Board games, free coffee, internet access and cheap, comfortable rooms – it has several bunks in dormitory rooms (**F**) – all add to the convivial atmosphere, but the Macondo's biggest asset is the wealth of information available on local activities and the chance to swap tales with the many backpackers who pass through.

Baricharà *p119, map p119*

A Hostal Misión Santa Bárbara, C 5, No 9-12, T7267163 (or Bogotá T2884949), www.hostalmisionsantabarbara.info. If you have the cash to splash this is the place to stay in town. Each room is individually decorated with great taste (1 even has stained-glass windows) and all open onto a delightful plant-filled courtyard. Has a good restaurant and a swimming pool.

B Coratá, Cra 7, No 4-08, T7267110. This delightful colonial building has a beautiful balustraded terrace looking down onto a courtyard with an impressive *saucellaron* tree. TV, and hot water in private bathrooms. No fans or a/c but the high ceilings keep you cool.

B La Mansión de Virginia, C 8, No 7-26, T7267170. Impeccable colonial house with rooms set around a lovely courtyard. Has fine, comfortable beds and private baths with hot water. Recommended.

D Chia-Ty, Cra 6, No 4-51, T7267727. A good, cheap option, run by a nice old couple. Rooms are simple but clean with private bath and look onto a pretty garden.

D La Posada de Pablo 2, C 3, No 7-30, T7267070. One of several places belonging to 'Pablo' in town. This one is next to the Iglesia de Jesús Resucitado and a gorgeous park. Has TV and good beds. Try for rooms 10 or 11, which have exquisite views across the rooftops to the cathedral.

E Los Tiestesitos, Cra 5, No 7-62, T7267224. The only real budget option in town – but it's a good one. Run by a couple of old ladies, you almost have to fight your way through a profusion of plants to reach your room. Clean rooms, own bath and comfortable beds. Also doubles as an *artesanías* shop selling ceramics.

Camping Just outside Baricharà on the road to San Gil is **La Chorrera**, a natural swimming pool, T7267422, US$0.30 to bathe, US$1.60 to camp, meals by arrangement, clean, attractive.

Guane *p120*

Guane has 2 delightful and economical hostals to stay in, both highly recommended.

D Posada Mi Tierra Guane, Parque Principal, opposite museum, T3156306878, hildaui@hotmail.com. Run by a nice woman, this small 6-room hostel is comfortable and charming with a pleasant courtyard and private bathrooms. Some rooms have bunk beds.

D Shia Shue, C Real, T7247753. Just off the plaza. Fine, comfortable rooms with private baths in a colonial house.

Bucaramanga *p121, map p122*

Since Bucaramanga has numerous national conventions, it is sometimes hard to find a room in more expensive hotels.

AL Chicamocha, C 34, No 31-24, T6343000, www.hotelchicamocha.com. Large hotel near the Zona Rosa. Has a pool, sauna, gym and Wi-Fi throughout, though you would expect more for your money.

A Guane, C 34, No 22-72, T6347014, www.hotel-guane.com. Smart hotel with large rooms that include reception areas. Has a pool and solarium. Breakfast included.

A-B Asturias, Cra 22, No 35-01, reservas asturias@hotelciudadbonita.com.co. Rooms are set around a sunny atrium and vary in quality. Downstairs require renovation but are consequently cheaper. Includes American breakfast in price and has a pizza restaurant attached. Guests can use next door swimming pool at La Ciudad Bonita for US$8.

B Ruitoque, Cra 19, No 37-26, T6334567, www.hotelruitoque.com. From the outside it may not be much to look at it has good-sized, clean rooms, a restaurant, Wi-Fi and is just a block from Parque Santander.

B El Pilar, C 34, No 24-09, www.hotelpilar.com. Good rooms and lots of extras: private parking, an internet room, restaurant and accident insurance. Cheaper with fan.

D Balmoral, Cra 21/C 35, T6303723. A good budget option with clean rooms, cable TV, hot water and good location a block from Parque Santander. Its downside is that street-facing rooms are noisy while back rooms have no windows and can be stuffy.

D Colonial Plaza, C 33, No 20-46, T6454125. Its certainly not colonial but its rooms are clean and it has hot water. Slightly cheaper with fan.

D Kasa Guane, C 49, No 28-21, T6576960, www.kasaguane.com. This new backpackers' hostel is the best budget option in town. Owned by paragliding instructor Richi Mantilla of Colombia Paragliding, it's decorated with Guane culture artefacts and has several private rooms as well as dorms with bunks. Additional services include internet, a kitchen for use by guests, table games, a pool table and good information on the local area.

F Hotel Carolina, Cra 18, No 30-56, T6802225. Good value at the price. Rooms are simple but clean and it offers laundry service. The area, nicknamed the Zona Roja, can be dangerous; be careful at night.

Girón *p124*

D-E Hotel Las Nieves, C 30, No 25-71, T6810144, www.hotellasnievesgiron.com. Delightful colonial buidling on the main plaza that expertly walks the tightrope between faded grandeur and disrepair. Each of its large rooms has a desk, TV and hot water. Ask for a street-facing room, all of which have balconies for people watching. Has Wi-Fi and an excellent, cheap restaurant. Rooms with fan are significantly cheaper than with a/c.

D Girón Chill Out, C 25, No 32-02, T6461119, www.gironchillout.com. This Italian-owned hostel has 3 private rooms in a colonial house with high ceilings. As well as Wi-Fi, cable TV and use of a washing machine, there is also a kitchen for use by guests, though you might be tempted by the excellent restaurant serving Italian food with ingredients imported from the mother country, also owned by the hostel, on the corner of the same street.

● Eating

San Gil *p117*

San Gil has a number of good eating options but it should be noted that here, as in much of this region, it is difficult to find places open in the evening.

The market on Cra 11 between C 13 and 14 is another great breakfast spot with lots of stalls selling fruit salads and juices. If you don't have a sweet tooth be sure to ask them to lay off the condensed milk and cheese on your salad.

♥ **Donde Betty**, Cra 9, C 12 esquina. Great little breakfast spot selling *arepas*, scrambled eggs and fruit juices. On the corner of the Parque Principal, hence an excellent place for people watching.

♥ **El Maná**, C 10, No 9-12. It would be difficult to leave this restaurant without feeling a little bloated what with the many set menu courses you get for less than US$4. Try the chicken stuffed with ham and cheese. Open at lunchtime and evenings except Mon.

♥ **Pizzeria Pierrot**, Cra 9, No 9-130. The best pizzas in town. Open in the evenings and does home delivery.

♥ **Rogelia**, Cra 10, No 8-09. Great little lunchtime place in a colonial building with large wooden beams. Serves local specialities such as *cabrito con pepitorio* and *carne oreada* (a bit like beef jerky). *Menú ejecutivo* US$2.50.

♥ **Saludable Delicia**, C 11, No 8-40. Excellent vegetarian restaurant with a wide choice of options including pumpkin soup, veggie burgers and *frijoles en salsa*. Also has many honey, nut and cereal products for sale.

♥ **Santander Alemán**, C 12, No 7-63. Part of the hostel of the same name. Excellent set menu, home-cooked food for just US$2. Open in the evenings.

Barichara p119, map p119

♥ **El Compa**, C 5, No 4-48. Family-run restaurant serving typical regional food, including *sobrebarriga* and *arepa santandereana*.

♥ **Color de Hormiga**, C 8, No 8-44. If you visit only one restaurant in Santander it should be this one. Billing itself as 'atypical' food, Color de Hormiga specializes in all things ant; the *hormiga culona* is a large-winged ant often eaten as a snack in the region. Here, the chefs have taken this to another level with fine steaks or chicken served in ant sauce. What's more, the restaurant's setting – on a terrace with a pretty garden and views onto the town below – is a delight.

Guane p120

There are 3 good restaurants on the plaza all serving typical regional food.

♥ **Guayubi**, to the left of the museum as you face it. Goat is a bit of a speciality as is the *chicha de maíz*, a mild alcoholic drink made from corn masticated by the local women.

Bucaramanga p121, map p122

Try the *hormigas culonas* (large-bottomed black ants), a local delicacy mainly eaten during Holy Week (sold in shops, not restaurants and also sold on main highways in Santander at that time).

♥♥♥ **La Carreta**, Cra 27, No 42-27. Established by local football legend Roberto Pablo Janiot nearly 50 years ago, this colonial building has been tastefully restored. *Parrillas* and seafood can be enjoyed around a courtyard of sculpted gardens and water features.

♥♥♥ **Mercagán**, C 45, No 33-47. The large photograph of a cow on the menu immediately tells you that this place is not for vegetarians. Steaks and hamburgers are the order of the day. Fine setting opposite the beautiful Parque San Pío.

♥♥ **DiMarco**, C 28, No 54-21. Top-notch steaks in pleasant surroundings.

♥♥ **El Viejo Chiflas**, Cra 33, No 34-10. Good restaurant in the heart of the Zona Rosa. Try the *cabrito* (goat), a local speciality.

♥♥ **La 22**, Cra 22, No 45-18. So popular is this local canteen that at weekends you will struggle to be seated. Paella and *sancocho* are some of their specialities.

♥♥ **Los Kioskos**, C 45, No 22-45. Los Kioskos consists of a series of thatched huts festooned with plants. Menu of regional food. There are often live *vallenato* bands to help you digest.

♥♥ **Los Tejaditos**, Cra 28, No 34. Popular with locals, with a varied menu of meats, seafood, pastas and salads.

♥ **La Pamplonesa**, C 35, No 18-29. Just off Parque Santander, this *panadería* does good breakfasts as well as sandwiches, cakes and fruit juices. For local sweets and delicacies, try Alba, Cra 10, No 41-01, a family-run *dulcería* more than 100 years old. It's so sweet you have to battle with a hive of bees that swarm around the shop.

ⓦ Tony's, Cra 33A-67 Not satisfied with their enormous breakfasts and lunches, *bumangueses* like to fit in an extra meal in between known as *onces*. Tony's caters for them all. Good *tamales* and *arepas*.

ⓝ Bars and clubs

Bucaramanga *p121, map p122*
When they want to party, most *bumangueses* head for the Zona Rosa in the eastern end of town, where hundreds of bars and clubs will jostle for your attention. **El Guitarrón** and **El Sombrero**, both on Carrera 33, have live mariachi bands.

⊛ Festivals and events

Bucaramanga *p121, map p122*
Jul The annual international piano festival is held in the Auditorio Luis A Calvo at the Universidad Industrial de Santander, one of the finest concert halls in Colombia. The university is worth a visit for the beautiful grounds.
Mar Feria de artesanías (Handicraft Fair) at the Centro de Exposiciones y Ferias (CENFER).

ⓞ Shopping

San Gil *p117*
Armando Palitos, Cra 11, No 9-44, T7243345. Excellent selection of *artesanías*, ranging from furniture and plates to *bolsos de fique* (woven bags).

Barichara *p119, map p119*
Artes y Variedades, C 6, No 7-40. Lots of locally made handicrafts, including *sandalias de fique* (woven sandels).

Tierrarte, C 6, No 7-81. Fine leather products such as belts and bags, as well as beautiful jewellry. Credit cards accepted. Also has shops in San Gil and Bucaramanga.

Bucaramanga *p121, map p122*
Camping equipment
Acampemos, C 48, No 24-70, last place in Colombia to get camping-gas cartridges before Venezuela.

Handicrafts
Try **Bosque**, near the Parque García Rovira, C 36, No 12-58 or opposite the market in barrio Guarin, C 33A, No 33-23. Also try **Girón** (see below) and typical clothing upstairs in the food market, C 34 y Cras 15-16. Similar articles (*ruanas*, hats) in San Andresito.

ⓐ Activities and tours

San Gil *p117*
Adventure sports companies
Colombia Rafting Expeditions, Cra 10, No 7-83, T7245800, www.colombiarafting.com. The best for rafting, with International Rafting Federation-qualified guides. Also does hydrospeed.
Exploracion Colombia Guides, C 8, No 10-38, T7238080, exploracol@hotmail.com. Offers paragliding, whitewater rafting, canyoning and caving.
Páramo Santander Extremo, Parque Principal, Páramo, T3112513785 (mob). Based in nearby Páramo, this company is best for abseiling and canyoning but also does caving, rafting and horse riding.

Cycling
Hire bikes for US$1 per hour from **El Ring**, C 7, No 10-14, T243189, or try at the **Macondo Guesthouse** or **Hostal Monkora** which both have a few bikes for hire (see Sleeping).

Bucaramanga *p121, map p122*
There are opportunities for parapenting at the nearby Mesa del Ruitoque and over the

Cañón de Chicamocha, to the south of the city. Good schools are **Las Aguilas**, Km 2 vía Mesa de Ruitoque, Floridablanca, T6352470, www.voladerolasaguilas.com, and **Colombia Paragliding**, T4326266, www.colombia paragliding.com, which also has a hostel, where you can stay while you take lessons.

◎ Transport

San Gil *p117*
Bus
Bus station 5 mins out of town by taxi on road to Tunja, the bus terminal for local destinations is on Cra 11 with C 15. To **Bogotá**, US$19. To **Bucaramanga**, US$6, 2½ hrs. To **Barichara** from C 12, US$1.40, 45 mins, every hour, taxi US$5. To **Bucaramanga**, Cotransangil has regular buses throughout the day, 2½ hrs.

Barichara *p119, map p119*
To **San Gil**, hourly bus from 0600, Cotransangil, 45 mins, US$1.50.

Bucaramanga *p121, map p122*
Air
To **Bogotá**, several flights a day with Avianca and AeroRepública. To **Cúcuta** 2 daily with Satena and Aires. To **Medellín** 2 daily with Satena and Aires.
 Airlines offices Avianca, C 37, No 15-03, T6426117. AeroRepública, Cra 35, No 54-14, T6430222. Aires, C 36, No 26-48, T6323938. Satena, C 36, No 15-56, T6707087.

Bus
The bus station is several miles outside the town. You can book tickets to all destinations here. Call T6371000 and you will be connected to all relevant bus companies. To **Bogotá**, 8-11 hrs, US$38 (Pullman) with Berlinas del Fonce (C 53, No 20-40, T6304468, www.berlinasdelfonce.com, or at bus terminal), at 0630, 0830, 2030, 2100, 2130, 2200, 2230, 2300 and 2330; with Copetran, www.copetran.com.co, US$38, 19 services a day starting at 1200 (this journey is

uncomfortable, there are no relief stops, and it starts off hot and ends cold in the mountains, be prepared) To **Barranquilla**, 13 hrs, US$50 with Berlinas. To **Cartagena**, US$55, 14 hrs, with Copetran, 7 services daily from 1630. or 1 with Berlinas. To **Santa Marta**, 11 hrs, US$45 with Copetran or Berlinas. To **Valledupar**, 10 hrs, US$15 with Copetran, 5 a day. To **El Banco** on the Río Magdalena, US$28, 7 hrs, several companies, direct or change at Aguachica, this journey should be made in daylight. To **Barrancabermeja**, 2 hrs, US$8, a scenic ride with 1 rest stop, this road is paved. Hourly buses to **San Gil**, 2½ hrs, US$10. To **Tunja**, 7½ hrs, US$40. To **Berlín**, US$6. To **Pamplona**, 3 a day, US$5 (Pullman), US$14 (*corriente*). To Cúcuta, 6 hrs, US$22 (Pullman), *colectivo* US$22. The trip to Cúcuta is spectacular in the region of Berlín. Other companies with local services to nearby villages on back roads, eg the colourful folk-art buses of **Flota Cáchira** (C 32, Cra 33-34), which go north and east.

◎ Directory

San Gil *p117*
Internet There are countless internet cafés dotted around the town. **Cofee em@il**, C 13, No 9-78, which has Skype and headphones.

Bucaramanga *p121, map p122*
Banks HSBC, Cra 19, No 63-41. BBVA, C 35, No 18-02. Bancafé, C 35, No 16-20, Visa agents. Bancolombia, by Parque Santander, will cash Thomas Cook and Amex TCs, long queues (cheques and passports have to be photocopied). Many other banks, many with ATMs. **Internet** Setelco, Cra 27, No 19-15. Iter-Mega, Cra 29, No 32-58. **Colombia On Line**, C 13, No 29-16. There is free Wi-Fi in all of Bucaramanga's parques and in many of the shopping centres. **Money exchange** Exprit, C 52, No 31-153, T6577747. Cambiamos, Centro Comercial Cabecera, Level IV, local 104, Cra 35A con C 49. **Post** office Servientrega, Cra 21 entre C 24 y C25.

Norte de Santander Department

The border between Santander and Norte de Santander departments is at the high pass near Berlín. Thereafter, the Cordillera Oriental slowly reduces in height to become a ridge, now the border with Venezuela, and ending at the peninsula of La Guajira and the Caribbean Sea. A spur, however, turns northeast, crosses the border at the Tamá National Park to become the Sierra Nevada de Mérida, the highest mountains of Venezuela. The northeast of the department is down in the Maracaibo basin, the hottest place in South America. This border country with Venezuela was intimately linked with the wars of independence, with both Bolívar and Santander. Parts of Norte de Santander, particularly along the Venezuelan border, still have some guerrilla activity. Pamplona and Cúcuta are safe but travellers should take advice before venturing into any other areas of the department.
▸▸ *For listings, see pages 134-137.*

Pamplona ⊖🏢🏪🏨🍴🛍 ▸▸ *pp134-137. Colour map 2, A6.*

→ *Phone code: 5. Population: 68,000. Altitude: 2200 m.*

Pamplona, set in a green valley and surrounded by mountains, is a more than worthwhile stopover between Bucaramanga and Cúcuta. It was founded in 1549 by Pedro de Orsúa and Ortún Velasco. During the colonial era it was as important as Bogotá. The independence movement was started here in 1810 by Agueda Gallardo. It became important as a mining town but is now better known for its university – students make up almost 40% of the population. While an 1875 earthquake destroyed large sections of the town it still manages to retain a certain colonial atmosphere. At 2200 m, it can get cold, especially at night when a jumper or even a coat is required.

Tourist office **Oficina de Turismo Pamplona**① *C 5, No 6-45, T5680960, cortour pamplona@yahoo.es*, next to *alcaldía*, off Plaza Central. Very helpful and friendly, organizes tours into surrounding area and guides for hiking in hills.

Sights
The severe earthquake of 1875 played havoc with the monasteries and some of the churches. There is now a hotel on the site of the former San Agustín monastery, but it is still possible to visit the remains of the ex-monasteries of San Francisco and Santo Domingo. The **cathedral** is in the spacious **Plaza Central** (Plaza Aguela Gallardo), a massive building with five naves. It dates from the 17th century but has been damaged by earthquakes and rebuilt over the years. The **Iglesia del Humilladero**, adjoining the cemetery also dates from the 17th century, is very picturesque and allows a fine view of the city. The sculpture *Cristo del Humilladero* came from Spain. In September, there is an annual festival celebrating the *Humilladero*.

  Museo de Arte Religioso ① *C 4/Cra 5, Mon-Fri 0800-1200,1400-1800; Sat 0800-1200, US$0.50*, is a collection from the region and has paintings by many Colombians including Vázquez de Arce y Ceballos. The fine **Casa Colonial**① *C 6, No 2-56*, is now an archaeological museum. It's a little gem, with artefacts from the Motilones and other indigenous communities still living in the north of the department.

  Casa Anzoátegui ① *Cra 6, No 7-48, Mon-Fri 0800-1200, 1400-1800*, is where one of Bolívar's generals, José Antonio Anzoátegui, died in 1819, at the age of 30, after the battle of Boyacá. The state in northeast Venezuela is named after him. The restored colonial

Simón Bolívar

Aside from Columbus, no single man has had a greater influence on South American history than Simón Bolívar. This Venezuelan aristocrat galvanized the many factions of the continent into a united army that succeeded in expelling the Spanish from present-day Colombia, Venezuela, Panama, Ecuador, Peru and Bolivia.

His campaign through the Departments of Norte de Santander, Santander and Boyacá remains one of his greatest achievements.

In May 1819, Bolívar marched into Colombia from Venezuela with a force of 2000 men, meeting with Santander's forces at Tame and proposing to cross the Andes using the rarely used route across the Páramo de Pisba, a barren, windswept section of the Cordillera Oriental whose lowest pass was over 3200 m. There were many deaths and few of his 800 horses survived but the audacious manoeuvre surprised the Spanish. The armies met near Paipa and Bolívar's troops inflicted a surprise defeat.

On 6 August, Bolívar marched into Tunja, but his route to the capital was blocked by the royalists at a bridge crossing the Río Boyacá, 16 km to the south. Despite the strength of their position, the Spanish were routed at the first attack and disintegrated. Over 1600 prisoners were taken and four days later, Bolívar entered Bogotá as the liberator of Colombia.

Four years later the First Congress of Gran Colombia met at Cúcuta on 6 May 1821. It was at this meeting that the plan to unite Venezuela, Colombia and Ecuador was ratified. It was the pinnacle of Bolívar's career.

house is now a museum covering the Independence period. **Museo de Arte Moderno** ① *C 5 on the Parque Central, Mon-Sat 0900-0000, 1400-1730, Sun 1200-1400, US$0.80*, principally exhibits the paintings and sculptures of Eduardo Ramírez Villamizar of Pamplona, who died in 2004. The colonial building is a notable local example and was declared a National Monument in 1975. Next to the Iglesia del Humilladero is the **Museo de Fotografía Antigua de Toto** ① *Cra 7, No 2-36*. Toto was the local undertaker and a prolific artist. The exhibition consists of hundreds of photographs sent in by the citizens of Pamplona, some dating back to the early 20th century and makes for a fascinating archive of local history. Sadly, Toto passed away but the space is maintained by some of his ten sons. It is open 'whenever possible' and is free.

Around Pamplona

Tamá National Park covers the point at which the Cordillera Oriental continues across into Venezuela, where there is also a National Park. It is high, rising to the Páramo de Santa Isabel with several sections above 3400 m, and extending over 48,000 ha. Access is from Herrán. From here take the minor road to El Tabor, cross the Río Táchira into Venezuela and go south through Villa Paéz-Betania to Palmazola, where you cross back into Colombia, with about 30 minutes to Orocué and the administrative centre of the Park.

There is a comparatively heavy rainfall (over 3000 mm per year on the lower slopes) which, combined with a wide range of altitude, produces a full set of forest habitats from jungle to high temperate woodland and *páramo* (moorland), with a vast variety of flora and fauna, including anteaters, deer and spectacled bears. It is reported that a waterfall has recently been discovered in the park about 820 m high. If this proves to be true, this would place the falls as the third or fourth highest in the world. Pamplona is surrounded by a number of rivers and lakes, including Laguna de Cácota and Laguna Camagueta, all within an hour's drive. Trips to the villages of Pamplonita, famous for flower cultivation and Mutiscua, renowned for its trout farms are also easily organised from Pamplona. Ask at tourist office next to *alcaldía* for details.

Cúcuta ▶▶ pp134-137. Colour map 2, A6.

→ *Phone code: 5. Population: 585,000. Altitude: 215 m.*

Cúcuta, capital of the Department of Norte de Santander, is only 16 km from the Venezuelan frontier. For a border town, it is a surprisingly pleasant place to visit, with plenty of green spaces and a bustling but non-threatening centre. It was founded in 1733 by Juana Rangel, severely damaged by the earthquake in 1875, and then elegantly rebuilt, with the streets shaded by trees. Anyone spending more than five minutes here will appreciate this latter fact, for Cúcuta is one hot place: the mean temperature is 29°C. It also lays claim to being one of the few cities in the world with a street grid system that begins at 0, as in Avenida 0.

Cúcuta

Sleeping
Arizona Suites 1
Bolívar 2
Casa Blanca 3
Cavalier 4
Hotel de la Paz 5
Lady Di 6

Lord 7
República Bolivariana 8
Tonchala 9

Eating
La Embajada Antioquena 1
La Mazorca 2

Londero's Sur 3
Pinchos & Asados 4
Rodizio 5
Venezia 6

Border essentials: Colombia–Venezuela

Cúcuta–San Antonio

Colombian immigration Exit and entry formalities are handled at the DAS office in the white house before the international border bridge. DAS also has an office at the airport, which will deal with land travellers. If you do not obtain an exit stamp, you will be turned back by Venezuelan officials and the next time you enter Colombia, you will be fined. DAS office in town at Avenida Primera, No 28-55, open 0800-1130, 1400-1700 daily. Take a bus from the city centre to Barrio San Rafael, southwards towards the road to Pamplona. Shared taxi from border US$3, will wait for formalities, then US$1 to bus station.

Entering Colombia by air All Colombian formalities can be undertaken at the airport. Visitors arriving by air may not need a visa: unfortunately, there are no local flights from Cúcuta to San Antonio or to Santo Domingo (San Cristóbal), the two nearby Venezuelan airports. In 2008, flights were suspended between San Antonio and Caracas and San Cristóbal and Caracas. The nearest airport with flights to Caracas was Mérida.

Entering Colombia by road You must obtain both a Venezuelan exit stamp and a Colombian entry stamp at the border. Without the former you will be sent back; without the latter you will have problems with police checks, banks and leaving the country. You can also be fined.

Leaving Colombia by private vehicle With all the right papers, the border crossing is easy and traffic normally flows smoothly.

Colombian customs Aduana office on the road to the airport (small sign); has a restaurant.

Entering Venezuela Passports must be stamped with an exit stamp at the white DAS building before the border crossing. If not you will have to return later to complete formalities. Expect very long queues. Venezuelan consulate Avenida Camilo Daza con, Calle 7, T713983/T712107, open 0800-1300, Monday to Friday. Car papers must be stamped at the SENIAT office in Venezuela.

Transport Bus to San Cristóbal, US$1.40 (**Bolivariano**), *colectivo* US$3; to San Antonio, taxi US$8, bus and *colectivo* from Calle 7, Avenida 4/5. From Cúcuta to or beyond, go to San Antonio or (better) San Cristóbal and change. On any form of transport which is crossing the border, make sure that the driver knows that you need to stop to obtain exit/entry stamps, etc.

Note There is a 30-minute time difference between Colombia and Venezuela.

Ins and outs

The **airport** is 5 km north of the centre, 15 minutes by taxi from the town and the border, US$4, $10 at night, $10 to border. Buses from Avenida 3 take rather longer. The notorious **bus station** is on Avenida 7 and Calle 0 (a really rough area). There is a private bus station belonging to Copetran on Avenida Camilo Daza, via Aeropuerto. Taxi from bus station to town centre, US$2.40. The new Berlinas del Fonce terminal is much safer; it is 2 km beyond the main terminal along continuation of Diagonal Santander. For more details see page 137. **Note** Cúcuta and the surrounding area is a great centre for smuggling. Be careful.

Tourist information

Corporación Mixta de Promoción de Norte de Santander ① *C 10, No 0-30, T5718981*, helpful, has maps and brochures. At the bus station (1st floor, currently under reconstruction), and at airport. Other maps obtainable from Instituto Geográfico, Banco de la República building, in the main plaza.

Sights

The **Catedral de San José** ① *Av 5 between C 10/11*, is worth a visit. Note the oil paintings by Salvador Moreno. The **Casa de la Cultura** ① *C 13, No 3-67*, also incorporates the **Museo del la Ciudad**, which covers the history of a city very much involved with the independence movement. The **international bridge** between Colombia and Venezuela is southeast of the city. Just beyond it is San Antonio del Táchira, the first Venezuelan town, and 55 km on is San Cristóbal.

Around Cúcuta

Just short of the border is the small town of **Villa del Rosario**, where the Congress met that agreed the constitution of Gran Colombia in the autumn of 1821, one of the high points of the career of Simón Bolívar. The actual spot where the documents were signed is now a park beside which is the **Templo del Congreso**, in which the preliminary meetings took place. Formerly a church, it was severely damaged in the 1875 earthquake and only the dome has been reconstructed.

Also nearby is the **Casa de Santander**, where General Francisco de Paula Santander, to whom Bolívar entrusted the administration of the new Gran Colombia in 1821, was born in 1792 and spent his childhood. It became a National Monument in 1959 and a museum in 1971 dedicated to the period of the independence campaigns and the contribution made then and later by General Santander. Open 0800 to 1800 daily.

◉ **Norte de Santander Department listings** → *Phone code: 5.*

For Sleeping and Eating price codes and other relevant information, see pages 31-36.

◉ **Sleeping**

Pamplona *p130*
Hotel accommodation may be hard to find at weekends, when Venezuelans visit the town.

Pamplona is famous throughout the region for its bread: there is a *panadería* on practically every corner. Particularly well known are **Panadería Chávez**, *Cra 6, No 7-36* and **Panadería Araque**. Try *pastel de horno, queso de hoja, pan de agua* or *cuca*, a kind of black ginger biscuit often topped with cheese. Pamplona even hosts a *cuca* festival in Sep/Oct of each year.

A-B El Solar, C 5, No 8-10, T5682010, miosolar@hotmail.com. Beautifully restored colonial building dating from 1776. Rooms upstairs are enormous and have their own kitchen and balconies looking onto the street. Rooms downstairs, without kitchen, are cheaper. Also has by far the best restaurant in town (see Eating, below).

B 1549 Hostal, C 8B, No 5-84, T5680451, 1549hostal@gmail.com. Another recent, lovingly restored colonial building. Rooms are light and airy and decorated with great taste by owners Ricardo and Kokis. Wi-Fi throughout. There is also a coffee bar and *panadería* in a large courtyard out back. Highly recommended.

B Cariongo, Cra 5/C 9, T5681515. A 1960s building that has seen better days, this was the best option in town until the recent opening of El Solar and 1549 hostel. Has a newer annex out back with comfortable rooms and a garden with playground but lacks character. Wi-Fi in lobby.

D-E Orsúa, C 5, No 5-67, T5682470. Probably the best budget option in town. Crumbling but characterful building east side of plaza central. Friendly owner and good restaurant. Rooms are cheaper if they don't look onto plaza.

E Imperial, Cra 5, No 5-36, T5682571. Large modern building on the plaza central with a youth hostel vibe. Rooms are a little grubby but staff are friendly. Cable TV and hot water.

E Santa Clara, Cra 6, No 7-21, T5684105. Rambling buidling in need of some tender loving care but is easy on the eye in a dilapidated sort of way and has hot water and a restaurant.

Cúcuta *p132, map p132*

AL Arizona Suites, Av 0, No 7-62, T5731884, www.hotelarizona-suites.net. Newly refurbished, centrally placed, the Arizona has all the mod cons including Wi-Fi, safety boxes and a restaurant serving Italian food.

AL Bolívar, Av Demetrio Mendoza, Barrio San Luis, T5710390, www.hotel-bolivar.com.

On the outskirts of town on the airport road, the Bolívar is an old colonial building with rooms in a series of modern bungalows set around peaceful gardens and 2 swimming pools. With a paddling pool and playground, it's ideal for children.

AL Tonchalá, C 10/Av 0, T5731891, www.hoteltonchala.com. A bit of an eyesore from the outside, the Tonchalá nevertheless has friendly, professional staff and lots of added extras including a large pool, a spa and beauty parlour an internet room and Wi-Fi throughout. Breakfast included in price.

A Casa Blanca, Av 6, No 14-55, T5722888. The reception area of the Casa Blanca has recently been refurbished and looks kind of grand with lots of glass and freshly painted white walls. The back, where the rooms are, is obviously still awaiting its facelift and is less slick. However, rooms are clean and it has a large pool and a restaurant serving regional and international food. Only hot water in the suites, which are more expensive.

B Lord, Av 7a, No 10-58, T5713609. On a busy street lined with stalls and opposite a shopping centre, the rooms are light and airy and it offers parking and laundry service. Cheaper with fan.

C Cavalier, Diagonal Santander C 6, No 1-28, T5830134. Basic but clean. Has a/c and offers laundry service.

D Hotel de la Paz, C 6, No 3-48, T5718002. Rooms are basic but at this price this hotel is recommended for having a pool and the delicious La Embajada Antioqueña restaurant next door. Offers 10% discount for stays longer than 5 days.

D Lady Di, Av 7, No 13-80, T5831922. With an enormous photo of Princess Diana above the doorway, you know this hotel will be kitsch but kind of fun. More photos feauture throughout. The rooms are clean but basic.

D República Bolivariana, Av 6, No 11-77, T5718099. Well placed near Parque Santander, this hotel is dedicated to Simón Bolívar and features lots of murals of the Liberator. Rooms are cheaper with fan.

🍴 Eating

Pamplona *p130*

🍴🍴 **Delicias del Mar**, C 6, No 7-60, T5684558. Popular lunchtime venue specializing in fish, particularly *robalo* and trout.

🍴🍴 **El Portón Pamplonés**, C 5, No 7-83. Specializes in locally caught trout and other fish.

🍴🍴 **El Solar**, C 5, No 8-10. By far the best in town. High quality fare served in the peaceful courtyard of this colonial hotel. Try the side of pork in honey. Highly recommended.

🍴🍴 **La Casona**, C 6, No 7-58, T5683555. Another local favourite serving meats and seafood. Try the *paella valenciana*.

🍴🍴 **Piero's Pizza**, C 9 / Cra 5. Pizzas cooked by an Italian family. Authentic.

🍴 **Calle Real Restaurante**, Cra 6, No 7-60. Family home that serves up a decent lunchtime *menú ejecutivo*.

🍴 **El Arriero**, C 6, No 7-18. Quirky little place serving basic fare.

Cúcuta *p132, map p132*

🍴🍴 **Londero's Sur**, Av Libertadores, No 0E-60, T5833335, Argentine grill serving *parrillas*.

🍴🍴 **Rodizio**, Av Libertadores, No 10-121, Malecon II Etapa, T5750095. Boasts 13 different types of meat as well as seafood.

🍴 **La Embajada Antioqueña**, C 6, No 3-48, T5731874. Local and antioquian food in a fine open-air setting.

🍴 **La Mazorca**, Av 4, No 9-67, T5712833. More comida criolla served in a pleasant courtyard decorated with hanging baskets and Antioquian paraphernalia. *Menú ejecutivo* US$3.50. Lots of fast food outlets on the 3rd level of the spanking new Centro Comercial Ventura Plaza, C 10 y 11 Diagonal Santander.

🍴 **Pinchos & Asados**, Av Libertadores, No 10-121, next to Rodizio, delightful setting on a terrace overlooking landscaped wooded gardens, delicious *brochettes*.

🍴 **Venezia**, Condominio La Riviera, Av Libertadores, T5750006. Oven-fired pizzas.

🎉 Festivals and events

Pamplona *p130*

Easter The town's Easter celebrations are famous throughout Colombia, with processions, and cultural presentations.

4 Jul Pamplona was the first town in Colombia to declare independence from the Spanish, a fact that is celebrated with bullfights, music concerts and art exhibitions.

14 Sep Dia del Señor del Humilladero is celebrated by *pamploneses*.

Oct Festival de la Cuca, local bakers compete to produce the tastiest ginger biscuit.

1 Nov Concerts and exhibitions are held to celebrate the foundation of the town.

🛍 Shopping

Pamplona *p130*

Pamplona is a good place to buy *ruanas*. There is a good indoor market 1 block west of the plaza central on C 6 (C del Mercado).

Cúcuta *p132, map p132*

Try C 10, Av 8 for leather boots and shoes.

Cuchitríl, Av 3 No 9-89, has a selection of the better Colombian craft work.

Centro Comercial Ventura Plaza, C 10 y 11 Diagonal Santander, has plenty of international brand shops, as well as *artesanías*.

Also try **Aquí Colombia**, C 10, No 1-46 or **Artesanías Franco**, Cra 7, No 5-10, Villa del Rosario.

🚌 Transport

Pamplona *p130*

Bus

To **Bogotá**, US$40, 13 hrs. To **Cúcuta**, US$5, 2½ hrs. To **Bucaramanga**, US$10, 4-5 hrs, great views. To **Málaga** from plaza central, 5 daily from 0800, 6 hrs, US$5. To **Berlín**, US$5. Buy tickets only at the official office upstairs. Do not accept help from 'intermediaries'. You can also take *colectivos* or shared taxis to

Bucaramanga (US$14) and Cúcuta (US$7), which usually cuts the journey by 1 hr and includes door-to-door pick up and delivery. Try **Cooptmotilon** on the north west corner of Plaza Central, C 5, T680291.

Cúcuta *p132, map p132*
Air
There are only domestic flights from Cúcuta airport. For flights to Venezuelan destinations you must cross the border and fly from San Antonio airport. **Note** Do not buy 'airline tickets' from Cúcuta to Venezuelan destinations. All flights go from San Antonio. Flights to **Bogotá**, AeroRepública has 2 a day, Avianca has 3 a day. To **Barranquilla**, daily, Avianca. To **Bucaramanga**, 3 a day, Avianca. To **Medellín**, 2 daily, Avianca and Aires.

   Airline offices Avianca, Av 0, No 13-84, T5712848 and at airport, T5874884, www.avianca.com. AeroRepública, C 15, No 0E-18, Los Caobos, T5833306, www.aerorepublica.com.co. Aires, Av 1E, No 18-12, Los Caobos, T5833941, www.aires.aero.

Bus
To **Bogotá**, hourly, 15-17 hrs, US$50, with Berlinas del Fonce, 13 a day and Copetran, both of whom have their own terminals (see Ins and outs), making 2 stops, 1 of which is **Bucaramanga**. There are frequent buses, even during the night (if the bus you take arrives in the dark, sit in the bus station café until it is light). To **Cartagena**, with Copetran, 4 a day at 0900, 1400, 1600 and 1730, with Berlinas, 1 a day, 16-19 hrs, US$59-72. To **Bucaramanga**, US$20, 6 hrs, with Copetrán and Berlinas del Fonce Pullman, hourly. There are good roads to **Caracas** (933 km direct or 1046 km via Mérida), and to **Maracaibo** (571 km). Bus to Caracas, 15 hrs, US$30, **Expreso Occidente**, or taxi *colectivo*.

   Warning Travellers have been reporting for years that the bus station is overrun with thieves and con-men, who have tried every trick in the book. This is still true. You must take great care, there is little or no police protection. On the 1st floor there is a tourist office for help and information and a café/snack bar where you can wait in comparative safety. Alternatively, go straight to a bus going in your direction, get on it, pay the driver and don't let your belongings out of your sight. Don't put your valuables in bus company 'safety boxes'. Make sure tickets are for buses that exist; tickets do not need to be 'stamped for validity'. For San Cristóbal, only pay the driver of the vehicle, not at the offices upstairs in the bus station. If you are told, even by officials, that it is dangerous to go to your chosen destination, double check. If the worst happens, report the theft to the DAS office, who may be able to help to recover what has been stolen.

⊙ Directory

Pamplona *p130*
Banks Banco de Bogotá, on the plaza central, gives Visa cash advances. There are several ATMs nearby. **Internet** Miscelánea Shekina, Cra 6, No 8B-13. Internet La Séptima, Cra 7, No 3-62. **Post office** Cra 6/C 6, in pedestrian passage. **Telephone** Telefónica Telecom, C 7 y Cra 5-79.

Cúcuta *p132, map p132*
Banks A good rate of exchange for pesos is to be had in Cúcuta, at the airport, or on the border. Banco Ganadero and Banco de Los Andes near the plaza will give cash against Visa cards. Bancolombia changes TCs. Banco de Bogotá, on Parque Santander, advances on Visa. There are money changers on the street all round the main plaza and many shops advertise the purchase and sale of bolivares. Change pesos into bolivares in Cúcuta or San Antonio as it is difficult to change them further into Venezuela. Similarly, do not take bolivares further into Colombia, change them here. There are also *casas de cambios*, Casas de Cambio Invercambios, Av 5, No 13-32, Casa de Cambio Unidas, Av 5, No 11-39, L-3 C.C. Cúcuta Plaza, El Bolívar de Oro, C 10, No 4-48.

Contents

142 Cartagena
142 Ins and outs
143 Background
144 Sights
151 Beaches
152 Listings

161 Around Cartagena
161 Volcán del Totumo
161 Islas del Rosario
162 South of Cartagena
168 Listings

174 Barranquilla
176 Listings

179 Santa Marta and around
180 Santa Marta
182 Around Santa Marta
185 Tayrona National Park
187 Ciudad Perdida
188 Sierra Nevada de Santa
Marta
189 Listings

195 East to Venezuela
195 Riohacha
195 Santuario Los Flamencos
196 Valledupar
197 Guajira Peninsula
200 Listings

**203 San Andrés and
Providencia**
204 San Andrés and around
206 Providencia
209 Listings

Footprint features

140 Don't miss ...
162 Mud volcanoes
184 Gabriel García Márquez
186 The Lost City
198 Música tropical
201 Hammocks
208 The black crabs of Providencia

Border crossing

Colombia-Venezuela
199 Maicao

Cartegena & the North Coast

At a glance

Getting around Walking in city centre. Buses and taxis between cities.
Time required 2-3 weeks to explore Cartagena, Santa Marta and other regions.
Weather Hot all year round; more rain Aug-Nov.
When not to go Very crowded during Christmas and Easter periods but most festivals occur during this time.

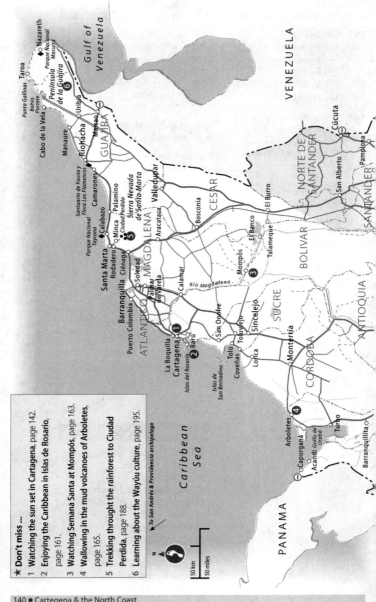

★ Don't miss ...
1 Watching the sun set in Cartagena, page 142.
2 Enjoying the Caribbean in Islas de Rosario, page 161.
3 Watching Semana Santa at Mompós, page 163.
4 Wallowing in the mud volcanoes of Arboletes, page 165.
5 Trekking throught the rainforest to Ciudad Perdida, page 188.
6 Learning about the Wayuu culture, page 195.

Descending on the lowlands of Colombia's Caribbean coast you enter another world. Steamy, colourful and lively, the entire area pulses to the rhythms of the omnipresent *vallenato*. *Costeños* may be looked down on by their more sombre countrymen, intimating that they lack the same sophistication and work ethic, but they certainly know how to enjoy themselves. There are almost endless fiestas and the Barranquilla carnival is held here, often cited as second best only to Rio for colour and size, and less commercialized.

Aside from drinking and dancing, there is also fine architecture and an impressive literary legacy, particularly in Cartagena, the emerald in the crown of Colombia. This stunning colonial city bursts with colour and history, and offers fine food, a lively nightlife and some sparkling coral islands within easy reach.

South from Cartagena is Mompós, a colonial town where the clocks stopped somewhere back in the early 20th century and which puts on one of the best Easter festivals in the world. Up the Gulf of Urabá, on the way to Panama are the villages of Acandí, Capurganá and Sapzurro, unreachable by road and boasting a wild shoreline of coral reefs and the virgin jungles of the Darién.

Travel east along the coast and you'll reach Santa Marta, Colombia's oldest city and gateway to the spectacular Tayrona National Park. Rising up from the shores is the Sierra Nevada de Santa Marta, the highest coastal mountain range in the world, and one of the few places that can boast tropical beaches and snow-capped mountains within 20 miles of each other. The Sierra Nevada was home to the indigenous Tayrona and a visit to one of their recently discovered cities, Ciudad Perdida, must come high on anyone's list of Latin American adventures.

Beyond Santa Marta is the arid landscape of the Guajira Peninsula, home to the indigenous Wayúu, enormous flocks of flamingos and the ethereal Cabo de la Vela, where turquoise waters lap against a desert shoreline.

Cartagena

→ *Colour map 1, B2. Phone code 5. Population: 1,090,000.*
Cartagena is one of the hottest, most vibrant and beautiful cities in South America. It combines superb weather, a sparkling stretch of the Caribbean and an abundance of tropical fruit. Nuggets of history can be found around every corner and in every palm-shaded courtyard of this most romantic of places. There are exquisitely preserved colonial mansions, excellent museums and fine dining, it's a place not to be missed. ▸▸ *For listings, see pages 152-160.*

Ins and outs

Getting there

Rafael Núñez **airport** is 1.5 km from the city in the Crespo district and it can be reached by local buses from Blas de Lezo, in the southwest corner of the inner wall. There is a *casa de cambio*, T656 4943, open Monday to Friday 0830-2030, Saturday 0830-1700 and Sunday 0830-2100. It cashes Amex TCs but not Bank of America and better rates are available in town. For tourist information, ask at the travel agent's offices on the upper level. There is also a good self-service restaurant. A bus from the airport to Plaza San Francisco costs between US$0.60 and US$0.80, depending on whether the bus is air conditioned. A taxi to the centre is US$4 (official price). Buses and taxis for the return trip can be found on Avenida Blas de Lezo close to Puerta del Reloj. Buses can be very crowded and if you have a lot of luggage, a taxi is recommended.

The **bus terminal** is 30 minutes from town on the road to Barranquilla, a taxi costs US$5, or you can take the city buses to the 'Terminal de Transportes', from between US$0.60 and $0.80. Agree your taxi fare before you get in.

Undoubtedly, the best way to arrive is by sea and a description of the approach is given below under Background. Regular lines are at present non-existent, but what is possible is detailed on page 159. Cartagena is, however, popular for cruise ships and those who have their own sea transport: around 200,000 passengers pass through the docks each year. Equally, many tourists take trips to the offshore islands.

Getting around

Local buses are crowded, slow, ramshackle but colourful, cheap and a good way to find out about the locals. As usual in Latin America, do watch your belongings. **Taxis** are also quite cheap and more convenient. There are no meters, journeys are calculated by zones, each zone costing about US$1.25, though the minimum fare is $2.50. Thus Bocagrande to Centro, two zones, is US$2.50. It is quite common to ask other people waiting if they would like to share, but, in any case, always agree the fare with the driver before getting in. By arrangement, taxis will wait for you if visiting more remote places. Fares go up at night.

Best time to visit

The climate varies little during the year. Temperatures rise marginally when there is more frequent rain (August-November), and there can be flooding. Freak weather (as in 1999 on the fringes of the Venezuelan disaster) is very unusual. Fiestas are taken seriously in Cartagena, and if you want a quiet time you might want to avoid certain times of the year. If you want to join in, be sure to plan in advance or be prepared to struggle for accommodation and expect higher prices. ▸▸ *For further information, see Festivals and events, page 157.*

Tourist information

Turismo Cartagena de Indias has three offices. The main office is in the Plaza de las Aduanas, T6601583, and there are kiosks in Plaza de los Coches and Plaza de San Pedro Claver. **The Colombian Tourist Board – Proexport** ⓘ *C 28, No 13A-15, p35, T5600100, www.visitcolombia.com*, are another useful source of information.

Security

Carry your passport, or a photocopy, at all times. Failure to present it on police request can result in imprisonment and fines. Generally, the central areas are safe and friendly (although Getsemaní is less secure), but should you require the police, there is a station in Barrio Manga. Beware of drug pushers on the beaches, pickpockets in crowded areas and bag/camera snatchers on quiet Sunday mornings. At the bus station, do not be pressurized into a hotel recommendation different from your own choice.

Background

The full name of Cartagena is *Cartagena de Indias*, a name that is quite frequently used and a reminder that the early Spanish navigators believed they had reached the Far East. It was founded by Pedro de Heredia on 13 January 1533. The core of the city was built by the Spaniards on an island separated from the mainland by marshes and lagoons close to a prominent hill, a perfect place for a harbour and, more important at the time, easy to defend against attack. Furthermore, it was close to the mouth of the Río Magdalena, the route to the interior of the continent. In 1650, the Spaniards built a connection to the river, 145 km long, known as the **Canal del Dique**, to allow free access for ships from the up-river ports. This waterway has been used off and on ever since, was updated in the early 19th century and it is still used, mainly by barges, today.

The great Bay of Cartagena, 15 km long and 5 km wide is protected by several low, sandy islands. There were then two approaches to it, Bocagrande, at the northern end of Tierrabomba island – this was the direct entry from the Caribbean – and Bocachica, a narrow channel to the south of the island. Bocagrande was blocked by an underwater wall after Admiral Vernon's attack in 1741, thus leaving only one, easily protected, entrance to the approach to the harbour. The old walled city lies at the north end of the Bahía de Cartagena.

Cartagena declared its independence from Spain in 1811. A year later Bolívar used the city as a jumping-off point for his Magdalena campaign. After heroic resistance, Cartagena was retaken by the royalists under General Pablo Morillo in 1815. It was finally freed by the patriots in 1821.

Cartagena today

Although Cartagena is Colombia's fifth largest city, the short term visitor will not be aware of the size of the place. Beyond and behind the old walled city, Bocagrande and Manga is a large sprawling conurbation that stretches 10 km to the southeast. People have been moving in to add to the pressure on the poorer neighbourhoods as everywhere else in this part of the world, but Cartagena is a long way from the more heavily populated parts of highland Colombia, to the city's advantage.

The city's fortifications

Cartagena was one of the storage points for merchandise from Spain and for treasure collected from the Americas to be sent back. A series of forts protecting the approaches from the sea, and the formidable walls built around the city, made it almost impregnable.

Entering the **Bahía de Cartagena** by sea through Bocachica, the island of Tierrabomba is to the left. At the southern tip of Tierrabomba is the fortress of **San Fernando**. Opposite it, right on the end of Barú island, is the **Fuerte San José**. The two forts were once linked by heavy chains to prevent surprise attacks by pirates. Barú island is separated from the mainland only by the Canal del Dique. In recent years, the city has been expanding down the coast opposite Tierrabomba and settlements can be seen as you approach the entrance to the inner harbour of Cartagena, protected by another two forts, **San José de Manzanillo** on the mainland and the **Fuerte Castillo Grande** on the tip of **Bocagrande** now the main beach resort of the city.

In the centre of the harbour is the statue of the Virgin with the port installations to the right on Manga island. There is a very good view of the harbour, cruise boats and port activity from the end of Calle 6/Carrera 14, Bocagrande, though access to Castillo Grande itself is restricted. Manga Island is now an important suburb of the city. At its northern end a bridge, **Puente Román**, connects it with the old city. This approach to the fortified city was defended by three forts: **San Sebastián del Pastelillo** built between 1558 and 1567 (the *Club de Pesca* has it now) at the northwestern tip of Manga Island; the fortress of **San Lorenzo** near the city itself; and the very powerful **Castillo San Felipe de Barajas** inland on San Lázaro hill, 41 m above sea-level, to the east of the city.

The first fortifications on the site were built in 1536 though the main constructions began in 1639 and it was finished by 1657. It is the largest Spanish fort built in the Americas. Under the huge structure is a network of tunnels cut into the rock, lined with living rooms and offices. Some are open and illuminated, a flashlight will be handy in the others; visitors pass through these and on to the top of the fortress. Good footwear is advisable in the damp sloping tunnels. Baron de Pointis, the French pirate, stormed and took it, but Admiral Vernon failed to reach it. In the **Almacén de Pólvora** (Gunpowder store) ① *daily 0800-1800, US$7, guides available*, there is an interesting 1996 reproduction of Vernon's map of the abortive attempt to take the city in 1741. On the statue of Don Blas de Lezo below the fortress, don't miss the plaque displaying the medal prematurely struck celebrating Vernon's 'victory'.

Yet another fort, **La Tenaza**, protected the northern point of the walled city from a direct attack from the open sea. The huge encircling walls were started early in the 17th century and finished by 1735. They were on average 12 m high and 17 m thick, with six gates. They contained, besides barracks, a water reservoir.

Around the old city

The old walled city was in two sections, outer and inner. Much of the wall between the two disappeared some years ago. Nearly all the houses are of one or two storeys. In the outer city, the artisan classes lived in the one-storey houses of **Getsemaní** where many colonial buildings survive. Today, there is a concentration of hotels and restaurants here. Immediately adjoining is the modern downtown sector, known as **La Matuna**, where vendors crowd the pavements and alleys between the modern commercial buildings. Several middle range hotels are in this district, between Avenidas Venezuela and Lemaitre.

In the **inner** city, the houses in **El Centro** were originally occupied by the high officials and nobility. **San Diego** (the northern end of the inner city) was where the middle classes lived: the clerks, merchants, priests and military. Today, the streets of the inner city are relatively uncrowded; up-market hotels and restaurants are sprinkled throughout the area.

Just under a kilometre from the old city, along a seafront boulevard, **Bocagrande** is a spit of land crowded with hotel and apartment towers. Thousands of visitors flock to the beach with its accompanying resort atmosphere, fast-food outlets, shops – and dirty seawater. See Beaches, page 151.

The old city streets are narrow. Each block has a different name, a source of confusion, but don't worry: the thing to do is to wander aimlessly, savouring the street scenes, and allow the great sights to catch you by surprise. However, if you do want to know what you are looking at, the maps are marked with numerals for the places of outstanding interest. Most of the 'great houses' can be visited. Churches are generally open to the public at 1800, some for most of the day. Weekends and holidays are the best time for photography when traffic is minimal. What follows is a walking route for the sights of the old city which you can pick up and leave wherever you wish. Note that the numbers below refer to the circled numbers on the Historical Centre map.

Outer city

The **Puente Román** (1) is the bridge which leads from Isla Manga, with its shipping terminals, into Getsemaní, characterized by its *casas bajas* (low houses). The chapel of **San Roque** (2), early 17th century, is near the end of Calle Media Luna, and the hospital of Espíritu Santo. Just across the Playa Pedregal (3) is the Laguna de San Lázaro and the **Puente Heredia**, on the other side of which is the Castillo San Felipe de Barajas, see above. In an interesting plaza, is the church of **La Santísima Trinidad** (4), built 1643 but not consecrated till 1839. West of the church, at No 10 Calle Guerrero, lived Pedro Romero, who set the revolution of 1811 going by coming out into the street shouting 'Long Live Liberty'. Along Calle Larga (5), Calle 25, is the monastery of **San Francisco**. The church was built in 1590 after the pirate Martin Côte had destroyed an earlier church built in 1559. The first Inquisitors lodged at the monastery. From its courtyard a crowd surged into the streets claiming independence from Spain on 11 November 1811. The main part of the monastery has now been turned into business premises – take a look at the cloister garden as you pass by. Handicrafts are sold in the grounds of the monastery, good value, fixed prices, and, at the back, is the Centro Comercial Getsemaní, a busy shopping centre. On the corner of Calle Larga, formerly part of the Franciscan complex, is the **Iglesia de la Tercera Orden**, a busy church with a fine wooden roof of unusual design and some brightly painted niche figures. The church and monastery front on to the Avenida del Mercado on the other side of which is the **Centro Internacional de Convenciones** (6). It holds gatherings of up to 4000 people and is frequently used now for local and international conventions. It was built in 1972 on the site of the old colourful market, now banished to the interior part of the city. Although the severe fort-like structure is more or less in keeping with the surrounding historic walls and bastions, not everyone believes this is an improvement. When not in use, ask for a guide to show you around.

Immediately to the north is **Plaza de la Independencia**, with the landscaped **Parque del Centenario** alongside. At right angles to the Plaza runs the **Paseo de los Mártires**, flanked by the busts of nine patriots executed in the square on 24 February 1816 by the royalist Pablo Morillo after he had retaken the city.

Cartagena historical centre

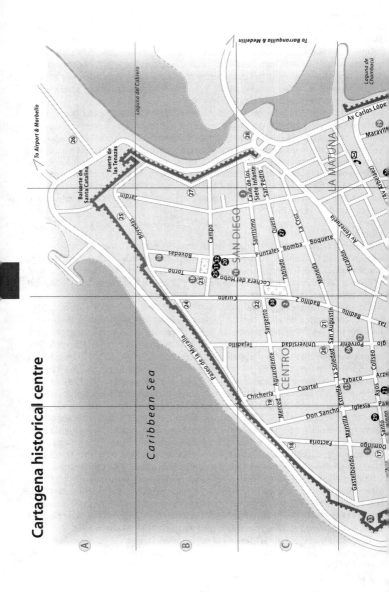

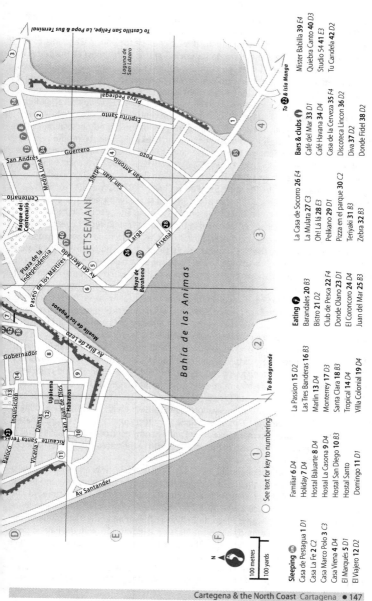

To Castillo San Felipe, La Popa & Bus Terminal

Laguna de San Lázaro

Playa Pedregal

Espíritu Santo

San Andrés
Guerrero
Media Luna
Centenario
Parque del Centenario
Plaza de la Independencia
Paseo de los Mártires
GETSEMANÍ
Sierpe
San Antonio
Pozo
San Juan
Av del Mercado
Larga
Arsenal
Playa de Barahona
Muelle de los Pegasos
Bahía de las Ánimas

Gobernador
Inquisición
Upalema
Damas
San Juan de Dios
Ricaurte
Santa Teresa
Vicaría
Baloco
Habanos
Av Santander

To Isla Manga
To Bocagrande

N
100 metres
100 yards

See text for key to numbering

Sleeping
Casa de Pestagua 1 D1
Casa La Fe 2 C2
Casa Marco Polo 3 C3
Casa Viena 4 D4
El Marqués 5 D1
El Viajero 12 D2
Familiar 6 D4
Holiday 7 D4
Hostal Baluarte 8 D4
Hostal La Casona 9 D4
Hostal San Diego 10 B3
Hostal Santo Domingo 11 D1
La Passion 15 D2
Las Tres Banderas 16 B3
Marlin 13 D4
Monterrey 17 D3
Santa Clara 18 B3
Tropical 14 D4
Villa Colonial 19 D4

Eating
Barandales 20 B3
Bistro 21 D2
Club de Pesca 22 F4
Donde Olano 23 D1
El Coroncoro 24 D4
Juan del Mar 25 B3
La Casa de Socorro 26 E4
La Mulata 27 C3
Oh! Lá lá 28 E3
Pelikano 29 D1
Pizza en el parque 30 C2
Teriyaki 31 B3
Zebra 32 B3

Bars & clubs
Café del Mar 33 D1
Café Havana 34 D4
Casa de la Cerveza 35 F4
Discoteca Lincon 36 D2
Diva 37 D2
Donde Fidel 38 D2
Mister Babilla 39 F4
Quiebra Canto 40 D3
Studio 54 41 E3
Tu Candela 42 D2

Inner City

At the western end of the Paseo is a tall clock tower, often used as the symbol of Cartagena. To the left is the **Muelle de los Pegasos** from where the tourist boats leave. Under the clock tower is the **Puerta del Reloj** and the three arches are the principal entrance to the inner walled city. Inside is the **Plaza de los Coches (7)**. As with almost all the plazas of Cartagena, arcades here offer refuge from the tropical sun. At one time, this plaza was the slave market, and later, it was from here that carriages (coches) could be hired for local journeys. On the west side of this plaza is the **Portal de los Dulces**, a favourite meeting place and where you can still buy all manner of local sweets and delicacies. **Plaza de la Aduana (8)**, with a statue of Columbus in the centre and the **Casa de la Aduana** along the wall, originally the tax office and now part of the city administration as the **Palacio Municipal**. Opposite is the **Casa del Premio Real** which was the residence of the representative of the Spanish King. In the corner of the wall is the **Museo de Arte Moderno** ① *Mon-Fri 0900-1200, 1500-1800, Sat 1000-1200, US$0.50*, a collection of the work of modern Colombian artists. There is a museum shop.

Past the museum is the **Plaza de San Pedro Claver (9)** ① *daily 0830-1700, US$2.20, reduction with ISIC, guides, $3 in Spanish, a little more in English*, and the church and monastery of the same name, built by Jesuits in 1603 and later dedicated to San Pedro Claver, a monk in the monastery, who died in 1654 and was canonized 235 years later. He was called *El Esclavo de los Esclavos*, or *El Apóstol de los Negros*: he used to beg from door to door for money to give to the black slaves brought to the city. His body is in an illuminated glass coffin set in the high marble altar, and his cell and the balcony from which he kept watch for slave ships are shown to visitors. There are brightly coloured birds in the small monastery garden. Several upstairs rooms form a museum, with many interesting items linked and not linked to Pedro Claver. In the pottery room, for example, is the chair used by the Pope on his visit to Cartagena in 1986. In another room there are several old maps, one of which shows the Caribbean maritime boundaries of Colombia, topical in that disputes with Nicaragua over San Andrés persist in 2008.

Following the wall round, it is well worthwhile climbing up the **Baluarte San Francisco Javier (10)** for a good view of the city and the Caribbean. There is a **Museo Naval del Caribe** ① *Tue-Sun (Mon during high season) 1000-17300, US$2.70, children ½-price*, with maps, models and display of armaments, near the Baluarte. On the corner of Calle Ricuarte is the convent of **Santa Teresa (11)**, founded in 1609 by a rich benefactor as a convent for Carmelite nuns. It had various uses subsequently, as a prison, a military barracks, a school and in the 1970s, was occupied by the police. It was recently purchased by the Banco Central as a heritage investment and has now been converted into a hotel. It is possible to visit the public areas of the hotel and admire the tasteful work of restoration. There is a great view from the roof.

El Bodegón de la Candelaria (12) ① *C Las Damas No 64*, was an elegant colonial residence. It has been faithfully restored and there is some fine panelling and period furniture to see. It is now a restaurant specializing in good seafood. A small shrine in one of the rooms marks the place where the Virgin appeared to a priest who was living there at the time. One block away is **Plaza de Bolívar (13)** with an equestrian statue of the Liberator in the centre. Formerly it was the Plaza de la Inquisición, with the Palacio de la Inquisición (see below), on its west side. The gardens of the plaza were given a face-lift in 2000 and is now an attractive corner of Cartagena.

On the opposite side of the Plaza de Bolívar to the Palacio de la Inquisición is the **Museo del Oro Zenú (14)** ① *Tue-Fri 0800-1200, 1400-1800, Sat 0900-1700, free*. Gold and pottery are very well displayed. Specially featured is the Zenú area to the south of Cartagena in the marshlands of the Sinú, San Jorge and Magdalena rivers, which is flooded by the river waters six to eight months of the year. Early drainage systems are featured, as is the advanced level of weaving techniques using the *cañafleche* and other fresh water reeds. This area was densely populated between the second to tenth centuries AD during which time the gold working skills of the people were developed to the high level that can still be seen today at Mompós, at the northern edge of the Zenú region.

The **Palacio de La Inquisición (15)** ① *Mon-Fri 0900-1700, US$2.75*, is on the other side of the Plaza Bolívar. The jurisdiction of this tribunal extended to Venezuela and Panama, and at least 800 were sentenced to death here. There is a small window overlooking the plaza where the public were informed of the sentences. The Palacio houses a modest historical museum, though some of the exhibits are in poor condition. Of special interest are the model of Cartagena in 1808, copies of Alexander Von Humboldt's maps showing the link he discovered between the Orinoco and Amazon rivers (*Canal de Casiquiare*) and of the Maypures rapids on the Orinoco – note that the longitude lines on the maps are west of Paris not Greenwich. The main attraction is the grisly collection of torture instruments. Historical books are on sale at the entrance.

The **Cathedral (16)**, in the northeast corner of Plaza de Bolívar, begun in 1575, was partially destroyed by Francis Drake. Reconstruction was finished by 1612. Great alterations were made between 1912 and 1923. A severe exterior, with a fine doorway, and a simply decorated interior. See the gilded 18th century altar, the Carrara marble pulpit and the elegant arcades which sustain the central nave. Although established in 1610, the present building dates from 1706 with modifications up to 1770. The stone entrance with its coats of arms is well preserved and the ornate wooden door is very notable. The whole building, with its balconies, cloisters and patios, is a fine example of colonial baroque.

Across the street is the **Palacio de la Proclamación** named for the declaration of independence of the State of Cartagena in November 1811. Before that it was the local Governor's residence, and later was where Simón Bolívar stayed in 1826. The building was restored in 1950.

The church and monastery of **Santo Domingo (17)**, built 1570 to 1579 is now a seminary. The old monastery was replaced by the present one in the 17th century. Inside, a miracle-making image of Christ, carved towards the end of the 16th century, is set on a baroque 19th-century altar. This is a most interesting neighbourhood, very little changed since the 16th century. In Calle Santo Domingo, No 33-29, is one of the great patrician houses of Cartagena, the **Casa de los Condes de Pestagua**, until recently the Colegio del Sagrado Corazón de Jesús, now a boutique hotel (see page 153). It has a fine colonnaded courtyard, marble floors and magnificent palm trees in the centre garden. Beside the church is the **Plaza de Santo Domingo**, one of the favourite corners of Cartagena, with popular restaurants, bars and cafés. A sculpture by Fernando Botero '*La Gorda*' is in the Plaza.

North of Santo Domingo at Calle de la Factoría 36-57 is the magnificent **Casa del Marqués de Valdehoyos (18)**, originally owned by the Marqués, who had the lucrative licences to import slaves and flour. The fine woodcarving is some of the best in Cartagena and the ceilings, chandeliers, wooden arches and balustrading are special. The views of the city from the fine upper floor balconies are also recommended. Currently the building houses a technical college and the Ministry for Foreign Relations. It is difficult to gain entry but on occasion tourists are permitted into the part owned by the college.

A short walk north is the Plaza, church and convent of **La Merced (19)**, founded 1618. The convent, a prison during Morillo's reign of terror, is now occupied by a private university (Jorge Tadeo Lozano), and its church has become the **Teatro Heredia**, which was beautifully restored recently.

Two blocks east is Calle de la Universidad, at the end of which is the monastery of **San Agustín (20)**, built in 1580, now the Universidad de Cartagena. From its chapel, now occupied by a printing press, the pirate Baron de Pointis stole a 500-pound silver sepulchre. It was returned by the King of France but the citizens melted it down to pay their troops during the siege by Morillo in 1815.

One block along Calle de San Agustín is **La Casa Museo de Simón Bolívar (21)**, a collection of memorabilia in the first Cartagena house he stayed in, now the Biblioteca Bartolomé Calvo owned by the Banco de la República.

One block along Badillo (Carrera 7) is the church of **Santo Toribio de Mongrovejo (22)**. Building began in 1729. In 1741, during Admiral Vernon's siege, a cannon ball fell into the church during Mass and lodged in one of the central columns; the ball is now in a recess in the west wall. The font of Carrara marble in the Sacristy is a masterpiece. There is a beautiful carved ceiling (*mudéjar* style) above the main altar with a rear lighted figure of Christ. Opens for Mass at 0600 and 1800, closed at other times.

The church and monastery of **Santa Clara de Assisi (23)** is close by. It was built 1617-1621, and has been spectacularly restored. It is now a hotel, but this is one you must see. Behind the hotel is the orange **Casa de Gabriel García Márquez (24)**, the most famous living Colombian author, on the corner of Calle del Curato.

Beyond the Santa Clara is the **Plaza de las Bóvedas (25)**. Towards the sea, before Las Bovedas, you will see a bank (*espiga*) leading to a jetty used in colonial times when the water came up to the walls, as shown on the 1808 map displayed in the **Palacio de la Inquisición**. All the land below the walls has since been reclaimed, with sports fields, recreational areas and the Avenida Santander/Paseo de la Muralla, a busy bypass to the city. The walls of Las Bóvedas, built 1799, are 12 m high and from 15- to 18-m thick. At the base of the wall are 23 dungeons, now containing tourist shops. Both an illuminated underground passage and a drawbridge lead from Las Bóvedas to the fortress of La Tenaza, which guarded the approach to the city from the coast to the northeast.

Casa de Núñez (26) ① *Mon-Fri 0800-1200, 1400-1800, there is also a monument to the 1886 constitution in the small park beside the lagoon*, just outside the walls of La Tenaza in El Cabrero district was the home of Rafael Núñez, four-time president of Colombia. He established the constitution of 1886 and wrote the national anthem. His grandiose marble tomb is in the delightful small **Ermita El Cabrero** church opposite.

Back along the lagoon is the old **Plaza de Toros (27)**, bull ring. It is an interesting wooden building but now abandoned and in a dangerous state. It cannot be visited.

Closer to the centre, where the main road leads into the city, is a roundabout, in the centre of which is the monument to **La India Catalina (28)**, Pedro de Heredia's indigenous interpreter in the early days of the Spanish conquest. A miniature of this statue is given to the winner of the annual Cartagena film festival – a Colombian 'Oscar'.

The ramparts

In addition to being a spectacular feature of Cartagena, the city walls make a great walk and are an excellent way to visit many of the attractions inside. A good place to start is the **Baluarte de San Francisco Javier (10)** from where, with a few ups and downs, it is continuous to **La India Catalina (28)**. From this point, there are two further sections along the lagoons to the **Puente Román (1)**. The final section along the Calle del Arsenal can be completed through the **Playa de Barahona**, a bayside park, which is busy at weekends.

The entire walk takes about 1½ hours, although if you take a camera it can take considerably longer. It is a spectacular walk in the morning around 0600 and equally at sunset. At many points you can drop down to see the sights detailed above in the tour of the old city.

Three of Cartagena's sights are off our map. Two of them, the Fortress of San Fernando and the Castillo San Felipe de Barajas, across the **Puente Heredia** (3) have been described above. The third is **La Popa hill** ① *daily 0800-1730, US$1.50, children US$0.75, guides available*, nearly 150 m high, from where there is a fine view of the harbour and the city. It is not recommended to walk up on your own; either take a guided tour or take a public bus to Teatro Miramar at the foot of the hill (US$0.50), then bargain for a taxi up, about US$7 return. If driving, take Carrera 21 off Avenida Pedro de Heredia, and follow the winding road to the top. The Augustinian church and monastery of Santa Cruz, and restored ruins of the convent dating from 1608 can be found here. In the church is the beautiful little image with a golden crown of the Virgin of La Candelaria, reputed as a deliverer from plague and a protector against pirates. The statue was blessed by the Pope on his visit in 1986. The Virgin's day is 2 February and for nine days before the feast thousands of people go up the hill by car, on foot, or on horseback. On the day itself people carry lighted candles as they go up the hill. There is an attractive bougainvillea-covered cloister with a well in the centre, and a museum with illuminated manuscripts, old maps, music books, relics and an image of the *Cabro de Oro* (golden goat) found by the Augustinians on the site, presumed to be an object of veneration of the indigenous people who previously inhabited the area. The name was bestowed on the hill because of an imagined likeness to a ship's poop deck.

Beaches

Take a bus south from the Puerta del Reloj, taxi US$2.20, or walk to **Bocagrande**, where the beaches can be dirty in parts and often crowded. You will also be constantly hassled. The sea is a little dirty, though better if you go as far as the Hilton at the end of the peninsula.

Marbella beach is an alternative, just north of Las Bóvedas. This is the locals' beach, and therefore quieter than Bocagrande during the week and good for swimming, though subject at times to dangerous currents.

The **Bocachica** beach, on Tierrabomba island, is also none too clean and you may be hassled here too. Boats leave for Bocachica from Muelle Turístico. The departure point is the two-storey glass building half-way along, which also has some tourist information. The round trip can take up to two hours each way and costs about US$10. *Ferry Dancing*, about half the price of the faster, luxury boats, carries dancing passengers. Boats taking in Bocachica and the San Fernando fortress include *Alcatraz*, which runs a daily trip from the Muelle Turístico. Alternatively, you can cross from Bocagrande, *lanchas* leave from near the Hilton Hotel and go to Punta Arena beach on Tierrabomba.

Boats to the Islas del Rosario (see page 161) may stop at the San Fernando fortress on Tierrabomba island and **Playa Blanca** on the Isla de Barú for one hour. You can bargain with the boatman to collect you later. Take food and water since these are expensive on the island. Barú, a long thin island, has mostly fine white-sand beaches which are slowly being exploited by up-market hotel complexes that will hopefully respect this fragile environment. The stopping place for tourist boats from Cartagena is Playa Blanca which is crowded in the mornings, but peaceful after the tour boats have left at around 1400.

Another alternative is to catch a fishing boat from the Mercado Bazurto (a short distance beyond *La Popa*) to Playa Blanca, leaving around 0830, US$3.50 one way, and take another one back when you choose. Many consider this to be the best beach in the region, with stretches of white sand and shady palm groves. There are several simple and cheap places to stay here and **Mama Root** is highly recommended. Other places include **Hugo's Place**, which has a campsite, restaurant and hires hammocks with mosquito nets, and **El Paraíso**. The **Wintenberg Camp** has good *cabañas*, although at the time of writing the owner was in a dispute with local authorities who want to build high rise hotels on his property. Remember to take water, as there is little on the island. You can also reach Playa Blanca by taking the bus to Pasacaballo, crossing the Canal del Dique by canoe and continuing by truck or jeep to the beach. If walking, allow 2½ hours in all. If staying the night at Playa Blanca in *cabañas* or tents, beware of ferocious sandflies. A *cabaña* will typically cost about US$12 per night. **Note** Pay for boat trips on board if possible, and be certain that you and the operator understand what you are paying for.

The little fishing village of **La Boquilla**, northeast of Cartagena, is near the end of a sandy promontory between the Ciénaga de Tesca and the Caribbean, about 20 minutes past the airport. There is a camping area with an attractive pool surrounded by palm trees and parrots, entrance US$2. There is a good beach nearby, El Paraíso, which is busy at weekends with people dancing, but quiet during the week, and where you can get good fish dishes. Visit the mangrove swamps nearby to see the birds.

◉ Cartagena listings → Phone code: 5.

For Sleeping and Eating price codes and other relevant information, see pages 31-36.

◉ Sleeping
Hotel prices rise for the high season, Nov-Mar, and Jun-Jul. From 15 Dec to 31 Jan they can rise by as much as 50% on Bocagrande beach; in town you will find not find much below **E**, but price increases are not as steep. Hotels tend to be heavily booked right through to Mar.

Around the old city *p144, map p146*
Getsemaní and La Matuna
Many cheap hotels on C Media Luna are brothels; this area is not advisable for women on their own.
AL Monterrey, Paseo de los Mártires, Cra 8B, No 25-103, T6648560, www.hmonterrey. com. Just outside the old city walls and with a view onto the Puerta del Reloj, this hotel has rooms in simple colours with balconies, TV and hot water. It also has a sunroof with a jacuzzi and access to internet.

D Hostal Baluarte, Media Luna, No 10-81, T6642208. A family-run, converted colonial house with a fine courtyard shaded by a mango tree and wrought-iron furniture, rocking chairs and hammocks in which to relax. Can arrange tours to the Islas del Rosario and has laundry service. Rooms a little small.
D Hostal La Casona, C Tripita y Media, Cra 10, No 31-32, T/F6641301, hostalla casona@hotmail.com. Has a breezy central courtyard and rooms with private bath. Laundry service provided.
D Hotel Marlin, C de la Media Luna, No 10-35, T6643507, www.hotelmarlin cartagenacol.com. Aquatic-themed hostel run by a friendly Colombian. Has fine balcony looking onto the busy C de la Media Luna. Rooms are clean but a little dark, offers internet access, free coffee and spare mattresses for children. Recommended.
D Villa Colonial, C de las Maravillas, No 30-60, T6644996, hotelvillacolonial@ hotmail.com. Pleasant, airy building with

clean rooms. Laundry service and TV. Also has a sister hotel on C de la Media Luna with slightly bigger rooms.

E Casa Viena, C San Andrés, No 30-53, T6646242, www.casaviena.com. A hub of information on activities in Cartagena, this hostel in Getsemaní is very popular with backpackers. Offers internet access, use of a kitchen, a TV room and very cheap dormitories.

E Familiar, C del Guerrero, No 29-66, near Media Luna, T6642464. Fresh and bright, family-run hotel with rooms set around a colonnaded patio. Has a good noticeboard full of information, a laundry service and use of a kitchen.

E Holiday, Media Luna, No 10-47, T6640948, www.holidayhostelcaribe.com. Rooms open on to a corridor patio with potted plants and tables. There's a small kitchen and a good information board. Some rooms with shared bath.

E Hotel Tropical, C 30, No 8b-58, T664 5479. A dirty, crumbling building with some partitioned bedrooms. Cheap.

El Centro and San Diego

LL Casa de Pestagua, C Santo Domingo, No 33-63, T6649510, www.casapestagua.net. Formerly home to the Conde de Pestagua, this historic house has been restored by architect Alvaro Barrera Herrera with great care. From the street it opens up into a magnificent colonnaded courtyard lined with enormous palm trees. Beyond is a swimming pool and spa, and on the top floor a sun terrace with jacuzzi and sea views.

LL El Marqués, C Nuestra Señora del Carmen, No 33-41, T6647800, www.elmarqueshotelboutique.com. Another house belonging to the Pestagua family, in the 1970s this boutique hotel was owned by New York film mogul Sam Green who was well known for throwing lavish parties. Guests included John Lennon, Robert de Niro and the Kennedy clan. The central courtyard, dominated by a large crumbling wall of draping ivy, features giant birdcages, hanging bells and large palm trees. The rooms are crisp, white and have Wi-Fi and iPod docks. Exquisite.

LL La Passion, C Estanco del Tabaco, No 35-81, T664 8605, www.lapassion hotel.com. In the heart of the old city, this grand building brings the concept of the Marrakech boutique hotel to Latin America. Its French owners have trawled the globe in search of exquisite furnishings. A mixture of colonial and Republican-era architecture, La Passion has cathedral-like rooms that providing modern, elegant and discreet comfort in the shape of plasma TVs, Wi-Fi and MP3 players. Breakfast is included in the price and served on the sublime roof terrace, next to the swimming pool.

LL Santa Clara, Cra 8, No 39-29, T664 6070, www.sofitelsantaclara.com. The French Sofitel group own this magnificently restored early 17th-century convent on the enchanting Plaza de San Diego.

Rooms, however, are in a modern annex and most have a balcony looking onto a large swimming pool, invariably with views of the sea. Has 2 restaurants, a bar and a spa.

AL Casa La Fe, Parque Fernández de Madrid, C 2a de Badillo, No 36-125, T6640306, www.casalafe.com, A republican-era house (c1930) on the delightful Parque Fernández de Madrid, the 11 en suite bedrooms of Casa La Fe have been restored by an English couple with great taste. It has a pool-jacuzzi on the roof and other services such as Wi-Fi, free bicycle use, and free breakfast served in a leafy patio.

A Casa Marco Polo, C de los Siete Infantes, No 9-89, T316 8749478, cantolindo1@ hotmail.com. Private rooms in a 450-year-old colonial mansion belonging to a local *cumbia* musician. 2 rooms, 1 cheaper (**B**), have a/c, cable TV and share a roof terrace with stunning views of Barrio San Diego. A 3rd room and swimming pool are still being converted, hence the excellent price. Highly recommended.

A Hostal San Diego, C de las Bóvedas, No 39-120, T660 1433, www.hostalsan diego.com. Near the delightful Plaza San Diego, this colonial building with its salmon pink exterior has modern rooms which open out onto a tiled courtyard.

A Las Tres Banderas, C Cochera de Hobo, No 38-66, T660 0160, www.hotel3 banderas.com. Another hotel in the bohemian district of San Diego, this old building is split over 2 breezy courtyards with water features. All rooms have a safe and come with breakfast included. Free internet access.

B Hostal Santo Domingo, C Santo Domingo, No 33-46, T664 2268, hsantodomingopiret@ yahoo.es. If you are looking for a budget option in the old town, this is your best bet. Rooms are simple but clean and open up on to a sunny patio. Breakfast is included, there is a laundry service and the gate is always locked, so security is good.

C Hotel El Viajero, C del Porvenir, No 35-68, piso 2, T6643289, hotelviajero664@ hotmail.com. Ideally located in the centre

of the old town, this 2nd floor hostel is more practical than attractive. Organizes tours, has a/c, TV and internet, and access to a kitchen.

Beaches *p151*

Bocagrande

LL Capilla del Mar, C 8, Cra 1, T665 3866. Resort hotel across the road from the beach, with swimming pool on top floor and 3 restaurants serving seafood and *parrillas*.

LL Cartagena Hilton, El Laguito, T665 0660. At the end of Laguito with a semi-private beach, the Hilton has everything you would expect of an international hotel, including 3 pools, a spa and a gym.

LL Hotel El Caribe, Cra 1, No 2-87, T665 3855. Enormous Caribbean-style hotel with 2 newer annexes, a/c, beautiful grounds and a swimming pool in the expensive restaurant. Has various tour agencies and a dive shop.

L Hotel Almirante, Av San Martín, No 6, T665 8811, reserves.halmirante@hotelesestelar. com. Popular with affluent Colombian tourists, this high-rise hotel has 250 rooms and all the usual resort facilities, including a half moon-shaped pool on the top floor with good views out over the beaches.

A Bahía, Cra 4a with C 4a, T665 0316. Has the feel of a 1950s hotel. Discreet, quiet, with fine pool and restaurant.

A Hotel Charlotte, Av San Martín, No 7-126, T665 9201, www.hotelescharlotte.com. Stylishly designed in cool whites. Has a pool, and Wi-Fi in the lobby. Smart restaurant serves up Italian food. Recommended.

A Hotel Playa, Av San Martín, No 4-87, T665 0112, www.cartagenahotelplaya.com. Some of the rooms are painted in lurid colours but are otherwise fine and it has an inviting pool and direct access to the beach. TV, a/c and breakfast included.

B Casa Grande, Av del Malecón, No 9-128, T665 6806. Yellow and blue house set back from the beach with spacious rooms off a tranquil garden at the back. Recommended.

C Ibatama, Av San Martín 7-46, T665 1127, hotelesibatamactg@yahoo.com. Has a

pleasant terrace looking out over 1 of the principal streets, with a/c and TV, though the rooms are quite small and few have windows.
C Leonela, Cra 3A, 7-142, T6654761, www.hostaleonala.com. A very helpful and friendly couple have run this hotel for more than 30 years. Has a family atmosphere and a small restaurant serving breakfast for US$4. Good value.
C Mary, No 6-53, T6652833. Basic rooms but pleasant and friendly. A/c or fan.

Eating

At cafés try *patacón*, a biscuit made of green banana, mashed and baked; also from street stalls in Parque del Centenario in the early morning. At restaurants ask for *sancocho* the local soup of the day of vegetables and fish or meat. Also try *obleas* for a snack, biscuits with jam, cream cheese or caramel fudge (*arequipe*), and *buñuelos*, deep-fried cheese dough balls. Fruit juices are fresh, tasty and cheap in Cartagena: a good place is on the Paseo de los Pegasos (Av Blas de Lezo) from the many stalls alongside the boats.

The city's fortifications *p144*
Club de Pesca, San Sebastián de Pastelillo fort, Manga Island, T6605863/T6607065. Wonderful setting, perhaps the most famous fish and seafood restaurant in Cartagena, though expensive. Warmly recommended.

Around the old city *p144, map p146*
Getsemaní and La Matuna
With spiralling property prices it won't be long before Getsemaní has the same gentrification treatment as Centro and San Diego, as is evidenced by an increasing number of smart restaurants opening up in the area.
Café Havana, C de la Media Luna y C del Guerrero. A fantastic Cuban bar and restaurant, which feels like it has been transported from Havana brick by brick. The walls are festooned with black-and-white portraits of Cuban salsa

stars and it has live bands playing most nights. Highly recommended.
El Coroncoro, C Tripita y Media, No 31-28. More typical of the area, very popular at lunchtime with locals. It's atmospheric and offers *comidas corrientes* from US$2.
La Casa de Socorro, C Larga, No 8B-112, T6644658. This seafood restaurant is popular with locals and does very good *bandejas de pescado* and *arroz con camarones*. Take note that there are 2 rival restaurants of the same name on the same street. The one mentioned is the original and better.
Oh! lá lá..., Callejón Vargas, No 9a-6. A new restaurant offering fine French food at reasonable prices.

El Centro and San Diego
Plaza San Diego has several good restaurants serving up a variety of international cuisines.
Donde Olano, C Santo Domingo with Inquición. Art deco restaurant serving French and Creole cuisine, cosy atmosphere, though a little overpriced. Try the *ceviche*.
Juan del Mar, Plaza San Diego, No 8-12. Offers 2 restaurants in 1: inside serves expensive seafood while outside cooks up fine, thin-based pizzas, though you are likely to be harassed by street hawkers.
Teriyaki, Plaza San Diego, No 8-28. Next to *Zebra*, serves sushi and Thai food in smart surroundings.
Zebra, Plaza San Diego, No 8-34. Café with wide selection of coffees, hot sandwiches and African dishes.
Barandales, C de Tumbamuertos, No 38-65, Piso 2. Small restaurant run by a lovely couple from Bucaramanga. They serve up typical dishes from Santander such as *cabrito* as well as delicious stuffed *patacones*. Has a great balcony overlooking the Plaza de San Diego.
Bistro, C de los Ayos, No 4-46. German-run restaurant with a relaxed atmosphere. Sofas, music, European menu at reasonable prices. Recommended.
La Mulata, C Quero, No 9-58. A popular lunchtime venue with locals, you get a

seletion of set menu dishes. Has Wi-Fi and offers 50% discount if it's your birthday.

Pelikano, C Santo Domingo, No 2-98. Atmospheric seafood and meat restaurant offering set menu of starter, main course and 2 glasses of wine for under US\$15.

Pizza en el parque, C 2a de Badillo, No 36-153. This small kiosk serves up delicious pizzas with some interesting flavours (pear and apple) which you can munch on while enjoying the delightful atmosphere of Parque Fernández Madrid.

The beaches p151
There are good fish dishes in La Boquilla.

Bocagrande
Carbón de Palo, Av San Martín, No 6-40. Steak heaven, cooked on an outdoor *parrilla*.
Restaurante Arabe, Cra 3A, No 8-83, T665 4365. Upmarket Arab restaurant serving tagines, etc. A/c, indoor seating or pleasant outdoor garden.
Jeno's, Av San Martín, No 7-162. Eat in or take away pizza.
Juan Valdez Café, Av San Martín, No 7-17, Starbucks-style chain serving various types of coffee and sandwiches. Has Wi-Fi.
La Fonda Antioqueña, Cra 2, No 6-164. Traditional Colombian, nice atmosphere.
Ranchería's, Av 1A, No 8-86. Serves seafood and meats in thatched huts just off the beach. *Comida corriente*, US\$8.

Bars and clubs

Cartagena boasts a lively dance scene and the atmosphere in the city after dark is addictive. A great place for a drink is any one of the cafés next to the Santo Domingo church.

Around the old city p144
Many of the hotels have evening entertainment and can arrange *chiva* tours, usually with free drinks and live music on the bus.
There are good local nightclubs in Bocagrande eg **La Escollera**, Cra 1, next to El

Pueblito shopping centre, with other places nearby including spontaneous musical groups on or near the beach most evenings.
Most places don't get going until after 2400, though the Cuban bar **Donde Fidel**, on Paseo de los Dulces, and **Café Havana**, on C de la Media Luna in Getsemaní start a little earlier and are highly recommended if you want to hear Cuban salsa. C del Arsenal host the majority of Cartagena's clubs and you will likely wind up there if you are really giving the city's nightlife a go. Most bars play crossover music.

Café del Mar, on Baluarte de Santo Domingo, El Centro. The place to go at sundown, where surrounded by ancient canons you can watch the sun set over the bay.
Casa de la Cerveza, at the end of C del Arsenal. Low sofas peppered around the battlements.
Diva, C del Arsenal. Next door to **Tu Candela**. A 3-level bar playing salsa and electronic music, 2000-0400.
Mister Babilla, C del Arsenal. The most popular and exclusive bar. Take something warm with you – they really like to blast the air conditioning here.
Quiebra Canto, C Media Luna at Parque Centenario, next to **Hotel Monterrey**, Getsemaní. The best place for salsa. Nice atmosphere, free admission.
Tu Candela, C del Arsenal. Where you can dance in the vaults to 'crossover'.

Gay bars
Discoteca Lincon, C del Porvenir.
Studio 54, C Larga, No 24, Getsemaní.

Entertainment

Cartagena p142, map p146
Cinema
There are many cinemas in Cartagena. In Bocagrande there is one in the **Centro Commercial Bocagrande**. Others are in the **Centro Comercial Paseo de la Castellana** on Av Pedro de Heredia and in **Centro**

Comercial La Plazuela in the same area.
Teatro Heredia, has recently been restored.

Dance
El Colegio del Cuerpo, C Larga, No 10-27, T6643184, www.elcolegiodelcuerpo.org. A classical dance studio that works with children from Cartagena's slums. They perform internationally and occasionally in Cartagena.

⊛ Festivals and events

Cartagena *p142, map p146*
2-6 Jan La Feria Taurina. Several days of bull fighting.
Jan Hay Festival Cartagena, www.hay festival.com. Franchise of the famous literary festival in the UK, takes place at the end of the month, with internationally renowned writers.
Jan-Feb La Candelaria (Candelmas).
Mar Caribbean Music Festival. Groups from all over the Caribbean region and beyond perform salsa, reggae, etc.
Mar International Film Festival, Beluarte San Francisco, C San Juan de Dios, T660 1701/2, www.festicinecartagena. com. The longest running festival of its kind in Latin America. Although mainly Spanish American films are featured, the US, Canada and European countries are represented in the week-long showings.
Nov Independencia. In the 2nd week of the month, to celebrate the independence of Cartagena. People in masks and fancy dress dance in the streets. There are beauty contests, battles of flowers and general mayhem.

○ Shopping

Cartagena *p142, map p146*
There is a good selection of *artesanías* at **Compendium** on Plaza Bolívar. **Galería Cano**, next to the Gold Museum has excellent reproductions of pre-Columbian designs. Pricey antiques can be bought in C Santo Domingo and there are a number of jewellery

shops near Plaza de Bolívar in Centro, which specialize in emeralds. Beware of 'Cuban cigars' sold on the street, **Habanos**, C San Juan de Dios, has a wide selection but in general you will pay less in Bogotá.
The handicraft shops in the Plaza de las Bóvedas (**25**) have the best selection in town but tend to be expensive – cruise ship passengers are brought here. Woollen *blusas* are good value; try the **Tropicano** in Pierino Gallo building in Bocagrande. Also in this building are reputable jewellery shops.
Abaco, C de la Iglesia with C Mantilla, No 3-86. A bookshop, which is a popular hangout for local writers and poets. Delightful atmosphere and a café serving juices and snacks.
Comercial Centro Getsemaní, C Larga between San Juan and Plaza de la Indepen-dencia. A large shopping centre. Good *artesanías* in the grounds of the convent.
H Stern, Pierino Gallo shopping centre and at the **Hilton Hotel**. Jewellery shop.
Instituto Geográfico Agustín Codazzi, C 34, No 3-37, Edificio Inurbe. Maps.
Libreria Nacional, Cra 7 (Badillo), No 36-27, T664 1448. Bookshop.
Magali París, Av Venezuela y C del Boquete. A supermarket, with a/c and cafeteria.
Santo Domingo, C Santo Domingo, No 3-34. Recommended for jewellery.
Upalema, C San Juan de Dios, No 3-99. A good selection of handicrafts.

Markets
The main market is to the south east of the old city near La Popa off Av Pedro de Heredia (Mercado Bazurto). Good bargains in the La Matuna market, open daily including Sun.

▲ Activities and tours

Cartagena *p142, map p146*
Bullfighting
Bullfights take place in the 1st week of Jan in the new Plaza de Toros at the Villa Olímpica on Av Pedro de Heredia away from the centre, T6698225.

Diving

Cultura del Mar, T6649312, www.cultura delmar.com. Organizes diving and snorkelling tours while aiming to promote responsible environmental practice. Well-informed guides take divers and snorkellers on educational tours of the islands' coral reefs and into mangrove swamps – a spectacular experience. Cultura del Mar works with local educational organizations to promote environmental responsibility in schools and organizes annual cleaning days to clear up the islands and their waters. Also have an eco-hotel on Isla Grande in the Islas del Rosario that supports the local community. Highly recommended.

La Tortuga Dive Shop, Edif Marina del Rey, 2-23, Local 4, Av del Retorno, Bocagrande, T6656995, www.tortugadive.com. A mini-course with 2 dives costs US$105. A faster boat, which allows trips to Isla Barú as well as Los Rosarios, is the same price at **Hotel Caribe Dive Shop**, T665 3517, www.caribe diveshop.com, caribediveshop@yahoo.com, though discounts are sometimes available if you book via the hotels, enquire.

Football

Estadio de Futbol Pedro de Heredia, Villa Olímpica, south of the city. Games are infrequent. Seats for matches cost between US$5 and US$13.50.

Horse-drawn carriage rides

Horse-drawn carriages can be hired for for a trip around the walled city from Puerta del Reloj, about US$16 for up to 4 people. Or from opposite Hotel El Dorado, Av San Martín, in Bocagrande, to ride into town at night (romantic but a rather short ride).

Tour operators

Aventure Colombia, C del Santísimo, No 8-55, T314 5882378 (mob), www.aventurecolombia.com. The only tour organizer of its kind in Cartagena, Frenchman Mathieu Perrot-Bohringer and his Colombian wife Angelica specialize in alternative tours of the Sierra Nevada de Santa Marta but also in local and national activities and expeditions. They aim to practice responsible tourism, working (wherever possible) with local and indigenous groups. For further information on boat trips they organize, see Transport, page 159. Highly recommended.

Ocean & Land, Cra 2, No 4-15, Local 6, Bocagrande, T6657772, oceanlandtours@ yahoo.com. Organizes city tours, rumbas in *chivas* and other local activities.

Travel Expert, Cra 1, No 2-87, Local 7, Bocagrande, T665 9086, travelexpert@ telecom.com.co. Full travel service for Cartagena and nationwide.

Yachting

Club Náutico, Av Miramar on Isla Manga across the Puente Román, T6605582. Good for opportunities to charter, crew or for finding a lift to other parts of the Caribbean.

⊕ Transport

Cartagena *p142, map p146*
Air
Direct flights daily to major Colombian cities and to smaller places in the north of the country. International flights direct daily to Miami and Panama. From Dec to Mar flights can be overbooked and even reconfirming and turning up 2 hrs early doesn't guarantee a seat; best not to book a seat on the last plane of the day if you can avoid it. Daily flights to all main cities and international destinations.
Airline offices AeroRepública, Cra 6, No 8-116 (Bocagrande), T6650428; **Avianca**, C del Arzobispado, No 34-52, T6641729, also in Bocagrande, C 7, No 7-17, L 7, T6655727 and at the airport; **CC Invercredito**, Local 18, T664 9077, Mon-Fri 0800-1800, Sat 0900-1300; **Copa**, C Gastelbondo, No 2-95, T0180 00112672.

Bus
Colectivos for **Barranquilla** leave from C 70, Barrio Crespo every 2 hrs and cost US$14 and are a good option as they do a centre-to-centre service. There is a regular bus to **Barranquilla**, every 15 mins, 2-3 hrs, US$8, Berlina; Brasilia; Concorde; La Costeña.To **Medellín**, 665 km, approximately 1 every hr starting from 0530, 13-16 hrs, US$60, **Brasilia**; **Copetran**; **Rápido Ochoa** (slightly cheaper, recommended), book early (2 days in advance at holiday times). The road is now paved throughout, but in poor condition. To **Santa Marta**, 1 every hr,4 hrs, US$13.50, **Berlina**; **Brasilia**; **La Costeña**.

To **Bogotá** via Barranquilla and Bucaramanga, 16 a day, 21-28 hrs (depending on number of check-points), US$75, with **Berlina**; **Brasilia**; **Concorde**; **Copetran**; **Rápido Ochoa**. To **Magangué** on the *Magdalena*, US$12, 4 hrs with **Brasilia**. To **Mompós**, 0700, 12 hrs including ferry crossing from Magangué, US$17, **Unitransco**. To **Riohacha**, US$22. Bus to **Maicao** on Venezuelan frontier, every hour 0500-1200, 2 in the evening, 12 hrs, US$27, with **Brasilia**.

Car hire
Several of the bigger hotels have car rental company offices in their foyers, such as Hotel Bahía, Bocagrande, C 14, No 3-59, local 1. There are several car rental companies in Edif Torremolinos, Av San Martín: **International Car Rentals**, T6655399; **National**, T6653336; **Rentacars**, T6652852. At the airport, try **Platinum** on 2nd floor, T666 4112.

Sea
Intermittent boats go from Cartagena to **Porvenir** in the San Blas Islands (Panama); the journey takes about 2 days and the 1-way fare is US$350 per person, including food and 3 nights touring the San Blas archipelago. The sailboats will normally end in **San Blas** from which you can continue your journey by air or overland to Panama City. The skippers will help with immigration paperwork.

There are 3 boats that provide a regular service between Cartagena and San Blas. Highly recommended is **Stella Luna**, T312 6817833 (Colombia) or T507 67686121 (Panama), captained by Hernando Higuera, a key figure in establishing Cartagena's sailing club, who has strong friendships with many of the indigenous Cuna of San Blas. Also try: **Tango**, run by French skipper David T314 558 8945 (mob) or German captain Guido T316 2436324 (mob), who also owns a backpackers' hostel in Panama. Take your time before choosing a boat. Some captains are irresponsible and unreliable. The journey is cramped and you do not want to make it with a captain you do not get on with.

Aventure Colombia, T314 5882378 (mob), www.aventurecolombia.com, can provide reliable information on trustworthy boats and skippers. Also organize 8-day tours to San Blas via the Islas del Rosario, Islas de San Bernardo, Isla Fuerte and Sapzurro in the Darién, costing US$500 per person, including food.

Also try noticeboards at backpacker hotels such as Hotel Casa Viena or ask around at the Yacht Club (Club Nautico). In Panama, the only reliable information is in Porvenir.

Taking a vehicle It is possible to ship a car from Cartagena to Panama. 3 companies that can arrange shipment of vehicles to Panama are: **Agencia Internacional Ltda**, Cra 2, No 9-145, Edif Nautilus, Bocagrande, T6647539, agents for King Ocean Services, 11000 NW 29 St, Suite 201, Doral, FL, T305- 591 7595, serving Cartagena, Panama and Miami; **Hermann Schwyn**, Edif Chambacu Business Center, Piso 6, PO Box 1626, T6503610, www.schwyn.com; **Mundinaves**, Edif City Bank, oficinas 13F y 13G, T6644188, www.mundinaves.com.

Note On the street, do not be tempted by offers of jobs or passages aboard ship. Jobs should have full documentation from the Seamen's Union office and passages should only be bought at a recognized shipping agency.

◑ Directory

Cartagena *p142, map p146*
Banks There are many ATMs, the most convenient are in the Plaza de la Aduana, where there are **BBVA**, **Bancolombia**, **Davivienda** and **Santander** offices. In Bocagrande a number of banks can be found around Av San Martín with C 8. If you are changing TCs make sure you have your passport with you or you will probably be charged the 3% tax applicable to residents. Never change money on the street in any circumstances. There are *cambios* in the arcade at Torre Reloj and adjoining streets which change Amex TCs; **Cambiamos**, Cra 2, No 1-100, Edif Seguros Bolívar, Bocagrande, T6651600; **Comisiones Las Bovedas**, C del Colegio, No 34-53, T6641692; **Comisiones Royal**, Cra 2, No 5-52, Centro Comercial Michel Center, Bocagrande, T655 1556; **Western Union**, Av Venezuela, No 8A-87, Edif City Bank. **Embassies and consulates** Austria, Cra 9, No 32A-50, Edif Concasa, La Matuna, T664 8490; **Belgium**, C 8, No 4-41, Bocagrande, T665 2741; **Canada**, Cra 3, No 33-08, Apto 201, C Santo Domingo, El Centro, T6647393; **France**, Cra 7, No 37-34, Plaza Fernández de Madrid, San Diego, T6646714; **Germany**, C Real, No 42-02, Ap 102, Cabrero, T6600309; **Norway**, C 32, No 8A-65, Edif Banco Central Hipotecario, La Matuna, T6645557; **Panama**, C 69, No 4-97, Crespo, T6662079; **Spain**, C de la Universidad, No 36-44, Centro, T6642658; **Sweden**, Cra 4, No 5A-19, Bocagrande, T6655832; **USA**, Cra 3, No 36-37, C de la Factoría, Centro, T6600415; **Venezuela**, Cra 3, No 8-129, Edif Centro Ejecutivo, Of 802, T6650382, Bocagrande, open to 1500, possible to get a visa the same day (US$30), you will need an onward ticket and 2 photos, but ensure you get a full visa not a 72 hrs' transit unless that is all you need.
Immigration DAS, just beyond Castillo San Felipe, Cra 20B, No 29-18, Plaza de la Ermita (Pie de la Popa), T6563007, helpful. DAS passport office is in C Gastelbondo, near the ramparts. Get free visa extensions here.
Internet Camilina, C de Coliseo, No 5-52, T6646866; **Conexion San Diego**, C de las Bóvedas, No 39-120, T6642382; **Game Over**, C San Andrés, No 30-47. **Language** The Nueva Lengua School, www.nuevalengua. com/cartagena offers courses ranging from half-day schedules to a scheme that arranges volunteer jobs. There's even a Spanish and dancing course. **Laundry** Chalet Suizo, Media Luna, No 10- 36, also email, information and tours arranged. **Medical services** There is a recompression chamber at the naval hospital, Bocagrande; **Hospital Bocagrande**, C 5/Cra 6, Bocagrande, T6655270. **Post office** In Centro, for airmail is at the Avianca office near the cathedral, Mon- Fri 0800-1830, Sat 0800-1500, and Av Lemaitre, La Matuna; **Adpostal**, C 32, La Matuna; **Deprisa**, La Matuna, C 33, No 8-20; **Envia Colvanes**, Av Principal del Bosque Diag 21, No 49-70. **Security** For loss of documents, etc, ask for a *denuncia* from the Policía-Inspección Urbana, Centro Comercial La Plazoleta, Matuna. The office is in the *Pasaje* leading to Av Carlos López. In Bocagrande there is a police station on Parque Flanaga. **Telephone** Next to Adpostal; long-distance phones behind this building.

Around Cartagena

Cartagena is surrounded on almost all sides by water and travellers will be drawn to the city's sparkling Caribbean coast. Islas del Rosario are glistening examples of what a tropical paradise should look like, and for those on a budget there is Playa Blanca on the Barú peninsula. To the northeast of Cartagena, the coastline is characterized by ciénagas (mangrove swamps), such as the Ciénaga La Caimanera, which provide plenty of opportunities to observe the wildlife that subsists in these remarkable ecosystems. A few kilometres further on is the Volcán del Totumo, an extraordinary crater-like mud hole where bathers can wallow before washing off in the nearby ciénaga.
▶▶ *For listings, see pages 168-173.*

Volcán del Totumo

Along the coast north of Cartagena, at La Boquilla, is the Ciénaga la Caimanera, a labyrinth of mangrove swamps full of wildlife. Canoe trips can be made to explore these (motorboats are not allowed). Local guides cost US$8 per person, and they will catch oysters for you to eat. Further north is **Galerazamba**, there is no accommodation but good local food. Nearby are the clay baths of **Volcán del Totumo** ① *entry to the cone US$1, the unusual experience will cost you US$2 and you wash off in the nearby Ciénaga*, in beautiful surroundings. Climb up steep steps to the lip of the 20-m high crater and slip into the grey cauldron of mud, about 10 m across, at a comfortable temperature and reputed to be over 500 m deep. Massages are available for a small extra fee. You can catch a bus from Cartagena to Galerazamba at the Mercado Popular, Carerra 2 with Calle 16, US$1.50, two hours, ask to be dropped off at Lomo Arena where the bus turns off to Galerazamba. Walk along the main road for 2 km to a right turn signposted to Volcán del Totumo which is 1.5 km along a poor road. Hitching is possible. Taking a tour from Cartagena will cost more but will save a lot of time. **Aventure Colombia** ① *C del Santísimo, No 8-55, Cartagena, T314 588 2378 (mob), www.aventurecolombia.com*, organizes tours to the volcano for US$22, including transport and lunch at La Boquilla or Playa de Manzanillo. A tour of both the volcano and the mangroves is US$38.

Islas del Rosario ●▲▲ ▶▶ *pp168-173.*

The National Park of Corales del Rosario embraces the archipelago of Rosario (a group of 30 coral islets, 45 km southwest of the Bay of Cartagena) and the mangrove coast of the long island of Barú to its furthest tip. **Isla Grande** and some of the smaller islets are easily accessible by day trippers and those who wish to stay in one of the hotels. Permits are needed for the rest, entrance fee US$2. These picture postcard islands represent part of a coral reef, low-lying, densely vegetated and with narrow strips of fine sand beaches. **Rosario** (the largest and best conserved) and **Tesoro** both have small lakes, some of which connect to the sea, and many of the smaller islets are privately owned. There is an incredible profusion of aquatic and bird life here and the **Aquarium** (*Oceanario*) ① *US$3*, in the sea is worth visiting. Look out for the huge catfish but note that the price of entry is not included in boat fares. The island has access to some of the best coral reefs on the archipelago and diving and snorkelling is available. The **Hotel El Caribe** in Bocagrande (see page 154) offers scuba lessons in its pool followed by diving at its resort on Isla Grande, for US$230 and upwards. ▶▶ *For further information on diving, see Activities and tours, page 172.*

Mud volcanoes

The Caribbean coast is peppered with several geological curiosities popularly known as 'mud volcanoes'. These large mud pools are believed to be the result of underground oil and gas deposits, which combine with water, forcing the mud to ooze to the surface. Often they form conical mounds, hence the name. Many of these pools can be found between the Gulf of Urabá and Santa Marta. Turbo has several in its proximity (Rodosalín, El Alto de Mulatos and Caucal), as does San Pedro de Urabá. The Volcán de Totumo is a popular day trip from Cartagena, but the pick of the bunch is Arboletes, where an enormous 30-m-wide lake has formed a stone's throw from the beach.

Wallowing in the grey-black mud is a strange experience. It's impossible to sink and attempts to swim are about as worthwhile as trying to battle your way across a vat of treacle. When you have had enough, clamber out and join the line of mud-caked figures waddling down to the Caribbean for a wash and a swim. The stuff is reportedly an excellent exfoliant and does wonders for the skin and hair.

Travel agencies and the hotels offer excursions from the Muelle Turístico, leaving 0700-0900 and returning 1600-1700, costing from around US$45, lunch included; free if staying at one of the hotels. Overnight trips can be arranged through agencies, but they are overpriced. Note that there is an additional 'port tax' of US$5 payable at the entrance to the Muelle or on the boat. Book in advance. For five or more, try hiring your own boat for the day and bargain your price. This way you get to see what you want in the time available. The tour boats leave you with plenty of time with the beach vendors. For the cheapest rates, buy tickets from the boat owners (make sure they are the boat owners!) at the dockside, but they may already be booked up. **Aventure Colombia** organizes sailboat tours of the islands.

If you wish to enjoy the islands at your leisure there are a number of hotels to stay in. Recommended are **Isla del Pirata**, which has a number of simple, comfortable *cabañas* and where fresh fish and lobster are served for lunch and dinner. On neighbouring Isla Grande is **San Pedro de Majagua**, owned by Hotel Santa Clara in Cartagena. Snorkelling and diving organizers **Cultura del Mar** also have an ecohotel here, where you can sleep in hammocks or beds, with cooking provided by a local family. ▶▶ *For further information, see Sleeping, page 168.*

South of Cartagena ⬤🅿⬤⬤⬤🄲 ▶▶ *pp168-173.*

Just a few years ago, the area south of Cartagena was a no-go zone. The road between Cartagena and Medellín was the scene of frequent kidnappings by guerrillas who could perform raids on passing traffic and quickly abscond into the region's network of densely vegetated hills. Today it's a different story, and locals no longer sweat before making what was once a perilous journey. However, a word of warning: this area is still very much active in drug trafficking. Towns such as Sincelejo and Montería are fine to pass through but we advise against staying there too long. As a precaution, we also advise against travel at night between Cartagena and Medellín.

The improvement in security also means that this area, rich in culture and natural wonders, has opened up to tourism. Southwest of Cartagena, on an island in the middle of the imperious Magadalena, is the equally regal town of Mompós. Due south is Tolú, gateway to the coral islands of San Bernardo, while further along the coast is Arboletes, location of the largest mud volcano in the area. Further still is Turbo, a rough frontier town from where boats can be caught to the emerald green coastline of the Darién.

Mompós → *Colour map 1, B3. Phone code: 5. Population 35,000.*

Ins and outs To reach Mompós from Cartagena there are three options: a direct bus leaves at 0700, US$17 (negotiable). Alternatively, take a bus to Magangue, a *chalupa* (motorized canoe), US$3.50, followed by *colectivo* from La Bodega, US$4 per person. Lastly, a *colectivo* direct from your hotel will cost US$19.50, call T312 622 5946 (mob).
▸▸ *For further information, see Transport, page 172.*

Sights Thanks to a geographical anomaly, Mompós (sometimes spelt Mompox and officially known as Santa Cruz de Mompós) retains much the same atmosphere you might have experienced visiting this sleepy town in the early 20th century. The grand old Magdalena River splits in two just before Mompós. When the town was founded in 1537, the Mompós branch of the river was the main tributary and it became a major staging port for travellers and merchandise going to the interior. But at the beginning of the 20th century it silted up with mud and became unnavigable for large boats, so traffic was diverted to the Brazo de Lobo. As a result, Mompós became a backwater and it has remained practically untouched ever since.

Mompós

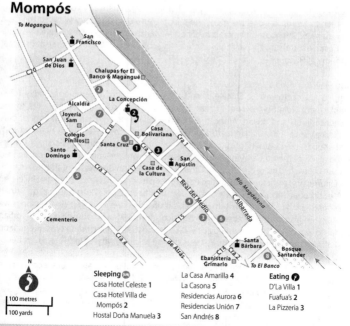

Sleeping		Eating
Casa Hotel Celeste 1	La Casa Amarilla 4	D'La Villa 1
Casa Hotel Villa de	La Casona 5	Fuafua's 2
Mompós 2	Residencias Aurora 6	La Pizzeria 3
Hostal Doña Manuela 3	Residencias Unión 7	
	San Andrés 8	

100 metres
100 yards

In 1995 UNESCO declared it a World Heritage Site for the quality of its colonial architecture and its fine churches, and it was the setting for the film adaptation of Gabriel García Márquez's *Chronicle of a Death Foretold*.

Today, in the evenings, as the soporific heat begins to lessen and the bats start to swoop from the eaves of the whitewashed houses, locals carry their rocking chairs out onto the streets to chat with neighbours and watch the world go by. Cars are rare here, the main forms of transport are bicycle, moped, auto-rickshaw – or on foot.

Mompós is still a difficult place to reach – while direct buses are possible, most journeys include a combination of bus, motorized canoe and car. But plans are afoot to improve transport connections. Hopefully, these changes won't detract from its languid charm.

The churches demonstrate the colonial origins of the town; five of the six are close to the centre. The church of **San Francisco** is probably the oldest, dating from the end of the 16th century, with an interesting interior. **Santo Bárbara**, on Calle 14 by the river, has a unique octagonal Moorish tower and balcony. **San Juan de Dios, La Concepción, Santo Domingo** and **San Agustín** are all worth visiting. You may have to ask around for the key to see inside, they are not normally open except during Mass. Among the old buildings are the Casa de Gobierno, once a home of the Jesuits and now the **Alcaldía**, and the **Colegio Pinillos**. The cemetery is of considerable historical interest, make sure to visit it on the Wednesday of Semana Santa when it is illuminated by thousands of candles lit by the locals to respect the dead. The town is well known in Colombia for hand-worked gold and silver jewellery, especially filigree, as well as its wicker rocking chairs.

Simón Bolívar held Mompós dear to his heart, for it was the site of one of the greatest victories in his campaign to expel the Spanish from South America. "If to Caracas I owe my life, then to Mompós I owe my glory," he said. He stayed in what is now called the **Casa Bolivariana**, which houses memorabilia of his times and also has some religious art exhibits. The **Casa de la Cultura** is a particularly interesting colonial building and home of the local Academy of History.

Tolú → *Colour map 1, B2. Phone code: 5.*

Tolú, 35 km northwest of Sincelejo, on the coast, is a fast developing holiday town popular with Colombians and, increasingly, foreign tourists attracted by visits to the offshore islands and diving. Along the *malecón* (promenade), there are plenty of bars and restaurants. A distinctive feature of the town are the bicycle rickshaws armed with loud soundsystems blasting out vallenato, salsa and reggaeton. The rickshaw drivers spend much of their time trying to outdo each other with the volume of their music. Tolú can also be reached more directly from Cartagena, though **San Onofre**, then, after 46 km from San Onofre, turn right for Tolú. Continue straight on from Toluviejo for 20 km to Sincelejo.

A good boat trip from Tolú is to the beautiful beaches of Múcura island or Titipán (D *cabañas*) in the **Islas de San Bernardo**, about US$20, three hours. Trips to the mangrove lagoons are also recommended. Club Náutico Mundo Marino, run daily tours to San Bernardo Islands at 0800, returning at 1600, which cost US$20, including the aquarium on Isla Palma. The tour includes a three-hour stay on Múcura, where there are a number of shacks serving seafood, including excellent barbecued lobster. The beach is of fine white sand with beautiful, clear water. Unfortunately, with four separate launch boats converging on the island at the same time, it gets very crowded and the number of beach vendors can detract from the beauty of the place. There is a charge for everything, including sitting at a table. To enjoy the islands at your leisure, it is better to stay overnight. ⯈ *For further information, see Activities and tours, page 172.*

There are better beaches at **Coveñas**, 20 km further southwest, the terminal of the oil pipeline from the oilfields in the Venezuelan border area. Coveñas is essentially a 5-km-long stretch of road peppered with *cabañas* and hotels. During high season (Easter, Christmas, June and July) it is very popular with Colombians eager to hit the beach and party. To get there, take a bus or *colectivo* from Tolú.

Further along the coast, turning right 18 km southwest of Coveñas at Lorica is **San Bernardo del Viento** from where launches can be arranged to **Isla Fuerte**, an unspoilt coral island with fine beaches and simple places to stay. A good place to dive, but there are very limited facilities on the island. Enquire at travel agencies in Medellín and elsewhere for inclusive trips or negotiate in San Bernardo.

Arboletes

Southwest of Tolú is the unremarkable town of Arboletes which nonetheless has an extraordinary attraction: the largest mud volcano in the area. Dipping into this swimming pool-sized mud bath is a surreal experience – like swimming in treacle. It's also very good for your skin. You can wash the mud off with a dip in the sea by walking down to the beach 100 m below. Arboletes is also a convenient stopover on the way to Turbo and the Darién coast.

The **Volcán de Lodo** is a 15-minute walk from town on the road to Montería or a two-minute taxi ride (US$5.50 return – the driver will wait for you while you bathe). A mototaxi costs US$1. There is a small restaurant and changing rooms (US$ 0.30), plus a locker room (US$1 per bag) and showers (US$0.50).

Turbo

At the mouth of the Gulf of Urabá is the port of Turbo, a hot, rough, frontier community with a lawless feel about it. It is a centre for banana cultivation. There is little reason to stop here except to catch a boat to Capurganá and the Panamanian border.

The Darién Gap

The Darién Gap has long held a special place in travellers' lore as the ultimate adventure – and with reason. This thin stretch of land, just 50 km wide and 160 km long, which links Central and South America, has some of the densest tropical jungle in the world – so dense that to date neither the Panamanians nor the Colombians have succeeded in building a road across. There are no roads of any kind, the only inland routes are by boat or on foot. At present, the Pan-American Highway from Canada to Tierra del Fuego in Chile stops at Yaviza in Panama, 60 km short of the frontier, and begins again 27 km west of Barranquillita, well into Colombia. The Darién is home to an incredible profusion of flora and fauna, as well as indigenous tribes who rarely see foreigners.

The trek across the Darién is held in high regard by adventurers but we strongly advise against it, not simply because it is easy and fatal to get lost, but also because bona fide travellers are not welcome (indigenous communities still living in Darién have never truly accepted trekkers passing through) and this area still has a heavy guerrilla presence. The Colombian government's successes against the FARC have pushed them to the extremes of the country, where they have retreated to lick their wounds. Those trafficking drugs from South to North America have found the density of the jungle a useful protection for running consignments. Both FARC and ELN guerrilla groups have infiltrated the region and paramilitaries regard this as a threat to their land. As a result this has become a violent war zone, virtually deserted now by police and the military, and it is a hostile environment for any tourist. As recently as 2008 there were reports of kidnappings in the Darién. For the moment only the foolhardy will attempt the land crossing. However, the Caribbean coastline, heavily patrolled by Colombian and Panamanian forces, is safe, though you should exercise caution if venturing into the forest beyond.

Acandí
Acandí is a small fishing village on the Caribbean side of the Darién. It has a spectacular, forest-fringed bay with turquoise waters. In April, thousands of leatherback turtles come here to lay their eggs. There are several cheap *residencias* to stay in. There are daily flights from Medellín with Aerolíneas de Antioquia (US$150 one way).

Capurganá
For many years, Capurganá and neighbouring Sapzurro have been one of the best kept secrets in Colombia. In this most isolated of Colombia's corners, a glistening, untouched shoreline of crystal waters and coral reefs backs on to quiet little villages where, at night, if you listen carefully, you can hear the howler monkeys calling to each other in the jungle-clad hills behind.

Capurganá has developed into a resort popular with affluent Colombians but is little visited by foreigners. This is partly due to the fact that it is either difficult or expensive to get to and that until recently it was an important point for smuggling drugs through to Panama and there was heavy guerrilla activity. But a strong army presence has put an end to that and it is now considered a safe place to visit. It is a quiet place: there are no cars and just two motorbikes. Taxi rides are provided by horse and carts, and someone has had the ingenious idea of attaching modified plastic seats.

There are two beaches in the village. La Caleta is at the northern end, beyond the pontoon, and is protected by a barrier reef, has golden sand and is the best for swimming. There are a couple of restaurants and several hotels and *cabañas* here. Playa de los Pescadores, south of the village, is fringed by palm and almond trees but has disappointing grey sand and is more pebbly. Ask the fishermen about fishing trips from here (US$ 15-20 in rowing boats).

Around Capurganá
Several half- and full-day trips can be made by launch boat to neighbouring beaches. Aguacate is a beautiful bay with clear, aquamarine water and a small beach. There is a rocky promontory with a blowhole and what locals call 'La Piscina', a natural jacuzzi amongst the rocks which you can lower yourself into using a rope. There is also a small restaurant serving fried fish for US$7. Aguacate has good snorkelling, but Playa Soledad is perhaps the most attractive beach in the area and was recently used as the location for a Colombian reality TV programme. The beach is white sand and fringed by palms.

A return trip by launch boat costs US$11 per person, minimum five people. You can also walk to Aguacate, 1½ hours along the coast, though not to Playa Soledad. Note that it can be difficult to obtain a return by launch if you walk.

Another trip is to Sapzurro, a few kilometres north (see below). Capurganá Tours organizes day trips to the San Blas archipelago in Panama, possibly some of the most beautiful islands in the Caribbean and launches stop at the island of Caledonia (US$55-60 per person with a minimum of 28 people).

There is excellent diving and snorkelling around Capurganá. You are likely to see nurse sharks, moray eels, spotted eagle rays, trumpetfish, jewfish, barracuda and hawksbill turtles, among other species, as well as large brain and elkhorn coral. Several of the hotels organize diving and the independent dive centre, **Dive and Green**, near the jetty is recommended.

A delightful half-day excursion is to **El Cielo**, a small waterfall in the jungle. You can walk there in 40 minutes through beautiful primary jungle. Take flip flops or waterproof boots, as you will have to cross a stream several times and it is muddy. Take the path to the left of the airport and keep asking for directions as it is easy to get lost. Just before the waterfall there is a small restaurant serving *patacones* and drinks. There is a swimming hole with a zip wire. Alternatively, you can hire horses to take you there (US$7). Entry to the waterfall is US$2.

Another horse-riding trip is to El Valle de Los Ríos, a valley in the jungle with several crystalline rivers and beautiful waterfalls. The primary forest in this area is rich in wildlife; you might see, among other animals, sloths, howler monkeys, toucans, parrots, fishing eagles and several types of lizard and iguana. You should take a guide for this. The trip includes lunch at a *ranchería*. For more details, enquire at **Capurganá Tours** in town, by the jetty, or at the football pitch (*cancha de futbol*) in the village centre.

Sapzurro

Sapzurro is a quiet little village in the Darién and the last outpost before Panama and Central America. Set in a shallow, horseshoe-shaped bay dotted with coral reefs, little happens in this village of less than 1000 inhabitants. There are no roads, let alone cars. The houses of this tiny village are linked by intersecting pathways bursting with tropical flowers. It has a couple of excellent little hostels and some good restaurants serving up home-cooked seafood. The bay is excellent for snorkelling, with a couple of underwater caves to explore.

Aventure Colombia organizes sailing trips from Cartagena to Sapzurro via the San Bernardo coral islands and Isla Fuerte. The passage of three days and three nights costs US$200, or US$250 with accommodation in Sapzurro and tours to El Cielo and the beaches of El Aguacate and Playa Soledad. There is an option to continue on to the San Blas islands in Panama for US$800.

You can make a day trip to the small village of **La Miel** over the border in Panama by walking up the forested hill behind the village. This could qualify as the most relaxed border crossing in the world. The Colombian and Panamanian immigration offiers share a hut and copy each other's notes. Be sure to take your passport; if only going to La Miel they won't stamp it but they will take your details. There are breathtaking views of Panama and back into Sapzurro at the border crossing on the brow of the hill.

La Miel has a gorgeous white-sand beach with beautiful, clear waters and a coral reef. The snorkelling is relatively good though a little low on fauna. There are a couple of shacks selling beer and food. Try the sea snails in coconut sauce. You can arrange for a launch to pick you up and take you back to Sapzurro or Capurganá.

For Sleeping and Eating price codes and other relevant information, see pages 31-36.

⦿ Sleeping

Islas del Rosario *p161*

AL Isla del Pirata, book through **Excursiones Roberto Lemaitre**, T6655622, www.hotel islapirata.com, hotelislapirata@yahoo.com. A number of simple, comfortable *cabañas* with activities that include diving, snorkelling, canoeing and petanque. Fresh fish and lobster are served for lunch and dinner. Prices start from US$140 and include transport to the island, food and non-guided activities. Highly recommended.

Isla Grande

LL Cultura del Mar, T6649312, www.cultura delmar.com. An eco-hotel, where you can sleep in hammocks or beds, with cooking provided by a local family. The price includes all meals, 2 days snorkelling and transport to and from the islands. Diving can also be arranged here.

AL San Pedro de Majagua, Calle del Torno, No 39-29, T6646070, www.hotelmajagua. com. Owned by **Hotel Santa Clara** in Cartagena. Prices start from US$130 per night.

Mompós *p163, map p163*

Almost all of the hotels in Mompós are located on C Real del Medio, the main thoroughfare through town which boasts beautifully preserved whitewashed houses with enormous iron grills. Note that most hotels in Mompós double in price over Semana Santa and other festival periods.

A Hostal Doña Manuela, C Real del Medio (Cra 2), 17-41, T6855612, mabe642@yahoo. com. A charming hotel converted from the largest colonial house in town, centred around a courtyard with an extraordinary banyan tree. The rooms are spacious and fresh, while its swimming pool at the back provides welcome respite from the soporific heat. With an art gallery and jewellery shop and its central position, it is often at the hub of the action. Accepts credit cards.

B-C Residencias Aurora, Cra 2, No15-65, T6855723. Dishevelled but with character. Some shared baths, big ceilings, kitchen available, security could be an issue.

C Casa Hotel Villa de Mompós, 500 m east of Parque Bolívar, T6855208. Charming family-run hotel, decorated with antique bric-a-brac. Internet access $1 per hr. Can also arrange rooms for families during festival periods.

C Casa Hotel Celeste, Cra 2, No 14-174, T6856875. Decorated with old photographs and fake oil paintings, this hotel is just the right side of chintzy. Rooms are a little small.

C Hacienda San Ignacio, a few kilometres out of town on the road to Talaigua. This modern hacienda, built on land belonging to Jesuit priests may offer welcome respite from the sometimes oppressive heat of Mompós. Rooms are clean and simple, it has a swimming pool and offers horse riding. It is managed by **Hostal Doña Manuela**; ask there for details.

C La Casona, Cra 2, No 18-58, T6855307, eusedeal@yahoo.es. Fine colonial building with delightful courtyards and plants. Has a billiard table, TV, a/c, laundry service and internet access. Just pips the rest of them for atmosphere.

C San Andrés, Cra 2, No 18-23, T855886. Another fine, restored colonial building. The patio has parrots and aquariums. Rooms have TV and bathroom. Has own water and electricity supply (useful during power cuts). Can arrange guides for local area.

D Residencias Unión, C 18, No 3-43, T6855723. The only hotel in Mompós in a modern building. The rooms are cheap but a little dark and likely to be noisy during festivities as hotel is near all the action. No double beds available.

D-E La Casa Amarilla, Cra 1, No 13-59, T6856326, www.lacasaamarillamompos. blogspot.com. 1 block up from the Iglesia Santa Bárbara on the riverfront, this new backpackers' hostel has 2 private rooms with bathrooms and a dorm, all decorated with beautiful murals by the internationally renowned artist stepmother of English owner Richard McColl. The hostel boasts 2 living rooms equipped with TV and DVD player, a book exchange and an information board while at the end of the garden there is an open-plan kitchen for guests' use. Thanks to his other job as a travel journalist, Richard is an excellent source of information on Colombia.

Tolú p164

B Alcira, Av La Playa, No 21-151, T288 5016, alcirahotel@yahoo.com. On the promenade, has a breezy courtyard and lots of balconies with rocking chairs. Has a/c, laundry service, parking and Wi-Fi. Breakfast included.

B Playamar, Av La Playa, No 22-22, T286 0587, playamar@yahoo.es. Large, white building on the *malecón* with beautiful lemon trees outside. Has all the mod cons, including Wi-Fi, a/c, minibar, parking and TV. Has a small restaurant serving breakfast for US$3-5.

D Altamar, Cra 3, No 17-36, T2885421. Bright rooms opening onto an open-air corridor. Has its own water and electricity supply (there are frequent power and water cuts in Tolú). Prices more than double in high season.

D Darimar, C 17, No 1-60, T2885153. Just off the beach front with small but clean rooms, private bathrooms, TV and parking. Friendly staff.

D Mar Adentro, Av La Playa, No 11-36, T2860079. Hotel belonging to tour agency of same name. Nice, clean rooms with private bathrooms. Rooms are cheaper (**E**) with fan.

E Villa Babilla, C 20, No 3-40, T2886124, www.villa babillahostel.com. Easily the best option in Tolú. Colombian-German couple Alex and Laffie have built a quiet little haven of simple, brightly painted rooms with a

thatched *cabaña* as a TV area and lots of hammocks. At time of writing it was being expanded and will include rooms with terraces and a communal area with hammocks, sofas and Wi-Fi throughout. Alex is a good source of information on activities in local area.

E El Turista, Av La Playa, No 11-20, T288 5145. The cheapest option in town and good value for money. On the promenade, next to all the tour agencies.

E Los Angeles, C 17, No 1-23, T300600 6107. Right on beach with TV, fan and private bathrooms, though the rooms are crammed with as many beds as possible.

Coveñas

A Villa Melissa, T288 0249, www.villa melissa.com. Large apartments on the beach each with their own balcony, a/c and TV, Also has a swimming pool.

D Cabañas del Morrosquillo, Km 9 Vía Tolú, T2800341. Not the prettiest concrete structures you have ever seen but have comfortable beds and fan. On a good, quiet stretch of beach.

Arboletes p165

E Ganadero, C Principal, T820 0086. Basic but clean rooms. Has a pleasant reception area under a thatched hut and a restaurant serving basic fare for US$3.50.

E La Floresta, C Principal, T820 0034. Opposite **Ganadero**, this small hotel has simple rooms with private bathrooms. It's best to ask for a street-facing room if you want a window.

Turbo p165

B Playa Mar, Av de la Playa, T827 2205. Good, but somewhat run down with a restaurant. Has a/c, TV and is cheaper with fan.

C Castilla de Oro, C 100, No 14-07, T827 2185. The best option in town, has a/c, safety box, minibar, a good restaurant and a swimming pool. Modern building with reliable water and electricity. Friendly staff.

C-E Hotel 2000, C 101, No 11-115, T827 2333. Next to bus terminal, rooms with TV and private bathrooms. Almost half the price if you choose a room with fan only.

C Simona del Mar, Km 13 Vía Necoclí, T824 5682, www.simonadelmar.com. Turbo is not a safe place in which to walk around at night, so this is a better, safer option for sleeping. A few kilometres outside town, this hotel has a number of *cabañas* in a tranquil setting and near the beach. Has good restaurant. The beach is nice enough, although like everywhere on this stretch of the coast, the sea is a muddy brown due to its proximity to the Gulf of Urabá. A taxi to and from Turbo is US$11. You can also ask *colectivos* to drop you there.

Capurganá *p166*

Accomodation and food are generally more expensive than in other parts of Colombia but it is possible to find reasonably cheap hostels and restaurants.

LL Almar, enquire through offices in Medellín, T4366262, almar@une.net.co. Luxury wooden *cabañas* amongst manicured gardens and right on the beach. Has Turkish bath, spa, jacuzzi and a pool.

AL Tacarcuna Lodge, T6828819 (Medellín), www.hotelesdecostaacosta.com. *Cabañas* around a garden pool. All meals included.

A Playa de Capurganá, T3318680 (Medellín) T316 4825781 (mob), www.jardinbotanico darien.com/condominio.htm. Set in tropical gardens, this breezy wooden house has comfortable rooms with private bathrooms and a fine veranda with hammocks from which to look out to sea, as well as a great swimming pool right on the beach. The price includes a home-cooked breakfast and dinner. Recommended.

B Marlin Hostal, T8243611, capurgana marlin@yahoo.es. The best mid-range option in town. A beautiful wooden chalet on Playa de los Pescadores with good rooms, private bathrooms and a patio with a mango tree and lots of plants and songbirds. Has

a good restaurant serving excellent fish. There are also bunks (**F**) available.

C Cabaña Darius, T314 6225638, www.cabanadarius.com. In the grounds of Playa de Capurganá, this little place is excellent value for money with simple, comfortable rooms in a wooden chalet set amongst acres of exquisite tropical gardens. Large balconies with hammocks. Rooms have fan, private bathroom and breakfast is included.

D Hostal Capurganá, C del Comercio, T3167433863, www.hostalcapurgana.net. Comfortable, clean rooms with private bathrooms. Has a pleasant patio and is well situated on the main street, next to the jetty. Recommended.

D Luz de Oriente, T8243719, luzdeoriente 999@hotmail.com. Right on the jetty, each of the rooms is named after a *Lord of the Rings* character. Rooms are a bit cramped with too many beds. Has a beautiful restaurant serving average food.

E Los Delfines, T6828788. A few blocks back from the jetty, rooms are very basic but there are pretty balconies with hammocks, a restaurant and TV.

Private houses There are several private homes for hire, including:

Cabaña de los Alemanes, a simple self-catering bungalow with a thatched hut for slinging hammocks and a small plunge pool. The *cabaña* is in a prime position, right on the waterfront – the sea laps against the edge of the garden. Sleeps 8 in bunks and single beds for US$130 per night. Enquire at **Dive and Green**, page 172, for more details.

Sapzurro *p167*

D Zingara Cañañas, Camino La Miel, T313 6733291. Pretty much the last building before you get to Panama, Zingara has 2 lovely *cabañas* with gorgeous views over the bay. The owners have a herb and vegetable garden and sell home-made chutneys. This also doubles up as the village pharmacy.

E Paraíso Sapzurro, T8244115/T3136859862, paraisosapzurro@yahoo.com. Right on the beach at the southern end of the village, this has a number of *cabañas*, a little more basic than Zingara's, run by a charismatic Chilean. Has an excellent thatched ranch full of hammocks for relaxing. Also has space for camping (US$3 or US$4 with tent hire). Ask for El Chileno and you will be directed here when you arrive.

🍴 Eating

Mompós p163, map p163
Good bakeries on C 18 and Cra 3 for coffee, cakes and snacks. A selection of fast food kiosks can be found at the Plaza Santo Domingo, next to the church.
🍴🍴🍴 **Restaurante Doña Manuela**, part of the hostel of the same name, probably the best restaurant in town (though pricey with it), fish is particularly good, try the Bagre Momposino.
🍴🍴🍴 **Fuafua's**, on Parque Bolívar, T6840609. Serves *comida corriente*, worth going to if just to experience its grand old dilapidated dining hall looking out over the square.
🍴🍴🍴 **La Pizzería**, opposite San Agustín Church. Good pizzas in a lovely setting.
🍴 **D'La Villa**, C 18, No 2-49, T6858793. For those tired of chicken and steak this bakery/ ice cream parlour also serves up a selection of crêpes.
🍴 **La Parcela**, a few kilometers out of town opposite the airport, open only on Sun. Mompósinos go here to sit under the shade of mango trees and eat *sancocho* and *ajiaco* while listening to *vallenato*.

Tolú p164
🍴 **La Atarraya**, C 15, No 1-38. Cheap fast food. Burgers, pizza and hotdogs.
🍴 **La 15**, Av La Playa, No 15 esquina. Good quality steaks with swift service. Recommended.
🍴 **La Red**, Av La Playa, No 20. Decorated with all things aquatic, including fishing nets, star fish, turtle shells, oars and model boats. Serves cheap but good seafood, steaks, burgers and hotdogs. Friendly staff.
🍴 **Punto B**, C 15, No 2-02. Cheap and cheerful restaurant and *panadería* serving the usual Colombian fare. *Comida corriente*, US$ 3.

Capurganá p166
🍴 **Donde Josefina**, Playa La Caleta, T316 7797760. Josefina cooks exquisite seafood, served to you under a shady tree on the beach. Try the lobster cooked in garlic and coconut sauce.
🍴 **El Patacón**, C del Comercio. Serves good, simple seafood.
🍴 **Luz de Oriente**, on the jetty. Lovely-looking restaurant decorated with lots of hanging shells, though the food is a bit bland.
🍴 **Pizzeria Mi Ciclo**, T314 789 1826. This isn't a restaurant as much as a lovely woman who will cook remarkably good pizzas from an oven in her bedsit and bring out a table and chairs for you to eat them on. Ask around for her on the C del Comercio, near Capurganá Tours.

Sapzurro p167
🍴 **La Negra**, C Principal. Serves home-cooked seafood.

🎭 Entertainment

Mompós p163, map p163
There are a number of bars and discos along the riverfront, among the best of which is the bohemian **Luna de Mompox**.

🛍 Shopping

Mompós p163, map p163
Mompós is famous for its filigree gold and silver jewellery and its wicker rocking chairs. You can visit workshops to see how they are made.

Jewellery
Joyería Sam, C18A No 2B, T6855829, www.joyeriasam.com. Fine selection of beautifully worked gold and silver earrings, bracelets and brooches.
Santa Cruz, Cra 2, No 20-132, T6856371, tallersantacruz@yahoo.com.

Rocking chairs
Ebanistería Grimarlo, Cra 2, No 13-29, T6855313.
Muebles Momposinos, Cra 2, opposite Monumento del Sagrado Corazón, T6855349.

▲ Activities and events

Islas del Rosario *p161*
Diving
A diving permit from MA costs US$31.
Cultura del Mar, Getsemaní C del Pozo, No 25-95, Cartagena, T6649312, www.cultura delmar.com. Offices in Cartagena, organizes snorkelling and diving, and various tours of the coral reefs and mangroves of the islands.
Excursiones Roberto Lemaitre, C 8, No 4-66, Bocagrande, T665 5622 (owner of **Club Isla del Pirata**). They have the best boats and are near the top end of the price range but **Yates Alcatraz** is more economical; enquire at the quay.

Tolú *p164*
Tour operators
Club Náutico Mundo Marino, Av La Playa, No 14-40, T2884431, www.clubnautico mundomarino.com. Have the best boat and do not overbook. They run daily tours to San Bernardo Islands at 0800, returning at 1600, which cost US$20, including the aquarium on Isla Palma. The tour includes a 3-hr stay on Múcura where there are a number of shacks serving seafood.
Mar Adentro, Av La Playa 11-36, T2860079, www.club nauticomaradentro.com. A good agency.

Capurganá *p166*
Diving
Dive and Green, near the jetty, T6828825, www.diveandgreen.com. The only dive centre in town that does PADI. Has a 27 ft boat with 200 horsepower. Excursions to San Blas. English spoken.

Tour operators
Capurganá Tours, C del Comercio, T682 8858, www.capurganatours.com. Organizes walking tours with knowledgeable guides to nearby beaches and into the jungle as well as horse riding, diving and birdwatching. Trips to San Blas islands in Panama arranged if sufficient people. Can assist in booking flights from Puerto Obaldía to Panama City. English spoken. Highly recommended.

⊙ Transport

Mompós *p163, map p163*
Air
Mompós has an airport but there have been no commercial flights for some years.

Bus
To **Cartagena** there are 3 options: with **Unitransco**, direct, US$17 (negotiable), bus leaves at 0600 from outside Iglesia Santa Barbara; or *colectivo* to La Bodega, US$4 per person, *chalupa* (motorized canoe) US$3.50, and finally bus to Magangué. **Asotranstax** runs a door-to-door *colectivo* service between Mompós and Santa Marta, $30; and Mompós and Valledupar. To **Medellín**, taxi to La Bodega, then *chalupa* to Magangué and finally bus with **Brasilia** or **Rápido Ochoa**, 10 hrs, US$45. Alternatively, take a bus to Santa Ana via Aracataca and Bosconia, then a *chalupa* to Talaigua, and finally a *colectivo*.
Unitransco has direct service to Barranquilla, leaving at 0600. To **Bogotá**, **Copetran** and **Omega** have services leaving from El Banco (4WD trip from Mompós) at 1600, US$27-39. To **Bucaramanga**, a Copetran bus leaves El Banco at 1000.

Return journey leaves Bucaramanga at 1000.

Tolú p164
Bus
Brasilia has buses every hour to **Cartagena** between 0715 and 1730. 12 a day to **Medellín** with Brasilia and Rápido Ochoa, US$40, via Montería except at night. **Bogotá**, 3 a day, US$55. To **Barranquilla**, **Santa Marta** and **Riohacha**, 5 a day, US$33. For **Bucaramanga** you must change at Sincelejo, 2 a day, US$55. To **Valledupar**, 1 a day, changing at Sincelejo, US$25.

Turbo p165
Sea
Launches for **Acandí**, **Capurganá** and **Sapzurro** leave daily at 0800, US$26 and take 3 hrs. It's a spectacular journey that hugs the Caribbean shoreline of the Darién. As passengers begin to embark you will notice a rush for seats at the back. You are well advised to join in the scrum as the journey is bumpy and can be painful in seats at the front. **Note** There is a 10 kg limit on baggage, excess is US$0.30 per kg. Between mid-Dec and the end of Feb the sea becomes very choppy and dangerous. We advise you not to make this journey during this period.

Capurganá p166
Air
1 flight daily to **Medellín** with Aerolineas de Antioquia (ADA), US$400 return. Twin Otter biplanes with16 passenger capacity. Be sure to book ahead. Baggage limit of 10 kg. Excess is US$2 per kg. You may be asked to allow your baggage to follow on a later plane if seriously overweight.

Sea
There's a launch to **Turbo**, daily, leaving at 0800, US$27. Be sure to get a seat at the back as the 3-hr ride is bumpy and can be excruciatingly uncomfortable at the front.

There are daily launches to **Puerto Obaldía** in Panama, US$20. From here it is possible to fly to **Panama City**, US$84 (1-way) with Aeroperlas. It is also possible to catch a further launch from Puerto Obaldía to **Mulatuto**, US$20, and from there on to **Colón**, US$66.

Sapzurro p167
You can walk to Capurganá in 4 hrs, a beautiful hike along the coastline through jungle rich in wildlife.

Sea
Launches to **Capurganá** cost US$11 (5 people minimum), 30 mins. Launches leave from Puerto Obaldía or La Miel to **Panama**.

⊕ Directory

Tolú p164
Banks There are several banks with cash-points on the parque principal. **Internet** Cyber Blue, C 15, No 2, headphones and camera.

Arboletes p165
Banks There is a Banco Agrario in the Parque Principal, though it doesn't have a cashpoint.

Capurganá p166
Banks There are no banks in Capurganá. It´s best to bring sufficient cash with you though **Capurganá Tours** will exchange cash on credit cards for a 6.5% commission. **Internet** Capurganá Tours, with Skype and headphones. **Immigration** DAS office, on the waterfront next to the police station, between the jetty and Playa de los Pescadores, Mon-Fri 0800-1500, Sat, Sun and holidays 0900-1600, T3117466234. If leaving for Panama you must get your passport stamped here. Requirements for entry into Panama are proof of US$600 in the bank and a yellow fever certificate.

Barranquilla

→ *Colour map 1, A2. Phone code: 5. Population: 1,109,000.*

Barranquilla, Colombia's fourth city, lies on the western bank of the Río Magdalena, about 18 km from its mouth. It's a seaport (though less busy than Cartagena or Santa Marta), as well as a river port, and a modern industrial city with a polluted but colourful central area near the river. First and foremost, however, Barranquilla is famed for its Carnival, reputed to be second only to Rio de Janeiro in terms of size and far less commercialized. In 2003 UNESCO declared it a "masterpiece of the oral and intangible heritage of humanity". Pre-carnival parades and dances last through January until an edict that everyone must party is read out. Carnival itself lasts from Saturday, with the Batalla de las Flores, through the Gran Parada on Sunday, to the funeral of Joselito Carnaval on Tuesday. The same families have participated for generations, keeping the traditions of the costumes and dances intact. Prepare for three days of intense revelry and dancing with very friendly and enthusiastic crowds, spectacular float processions, parades and beauty queens. The main action takes place along Calle 17, Carrera 44 and Vía 40. ▸▸ *For listings, see pages 176-178.*

Ins and outs

Getting there **Ernesto Cortissoz airport** is 10 km from the city. A city bus from the airport to town costs US$0.35 (US$0.40 on Sunday). Only take buses marked 'centro', you can catch them 200 m from the airport on the right. A taxi to town costs US$7 (taxis do not have meters, so agree on the fare in advance). The main **bus terminal** is south of the city near the Circunvalación. Some bus companies have offices around Calle 34 and Carrera 45. If arriving into Barranquilla by boat and shipping your car, allow two days

Barranquilla centre

⇒ **Barranquilla maps**
1 Barranquilla centre, page 174
2 Barranquilla – El Prado, page 175

Sleeping
del Mar 2
Girasol 3
Horizonte 4
San Francisco 5

Eating
Pescadero El Centro 1

to complete all the paperwork you'll need to retrieve your car from the port. ▸▸ *For more information, see Transport, page 178.*

Getting around Taxis for trips within town cost US$1.60.

Tourist information Tourist information is available at the main hotels and from the **tourist police** ① *Cra 43, No 47-53, T351 0415, T3409903.*

Sights

The city is surrounded by a continuous ring road called the 'Vía Cuarenta' from the north along the river to the centre; 'Avenida Boyacá' to the bridge (Puente Pumarejo), which crosses the Río Magdalena for Santa Marta; and 'Circunvalación' round the south and west of the city. The long bridge over the Río Magdalena gives a fine view of Barranquilla and the river.

In the centre the principal boulevard is **Paseo Bolívar** leading to **Parque Simón Bolívar**. Two blocks south is a handsome church, **San Nicolás**, formerly the cathedral, in Plaza San Nicolás, the central square, and before it stands a small statue of Columbus. The new **Catedral Metropolitana** ① *Cra 45, No 53-120*, is opposite Parque la Paz. There is an impressive statue of Christ inside by the Colombian sculptor, Arenas Betancourt.

② Barranquilla – El Prado

➡ **Barranquilla maps**
1 Barranquilla centre, page 174
2 **Barranquilla – El Prado, page 175**

400 metres
400 yards

Sleeping 🛏
Barranquilla Plaza 1
Bulevard 58 3
El Prado 2
Majestic 4

Eating 🍴
Don Pepe 1
Jardines de Confucio 2
La Fonda Antioqueña 3
Loca 4

Los Helechos 5

Bars & clubs 🍸
Froggs Leggs 6
Henry's 7

Further along is the small **Museo Antropológico** ① *C 68, No 53-45*, which has a big physical relief map on the front lawn, and the **Museo Romántico** ① *Cra 54, No 59-199*, which covers the history of Barranquilla, including the establishment of air services and radio in Colombia, with an interesting section on the local Carnival and a replica of 'Camellón Abello', an old street of Barranquilla.

The commercial and shopping districts are round the Paseo Bolívar, a few blocks north of the old cathedral, and in Avenida Murillo. The colourful and vivid **market** is between Paseo Bolívar and the river, the so-called Zona Negra on a side channel of the Magdalena. Nearby is one of the biggest and best maintained **zoos** ① *C 77/Cra 68, take bus 'Boston/Boston' or 'Caldes/Recreo'*, in the country, however many of the animals (some rarely seen in captivity) are kept in small cages. There are good parks to the northwest of the centre, including **Parque Tomás Suri Salcedo** on Calle 72. Stretching back into the northwestern heights overlooking the city are the modern suburbs of **El Prado**, Altos del Prado, Golf and Ciudad Jardín, where you'll find the **El Prado Hotel**.

There is a full range of services including commercial and shopping centres, and banks between Bulevar Norte and Avenida Olaya Herrera towards the Country Club. There are five stadiums in the city, a big covered coliseum for sports, two for football, and the others cater for basketball and baseball. The metropolitan stadium is on Avenida Murillo, outside the city where it meets the south stretch of the Circunvalación.

Around Barranquilla

Regular buses from Paseo Bolívar and the church at Calle 33/Carrera 41 go to the attractive bathing resort of **Puerto Colombia**, 19 km, with its pier built around 1900. This was formerly the ocean port of Barranquilla, connected by a railway. The beach is clean and sandy, though the water is a bit muddy. Nearby are the beaches of **Salgar**, and north of Barranquilla is **Las Flores** (2 km from the mouth of the Río Magdalena at Bocas de Ceniza), both good places for seafood.

South along the west bank of the Magdalena, 5 km from the city, is the old colonial town of **Soledad**. The cathedral and the old narrow streets around it are worth seeing. A further 25 km south is **Santo Tomás**, known for its Good Friday flagellants who symbolically whip themselves as an Easter penance. There are also street theatre presentations at this time. The small town of Palmar de Varela is a little further along the same road, which continues on to Calamar.

⊛ **Barranquilla listings** → *Phone code: 5.*

For Sleeping and Eating price codes and other relevant information, see pages 31-36.

⊜ Sleeping

Barranquilla *p174, maps p174 and p175*
Hotel prices tend to double during Carnival. Watch out for thieves in downtown hotels.
LL El Prado, Cra 54, No 70-10, T369 7777, www.hotelpradosa.com, reservas@hotel pradosa.com. A landmark in Barranquilla, this enormous hotel with 200 rooms has been around since 1930 and still retains some of of its old-fashioned service. It has a fantastic pool shaded by palm trees, various restaurants, tennis courts and a gym.
AL Barranquilla Plaza, Cra 51B, No 79-246, T361 000, www.hbp.com.co. A deluxe hotel popular with Colombian businessmen, it's worth visiting just for the 360° view of the city from its 26th floor restaurant. It has all the other amenities you would expect of a hotel of this standard, including gym, spa, sauna and internet.

A Hotel Majestic, Cra 53, No 54-41, T349 1010, hotelmajestic@metrotel.net.co. An oasis of calm from the bustle of Barranquilla, the Majestic has a fine pool and large, fresh rooms as well as a restaurant serving the usual fish and meat dishes and sandwiches.

B Hotel Bulevard 58, Cra 58, No 70-41, T368 0810, www.cotelco.org/boulevard58. It has an 1980s feel about it even though it was apparently only converted from a residential home in the 1990s. Breakfast is included, and it has a pool, and Wi-Fi available in all rooms.

C Hotel San Francisco, C 43, No 43-128, www.sanfranciscohoteles.com. With modern, bright, clean rooms, and a courtyard full of songbirds, this is a good, safe bet. It also offers laundry, a restaurant and internet services,

D Hotel Girasol, C 44, No 44-103, T379 3191, www.elhotelgirasol.com. It's clean, safe and has a restaurant and Wi-Fi in all rooms, but it doesn't offer much in terms of character.

E Hotel del Mar, C 42, No 35-57, T341 3703. Popular with locals, this is probably the best option for those on a budget. The rooms are clean and bright, the service friendly and the food in its restaurant cheap. Good value.

F Horizonte, Cra 44, No 44-35, T341 7925. Dingy and dark but just about passes.

🍴 Eating

Barranquilla *p174, maps p174 and p175*
In Barranquilla you'll find places to suit all tastes and budgets. There are Lebanese restaurants with belly-dancers, Chinese restaurants and pizzerías. The best selection is on C 70 from **Hotel El Prado** towards Cra 42. At C 70 y 44B you'll find several *estaderos*, bars with snacks and verandas.

♦♦ Jardines de Confucio, Cra 54, No 75-44. Classy Chinese restaurant with a large menu and a good atmosphere.

♦ Don Pepe, Cra 53, No 53-90, T379 9234. Opposite the **Hotel Majestic**, it has a breezy outdoor patio serving up *comida santandereana*.

♦ La Fonda Antioqueña, Cra 52, No 70-73, T360 0573. Just across the road from **Los Helechos** and serving the same fare, but it has a fine patio with draping flowers.

♦ La Pizza Loca, Cra 53, No 70-97, also at C 84, No 50-36. Pizzería.

♦ Los Helechos, Cra 52, No 70-70, T356 7493. Around the corner from **Hotel El Prado**, this popular restaurant serves up typical *comida antioqueña*, including *sancochos* and *ajiacos*, in a good atmosphere.

♦ Pescadero del Centro, Cra 44, No 42-43. A favourite, seving local seafood.

🍸 Bars and clubs

Barranquilla *p174, maps p174 and p175*
Froggs Leggs, C 93, No 43-122. Popular bar, good atmosphere.
Henry's Bar, C 80, No 53-18, CC Washington. Open daily from 1600. Popular US-style bar, with pizzería downstairs.

🎭 Entertainment

Barranquilla *p174, maps p174 and p175*
Theatre
Teatro Amira de la Rosa. This is one of the most modern theatres in Colombia, and it offers a full range of stage presentations, concerts, ballets, art exhibitions, etc. These run throughout the year.

🎉 Festivals and events

Barranquilla *p174, maps p174 and p175*
Mar/Apr Carnival, tickets for the spectator stands are sold in major restaurants and bars, eg **Froggs Leggs** (see Bars and clubs, above). La Casa de Carnaval, Carrera 54, No 49B-39, T379 6621, www.carnavaldebarranquilla.org, is the official office and the best place to get information. Carnival is a long-standing tradition in Barranquilla, lasting for the 4 days before Ash Wed, comparable, some say, with

the carnivals of Rio de Janeiro and Trinidad.
There are parades, floats, street dancing,
beauty contests and general mayhem.
As normal on such occasions, take special
care of your valuables.

⊙ Shopping

Barranquilla *p174, maps p174 and p175*
Bookshop
Librería Nacional, CC Buenavista, Cra 53,
No 98. Has a small selection of English books.

Markets
San Andrecito, or 'Tourist Market', Vía 40.
Where smuggled goods are sold at very
competitive prices. Picturesque and reasonably
safe. Any taxi driver will take you there.

Shopping centres
Centro Comercial Buenavista, Cra 53,
C 98. Has a good selection of shops,
cinemas and fast food outlets.

▲ Activities and tours

Barranquilla *p174, maps p174 and p175*
Tour operators
Aviatur, Cra 54, No 72-96, local 3, T361
6000, aviatur@metrotel.net.co. Organize tours
to Parque Tayrona and other destinations.

⊖ Transport

Barranquilla *p174, maps p174 and p175*
Air
The bus to the airport (marked 'Malambo')
leaves from Cra 44, goes up C 32 to C 38,
and then C 30 to the airport.
   Daily flights to **Bogotá**, **Cartagena**,
Medellín, **Bucaramanga**, **Montería** and
Valledupar. International flights to **Aruba**,
Curaçao, **Miami** and **Panama City**.
   Airline offices AeroRepública, C 72,
No 54-49, local 1 y 2, T3608239.

Bus
To **Santa Marta**, about 2 hrs, US$3.25,
Pullman (less in non-a/c, Coolibertador),
also direct to Santa Marta's Rodadero beach.
To **Valledupar**, 5-6 hrs, US$10. To **Montería**
direct, 7-8 hrs, US$11. To **Medellín**, 16 hrs,
US$40, Pullman. To **Bucaramanga**, 1130
most days, 9 hrs, US$27 with Copetran
(a/c, 1st class). To **Bogotá**, frequent, 24 hrs,
US$45, direct with Copetran. To **Caucasia**,
8-11 hrs, US$17. To **Maicao**, every 30 mins
from 0100-1200, 6 hrs, S$14.50, Brasilia.
To **Cartagena**, 2 hrs by colectivo US$7, 2½-
3 hrs, US$4.50 with Transportes Cartagena;
US$6 with Expreso Brasilia; Brasilia Van Tours
minibus, from their downtown offices as well
as the bus terminals.

Taxi
Avianca, C 72, No 57-79, T3534691.
   To **Cartagena**, US$15 per person, leaves
when full.

⊙ Directory

Barranquilla *p174, maps p174 and p175*
Banks There are a number of banks,
inlcuding **Bancolombia** and **Banco de
Bogotá**. ATMs are also readily available. For
currency exchange, **El Cairo**, C 76, No 48-30,
T3606433, and at C 34, No 43-177; **Paseo
Bolívar**, T3799441, TCs, euros, dollars but
not sterling, Mon-Fri and Sat 0900-1200.
Embassies and consulates Germany,
C73, Vía 40-270, T3532078; **Netherlands**,
Cra 77B, No 57-141, of 806, T3688387; **USA**,
C 77B, No 57-141, of 511, T3532001 (visas
obtainable only in Bogotá); **Venezuela**, Edif
Bancafé, Cra 52, No 69-96, p 3, T3682228,
T3682207, 0800-1500, visa issued same
day, but you must be there by 0915 with
photo and US$30 cash; proof of onward
travel may be required. **Internet** Chatnet,
Cra 54, No 72-111, local 3. **Post office**
Plaza Bolívar. **Security** DAS, C 54, No 41-133,
T3717500; Tourist police, Cra 43, No 47-53,
T3510415, T340 9903.

Santa Marta and around

→ Colour map 1, A3. Phone code: 5. Population: 309,000.

Santa Marta, the capital of Magdalena Department, is the third Caribbean port, 96 km east of Barranquilla. Unlike Cartagena, it is no colonial beauty but what it lacks in architecture it makes up for in character and bustle, and the Sanmarios are some of the most welcoming and gregarious people you will find anywhere in Colombia. The area around Santa Marta has much to offer, including a number of beaches. Head west to the family resort of Rodadero, or north to the fishing village of Taganga. Backpackers will love Taganga's lazy charm, and it's a convenient stopping point en route to Tayrona and a good place to organize treks to Ciudad Perdida mountain range. Southeast is Ciénaga de Santa Marta, 4000 sq km of wetlands with all types of waterbirds, and from here you can reach Aracataca, birthplace of Colombia's most famous writer, Gabriel García Márquez, and believed to be the inspiration for the village of Macondo which features in so many of his books.

When leaving Santa Marta, most travellers will make a beeline for Tayrona National Park and its wild coastline of golden sands, secluded coves and tropical jungle. But there are other options. If the heat of the coast becomes too much, the rural village of Minca in the foothills of the Sierra Nevada, will provide welcome respite. ▶▶ *For listings, see pages 189-194.*

Ins and outs

Getting there The airport, Simón Bolívar, is 20 km south of city. A bus to town costs US$0.35 and a taxi to Santa Marta is US$7, or US$4 to Rodadero. If you arrive by bus, beware of taxi drivers who take you to a hotel of their choice, not yours. The bus terminal is southeast of the city, towards Rodadero, and a minibus to the Santa Marta costs US$0.30, a taxi US$2.50. To Rodadero a taxi is US$3.50.

Although cruise ships from various places (eg USA, Puerto Rico, Panama and even Europe) visit Santa Marta from time to time, it is difficult to find a passage here from overseas. Without a *carnet de passages*, it can take up to four working days to get a car out of the port, but it is usually well guarded and it is unlikely that anything will be stolen. ▶▶ *For further information, see Essentials, page 26.*

Getting around Local bus services from Santa Marta to Rodadero cost US$0.60, and a taxi is US$3. Many of the buses coming from Barranquilla and Cartagena stop at Rodadero on their way to Santa Marta.

Tourist information The tourist office ① *Alcaldía Distrital de Santa Marta, C 17, No 3-120, T300 816 1695, turismo@santamarta.gov.co,* is helpful and has lots of maps and brochures. The online magazine www.tumbacuatro.com, is an excellent source of information on cultural events, activities, new restaurants and bars in Santa Marta and around.

Climate This area is relatively humid but the on-shore winds moderate the temperature much of the time. February and March are pleasant months to visit.

Security The north end of town near the port and beyond the old railway station, and areas south of Rodadero beach are dangerous and travellers are advised not to go there alone. Beware of jungle tours, or boat trips to the islands sold by street touts.

Background

This part of the South American coastline was visited in the early years of the 16th century by the new Spanish settlers from Venezuela. At this time, many indigenous groups were living on and near the coast, and were trading with each other and with communities further inland. The dominant group were the Tayrona.

Santa Marta was the first town created in Colombia by the *conquistadores*, in 1525. The founder, Rodrigo de Bastidas, chose it for its sheltered harbour and its proximity to the Río Magdelena and therefore its access to the hinterland. Also, the *indígenas* represented a potential labour force and he had not failed to notice the presence of gold in their ornaments.

Within a few years, the Spanish settlement was consolidated and permanent buildings appeared (see the Casa de la Aduana, below). Things did not go well, however. The *indígenas* did not 'collaborate' and there was continual friction amongst the Spaniards, all of whom were expecting instant riches. Bastidas' successor, Rodrigo Alvarez Palomino, attempted to subdue the *indígenas* by force, with great loss of life and little success. The *indígenas* that survived took to the hills and their successors, the Kogi, are still there today.

By the middle of the 16th century, a new threat had appeared. Encouraged and often financed by Spain's enemies (England, France and Holland), pirates realised that rich pickings were to be had, not only from shipping, but also by attacking coastal settlements. The first raid took place around 1544, captained by the French pirate Robert Waal with three ships and 1000 men. He was followed by many of the famous sea-dogs – the brothers Côte, Drake and Hawkins – who all ransacked the city in spite of the forts built on a small island at the entrance to the bay and on the mainland. Before the end of the century more than 20 attacks were recorded and the pillage continued until as late as 1779, the townsfolk lived in constant fear. Cartagena, meanwhile, became the main base for the *conquistadores* and much was invested in its defences. Santa Marta was never fortified in the same way and declined in importance as a result, this accounts for the poverty of the colonial heritage here. Over the years caches of treasure have been unearthed in old walls and floors – grim testimonies to the men and women of those troubled times who did not survive to claim them.

Two important names connect Santa Marta with the history of Colombia. Gonzalo Jiménez de Quesada began the expedition here that led him up the Río Magdalena and into the highlands to found Santa Fe de Bogotá in 1538, and it was here that Simón Bolívar, his dream of Gran Colombia shattered, came to die. Almost penniless, he was given hospitality at the *quinta* of San Pedro Alejandrino, see below. He died there on 17 December 1830, at the age of 47.

Santa Marta ⊜🟠🟠⊛🟠🔺🟠🟢 ➡ *pp189-194.*

Orientation

Santa Marta lies at the mouth of the Río Manzanares, one of the many rivers that drain the Sierra Nevada de Santa Marta, on a deep bay with high shelving cliffs at each end. The city's fine promenade offers good views of the bay and is lined with restaurants, accommodation and nightlife, though none of a very high quality. At the southern end, where the main traffic turns inland on Calle 22, is a striking sculpture dedicated to the indigenous heritage of the region, La Herencía Tairona. The main commercial area and banks are on Carrera 5 and Calle 15.

Sights

The centre of Santa Marta is the pleasant and leafy Plaza Bolívar, which leaads down to the beach. It is complete with statues of Bolívar and Santander, and a bandstand. On the north side is the **Casa de la Aduana** ① *C 14/Cra 2*, which became the Custom House when Santa Marta was declared a free port in 1776. Previously it belonged to the Church and was used as the residence of the Chief Justice of the Inquisition. The house dates from

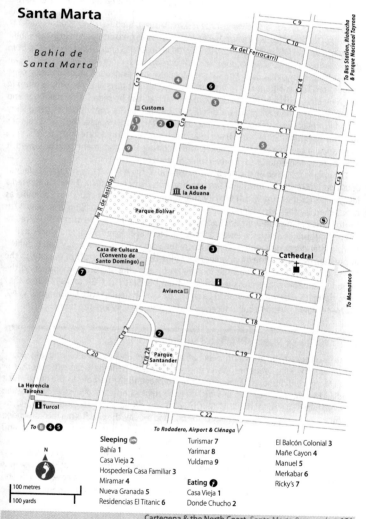

Santa Marta

Bahía de Santa Marta

To Bus Station, Riohacha & Parque Nacional Tayrona

Av del Ferrocarril

Customs

Casa de la Aduana

Parque Bolívar

Av R de Bastidas

Casa de Cultura (Convento de Santo Domingo)

Avianca

Cathedral

To Mamatoco

Parque Santander

La Herencia Tairona

Turcol

To 8 4 5

To Rodadero, Airport & Ciénaga

N

100 metres
100 yards

Sleeping
Bahía **1**
Casa Vieja **2**
Hospedería Casa Familiar **3**
Miramar **4**
Nueva Granada **5**
Residencias El Titanic **6**

Turismar **7**
Yarimar **8**
Yuldama **9**

Eating
Casa Vieja **1**
Donde Chucho **2**

El Balcón Colonial **3**
Mañe Cayon **4**
Manuel **5**
Merkabar **6**
Ricky's **7**

1531 and was probably the first built of brick and stone in Colombia. An upstairs garret, added in 1730, offers an excellent view of the city and the bay. Simón Bolívar stayed here briefly in December 1830 and he lay in state on the second floor from 17 December to the 20 December before being moved to the cathedral. The Custom House now displays an excellent archaeological collection, with four rooms of exhibits mainly dedicated to the indigenous Tayrona. Especially interesting is the model of Ciudad Perdida, the most important of the Tayrona cities. A visit here is strongly recommended. Also housed here is one of the Banco de la República's **Museos de Oro** (Gold Museums) ① *Tue-Sat, 0800-1200, 1400-1800, Sun and holidays, 0800-1200 (tourist season), Mon-Fri, 0800-1200, 1400-1800, (the rest of the year), free*, with a number of pre-Columbian gold artefacts held in the vault.

Quinta de San Pedro Alejandrino ① *daily 0930-1630; US$3, take a bus or colectivo from the waterfront, Cra 1C, to Mamatoca and ask to be dropped off at the Quinta, US$0.25*, an early 17th-century villa, is 5 km southeast of the city and dedicated to sugar cane production. This is where Simón Bolívar lived out his last days and the simple room in which he died, with a few of his personal belongings, can be seen. Other paintings and memorabilia of the period are on display in the villa, and a contemporary art gallery featuring works by artists from Venezuela to Bolivia (the countries associated with Bolívar's life), and an exhibition hall have been built on the property. The estate and gardens, with some ancient cedars, *samanes*, dignified formal statues and monuments, can be visited. It is an impressive memorial to the man most revered by Colombians.

The original building on the site of the **cathedral** ① *Cra 4, C 16/17, open for Mass daily at 0600 and 1800 (more frequently on Sun), and you may find it open at 1000*, was completed a few years after the founding of the city and was probably the first church of Colombia as proclaimed by the inscription on the west front. The present building is mainly 17th century with many additions and modifications, hence the mixture of styles. There are interesting shrines along the aisles, a fine barrel roof and chandeliers, and a grey Italian marble altar decorated with red and brown, the whole giving a light, airy and dignified impression. Notable is the monument to Rodrigo de Bastidas, founder of the city, to the left of the main entrance and the inscription by the altar steps commemorating the period when Bolívar's remains rested here from his death in 1830 to 1842 when they were transferred to the Pantheon in Caracas. The **Convento de Santo Domingo** ① *Cra 2, No 16-44*, now serves as a cultural centre and houses a library and the tourist office.

Around Santa Marta ⊜❷↟▲❻ ›› *pp189-194.*

There are rocky headlands and beaches in the bays and coves all along this coast, surrounded by hills, green meadows and shady trees. The largest sandy bay is that of Santa Marta, with Punta Betín, a promontory, protecting the harbour to the north and a headland to the south on top of which are the ruins of an early defensive fort, Castillo San Fernando. The rugged Isla El Morro lies 3 km off Santa Marta and is topped by a lighthouse. Because of the proximity of the port and the city, the beach is not recommended for bathing. There is marine eco-system research science centre, run by Colombian and German universities near the end of Punta Betín.

In addition to those listed below, there are more beaches in the bays near the Cabo and Isla de la Aguja. Villa Concha has a nice beach, popular with the locals at the weekends and a good day trip during the week. The bay is surrounded by tree-covered hills and there are a number of restaurants nearby.›› *For further information on nearby beaches, see Tayrona National Park, page 185.*

Rodadero and around

Rodadero beach, 4 km southwest of Santa Marta, is one of the best along this coast. It is part of the municipality of **Gaira**, a small town 2 km away, alongside the main road, on the Río Gaira which flows into the Caribbean at the southern end of Rodadero beach. The main part of the beach has high rise hotels of all standards, but it is attractive, tree lined, relatively clean and pleasant for bathing. Behind the promenade are the restaurants, cheaper accommodation and services. Nearby are a number of holiday flats and other holiday centres operated by public and social entities. Rodadero is a popular destination for family holidays. **Fondo de Promoción Turística** ① *C 10, No 3-10, T/F422 7548*, can provide local information and advice on hotels.

Launches leave Rodadero beach for the 10-minute trip to the **Aquarium**, north along the coast at Inca Inca Bay, where you'll find sharks, seals and many colourful fish of the Caribbean. The aquarium is linked to a small museum housing relics from Spanish galleons sunk by pirates, and a collection of coral and seashells. The boats leave from Carrera 2, Calles 10/11 every hour from 0800, and charge US$2.50 including admission. The last boat back leaves at 1600. From the aquarium, you can walk (10 minutes) to the Playa Blanca and swim in less crowded conditions than elsewhere. There is also food available at this beach.

Taganga and around

Close to Santa Marta is the fishing village and beach of **Taganga**, 15-20 minutes away by minibus (US$0.60) or taxi (US$3). Set in a tranquil semi-circular bay surrounded by scorched hills dotted with cacti, Taganga attracts its fair share of backpackers and yet, at

Around Santa Marta

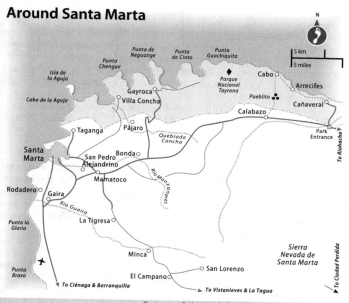

Gabriel García Márquez

More than any other Colombian, Gabriel García Márquez, or Gabo as he is affectionately known, has shaped the outside world's understanding of Colombian culture. His books champion the genre of magical realism where reality and the fantastical blur so naturally that it is difficult to discern where one ends and the other begins.

But is this what life in Colombia is really like? Schoolteachers-turned-dictators who fashion a town's children into an oppressive army, a woman so beautiful she causes the death of anyone who courts her and a child born with his eyes open because he has been weeping in his mother's womb seem improbable, especially to sceptical Western sensibilities. Yet many of the places, events and characters are based on real life. Macondo, a place which features in so many of his stories, is modelled on his birth town of Aracataca. Cartagena is easily recognizable in the unnamed port that is the setting for *Love in the Time of Cholera* while Fermina Daza and Florentino Ariza's love affair is based on his own parents' marriage. Events in *Chronicle of a Death Foretold* and *The Story of a Shipwrecked Sailor* were inspired by real life stories lifted from newspaper articles.

"Owing to his hands-on experience in journalism, García Marquez is, of all the great living authors, the one who is closest to everyday reality," wrote the American literary critic Gene H Bell-Villada, and who can challenge Gabo's interpretation of the truth when Colombia has produced real life characters like Pablo Escobar? Where else in the world would have villages that host donkey beauty contests or elect a mayor who dresses up as a superhero? Sometimes Colombian reality is stranger than Gabo's fiction.

least for now, it manages to retain its spirit as a fishing village while still catering for the demands of tourists. The swimming is good, especially on Playa Grande, 25 minutes' walk round the coast, but do not leave your belongings unattended. Taganga is quiet during week, but it is popular at weekends. Boat trips along the coast for fishing, and to the many bays and beaches are run by Hotel Ballena Azul and by a syndicate of boatmen along the beach.

Half an hour north of Taganga is Isla de la Aguja, a good fishing zone, and nearer is Playa Granate, with excellent places to snorkel and dive around the coral reefs, although lately the reefs have been showing signs of bleaching.

Ciénaga de Santa Marta

The paved coast road to Santa Marta from Barranquilla passes salt pans and skirts the Ciénaga de Santa Marta, where all types of water birds, plants and animals may be seen. Cutting off the egress to the sea to build the coast road caused an ecological disaster, but a National Environment Programme is working to reopen the canals and restore the area. There are several villages built on stilts in the lake. On the east shore of the lagoon is **Ciénaga**, famous for *cumbia* music.

Aracataca

Aracataca, 60 km south of Ciénaga and 7 km before Fundación, is the birthplace of Gabriel García Márquez. It was fictionalized as Macondo in some of his novels, notably in *One Hundred Years of Solitude*. His home is now a modest museum; it is 1½ blocks from the plaza, ask for directions. There are *residencias*, try **Hospedaje El Porvenir**, and a restaurant, but it is better to stay in Fundación. In 2007 a new train was inaugurated, **El Tren Amarillo de Macondo**, between Santa Marta and Aracataca. García Márquez himself, with a large entourage, joined the first run on 30 May 2007; however, a regular service has yet to come into operation.

Tayrona National Park ●▲» *pp189-194. Colour map 1, A3.*

The beaches of Tayrona National Park are what you would expect of a tropical paradise; thick jungle teeming with wildlife spills over onto golden sand beaches with pounding surf and there are small, secluded bays, excellent for swimming and sun bathing. There is something of the prehistoric about Tayrona. Squint your eyes and with a little imagination the flocks of pelicans that glide overhead become pterodactyls, the bright-tailed lizards that scurry underfoot as you walk through the forest paths reminders of their extinct cousins and the enormous boulders that stand guard over the beaches look like they have been there since the beginning of time. However, time and tourism have caught up with Tayrona and it is becoming increasingly popular. Prices have rocketed in the past ten years and there is now a steady stream of visitors, especially during national holidays. If you want to enjoy this corner of paradise in isolation then you should avoid going there during Semana Santa, July, August and December.

The park is named for the Tayrona (also spelt Tairona) culture, one of the most important of pre-colonial Colombia. It extends from north of Taganga for some 85 km of rugged coastline much of it fringed with coral reefs. You will see monkeys, iguanas and maybe snakes.

Ins and outs

Getting there To get to the park entrance, take a minibus from the market ① *Cra 11/ C 11*, in Santa Marta. The services are frequent and start from 0700, with the last minibus back at 1630. The journey will take 45 minutes and cost about US$2. Alternatively, go to the Riohacha road police checkpoint (taxi US$1 or bus to Mamatoca) and catch any bus there going towards Riohacha.

Park information Entry to the park is US$13 per person, US$1 for a motorcycle, US$3.50 for a car. It opens at 0800. If you arrive earlier, you may be able to pay at the car park at Cañaveral. Check with MA in Santa Marta before visiting and obtain a permit if necessary. Visitors normally stay overnight and hotels can help in arranging tours. Normally, you are advised to book accommodation before going, especially at holiday times. However, in the past few years, the park has been closed for safety, water shortages, local staffing and other reasons, only to be reopened after a short break. Unfortunately, this has given rise to confusion and contradiction. The best place for information is Santa Marta, and hopefully you will find that the park is open when you wish to visit. Information can also be found on the **Colombian Tourist Board – Proexport**'s website, www.visitcolombia.com.

It is advisable to inform park guards when walking in the park. Wear hiking boots and beware of bloodsucking insects. Take your own food and water, but no valuables as robbery has been a problem. You can hire horses to carry you and your luggage from Cañaveral to Arrecifes (US$8) and El Cabo de San Juan (US$18). Generally, there is litter everywhere along the main trails and around the campsites. In the wet, the paths are very slippery. There is no need to take guides, who charge US$20 or more per person for a day trip.

The Lost City

From the first day we set out on the trail toward the mysterious Colombian Lost City, until day six when the remarkable adventure into the heart of the sierra came to its end, I was blown away by the crystal-clear rivers that cascaded down from the upper reaches of the mountains and treated us to amazing swimming holes, beautiful falls and a much welcomed respite after hours of hiking amidst the endless jungle landscape. There are 18 or so river crossings en route to the Lost City, river pools to swim in each day and 1300 stone steps to climb at the very end of the third day that take you above the gorgeous river valleys to the high ridges blanketed in green. While the site alone is impressive, and its mysterious history and late discovery only add to its splendor, the surrounding mountain peaks dominate the endless landscape. What else lies undiscovered and hidden among such wild, rugged and beautiful terrain?

Despite the unsettling events in 2003, when eight foreigners were kidnapped along the Lost City trail, the region is currently considered safe and is heavily patrolled by the Colombian Army. The site is guarded day and night by about 40 friendly soldiers who pass their two month assignment on site by asking visitors for cigarettes in exchange for odd looking nuts that they have picked up off the jungle floor. They will also obligingly pose for photos, which they seem to enjoy more than anything else.

There is more than one option when it comes to choosing a route, some a little more difficult and with longer days, but the rewards will outweigh the fatigue. Starting and finishing the hike in different places will give you the chance to see more of the remote landscape and travel to less visited parts of this unique mountain range. For more information on trekking, see the page 188.

Craig Weigand

Out of high season the park is relatively empty and you will usually find beaches with barely a soul on them. But beware, during holiday periods, especially during Semana Santa, the amount of visitors can increase fivefold.

Around the park

There are various places where there is access to the bays and beaches by road, including an unsurfaced road from the eastern edge of Santa Marta at Bastidas north 5 km to the beach at Villa Concha (see below). On towards Riohacha beyond Bonda there is a road in poor condition to Gayraca and Neguange (where indigenous peoples had an important settlement to exploit marine salt resources), to a point near Ancón Cinto. You can reach Negangue beach by *colectivo* from Santa Marta Enquire also for transport to Villa Concha. Alternatively, take a boat from Taganga.

The normal entry to the park today is further on, turning off the main road at El Zaino, 35 km from Santa Marta and at the eastern end of the park. From there, a road leads within the park 4 km to the administrative and visitor centre with car park at **Cañaveral**, about one hour walk into the park from the gate. About 40 minutes west of Cañaveral on foot is **Arrecifes**, from where it is a 45-minute walk to El Cabo de San Juan, then up inland along a stream (La Boquita) 1½ hours on a clear path to the archaeological site of **Pueblito**. A guided tour around the site is free, but check at the entry if it is available. There are many other smaller Tayrona settlements in the park area and relics abound. At

Pueblito there are indigenous people; do not photograph them. From Pueblito you can either return to Cañaveral, or continue for a pleasant two-hour walk to Calabazo on the Santa Marta–Riohacha road. A circuit of Santa Marta, Cañaveral, Arrecifes, Pueblito, Calabazo, Santa Marta in one day is arduous, needing an early start.

Bathing is not recommended near Cañaveral or Arrecifes as there is often heavy pounding surf and the currents are treacherous. About 5 km east of Cañaveral are splendid, deserted sandy beaches. You have to walk there, but take care as the park borders marijuana-growing areas. The beach at **Villa Concha** is one of the most beautiful beaches of the area, with camping and several places to eat. Beyond Arrecifes (the sea can be dangerous on this beach) near **Cabo de San Juan** is La Piscina, a beautiful, safe natural swimming pool, excellent for snorkelling. Other safe bathing beaches can be found further along the shore but the going is difficult.

East from Tayrona

Approximately 3 km beyond Cañaveral and Guachaca along the coast is Los Angeles (Km 33.5 on the Santa Marta–Riohacha road), a camping site which offers access to fine empty beaches, excellent for surfing, at a fraction of the cost of a stay in Tayrona. Charming owner Nohemi Ramos hires out hammocks or tents for around $10 (less if you bring your own) and can cook up simple meals of freshly caught fish. She also offers guided tours of Tayrona, Pueblito and other local sights (for Spanish speakers and can put you in touch with English-speaking guides). A *cabaña* with splendid views out to sea was under construction at time of writing.

A 10-minute walk west from Los Angeles brings you to the mouth of the Río Piedras, the border of Tayrona Park, where you can bathe in the company of egrets and enjoy sights to rival any of those seen in the park. The paved coastal road continues from Tayrona and crosses into Guajira Department at Palomino, 80 km from Santa Marta, which has a fine beach and cheap *cabañas* as accommodation; 72 km from Palomino is Los Camarones and the entry to Santuario Los Flamencos, 25 km short of Riohacha.

Ciudad Perdida ▲ ▸▸ *pp189-194. Colour map 1, A3.*

Ciudad Perdida, (Lost City) is the third of the triumvirate of 'must-sees' on Colombia's Caribbean coast (the other two being Cartagena and Tayrona). The six-day trek is right up there with the Inca Trail in Peru and Roraima in Venezuela, as one of the classic South American adventures and is a truly memorable experience.

The site

Discovered only as recently as 1975, Cuidad Perdida was founded near the Río Buritaca between 500 and 700 AD and was surely the most important centre of the Tayrona culture. It stands at 1100 m on the steep slopes of Cerro Corea, which lies in the northern part of the Sierra Nevada de Santa Marta. The site, known as Teyuna to the indigenous locals, covers 400 ha and consists of a complex system of buildings, paved footpaths, flights of steps and perimetrical walls, which link a series of terraces and platforms, on which were built cult centres, residences and warehouses. Juan Mayr's book, *The Sierra Nevada of Santa Marta* (Mayr y Cabal, Bogotá), deals beautifully with Ciudad Perdida.

Archaeologists and army guards will ask you for your permit (obtainable in Santa Marta, MA, Turcol or ask at tourist office). Don't forget that Ciudad Perdida is in a National

Park: it is strictly forbidden to damage trees and collect flowers or insects. Note also that there are over 1200 steps to climb when you get there.

Trekking
Six-day trips can be organized by the tourist office and Turcol in Santa Marta (see page 193). Price includes transport, mules or porters, guide and food. It is three days there, one day (two nights) at the site, and two days back. The route goes beyond Parque Tayrona on the road to Riohacha, then past Guachaca turns inland to the roadhead at El Mamey. The climb broadly follows the Río Buritaca, and apart from crossing a number of streams, is up all the way. Ciudad Perdida is on a steep slope overlooking Río Buritaca.

Ask at hotels in Santa Marta (eg **Hotel Miramar**) or Taganga, or at the Santa Marta market for alternative tours. If you are prepared to shop around, and cook and carry your supplies and belongings, a tour could cost you less. Under no circumstances should you deal with unauthorized guides, check with the tourist office if in doubt, and try to get views of the quality of guides from travellers who have already done the trip.

You will need to take a tent or a hammock and mosquito net (on organized tours these may be supplied by the guide), a good repellent, sleeping bag, warm clothing for the night, torch, plastic bags to keep everything dry, and strong, quick-drying footwear. Small gifts for the indigenous children are appreciated.

Be prepared for heavy rain – the northern slopes of the Sierra Nevada have an average rainfall of over 4000 mm per year. Check conditions, especially information on river crossings, and ensure you have adequate food, a water bottle and water purifying tablets before you start. Try to leave no rubbish behind and encourage the guides to ensure no one else does. Going on your own is discouraged and dangerous. Route finding is very difficult and unwelcoming *indígenas*, paramilitaries and drug traders increase the hazards. Properly organized groups appear to be safe.

Sierra Nevada de Santa Marta ⊜ ›› *pp189-194.*

Minca
ⓘ *Catch a bus from C 11 with Cra 11 in Santa Marta (30 mins, $1.50). A taxi will cost about $10.*
If the heat of the coast becomes too much then a stay up in Minca is a refreshing alternative. Some 20 km from Santa Marta in the foothills of the Sierra Nevada, this small village, surrounded by coffee *fincas* and begonia plantations, is becoming increasingly popular and offers several cheap and truly charming places to stay. Horse riding, birdwatching and tours further into the Sierra Nevada can be arranged from here.

About 45 minutes walk beyond the village is **El Pozo Azul**, a local swimming spot under a waterfall, popular at weekends but almost always empty during the week, well worth a visit. El Pozo Azul was a a sacred indigenous site where purification rituals were performed and on occasion it is still used by the Kogi of the Sierra Nevada.

San Lorenzo
Beyond Minca, the partly paved road rises steeply to San Lorenzo which is surrounded by a forest of palm trees. On the way to San Lorenzo is La Victoria, a large coffee *finca* which offers tours to demonstrate the coffee-making process. It is possible to stay in *cabañas* run by the park authorities near San Lorenzo. **Aventure Colombia** organizes tours with guides, transportation, food and lodging to this section of the park.

For Sleeping and Eating price codes and other relevant information, see pages 31-36.

⊖ Sleeping

Santa Marta *p180, map p181*
Av Rodrigo de Bastidas (Cra 1) has several seafront holiday hotels while Cra 2 and connecting calles have many budget *residencias*. For groups of 4 or more, consider short-letapartments.

B Yuldama, Cra 1, No 12-19, on the seafront, T4210063, F4214932. Modern but a bit sterile, with clean rooms, a/c, cable TV and breakfast included.

C Hotel Casa Vieja, C 12, No 1-58, T4311606, www.hotelcasavieja.com. Has a Spanish feel about it with white tiling and simple, clean rooms and a/c. Prices cheaper with fan. Has friendly staff and a restaurant serving delicious Colombian food.

C Nueva Granada, C 12, No 3-17. This charming old building in the historic quarter has a peaceful courtyard with palm trees, hanging baskets, parakeets and a plunge pool. It hires bikes and has internet access. The pick of the bunch.

D Hotel Bahía, C 12, No 2-70, T4214057. Clean and modern but lacking character, it has its own restaurant and offers a safe, parking service and the option of a/c or fan.

D Turismar, Cra 1a, No 11-41, T4212408. A good option if you opt for a dorm but individual rooms are dark and spartan. Beachside, with pleasant courtyard.

E Hospedería Casa Familiar, C 10, No 2-14, T4211697, www.hospederia casafamiliar.freeservers.com. An extremely friendly and helpful family run this hostel. Offers rooms with a private bath and fan, and has a roof terrace where you can cook your own food. Has its own dive shop and organizes trips to Tayrona and Ciudad Perdida. Recommended.

E Yarimar, Cra 1, No 26-61, T4212713. A 10-min walk from the centre on the south side of town. Ramshackle but with charm, has a roof terrace of sorts and a good restaurant serving seafood.

F Miramar, C 10C, No 1C-59, T4214756. Its reputation as the ultimate backpacker's hotel precedes it. Basic but cheap rooms, a good restaurant serving delicious fruit juices, has a number of computers and Wi-Fi, and organizes tours to Tayrona Park and Ciudad Perdida.

F Residencias El Titanic, C 10C, No 1C-68, T4211947. Opposite the **Miramar**, offering similar rooms with own bath and cable TV. Clean but a little dark.

Rodadero *p183*
There are various short-let apartments available. You will probably be approached while strolling along the beach or try **Mayito Arrieta**, T4227192, T310 642 2921 (mob), mayitoarrieta@telecom.com.co. Prices start from US$40 for 2 people with a/c, TV and balcony, near the beach.

L Tamacá, Cra 2, No 11A-98, T4227016, F4227028. Resort-style hotel with fine pool, casino, large reception area and direct access to beach. All rooms have balcony with sea view, hot water and a safe but are a little sterile.

AL Cañaveral, Cra 2, No 11-65, T4227146, F4228076, **Tamacá**'s sister hotel, offering much the same but with no pool. It's further from the beach.

A Hotel La Sierra, Cra 1, No 9-47, T4227960, lasierra@germanmoraleshijos.com. Fine hotel with pleasant terrace set back from beach, rooms with balcony and Wi-Fi. Recommended.

B El Rodadero, C 11, No 1-29, T4228323, www.hotelrodadero.com. Stylish, modern building with a touch of art deco. Excellent pool, rooms with fine views of the beach and breakfast is included.

C Hotel Bariloche, C 13, No 2-59, 500 m from the beach, T422 8692, hotelbariloche

77@hotmail.com. Leafy, tiled courtyard with fountain. Rooms are clean but a little musty.
C Hotel Nashama, C 13, No 2-41, T422 5985, F422 8253. Clean but unspectacular rooms, with a/c and TV. Discounts are available for groups.
C Tucuraca, Cra 2, No 12-43, 2 mins' walk from the beach, T422 7493, hoteltucuraca@ yahoo.com. Rooms are clean with cable TV and a/c or fan, but they lack character. For groups of 4 or more, ask for apartments.

Taganga p183
A La Ballena Azul, Cra1, C 18, T4219009, www.hotel ballenaazul.com. Right on the beach, this stylish hotel offers friendly service, a fine restaurant and a terrace bar. Decorated in cool blues and whites, rooms open onto a central atrium with hanging bougainvillea and a palm tree. If you are prepared to spend a little more this is easily the best option in town. Rooms with fan or a/c, breakfast included, Wi-Fi available.
B Bahía Taganga, C 2, No 1-35, T4217620. If you want to get away from the backpacker crowd and can't afford **La Ballena Azul**, then this is your place. Up on a hill at the north end of the bay it has commanding views over the village and is tastefully decorated with clean rooms. Friendly owner.
B Casa Blanca, Cra 1, No 18-161, at the southern end of the beach, barbus85@ latinmail.com. Crumbling but has character. Each room has its own balcony with a hammock and the roof terrace is a fine place to pass the evening drinking beer with fellow guests.
C Techos Azules, Sector Dunkarinca, Cabaña 1-100, T4219141, www.techos azules.com. Off the road leading into town, this hostel is a collection of *cabañas* with good views over the bay. Offers internet, free coffee and a laundry service.
D Casa de Felipe, Cra 5A, No 19-13, 500 m from beach behind football field, T4219101, www.lacasade felipe.com. The true backpackers' choice. Has a shady garden

of bougainvillea, cacti and hammocks, its own kitchen and Wi-Fi. Some dorms available.
E Bayview Hostel, Cra 4, No 178-57, T421 9128, www.bayviewhostel.com. With a technicolour façade, it offers pleasant rooms with balconies or cheaper dorms with bunk beds out back. It has a kitchen, 2 lounges with DVD player and rocking chairs,and Wi-Fi.
E Hotel Pelikan, Cra 2, No 17-04, T421 9057. Has character and offers rooms with fan and private bath. Laundry service available.

Tayrona National Park p185
Thatched 'ecohabs' (**LL**) are available in the park, they are circular cabins built in the style of indigenous *bohíos*, which hold 2-6 people. These cost US$300 in high season for 2-4 people, US$240 in low season, and the price includes breakfast, cable TV, phone, safe and hot water. There is also a spa offering various massages and treatments. The eco in ecohabs refers more to proximity to nature than any strict environmental policy, although they do recycle. Great views over sea and jungle and a good restaurant.

Camping campsite US$15 for a 5-person tent, or US$4 for a hammock. There are facilities, but only a tiny shop, take all supplies or eat in the restaurant. An attractive site but plenty of mosquitoes. Beware of falling coconuts and omnivorous donkeys.

Arrecifes
LL Yuluca, Arrecifes beach. Huts with TV, safe, minibar, fan and ultra sonic insect repellent. US$225 for 2-4 people in high season; US$170 in low season.

Camping Yuluca (see above) charges around US$3 for a tent, US$8 for a hammock, and offers fresh water showers and toilets, very clean. There is a good restaurant, though bringing your own food is recommended, as it is expensive.

Cabo de San Juan

Camping On the path to Pueblito, there is a campsite at this beautiful double bay divided by a thin strip of sand and a large rock, where there is excellent bathing. There is also a small restaurant and hammocks for hire (US$13 in high season or US$10 in low season); there are 2 *cabañas* built on the rock that divides the 2 bays (US$50 in high season or US$43 in low season); pitching your own tent will set you back US$7, while hiring a tent for 2 persons costs $19. There are other camping and hammock places en route. There is nowhere to stay at Pueblito.

Minca *p188*

C Sierra's Sound, C Principal, T4219993, www.sierra sound.es.tl. With a veranda overlooking a rocky river, pasta home-made by its Italian owner, hot water, TV and organized tours into the Sierra Nevada, this is perhaps the most sophisticated place to stay in Minca.

D La Casona, on the hill to the right as you enter the village, T4219958, lacasona@ colombiaexotic.com. With commanding views of the valley below, this is a converted convent with a wraparound veranda. The art is by the owner, a sculptor from Bogotá, who runs the hostel with his family. Magical.

D Sans Souci, T4219968, sanssouciminca@ yahoo.com. Rambling house in beautiful garden of bamboo and exotic flowers. German owner Chris provides rooms in the house or separate apartments. Has rustic swimming pool, football pitch, kitchen and the option of a discount in exchange for gardening services. Stunning views.

⊘ Eating

Santa Marta *p180, map p181*

⫻ **Mañe Cayon**, Cra 1a, No 26-37. Next to **Manuel** on the affluent south side of town. Quality seafood in a good atmosphere.

⫻ **Manuel**, Cra 1, No 26-167, T4231449. Pricey but very good-quality seafood, popular lunchtime spot for *Samarios*.

⫻ **Donde Chucho**, Cra 2, No 16-39. A little expensive but well situated in the corner of Parque Santander. Serves seafood and pasta.

⫼ **Ricky's**, Cra 1a, No 17-05. Beachside restaurant serving international food, including Chinese. Reasonably priced.

⫼ **Merkabar**, C 10C, No 2-11. Pastas, great pancakes, good juices and specializes in seafood. Family-run, good value and provides tourist information.

⫼ **Restaurante Casa Vieja**, C 12, No 1-58. Part of the hotel, see Sleeping. Serves delicious *comida criolla*.

⫼ **Restaurante El Balcón Colonial**, C 15, No 3-35. Serves typical and cheap food.

⫼ **Yarimar**, Cra 1, No 26-37. Good seafood.

Rodadero *p183*

There are fast-food restaurants and very good juice kiosks along the seafront.

⫼ **El Banano**, Cra 2, No 8-25, also Cra 2, No 7-38. Good meat dishes and light meals, try their *carne asada con maduro* (banana) *y queso crema*, delicious. Recommended.

⫼ **El Pibe**, C 6, No 1-26. Argentine-run restaurant, serving steaks.

Taganga *p183*

Fresh fish is available along the beach and good pancakes can be found at the crêperie at the **Hotel La Ballena Azul**.

⫼ **Bitácora**, Cra 4, No 17-03, just off the beach. Serves seafood, pastas, burgers, steaks and salads.

⫼ **Donde Juanita**, Cra 1, No17-1. Serves fine home-cooked food, including fish and meat. Very cheap, with good vegetarian options.

⫼ **Yiu Nu Sagu**, C 12, No 1-08. Beachside pizzería, large helpings.

🅞 Bars and clubs

Santa Marta *p180, map p181*
Santa Marta is a party town with many new clubs, discos and bars opening every week. The website www.samarios.com, is an excellent resource for finding out what's going on at night.
Barrio Sumario, C 17, between Cra 3 and 4 (on same road as **La Puerta**). A popular bar playing local music.
La Escollera, C 5, No 4-107, outside of town at El Lago. Huge club under an open straw roof. Concerts are staged here.
La Puerta, C 17, between Cra 3 and 4. Excellent bar and atmosphere in a colonial house. Highly recommended.

Rodadero *p183*
There are many bars and nightclubs here.
Burukuka, Vía al Edif Cascadas del Rodadero, T3013746620, www.burukuka.com. Steak bar looking out over Rodadero beach.
La Escollera, C 5, No 4-107, Lagunita, T422 9590, www.la-escollera.com. One of the best, open till late.

Taganga *p183*
El Garaje, T4219003. Plays hip hop and other forms of electronic music. Starts late, finishes late.
Mojito Net, C 14, No 1b-61. Open 0800-0200, happy hour 1400-2100. Live music, open mic sessions, wine, cocktails, food and internet.

🅔 Festivals and events

Santa Marta *p180, map p181*
Jun/Jul Festival Patronal de Santa Marta. Celebrates the founding of the city with parades and musical performances.
Aug Fiesta del Mar Aquatic events and a beauty contest.
Sep International Caribbean Theatre Festival. Contributions from many of the Caribbean countries.

🅞 Shopping

Santa Marta *p180, map p181*
Look around for small artefacts and figurines in the indigenous tradition, sometimes sold on the beach. Best if you can find the artists who live in and around Santa Marta.

Artesan shops
The market is at C 11/Cra 11, just off Av del Ferrocarril and has stalls with excellent selections of hammocks.
Artesanías La 15, C15 with Cra 9, T310 730 9606, good selection of typical handicrafts;
Artesanías Sisa, Cra 4, No 16-42 on the Plaza Catedral, T4214510, local handicrafts including bags, hammocks and sombreros;
José Pertuz, C 38, up the hill beyond Cra 17.

Shopping malls
El Barco, C 13, No 5-22; **El Emporio**, Cra 9, C 11/12; **La Revelación**, C11 opposite Cacharrería Estrella de la Moda.

🅰 Activities and tours

Santa Marta *p180, map p181*
For guided trips to Quinta San Pedro Alejandrino and other local points of interest, ask at your hotel, travel agencies or the tourist office. Similarly, if you wish to visit the Marine Centre at Punta Betín you will need a boat or a permit to pass through the port area, so ask for guidance. For trips to Tayrona National Park, Ciudad Perdida and the Sierra Nevada, see under the relevant destination. Coach tours also go to Aracataca and Ciénaga de Santa Marta from Santa Marta.

Tour operators
Aviatur, C 23, No 4-17, T421 3848. Good service.
Innova Aircraft de Colombia, T466 5875, www.innovaaircraftdecolombia.com. Offers flights over the Sierra Nevada, Tayrona Park and other destinations.

Nohemi Ramos, Tierra Mar Aire, C 15, No 2-60, T421 5161. Amex agent and full tourist travel agent.

Sendero Tairona, Cra 3, No 18-46, T4229505, clubsenderotayrona@gmail.com. A hiking club, offers trips into Tayrona Park and the Sierra Nevada from US\$130, which includes transport, food, guides and accommodation.

Sierra Tours, C 22, No 16-61, Santa Marta, www.sierratours-trekking.com. Come highly recommended for tours.

Turcol, Cra 1C, No 20-15, T/F421 2256. Arranges trips and provides a guide service.

Rodadero *p183*
Diving shops

Caribbean Divers, Cra 1, No 5-113, T422 0878, info@carribbeandiverscol.com. Offers PADI and NAUI qualifications. A mini course costs US\$100.

Taganga *p183*
Diving shops

There are 4 dive shops in Taganga.

Oceano Scuba, Cra 1A, No 17-07, T4219004, www.oceano scuba.com.co. PADI courses, 2, 3 and 4 days from \$70.

Octopus Diving Center, C 15, No 1b-14, T3173277570, octopusdivingcenter@ gmail.com. PADI, NAUI and BIS courses. Night and wreck dives are offered. English spoken.

Poseidon Dive Center, C 18, No 1-69, T4219224, www.poseidondivecenter.com. PADI courses at all levels and the only place on the Colombian Caribbean coast to offer an instructor course. Offers a tourist package with no sales tax (16%). German owner, with English and Croatian spoken. Own pool for beginners, also has rooms to rent.

Tayrona Dive Center, Cra 2, No 18a-22, T4219195, www.tayronadivecenter.com. Mini course with 2 dives is US\$77.

Tour operators

Sierra Tours, C 17, No 1-18, www.sierra tours-trekking.com. Highly recommended for tours.

Tayrona National Park *p185*

Ecoturt come highly recommended for guided tours of Pueblito and other parts of the park. Speak to Nohemi Ramos or Jarven Rodríguez, T3163738846, ecoturt@ latinmail.com. Some English spoken.

Ciudad Perdida *p187*

Recommended guides:

Magic Tour Taganga, T4219432, www.magic tourstaganga.com. Work closely with La Ballena Azul.

Sierra Tours, C 22, No 16-61, Santa Marta and C 17, No 1-18, Taganga, T421 9401, T420 3413, www.sierratours-trekking.com, info@sierratours-trekking.com. Are highly recommended and prices start at \$250 for a minimum of 5 people.

⊕ Transport

Santa Marta *p180, map p181*
Air

There are daily flights to Bogotá and Medellín; and connections to other cities. During the tourist season get to the airport early and book well ahead (the same goes for bus reservations).

Airline offices Avianca, Edif de los Bancos, Cra 2B y C 14, T214 4018, T432 0106 at airport; Centro Comercial Rex, Cra 3, No 17-27, Local 102, T421 0120; and at C 7, No 2-15, T422 0118.

Bus

To **Barranquilla**, 7 daily, 2 hrs, US\$5.50, Brasilia. To **Medellín**, 6 daily, 15 hrs, US\$52, Brasilia or Copetran. To **Bogotá**, 7 daily, 16 hrs, US\$67, Brasilia or Copetran. To **Cartagena**, 5 hrs, US\$10-11, Brasilia. To **Riohacha**, 4 hrs, US\$11.50. Frequent buses to **Maicao**, 4-5 hrs, US\$17 for a/c or cheaper for buses without. Brasilia runs a bus through to **Maracaibo**, daily, US\$28. To **Bucaramanga**, 9 hrs, US\$45, Brasilia or Copetran. To **Mompós** there's a door to door *colectivo* service, US\$30 with Asotranstax, C 23, No 4-27.

Sea

Although cruise ships stop here, it is difficult to find onward passage.

---

❶ Directory

Santa Marta *p180, map p181*
Banks Most banks and ATMs are in Plaza Bolívar eg **Banco Occidente**, good rates for MasterCard. There are plenty of cash machines. For currency exchange, 3rd block of C 14, many others on this street. In Rodadero, Apto 201, Cra 1, No 9-23. Santa Marta is a good place to exchange pesos into Venezuelan bolivares. **Emergencies** Police, T112. **Immigration** DAS Office, Cra 8, No 26A-15, T421 4917, Sr Chávez (DAS director at Santa Marta) runs a tight ship and is not flexible. **Internet** Tama Café, C16 with Cra 13, open 0800-1230 and 1400-1830, sells delicious food too. **Telephone** Telecom, C 13, No 5-17.

Rodadero *p183*
Banks For currency exchange, Apto 201, Cra 1, No 9-23.

Taganga *p183*
Internet Playanet, Cra 1, No 15-9, T421 9296, also sells credit for mobile phones.

East to Venezuela

Along the coast from Santa Marta the lush vegetation of the foothills of the Sierra Nevada gives way to flat expanses of scorched earth where only a scrub-like tree known as trupillo and the cactus survive. The change in landscape marks the beginning of La Guajira peninsula, home to the Wayúu. It is also the northernmost tip of South America and it certainly feels like the end of the world; an arid and unforgiving terrain which nonetheless offers a home to vast flocks of flamingos and other birds and a chance to mingle with one of Colombia's best-preserved indigenous cultures. Riohacha may be a departmental capital but it feels more like a sleepy fishing village, though it livens up somewhat at the weekend. Musichi and Manaure with their flocks of flamingos and salt works will be of interest to nature lovers and Cabo de la Vela with its turquoise waters that lap against a desert landscape is a sight to behold. If you have the time and energy then Parque Natural Nacional Macuira, an oasis of tropical green sprouting out of the semi desert, and Punta Gallinas will cap off a trip into this strange and sometimes ethereal land. The difficulties in transport only add to the sense of adventure this peninsula presents. » *For listings, see pages 200-202.*

Riohacha » ⬤🅑🅕🅞🔺🅑🅖🅒 » *pp200-202. Colour map 1, A5.*

Riohacha, 160 km east of Santa Marta, is capital of Guajira Department. Formerly a port, today it has the ambience of a provincial fishing town. The city was founded in 1545 by Nicolás Federmann. One of Riohacha's resources of those days were oyster beds, and the pearls were valuable enough to tempt Drake to sack it. Pearling almost ceased during the 18th century and the town was all but abandoned. José Prudencia Padilla, who was born here, was in command of the republican fleet that defeated the Spaniards in the Battle of Lago Maracaibo in 1823. He is buried in the **cathedral**, and there is a statue in the central park which bears his name. *Riohacha y Los Indios Guajiros*, by Henri Candelier, a Frenchman's account of a journey to the area 100 years ago, is very interesting on the life of the Wayúu.

The **airport**, José Prudencio Padilla, is south of the town towards Tomarrazón and the main **bus terminal** is on Calle 15 (Avenida El Progreso)/Carrera 11. It has good white-sand beaches lined with coconut palms and a bustling market. At weekends it fills up, and bars and music spring up all over the place. The sea is clean, despite the red silt stirred up by the waves and it is a good place to take stock before pushing through into the more remote areas of La Guajira. There is a tourist office, **Cortguajira** ① *Cra 7/C 1, Av La Marina, T727 2482, F727 4728*, which is well organized.

Santuario Los Flamencos » *Colour map 1, A5.*

The Santuario de Fauna y Flora Los Flamencos is 7000 ha of saline vegetation including some mangroves and lagoons. There are several small, and two large, saline lagoons (Laguna Grande and Laguna de Navío Quebrado), separated from the Caribbean by sand bars. The latter is near Camarones (take a *colectivo* from Riohacha), which is just off the main road. Some 3 km beyond Camarones is 'La Playa', a popular beach to which some *colectivos* continue at weekends. The two large lagoons are fed by several intermittent streams which form deltas at the south point of the lakes and are noted for the many colonies of flamingos, some of whom are there all year, others congregate between November and May, during the wet season when some fresh water enters the lagoons.

A zoom lens is recommended for photographs. The birds are believed to migrate to and from the Dutch Antilles, Venezuela and Florida.

Across Laguna de Navío Quebrado is a warden's hut on the sand bar, ask to be ferried across by local fishermen or the park guards who are very helpful. There is a visitor centre and some accommodation. Camping is permitted near the centre. Take plenty of water if walking. The locals survive, after the failure of the crustaceans in the lagoons, on tourism and ocean fishing. There are several bars/restaurants and two shops on the beach.

Valledupar ⬤❀⬤⬤ ▸▸ pp200-202. Colour map 1, B4.

→ Phone code: 5. Population 348,000.

Some 125 km south of Santa Marta the main road to Bucaramanga and Bogotá crosses from Magdalena into César Department. Several roads lead east to Valledupar, the best of which goes from Bosconia, 157 km from Santa Marta. At Km 303, El Burro, is the unpaved

Riohacha

Sleeping
Arenas 3
Almirante Padilla 1
Arimaca 2

Gimaura 7
Internacional 4
Tunebo 5
Yalconia del Mar 6

Eating
Papillon 1
El Malecón 2
Monik 3

road to Talameque and El Banco on the Río Magdalena, and 31 km beyond is La Mata where the oil pipeline from the border area with Venezuela crosses on its way to Coveñas on the Caribbean coast. At San Alberto, 437 km from Santa Marta, the new highway goes right to follow the Río Magdalena to Honda and is now the quickest way to the centre of the country and Bogotá. The old road continues to Bucaramanga, 530 km from Santa Marta. A paved road also comes from the northeastern towns of Maicao and Riohacha to Valledupar, capital of César Department. The town is on the Río Guatapurí which rises in the heart of the Sierra Nevada de Santa Marta.

The Alfonso López **airport** is on the southern outskirts of the city, 3 km from the centre, and a short walk from the bus terminal. A taxi to the centre will cost US$3. The **bus terminal**① *Av Salguero (Cra 7A)*, is 3 km down the road to Robles and Maicao.

One of the few old buildings in the town, which was founded in the middle of the 16th century, is the **Iglesia La Concepción** which overlooks the central plaza named after a past president, Alfonso López Pumarejo. Nearby is a fine balconied colonial façade of the **Casa del Maestre Pavejeau**, and there is an interesting display of indigenous cultures in the **Casa de la Cultura**① *Cra 6, No 16A-24, T572 3271*. Valledupar claims to be the home of the *vallenato* music.

Guajira Peninsula ▶▶ ◉❶❷ *pp200-202. Colour map 1, A6.*

Beyond Riohacha to the east is the arid and sparsely inhabited Guajira Peninsula, with its magnificent sunsets. The indigenous peoples here, the Guajiros, collect *dividivi* (pods from a strangely wind-bent tree, the *Caesalpina coriaria*, which are mainly used for tanning), tend goats and fish. Look out for the coloured robes worn by the women.

Ins and outs

To visit a small part of the Peninsula you can book a tour with one of the many tour companies in Riohacha (see Activities and tours, page 201). Alternatively, you can catch a ride in a *carrito*, a taxi shared with three others, to Uribia or Manaure (US$7) and from there on to Cabo de la Vela.

Manaure and around

Manaure is known for its salt flats southwest of the town. Hundreds of workers dig the salt and collect it in wheelbarrows, a bizarre sight against the glaring white background. If you walk along the beach for an hour, past the salt works, there are several lagoons where flamingos congregate. Around 14 km from Manaure in this direction is **Musichi**, an important haunt of the flamingoe, sometimes out of the wet season. Note that they may be on the other side of the lagoon and difficult to see. You can hire a moto-taxi in Manaure that will take you towards Musichi to see the flamingos.

From Manaure there are early morning busetas to **Uribia** (20 minutes, US$1), and from there to Maicao, another hour. In Uribia, known as the indigenous capital of Colombia, you can buy authentic local handicrafts by asking around. There is a **Wayúu festival** here annually in May, and *alijunas* (white people) are welcome, but ask permission before taking photographs. You can get *camionetas* from Uribia to to **Cabo de la Vela** (about two hours once everyone has been dropped off at their various *ranchitos*, US$3). The drive is spectacular with the final few kilometers involving a bumpy ride across a shimmering, dried-out salt lake that generates mirages. Cabo de la Vela is where the Wayúu believe their souls go after death, and is known as Jepira. It consists of a number of shacks haphazardly

Música tropical

No country in South America has a greater variety of musical genres than Colombia, and nowhere is music more abundant than in the fertile breeding grounds of the North Coast. The diversity of musical expression comes from a mixture of African, indigenous and European influences.

On the coast, *música tropical* is an umbrella term used to encompass the many hybrids that have arisen over the years. Most popular among these is *vallenato*, a form of music which originated with farmers around Valledupar and which primarily uses the accordion, *guacharaca* (a tube with ridges carved into it, which when scraped with a fork produces a beat) and the *caja vallenata* (a cylindrical drum brought over by African slaves) as its instruments.

Vallenato is the current favourite but it has its roots in a more ancient genre, *cumbia*. *Cumbia* began as a courtship dance practiced among the slave population – it is believed to derive from Guinean *cumbe* – and later mixed with European and indigenous instruments, such as the guitar, the accordion and the gaita, a type of flute used by the *indígenas* of the Sierra Nevada de Santa Marta. *Cumbia* is celebrated for bringing together Colombia's three main ethnic groups and it was used as an expression of resistance during the campaign for independence from the Spanish. *Cumbia* has many other derivatives, such as *porro*, *gaita*, *fandango* and *bullerengue*.

The newest genre to emerge is *champeta*. This is the most African of the genres, it takes its influence from *soukous* and *compas*, and is characterized by very sensual dancing. It gained popularity among the black population of Cartagena and San Palenque de Basilio in the 1980s.

---

scattered round a two-mile bay. The barren landscape of shrubs and cacti only serves to accentuate the colour of the water, which glimmers in a dozen shades of aquamarine.

Getting to Cabo de la Vela independently is a time-consuming and at times uncomfortable experience, but that's also part of the fun. It is far easier (but more expensive) to book a tour from Riohacha.

Macuira National Park

ⓘ *Entry is free.*

Towards the northeast tip of the Guajira peninsula is the Serranía de Macuira, named after the Makui people, ancestors of the Wayúu. The 25,000-ha park is entirely within the Wayúu reservation. It consists of a range of hills over 500 m, which have a microclimate of their own creating an oasis of tropical forest in the semi-desert. The highest point is **Cerro Palúa**, 865 m, and two other peaks are over 750 m. Moisture comes mainly from the northeast, which forms clouds in the evening that disperse in the early morning. The average temperature is 29°C and there is 450 mm of mist/rain providing water for the streams that disappear into the sand once they reach the plains. Macuira's remoteness gives it interesting flora and fauna and notable wildlife includes the Cardinal bird and 15 species of snake, including coral snakes. There are also Wayúu settlements little affected by outsiders, where the indigenous people cultivate cashew nuts, coconuts and plantains, as well as collecting dividivi pods. The rangers are all locals and are very friendly. A recommended walk in the park is a visit to the 40 m-high El Chorro waterfall, a delightful lush, green area.

Border essentials: Colombia–Venezuela

Maicao

Note that there is no Venezuelan consul in Maicao. If you need a visa, get it in Barranquilla, Cartagena or Riohacha. Entering Venezuela, a transit visa will only do if you have an confirmed ticket to a third country within three days.

Transport *Colectivos*, known as *por puestos* in Venezuela, run from Maicao to Maracaibo, US$6 per person, or there is an infrequent *microbus*, US$3.50. There are very few buses to Venezuela after 1200. **Brasilia** bus company has its own security compound, non-passengers are not allowed in. You can change money, buy bus tickets and food before your journey. *Por puestos* wait here for passengers to Maracaibo; it is a very easy transfer.

Paraguaipoa

If travelling by *por puesto* make sure the driver stops at the Colombian entry post. If not you will have to return later to complete formalities. With all the right papers, border crossing is easy.

Transport Minibuses or *busetas* can be caught from the terminal de Maracaibo (T0261 7225649) to Maicao for US$13, but they only run from 0400 to 0800. *Carritos*, taxis shared with three other passengers, continue to leave Maracaibo until 1500 (US$18 per person).

Beyond Macuira is **Punta Gallinas**, the northernmost point in South America and a spectacular location. Nearby is Taroa, where sand dunes drop directly into the sea.

Ins and outs To reach the Parque Natural Nacional Macuira you must travel northeast from Uribia along the mineral railway, then either round the coast past Bahía Portete, or direct across the semi-desert, to Nazareth on the east side of the park. There are no tourist facilities anywhere nearby and no public transport, though trucks may take you from the Bahía Portete area to **Nazareth** (six to eight hours), if you can find one. Nazareth is a Wayúu village where you can stay the night, where food is available and where you can find local guides. The best way to visit is to contract your own jeep and guide, recommended is **Kaí Eco Travel** ① *T7177173, www.kaiecotravel.com*, run by a network of indigenous families. A full tour of the peninsula, with visits to Cabo de la Vela, Parque Natural Nacional Macuira and Punta Gallinas costs US$540 per person, including transport, accomodation and food. Beyond Cabo de la Vela we strongly advise you take a tour (see page 201) as there is no public transport, little Spanish is spoken and the locals can be hostile. **Eco-Guías** in Bogotá and **Aventure Colombia** in Cartagena also arrange trips here from time to time.

Note The Guajira peninsula is not a place to travel alone, parties of three or more are recommended. If going in your own transport, check the situation before setting out. Also remember it is hot, it is easy to get lost, there is little cover and very little water. Locals, including police, are very helpful in giving lifts.

Maicao → *Phone code: 5. Colour map 1, A5.*

The paved Caribbean coastal highway, continues from Riohacha inland to Maicao, 78 km, close to the Venezuelan border. Now that there are no flights from Barranquilla to

Maracaibo, taxi or bus to Maicao and *colectivo* to Maracaibo is the most practical route. There is a new bus terminal to the east of town.

Maicao, is full of Venezuelan contraband, and is still at the centre of the narcotics trade It has a real Wild West feel to it. Most commercial premises close before 1600, and after 1700 the streets are unsafe, though in recent years security has improved somewhat.

⊙ East to Venezuela listings → Phone code: 5.

For Sleeping and Eating price codes and other relevant information, see pages 31-36.

⊜ Sleeping

Riohacha *p195, map p196*
A Arimaca, C 1, No 8-75, T7273481, arimaca@col3.telecom.com.co. Impressive high tower with clean, light and spacious rooms, some with reception room, all with balconies and magnificent sea views. There is a fine swimming pool on 2nd floor. Could do with a lick of paint.
B Hotel Arenas, Cra 5, No 1-25, T7275424. Clean rooms if a little dark, with cable TV and a/c. Helpful staff and near the beach.
B Gimaura (state-owned), Av La Playa, T272 266. Rooms are light and airy, with balconies looking out to sea. Breakfast is included and the staff are helpful. Has a swimming pool and its own tour agency. 5-min walk to town.
D Tunebo, Cra 10, No 12A-02, T7273326, marytunebo@hotmail.com. Friendly staff, some a/c. Rooms are a little dark and far from the action.
E Almirante Pedilla, Cra 6/C 2. Crumbling but with character, has an inviting patio and a restaurant with cheap *almuerzo*. It's clean, friendly and very central.
E Internacional, Cra 7, No 13-37, T7273483. Down an alleyway off the market, friendly with a pleasant restaurant on the patio. Free iced water. Recommended.
E Yalconia del Mar, Cra 7, No 11-26, T7273487. Private bath, clean, safe, helpful, halfway between beach and bus station.

Valledupar *p196*
B Vajamar, Cra 7, No 16A-30, T5743939. With breakfast, pool and expensive food.

E Hotel/Restaurant Nutibara, C19, No 9-19, T5743225. Rooms with a/c, reakfast included.
F Residencia El Triunfo, C 19, No 9-31. Small rooms with fan, clean and with bath.

Manaure and around *p197*
Manaure
D Palaaima, Cr 6, No 7-25, T7178195. Comfortable, cool rooms with a/c or fan, helpful. There are always Wayúu locals hanging around the hotel who are eager to talk about their culture and traditions.

Uribia
G Flamingo, G Uribia and 1 basic *residencia* with no running water.

Cabo de la Vela
Along the coast, ask anyone and you will probably be able to get fried fish, coconut rice and a place to hang a hammock (US$4).
D Iguaran. Conchita hires out *cabañas* made in the traditional Wayúu style.
E Mamicha. Good beds and flushing toilets.
E-G El Caracol. You can hire a basic *cabaña* or sling a hammock.

Maicao *p199*
B Hotel Maicao Internacional, C 12, No 10-90, T7267184. Good rooms with a/c, friendly staff and a rooftop swimming pool and bar. A good option in Maicao.
B Maicao Plaza, C 10, No 10-28, T7260310. Clean and spacious, this hotel offers a/c, cable TV, and en suite bathrooms with cold water.
C Los Medanos, Cra 10, No 11-25, T7260467. This hotel has clean, large rooms, though they are a bit dark. Extras include a/c, cable TV, minibar, a restaurant and a disco. Its private bathrooms have cold water only.

Hammocks

There's no better way to enjoy Colombia's beaches than to relax in a hammock, and there are abundant conveniently located palm trees to use as supports. Plenty of places hire them out but for true comfort its best to buy your own.

The hammocks developed by the Wayúu are made up of intricately woven threads of cotton that form a crocheted net. These are known as *chinchorros* and they often feature elaborate tassels.

The other most common style, uses brightly coloured woven cotton or wool to form a large stretch of material.

San Jacinto, a couple of hours south of Cartagena, is the capital of Colombia's hammock industry and the best place to find a bargain, but the market in Santa Marta also has a good selection. For *chinchorros*, the best places are the market in Riohacha and Uribia's handicraft shops in La Guajira.

D El Dorado, Cra 10, No 12-45, T7267242. A little dilapidated, but it has a/c, TV and a good water supply.

🍴 Eating

Riohacha *p195, map p196*
Many ice cream and juice bars, and small *asados*, serving large, cheap selections of barbecued meat can be found at the western end of the seafront.

El Malecon, C 1, No 3-43. Good selection of seafood and meats served in a palm-thatched barn looking out to sea. There is music and dancing in the evenings. A good place for people watching.

Papillon, Cra 7, No 3-27. Selection of crêpes, salads and sandwiches, served on a peaceful, brightly coloured patio. The owner is a knowledgeable, Belgian ex-photojournalist.

Restaurante Monik, Cra 7, No 5-16. Cheap and cheerful, serving typical Guajira dishes.

Manaure and around *p197*
Cabo de la Vela

El Caracol. Expensive but good, serving catch of the day (try the *langostina al ajillo*).

Valledupar *p196*
Hotel/Restaurant Nutibara, next door to Residencia El Triunfo. Cheap meals, excellent fruit juices.

✦ Festivals and events

Valledupar *p196*
Apr Festival de la Leyenda Vallenata, www.festivalvallenato.com. One of the most important music festivals in Colombia.

○ Shopping

Riohacha *p195, map p196*
Good hammocks sold in the market. The best places for buying local items are **La Casa de la Manta Guajira**, Cra 6/C 12, be prepared to bargain; **Ojo de Agua**, C 2/Cra 9; and **Rincón Artesanal Dicaime**, C 2, No 5-61, T7273071.

⛰ Activities and tours

Riohacha *p195, map p196*
Tour operators
Guajira Total, stand in front of **Hotel Almirante Padilla** on seafront, T7272328, T3157148057 (mob). Trips to Wayúu *rancherías*, Manaure and Cabo de la Vela.
Guajira Viva, C 3, No 5-08, loc 1, T7270607. 5-day tours to Alta Guajira, Cabo de la Vela, Santuario de Fauna y Flora los Flamencos.
Lucho Freyle, T728 2885, T3126471434 (mob). Wayúu guide in Riohacha, jeep tours around La Guajira and Cabo de la Vela.

Operadora Turística Wayúu, C 1A, No 4-35, T311-400 7985 (mob). Wayúu-run and can be found on the seafront. Sells beautiful, colourful Wayúu *mochilas*. Organizes tours to *rancherías* and Cabo de la Vela.

Uribia
Kaí Eco Travel, T7177713, T3114362830 (mob), www.kaiecotravel.com. Run by a network of Wayúu families, organizes tours to Cabo de la Vela, Parque Natural Nacional Macuira, Punta Gallinas. Highly recommended. **Kaishi**, T3114296315, T3164296315 (mob). Speak to Andrés Orozco, this company organizes jeep tours around La Guajira.

● Transport

Riohacha *p195, map p196*
Early morning is best for travel, transport is scarce in the afternoon.
Air
1 flight a day **Bogotá**, Avianca; where connections to other cities can be made.

Bus
It is best to travel from Riohacha in a luxury bus, in the early morning, as these are less likely to be stopped and searched for contraband. Brasilia runs Pullman buses to **Maicao**, every 30 mins from 0630-1700, US$5.50.

No direct buses to **Cabo de la Vela**: travel to Uribia and wait for a jeep (leaves when full). It's a long and uncomfortable journey.

Some *colectivos* for **Uribia** and the northeast leave from the new market, 2 km southeast on the Valledupar road.

Taxi
Coopcaribe Taxis travel throughout the region and can be picked up almost anywhere in town, especially close to the old market area near the Hotel Internacional or outside Drogas La Rebaja. Daily to **Uribia**, 1½ hrs, US$7; **Manaure**, 1¾ hrs, US$8. They leave when full (4 people), be prepared to pay slightly more if there are no travellers.

Valledupar *p196*
Air
There are flights Mon-Fri to **Barranquilla**.

Bus
To **Barranquilla**, 5-6 hrs, US$11; **Bucaramanga**, 8 hrs US$30; **Santa Marta**, 4 hrs; **Cartagena**, US$13 with Expreso Brasilia.

Maicao *p199*
Bus
Brasilia has a service every 30 mins from 0630-1700 to **Riohacha**, US$5.50; **Santa Marta**, 3 hrs, US$17; **Barranquilla**, 4-5 hrs, US$22; **Cartagena**, 6 hrs, US$27.

1 bus daily to **Bogotá** at 1345, US$72; to **Medellín**, 3 daily, 0915, 1330, 1615, US$77. Regular service to **Barranquilla**, US$22.

● Directory

Riohacha *p195, map p196*
Banks Most are on Parque Almirante. Banco de Bogotá, Cra 7, between C 2/3, for Visa, Mon-Fri, 0800-1600, Sat, 0900-1200. **Embassies and consulates** Venezuela, Cra 7, No 3-08, p7-B, T727 4076, F727 3967, Mon-Thu 0900-1300, Fri 0900-1500, if you need a visa, you should check all requirements for your nationality before arriving at this consulate. Travellers report it is easier to get a Venezuelan visa in Barranquilla. **Immigration** DAS Office (immigration) C 5 y Cra 5, open 0800-1200, 1400-1800. **Internet and telephone** On Parque Almirante. **Post office** C 2, Cra 6/7.

Valledupar *p196*
Banks You can change money at *casas de cambio* on Calle 16.

San Andrés and Providencia

San Andrés and Providencia are destinations most Colombians dream about visiting at least once in their lifetime. Closer to Nicaragua than to the Colombian mainland – there is a running dispute between the two countries over sovereignty – these Caribbean islands have what locals have dubbed 'the sea of seven colours', though it often seems like more. The waters around this archipelago play host to a variety of marine life, and the clarity of the sea makes this one of the best diving destinations in the Caribbean. In 2000, UNESCO declared the archipelago a World Biosphere Reserve, christened The Seaflower. At 32 km in length, the Old McBean Lagoon barrier reef off Providencia is the third largest in the world. ▸▸ *For listings, see pages 209-212.*

Background

San Andrés and Providencia share a coastline rich in coral reefs, white sand cays and waters of extraordinary colours, but are in fact very different. San Andrés, the larger island, is a popular mass tourism destination, replete with resort hotels and discos. Providencia has quietly observed its big sister's development, decided it does not want to follow the same path, and has put in place certain restrictions to halt the encroachment of package tourism.

The original inhabitants are mostly the descendants of Jamaican slaves brought over by English pirates such as Henry Morgan, and with the arrival of English, Dutch, French and Spanish settlers over the years this has led to an extraordinary genealogical mix. Today, especially in San Andrés, much of the original culture has been diluted and about 50% of the population is now made up by immigrants from mainland Colombia. The remainder are locals and there are some Lebanese and Turkish communities. Immigration is less pronounced in Providencia.

San Andrés and Providencia are famous in Colombia for their music, styles include the local form of calypso, soca, reggae and church music, as well as schottische, quadrille, polka and mazurka, the musical legacies of the various European communities which settled here. A number of good local groups perform on the islands and in Colombia. Concerts are held at the **Old Coliseum** (every Saturday at 2100 in the high season). There is a cultural centre at Punta Hansa in San Andrés town.

San Andrés Island

Punta Norte
Johnny Cay
Bahía Sardinas
San Andrés
Punta Hansa
Roca del Pescador
Punta Paraíso
Bahía de San Andrés
Baptist Church
Bahía Baja
Seaquarium
La Loma (104m)
El Acuario
La Laguna
Haynes Cay
Cueva de Morgan
Rocky Cay
Caribbean Sea
San Luis
El Cove
Bahía Sonora
N
1 km
1 miles
Monte Derecho
La Piscinita

Sleeping 🛏
Casa Harb 1
Marazul 2
Sunset 3

Eating 🍴
Bibi's Place 1

Hoyo Soplador
Punta Sur

After their discovery by Colombus on his fourth trip to the Caribbean, their early colonial history was dominated by the conflicts between Spain and England, though the Dutch occupied Providencia for some years. English Puritans arrived on Providencia from Bermuda and England in 1629 and later moved to San Andrés. The English left in 1641, but Creole English remained the dominant language until recent times and is still widely spoken. Surnames such as Whittaker, Hooker, Archbold, Robinson, Howard and Newell are also common. Providencia later became a pirate colony, shared between the Dutch and the English before it was taken back by the Spanish and assigned to the Vice Royalty of New Granada (modern day Colombia) in 1803. In 1818 French Corsair Louis-Michel Aury successfully invaded Providencia and declared it part of the United States of Argentina and Chile, using it to capture Spanish cargo to bolster the burgeoning Latin American independence movement. Finally, in 1822 San Andrés, Providencia and Santa Catalina were adhered to the newly independent state of Gran Colombia.

The islands are 770 km north of continental Colombia, 849 km southwest of Jamaica, and 240 km east of Nicaragua. This proximity has led Nicaragua to claim them from Colombia in the past. Three battleships patrol San Andrés to guard against any invasion by the Nicaraguans.

San Andrés and around ▸ ⊖❼❼❀▲⊖❶ pp209-212. Colour map 1, inset.

→ Phone code: 8. Population: 77,000.

San Andrés, a coral island, is 11 km long, rising at its highest to 120 m. The town, commercial centre, major hotel sector and airport are at the northern end. A good view of the town can be seen from **El Cliff** (see below). San Andrés is a popular, safe and local holiday destination for Colombians.

Ins and outs
Getting there A cheap way to visit San Andrés is by taking a charter flight from Bogotá or another major city for a weekend or a week, with accomodation and food included. See the

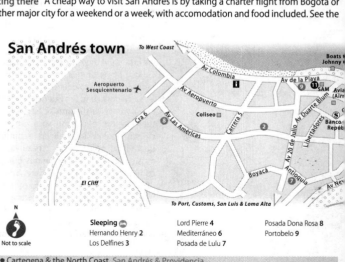

San Andrés town

Sleeping ●
Hernando Henry **2**
Los Delfines **3**

Lord Pierre **4**
Mediterráneo **6**
Posada de Lulu **7**

Posada Dona Rosa **8**
Portobelo **9**

newspapers, which usually have supplements on Wednesday or Thursday. However, the hotel and a restaurant may not be satisfactory. You may wish to go for a cheap airfare and choose where to stay on arrival. The airport is 15 minutes' walk from town. Buses to the centre and San Luis go from across the road. A taxi is US$5.50, a *colectivo* US$0.70. Cruise ships and tours go to San Andrés but there are no other, official passenger services by sea. ▸ *See Transport, page 212.*

Getting around Buses run every 15 minutes on the eastern side of the island, US$0.30, and more often at night and during the holidays. Taxis around the island cost US$11, but in town fares double after 2200.

Bicycles are easy to hire but are usually in poor condition, so choose your own bike and check all parts thoroughly. Motorbikes and golf buggies are also easy to hire.

Tourist information There is a tourist office at the airport and at ① *Circunvalar Av Newball, diagonal Club Náutica, Mon-Fri 0800-1200, 1400-1800,* staff are helpful and English is spoken. They can also provide maps and hotel lists. On arrival in San Andrés, you must buy a tourist card, US$9, which is also valid for Providencia so don't lose it. You must also have an onward or return ticket.

Sights

Besides the beautiful cays and beaches on the eastern side, see **Hoyo Soplador** (South End), a geyser-like hole through which the sea spouts into the air when the wind is in the right direction. The west coast is less spoilt, but there are no beaches on this side. Instead there is **El Cove** (The Cove), the island's deepest anchorage, and **Cueva de Morgan** (Morgan's Cave), reputed hiding place for pirate's treasure, which is penetrated by the sea through an underwater passage. Next to Cueva de Morgan is a **museum** ① *entry US$2.70,* with exhibitions telling the history of the coconut, lots of paraphernalia salvaged from wrecks around the island and a replica pirate ship. The museum is run by Jimmy Gordon, author of *Legado de Piratas,* who has extensive knowledge of the island's history. About 1 km south from Cueva de Morgan is **West View** ① *daily 0900-1700, entry US$1.10 including bread to feed the fish,* an excellent place to see marine life as the sea is very clear. There is a small jetty with a diving board and slide, and you can hire Aqua Nauta equipment (US$50 for 30 minutes), old-fashioned diving equipment with oxygen piped through a tube to a helmet. There is a small restaurant opposite the entrance.

At El Cove, you can continue round the coast, or cross the centre of the island back to town over **La Loma**. This is the highest point on the island and nearby is **La Laguna**, a fresh water lake 30 m deep, home to many birds and surrounded by palm and mango trees. On the town side of La Loma is the first **Baptist Church** to be built on the island (1847), acting as a beacon to shipping. The

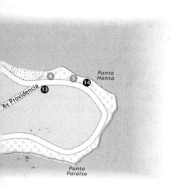

Eating ●
Guillos Café **11**
La Fonda Antioqueña **12**

Margherita e Carbonara **13**
Niko's **14**

church has a Sunday service from 1000-1300 with gospel singing. If you take a turning just before the church you will reach the **Mirador Escalona**, a lookout point on someone's unfinished roof (US$1), from which there are spectacular views of the island. In the centre of the island you will find some life as it was before San Andrés became a tourist destination, with clapboard houses and traditional music.

Excursions
Boats leave from San Andrés in the morning for El Acuario and Haynes Cay, and continue to Johnny Cay (frequently spelt Jhonny) in the afternoon, which has a white beach and parties all day Sunday (US$16.60 return). El Acuario has crystalline water and is a good place to snorkel, and see eagle and manta rays. You can wade across the water to Haynes Cay where there is good food and a reggae bar at **Bibi's Place**. These are popular tours; if you want to avoid the crowds a good option is to hire a private boat (US$110 for the day) and do the tour in reverse. Boats for the cays leave from Tonino's Marina between 0930 and 1030, returning at 1530, or from Muelle Casa de la Cultura on Avenida Newell.

Apart from those already mentioned, other cays and islets in the archipelago are Bolívar, Albuquerque, Algodón (included in the Sunrise Park development in San Andrés), Rocky, the Grunt, Serrana, Serranilla and Quitasueño. On San Andrés the beaches are in town and on the eastern coast. Perhaps the best is at San Luis and Bahía Sonora (Sound Bay).

Diving
Diving off San Andrés is very good; the depth varies from 3-30 m, visibility from 30-60 m. There are three types of site: walls of seaweed and minor coral reefs, large groups of different types of coral, and underwater plateaux with much marine life. It is possible to dive in 70% of the insular platform. The Blue Wall (Pared Azul) is excellent for deep-water diving. Black Coral Net and Morgam's Sponge are other good sites. ▸▸ *For further information, see Activities and tours, page 211.*

Providencia ▸▸ ◐❶❀▲◐❻ *pp209-212. Colour map 1, inset.*

→ *Phone code: 8.*
Providencia, also called Old Providence, 80 km to the north-northeast of San Andrés, is 7 km long and 3.5 km wide. The island is more mountainous and considerably more verdant than San Andrés, rising to 360 m, due to its volcanic origin and is much older. There are waterfalls, and the land drops steeply into the sea in places.

Providencia is striving to retain its cultural identity. Hotels must be constructed in the typical clapboard style of the island and cannot be built higher than two storeys, while mainland operators cannot manage them directly; they must work in partnership with local owners. Only locals are allowed to buy property on the island and outsiders can stay no longer than six months at a time.

Ins and outs
Getting there Visitors can arrive by air from San Andrés or by sea on one of the cargo boats that ferry goods over to Providencia three times a week.

Getting around *Chivas* circle the island at more or less regular intervals, the standard fare is US$1.60. *Colectivos* can also be found on the island and charge much the same.

Around the island

Day tours are arranged through hotels around the island, stopping typically at Cayo Cangrejo to swim and snorkel, they cost about US$17. Snorkelling equipment can be hired and diving trips arranged: the best places are Aguadulce and South West Bay.

In 1996 part of the east coast and offshore reefs and coral islands were declared a National Park (**Parque Nacional Natural Old Providence – McBean Lagoon**). The land position includes Iron Wood Hill (150 m), mainly small trees but including cockspur (*Acacia colinsii*) which has large conical-shaped needles, home to a species of ant (*Pseudo-myrmex ferruginea*) with a very painful sting. There are superb views from Casabaja (Bottom House) or Aguamansa (Smooth Water), a climb to the summit will take about one hour, and with a guide will cost US$13.80. You will see relics of the fortifications built on the island during its disputed ownership.

Providencia

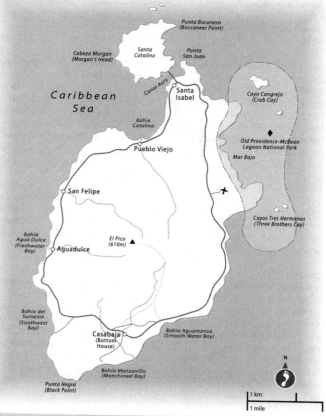

The black crabs of Providencia

With the arrival of the first rains between April and June, Providencia is the scene a spectacular natural phenomenon. Each night during the wet season thousands of black crabs (*Gecarcinus lateralis*) descend from the forests of High Hill and release their eggs in the waters between South West Bay and Freshwater, wriggling their abdomens in the surf to deposit their eggs. The hatchlings are born in the sea and return to the hills one month later.

During the migration the road that encircles the island is closed to traffic, thus allowing the crabs free access to the beaches without the risk of being run over. Coralina, the government's environmental agency on the archipelago, has banned the capture and eating of crabs during the breeding season and anyone caught disobeying the ban risks a heavy fine equivalent to the three-month minimum wage.

Many of the islanders make a living from crab fishing but during this time hunters turn protectors as they are employed as enforcers of the ban, thus ensuring that Providencia's black crab population will continue to thrive.

Horse riding is available, and boat trips can be made to neighbouring islands such as **Santa Catalina**, an old pirate lair separated from Providencia by a channel cut for their better defence. To the northeast is Cayo Cangrejo (Crab Cay), a beautiful place for swimming and snorkelling, and Cayos Tres Hermanos (Three Brothers Cay). Boat trips leave from 1000-1500 and cost about US$17 per person, with a two hour lunch in South West Bay. Santa Catalina is joined to the main island by a 100 m wooden bridge, known as the Puente de los Amantes (Lovers' Bridge). On the west side of Santa Catalina are the ruins of an old fort, built by the English to defend their pirate colony. Formerly known as Fort Warwick, it was rechristened Fuerte de la Libertad after the island was taken back by the Spanish in the 17th century. The fort still has the original canons and it is rumoured that there is a secret cave which was used by Henry Morgan to escape to the sea below (most probably untrue). Beyond the fort is a fine beach, excellent for snorkelling, with caves with air chambers and lots of starfish. Further still is a rock formation called Morgan's Head; seen from the side it looks like a man's profile. The path beyond Morgan's Head leads through thick forest to the top of the mountain and an abandoned house formerly belonging to a drug trafficker.

The beaches

Bahía Manzanillo (Manchineel Bay) is named after the manzanillo trees found on its edges (the fruit is like a miniature apple, sweet smelling but with an acid taste – and dangerous, do not eat), and is the largest, most attractive and least developed, with a couple of restaurants, including Roland's Reggae bar (see page 210). **Bahía del Suroeste** (South West Bay) is fringed by almond trees, palms and has bottle green water, and on Saturday afternoons the local boys put on bareback horse races. **Bahía Agua Dulce** (Freshwater Bay) has a small strip of beach and the sea laps at the fronts of the many hotels in this small bay. Two smaller beaches are Alan's Bay, between Aguadulce and San Felipe, which is very secluded and seldom visited, and Playa del Fuerte, underneath the fort on Santa Catalina, which has excellent snorkelling and lots of starfish.

For Sleeping and Eating price codes and other relevant information, see pages 31-36.

⊜ Sleeping

San Andrés *p204, maps p203 and p204*
LL Casa Harb, C 11, No 10-83, T5126348, www.casaharb.com. Just outside town, this boutique hotel takes its inspiration from the Far East and is the most stylish location on the island. Each room is individually decorated with antique furniture. The baths, made of solid granite, are enormous. A former family home, this mansion has a an infinity pool and offers homecooked meals.
LL Lord Pierre, Av Colombia, No 1B-106, T512 7541, www.lordpierre.com. While it may boast a magnificent pier on the tip of the *malecón*, this is a hotel that needs a rehaul. Rooms are large but a little dated, with heavy furniture.
LL Marazul, Cra San Luis, No 30-45, T513 2678. This enormous chain resort hotel sits on the southern end of town on the way to San Luis. It has a private beach, pool, 3 restaurants and a disco. Non-guests can use the facilities for US$40 per day.
AL Los Delfines, Av Colombia, No 1B-86, T5121800, www.decameron.com. Another hotel in the Decameron chain, this one achieves some individuality. The rooms are particularly comfortable, all painted a cool white and set around a fine pool. There is also a restaurant on a jetty, under which large schools of fish congregate for feeding.
A Sunset Hotel, Carretera Circunvalar Km 13, T5130433, sunsetsai@hotmail.com. On the western side of the island, this is the perfect place to stay if you want to do some serious diving – or if you just want to get away from the crowds. It has bright, fresh rooms with high ceilings, all set around a salt water swimming pool. With a restaurant serving a mixture of international and regional food in a typical clapboard house and a dive shop next door, this is one of the best places to unwind in San Andrés.

B La Posada de Lulu, Av Antioquia, No 2-18, T5122919, www.laposadadelulu.descanso rural.com. This brightly coloured hostel with its clean and comfortable rooms is one of the best mid-range options in town. There are 2 apartments to rent for longer stays and an excellent restaurant serving home cooked food for US$3. Recommended.
B Portobelo, Av Colombia, No 5A-69, T512 7008, www.portobelohotel.com. Occupies a couple of buildings on the western end of the *malecón*. Rooms have large beds, a/c and cable TV. Breakfast included.
B-C Hernando Henry, Av Las Américas, No 4-84, T5123416. At the back of town, this hotel has shoddy but passable rooms. TV and laundry service. Rooms are significantly cheaper with fan.
C Posada Doña Rosa, Av Las Américas con Aeropuerto, T5123649. A 2-min walk from the airport, this is a reasonable and economical option. It has clean rooms with private bathrooms and a small patio with potted plants. There is a kitchen and TV room, and it's a short walk from the beach. Also has 2 apartments to rent.
D Mediterráneo, Av Colón, T512 6722. Noisy, crumbling building near the beach. Rooms just about pass for cleanliness. TV and fridge provided.

Private houses
D pp Red Crab, Av Circunvalar, San Luis, T513 0314, www.arriendos. biz/RedCrab.html. A villa on the beach with 4 independent apartments, each with a capacity of up to 6 people. Price includes use of a swimming pool and the services of a housekeeper.

Camping
You can camp on Hayes Caye for US$100 per person (includes transport, food and drinks), but you must ask the Port Authority for permission through **Bibi's Place** (see Eating, below).

Providencia *p206, map p207*
There are several rooms available for rent at affordable prices in local houses or *posadas nativas*. Try Captain 'Hippie', T5148548/T311 4854805 (mob), who offers home-cooked food and lodging in his house (**E** pp).
AL Cabañas Miss Elma, Aguadulce, T514 8229, philhuffington@yahoo.es. Wood-panelled *cabañas* with terraces, right on the beach. Large rooms, some with reception rooms and baby cots. Cable TV and a/c.
A Cabañas Miss Mary, South West Bay, T514 8454, www.missmaryhotel.com. On the beach at South West Bay, Miss Mary has clean, comfortable rooms with cable TV and hot water. Breakfast is included.
A Hotel Sirius South, West Bay, T5148213, www.siriushotel.net. Large, colourful house set back from the beach, run by a Swiss family. The rooms are large and light, some have balconies with hammocks. Kitchen available for guests. Prices negotiable.
A Posada del Mar, Aguadulce, T514 8168, posadadelmar@latinmail.com. Pink and purple clapboard house with comfortable rooms, each with a terrace and hammock looking onto the bay. The sea laps at the edge of the garden. Has cable TV, a/c, minibar and hot water. Recommended.
C Hotel Old Providence, Santa Isabel, T5148691. Above supermarket **Erika**, rooms are basic but clean and have a/c, cable TV, fridge and private bathroom.

Camping
Roland's Reggae bar, Playa Manzanillo, T5148417, rolandsbeach@hotmail.com. Hires tents for camping (**F**).

❶ Eating

San Andrés *p204, maps p203 and p204*
🍴 **Bibi's Place**, Haynes Caye, T513 3767, caritoortega@hotmail.com. Reggae bar and restaurant on cay next to El Acuario serving seafood, including crab and lobster. Organizes full moon parties and civil and rasta weddings.

🍴 **Margherita e Carbonara**, Av Colombia, opposite the Lord Pierre Hotel. Italian-owned restaurant decorated with photographs from Italian films. Good pizzas.
🍴 **Niko's**, Av Colombia, No 1-93. Bills itself as a seafood restaurant though its steaks are actually better. Lovely setting by the water.
🍴 **Guillos Café**, Av Peatonal next to **Portobelo** Hotel. Fast-food restaurant serving sandwiches and burgers, as well as local specialities.
🍴 **La Fonda, Antioqueña**, Av La Playa, No 1-16. On the main beach in San Andrés town, this *paisa* restaurant serves good, cheap food.

Providencia *p206, map p207*
Local specialities include crab soup and *rondón*, a mix of fish, conch, yucca and dumplings, cooked in coconut milk. Corn ice cream is also popular – it tastes a little like vanilla but a little sweeter. Breadfruit, a grapefruit-sized fruit with a taste similar to potato, is the archipelago's official fruit.
🍴 **Caribbean Place** (Donde Martín), Aguadulce. *Bogoteño* chef Martín Quintero arrived for a brief stay in 1989 and has never left. He uses local ingredients. Specialities include lobster in crab sauce, fillet of fish in ginger and corn ice cream.
🍴 **Roland's Reggae Bar**, Playa Manzanillo, T514 8417, rolandsbeach@hotmail.com. Roland is a legend on the island, as are the parties at his bar-restaurant on Manzanillo Beach. The menu is mainly seafood, with fried fish and ceviches.
🍴 **Pizza's Place**, Aguadulce. Basic pizzas and pastas.

✪ Festivals and events

San Andrés *p204, maps p203 and p204*
Jun Jardín del Caribe. A folkloric festival.
20 Jul Independence.
Dec Rainbow Festival. Reggae and calypso music.

Providencia *p206, map p207*
Jun Carnival.

▲▲ Activities and tours

San Andrés *p204, maps p203 and p204*
From Toninos Marina there are boat trips to the nearby cays, US$17 with lunch included.

Canopying
Canopy La Loma, Vía La Loma-Barrack, T3144479868 (mob). Has a site at the top of the hill in San Andrés. 3 'flights' over the trees at heights of 450 m, 300 m and 200 m above sea level with spectacular views out to sea and costs US$17. Safety precautions and equipment are good.

Diving
Banda Dive Shop, Hotel Lord Pierre, Local 102, T5122507, www.bandadiveshop.com. PADI qualified, mini courses from US$83. Fast boat and good equipment.
Sharky Dive Shop, Carretera Circunvalar Km 13, T513 0420, www.sharkydiveshop.com. Next to **Sunset Hotel**, Sharky's has good equipment and excellent, English-speaking guides. PADI qualifications and a beginner's course held in the Sunset Hotel's saltwater swimming pool.

Fishing
Cooperativa Lancheros, on the beach in San Andrés town. Can arrange fishing trips. Windsurfing and sunfish sailing rental and lessons are also available from Bar Boat, on the road to San Luis (opposite the naval base), 1000-1800 daily (also has floating bar, English and German spoken), and Windsurf Spot, Hotel Isleño; water-skiing at Water Spot, Hotel Aquarium, and Jet Sky.

Watersports and boat trips
Snorkelling equipment can be hired for US$10.
Bar Boat, on the road to San Luis (opposite the naval base), daily 1000-1800. Wind-surfing, and sunfish sailing rental and lessons. Also has floating bar, English and German spoken.
Centro Comercial New Point Plaza, No 234, T5128787. Morning boats to El Acuario Cay, off Haynes Cay. The trip takes 20 mins and costs

US$16 return. Using a mask and wearing sandals as protection against sea-urchins, you watch the colourful fish. They also run the Nautilus, a glass hull semi-submarine, US$17.
Cooperativa Lancheros, on the beach in San Andrés town. Can arrange windsurfing, jet skiing and kite surfing.
Also try **Windsurf Spot**, Hotel El Isleño, Av Colombia, No 5-117; and **Water Spot**, Decameron Aquarium, Av Colombia, No 1-19, www.decameron.com.

Providencia *p206, map p207*
Diving
Recommended diving spots on the Old McBean Lagoon reef are Manta's Place, a good place to see manta rays; Felipe's Place where there is a submerged figure of Christ; and Stairway to Heaven, which has a large wall of coral and big fish.
Felipe Diving, South West Bay, T8518775, www.felipediving.com. Mini courses from US$80, also rents snorkel equipment. Owner Felipe Cabeza even has a diving spot on the reef named after him. Warmly recommended.
Sirius Diving, South West Bay, T514 8213, www.siriusdivecenter.com. PADI qualifications, mini course US$80.

Snorkelling and boat trips
Recommended snorkelling sites include the waters around Santa Catalina, where there are many caves to explore as well as Morgan's Head and lots of starfish; Hippie's Place, which has a little bit of everything; and El Faro (The Lighthouse), the end of the reef before it drops into deep sea, some 14 km from Providencia.
Valentina Tours, T5148 548. Lemus Walter, aka Captain 'Hippie', organizes snorkelling, and boat trips (US$17 per person) to the outlying cays and reefs. He has a section of the reef named after him. He charges US$140 for a day's hire of the boat.

Tour operators
Body Contact, Aguadulce, T514 8283. Owner Jennifer Archbold organizes excursions,

fishing and hiking trips, currency exchange, accommodation, and more. Recommended.

Walking

There is a good walk over Manchineel Hill, between Bottom House (Casa Baja) and South West Bay, 1.5 km through tropical forest, with fine views of the sea; many types of bird can seen, along with iguanas and blue lizards. Guided tours depart twice a day at 0900 and 1500 from Bottom House. Enquire at **Body Contact**, see above, or Coralina, T514 9003.

● Transport

San Andrés *p204, maps p203 and p204*
Air Flights to **Bogotá, Cali, Medellín** and **Cartagena** with AeroRepública; Avianca; Satena; and Searca (booked through Decameron). **Copa** runs 1 flight daily to **Panama City**. To **Providencia** 2 times a day with **Satena** and **Searca**. Bookable only in San Andrés.
Sea Cargo ships are not supposed to carry passengers to the mainland, but many do. It's possible to catch a ride on one of the cargo boats to **Providencia** 3 times a week. The journey takes 7-8 hours and is uncomfortable. Normal price is US$22. They usually leave at 2200, arriving in the early morning. *Miss Isabel, Doña Olga* and *Raziman* are 3 boats that make the trip regularly. Speak directly to the captain at the port in San Andrés, or enquire at the Port Authority (*Capitanía del Puerto*) in San Luis. Any other offer of tickets on ships from San Andrés, or of a job on a ship, may be a con. The sea crossing to **Cartagena** takes 3-4 days, depending on the weather.

Vehicle and bicycle hire

Motorbikes are easy to hire, as are golf buggies. Cars can be hired for US$22 for 2 hrs, US$65 for a day. Passport may be required as deposit.
   Bikes are a popular way of getting around on the island and are easy to hire, eg opposite **Los Delfines Hotel** on Av Colombia, US$2 per hr or US$7 per day.

Providencia *p206, map p207*
Vehicle and bicycle hire
Mopeds can be hired for US$27 per day from many of the hotels (eg **Posada del Mar** in Aguadulce) and golf buggies are a lso available for US$83 per day.

● Directory

San Andrés *p204, maps p203 and p204*
Banks Banks close 1200-1400. **Banco de Bogotá**, will advance pesos on a Visa card. **Banco Occidente**, for MasterCard. ATMs available in town and at the airport (Davivenda, in the lobby at the foot of the stairs). Some shops and most hotels will change US$ cash; it's impossible to change TCs at weekends. **Titan casa de cambio**, inside CC Leda, Av de las Américas, open Mon-Fri, and Sat, 0830-1200, changes TCs, US$ and euros. **Immigration** DAS, right next to airport, T512 7182/T512 5540. **Internet and telephone** Bistronet, Av Colón, Edif Bread Fruit, Local 105, headphones and Skype, also, international calls; Varieteam Shop, Av Providencia, Centro Comercial Leda, Local 111, headphones and Skype, photocopying, fax and scanner, CDs and DVDs sold. **Post office** Deprisa at the airport and Av Colón, Edif Salazar.

Providencia *p206, map p207*
Banks Banco de Bogotá, Santa Isabel, Mon-Thu 0800-1130, 1400-1600, Fri 0800-1130, 1400-1630, exchanges cash; and **Banco Agrario**, Santa Isabel, exchanges cash. An ATM is tucked away just before the Lover's Bridge, on the road to Santa Catalina. Exchange rates from shops and hotels are poor. **Emergencies** Police: T2. **Internet** Bodycom, in CC Newball, next to super-market Hamilton. **Medical services** Ambulance, T514 8016 at hospital; Medical emergencies, T11. **Telephone** Telecom in Santa Isabel (centre), Mon-Sat 0800-2200; Sun 0900-1230, 1400-1900.

Contents

216 Medellín
216 Ins and outs
217 Background
220 Central Medellín
225 North of the centre
227 South of the centre:
El Poblado
227 West of the centre
227 Around the city
228 Listings

238 Around Medellín
238 East of Medellín
242 South of Medellín
243 North of Medellín
244 Santa Fe de Antioquia
and around
245 Listings

249 Chocó
249 Quibdó
249 Along the Pacific Coast
251 Listings

253 La Zona Cafetera
253 Manizales
256 Around Manizales
257 Marmato
260 Parque Nacional
Los Nevados
262 Santa Rosa de Cabal
262 Pereira
264 West of Pereira
267 Armenia
268 Parque Nacional
del Café
269 Ibagué and around
270 Cartago
270 Listings

Footprint features

214 Don't miss ...
221 Pablo Escobar
225 Tango in Medellín
228 Sculptures
235 The Metrocable
239 The zócalos of Guatapé
241 Discovering Reserva Natural
Cañón del Río Claro
257 Staying on a coffee finca
258 The legends of Marmato
269 Love hotels

At a glance

⊖ **Getting around** Metro or taxi in Medellín; buses between towns in rest of region. Car hire recommended for exploring coffee *fincas* of Zona Cafetera.

⊘ **Time required** 3-4 days in Medellín; 1 week to explore villages and towns of Antioquia; 1 week to explore Zona Cafetera; 3-4 days trekking in Los Nevados.

☼ **Weather** Spring-like all year round. Prone to more rain (and mudslides on roads) Mar-May and Sep-Nov.

✕ **When not to go** Good all year.

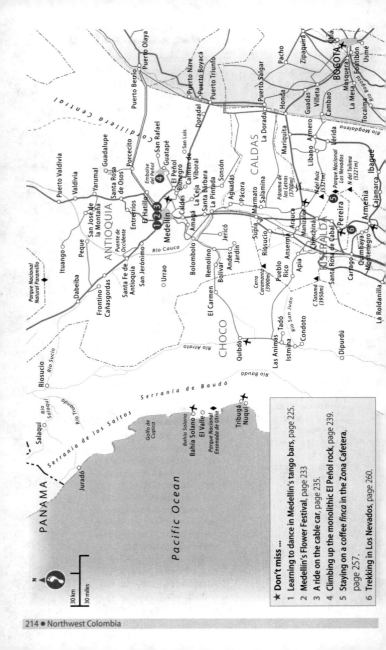

★ **Don't miss ...**

1 Learning to dance in Medellín's tango bars, page 225.
2 Medellín's Flower Festival, page 233.
3 A ride on the cable car, page 235.
4 Climbing up the monolithic El Peñol rock, page 239.
5 Staying on a coffee *finca* in the Zona Cafetera, page 257.
6 Trekking in Los Nevados, page 260.

The people of Antioquia have made this corner of Colombia the country's industrial capital and *paisas*, as people from here are known, are enterprising, business-savvy individuals, known for their pride in their distinctive accent, gregarious nature and generous hospitality. Their boundless optimism has seen Medellín, for so long associated with Pablo Escobar and his drug cartel, undergo an extraordinary renaissance into a city buzzing with new ideas, art and culture. Outside of Medellín there are delightful typical villages such as Santa Fe de Antioquia, which have unique characters that locals will tell you are pure *paisa*.

El Chocó could not be more different. This area's relentless rainfall and dense jungles have hampered attempts to build any significant roads and as a result, the area is one of the poorest economically but one of the richest culturally. Its population is proud of its African heritage, reflected in their distinctive music. Travellers should take advice before going, but Bahía Solano and Nuquí are relatively safe and boast some of the most beautiful, untouched beaches in Colombia and a chance to see one of the great whale migrations.

The Zona Cafetera is Colombia's main coffee-producing region. The bamboo forests, chattering brooks, banana groves and coffee plantations that make up its landscape create a bewildering spectrum of greens. The three main cities – Manizales, Pereira and Armenia – are relatively new and their susceptibility to damage from earthquakes has left them lacking in architectural charm. But the surrounding countryside is brimming with delightful *fincas* and pretty villages. Moreover, the icy peaks of Los Nevados, the eerie wax palms of the Valle de Cocora, or the incredible volume of birdlife at the Río Blanco reserve make this an excellent destination for nature lovers.

Medellín

→ *Colour map 2, B3. Phone code: 4. Population: 2,200,000 (city). Altitude: 1487m.*

Medellín, capital of Antioquia Department, is a dynamic, contemporary city, considered by many to be the engine of Colombia. Previously the home and headquarters of notorious narco-trafficker Pablo Escobar, Medellín has since shaken off its association with drugs and violence in what is one of the most remarkable turnarounds in Latin America. Medellín is now a fresh, vibrant and prosperous city known for its progressive social politics, art, culture and partying. It is one of the main industrial cities of Colombia, and paisas are known for their canny business sense as well as the pride they take in their city. In the centre, the new has driven out much of the old and few colonial buildings remain. However, large new buildings must, by law, incorporate modern works of art which, together with plazas and parks that feature monuments and sculptures, makes for an interesting walking tour. Music and arts festivals attract many visitors and the flower festival, the Desfile de Silleteros, *in August, is the most spectacular parade in Colombia. Known as ´The City of Eternal Spring´, Medellín has a pleasant, temperate climate; warm during the day and cool in the evening.* ⟫ *For listings, see pages 228-237.*

Ins and outs

Getting there

Air The **José María Córdova international airport** (sometimes called Rionegro airport), is 28 km from Medellín by the new highway, and 9 km from Rionegro. A taxi to town is US$27 (rising by 10% every year), *buseta* to centre, US$4, frequent service from 0400-2100, taking about one hour to the small road (Carrera 50A/Calle 53) next to **Hotel Botero Plaza**. To Rionegro from the airport is US$0.20 bus, US$8 taxi.

There is also the **Enrique Olaya Herrera metropolitan airport** in the city, where some internal flights arrive. Taxis between the airports are US$27. From Enrique Olaya Herrera to the centre or El Poblado, US$3.30.

Bus Long-distance buses arrive either at **Terminal del Norte** or **Terminal del Sur**. A taxi from either costs US$2.70 to the centre, or there are local buses and the metro.

Getting around

The best way to get around the city is by metro, which serves the three main sectors of Medellín: centre, south and west. It is efficient and safe. A single ticket, US$0.65, is valid for the Metrocable as well. The town bus services are marginally cheaper but slower. There are plenty of taxis.

Orientation

Medellín is set in the comparatively narrow Aburrá valley surrounded by high mountain barriers of the Cordillera Central in nearly all directions. The built-up metropolitan area now extends from Copacabana in the north to Sabaneta in the south, more than 25 km.

The city is centred around the old and the new cathedrals, the former on **Parque Berrío** and the latter overlooking **Parque de Bolívar**. The main commercial area is three blocks away on Carrera 46, with shopping and hotels throughout the area. Some streets have been pedestrianized.

Footprint Mini Atlas
Colombia

Caribbean Sea

N

100 km

100 miles

1 inset
*Providencia
San Andrés*

PANAMA

1

Riohacha
Santa Marta
Maicao
Barranquilla
Maracaibo
Valledupar
Cartagena

Sincelejo

PANAMA
Montería
Río Cauca

2
Turbo
Cúcuta

Barrancabermeja

VENEZUELA

Pacific
Ocean
Bucaramanga
Aracua
Puerto
Carreño

Medellín
Río Meta
Bahía Solano
Villa de
Leiva
Tunja
Puerto Ayacucho
Quibdó

Istmina
Manizales
Yopal
Río Orinoco

Cartago
Pereira
Armenia
Ibagué
□ BOGOTA

Buenaventura
Villavicencio
Puerto
Inírida

3
Isla
Gorgona
Cali
Río Guaviare

Guapi
Neiva
San José del
Guaviare
Río Guainía

Popayán
La Plata
Garzón
San Agustín
Florencia
Río Vaupés
Mitú

Tumaco
Pasto
Mocoa
Río Apaporis

Ipiales
Puerto Asís
Tulcán

Leguizamo
Río Caquetá

ECUADOR

BRAZIL

Río Putumayo

PERU
Tarapacá

Río Amazonas
Leticia

Benjamin
Constant
4

Altitude in metres	Paved road
4000	
3000	Unpaved all
2000	weather road
1000	Seasonal
500	unpaved road
200	Track
0	
Neighbouring	Rail
country	

Map 1

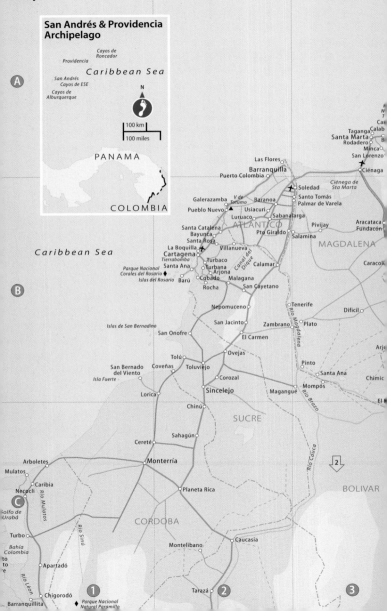

San Andrés & Providencia Archipelago

Cayos de Roncador

Providencia

Caribbean Sea

San Andrés
Cayos de ESE

Cayos de Alburquerque

N

100 km

100 miles

PANAMA

COLOMBIA

Caribbean Sea

Tanganga Calab
Santa Marta
Rodadero B
Minca
San Lorenzo Ciénaga

Las Flores
Barranquilla *Ciénaga de Sta Marta*
Puerto Colombia Soledad
Santo Tomás
Galerazamba *V de Totumo* Baranoa Palmar de Varela
Pueblo Nuevo Usiacurí
Luruaco Sabanalarga Pivijay
ATLÁNTICO Pto Giraldo
Santa Catalena Salamina Aracataca
Bayunca Villanueva Fundación
Santa Rosa
La Boquilla **MAGDALENA**
Cartagena
Tierrabomba Turbaco Caracolí
Santa Ana Turbana
Parque Nacional Arjona
Corales del Rosario Cubado Calamar
Islas del Rosario Barú Rocha Malagana
San Cayetano

Nepomuceno Tenerife
Dificil
San Jacinto
Islas de San Bernadino Zambrano Plato
San Onofre El Carmen
Arje
Tolú Ovejas
San Bernado Coveñas Toluviejo Pinto
del Viento Corozal Santa Ana
Isla Fuerte Sincelejo Chimic
Lorica Magangué Mompós
Chinú **SUCRE** El

Cereté Sahagún

Arboletes
Mulatos Monterría 2
Caribia **BOLIVAR**
Necoclí
Golfo de Planeta Rica
Urabá **CÓRDOBA**
Turbo
Bahía
Colombia
to
to Montelíbano Caucasia
Apartadó
Barranquillita 1 Tarazá 2 3
Chigorodó *Parque Nacional*
Natural Paramillo

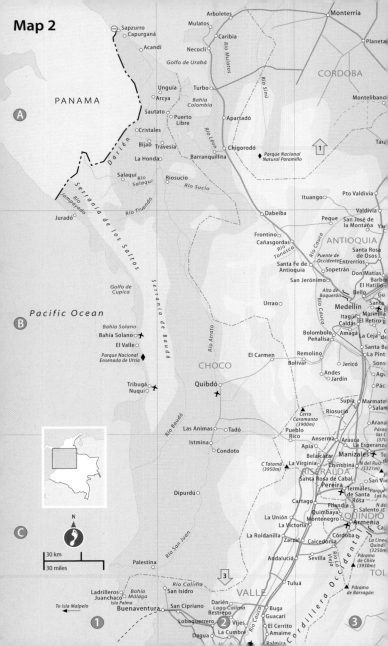

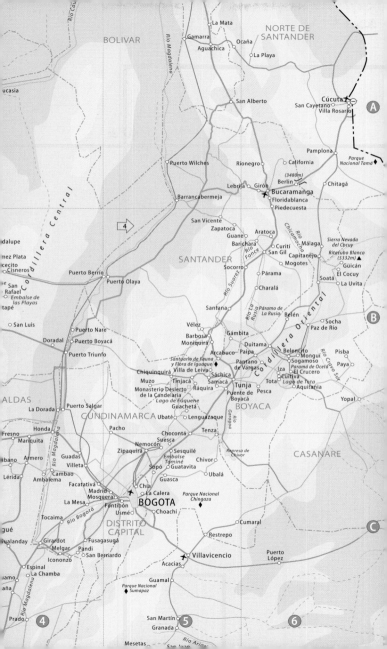

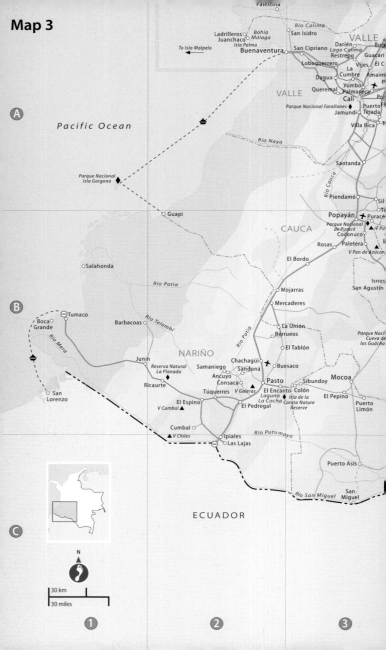

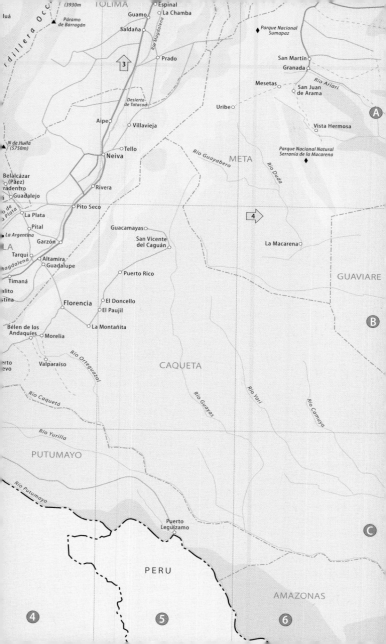

In the south, El Poblado has become an upmarket commercial and residential area and many companies have moved their headquarters there from the centre. The best hotels and restaurants are in or near El Poblado. The area around Parque Lleras, known as the Zona Rosa, is where most of the bars and nightclubs are situated.

Also favoured is the area west of the centre between Cerro El Volador and the Universidad Pontificia Bolivariana. Around Carrera 70 and Calle 44 are busy commercial and entertainment sectors with many new hotels, shopping centres and the huge **Atanasio Girardot** sports stadium nearby.

A new feature of Medellín is the pedestrianization in the centre. Pasaje Junín (Carrera 49) is now closed to traffic from Parque de Bolívar to Parque San Antonio (Calle 46). This gives walkers pleasant relief from traffic in the busy heart of the city. If driving out of Medellín, check routes carefully before leaving. There are few signs and information from officials and petrol stations is often less than clear.

In Listings (pages 228-237), we give the Calle (C) and Carrera (Cra) numbers for easy reference. Unlike most other Colombian cities, most central streets are named, and locally these are normally used. Refer to the maps which show both numbers and names. Particularly important are: Carrera 46, part of the inner ring road, which has several names but is known popularly as 'Avenida Oriental'; Carrera 80/Carrera 81/Diagonal 79, the outer ring road to the west, which is called 'La Ochenta' throughout; Calle 51/ 52, east of the centre is 'La Playa'; and Calle 33, which crosses the Río Medellín to become Calle 37, is still called 'La Treinta y Tres'.

For your first general view of the city, take the metro. Most of the track in the centre is elevated, none of it is underground and you can ride the whole system on one ticket for US$0.65.

Tourist information

Oficina de Turismo de Medellín ① *C 41, No 55-80, oficina 302, T2616060*. For information on the city, helpful staff. **TURISA** office ① *in the Centro Administrative La Alpujarra, Of 1034, T3859070*. There are tourist booths at both airports andthe bus stations.

Best time to visit

Medellín's climate is generally warm and pleasant though it is often cloudy and rain can come at any time over the Cauca valley from the Chocó, which is only 100 km to the west. The city's festivals draw many visitors from the rest of Colombia and abroad and the *paisas* know how to have a good time. ▸▸ *For details, see Festivals and events, page 233.*

Safety

Travellers should take the same safety precautions as they would in any large city, particularly at night. Medellín is, nevertheless, a friendly place. For all police services: T112.

Background

Though the Valle de Aburrá was discovered early on by the Spaniards (1541), there were few settlements here until early in the 17th century. The founding of the town is thought to be in 1616 as 'San Lorenzo de Aburrá', on the site of what is now El Poblado. It was given the official title of town (*villa*) in 1675 by Queen Mariana of Austria and named after Don Pedro Portocarrero y Luna, Count of Medellín, who achieved this recognition of the town by Spain. It was declared a city in 1813 and in 1826 it became the capital of Antioquia, by which time the city had become established around the **Basílica de La Candelaria** (now known as the Old Cathedral), which was built at the end of the 17th century.

The industrialization of Medellín followed the coffee boom. The first looms arrived in 1902. Today the city produces more than 80% of the textile output of the country, and textiles account for only half its industrial activity. Other major local industries are brick

1 **Medellín**

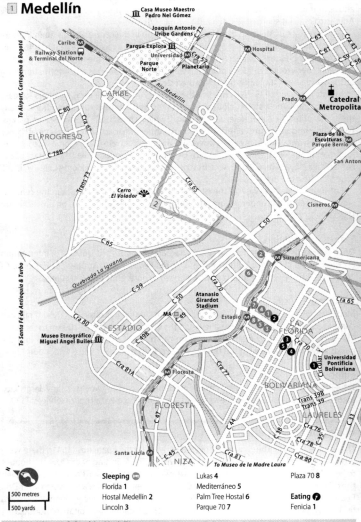

Sleeping 🛌	Lukas **4**	Plaza 70 **8**
Florida **1**	Mediterráneo **5**	
Hostal Medellín **2**	Palm Tree Hostal **6**	Eating 🍴
Lincoln **3**	Parque 70 **7**	Fenicia **1**

making, leather goods and plastics. There has been limited immigration from overseas since the original settlement, but the natural growth in population has been extraordinary. Recently, the city has continued to expand at a great pace, a manifestation of which is the fine metro, giving easy communication across the city.

To Santa Elena & Airport

To Las Palmas & Airport

➡ **Medellín maps**
1 **Medellín, page 218**
2 Medellín centre, page 222
3 El Poblado, page 226
4 Medellín metro, page 236

Teatro Pablo
Tobón Uribe

BUENOS
AIRES

C 51
C 50
C 49
Cra 29
Cra 35
Cra 32
Cra 36A

Morro El
Salvador

C 32

Variante Las Palmas

Alpujarra

Variante Las Palmas

Variante Las Palmas

Cra 25

Exposiciones

C 44
Cra 45
Cra 43A
C 29

Cra 24

6

3

7

Av El Poblado

Cerro
Nutibara

Industriales

Cra 43F

Cra 57

Cra 48

Río Medellín

Plaza del
Poblado

San José

EL POBLADO

C 10

MALIBU

Cra 66B

Cra 30

C 29

C 25

C 23

Cra 54

Parque
Zoológico
Santa Fe

SANTA
FE

C 20

C 16

Poblado

Autopista Sur

To Envigado

Cra 73

Terminal
del Sur

C 10

Cra 4

C 2

CRISTO
REY

C 15

C 25

GRANADA

Cra 70

Olaya Herrera
Airport

Cra 65

Cra 52

To Cali

La Margarita No 2 **2**
Opera Pizza **3**
¡Orale ! **4**
Pomodoro **5**

Bars & clubs 🍸
Babylon **6**
Trilogia **7**

Central Medellín

The focus of the city is the **Plaza de las Esculturas** (also known as the Plaza Botero), Calle 52 y Carrera 52, which has 23 sculptures donated by Frenando Botero, Colombia's leading contemporary artist, as well as two fountains designed by him. Botero made these sculptures to be touched and his sensuous pieces of rotund characters certainly invite this. On the north side of the plaza is **El Palacio de la Cultura Rafael Uribe**, an extraordinary Flrod Gothic building, built by Belgian architect Agustín Goovaerts between 1929 and 1937, which was formerly the governor's office and is now a cultural centre and art gallery (free entry). Opposite is the **Museo de Antioquia** ① *Cra 52, No 52-53, T2513636, open Mon, Wed-Fri, 0930-1700, Sat and holidays, 1000-1600, US$4.40. metro stop: Parque Berrío.* It has contemporary pictures and sculptures, including the best collection of works by Botero, and a room of paintings of Francisco Antonio Cano. With auditorium, film shows, etc. There is a good gift shop selling clothes by up-and-coming Colombian fashion designers as well as postcards and molas. Three blocks away, the **Parque de Berrío** is bounded on one side by the **Señora de La Candelaria** church. The original building on this site dated from the latter part of the 17th century. The present church was finished around 1767 and became the original cathedral of the city, consecrated in 1776, with the towers built five years later and the cupola in 1860. The clock was donated by Tyrell Moore (see below) in 1890. It remained the city's cathedral until 1931. It has a fine flat-roofed nave and interesting altar gilding by local artisans dedicated to the patron of Medellín.

Overlooking Parque Berrío is **Museo Filatélico** ① *4th floor of Banco de la República building, C 50, No 50-21, T5767402, Mon-Fri 0830-1100, 1400-1800, metro stop: Parque Berrio,* with an interesting stamp collection and special displays connected with postal services. Also music room with concerts on video in afternoons.

Parque de Bolívar, four blocks away, is dominated by the new **Catedral Metropolitano**, one of the largest (sun dried) brick structures in the world, built between 1875 and 1931. It is also claimed to be the largest cathedral in South America. It is impressive inside, with marble used only for the pulpit, the altar canopy and some statuary around the nave. The Spanish stained-glass windows are a good example of the period. There are several paintings of Gregorio Vázquez de Arce. There is a plaque in the square to Tyrell Moore, the Englishman who dedicated the land to the city for the park, in the centre of which is a statue of Bolívar. On the first Saturday of the month there is a craft market known as the *Mercado de San Alejo* in Parque de Bolívar.

The oldest church in the centre of Medellín is believed to be the **Iglesia de la Veracruz**, originally started in 1682 by early Spanish settlers. It was only finally completed around the end of the 18th century. Pablo Chávez was commissioned to decorate the interior and the main altar was brought directly from Spain. It has an attractive *calicanto*-style façade. In the square outside, there is a statue of Atanasio Girardot, a hero of the war of Independence.

Further south, the **Iglesia de San Benito** was also founded about 1685 but its present baroque style dates from 1802. Another old foundation is the **Iglesia de San José** begun in the 17th century but modified several times up to 1903, the last work done by the Nicaraguan architect Félix Pereira. It houses the oldest painting in Medellín – of San Lorenzo, the first patron saint of Medellín. The painting of San José is by Carlos Hefritter.

Three other churches are worth a visit. **San Ignacio**, a Franciscan church in Plaza San Ignacio, begun in 1793, has a colonial interior with a barrel vaulted central nave and a splendid red and gold altar. It was later taken over by the Jesuits forming part of the

Pablo Escobar

Not since the assassination of presidential candidate Jorge Eliécer Gaitán has a man held such a powerful hold over Colombia.

Pablo Emilio Escobar de la Vega, who gained world infamy as one of the world's most notorious outlaws, was born in 1949 into a middle-class family in the Antioquian town of Rionegro. He began his criminal career stealing tombstones and selling them on. He progressed to car crime and then muscled his way into the drug business, eventually becoming the head of the most powerful drug cartel in the world.

He developed a reputation for casual, lethal violence, often kidnapping his enemies and holding them for ransom. His trademark technique for dealing with the authorities became known as *plata o plomo* (cash or lead); any judge or official who refused his bribes was shot.

By the mid-1980s his drug organization was so lucrative that he owned 19 residences in Medellín alone, each with its own heliport, as well as boats, planes, banks and properties throughout the word. In 1989, Forbes magazine listed him as the 7th richest man on the planet, estimating that the Medellín cartel was pulling in US$30 billion a year.

Yet despite the brutal assassinations, he was incredibly popular. He was a master at manipulating public opinion and actively cultivated an image as the *'paisa* Robin Hood'. He raised money to build roads and put up electricity lines and built roller-skating rinks, football pitches and even a housing development for the poor known as Barrio Pablo Escobar.

At the height of his popularity he ran and was voted into Congress. But his forays into public life also brought attention to his nefarious activities and after the assassination of presidential candidate Luis Carlos Galán (in which he is believed to have been involved), President Cesar Gaviria ordered his arrest. He went on the run for several years, using a string of hideouts in Medellín and Antioquia before he eventually tired and negotiated very favourable terms of surrender.

He was allowed to design and construct a luxurious prison on a hill outside Medellín that came to be known as La Catedral. It had a football pitch and gym and the rooms were like hotel suites, with jacuzzis, giant TVs and bars. He hosted lavish parties, while he came and went as he pleased, often attending football matches in Medellín, his motorcade accompanied by a police escort that blocked traffic to ensure smooth passage.

Eventually the government decided to transfer him to a 'real' prison but in the resulting siege of La Catedral, Escobar slipped through the cordon of an entire army battalion and went on the run for a further 18 months.

In the meantime a vigilante group known as Los Pepes (Los Perseguidos por Pablo Escobar – People Persecuted by Pablo Escobar), believed to be funded by his rivals, the Cali Cartel and to be colluding with the government, began a campaign in which 300 of his business associates were assassinated, severely hampering his cash flow. He was eventually tracked down and shot by special forces in December 1993 while attempting to escape across the rooftops of a Medellín suburb.

During his three-decade career he is believed to have been responsible for the death of more than 4000 people, including 30 judges and 457 policemen, while he is also charged as the single figure who most developed Colombia's reputation as nation synonymous with drugs, kidnappings and pitiless violence.

original group of buildings of the Universidad de Antioquia: this complex includes the auditorium (*paraninfo*) of the university, which was declared a National Monument in 1982 and over a period of eight years was tastefully renovated and reopened in 1997 – there is a great view of the city from the top of the tower. The two others are **San Juan de Dios**, in colonial style, and **San Antonio**, designed by Benjamín Machiantonio and built

2 Medellín centre

Sleeping	Gran **3**	Eating
Botero Plaza **1**	Nutibara **4**	1,2,3... Cazuelas **5**
Casa Dorada **2**		Café Botero **6**

between 1884 and 1902. It was inspired by San Antonio de Padua, a 13th-century Venetian church. This church has one of the biggest domes in the country.

The city's main business area is **Villanueva**, named after the nunnery which has now been converted into a commercial centre. It is interesting for its blend of old and modern architecture, including many skyscrapers. To the north across Calle 58, is El Prado section,

➡ **Medellín maps**
1 Medellín, page 218
2 **Medellín centre, page 222**
3 El Poblado, page 226
4 Medellín metro, page 236

Chung Wah **1**
Deli Lunch **8**
Hato Viejo **9**

Fonda Parque Boívar **10**
Salon de Té Astor **11**
Versalles **12**

Bars & clubs 🍸
La Boa **13**
Guanábano **14**

originally a *finca* named La Polka, where there were many fine old houses, most of which have been replaced or are in decay. Some however have been restored and the area attracts artists and musicians. There are many sculptures in the city (see below). One collection not to be missed is of the works of Fernando Botero in **Parque San Antonio** ① *between C 44/46 and Cra 46*, including the *Torso Masculino* (which complements the female version in Parque Berrío), *La Mujer Inclinada* and the *El Pájaro de Paz (Bird of Peace)*, which was severely damaged by a guerrilla bomb in 1996. At the request of the sculptor, it has been left unrepaired as a symbol of the futility of violence. A new *Bird of Peace* has been placed alongside to make the point yet more dramatic. There is a garden beyond the plaza with the sculptures and a useful footbridge to cross the busy Calle 44 (San Juan).

On the other side of the metro is the **Palacio Cultural** ① *Cra 52, C 48*, designed by Agustín Goovares in the Romantic style. Built in 1925, it is now a commercial centre, recognisable by its brass-coloured domes, stylishly renovated with sweeping marble staircases and spacious hallways. Government of the city and department is now conducted from **La Alpujarra** administrative centre, a nine-block area from Calle 44/Carrera 52. Within the complex is the fine old Medellín railway station building designed in 1914 by Enrique Olarte.

Also in the centre is **Casa Museo Maestro Pedro Nel Gómez** ① *Cra 51B, No 85-24, T2263333, free, Mon-Fri 0900-1200, 1400-1700, Sat 0900-1400, may be closed during school holidays, metro station: Universidad*, house of the Colombian painter and sculptor (1899-1984) with many of his artworks, and a specialist library. **Archivo Histórico de Antioquia** ① *Cra 51, No 52-03, T2510823*, is a research library for the department with over 30000 volumes.

Of the modern buildings, the **Edificio Coltejer** deserves a mention. It is the tallest building in Medellín (35 floors) and was built as the headquarters of the Compañía Colombiana de Tejidos, thus symbolising the importance of textiles to the city. It is in the form of a needle with the 'eye' clearly visible near the top. The building contains offices, a commercial centre, two cinemas and various other public facilities for cultural events.

An unusual attraction is the **Punto Cero** (Point Zero), an elegant steel double arch with a pendulum marking the 'centre of the city'. It was the initial idea of students at the neighbouring Universidad Nacional. It straddles the river where it is crossed by Calle 67.

The **Edificio Inteligente** ① *C 43, No 58-01*, was completed in 1996. All the main public services in Medellín concentrate their administrative operations here in a highly energy-efficient building. Nearby is the **Parque de los Pies Descalzos** (Barefoot Park) ① *C 42B, No 55-40*, an excellent example of urban planning. It is designed to encourage local workers to relax during their lunchtime and, as the name suggests, sand pits, fountains, a Zen garden and a bamboo forest actively promote strolling about shoeless. It has several restaurants and, internet cafés as well as the **Museo Interactivo EPM** ① *US$3.50, Tues-Fri 0800-1830, Sat 1200-1830, Sun and hols 1000-1830*, an interactive science and technology museum with 22 rooms on 4 levels.

One of the city's more unusual sights is the **Cementerio San Pedro** ① *Cra 51, No 68-68, T2120951, near the Hospital metro station, daily 0700-1800*. Built in 1828, it has the dubious honour of being the resting place of many notorious drug dealers, guerrillas and the like, as well as of the richest families of Medellín. One particularly elaborate tomb is reserved for the Muñoz family who were some of Pablo Escobar's most ruthless *sicarios* (assassins). Up until 2004 this had *mariachi* music playing from speakers but it was later removed. Also of note is the tomb of Jorge Isaacs, celebrated author of the romantic novel *Maria*. Even for Latin America, some of the tombs are spectacular, and the small chapel has some

Tango in Medellín

Tango may have originated in the *barrios* of Buenos Aires and Montevideo but it has been adopted in Medellín as one of its own.

How tango arrived in Medellín is unclear but by 1919 it is evident that it was gaining widespread popularity. A short story written by local poet Ciro Mendía references tango star Carlos Gardel's *Mi Noche Triste* in a tale that revolves around a fallen woman who is assassinated by her jealous lover in the red-light district of the city.

By 1922, North American record companies such as RCA Victor and Columbia had picked up on tango's increasing popularity and began to distribute tango songs for the Colombian market, while tango films featuring Argentine starlets such as Libertad Lamarque drew large crowds to the city's cinemas. In Medellín, tango was concentrated around the working-class barrio of Guayaquil, where cantinas and cafés played songs by Argentine stars.

It was after the tragic death of Carlos Gardel in 1935 in a plane accident at Medellín's Olaya Herrera airport that tango really took off. The death in their city of its biggest star crystallized tango's connection with the local imagination and during the 1940s, 1950s and 1960s, tango gained increasing clout as a form of music intrinsic to Medellín's distinctive culture.

By the 1950s Medellín was hosting large-scale tango concerts and many of Argentina's biggest tango stars came to perform and even settle in the city.

Today, tango culture is still strong in Medellín. Bars such as Salón Málaga and La Boa (where the novel *Aire de Tango* was written) are popular venues for tango aficionados, while the city hosts monthly *Tangovías*, in which entire streets are given over to tango dancing events. Each June, the Festival de Tango takes place with over 60 events, including dance competitions and concerts.

of the most colourful stained glass in Antioquia. It is also a place for some unique sculptures such as *Dolor de Madre*, depicting the anguish of a mother losing a young son, a replica of Michelangelo's *La Pietà*. Each month during the full moon there are nocturnal tours of the cemetery with violin music, dancing and storytelling.

South of the Río Medellín, in the Suramericano district, is the **Museo de Arte Moderno** ① *Cra 64B, No 51-64, T2302622, Mon-Fri 1000-1900, Sat 1000-1700, free*. It has a small collection of paintings, collages, photographs etc. Particularly good Débora Arango. Foreign films daily except Wednesday. There is also a coffee shop.

Nearby is the **Biblioteca Pública Piloto para América Latina** ① *Cra 64, No 50-32, T2302382/T2302422, Mon-Sat 0800-1800*. This is one of the best public libraries in the country, set up by UNESCO and the Colombian government in 1952. There is also art and photo exhibitions, authors reading their own work, and foreign films. There are several branches in Medellín and it has links to the **Biblioteca Luis Angel Arango** in Bogotá.

North of the centre

Joaquín Antonio Uribe gardens ① *Cra 52, No 73-298, T2337025/T2115607, gardens daily, 0800-1730, adult US$2.70, children US$1; the public entrance is at Cra 52/C 78 about 300 m away from metro station Universidad,* was formerly the **Finca Edén** turned into a garden by the owner, the botanist, Joaquín Antonio Uribe. It was rescued from developers in 1972 and converted into a public garden with 5500 species of plants and trees. There is a lake with various lilies on display – a cool and restful place. In March there is an international orchid show in the gardens in a covered exhibition area. There is a new restaurant (♔♔♔) **In Situ**, serving salads, soups, pastas and steaks, with beautiful views of the gardens, as well as a more economical restaurant for lunches and snacks, facilities for children, a library and an open-air auditorium.

Opposite the botanical gardens is the brand new **Parque Explora** ⓘ *Cra 52, No 73-75, T5168300, www.parqueexplora.org, Tue-Fri 0830-1800, Sat and Sun 1000-1800, US$4 to US$14 depending on how many rooms you plan to see, full tour approximately 6-8 hrs,* a science and technology museum. With 20,000 square metres of more than 300 interactive scientific puzzles and games, this is fun for adults and heaven for kids. It has four state-of-the-art rooms, each of which take one to two hours to explore. **Territorios Digitales** features the latest technological advances. You can make your own radio or TV programme, find out about stop-motion animation and play around with shadow photography. In **Colombia Geodiversa** you can learn all about seismic activity and the forces of nature in the earthquake and tornado simulators. The **Conexión de la Vida** room has enormous leaves plucked from the Amazon as well as a large display of insects. You can also simulate a race

El Poblado

➡ **Medellín maps**
1 Medellín, page 218
2 Medellín centre, page 222
3 **El Poblado, page 226**
4 Medellín metro, page 236

500 metres
500 yards

Sleeping	Eating	Bars & clubs
Black Sheep Hostal **1**	Bagels & Brunch **1**	B-lounge **8**
Casa Kiwi **2**	Basílica **2**	Blue Rock **9**
Dann Carlton **3**	Donde Paco **3**	Niagara 5 Puertas **10**
Global Hostel **4**	Le Bon **4**	
La Habana Vieja **5**	Triada **5**	
Park 10 **6**	Thaico **6**	
Provenza **7**	Tony Roma's **7**	

with a cheetah or an elephant. In **Física Viva**, lots of interactive games teach you about how birds sing and how fish swim. There is also a 3D cinema. Only recently opened, this has to be one of the highlights of a visit to Medellín.

Nearby is the **Parque Norte** ① *Cra 55, No 76-115, Mon-Sat 0900-2000, US$12, metro station: Universidad*, a recreational park with a lake and children's playground.

Next to it is the old railway station **El Bosque**, now restored and converted into a recreation centre for the elderly. Also in this area is the **Planetario** ① *Cra 52, No 71-117, T5272222, Tue-Fri 1100-1600, Sat, Sun and holidays, 1100-1700*, with a 300-seat projection room, an auditorium for 200, library and exhibition hall.

The **Parque Zoológico Santa Fe** ① *Cra 52, No 20-63, T2351326, daily 0900-1700, US$3.30, take the metro to Industriales, cross the river and walk along Cra 52 about 10 mins*, mainly houses South American animals and birds and is concerned with the protection of threatened local species including the spectacled bear and the Andean condor. There are special exhibits of Caribbean fauna and a butterfly section. Within the complex is the **Museo Santa Fe** with exhibition halls including displays of furniture and pictures of Medellín's past, including the Antioquia railway and the construction of La Quiebra Tunnel (additional charge US$0.50).

South of the centre: El Poblado

Museo El Castillo ① *C 9 Sur, No 32-269, T2660900, Mon-Fri 0900-1130, 1400-1730, Sat 0900-1100, free*, formerly a landowner's home, constructed in 1930 in neo-Gothic style, has interesting collection of painting, sculptures, porcelain and furniture. The house is set in beautiful grounds. There is also a 250-seat concert hall. Take a bus to Loma de los Balsos, El Poblado, then walk 1 km up the hill until you see the road lined with pine trees to the right.

The church **Iglesia San José** is on the central park of Poblado in the south of the city where the Spanish first settled in the Aburrá valley in 1616. The present church is the third on the site, in which the architect Agustín Goovares was involved. There are commemorative plaques in the park.

West of the centre

Museo Etnográfico Miguel Angel Builes ① *Cra 81, No 52B-120, T2642299/T4216259, www.yarumal.org, Mon-Fri, 0800-1200, 1400-1700, Sat 0900-1200, free but voluntary contributions appreciated*, was originally founded in 1963 in Yarumal, Antioquia by missionaries and moved to Medellín in 1972. It has an extensive collection of artefacts from indigenous cultures, two floors dedicated to Colombia, one to other Andean countries including Peru and Bolivia and another floor to Africa. There are models of indigenous houses in a fine building with a library and bookshop.

Take the metro to Floresta and walk along Carrera 81 (about 10 minutes). The **Museo de la Madre Laura** ① *Cra 92, No 34D-21, T2523017, Tue-Fri 0800-1200, 1400-1700*, has a good collection of indigenous costumes and crafts from Colombia, Ecuador and Guatemala collected by a community of missionary nuns.

Around the city

You will notice three prominent hills within the Aburrá valley. They are first, **Cerro Nutibara** (across the river from Industriales station), where there is an outdoor stage for open-air

Sculptures

Sculptures are hard to miss in Medellín. The best of Rodrigo Arenas Betancur are the *Monumento a la Vida*, in the forecourt of the **Edificio Suramericana de Seguros**, Calle 50/Carrera 64, where exhibitions of work by leading South American artists are held. More examples of his work, the *Energía Creadora* and *El Cristo Cayendo*, are on display at the new campus of **Universidad de Antioquia**, Calle 67, No 53-108.

Fernando Botero, another major artist, is well represented in the city parks and in the Museo de Antioquia. There are many others, also murals, paintings, mosaics and so on, very much helped by the 1983 decree that requires all constructions in the city of over 2000 sq m to incorporate a work of art. A notable colourful mosaic can be seen on the façade of the **Clínica Soma**, Carrera 46/Calle 51.

concerts, sculpture park (the idea of former President Belisario Betancur) with exhibits from other Latin American countries, a miniature Antioquian village (known as Pueblito Paisa), souvenir shops and restaurants. There is a statue of Chief Nutibara near the village. Every month, on the night of the full moon, there is a party here with music, dancing, food stalls, tango show etc, organised by the Department of Sports and Recreation. To get there, take a 301 bus from Carrera 43/Calle 54, which takes you to the bottom of the hill with 1½ km to walk, or a taxi from Industriales or Exposiciones metro stations to the village, US$1. Second is **Cerro El Volador** (seen as the metro turns between Universidad and Caribe stations), tree covered and the site of an important indigenous burial ground; and third, **Morro El Salvador** (to the east of Alpujarra station), with a cross and statue designed by Arturo Longas in 1950 on top. This hill and its small public park have been absorbed into building developments and is not recommended for visits on foot.

No visit to Medellín would be complete without a ride on the Metrocable, one of the city's proudest achievements. Take the metro north to Acevedo and transfer to the cable-car line up to Santo Domingo Savio, formerly one of the city's most dangerous and crime-riddled barrios. You can now walk around the neighbourhood perfectly safely (although it's best not to flash your cash or expensive cameras). The new library, **Parque Biblioteca de España**, a short walk down from the metro station, opened by the King and Queen of Spain in March 2007 is worth a look. Designed by Colombian architect Giancarlo Massanti it has seven floors with 14,000 donated books and 108 computers. All this in what was once one of the most feared areas of Medellín (see box, page 235).

◉ Medellín listings → *Phone code: 4.*

For Sleeping and Eating price codes and other relevant information, see pages 31-36.

● Sleeping

Central Medellín *p220, map p222*
Medellín has transformed beyond recognition in the last decade and one of these changes is that much of the

accommodation has moved out of the centre. Many of the cheaper hostels in this part of town are *acostaderos* or pay-by-the-hour brothels with questionable security that we advise you to avoid.
A Gran, C 54, No 45-92, T5134455, www.granhotel.com.co. A 1970s modern structure often used for business conventions, the Gran is just 5 blocks from

Parque de Las Esculturas. It has a swimming pool, room service and a restaurant serving steak, fish and pastas.

A Nutibara, C 52A, No 50-46, T5115111, www.hotelnutibara.com. The grand old lady of Medellín, the Nutibara was the city's first major hotel, built in 1945. Its best days may be behind it but it retains a certain art-deco charm and has all modern amenities, including a pool, sauna, Turkish bath, an internet room and Wi-Fi in the lobby.

B Botero Plaza, Cra 50A, No 53-45, T5112155, www.hotelboteroplaza.com. Just 1 min's walk from Parque Botero, this hotel is also convenient as it is on the same street where the *busetas* leave for the airport. It has clean rooms, an internet café, sauna, gym and Turkish bath but is also located in a slightly seedy area that can be dangerous by night.

D Casa Dorada, C 50, No 47-25, T5125300, casadorada@granhotel.com.co. Part of the Gran Hotel, this is one of the few safe budget options in the centre. It has hot water and TV but the rooms are a little dark and musty.

El Poblado and around *p227, map p226*
L Park 10, Cra 36B No 11-12, T3106060, www.hotelpark10.com.co. In a quiet and green corner of El Poblado, the Park 10 has a cultured air with wooden floorboards and smartly dressed bellboys. All rooms have a reception area and safes. It also has a sauna,

gym, Wi-Fi and the travel agency **Aviatur** in the same building.

L Dann Carlton, Cra 43A, No 7-50, Av El Poblado, T4445151, www.danncarlton.com. Enormous block of brick that towers over Av El Poblado, the Dann Carlton has all the usual amenities, including a pool, spa, sauna, beauty parlour and Wi-Fi throughout. Features include a computer in every room and a revolving restaurant on the top floor.

A Provenza, Cra 35, No 7-02, T3265600, provenzahostal@gmail.com. This relatively new hotel just a couple of blocks from the Zona Rosa has a fresh and airy feel with lots of white colours. Has Wi-Fi, TV and a laundry service.

A La Habana Vieja, C 10 Sur, No 43A – 7, T3212557, www.hotellahabanavieja.com. Tucked away just off Av Poblado, this is about the only colonial hotel you will find in Medellín. Has TV, minibar and balconies for rooms on 2nd floor. Breakfast included.

B Global Hostel, Cra 35, No 7-58, www.globalhostelcolombia.com. In a city that has a poor selection of midrange hotels, this is an excellent option. The owners have gone for a minimalist, boutique look and generally succeed. Close to the Zona Rosa, with breakfast included and Wi-Fi throughout. Highly recommended.

D Casa Kiwi, Cra 36, No 7-10, T2682668, www.casakiwihostel.com. A maze of living

areas, games rooms and outdoor patios, Casa Kiwi is one of the most comfortable backpackers' hostels you will find in Colombia. The rooms are tastefully decorated while a couple of dorm rooms with bunks (F) provide an economical alternative. Has Wi-Fi, several computers, a pool table, DVD collection and is just a couple of blocks from the bars and restaurants of Parque Lleras.

D The Black Sheep Hostal, Transversal 5a, No 45-133, T5807837, www.blacksheep medellin.com. Run by New Zealander Kelvin, The Black Sheep is another very comfortable backpackers' hostel on the site of an ex-hospital. With 5 internet-connected computers, a kitchen, Spanish classes and a Sun BBQ, it is an excellent place to unwind and plot excursions around Antioquia. Kelvin also writes an excellent blog on his website, full of invaluable information on the rest of Colombia. Bunks in dorms (F) also available.

West of the centre p227, map p222

A Mediterráneo, Cra 70, No 5-23, T4102510, www.mediterraneomedellin.com. Smart hotel with lots of glass and airy rooms. The sauna and Turkish bath on the roof are included in the price as is Wi-Fi. Good restaurant serving up economic meals. Recommended.

A Lincoln, Circular 3a, No 70-28, T4091200, www.hotellincoln.com.co. Boutique hotel with excellent rooms with large windows. TV, stereo, safe and Wi-Fi in every room. Popular with businessmen, hence discount negotiable at weekends.

A Florida, Cra 70, No 44B-38, T2604900, www.hotelfloridamedellin.com. Standard hotel on Carrera 70. Has internet room, Wi-Fi, laundry service, car park and restaurant. Some rooms lack windows.

A Lukas, Cra 70, No 44A-28, T2601761, www.lukashotel.com. Clean and crisp rooms with all the necessary amenities, including safe, a/c, cable TV, an internet room and Wi-Fi throughout. Breakfast included.

B Parque 70, C 46B, No 69A-11, T2603339. Good little mid-range hotel in a quiet cul-de-sac off the Carrera 70. Clean rooms

with minibar, stereo, TV and Wi-Fi. Just 1 block from the Estadio metro station.

C Plaza 70, Cra 70, No 45E-117, T4123266. This functional hotel has clean but dark and small rooms with cable TV. Internet access.

D Hostal Medellín, Cra 65, No 48-144, www.hostalmedellin.com. Spacious hostel run by a German and Colombian couple, popular with bikers for its large garage. Has a fine little garden with a hammock and organizes tours to Guatape and Santa Fe de Antioquia. 2 rooms have private bathrooms.

D Palm Tree Hostal, Cra 67, No 48D-63, T2602805, www.palmtreemedellin. Another backpackers' hostel which ticks all the boxes in terms of facilities, including a kitchen, Wi-Fi, TV and DVD room, bike hire, book exchange and hammocks. Private and dormitory rooms (F) available.

🍴 Eating

Central Medellín p220, map p222

🍴 **Café Botero**, Cra 52, No 52-43 Esquina. Excellent lunchtime venue next to the Museo de Antioquia. Fish, fine steaks and delicious puddings. Recommended.

🍴 **Hato Viejo**, Cra 47, No 52-17. Overlooking Av La Playa, Hato Viejo serves typical dishes such as *ajiaco*, *sudao* and *mondongo* as well as the usual steaks and fish.

🍴 **Versalles**, Pasaje Junín, No 53-59. Argentine-run restaurant famous in Medellín for being the epicentre of the Colombian nihilism movement of the 1960s. *Parrillas*, pastas and pizzas in a room filled with photographs of renowned Latin American philosophers.

🍴 **Chung Wah**, C 54, No 49-75. The oldest and best Chinese restaurant in town.

🍴 **1,2,3… Cazuelas**, CC Unión, Cra 49, No 52-107, local 219fast food *cazuelas* in what was once the Union Club, Medellín's most exclusive social club.

🍴 **Deli Lunch**, Cra 49, No 52-81, local 99. Creole food at economic prices. *Menú ejecutivo* US$4. Several similar places nearby.

♥ **Fonda Parque Bolívar**, C 55, No 47-27. Just off the Parque Bolívar, this popular lunchtime venue is festooned with antiques. *Menú ejecutivo* US$2.

♥ **Salón de Té Astor**, Cra 49, No 52-84. Excellent pastries, a delightful traditional tea house, famous throughout Colombia for its chocolate delicacies. Try the *besitos de negro*. Lasagna, sandwiches and salads also served.

El Poblado *p227, map p226*

♥♥♥ **Basílica**, Cra 38, No 8ª-42, Thick Argentine steaks and sushi on an open terrace on Parque Lleras.

♥♥♥ **Tony Roma's**, Cra 43, No 7-50. Revolving restaurant on top of the **Hotel Dann Carlton**, serving ribs and steak. Worth visiting just for the view.

♥♥♥ **Triada**, Cra 38, No 8-08. Enormous restaurant/bar/club in the heart of the Zona Rosa. Huge steaks, sushi, salads and Tex Mex are the order of the day. It even has a bell on each table for calling the waiter. Good atmosphere with open terrace.

♥♥ **Thaico**, C 9, No 37-40. Good Thai food with fresh ingredients. A popular spot for watching televised sports (or just people strolling through Parque Lleras).

♥ **Le Bon**, C 9, No 39-09. French café serving omelettes, pancakes, fruit salads and coffees and teas from around the world. Lovely atmosphere on terrace surrounded by plants on Parque Lleras. Often has jazz bands in the evening.

♥ **Donde Paco**, Cra 35, No 8A-80. Economic Colombian or oriental food in a good atmosphere. *Menú ejecutivo* US$4.

♥ **Bagels & Brunch**, C9, No 38-26. 0% fat free boasts the slogan of this breakfast venue, but it's a hearty start to the day all the same with stuffed bagels, pancakes with maple syrup and fruit smoothies.

West of the centre *p227, map p222*

♥♥ **La Margarita No 2**, Cra 70, No 45E-11. Antioquian dishes in a pleasant atmosphere – *bandeja paisa* and *cazuelas*.

♥ **Fenicia**, Cra 73, No 2-41. Family-run Lebanese restaurant serving kebabs, tabouleh, *pide* and falafel. Part of the restaurant is in what used to be the family home garage. Takeaway service available.

♥ **Opera Pizza**, C 42, No 70-22. *Paisas* swear these are the best pizzas in town. Italian-owned restaurant with a wood-fired oven. Recommended.

♥ **¡Orale!**, C 41, No 70-138. Excellent little Mexican canteen with tables on the street. Burritos, tacos and fajitas.

♥ **Pomodoro**, C 42, No 71-14. This little Italian restaurant serves lots of different types of pastas and sauces at reasonable prices.

⚭ Bars and clubs

Medellín *p216, maps p218 and p222*

In the **centre**, the area around the Parque de Los Periodistas attracts a more bohemian crowd with Goths, punks, and students. Be careful how you go, however, as this area is considerably more seedy than the upmarket Zona Rosa. Try **La Boa**, C 53, No 43-59, which has been around for more than 40 years and is famous for its tango and jazz. The book *Aire de Tango* by Manuel Mejíor Vallejo was written here. It claims to be the only bar in Medellín where there has never been a fight! Also try **Guanábano**, Cra 43, No 53-21, which has an atmosphere reminiscent of the edgier parts of East London or East Berlin, lots of Rolling Stones album covers decorate the walls of an old building with a *caña brava* roof.

In the **south**, the best are in the centre of **El Poblado**, in what is commonly known as the Zona Rosa, around Parque Lleras. **B-Lounge**, Cra 35, No 10-38. The place to go on Wed nights, with karaoke and lots of beautiful women.

Babylon, Cra 38, No 19-60. On Thu it's all you can drink for US$17.

Blue Rock, C 10, No 40-20. Open Thu-Sat, plays rock and Colombian music. Small and crowded, entry often includes a free drink.

Niagara 5 Puertas, Cra 38, No 8-11.
Triada, Cra 38, No 8-08, is a popular spot
with a bar and disco upstairs.
Trilogía, Cra 43G, No 24-08, T2626375,
This club in Barrio San Diego attracts an
older crowd and has live cover bands
playing a mix of rock and Colombian
music. Arrive before 2230 on Fri and Sat.

In **west** Medellín, you will find plenty of
bars along Cra 70 and the adjacent streets.

If the prices and plastic people of the
Zona Rosa get too much, an alternative
after-hours location is Sabaneta, 11 km from
the centre of Medellín. This suburb has an
attractive plaza and fills up in the evenings
with a mixed crowd of young and old. There
are several excellent bars and restaurants
with lots of local history. The best way to get
there is by taxi, US$5.50 from El Poblado.
Canalón, Cra 40, No 75S-25. A popular
club in this area, open Fri and Sat.
La Herrería, Cra 45, No 70 Sur-24. Crammed
to the ceiling with pictures of local characters,
Mexican sombreros, horse saddles and
banana bunches, this bar also serves popcorn
and fruit salad to accompany your drinks.
El Viejo John, Cra 45, No 70 Sur-42. A popular
local spot with strings of chorizo hanging
from the ceiling. Also serves *bandeja paisa*
and other typical dishes.
Fonda Sitio Viejo, C 70 Sur, No 44-33.
Another bar full of character. This one
has a jumble of photographs of every
church in Medellín.

🞄 Entertainment

Medellín p216, maps p218 and p222
Cinema
The shopping centres **CC Oviedo**, Cra 43A, No
6 Sur-15, T3216116, **CC Unicentro**, Cra 66B,
No 34A-76, T2651116, **Parque Comercial El
Tesoro**, Cra 25A, No 1A Sur-45, T3211010, and
CC Los Molinos, C 30A, No 82A-26, T2383505
all have multiplexes showing the latest
releases. Free foreign/cultural films at
Universidad de Antioquia, or **Universidad de**

Medellín. The **Centro Colombo Americano**,
Cra 45, No 53-24, T5134444, shows foreign
arthouse films, check the local press.

Music
Monthly concerts by the **Antioquia Symphony
Orchestra** in the **Teatro Metropolitano** (see
below). Band concerts and other entertain-
ments in the Parque de Bolívar every Sun.

Universidad de Medellín theatre
has monthly tango shows. Tango also
at **Vos Tango**, C 34, No 66A-13, opposite
the **Super Ley** supermarket in Unicentro,
T2659352, US$5.

Carlos Gardel, the legendary tango singer
died in 1935 in an air crash in Medellín and
was commemorated in a museum in Barrio
Manrique in the northeast of the city.
Unfortunately, it was closed when the owner
retired in 1997. The contents of the museum
are at the University of Antioquia except for
a small exhibition at the Enrique Olaya
Herrera airport, which is where Carlos Gardel
died. *Tangovía* is a general term for occasions
when streets, especially in Barrio Manrique,
are closed to traffic for tango dancing. Cra 45
(Av Carlos Gardel), leads north east into the
centre of Barrio Manrique and is normally the
centre of activity. Enquire at the **Oficina de
Turismo**, T2616060 when the next fiesta will
be, usually 1 per month.

Theatre
Teatro Metropolitano C 41, No 57-30,
T2324597, www.teatrometropolitano.com.
 A modern-style brick building close to the
river, 1600 capacity, symphony concerts,
opera, ballet, tango shows, etc.
Teatro de la Universidad de Medellín,
Cra 87, No 30-65, T2567500, www.teatro
pablotobon.com. Home of the other Medellín
symphony orchestra, the Philharmonic, also
gives a wide range of cultural presentations.
Teatro Pablo Tobón Uribe, Cra 40,
No 51-24, T2392674. Traditional theatrical
presentations, 880 capacity. There are many
other theatres of all types in the centre and
barrios of the city. See local press for details.

⊛ Festivals and events

Medellín *p216, maps p218 and p222*
Easter Semana Santa (Holy Week) has special Easter religious parades.
Apr Exposición Equina de Medellín (equestrian show), takes place annually in the Coliseo Aurelio Mejía, a short distance from Tricentenario metro station.
Jul International Poetry Festival, held annually, on Cerro Nutibara in the open-air Carlos Vieco. For information, see www.festivaldepoesiademedellin.org.
17-26 Jul Feria de Artesanías, handicrafts of all kinds from all over the country, held in the Atanasio Girardot stadium complex.
Aug Feria de las Flores/Desfile de Silleteros (flower fair), held annually in the first half of the month, for several days ending on the Sat with parades and music. The parade goes from Cra 55 across the Puente Colombia to the Atanasio Girardot Stadium. The flowers are grown at Santa Elena in the Parque Ecológico de Piedras Blancas, 14 km from Medellín (bus from Plaza Las Flores). It has been growing in popularity since 1957. A horse *Cabalgata* is a special feature – in 2006, 8223 riders took part, taking 4 hrs to pass by: a Guinness World Record.
2nd Sat in Sep Amor y Amistad, in true *paisa* style, this equivalent of St Valentine's day lasts for a whole week!
Dec Christmas starts with a fantasy parade and dancing on Dec 7 to coincide with the switching on of illuminations.

○ Shopping

Medellín *p216, maps p218 and p222*
Handicrafts
Try the *artesanía* shops on the top of Cerro Nutibara, or **Salvarte** in CC Oviedo, Almacén de Turantioquia in the Plaza Mayor.

Markets
There is a small handicrafts market at C 52 near Cra 46 with many hippy stalls.

Mercado San Alejo, Parque Bolívar, open on the first Sat of every month except Jan, 0800-1800. Before Christmas, it is there Sat and Sun with handicrafts on sale at good prices. Good shopping generally around Parque Bolívar.

Textiles
Many of the textile mills have discount-clothing departments attached where good bargains can be had. For more information, ask at your hotel.
Aluzia Correas y Cinturones, Oviedo Shopping Center, Poblado, Unicentro Medellín (also in Bogotá), for an incredible selection of belts.

Shopping centres
Shopping centres *(Centros Comerciales)* are in all the main areas of the city, of which the most notable are:
San Diego, C 34/Cra 43; **Camino Real**, Cra 47/C 52; **Villanueva**, C 57/Cra 49; **Oviedo**, Cra 43A/C 6 Sur; **Monterrey**, Cra 48/C 10; **La Candelaria**, Cra 43A/C 11; **Unicentro**, Cra 66B/C 34A; **El Diamante**, C 51/Cra 73; **Obelisco**, Cra 74/C 48; **Makro** (1996) at C 44/Cra 65. New.

Bookshops
Librería Continental, Cra 50/C 52; **Librería Científica**, C 51, No 49-52, T2314974. Large selection, some foreign books; **La Anticuaria**, C 49, No 47-46, T5114969. Antique and 2nd-hand books, including in English, helpful; **Centro Colombo Americano**, Cra 45, No 53-24, T5134444, www.colomboworld.com. Good selection of books in English for sale (including Footprint).

Maps
Virtually nothing in the bookshops. Good map of the city centre from the **Oficina de Turismo** (see page 217). Local and national maps from **Instituto Geográfico Agustín Codazzi** in Fundación Ferrocarril building, Cra 52, No 14-43, T3810561, office in the basement.

▲ Activities and tours

Medellín *p216, maps p218 and p222*
Bullfighting
At the bull-ring of La Macarena, C 44/Cra 63,
T2607193, in Jan and Feb; cheapest US$12,
usually fully booked.

Dance lessons
Academia Dance, Cra 46, No 7-9, T2661522.
Salso lessons. Black Sheep Hostal guests get
a 10% discount. Individual classes US$6.
Good reports.
Salón Malaga, Cra 51, No 45-80, T2312658.
This is one of Medellín's oldest tango bars.
It celebrated its 50th anniversary in 2008.
Owner Gustavo Arteaga is considered one of
the principle collectors of tango in Colombia.

Spanish classes
Eafit University, Cra 49, No 7 Sur 50, Av Las
Vegas, T261 9500. US$265 for 2½ months,
2 hrs a day, popular, well-organized Spanish
courses, good reports.
Medellín Spanish School (part of Black Sheep
Hostal), Transversal 5A, No 45-133, T3111589,
Spanish classes from US$6.50 per hr.

Sports complex
Estadio Atanasio Girardot, is a sports
complex at Cra 74, C 50. It was enlarged in
1978 for the Pan American games and has
facilities for over 50 sports including football,
baseball, olympic swimming pool, velodrome,
etc. It is next to the Estadio metro station.

Tour operators
Destino Colombia, C 50, No 65-42, Centro
Comecial Contemporáneo, Local 225,
T2606868, www.destinocolombia.com. Tours
to nearby attractions in Antioquia and
nationwide. Very well-informed
English-speaking guides. Can also arrange
flights. Very helpful. Recommended.
Turixmo, C 9, No 43A-31, turixmo@geo.
net.co. City and regional tours. Airport
pick-ups. Helpful and professional.

Trekking
Instituto de Deportes y Recreación
(Inder), T2606611. Organize walking tours
around Medellín on Sun, T576 0780.

⊖ Transport

Medellín *p216, maps p218 and p222*
Local
Bus Slow because of the volume of traffic,
but many are smart and comfortable – a
reaction to the new metro. *Colectivos*,
operating on certain main routes, US$0.35.

Car hire Milano, Cra 25, No 9A Sur-182,
T3174928, www.milanocar.com.
Hertz, C 1A Sur, No 43A-31, T3119262.
National, Cra43A, No23-08, T2610572. Also
offices and vehicles at International airport.
If driving in Medellín, check if there are any
restricted routes (eg car-sharing, bus lanes,
rush-hour restrictions) that apply to hire cars.

Metro The metro has 2 lines: Línea A from
Niquía to Itagüí; and Línea B from San Javier to
San Antonio, where they intersect, which
connect up with 2 cable car lines, Linea K and
Linea J. 1 journey (anywhere on the system)
US$0.72. The system operates from 0500-2300
on weekdays, 0700-2200 Sun and holidays.

Taxis Taxis have meters, make sure they are
used, minimum charge US$2. Radio taxis
include **Taxi Bernal**, T4448882 and **Taxi
Andaluz**, T4445555. For airport pickups, try
Turixmo, T2662846.

Long distance
Air The Aeropuerto José María Córdova,
28 km from Medellín, T5622828, has a
Presto restaurant, shops, Telecom with
email and fax service, no left luggage,
but the tourist office may oblige. It is
reached by the toll road or by 2 other
routes, 1 of which enters the city along
Variante Las Palmas through the south
of the city. This is normally used by *busetas*

The Metrocable

Medellín's cable car, the Metrocable, has become one of the symbols of this city's remarkable renaissance. It is the first cable car in the world designed primarily as a public transport system. Its success as a tool for social change has made it a popular tourist attraction.

The Metrocable connects the *comuna nororiental* (northwestern community), a slum full of brick- and corrugated iron-shack communities constructed haphazardly on the side of the hill, with the metro station at Acevedo. During the 1980s and 1990s this was one of the most notorious slums in Latin America, the *zona de cultivo*, or cultivation area, for drug trafficker Pablo Escobar's army of *sicarios* (assassins).

In terms of transportation, it was a difficult place to leave. Narrow streets clogged with traffic meant that it could take someone up to two hours to get into town by bus. Back in the 1990s the area was highly segregated, with sectors at war with each other. For example, the bridge between the communities of La Francia and Andalucia was a no-go area. Today, residents walk freely between the two neighbourhoods over what has been rechristened the 'Bridge of Reconciliation'.

Part of the local government's drive to propagate 'participatory democracy', the Metrocable's aim is to allow the city's very poorest to take an active role in society and to 'de-ghettoize' the area. Commuting time has been reduced to 45 minutes, allowing easier access for those looking for employment in the centre, and it has significantly improved congestion in the area. Most importantly, it has restored a sense of pride to the community.

The Metrocable is just one cog in a movement that has allowed the people of this neighbourhood to reclaim public space from criminals. Other initiatives include public libraries such as the recently opened **Biblioteca de España**, which brings books, computers and spaces for social and artistic activities to one of Latin America's most deprived communities.

The success is measurable. Violent deaths in the neighbourhood have fallen from 6349 in 1994 to 373 in 2005, while individual living space has grown from less than half a square metre to between two and three square metres per person.

The cable car's success is being replicated across Colombia and the region. A second line was inaugurated in 2008 to link La Aurora district with San Javier metro station, and a third is under construction, which will continue from Santo Domingo Savio as far as Lake Guarne. There is even talk of building a connection with the airport in Rionegro. Elsewhere in Colombia, the villages of Guatape near El Peñol and San Agustín in Huila have expressed an interest in building their own systems while Caracas, Venezuela already has one under construction.

---

and you can be dropped at a convenient point for transport to hotels in El Poblado.

Flights from **Aeropuerto José María Cordova** (sometimes called Rionegro airport). To **Bogotá**, 45 mins with **Avianca**, or **AeroRepública**, everty 40 mins. To **Cali**, 1 hr, **Avianca** 5 daily and **AeroRepública** 2 daily. To **Barranquilla**, **Bucaramanga**, **Cartagena**, 1hr, 1 daily, **Avianca**. Flights from **Aeropuerto Enrique Olaya Herrera** to **Bogotá**, 8 a day with **Satena**, also with **easyfly** (sometimes via Armenia, cheapest). To **Cali**, 2 a day with **Satena**. To **Quibdó**, with **easyfly** or **Aerolíneas de Antioquia** (ADA). To **Bucaramanga**, with **Satena**. To **Acandí** and **Capurganá**, 1 a day with **ADA**.

Airline offices AeroRepública, C 5A, No 39-141, T2684500. Aires, Cra 65A, No

13-157, T3611331. **Avianca**, Cra 43A, No 1A Sur-35, T3115833 and at both airports. **Satena**, Olaya Herrera airport, or C 9, No 41-56, T2662185. **Aerolíneas de Antioquia**, C 10, No 35-32 or at Olaya Herrera airport.

In addition, there are non-scheduled charter flights to coastal resorts eg San Andrés, and elsewhere, check with travel agents. To get the best price, shop around. Special offers can mean substantial savings. With difficulties on the road network from time to time, air services have become more comprehensive.

Note When leaving by air, make sure you go to the correct airport.

Bus The terminal for long-distance buses going north and east is **Terminal del Norte** at Cra 64 (Autopista del Norte) y Transversal 78 (full address Cra 64C, No 78-580), T2308514, about 3 km north of the centre, with shops, cafés, left luggage, 2 Visa/MasterCard ATMs and other facilities. It is well policed and quite safe, though best not to tempt fate. metro stop: Caribe. Taxi to or from the centre about US$2.70-US$4.40.

To **Bogotá**, 9-12 hrs, US$25, every 40 mins or so, with 5 companies. To **Cartagena**, Brasilia, Rápido Ochoa, Bolivariano or Copetran, 15 hrs, US$44-52, road paved throughout but poor. To **Santa Marta**, 18 hrs, US$51-58. To **Sincelejo**, 9½ hrs, US$23. To **Arboletes**, Rápido Ochoa, US$35, 12 hrs. To **Turbo**, US$27 with Gómez (the best), 14 hrs. To **Santa Fe de Antioquia**, 1½ hrs, US$5 with Sotrauraba or Gómez Hernández. To **Magangue**, US$41, with Rápido Ochoa or Brasilia.

The **Terminal del Sur**, Cra 65, No 8B-91, is alongside the Enrique Olaya Herrera airport. There are similar services to those of Terminal del Norte. To get there, take a bus No 143 marked 'Terminal del Sur' from C 51 (in front of the Banco Popular) along Cra 46 or the metro to Poblado on Línea A, from where you will probably need a taxi for the remaining 1.5 km to the bus station.

Frequent buses to **Manizales**, 7 hrs US$15, hourly 0430-1930 with **Empresa Arauca**. To **Pereira**, 8 hrs, US$16 by **Flota Occidental Pullman** or **Empresa Arauca** 0430-2330. Many buses to **Cali**, eg Flota Magdalena, US$20, 10-12 hrs. To **Popayán**, US$31, 12 hrs, **Expreso Bolivariano** at 1430

4 Medellín Metro

➡ **Medellín maps**
1 Medellín, page 218
2 Medellín centre, page 222
3 El Poblado, page 226
4 **Medellín metro, page 236**

and 2315. To **Ipiales**, US$42, 22 hrs, **Expreso Bolivariano**. To **Quibdó**, 11-13 hrs, US$25, with **Rapido Ochoa**. To **El Retiro**, US$2, with **Sotra Retiro**. To **La Ceja**, US$3, half hourly 0600-2000, with **Transportes Unidas La Ceja**. To **Jardín**, 4-5 hrs, US$9, with **Rápido Ochoa** or **Transportes Suroeste**.

⊙ Directory

Medellín p216, maps p218 and p222
Banks Most banks, opening hours 0800-1130 and 1400 to 1600, in the business zones have ATMs. Many accept international cards. **Bancolombia**, in El Poblado, cash against MasterCard, Amex, good rates for TCs and cash. Many banks open late and on Sat. Main hotels will cash TCs for residents when banks are closed, but at less favourable rates. Most *casas de cambio* are found in the shopping malls, eg CC El Tesoro. **Cultural centres** Centro Colombo Americano, Cra 45, No 53-24, T5134444. English classes, library, bookshop (including Footprint Handbooks), daily films, gallery for monthly exhibitions, very helpful. **Alianza Francesa**, Cra 49, No 44-94, Local 258, T5760780, www.alianzafrancesa.org.co, near San Antonio church. **Biblioteca Público Piloto**, library. **British Council**, Cra 42, No 16A Sur-41, T3131867. English lessons and cultural centre. **Embassies and consulates** Austria, Cra 43A, No 1 7-50, Of 701, T3121289. Belgium, Diagonal 75B, No 2A-120, Of 309, T3416060. Brazil, Cra 42, No 54A-155, interior 700, T3720022. Chile, Cra 48, No 12 Sur-70, Of 401, T3132209. Ecuador, C 50, No 52-22, Of 802, T5121193. Finland, C 17A Sur, No 48-35 T3263481. France, Cra 65, No 35-71. T3734771. Germany, Cra 48, No 26 Sur-181, Local 106. T3484040. Guatemala, Cra 42, No 33-173, T3722000. Italy, C 31, No

43A-172, T2620707. Mexico, C 36, No 66A-70. T3514812. Netherlands, C 52, No 47-42, piso 10, Of 1001. T5140756 Panama, C 10, No 42-45, Of 266, T3124590. Peru, Cra 43A, No 16A Sur-38, Of 601. T3136075. Spain, C 70, No 43A-99, T3524100. Sweden, C 16A Sur, No 30-53 T3141338. Switzerland, C6 Sur, No 43A-96, Of 802. T3113314. UK, Cra 42 No 53-26, T3779966. Venezuela, C 32B, No 69-59, T23503593511614. Note the Venezuelan consul will not issue visas. **Immigration** DAS, C 19, No 80A-40 in Belén La Gloria section, T2381728 and at main airport.
Internet There are plenty of internet cafés in El Poblado, travellers' hostels and most shopping centres. **Language** Eafit University, www.eafit.edu.co, has popular 10-week courses with 2 hrs of lessons a day, from US$265. The Black Sheep Hostal, www.spanishin medellin, offers 1-on-1 lessons.
Media The local daily newspaper is El Colombiano. There is also a weekly El Mundo. 2 TV stations are Telemedellín and Teleantioquia. **Medical services** Hospital General de Medellín, Cra 48, No 32-102. T3847300. Hospital Pablo Tobón Uribe, C78B, No 69-240, T4459100. Hospital Universitario San Vicente de Paul, C64, No 51D-00, T4441333. Clínica Soma, C 51, No 45-93 T5768400. Clínica Medellín, C 53, No 46-38, T3568585. Clínica Las Américas, Diagonal 75B, No 2A-80, T3421010. Clínica Oftalmológica de Antioquia, C 57, No 46-43, T513 3531. Clinica Oftalmológica Laureles, Transversal 74C, No 1-23, T4111000. **Dentist** Dra Marcela Madrid, Universidad CES, T3127914401, 24 hrs for emergencies. **Police** Local police T112. **Post office** Main Deprisa office, C 10, No 56-06, Mon-Fri 0730-2100, Sat, 0730-1800. Also Cra 46, No 52-36 and in all Exito supermarkets.
Telephone Telecom Cra 48, No 54-62, on Parque Bolívar, for international telephones and fax.

Around Medellín

By the time they reach Antioquia, the Andes have almost petered out yet their foothills can still reach heights of up to 3000m. This gives the rolling green countryside around Medellín an agreeable temperate climate in which all types of flowers and fruit thrive, and the typical villages of the region make for popular daytrips from the departmental capital. One such excursion is known as the Circuito del Oriente and involves a tour through typical paisa villages such as El Retiro, La Ceja and Río Negro. Further on is the network of artificial lakes known as the Embalse del Peñol, towered over by an extraordinary granite rock that bears an uncanny resemblance to Río de Janeiro's Sugar Loaf Mountain. On the shores of the lake is Guatape, a sleepy town that livens up at weekends.

Further east still, as the road drops down towards the Río Magdalena, temperate turns to tropical and hidden in the jungle is the Río Claro Nature Reserve, where a crystalline river with a marble bed has cut a path through an enormous rock, creating a 150-m canyon. Just a few kilometres on is Hacienda Napoles, former home of drug baron Pablo Escobar, now a theme park with pretensions to be the new Jurassic Park. Due south is the beginning of coffee country. Enchanting villages such as Jardín, Jerico and Andes are seldom visited, a just reward for the intrepid traveller. Santa Fe de Antioquia, to the north, was once the departmental capital, but fortunately for architecture lovers it was eclipsed by Medellín, allowing it to take on a new role as Antioquia's very own time vacuum.

▶▶ *For listings, see pages 245-248.*

East of Medellín ⊜❼♠▲ ▶▶ *pp245-248.*

Climbing east out of the valley of Medellín, the landscape becomes increasingly more attractive with carefully cultivated hills bursting with an abundance of coffee, tomatoes, corn and beans. This is Antioquia´s breadbasket and its many colonial towns are a popular weekend excursion for Medellín´s well-heeled. Known as the **Circuito de Oriente**, the one-day tour includes the towns of El Retiro, La Ceja and Rionegro and passes through some of the most expensive property in Colombia, including that of current Colombian president Alvaro Uribe.

El Retiro → *Colour map 2, B3, Phone code: 4. Altitude: 2175m. Population: 17,900.*

El Retiro, 33 km from Medellín, is a quiet colonial town with a fine plaza dominated by a 100-year-old ceiba tree. The pretty church, Nuestra Señora del Rosario, built in 1774, has an interesting stained-glass dome. There is an even older adobe mud chapel, the Capilla de San José, where a document to free local slaves, the first in South America, was signed in 1813. The Fiesta de los Negritos is held in late December to mark the event. El Retiro is also known for its furniture making and you can have almost anything copied here.

Beyond El Retiro is the pretty town of **La Ceja**, which has an attractive church dedicated to Nuestra Señora de Chiquinquirá. The main industry in town is flower-growing and a local flower festival is held annually in December. Any of the surrounding hills offer excellent views of the area, one of the best known is Cerro Capiro. The Circuito de Oriente continues its loop through several pretty colonial towns including **Carmen de Viboral**, known for its pottery; there are several factories north of the market place.

Five kilometres from Medellín airport is **Rionegro** (phone code: 4) in a delightful valley. The Casa de Convención and the cathedral are worth a visit. There are colourful processions in Easter Week. There are various hotels (**C-F**) and many places to eat in and near the plaza.

The zócalos of Guatapé

Walk through the streets of Guatapé and you will notice a curious feature about its buildings. The lower half of many houses is painted in bright colours and sport ornate sculptures depicting everyday scenes. These are the zócalos of Guatapé.

The zócalos have a practical use. They date back to 1918 when concrete first arrived in Colombia. Previously many houses suffered from deterioration due to wear and tear. Jesús Porras, a well travelled *guatapeño*, brought the idea back from Spain of fortifying the lower half of buildings with cement. But he added a new idea of embellishing the zócalos with sculptures.

The very first featured a sheep looking backwards while moving forwards, symbolizing Colombia's need to reflect on its troubled past while also looking forward to future progress. Many of the designs refer to local families, while in some eras a certain style prevailed that reflected national events. For example, during President Pastrano's talks with the FARC in the late 1990s, many of the frescoes incorporated doves – the sign of peace – into their designs.

The tradition continues today. The local municipality employs local artists to depict local characters. In the local bar, for example, the zócalos show men playing dominos. Step inside and you will likely see the same scene in real life. Guatapé's mayor has announced plans to have every house in town sport its own sculpture by 2011. That's an ambitious proposition: Guatapé's sculptors will have to produce about 200 a year to make the deadline.

Near Rionegro on the road southwest to El Retiro is **La Fe** reservoir, with a fine public park, **Parque de los Salados**, popular at weekends for aquatic sports amid pine forests.

El Peñol and around → *Colour map 2, B3. Phone code: 4. Population: 13,000. Altitude: 2250 m.*
At Rionegro, the western circuit loops back towards Medellín, but beyond, and not to be missed, is El Peñol, an extraordinary, 200-m-high, bullet-shaped granite rock, which towers above a countryside of interlocking artificial lakes known as the Embalse del Peñol. A spiral staircase has been built into a crack from the base to the summit. You can climb the 649 steps to the top in 30 minutes, where there are impressive views across the aquamarine lakes, as well as several tourist stalls and a snack bar. On the side of the rock you will notice the letters GI carved in white. This was originally meant to spell 'GUATAPE', an effort by residents of that town to claim it as their own and a view that is vociferously rejected by the residents of El Peñol. The painters were caught in the act and prosecuted, though the graffiti is yet to be removed.

The original town of El (Viejo) Peñol was founded in 1714 on an indigenous site known as Sacatín. In 1978, however, it was submerged under water when the reservoir was created. El Peñol Nuevo, built to replace it about 1 km from the original site is of little interest, although it does have a strange-looking church modelled on the rock. If you walk down to the lake you can still see the spire of the original church sticking out of the water.

Guatapé

An entirely more agreeable place to stay in is Guatapé, 3 km beyond the rock, a pretty lakeside town with brightly coloured colonial houses and a pleasant plaza with a white and red Greco-Roman church, the **Parroquia Nuestra Señora del Carmen**. If you look closely you will notice a gaping mistake on the church clock. The Roman numeral for '4' has been executed incorrectly.

At the weekend Guatapé transforms with the volume of visitors from Medellín and the *malecón* (promenade) along the lake shore tends to fill up with pleasure boats blasting out music. There is also a zip wire (known as 'canopy') across a section of the lake. During the week its a quiet town with several economical accommodation options.

Around Medellín

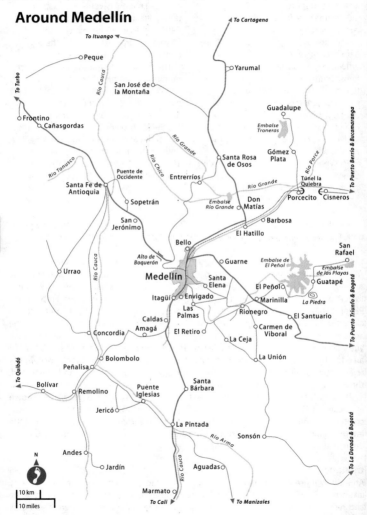

Discovering Reserva Natural Cañón del Río Claro

Before the main Bogotá–Medellín trunk road was completed, this majestic 150-m-deep limestone canyon was known only to jaguars and other animals of the forest.

Eduardo Betancourt, a *campesino* from a nearby *finca*, first discovered the gorge in 1964. Tracking a jaguar that had been killing his livestock, it took him six weeks to follow it back to the canyon. The animal eventually escaped him but not before leading him to the site, which locals refused to enter, believing it to be bewitched.

He returned home empty-handed but told his landowner Juan Guillermo Garcés about the canyon. Garcés was fascinated but nothing was done for a further six years until in 1970 a government engineer spotted it from a helicopter while searching for a suitable place to build a bridge across the river for the new road.

Garcés was inspired to see it for himself, so he set out with his brother and Betancourt. It took them two days to hack through the jungle and they had to enter the canyon itself by pulling themselves upriver on a raft.

They remained at the site for several months, building shelters in the caves under the steep walls of the canyon, and the diversity of species Garcés discovered during his stay inspired him to develop it into a private nature reserve to ensure its protection.

Fears that the building of the road would threaten the site were confirmed when 1500 visitors came on the first weekend of the completion of its construction. The canyon had gained some fame because journalists coming to stake out the nearby Hacienda Nápoles belonging to Pablo Escobar had made reports about this special place.

Garcés decided that it would be impossible to keep people away that the best way of protecting the canyon was to develop a sustainable tourism reserve. He named it 'El Refugio', in memory of its former role as a jaguar refuge.

Aside from the rock and the pleasure boats, Guatapé is known for its zócalos, the brightly painted skirting boards that adorn many of the houses. While originally a Spanish import, Guatapé is unique in that the residents have chosen to embellish theirs with intricate sculptures depicting local families and political events. Calle de los Recuerdos, a couple of blocks from the main plaza, has the best examples of these fascinating public works of art.

Guatapé has two convents nearby. One is a Benedictine monastery, which holds Eucharistic services with Gregorian chanting every Sunday at 1100. Las Adornadas del Divino Paraclito, a convent 6 kms away, holds 24-hour vigils. The nuns produce and sell honey and royal jelly. You can visit both by taking a mototaxi from the parque principal. **Note** There are no banks in Guatapé; the nearest bank with a cashpoint is at El Peñol.

Reserva Natural Cañón del Río Claro

ⓘ *www.rioclaroelrefugio.com.*

The Medellín–Bogotá road eventually descends into hot tropical forest before it meets the Río Magdalena at Puerto Triunfo. About three hours' drive and 152 km from Medellín is Reserva Natural Cañón del Río Claro, one of Colombia's first national parks, founded in 1970 by local landowner Juan Guillermo Garcés. A 450-ha conservation area based around a 150-m-deep limestone canyon, the nature reserve has spectacular walks through jungle paths alongside a crystal clear river with a marble bed. There are several caves that show the geological history of the area and a couple of sandy beaches. The reserve is noted for its incredible biodiversity with over 50 new species of plants discovered and more than 370 different species of bird identified since its foundation.

Doradal

About 15 km beyond Río Claro is Doradal, which has several hotels and restaurants alongside the busy Medellín–Bogotá trunk road but has an attractive plaza with palm trees and a beautiful church if you venture into the town proper. It is a convenient place to stay for visits to both the Río Claro Nature Reserve and Hacienda Nápoles.

Ins and outs Buses from the Terminal del Norte in Medellín to Doradal take three hours and cost US$14.

Hacienda Napoles

① *www.haciendanapoles.com, US$6.*

About 20 km beyond Río Claro is Hacienda Napoles, former country retreat of the notorious drug baron Pablo Escobar, now a theme park with a wildlife reserve full of exotic animals. Hacienda Nápoles was infamous throughout Colombia for the private zoo that Escobar put together and opened up for free to the public. Many of the animals – along with huge quantities of drugs – were flown in to the estate's private runway which with a length of 1280 m can land a Boeing 747. As the war between Escobar and the Colombian government escalated in the late 1980s, the estate was abandoned and was pillaged for secret stashes of money and drugs. It was repossessed by the government in 1989 and many of the animals died or were stolen. Some even escaped; it is believed that two of the hippos are now roaming free in the Magdalena river.

The estate consists of 2800 ha and is divided in four parts. One section houses a low-to-medium security prison with 1600 inmates. Another part has been given over to agricultural projects to provide employment for people displaced by the war. The rest of the estate has been handed over to a private firm to develop into a tourist attraction. The nature reserve is home to a herd of hippos – including 'El Viejo', who was part of Escobar´s collection – as well as water buffalo, ostriches, llamas, wild cats, monkeys and a butterfly sanctuary. In a slightly surreal turn, there is a collection of life size dinosaur models, rebuilt by the same model makers who built similar replicas for Escobar. You enter the reserve through gates with lettering uncannily similar to that used for the film of Jurassic Park.

It is also possible to visit Escobar´s old house, left in a state of disrepair, with holes in the swimming pool where bounty hunters excavated for buried treasure. The house, especially Escobar's bedroom, is remarkably small considering analysis by Forbes magazine placed Escobar as the seventh richest man in the world in his heyday. Other attractions include a Coliseum, used by Escobar as his private bullring, which now holds cultural events and exhibitions, and the runway.

At the time of writing there were several five-star hotels under construction as well as a camping zone but there are also several hotel options in nearby Doradal (see above).

South of Medellín ⊖⊖ ▶▶ pp245-248.

Santa Bárbara (Altitude 1857 m) is 57 km south of Medellín on the main road via the town of Caldas, with stunning views in every direction of coffee, banana and sugar plantations, orange-tiled roofs and folds of hills. There are hotels and restaurants on main plaza; the bus from Medellín costs US$1.20. A further 26 km is **La Pintada** (camping; hotels **F-G**). Here the road crosses the Río Cauca, then splits. To the left is the particularly attractive road through Aguadas, Pácora and Salamina, all perched on mountain ridges, to Manizales.

Alternatively, from La Pintada, the main road goes up the Cauca valley through **Riosucio**, a delightful town with fine views, a large church and many restaurants and shops. At Anserma the road turns east to Manizales via Arauca. There is beautiful country on the west side of the Río Cauca.

Shortly after Caldas, a road to the right (west) descends through Amagá to cross the Cauca at Bolombolo. From here, several attractive towns can be visited. **Jericó** is an interesting Antioquian town with a large cathedral, several other churches, two museums and a good view from Morro El Salvador. **Andes** is a busy coffee-buying centre, several places to stay and to eat, all on Carrera 50/51, with pretty waterfalls nearby.

Jardín is 16 km southeast of Andes. This pretty Antioquian village is surrounded by cultivated hills and trout farms. The plaza is full of flowering shrubs and trees. It was founded in 1863 on the site of an indigenous settlement (of the Embera-Katío group), who worked the naturally iodised salt in the river there. There is still a reservation of the Cristianías community in the locality. It is a delightful place with an attractive fountain in the plaza full of flowering shrubs and trees, living up to its name. The neo-gothic church, **Templo Parroquial de la Inmaculada Concepción**, has a fine façade built of dark, dressed stone. It is a National Monument. It has an elegant, striking altar of Italian marble and an eight-pointed star in the ceiling of the apse. There is a delightful festival (Fiesta de las Rosas) in January. The small museum in the Casa Cultura has paintings and local artefacts, and a bank that accepts Visa cards.

North of Medellín

The main road north from Medellín leads to Cartagena, 665 km. About 21 km north is **Santa Rosa de Osos**, 2550 m, founded in 1636 and with several surviving colonial buildings including the Humildad chapel. There are sculptures of Rodrigo Arenas Betancur and Marco Tobón Mejía. About 15 km southwest from Santa Rosa is **Entrerríos**, between the Río Grande and the Río Chico in attractive steep country, somewhat extravagantly called the 'Switzerland of Colombia', though the fishing is reported good. Nearby there is a 75 m *peñón*, El Monolito, which has proven to be of archaeological interest.

About 25 km north of Santa Rosa, a road to the west leads to **San José de la Montaña**, 2550 m, in the Páramo de Santa Inés, with cloudforest, caverns and waterfalls. 75 km beyond, over the gorge of Río Cauca, the rough road climbs again to **Ituango**, 1550 m, a town with simple accommodation, banks, pharmacies and a supermarket. Bus to Medellín.

From Ituango, rural transport is available to Badillo in the **Parque Nacional Natural Paramillo**, 460,000-ha of forest from the plains of the Río Sinú and the Río San Jorge to the headwaters of both rivers. There is páramo over 3000 m, the highest point, 3960 m, and a wide range of flora and fauna to see; caiman and turtles in the lower areas, monkeys, and many varieties of trees and birds at all levels.

The main road then climbs over to **Yarumal**, 122 km from Medellín, a friendly town in a cold mountain climate with fine views from Parroquia La Merced. There is a museum of religious art in the town hall and an interesting chapel, **Capilla de San Luis** nearby. There is a natural bridge 1 km from the town and several *peñoles* in the neighbourhood. There are many *hosterías* on the main plaza and Calle Caliente. A further high pass, Alto de Ventanas follows, then a drop to **Valdivia**, 159 km from Medellín. There are a number of good walking and riding trails here including to the gorges of Quebrada Valdivia and Quebrada El Oro and two waterfalls, Casacadas de Santa Inez and Chorros Blancos. There are *residencias* (**D-E**) to stay on the main road and several restaurants.

Santa Fe de Antioquia and around ⊜🚲🛏🛌⚠🛎🍴 ⟩⟩ pp245-248.
Colour map 2, B3.

→ *Phone code: 4. Population: 12,000. Altitude: 530 m.*

About 78 km northwest of Medellín is Santa Fe de Antioquia, or Santa Fe as it is frequently called. It was founded as a gold mining town by Mariscal Jorge Robledo in 1541, the first in the area, and still retains its colonial atmosphere, with interesting Christmas and New Year fiestas. For a time in the 19th century it was the capital of the department, and retains much of its grandeur and character, little affected by the changing times since then. It has some beautiful colonial mansions with wooden balconies and narrow cobbled streets. The plaza mayor is particularly attractive with an imposing cathedral and *artesanía* stalls selling tamarind products, nuts, honey and dried fruits. Its preservation was assured when it was given National Monument status in 1960.

Ins and outs
The bus station is on the road to Turbo at the north end of Carreras 9 and 10.

Sights
The **Catedral Metropolitano** is on the site of the first modest church in the town, built in the late-16th century. A second church was completed in 1673, with three naves, and other embellishments including chapels were added in the next 100 years. This in turn was replaced, in 1799, and the present building consecrated in 1837. It has an imposing white and coloured stone/brick façade (style called *calicanto* seen in a number of local buildings) overlooking the main plaza. There is a fine 17th-century Christ figure as the centrepiece of the high altar, and a notable Last Supper sculpture from the 18th century. The shrine with embossed-silver ornamentation was the work of local artists, but unhappily, several fine gold pieces, also of local workmanship, were stolen from the Treasury in 1986. The tower was used as a prison in times past.

The **Plaza Mayor** is dominated by the fountain, which has been supplying water

Santa Fe de Antioquia

Map labels:
To Turbo
To Coliseo & Puente de Occidente
Nuestra Señora de Chiquinquirá
Cra 13
Plaza José María Martínez Pardo
Palacio Arzobispal
Cra 12
La Casa Negra
Cra 11
Cra 10
Cathedral
Plaza Mayor
Cra 9
Museo de Arte Religioso
Santa Bárbara
Cra 8
Plazuela de Santa Bárbara
Casa de la Cultura
Cra 7
Cra 6
Jesús Nazareno
To Río Cauca & Medellín
To Río Cauca & Medellín
To Río Cauca & Medellín

100 metres
100 yards

Sleeping 🛏
Alejo 1
Caserón Plaza 2
Guaracú 3
Hostal Tenerife 4
Hostería de la Plaza Menor 5
Hostal Plaza Mayor 6
Las Carnes del Tío 7
Mariscal Robledo 8

Eating 🍴
Don Roberto 9
La Comedia 10
Macías 11
Napoli Pizzaría 12

to the town for 450 years and has a bronze statue of Juan del Corral, the President of Antioquia during its few years of independence between 1813 and 1826.

The **Iglesia de Santa Bárbara** ① *Cra 8 y C 11*, is also on the site of at least one previous building, which was passed to the Jesuits in 1728. They found it too small, and the present three-nave church was finished by Juan Pablo Pérez de Rublas at the end of the 18th century. The broad west front, also of *calicanto* style as are the interior walls and arches, is crowned with turrets and bells. An interesting woodcarving of the Virgin is enshrined in the Altar of San Blas, which is the oldest altar in Santa Fe. The font, in rococo style, is also older than the building.

The church of **Jesús Nazareno** is another classical style building, this from the 19th century, and is notable for the wood sculptures of Jesus on the cross and the representation of the Crown of Thorns. The church of **Nuestra Señora de Chiquinquirá** is across the José María Martínez Pardo square from the **Hotel Mariscal Robledo**, whose statue stands in the centre. The present church was built in the late 19th century on the site of a 17th-century Franciscan temple. An old painting of the Virgin of Chiquinquirá is built into the modern marble altar. This church too was used in the past as a prison. On the south side of the square is the **Palacio Arzobispal**, in republican style, well worth a look inside. Opposite is a music school, further evidence of the cultural life of the town.

The Museo Juan del Corral has been incorporated into the **Museo de Arte Religioso** ① *open weekends and holidays, 1000-1700*, next to the Iglesia de Santa Bárbara on Calle 11, which is being reorganized. There is an interesting collection of historical items, paintings, gold objects etc from colonial and more recent times. There are many fine colonial houses in the town, take a look inside where you can. Typical of the *calicanto* style are the *Casa de la Cultura*, and *La Casa Negra* (the birthplace of Fernando Gómez Martínez).

Around Santa Fe de Antioquia

A trip to the **Puente de Occidente** is well worthwhile. It is about 3 km downstream from the main (new) bridge and about 6 km from the centre of Santa Fe. You can walk, drive or take a taxi. Hitching is difficult as there is very little traffic. Leave the town northeast on Carrera 9, cross the main Turbo road, and follow the signs to the 'Coliseo'. The paved road winds through the suburbs of the town, then drops down steeply through dry scrub country to the river. The fine slender suspension bridge across the Cauca was designed and constructed by José María Villa, who studied in the USA, between 1887 and 1895. It is single track with wooden cross slats, 300-m long. Small vehicles are allowed to cross the bridge but are not encouraged: have a look – you will see why very few do so. The bridge was declared a National Monument in 1978.

⊕ Around Medellín listings → *Phone code: 4.*

For Sleeping and Eating price codes and other relevant information, see pages 31-36.

⊖ Sleeping

El Retiro *p238*
B El Gran Chaparral, Km 2 Vía La Fe, T5412451. Just outside El Retiro, this beautiful horse ranch and trout farm has fine rooms in

a converted stable. The horses across the yard are not for hire but alternative ones can be arranged on request. There is a large pond full of rainbow trout for fishing and a restaurant serving enormous Angus beef steaks or fish while horses are paraded past hungry diners. Rooms have cable TV and hot water.
C El Zaguán, C 21, No 22-08, T5412534. Modern brick building with 6 large and very

clean rooms. Has a rooftop with good views of the town and a small bar with occasional films shown on a video projector. Laundry service, TV and hot water.

E Casa Campesina, Cra 20, No 22-43, T5410692. This slightly run-down establishment near the parque principal has an extraordinary pulley system for opening the front door. Despite being a bit shabby it has good beds and several dorms.

Guatapé p239

B Hotel Guatatur, C 31, No 31-04, T8611212, www.hotelguatatur.fincasagroturisticas.com. Newish hotel in modern building just off the parque. Crisp, airy rooms with large windows and comfortable beds. The suites have lovely elevated jacuzzis with good views out to the lake. Restaurant, plasma-screen TV, minibar, room service. Breakfast included.

D El Descanso del Arriero, C 30, No 28-82, T8610878. An *arriero* is a mule driver and this pleasant hostel has a suitably rustic feel. It has good, clean rooms with private bath and hot water, some with a view to the church.

E La Florida, Cra 30, No 29-47, T8610600. On the main plaza above the bar of the same name. Simple but clean rooms. Rooms for hire in houses (**E**) can be found through calling the local tourist office on T8610555 ext 30 or T3128730302 (mob).

Reserva Natural Cañón del Río Claro p241

A El Refugio, T2688855 (Medellín), rioclaroelrefugio.une.net.co. Swiss Family Robinson-style wooden structures perched high above the river. All rooms have a balcony open to the elements and include all meals. There is also a small hostel (**D**) at the entrance to the reserve, with rooms with private bath, as well as a campsite (**F**). El Refugio also organizes rafting expeditions, Class I and II, more scenic than adventure sport. There is a series of zip wires (known in Colombia as 'canopy') which zig zag across the canyon and you can hire rubber rings to float down the river on.

Doradal p242

A Doradal Mediterráneo, Aldea Doradal, T8342129, http://hoteldoradalmediterraneo.blogspot.com. Aldea Doradal, a small community a couple of kilometres from Doradal could be a theme park nightmare. The whole village has been modelled on a Greek town, complete with whitewashed houses and narrow, windy streets. Somehow it works, partly due to the fact that locals have bought properties and injected some life into the place. The hotel, at the top of the village, has airy, a/c rooms with tiled bathrooms, a swimming pool and jacuzzi and Wi-Fi. Breakfast included.

B El Lago, 200 m east of Doradal on main road, T8342126. *Cabañas* with a/c and private bathrooms and a fine pool, though a little noisy with all the traffic.

E Hotel Yahaya, T8342177. On the main road but has clean, comfortable rooms with fan, TV, private bathroom and balcony as well as a good swimming pool. Has a restaurant serving typical dishes.

South of Medellín p242

There are several residencias and restaurants by the plaza.

A Hacienda Balandú, Vía Jardín Río Sucio, 800 m from town, T845 6850. Comfortable rooms, pool, gardens, lake, spa, sports, good restaurant.

Santa Fe de Antioquia p244, map p244

A Mariscal Robledo, C 10, No 9-70, T8531111. Former home of José María Martínez Pardo, former governor of Antioquia, this colonial mansion has a large swimming pool and commanding views across the valley. Staff can organize horse-riding trips and guided tours of the town.

A Guaracú, C 10, No 8-36, T8531097. Gorgeous colonial mansion with a restaurant set around a courtyard full of mango trees and palms. Beautiful antique furniture, gramophones, cameras and pistols interspersed throughout the building. There is even a large pet tortoise that wanders around the corridors. Rooms are very comfortable with TV and stereo. If not a guest you can pay for a *día de sol*, US$20, which includes lunch and a towel for relaxing by the delicious swimming pool.

A Hostal Tenerife, Cra 8, No 9-50, T8532261. This beautifully decorated colonial house has 7 rooms, each equipped with a/c, cable TV, and a minibar. There's free use of house bikes, internet access and a gorgeous swimming pool in one of its courtyards. Breakfast is incuded in the price. Recommended.

B Caserón Plaza, C 9, No 9-41, T8532040, www.hotelcaseronplaza.com.co. Large colonial building decorated with African carvings and potted plants. Comfortable rooms, some with balconies looking onto large pool. Has a fine sun deck with fantastic views across the valley. Internet room, Wi-Fi, bike hire, a/c and can arrange guides for local tours.

B Hostería de la Plaza Menor, C 9A, No 13-21, T8531133. Tucked away round the corner from the Plaza Menor, this hotel has 26 comfortable rooms and offers a swimming pool, Turkish bath, gym and a children's playground. A *día de sol* costs US$15.

C Las Carnes del Tío, C 10, No 7-22, T8533385. A restaurant that also offers some good rooms with vaulted ceilings and enormous bathrooms. Some dorms and shared baths.

D Hostal Plaza Mayor, Parque Principal, T8533448. Right on the main square, this is a popular choice with backpackers. There are hammocks, a small pool and a small *cabaña* with bunk beds (**E**). The owner also has a Mexican ranch outside town where he will take guests for a BBQ.

E Alejo, C 9, No 10-56, T8531091. Well placed at just 1 block from the Parque Principal, it has small and basic but clean rooms with their own TV and bathroom. Has a restaurant serving cheap food.

🍴 Eating

El Retiro *p238*
In addition to El Gran Chaparral (see above), there are several good places to eat on the Parque Principal, where there is also an ATM.

¶ Fonda de los Recuerdos, T5411605, at the entrance to town on the main road to Medellín, more antique junkyard than restaurant, which plays old boleros, tango and 1940s ballads and is reportedly a favourite with local politicians (there is a photograph of President Alvaro Uribe with eccentric owner Chepe on the wall).

Guatapé *p239*
There are several places to eat on the Parque Principal. Trout is a local speciality.

Doradal *p242*
¶¶ Asados del Camino, on main road at entrance to Doradal. *Bandeja paisa*, burgers and hotdogs in a large ranch.

Santa Fe de Antioquia *p244, map p244*
¶¶ Guaracu, C 10, No 8-36. In the hotel of the same name, the house speciality is fish especially trout. A *día de sol*, which includes a set menu lunch, use of the swimming pool 0900-1700 and a towel, cost US$17.

¶ Don Roberto, C 10, No 7-37. In a large colonial building with a swimming pool out the back, this restaurant has a simple menu of typical dishes such as *bandeja paisa* and *sancocho de bagre* as well as fast food. Delicious juices: try the *guandolo* – bitter orange with brown sugar. For use of the pool all day: US$4.50.

¶ La Comedia, C 11, No 8-03. On the corner of Parque Santa Bárbara, this restaurant has a novel concept: you can buy any of the furniture or utensils you use while you eat, all of which are made by *artesanos* from Barichara. Jazz music and exhibitions of work by local artists give it a Bohemian atmosphere. Colombian and international arthouse films are shown every Thu evening, projected either in the bar or in the parque.

♥ **Las Carnes del Tío**, C 10, No 7-22. Steaks and fish in the sunny courtyard of a fine colonial building.

♥ **Macías**, Parque Principal. On the main plaza, this small restaurant has been serving locals for over 35 years, so it must be doing something right. The menu is a mixture of regional and national dishes.

♥ **Napoli Pizzeria**, Cra 9, N0 10-61. Cheap and cheerful pizza by the slice.

⊛ Festivals and events

Santa Fe de Antioquia *p244, map p244*
Holy Week This is a major celebration here, and is followed by another week of festivities between the 2nd and 3rd Sun of Easter when there are many children's parades. This is known as Semana Santica.
Apr The Festival of Photography.
Oct A music festival is held in the Coliseo.
Dec Film festival for 5 days at beginning of the month.
22-31 Dec Fiesta de los Diablitos Folk dancing, parades, bullfights, etc.

❍ Shopping

Santa Fe de Antioquia *p244, map p244*
Guarnielería, C 10, No 7-66. Leather products, especially *carriel paisa*, a man's handbag replete with secret pockets for hiding your gun, now often used by women too.
Artesanías Antiguedades, Cra 10, No 10-71. Antique clocks, locks, cameras and typewriters as well as beautiful pâpier mache figurines.
Joyería Leydi, C 10, No 8-58. Excellent filigree gold jewellery.

▲ Activities and tours

El Retiro *p238*
Club Hípico Los Malos, Cra Santander, No 18-07, T5410436. Hire horses from US$22 per day with optional *burroteca* (a donkey with a music sound system attached).

Santa Fe de Antioquia *p244, map p244*
Gimnasio Life, C 10, No 7-09, T8534177. Only in Santa Fe can you get a gym housed in the courtyard of a beautiful colonial building. Exercise bikes and weights. US$2 for a half day.

For horse-riding excursions around local countryside, try **Carlos López Correa** T8531148 /T3113525213).

⊘ Transport

South of Medellín *p242*
Bus from **Medellín** (Terminal Sur), 4-5 hrs.

Santa Fe de Antioquia *p244, map p244*
Bus
To **Medellín** US$5 (Sotraurabá), 1hr.
Colectivos, US$7. To **Turbo**, US$20, 8 hrs, every 2 hrs or so.

ⓘ Directory

Santa Fe de Antioquia *p244, map p244*
Internet Comunícate sin límites, C 9, No 9-33 (Parque Principal). Internet and fax services.

Chocó

Undoubtedly one of the rainiest and most bio-diverse locations on the planet the Pacific coast of Colombia's Chocó region is overlooked and under-visited. Fearing the very real yet ubiquitous tales of kidnapping and guerrilla activity in this region, tourists understandably are quick to avoid coming this far west into Colombia – but with a little research and some good faith there are parts of the Pacific Chocó that are not completely out of bounds. For the most part it is recommended that you check in with the local authorities to find out what might be going on here before taking the plunge.

Stretching like a ribbon for 400 km between the Cordillera Occidental and the Pacific coast, from Panama to Valle del Cauca, Chocó is one of Colombia's least-developed and most beautiful departments. In the northern three-quarters of the department, the mountain ranges of the Serranía de Los Saltos and Serranía del Baudó rise directly from the ocean to reach a height of about 500 m. The scenery of pristine rainforest descending the mountain slopes to the sea is spectacular.
➤➤ *For listings, see pages 251-252.*

Ins and outs

The easiest and most convenient way to get out to the coast is to fly from Medellín or Bogotá via Quibdó to either Nuquí or Bahía Solano. **Satena**, www.satena.com, and **Aires**, www.aires.com.co both cover the routes. You can travel overland from Medellín with **Rápido Ochoa** but the road is currently unpaved, perilous and runs through the heart of the conflict.

Quibdó ☺☺☺ ➤➤ *pp251-252. Colour map 2, B2.*

➔ *Phone code: 4. Population: 131,000. Altitude: 50 m.*

Quibdó, the capital of the department, is an unlovely and underwhelming city on the frontline where the few western faces you are likely to see are aid workers or delegates from Medecins Sans Frontiéres. There is little to keep you here save for the unstoppable partying during the city's fiestas and the warmth and curiosity of the locals regarding your choice of tourist destination. Quibdó is the jumping-off point for most military operations in this stretch of the country and it is not uncommon to see brigades of soldiers returning war weary from the jungle here while the new batch ready themselves for their next outing.

Ins and outs

Travelling on from Quibdó you are strongly recommended to fly to Nuquí or Bahía Solano. In July 2008 a dozen or so Colombians travelling the Atrato River from Quibdó to the coast were kidnapped by the FARC guerrillas. They have since been released.

Along the Pacific coast ☺☺☺ ➤➤ *pp251-252.*

Nuquí ➔ *Colour map 2, B1.*

Nuquí town has very little to offer the visitor aside from a serviceable runway and some poorly stocked shops. It is to the north and south of the town where the real attractions lie in the form of award-winning ecolodges. ➤➤ *For further information, see Sleeping, page 251.*

El Valle → *Colour map 2, B1.*

Some 50 km north of Nuquí along the coast, El Valle has the best bathing and surfing beaches in the area. With tourism development there has been a decline in friendliness. El Almejal, north of town, is the best beach. The entrance to El Valle's harbour is very tricky at ebb tide and many boats have been swept onto the rocks here. As yet there is no access for regular vehicles. If hiring boats privately, check carefully before accepting offers. Make sure there are life jackets for any sea journeys. Solomon and his son Absolom are recommended.

A local product is *borojo* marmalade, made from a local fruit tasting like tamarind. Guides are available for tours by canoe up the Río Baudó, and to other places of interest along the coast. El Nativo has been recommended. A beautiful isolated beach, El Tigre can be visited by boat, or a three hour walk. Near El Valle the Fundación Natura have a Tortugario where they protect turtle eggs from predators in season. Visits are possible.

Parque Nacional Ensenada de Utria → *Colour map 2, B1.*
① *Entry is US$1.50 with a US$2 embarkation/disembarkation charge.*

Between Nuquí and El Valle is Parque Nacional Natural Ensenada de Utria. This 54,000-ha Park was created in 1987 to preserve several unique aquatic and terrestrial habitats. Steep, heavily forested mountains come down to the ocean to create dramatic scenery. Day trips may be arranged from El Valle, Nuquí, or Bahía Solano and special permits are sometimes granted for longer stays by MA in Bogotá. A (free) permit must be obtained from a MA office. The ranger welcomes volunteers to help in clearing rubbish from the beaches and other tasks (also best arranged in advance from Bogotá).

Getting there Boats hired from El Valle take one hour and cost approximately US$16 return, from Nuquí 1½ hours, US$24. Boats will not leave when the sea is too rough, which may be for several days. The launch that runs from Nuquí to El Valle can sometimes (depending on tides) leave you at Playa Blanca, a small, privately owned island near the park boundary. Here Sr Salomón Caizamo has a simple restaurant, but the food is good and he rents space, US$2 for up to five hammocks (a nice spot). There is good snorkelling and fishing. The park headquarters are five minutes away by motorboat and you can generally hitch a ride with fishermen or park employees. There are also a road and trail leading through the jungle from El Valle to the head of the inlet (9 km, four to five hours, can be very muddy), but you must arrange for a boat to pick you up as it is not possible to reach the park headquarters on foot.

The park is named after a large inlet (*ensenada*) at its centre, which is home to two varieties of whales, corals, needlefish, and many other aquatic species. This is one of the best places on the west coast of South America to see humpback whales migrating from late July to mid October. Motorboats are not allowed past the park headquarters, located halfway up the inlet, and the area is best appreciated if you paddle through in a canoe (try to rent or borrow). The surrounding hillsides are covered with pristine rainforest and there are several magnificent white sand beaches.

At the park headquarters and visitor centre there are maps, good information and a display of whale bones and other exhibits, plus a small restaurant. There are several well-marked trails. There is simple but comfortable accommodation for about 15 people in a guest house at US$6 per night and an outdoor kitchen with a wood stove, meals US$3, but camping is prohibited. Fresh fish can sometimes be purchased, but all other provisions should be brought from town. Mosquito nets are essential for protection against insects and vampire bats. Across the inlet from the headquarters is a private research station run by Fundación Natura as a base for biologists.

Bahía Solano → Colour map 2, B1.

Bahía Solano should be a much bigger tourist destination than it is given its levels of security and infrastructure. During the annual migration of the humpback whales – their breaching can be seen from the shore – the town in overrun with holidaymakers from Medellín. Outside of this period Bahía Solano is a functional fishing town with a side trade in collecting discarded keys of cocaine on their way north. This industry is so lucrative to local fishermen, who stand to earn a lifetime's pay in one swoop, that it has become a principal activity and at times this fishing village is often bereft of fish! Diving to a scuttled Naval Ship, hiking to waterfalls, sports fishing and visiting neighbouring beaches are just some of the attractions that can be enjoyed here. Drop in to the **Hotel Balboa Plaza**, you can't miss it as the only three-storey building in town, a folly and luxury pad built by Pablo Escobar falling into disrepair.

◉ Chocó listings

For Sleeping and Eating price codes and other relevant information, see pages 31-36.

◉ Sleeping

Quibdó *p249*
Quibdó is not overwhelmed with decent places to stay, but centrally located and safe is the **Hotel Malecón**, T4-6714662.

Nuquí *p249*
The **Piedra Piedra** (T5728931258, www.piedrapiedra.com), **Pijiba Lodge** (T5744745221, www.pijibalodge.com), and **Morromico** (T5785214172, www.morro mico.com) are environmentally aware, award-winning and design-oriented locations that can organize fishing trips, surfing outings and kayak rental. As communication is scant out here and usually by radio it is imperative to book ahead through the main offices in Medellín as the staff will be providing you with 3 sumptuous meals and will need to stock up in advance.

In 2007, several Colombians and 1 Norwegian were kidnapped from the Morromico lodge by FARC guerrillas. It is believed that a ransom was paid that resulted in the captives being liberated.

El Valle *p250*
Several large but simple tourist complexes at El Almejal, with rooms and cabins

(D-E range), as well as bars and restaurants (deserted on weekdays off-season).
AL Cabañas El Almejal, cabins with private bath, the best, clean, friendly, full board, reservations T2306060 (Medellín). Price depends on the package arranged, eg 3 nights/4 days, US$200.
L Las Gaviotas Centro Vacacional, T3413806 (Medellín). Cabins, good facilities.
C El Morro, full board, **D** with breakfast.
F Cabinas Villa Maga, between El Valle and El Almejal. Friendly, safe, family-run.
There is other accommodation in **E** and **F** categories, for example **Carmen Lucía** or **El Nativo y Rosa.** Ask around.

Bahía Solano *p251*
Las Brisas del Cabo Marzo, www.mapara crab.com, T573154887679. Run by the affable and knowledgeable Nancy and Enrique Ramírez, this is a small, comfortable family enterprise offering private rooms with fan and breakfast. Enrique is a master sports fisherman and diving enthusiast.

◉ Eating

Nuquí *p249*
Several small restaurants on the road to the airport serving mostly fish. Shops are well stocked with basic goods, prices somewhat higher than in Quibdó.

Bahía Solano *p251*
Good food at **Las Delicias** and at the restaurant run by Señora Ayde near the **Balboa** hotel.

🔘 Transport

Quibdó *p249*
Air To **Medellín**, Aces and SAM daily flights, US$40. To **Bogotá**, Aces daily; to **Bahía Solano** and **Nuquí**, daily, Aces and SAM. Enquire about other non-scheduled flights at holiday times.

Boat From Buenaventura up the Río San Juan to **Istmina** and on by road; infrequent services. Irregular cargo service down the Río Atrato to **Turbo** and **Cartagena** takes passengers. Cost to Turbo US$26, food included; to/from Cartagena US$40-55, 4 days, take drinking water. Deal directly with boatmen. Also 20-seater power boats, 7 hrs to Turbo, about US$30. The lower Atrato was a very dangerous area in 2000 (guerrillas, kidnappings, drug running). Much caution and detailed advance enquiry are strongly recommended.

Bus Transportes Ochoa to **Medellín** via El Carmen and Bolívar, 5 daily, 10-12 hrs, US$14 luxury coach, cheaper by regular bus. Transportes Arauca to **Manizale**s via Tadó, Pueblo Rico, La Virginia and Pereira, Tue, Thu, Sat, Sun at 0600, 14-17 hrs, US$16. Flota Occidental along same route to Pereira, daily at 0700, 8-10 hrs, US$15. Occasional buses to **Cali**, US$22 otherwise change at La Virginia. To **Bogotá**, US$27. Local service to **Santa Cecilia** and **Tadó**.

Nuquí *p249*
Air To **Quibdó**, Aces, 20 mins; to **Medellín**, Aces and SAM, US$70, 50 mins. All flights on Mon, Wed, Fri, and Sun only, return same day. Some extra flights Christmas and Easter time.

Overland Construction is continuing on a road from Las Animas to Nuquí, which will eventually connect the port planned for Tribugá with the interior. It is presently a strenuous 3-day trek along a jungle trail, through several indigenous villages, to Nuquí.

Sea There are launches south to Arusi (Mon, Wed, Fri), and, north to El Valle, there is a new twin engined boat, the *Magdalena* Mon, Wed and Fri calling at Jurubidá, US$4, La Esperanza, US$4, and El Valle, US$8, returning Tue, Thu and Sat, as well as occasional coastal vessels (small fuel barges) to Buenaventura, cost to Buenaventura about US$40. Sea taxis will take you to beaches and villages along the coast.

El Valle *p250*
Jeep A road runs 18 km from El Valle to Bahía Solano (passes by the airport before town). Jeeps leave every morning, 1-hr ride, US$2.50, tickets can be purchased 1 day in advance.

Bahía Solano *p251*
Air To **Medellín**, daily flights with Aces, 4 a week with SAM, US$65. To **Quibdó**, daily with SAM, US$35. Reconfirm return flights and arrive early when leaving.

Sea Some coastal cargo vessels north to **Juradó** and south to **Buenaventura**, eg M/V Fronteras, US$45, including food, 36 hrs, cramped bunks.

ℹ️ Directory

Quibdó *p249*
Banks Banco de Bogotá, cash against Visa, other banks do not change money. Restaurant El Paisa, Farmacia Mercedes, and a few shopkeepers sometimes change US$ cash, but rates are poor. Best to buy pesos in larger centres before arriving. **Immigration DAS office** C 29, Cra 4. No entry or exit stamps.

La Zona Cafetera

The three departmental capitals of La Zona Cafetera are in a north-south line, Manizales (Caldas) in the north, Pereira (Riseralda) 50 km away in the centre and Armenia (Quindío) a similar distance to the south, flanked to the east by the massif of Los Nevados. Because of the altitude, the climate is very agreeable and the road and transport facilities are good. There is much to see and enjoy and this is an excellent part of Colombia to visit with good services in the three cities. Much of the local transport in this region is by chiva (literally 'goat'), which are old, simple, brightly coloured buses, and jeeps, often called by the historic name 'Willys', also ancient but lovingly maintained. You will see that this area would be much the poorer without them.

All three can be reached from Bogotá by a road (309 km) passing through Facatativá and Honda and then over the Páramo de las Letras pass (3700 m, the highest main road pass in Colombia), or through Girardot to Ibagué and over the high crest of the Quindío pass (3250 m). ▸▸ *For listings, see pages 270-280.*

Manizales 🔘 ▸▸ *pp270-280. Colour map 2, C3.*

→ *Phone code: 6. Population: 335,000. Altitude: 2153 m.*

Manizales is a comparatively new city, founded in 1848 by a group of settlers from Antioquia looking for a peaceful place at a time of civil disturbances further north. As a result, Manizales has the feel of a late 19th-century city with 'republic' period architecture and a fierce pride in Los Fundadores, the founders of the city. However, this area is unstable geologically and was struck by severe earthquakes in 1875 and 1879 only to be followed by fires that swept through the city in 1925 and especially 1926, severely damaging the centre. The city is now dominated by its enormous cathedral, not unreasonably of reinforced concrete, and still to be finished. Two previous cathedrals on the site were destroyed and even this one suffered during an earthquake in 1979. Yet another threat to the city is the Nevado del Ruiz volcano seen to the southeast, which erupted in November 1985, but most of the damage done was to communities on the side away from Manizales.

Ins and outs

Getting there La Nubia airport is to the southeast overlooking the city. Buses to the centre US$1, taxi US$4. There are several daily flights from Bogotá, Cali and Medellín with **Avianca, Aires** and **Aerolíneas de Antioquia** (ADA), though due to the altitude and humidity, services are often delayed by fog. The bus terminal is seven blocks from the centre of the city. Travellers should take care around the station at night as crime is high in this area. There are good roads and comfortable bus services from the main cities of Colombia. From Bogotá and the east the Cordillera Central must be crossed, the most direct route via Honda crosses at 3700 m. Alternatively, via Girardot and Pereira, the pass is lower at 3250 m. Both are long winding climbs and descents.

Getting around The centre of Manizales is pleasant and convenient for walking, though narrow streets create traffic problems. An added attraction is the extensive views often seen over the local countryside. The key thoroughfare is Carrera 23, which runs the full length of the city, also called Avenida Santander in the east. It is the road to La Nubia airport, Honda and Bogotá. East of the centre is **El Cable**, centred around one of the pylons that made up the old cable car route It's the city's Zona Rosa and has the best restaurants and bars. Further east again is **Barrio Milán**, another popular nightime area.

Tourist information
Fomento y Turismo ① *C 29, no 20-25, T8846211, guidebook and maps available, open 0800-1200, 1400-1800, Mon-Fri*. For Los Nevados and other national parks, try **Unidad de Parques Nacionales** ① *C 76B, No 18-14, T8864104*.

Sights
The city was founded on a narrow saddle that falls away sharply to the north, west and south into adjacent valleys. Expansion has been to the east, along precipitous ridges between the Río Chinchiná and Quebrada Olivares using every available piece of flat land. Villages in the valleys are gradually being absorbed by the city, though a spectacular site for the visitor, the terrain causes significant travel difficulties. The climate is extremely humid (average temperature is 17°C, and the annual rainfall is 3500 mm), encouraging prodigious growth in the area around the city including the flowers that line the highways to the suburbs north and south. Frequently the city is covered in cloud but when it is clear, there are brilliant views in every direction. With luck, you may see the snows of the Nevados to the southeast. The best months of the year are from mid-December through to early March. The city looks down on the small town of Villa María, 'the village of flowers', now almost a suburb. Due to the earthquakes and fires, much of the architecture is predominantly modern with high-rise office and apartment blocks. Traditional 19th-century architectural styles are still seen in the suburbs and the older sections of the city.

The centre of the city is the **Plaza de Bolívar** with two ceramic murals by Guillermo Botero and a central plinth on which stands an extraordinary bronze statue of Bolívar Condor (1991) by Rodrigo Arenas Betancur, which depicts Bolívar as a condor, his head dismembered from his body and protruding into the plaza. On the north side of the plaza is the departmental government building, **La Gobernación**, an imposing example of neo-colonial architecture, built in 1926 around a central garden patio. The building was declared a National Monument in 1984.

Opposite is the **cathedral**, a new building constructed after the fires of 1925 and 1926 mainly of reinforced concrete, neo-gothic in style, with an elegant spire over 100 m high. It was designed and built by Italian architects between 1928 and 1939, although some work still continues, including strengthening the cupola. It now has four towers, one each dedicated to saints Inés, Francis, Mark and Paul. Inside look for the fine decorated altar cover with a suspended cross above, the wooden choir stalls and colourful stained-glass windows including a fine rose window at the west end. There is also a simple but elegant marble font to the left of the west door.

Nearby, the **Banco de la República** ① *Cra 23, No 23-06, 0900-1000, 1100-1130, 1430-1830 (yes, really), Mon-Fri, free*, has a gold and anthropology museum, with classical music every afternoon, a good reference library, and records and videos.

The **Iglesia de la Inmaculada Concepción** ① *Cra 22/C 30*, overlooks **Parque Caldas**, again in neo-Gothic style with cedarwood pillars, roof arching inside and stained-glass windows. It was built 1903-1921. **Iglesia de los Agustinos** ① *Cra 18, near the bus station*, has a colonial-style façade and many spires around the building.

The **bull-ring** ① *Av Centenario*, built around 1950, is an impressive copy of the traditional Moorish style, based on the one in Córdoba, Spain. It holds 20,000 people. Bullfights take place in late January, early Febuary, tickets US$8-27 depending on whether they are in *sol* or *sombra*. There are also fights in June and July with young bulls with no kills. The **University of Manizales** ⓘ *off Cra 23 at C 40*, is housed in a fine building (originally the railway station) of considerable historic interest. **Universidad de Caldas** ⓘ *C 65 No 26-10, Mon-Fri 0800-1200, 1400-1800 (take a 'Fátima' bus to the University)*, has a natural history museum with a good selection of butterflies, moths and birds. The **Centro de Museos** ⓘ *Cra 23, No 58-65, T8851374, Mon-Fri, 0800-1200, 1400-1600*, also part of Caldas University, has an art gallery and exhibitions on geology and archaeology. **The Teatro de los Fundadores** ⓘ *Cra 23/C 33*, at the eastern entrance to the city centre is a good example of local architecture. This is well worth a visit with some fine murals and metal sculptures in the foyer and upper floors, including works by Guillermo Botero (see below).

La Galería del Arte ⓘ *Av Santander (Cra 23) at C 55*, which has exhibitions of work by local artists. These can be bought. Further out on the road to Bogotá at Calle 65, you will see the tower of the Manizales terminal of the aerial cableway that went 75 km to Mariquita from 1922 till the 1960s carrying coffee, thus avoiding the difficult grind up to the Alto de Las Letras pass (3700 m) and down the other side. From Mariquita the coffee was taken by road and rail to the Río Magdalena for shipment and export.

Chipre is a suburb in the northwest of the city and has, in its centre, the **Nuestra Señora del Rosario church**, which is a replica of the previous city cathedral. Along Avenida 12 de Octubre, the west side is an open park with magnificent views over coffee country down towards the Río Cauca. Across to the east are views of the city. It is much frequented by locals at weekends. Stalls along promenade sell *obleas*, large wheat wafers, served with *arequipa*, coconut or *dulce de leche*, well worth a try. The large water tower,

Manizales

To Medellin
CHIPRE
Nuestra Señora del Rosario
El Tanque
To Monumento a los Colonistas
Av 12 de Octubre
To Plaza de Toros & Pereira
Av Centenario
Transversal 10
Los Agustinos
Av Santander Cra 18
La Gobernación
Plaza de Bolívar
Cathedral
Banco de la República
Teatro de los Fundadores
Parque Caldas
Inmaculada Concepción
To El Cable, Universidad de Caldas, Centro de Museos, La Galería del Arte, Airport & Bogotá
To University of Manizales

N
200 metres
200 yards

Sleeping		Eating
Bolívar Plaza 1	Mountain House 7	Chung Mi No 2 1
Bolívar 2	Roma Plaza 9	Las Vegas 2
California 3	Regine's 10	Pollo y Asado 3
Carretero 4	Tama Internacional 11	
Escorial 5	Varuna 12	
Las Colinas 6		

known as **El Tanque** is a local landmark. At the end of the avenue, is a new impressive sculpture, **the Monumento a los Colonistas**.

Excursions

Visits to coffee farms in the area are warmly recommended. They are often included in local tours arranged by agencies or through hotels. You will also see the spectacular local countryside. For staying on coffee farms, see box, opposite. For visits to Los Nevados National Park, see page 260.

Around Manizales ⏺ ➤ pp270-280.

About 8 km from Manizales is the **Parque Ecológico Río Blanco**, a 4343-ha protected cloudforest, considered by the World Wildlife Fund the best place for birdwatching in Colombia. To date, 335 species of bird have been identified, including 33 species of hummingbird. There are also 350 species of butterfly as well as 40 types of orchid and mammals such as spectacled bears, ocelots and the white-tailed deer. Some of the rarer birds that can be seen include a sub species of the rusty-faced parrot, the royal woodpecker and four types of toucan. The park is owned by **Aguas de Manizales** ① T8867777, which manages the water from the Río Blanco, providing Manizales with 35% of its drinking water, believed to be some of the purest in the world.

There are several hikes of between 20 minutes and eight hours as well as a rangers' hut where 22 species of hummingbird come to feed, managed by the **Fundación Ecológica Gabriel Arango Restrepo** ① www.fundegar.com, which conducts scientific flora and fauna investigation in the park with the support of WWF.

Before the area was turned into a reserve it was inhabited by campesino farming families. These have been allowed to stay and have been trained as rangers.

Entry is free but you must take a guide (recommended tip US$10) and you must get permission from Aguas de Manizales – ask for the Oficina de Recursos Naturales. Birdwatchers, photographers and hikers can stay at the Fundación Ecológica Gabriel Arango Restrepo's **rangers' hut** ① contact Technical Director Sergio Ocampo, T8867777, ext 1164, sergiofundegar@gmail.com. There are basic dormitories with bunk beds, US$17 per person, food US$12.50.

North of Manizales

The Pan-American highway runs north from Manizales to Medellín through some picturesque countryside dotted with small villages perched on the fertile montainsides of the Cordillera Occidental. As the road crosses the Río Cauca it reaches a fork: you can take the left turn to Supía and Río Sucio, or turn right to Medellín via Marmato.

Supía → Colour map 2, B3. Phone code: 6. Population: 30,000. Altitude: 1183 m.

With its backdrop of resplendent rolling green hills and an agreeable temperate climate, the small town of Supía, 77 km from Manizales, is worth a visit. It has a picturesque Parque Principal with palms and *ceiba* trees covered in Spanish Moss or *tillandsia*, as well as several attractive bird houses. A mixture of colonial and modern architecture, the town has an impressive church with two imposing towers.

It is known throughout the region for its *colación*, a sweet delicacy made from sugar cane; the **Feria de Colación** is celebrated every two years around the end of June/ beginning of July.

Staying on a coffee finca

The severe coffee crisis that hit the world in 1992 and has to some extent continued to this day, severly affected the coffee region of Caldas, Risaralda and Quindío. The emrgence of new coffee-growing nations such as Vietnam pushed up production levels to unprecedented levels while demand has not kept pace.

Colombia, with its emphasis on quality over quantity, has struggled. Coffee growers in the region have been forced to diversify into other crops. In 1994, Quindío's tourism board, emulating the success of Spain's countryside haciendas, proposed to the region's *finca* owners an alternative source of income, and the the idea of opening up coffee farms to tourism was born.

From stately post-colonial Antioquian mansions to some pretty primitive accommodation, no two *fincas* are the same. Some still produce their own coffee – and offer tours in which you can learn about the process of coffee-growing – while others have retired that part of the business and give guests the chance to relax, lounge around pools and appreciate the incredible richness of flora and fauna of the region.

There are over 980 registered coffee farms in the Department of Quindío alone. Below are just a few recommendations.

L Hacienda San José, see page 272, simply breathtaking.
L Hacienda Bambusa, see page 274, an enchanting traditional hacienda.
AL Finca Villa Nora, see page 274, a working coffee farm.
A El Delirio, see page 274, a beautiful, traditional *finca*.
A-B Hacienda Guayabal, see page 271, one of the best places to do a coffee tour in the region.
C El Carriel, see page 274, runs an excellent coffee tour.

For further details on staying in coffee *fincas*, visit www.clubhaciendas delcafe.com.

It is an excellent place for hiking in the hills. A particularly interesting trip is to Marmato, a town where gold is still mined as it was during the time of the Spanish conquistadors (see below), which can be reached by walking over the mountain or by *chiva* or jeep via a spectacular unpaved road.

There is an interesting little museum displaying religious artefacts at the back of the church, where there is also useful tourist information on the surrounding area.

Marmato ● ›› pp270-280. Colour map 2, B3.

→ *Phone code: 6. Altitude: 1350 m.*

Sat on top of a mountain, up an unpaved road some 7 km off the Manizales–Medellín highway and 80 km from Medellín, is Marmato, a village with a colourful history steeped in myths and legends. Since the 16th century, Marmato has been the focus of foreign exploitation by the Spanish, German and English because of its gold mines. Today local gold prospectors dynamite and excavate the mountain much in the same way they would have done 400 years ago. The locals still tell stories of witches, curses and ancient religious practices carried out by the black slaves who were brought to Marmato to extract gold for their foreign masters (see box, page 258, for more details).

The legends of Marmato

Known as the 'cradle of Colombian gold', it is believed that gold has been mined in Marmato for more than 500 years. When Sebastian de Belalcazar and Jorge Robledo arrived with their Spanish *conquistadores* in 1536 they found the local indigenous Cartamas already mining the mountain and fashioning beautiful *huacas* out of its gold.

Belalcazar and Robledo promptly disappeared (taking the Cartamas' bounty with them) but marched back in 1539 bringing black slaves from Cartagena to work the mines. Word spread about the fortune under the mountain and shortly afterwards German mercenaries, who had joined the Spanish hunt for El Dorado, arrived. They built their own mines in San Juan, a village just up the mountain from Marmato. In the 19th century, the British arrived on the invitation of the Colombian government, which used Marmato as collateral to secure funding for its fight for independence against the Spanish. Most recently, most of the mining rights have been bought by the Canadian company, Colombian Goldfields, which plans to exploit the mountain's vast reserves of gold and mine it on a commercial basis.

Marmato is a place steeped in myth, legend and superstition. Witches are said to live in the hills above; a cross at the mountain's peak is meant to ward off flying witches. The witches are said to be beautiful and have the power to entrance any man. In former times, the locals say they persuaded the foreign gold prospectors who came to Marmato to drink from the enchanted waters of the Cascabel spring. This was supposed to make them fall in love with the women of Marmato and never want to leave.

The slaves brought in by the Spanish to work the mines had their own distinct culture. Legend has it that they practised a sacred ritual under an ancient *ceiba* tree in which they formed a ring around the most beautiful slave girl and made her drink the blood of a sacrificial goat while she undressed. The local Catholic priest, shocked by the practice, denounced the slaves as devil worshippers and cursed them. The *ceiba* tree is believed to have fallen away in a landslide following the priest's damnation.

This is not the only example of divine intervention. The 16th-century **Iglesia de Santa Bárbara** has collapsed and been rebuilt several times, some say because the town priest cursed the village for of its liking for heavy drinking and prostitution; there is a belief in Marmato that the more you drink, the more gold you will find. The curses appear to continue to this day: in 2006 the town plaza and *alcaldía* were buried under a landslide. Luckily, no-one was killed.

Marmato has continued in its mining tradition to the present day. Many of the techniques used are little different to those used 400 years ago and most of the work is done by small teams of miners working for individually owned mines. There are currently 117 individual mining concessions in the Zona Alta (the area immediatley above Marmato) alone.

But all this looks set to change. In 2005, the Canadian-owned mining company Colombia Goldfields began acquiring concessions with the approval of the Colombian government. Thus far they have bought up 111 of the 117 concessions in Zona Alta, and the remainder of the individual owners look likely to be forced to capitulate.

Marmato is something of a paradox. While some of its houses have retained their traditional *tapia pisada* architecture and afford spectacular views down into the valley below; other parts are not so picturesque but are nonetheless fascinating to behold. Entire chunks of the mountain have been gouged out in the pursuit of gold, or have fallen away in frequent landslides; in 2006 the plaza mayor and the alcaldía were buried under tonnes of mud which at the time of writing had yet to be cleared. Buckets full of gold ore extracted from the mines zip up and down on wires that criss-cross the valley, while lorries trundle through its steep, narrow streets.

Marmato has a reputation for heavy drinking and philandering. The **Feria de Oro** in October is a raucous event involving copious consumption of beer and *aguardiente*. On Friday afternoons, busloads of prostitutes are shuttled in to satisfy the miners' needs.

Sights

The most interesting sights are above the village. Walk past the church and its square, along the main street. Beyond a row of shops there is a narrow cobbled street to the left. Keep climbing past the primary school and you will reach the secondary school where they will hire out helmets and Wellington boots (essential if you are going to visit one of the mines).

Beyond the school you will reach the main plaza and alcaldía (currently abandoned). Here there are spectacular views down into the village and the valley below, and some interesting murals depicting the legends of Marmato.

Exiting the plaza to the right you will notice several abandoned houses. Step inside to see how these homes incorporated former mines built by the Germans – some were used as kitchens or pantries. If you continue walking along a narrow path – be mindful how you go as this path is prone to landslides – you will reach a viewpoint from which you can see a stream running down a muddy gully. This is the source of the **Aguita de Cascabel**, a spring whose water the witches of Marmato fed to unsuspecting foreigners to make them fall in love with the village and its women. It is said that once someone drank from its waters they would never leave Marmato. From here, looking further down, beyond a former water mill, you can also see several stone buildings pegged to the side of the hill opposite. These were prison cells used to punish slaves.

From the plaza's lookout point, down below to your left you will notice a colonial building with a small park. This is the **Parque de los Mineros**, which houses a small library and several ingenious statues – a miner, a witch and a slave girl – made from miners' tools and nuts and bolts. It also has the original bell that was used to call the slaves to work, although someone has stolen the clapper! You can reach the park by leaving the plaza opposite the alcaldía and turning right beyond a group of buildings.

In these buildings there is a small silver studio. The workers will sell pieces of sillver at reasonable prices. Retracing your footsteps from the Parque de los Mineros, past the silver studios you will reach a small gold mine, owned by the town mayor. Here there are several pulley systems bringing down gold ore from mines further up. You can observe how the crushed rock is siphoned off with water to separate the gold. Here you can ask one of the miners to take you into the mine. The miners can provide head torches. There is no charge but a tip of US$5 would be appreciated. Health and safety is not a priority in Marmato. The mines are narrow, muddy and there is little oxygen. Do not enter if you suffer from claustrophobia. This is a working mine; you are likely to hear dynamite blasts in other parts of the mountain. You enter at your own risk.

ⓘ *Entry to the park is US$17 for non-Colombians.*

Los Nevados are a compact range of volcanic peaks in central Colombia and the nearest and most accessible mountains to Bogotá. This is a park with all the savage beauty associated with mountains, dormant volcanoes, hot springs and recent memories of tragic eruptions. The park is home to the huge volcanos of **Nevado del Ruiz**, **Nevado de Santa Rosa** and **Nevado del Tolima**. The highest of the three, Nevado del Ruiz (5321 m) erupted in 1985, completely destroying the village of Armero under a mud stream. In total the eruption killed more than 25,000 people. Nevado del Tolima is also still active but hasn't shown major changes in activity recently. The high-altitude volcano vegetation with *frailejones* up to 12 m, the volcanic lakes and the active volcanoes are all absolutely worth visiting.

All three volcanoes can be climbed and there are several treks within the park. The longest and toughest trek is from south (Ibaqué) to north (Manizales) in the park in six days. From Manizales you can take a 4WD up to Laguna de Otún, but deeper into the park it is hard to find any trails at all and therefore it's highly recommended that you hire a guide who knows the area well. A number of treks and hikes are available. ⤻ *For further information, see Activities and tours, page 277.*

Sights

Nevado del Ruiz is the highest of the three volcanoes. From Manizales it is easy to climb to 5100 m (after being dropped by car at 4800 m), which is a popular day tour, but with a special permit and gear it is also possible to climb to the top (5321 m). On peak days, the easier climb may be very crowded. **Laguna Verde Encantado** is a beautiful green lake between Paramillo el Cisne and **Nevado de Santa Isabel**. Nevado de Santa Isabel is the lowest of the three volcanoes and inactive. At the summit (5000 m) there is an amazing view (weather permitting), with Nevado del Ruiz to the north and Nevado del Tolima to the south. **Laguna Otún** is the biggest lake of the park and full of trout, fishing gear is available to rent. It is also one of the base camps to climb up Nevado de Santa Isabel. **Laguna Leona** is another large lake, but it has almost completely dried up. It sits at the feet of **Paramillo de Quindío**, which used to be the source of the lake. **Valle del Placer** is a big valley covered with *frailejone* plants. **El Rancho** (2600 m) is an area of hot springs and is a good place to start and end any attempt to climb **Nevado del Tolima**. Nevado del Tolima is the most beautiful but also the toughest summit in the park. From El Rancho it is a long climb to the summit (5215 m). The crater is spectacular; a walk around it in the snow is impressive. There are several routes to climb to the top but some are only for experienced climbers, otherwise it is recommended to go with a guide with good equipment.

Ins and outs

From Manizales it is possible to access the park by car. The main route is from the road between Manizales and Bogotá. At La Esperanza you take the right fork, then it is 17 km to the main park entrance/office. From this point you must enter the park with an official guide. If you don't come with an organized group you will have to pick and pay the guide at the entrance office. It is also possible to enter the park by car from the Termales de Otoño. By foot or on horse you can enter the park from Santa Rosa, Pereira (following Río Otún), Salento (Valle de Cocora) and Ibaqué (following Río Combeima).

When to go

For trout fishing the season is April to August. The dry seasons are January to February and June to September, but even in those months it can rain for days or be very foggy. There has been no problem with safety in recent years.

Los Nevados National Park

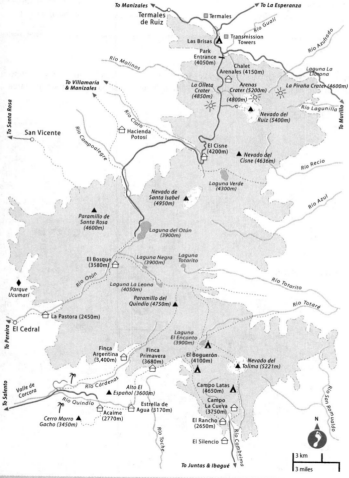

Santa Rosa de Cabal and around ›› *Colour map 2, C3.*

Some 22 km southwest of Manizales is **Chinchiná**, one of the main coffee-producing towns in Colombia. The surrounding hills are carpeted with coffee bushes and on roasting days the smell of coffee hangs in the air. Just outside the town (taxi US$3.30) is the **Hacienda Guayabal**, a coffee *finca* owned by the Londoño family since 1959. This is one of the best places to observe the growing and production process (see box, page 257). Halfway to Pereira, 15 km from Chinchiná, is Santa Rosa de Cabal, from where several thermal pools can be reached, including **Termales de Santa Rosa/Los Arbeláez** ① *0800-2400, US$8.* A 9-km unpaved road from Santa Rosa leads to the hot baths (early morning *chiva* or taxi, US$9 to entrance). They are surrounded by forests, with waterfalls. It's packed at the weekend.

Pereira ›› *pp270-280. Colour map 2, C3.*

→ *Phone code: 6. Population: 576,000. Altitude: 1411 m.*

Capital of Risaralda Department, 56 km southwest of Manizales, Pereira, stands within sight of the *Nevados* of the Cordillera Central. Pereira is situated on a small plateau,

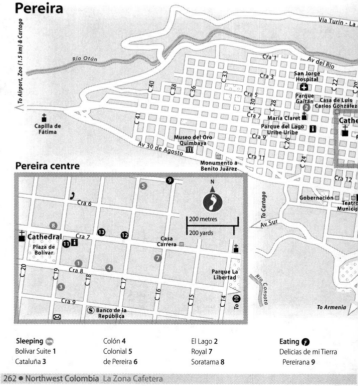

Sleeping 😴
Bolívar Suite **1**
Cataluña **3**

Colón **4**
Colonial **5**
de Pereira **6**

El Lago **2**
Royal **7**
Soratama **8**

Eating 🍴
Delicias de mi Tierra
Pereirana **9**

bounded to the south by the Río Consota and to the north, the Río Otún, about 140 m below. Beyond the Otún is **Dosquebradas**, an industrial town, now virtually part of the city, and dramatically linked by a viaduct. It is the largest city in this part of Colombia and acts as the centre of the Zona Cafetera with the appropriate range of official and commercial institutions and services. It has a very pleasant climate, though the green countryside around indicates a regular rainfall, usually short, sharp showers. Apart from coffee and cattle, there is a wide variety of local agricultural produce and you will notice the high quality of the food available here. Unfortunately this is an active seismic zone and earthquakes periodically damage Pereira. In 1995 significant damage was done to some buildings in the centre and again in January 1999 it was affected by the serious quake that devastated Armenia.

Getting there

Air The airport is 5 km west of the city. Daily flights from Bogotá, Cali, Ibagué and Medellín. Less frequent to other cities.

Road The bus terminal is 12 blocks south of the centre. Main roads are good in the Zona Cafetera. Frequent bus services from the main cities of Colombia. The direct road via Armenia to Ibagué, Giradot and Bogotá goes over La Línea pass (3250 m).

To Manizales
To Manizales

DOSQUEBRADAS

LA POPA

Viaducto Gaviria Trujillo

C 14
C 12
C 10

Parque La Libertad

Av del Ferrocarril

Cra 8

Cra 10

Nuestra Señora del Carmen

Cra 12

Monumento a Los Fundadores

Av Circunvalar

Av Ricaurte

14

N

1 km
1 mile

Delight **10**
Frisby **11**
La Terracita Paisa **12**

La Tienda del Recuerdo **13**
Mediterráneo **14**

Getting around

The city is centred around Plaza de Bolívar and most points of interest are within walking distance. The centre is safe (subject to the usual common sense precautions) but the semi-derelict area between Carrera 10 and 12 is not a place to linger. Local taxi and bus services are of good quality.

Tourist information

Oficina de Fomento al Turismo ⓘ *Cra 7, No 18-55, 6th floor, T3248030, www.pereira culturayturismo.gov.co*. **Corporación Autónomo Regional de Risaralda (Carder)** ⓘ *Av de las Américas, C 46, T314 1456*, has information but does not deal with park permits. Contact **Aviatur** ⓘ *Av 30 de Agosto, No 34-38 L1/15, T3263630, www.aviatur.com*, for park permits. **Turiscafé** ⓘ *C 19, No 5-48, office 901 (inside Novacentro), T3254157/58, www.turiscafe.net*, for good information on coffee farms in Risaralda.

Background

A settlement was established here around AD1541 by Mariscal Jorge Robledo but around 1700 it was moved to the present site of Cartago on Río La Vieja after continuing difficulties with a tribe of indigenous Quimbaya. Francisco Pereira from Cartago set out to re-establish a town here in the 19th century but died before achieving his objective. Remigio Antonio Cañarte, a priest and friend of Pereira, with a group of settlers, succeeded in 1863 and named the town after him.

Sights

The central square is the **Plaza de Bolívar**, noted for its *El Bolívar Desnudo*, a striking sculpture of the nude General on horseback by Rodrigo Arenas Betancur to commemorate the city's centenary in 1963. It caused a stir when unveiled, and brought a whole new meaning to the term 'liberator', but it is now accepted with pride by the local citizens. Enthusiasts of Arenas Betancur can find three of his other works in the city, *Monumento a los Fundadores* on Avenida Circunvalar/Calle 13, *El Prometeo*, in Universidad Tecnológico de Pereira (South on Calle 14), and *Cristo Sin Cruz* in the **Capilla de Fátima**, Avenida 30 de Agosto/Calle 49, towards the airport. There are many other examples of public art on display; look for works by Jaime Mejia Jaramillo and Leonidas Méndez. There is an interesting bronze of Benito Juárez, the Mexican patriot on Avenida 30 de Agosto. Also in Plaza de Bolívar is the **cathedral**, drab and unimpressive from the outside but with an elegant interior, fine chandeliers down the central nave, two large mosaics depicting baptism and the eucharist and a fine dome with roof paintings. Also interesting are the two Lady Chapels and the stained-glass windows.

There are three other parks with their churches. The **Parque del Lago Uribe Uribe** is the most picturesque with an artificial lake and a fountain illuminated at night. **Parque Gaitán** and **Parque La Libertad** (with its striking mozaic by Lucy Tejada) are also worth a visit. Opposite the Meliá Pereira hotel is the **Templo Nuestra Señora del Carmen**, a Gothic-style church with a dull grey concrete finish outside but inside it has some good sculptures and stained glass.

Two early-20th-century houses of architectural interest are **Casa de Luis Carlos González** ① *Cra 6, No 21-62*, and **Casa Carrera** ① *Cra 7, No 15-58*. Both have been declared national monuments. The impressive road bridge over the Río Otún connecting Pereira with Dosquebradas, is known as **El Viaducto Gaviria Trujillo**. It was built by Colombian, German and US contractors to Italian designs. The Interamerican Development Bank (BID) contributed to the US$50 million cost.

An interesting old Spanish service is to be found in the centre of Pereira; *Los Escribanos*. These scribes help locals with legal documents and filling in official forms, working on the street with their typewriters. They are found, in office hours, on Calle 19 by the post office.

Some way from the city centre, but worth a visit, is the small **Museo del Oro Quimbaya** ① *Av 30 de Agosto, No 35-08*. It features many Quimbaya pottery and gold items including three exquisite 2-cm-high face masks. Alongside is a library and a music auditorium with a daily programme of classical music. Free entry. The **botanical garden** ① *on the campus of Universidad Tecnológica de Pereria, T3212523, US$4.50, Mon-Sat, 0700-1600, must book a visit in advance and use a guide*, is good for birdwatching and has bamboo forests and two-hour nature walks.

West of Pereira ● ↦ *pp270-280.*

Northwest of Pereira, 30 km towards the Río Cauca, is **Marsella**, and the **Alexander von Humboldt Gardens**, a carefully maintained botanical display with cobbled paths and bamboo bridges. Just outside the town is the Ecohotel Los Lagos (**AL**), T3686529, www.ecohotelloslagos.com, previously a gold mine, then a coffee hacienda, and now restored as a hotel and nature park with lakes.

Parque Ucumari

ⓘ *park office T3254781, open daily for good information.*

From Pereira it is possible to visit the beautiful Parque Ucumari. If you're just visiting for the day and not staying overnight, entrance is free. It's one of the few places where the Andean spectacled bear survives. From Pereria, a *chiva* leaves daily (0900, 1500, more frequently during high season) with **Transporte Florida** from Calle 12, No 9-40 to the village of El Cedral. From El Cedral it is a two or 2½-hour walk to La Pastora, the park visitor centre and refuge. There is excellent camping, US$2.20 per person or US$6 at a refuge, meals extra. From La Pastora it is a steep, rocky one- to two-day hike to Laguna de Otún through beautiful scenery of changing vegetation. The Otún Quimbaya flora and fauna sanctuary forms a biological corridor between Ucumari and Los Nevados; it protects the last remaining area of Andean tropical forest in Risaralda. There are marked paths as well as *cabaña* accommodation, camping and meals available.

Pereira to Armenia

Along the road from Pereira to Armenia are some pleasant places to eat, art galleries and craft centres. This is the heart of the Zona Cafetera. The coffee grows here up to about 2000 m, above which is forest providing some communities with wood products as a livelihood. One such place is **Filandia**, a pleasant village 7 km off the main road, which has excellent examples of *paisa* with doorways, windows and balconies painted in primary colours. Unhappily, fire destroyed a corner of the town near the central plaza in 1996, but the unusual grey and white **Iglesia de la Imaculada Concepción**, dating from 1892, was not harmed.

Founded in 1878 by colonizers from Antioquia, its original name is believed to have been Finland, after the Scandinavian country. The village was used for the popular local *telenovela* – TV soap – called *Café con Aroma de Mujer*. Baskets for coffee picking and many other uses are made here. Because it is higher than the intervening land to the east, there are splendid views of the Nevados, especially dramatic if the weather is unsettled, and if there has been a recent storm, you may well see snow on the mountains well below the normal permanent snowline of about 4800 m. A **mirador** ⓘ *entry US$1.60, open 1000-2100*, has been constructed recently next to the cemetery, 1 km from the Parque Principal, a bit of an architectural disaster made from mangrove wood imported from San Bernardo del Viento, but which nonetheless has expansive views of Pereira, Armenia, Cartago and Quimbaya.

There are frequent buses from Pereira and Armenia, though none direct from Salento; take a bus to Pereira and change at Las Cruces on the main Pereira–Armenia highway.

Salento → *Phone code: 6. Population: 9400 Altitude: 1985 m.*

Well into the foothills of the Cordillera and on a promontory above the valleys that leads up to the Nevados of Quindío and Tolima, is the little town of Salento. The oldest settlement in Quindío, established on 5 January 1842 as the epicentre of the Antioquian colonisation of the region, sleepy Salento is the kind of place where you can hear a dog's bark resonate across the valley and the greatest obstacle to a good night's sleep is an overenthusiastic cockerel. It has some of the best examples of bahareque architecture of any town in the coffee region. On a clear day – especially in the mornings – you can see the snowy peaks of Los Nevados. It's also prone to a lot of rain, as evidenced by the abundance of crops and flowers grown in the region, and it often has low-lying clouds that drape over the mountains like loosely flung scarves.

The main plaza is especially impressive with a curious grey and white church, **Nuestra Señora del Carmen**, which sets off the nature of the rest of the square's architecture.

From the plaza, a walk up the Calle Real (Carrera 6), which has further beautiful examples of post-colonial architecture, The street leads to a 250-step climb, with 14 stations of the cross to measure your progress, to an outstanding viewpoint, overlooking the upper reaches of the Quindío and Cardenas rivers known as the Corcora valley. To the west many kilometres of the Cordillera Occidental can be seen. This is some of the finest countryside and mountain views in Colombia. It is a popular weekend resort for Colombians for walking, riding and trekking but quiet during the week. The local fiestas are held in the first week of January.

Tourist information Alcaldía de Salento ① *Parque Principal, T7593183*. **Plantation House** is also an excellent resource for information.

Valle de Cocora

Above Salento is the Cocora valley, part of the upper reaches of the Río Quindío. This fertile valley has an enchanting landscape of pines and eucalyptus towered over by the famous wax palms, Colombia's national tree. It makes for an extraordinary sight, the palms looming over the valley like sentinels on guard. With the crystal-clear waters of the Río Quindío, rich in freshwater trout, dissecting the valley, this beautiful spot has some breathtaking walks.

Getting there The centre of the valley (known as 'Cocora') is 12 km up from Salento along a rough track. Jeeps from Salento's plaza take about 35 minutes, US$1.60. Monday to Friday at 0610, 0730, 1130 and 1600, returning at 0830, 1230,1500 and 1700, with extra services at weekends and public holidays. Jeeps also leave when there are eight people waiting or someone willing to pay for eight people.

It is possible to hire a jeep (one way 24,000 pesos or 3000 pesos per person, whichever is the greater). It is also possible to arrange with the driver to collect you (same price).

About 5 km beyond Cocora is the **Acaime Natural Reserve**, at 2770 m, a 2½-hour walk, with a visitor centre, ponies for hire, accommodation for 20, US$5.50 per person, and a small restaurant. This is the most important wax palm zone in Colombia (see previous page), one of the reasons for the many varieties of humming birds, parrots, toucans and other wild life that can be seen feeding on the fruit of the palm.

A little before Acaime is **Finca La Montaña**, the end of the vehicular track, where there is a nursery for the wax palm. It is overlooked by Morro Gacho (see below). Jeeps take 20 minutes from Cocora, and the remaining 2 km to Acaime is a steep walk down across the infant Río Quindío and up the other side; approximately one hour.

Above Acaime there are many trails into the high mountains. Day trips include **Cerro Morro Gacho**, 3450 m and **Alto El Español**, 3600 m, both steep walks through the forest of the Natural Reserve. The trip to **Paramillo del Quindío**, 4700 m, one of the principal mountains of Los Nevados, takes three to four days, via **Finca Argentina** (3400 m, private *finca*, camping) and a total of 12 hours' ascent from Cocora to the top. This is an exposed rocky summit but not technically difficult. There are the remnants of a crater on the summit and climbers occasionally pitch their tents here on the grey/yellow sand. There are other *fincas*/camping sites that can be used on this trip.

Nevado del Tolima

The ascent of Nevado del Tolima 5221 m, normally takes three days up, staying at Finca Primavera (3680 m), and a two-day descent. This area is known as the Valley of the Lost as it is easy to wander off the track. It is best to call ahead to Finca Primavera and request a guide (US$8-14) to shepherd you through this section. Again there are variants, including camping at **Laguna El Encanto** midway between Tolima and Quindío, from which both can be climbed. You will need snow equipment for Tolima, ice axe and crampons recommended, but this too is not difficult.

The whole upland area is subject to wide temperature changes during the day depending on cloud cover and very cold nights. Route finding in this featureless country can be especially difficult in mist and guides are strongly recommended.

Details of what is available, prearranging places to stay, guides, transport, etc can be found in Salento. Guides cost around US$44 per day, mules US$20 per day.

Armenia ⬤ ⇥ *pp270-280. Colour map 2, C3.*

→ *Phone code: 6. Population: 324,500. Altitude 1838 m.*

Armenia, capital of Quindío Department, was named in memory of the massacres that took place in Armenia by Turkish Ottomans in the 19th century. Armenia, Colombia also has a tragic recent past. It has been affected by some of the worst earthquakes in the area, with that of January 1999 being particularly devastating. Most buildings in the centre of the city were damaged; about 30% were destroyed.

In spite of this, Armenia is a busy place, busier than either Pereira or Manizales. The Rodrigo Arenas Betancur **Monumento al Esfuerzo** in the Plaza de Bolívar poignantly portrays the present attitude of the local population. New construction is of high quality and hotels and restaurants are fresh and comfortable.

The surrounding Quindío countryside is a major coffee zone, and the slopes of the Cordillera here are home to the wax palm (see under Salento, page 265). Armenia, founded in 1889, suffers when international coffee prices fall and they have been low since the mid 1990s, but this is an enterprising sector of Colombia and you will see many new and different agricultural crops and activities developing. One of particular interest is the opening of many fine *fincas* to visitors for holidays; see box, page 257.

Ins and outs

Getting there To Bogotá, several flights daily with **Avianca**, easyfly and Aires. Aires and easyfly also fly to Medellín. Comprehensive bus services run to Armenia from major Colombian cities. The bus station is at Carrera 19, Calle 35, south of the city.

Getting around The interesting part of the city is within walking distance of the Plaza de Bolívar. There are important attractions in Quindío outside the city for which buses, taxis, tours or your own transport will be required.

Tourist information

Fondo Mixto de Promoción del Quindío ① *C 20, No 13-22, T7412810, www.turismo cafeyquindio.com.* **Corporación Autónomo Regional de Quindío (CRQ)** ① *C 19, No 19-35, T7460600,* for information on parks and natural reserves. Also for maps and information, **1C Instituto Geográfico Agustín Codazzi** ① *Cra 17, No 19-29, piso 2, open Mon-Fri 0730-1130, 1400-1630.*

Sights

The central square, **Plaza de Bolívar**, has a fountain and two bronze sculptures, a conventional Bolívar by Roberto Henau Buritacá, and a fine example of Rodrigo Arenas Betancur's work, the *Monumento al Esfuerzo*. The plaza has lost many of the surrounding buildings including part of the Quindío administration building (services relocated to the outskirts of the city). The striking modern **cathedral** was badly damaged but repairs are well advanced and we understand no changes will be incorporated, and, if so, the following description will stand: the façade is triangular in shape with a tall clock tower on the right. Inside, the nave continues the form and leaves a light airy feeling, accentuated by the fine modern stained glass. There is also an impressive bronze figure of Christ. Well worth a visit. Also of interest is the **San Francisco church**, with some notable stained-glass windows that overlook the market, covering four blocks in the centre of the city (this church is also closed as a result of the earthquake). There are many stalls of local artesanía, basket work is a local speciality, good prices. **Parque Sucre** is a colourful square with an ancient *ceiba* tree and a bust of Marshal Ayacucho. To the south is the oldest part of the city is **Parque Uribe Uribe** where concerts are held from time to time. Carrera 14, from Plaza Bolívar to Parque Sucre, has been pedestrianized.

The **Museo Quimbaya** ① *Av Bolívar, C 40 Norte, US$0.50*, is on the edge of town on the road to Pereira, take a city bus or taxi. It was designed by Rogelio Salmona and opened in 1986 and has a fine collection of ceramics and gold pieces from the local Quimbaya culture, well displayed. There is a cafetería and an open-air theatre for cultural presentations. There is also the **Museo del Oro Quimbaya** ① *Banco de República, Carrera 23, No 23-14, Tue-Sat, 0900-1630, Sun and holidays, 1000-1630*. Parque de la Vida, in the north of the city has bamboo structures, waterfalls and a lakeside theatre.

Parque Nacional del Café

Some 12 km northwest of Armenia is **Montenegro** (see under Armenia for Sleeping) near which is the **Parque Nacional del Café** ① *1 km from Pueblo Tapao, T7417417, in high season, daily 0900-1600, low season, Wed-Sun and public holidays, 0900-1600, general entrance, US$5.50, or US$12-21 for extra activities and rides, parking US$1; take a bus or colectivo*

Armenia

To ❷❶❷❸❹❺❻❼
Museo Quimbaya & Pereira

To Calarcá & Bogotá

San Francisco

Plaza de Mercado

Parque Sucre

Cathedral

Plaza de Bolívar

Parque Cafetero

Parque Uribe Uribe

To Bus Station (7 blocks) & Airport

To Cali

200 metres
200 yards

Sleeping 🛏
Alferez 1
Armenia 2
Bolivar Plaza 3
Café Plaza 4
Café Real 5
Centenario 6
Imperial 7
Zuldemayda 8

Eating 🍴
Anis 1
Café Quindio 2
Donde Nelson 3
El Rancho Argentino 4
Keizaki 5
La Fogata 6
La Fonda Antioqueña 7
La Puerta Quindiana 8
Natural Food Plaza 9

Love hotels

Every town has one but they are not what they seem. Colombia's motels are not cheap hotels for the weary motorist, but rather love hotels – convenient hideouts for illicit lovers that provide rates by the hour and the ultimate in discreet service.

You can recognize them by their suggestive nomenclature – names such as 'Hotel Seed' or 'Passion Hotel' – and by their lurid paintjobs, a mixture of electric blues or Pepto Bismol pinks, like sorry cast-offs from Miami's South Beach. Most have drive-in garages so that customers never have to show their faces at reception. Inside, a revolving dumb waiter allows the client to receive food, drinks, condoms and sex toys without ever having to meet the staff face-to-face. Some have jacuzzis, mirrored ceilings and pornography on TV, while others have special Saturday-night discounts.

Who goes there? Mainly teenagers and twenty-year-olds still living at home, but also adulterous couples and, of course, prostitutes with their clients. Colombia is a highly sexualized nation but also a predominantly Catholic country with strict moral codes. Motels are a convenient way of satisfying these conflicting desires and standards. You can measure how traditional a town is by the number of motels it has. For example, Armenia, in the heart of coffee country, has so many on its outskirts that the area has been nicknamed the Bermuda Triangle – no doubt because it's an easy place in which to lose yourself in passion.

(US$0.45) from Armenia to Montenegro and then a jeep marked 'Parque' (US$0.25) or taxi (US$2) to the entrance. There are restaurants, a Juan Valdez coffee shop, a botanical garden, ecological walks, a Quimbaya cemetery, a tower with a fine view and an interesting museum which covers all aspects of coffee. A cableway links to a children's theme park (rollercoasters, water rides, etc).

Beyond Montenegro is **Quimbaya**, known for its **Festival of Light** (Fiesta de Velas y Faroles) in December each year. About 7 km away is the **Parque Nacional de la Cultura Agropecuaria** (**PANACA**) ① *T7582830, Tue-Sun 0900-1800, US$18*, an educational theme park, with many varieties of horses (and a very good show/display), cattle and other animals. A good family outing.

Ibagué and around ⬤🔵⬤⬤⬤ ▸▸ pp270-280. Colour map 2, C3.

→ *Phone code: 8. Altitude: 1248 m.*

Ibagué, capital of Tolima Department, lies at the foot of the Quindío mountains. Parts of the town are old: see the **Colegio de San Simón** and the market (good *tamales*). The **Parque Centenario** is pleasant and there is a famous **Conservatory of Music**. Try the local alcoholic drink called *mistela*.

Just outside, on the Armenia road, a dirt road leads up the Río Combeima to El Silencio and the slopes of the Nevado del Tolima, the southernmost Nevado in the Parque Nacional Los Nevados. The climb to the summit (5221 m) takes two to three days', camping at least one night over 4000 m, ice equipment necessary. For safety reasons, it is recommended to visit the Nevado del Tolima only from Ibagué and not Manizales. A *lechero* (milk truck) leaves Ibagué marketplace for El Silencio between 0630 and 0730, US$2.50, two hours. A guide in Ibagué is **Maklin Muñoz** ① *Cra 1, No 5-24, T2615865, T3006756216 (mob)*.

Quindío Pass, 3350 m (known as La Línea after the power lines that cross the mountains) is on the Armenia to Ibagué road (105 km), across the Cordillera Central. On the east side of the Pass is **Cajamarca**, a friendly town in a beautiful setting at 1900 m. There's accommodation at **Residencia Central** (**F**) and **Nevado**, both on same street. **Bar El Globo** is on the corner of the main plaza serves excellent coffee. Interesting market on Sunday.

Cartago ⬤⬤ ⟩⟩ pp270-280. Colour map 2, C3.

→ Altitude: 920 m.

From Pereira and Armenia roads run west to Cartago, at the northern end of the rich Cauca Valley, which stretches south for about 240 km but is little more than 30 km wide. The road, the Pan-American, goes south along this valley to Cali and Popayán, at the southern limit of the valley proper. There it mounts the high plateau between the Western and Central Cordilleras and goes through to Ecuador.

Founded in 1540, Cartago, 25 km southwest of Pereira, still has some colonial buildings, particularly the very fine **Casa del Virrey** ① C 13, No 4-29, and the **cathedral**. Cartago is noted for its fine embroidered textiles.

ⓘ La Zona Cafetera listings → Phone code: 6 (unless otherwise indicated).

For Sleeping and Eating price codes and other relevant information, see pages 31-36.

⬤ Sleeping

Manizales p253, map p255
In Jan, during the fiesta, hotel prices are considerably increased.
AL Las Colinas, Cra 22, No 20-20, T8842009, www.hotelesestelar.com. Part of the Estelar Caín of hotels, Las Colinas has large rooms with cable TV and Wi-Fi. It also has a sauna.
A Hotel Carretero, C 23, No 35A-31, T8840255, www.hotelcarretero.com. Well placed, halfway between the centre and El Cable, the Carretero has a smart, glassy lobby and large, comfortable rooms. Breakfast is included in the price and it has Wi-Fi throughout as well as a sauna. Can also organize car hire.
A Hotel Escorial, C 21, No 21-11, T8847696, escorial@une.net.co. Smart hotel with good, clean rooms. Extra services include Wi-Fi, parking, cable TV and a restaurant serving local and international food. Breakfast is included in the price.
A Recinto del Pensamiento, Km 11 Vía al Magdalena, T8747494. Formerly a children's

holiday camp, this large 1-storey hotel is spread over acres of lovely gardens which form part of the headquarters of the Comité de Café's headquarters in Manizales. It has a lake with koi carp and an enormous pavilion made from *guadua bambusa*, but its biggest draw is the forested hills behind which make for pleasant walks and birdwatching.
B Bolívar Plaza, C 22, No 22-40, T8847777, bolivarplaza@hotmail.com. Just round the corner from Plaza Bolívar and the cathedral, this hotel has cable TV, Wi-Fi, laundry service and a restaurant.
B Roma Plaza, C 21, No 22-30, T8828440, www.hotelesmanizales.com. Around the corner from the Bolívar Plaza with simple, clean rooms, cable TV, Wi-Fi and breakfast included.
C Tama Internacional, C 23, No 22-43, T8842124. Cavernous, Republican-era building off the Plaza Bolívar with a popular restaurant. Rooms are a little small and dark.
D Hotel California, C 19, No 16-39, T8973487, lgt71@hotmail.com. Opposite the bus station, 42 clean and simple rooms with private bathrooms, TV, hot water, Wi-Fi and good mattresses. Avoid noisy front rooms facing

the station and bring a padlock as some windows don't lock properly.

D Hotel Bolívar, Cra 20, No 23-09, T8844066 or 8836486. Small and basic but clean rooms, all with en suite bathrooms and TV. As with all hotels in centre, be careful at night and avoid the area called 'La Galería'.

El Cable

AL Varuna, C 62, No 23C-18, T8811122, www.varunahotel.com. The newest hotel in town, has a slick, minimal look and a good restaurant serving international food. The rooms are large and comfortable with hydro massage showers and Wi-Fi throughout.

A-B Regine's Hotel, C 65A, No 23B-113, T8875360, regineshotel@hotmail.com. Located in a quiet suburban street behind Cable, Regine's has good, clean rooms and has computers for internet access, Wi-Fi, cable TV and laundry service. The free breakfast can be served in a small garden out the back where there are also some smaller, cheaper rooms. An excellent mid-range option.

D-F Mountain House, C 66, No 23B-137, T8874736, www.mountainhouse manizales.com. The only backpacker option in town, Mountain House is a suburban home with 3 private rooms and several dorms with bunks. It has a pool table and a terraced garden with a BBQ, also offers use of a kitchen and access to an internet-enable computer. There is Wi-Fi throughout and the price includes a breakfast of eggs on toast.

Supía p256

D El Diablito, C 18, No 6-10, T8560504, www.fincahoteldiablito.com. A few blocks outside town, next to the bullring, this family-run *finca* has a large garden full of fruit trees and a lake with fish and turtles. It has good, comfortable rooms with cable TV and fans as well as a *cabaña* next to a swimming pool.

D Hotel Plazazul, Cra 9, No 34-15, T8561038. This spanking new hotel is excellent value with very comfortable beds with crisp white sheets. It has a roof terrace with hammocks, a BBQ and

great views of the hills as well as 2 computers for internet access. The suites, a little more expensive, have enormous jacuzzis.

D Hotel Premium Biss, Av Guayabal, T3116317032. Another good-value new hotel with very clean rooms with a/c and cable TV. You pay a little more (**C**) for rooms with windows that look out onto the street.

F Hostal Santa Ana, C 34, No 6-28, T3128160661. This hostel, 1 block behind the Parque Principal, is very basic but has friendly staff and is housed in a beautiful colonial building.

Marmato p257

There is no accommodation available in Marmato but nearby Supía has several excellent options. There is a small restaurant in the plaza opposite the church, serving whatever is available.

Parque Nacional Los Nevados p260

C pp Cabañas el Cisne, comfortable, or camp outside (**G** pp). From here it is easy to reach Laguna Verde Encantada.

Camping It is possible to camp at **Chalet Arenales**, which is the starting point for climbing to the summit of Nevado del Ruiz. Besides the **Cabañas el Cisne** there is no accommodation inside the park, so you will need to bring all equipment yourself. Temperature can drop below 0°C at night as most of the park lies above 3800 m.

Santa Rosa de Cabal p262

A Hotel Termales de Santa Rosa de Cabal, attached to the hot baths, T3641322. Comfortable, chalet style, with restaurant.

A-B Hacienda Guayabal, Km 3 Vía Chinchiná-Santa Rosa, T8401463, www.haciendaguayabal.com. Working coffee *finca* 30 mins outside Manizales. Set in 64 ha of gorgeous rolling fields brimming with coffee plants well as a botanist's notebook full of flowers and trees. One of the best places to do a coffee tour in the region, guests can stay at the Londoño family home in private bedrooms or dorms. The price includes accommodation, 3 excellent home-cooked meals, a fine swimming pool and the tour. Coffee is free, of course (see box, page 257).

Pereira *p262, map p262*

L Hacienda San José, Entrada 16 cadena El Tigre, Km 4 Vía Pereira–Cerritos, T63132615, www.haciendahotelsanjose.com, US$160, breakfast included, 2 people sharing. One of the oldest houses in the region, this *bahereque* building built by Franciso Mejía Jaramillo in 1888 is simply breathtaking. Today it is run as a hotel and almost all of the features have been painstakingly preserved. Popular activities include horse riding through sugarcane, coffee and livestock fields and visits to one of the largest bamboo reserves in the region and a trapiche where you can see how *panela*, a sugarcane derivative, is processed (see box, page 257).

L Hotel de Pereira, Cra 13, No 15-73, T3350770, www.hoteldepereira.com. Pereira's grandest hotel with a spacious lobby and excellent service. Well located 3 blocks from the centre, it has good rooms with plasma TVs, Wi-Fi and a great pool. It has a travel agency within the building and a sauna, gym and Turkish bath under refurbishment at time of writing. Discounts available at weekends.

AL Soratama, Cra 7, No 19-20, T3358650, www.hotelsoratama.com. Recently refurbished hotel on the Plaza Bolívar with helpful staff and lots of services available, including parking, free local calls, Wi-Fi, massage therapist and an internet room. Breakfast included. Discounts available at the weekend.

C El Lago, C 25, No 6-39, T3346643. Clean rooms with private bathrooms and hot water. Has laundry service, an internet room and international call cabins and Wi-Fi.

C Hotel Cataluña, C 19, No 8-61, T3354527. The Cataluña has clean and airy rooms with balconies and private bathrooms with hot water. With cable TV and a popular restaurant serving fixed meals for US$2.50, it's good value for money.

C Hotel Royal, C 16, No 5-78, T3352501, hotelroyal@yahoo.com. Near the Plaza Bolívar, this hotel has clean, basic rooms with cable TV.

D Bolívar Suite, Cra 8, No 18-54, T3330505. Clean rooms with good light near the Parque Bolívar. All have cable TV and en suite bathrooms with hot water.

D Hotel Colonial, C 17, No 5-50, T3337206. Hotel with clean rooms and good security, though none have windows.

D-E Hotel Colón, Cra 8, No 17-30. Offers rooms with or without private bathroom. They're a bit grotty but will do. Mind the wobbly stairs on the way in.

West of Pereira *p264*

A-D La Posada del Compadre, Cra 6, No 8-06, T3685792, posadadelcompadre@ yahoo.com. This beautifully preserved *paisa* building has several good rooms of variable price depending on size and a gorgeous terrace with fine views out toward Salento. All rooms have en suite bathrooms that jar a bit with the rest of the architecture. Cable TV and breakfast included. Recommended.

C Hostal Tibouchina, C 6, No 5-05, T7582646. Fine old hostel on the corner of the plaza with a beautiful gallery looking out on the street. Comfortable, wooden panelled rooms with private bathrooms, cable TV and breakfast included.

D-F Cabaña del Recuerdo, Km 5 Vía Filandia-Montenegro, T3116285149, reservaselrecuerdo@hotmail.com. A few kilometres outside Filandia, this chalet on a Colombian family's *finca* is surrounded by banana and coffee plantations. It has a swimming pool, ping pong table and great walks in a *guadua* bamboo forest with a swimming hole in its midst. Free pick up from Filandia with enough forewarning.

Salento *p265*

B Casa Alto del Coronel, Cra 2, No 7 Esquina, T7593760, casadecampoaltodecoronel@ hotmail.com. Obscured by bushes of bougainvillea, this *bahereque* house has beautifully kept gardens and a summerhouse with fine views over the town and surrounding area. The rooms are good if a bit overdone with heavy floral wallpaper. Breakfast is included.

B Posada del Café, Cra 6, No 3-08, T759312, malenacafe@yahoo.com. On the gorgeous Calle Real, this traditional house has rooms set around a garden brimming with flowers, and has a friendly owner. Recommended.

C Balcones del Ayer, C 6, No 5-40, T7593273. Great position half a block from the plaza but the rooms are sparse and have windows that open onto a corridor. Good restaurant.

C Las Nubes, Cra 9, No 7-31, T3213522. The brass bell you have to ring to gain access to this beautiful house sets the tone. Another traditional *bahereque* building with painted doors and railings – this time the colour theme is red. Simple rooms with character and one of the best views in Salento.

C Posada del Angel, C 6, No 7-47, T7593507. Sweet little place with clean rooms and a great balcony with fine views.

D-F Camping Monteroca, Km 4 Vía Pereira–Salento, T3154136862 (mob), www.geocities.com/campingmonteroca. Sitting at the bottom of the hill next to the Río Quindío, Camping Monteroca offers something a little different. Owner Jorge has run the site for 30 years and knows the area, its history and wildlife well. The place is well maintained with clean bathrooms, showers, a communal cooking area and TV lounge. There is an eclectic museum filled with fossils and meteorites as well as a room dedicated to Simón Bolívar, who is reported to have stayed a night there. There's also a serpentarium. While the normal campsite is fine, what makes this place special is the themed cabins. Among others, you can sleep in your own jungle tree house or step into the past with a Beatles-themed cabin complete with waterbed. All cabins offer good privacy, a stove and hot showers.

D-F The Plantation House, C 7, No 1-04, T3162852603, www.theplantation housesalento.com. Popular backpackers'

hostel with 7 private bedrooms and several dorms with bunks. This traditional *behereque* house has fine views out toward the town cemetery and an excellent book exchange. English owners Tim and his Colombian wife have the best information in town on the local area and have recently bought a coffee plantation to which they offer tours.

E Las Palmas, C 6, No 3-02, T7593065. This small, traditional hostel has 8 comfortable rooms with en suite bathrooms and hot water. With a kitchen available and cable TV as well as a roof terrace with a table and chairs it represents good value for money.

Valle de Cocora *p266*

B Las Palmas de Cocora, Km 10 Valle de Cocora, T7593190. Wooden, 2-storey chalet with comforable rooms. Each of the 2 rooms has space for more, with various bunk beds, but they will hire for couples if demanded. Also has a restaurant serving trout (¶¶). Horses for hire (US$5.50 per hr, guide US$5.50 per hr).

E Finca San José, Km 11 Vía Cocora, T3102275091 (Mariela Pérez in Armenia). *Finca* San José is a 100-year-old mil farm, which sits above the hamlet of Cocora. With basic but characterful rooms and a delightful veranda with shuttered windows opening up onto spectacular vistas, this is an excellent place to stay while hiking the hills of the Cocora valley.

E Bosques de Cocora, Km 11 Vía Cocora, T7496831, juanb@valledecocora.com. Restaurant, hires out tents, mattresses, sheets, blankets and pillows. Shower facilities and free coffee and hot chocolate offered.

Armenia *p267, map p268*

AL Armenia, Av Bolívar, No 8N-67, T7460099, www.armeniahotelsa.com. Impressive new hotel in the northern part of Armenia. It has a cavernous lobby and enormous rooms with beds made from *guadua* bamboo as well as all the usual services expected from an international hotel – sauna, gym, swimming pool, Wi-Fi and a restaurant with Chilean and Argentine wines. Opposite is the Parque de la

Vida, a verdant space with waterfalls. Discounts available at weekends. English spoken.

AL Hacienda Bambusa, T3115069915, bambusa@haciendabambusa.com. Not strictly a coffee *finca* – this enchanting traditional hacienda sits hidden in a labyrinth of banana plantations – but the 160 ha are so beautiful that visitors are unlikely to be bothered by such details. This is very much a place to relax but there are plenty of activities for the restless, including canopying in a bamboo forest, horse riding, birdwatching or simply relaxing by the majestic pool. Has cable TV, restaurant and free pick up from airport or bus station (see box, page 257).

A Bolívar Plaza, C 21, No 14-17, T7410083, www.bolivarplaza.com. Just off the Plaza Bolívar, this hotel's rooms are a bit dark and musty, though they do have large beds. It also has parking, Wi-Fi and an internet room, free local calls and free breakfast.

A Centenario, C 21, No 18-20, T7443143, www.hotelcentenario.com. Modern hotel with airy, bright rooms and attentive staff. Has Wi-Fi throughout and a small internet room as well as cable TV, parking and breakfast included.

A Finca Los Alamos, Km 3 vía nueva al Caimo, T7466129, finca_losalamos@hotmail.com. Traditional house with simple, tasteful rooms and a large veranda. Set in landscaped gardens surrounded by banana plantations and with a good pool, the only downside is its proximity to a major road.

B Zuldemayda, C 20, No 15-38, T7410580, hzuldemayda@telecom.com.co. Popular business hotel with facilities such as Wi-Fi, internet room and parking. The rooms are a little dated but were under refurbishment at time of writing. Breakfast included.

B Café Real, Cra 18, No 21-32, T7443055, www.hotelcafereal.com. Modern hotel with bright but slightly pokey rooms. Has sauna, gym, Turkish bath and jacuzzi, Wi-Fi and breakfast included in the price.

C Café Plaza, Cra 18, No 18-09, T7411500, hotelcafeplaza@hotmail.com. Near the Plaza

Bolívar, this hotel is a little noisy but has simple but clean rooms with en suite bathrooms, cable TV and breakfast included.

E Imperial, C 21, No 17-43, T7449151. This hotel has basic but clean rooms with cable TV and good security. No hot water, however.

F Alferez, Cra 17, No 17-47, T74434096. Hotel with very basic rooms but nonetheless secure and with TV and laundry service.

Quimbaya

AL Finca Villa Nora, Km 1 carretera antigua Quimbaya, T7415472, fincavillanora@hotmail.com. The rooms all have the same fittings as they would have when Antioquian settlers built it in the 19th century and its spacious veranda is decorated with original Quimbaya artefacts. It has an excellent kitchen serving up home-cooked food and a pleasant pool for relaxing after a tour of its working coffee farm. Also has Wi-Fi (see box, page 257).

B Hostería Mi Monaco, Km 7 vía Armenia–Pueblo Tapao, T3103745643, www.mimonaco.net. On the side of a hill with a bamboo copse that plunges down to a stream, Mi Monaco has comfortable rooms with crisp, white sheets in a traditional 60-year-old *bahareque* house. With a good pool, jacuzzi, and professional mountain bike guides, it's an excellent place to relax.

C El Carriel, Km 1 vía Quimbaya-Filandia, T7463612, elcarriel@hotmail.com. This is an excellent option if you are looking for an economic way to stay on a working coffee *finca*. The rooms are simple but comfortable with private bathrooms and hot water and a good little restaurant, all in a traditional house. There's an excellent coffee tour in which you are encouraged to pick coffee grains and follow the whole coffee-making process from plant to cup (see box, page 257).

Montenegro

A Hotel del Campo, Km 7 contiguo a Panaca, T7415222, www.hoteldelcampo.com.co. Set on the lip of a steep valley surrounded by banana, yucca and alfalfa plantations, this hotel is ideally located just 500 m from the

Panaca park. It has good rooms with interesting bathrooms and a kidney-shaped pool. It has Wi-Fi in reception and a restaurant.

A El Delirio, Km 1 vía Montenegro-Parque del Café, T7450405, casadelirio@hotmail.com. This beautiful, traditional *finca* has been restored with immaculate taste with original mahogany furniture, wrought-iron beds and black-and-white photographs of bullfighters. It's a perfect place to unwind, boasting a pool, large gardens with a coffee plantation at the bottom and delicious home-cooked food (see box, page 257).

Ibagué and around *p269*
B Ambala, C 11, No 2-60, T8-2613888. Includes breakfast, and has rooms with TV, a pool, sauna, parking, and a restaurant.
F Sandremo, C 16, No 2-88, T8-2613339. Rooms with fan and TV.

Cartago *p270*
Many hotels in area around bus terminals (Cra 9) and railway station (Cra 9 y C 6).
C Don Gregorio, Cra 5, No 9-59, T211 5111. Rooms with a/c (cheaper with fan). Also has pool, sauna and includes breakfast.
F Río Pul, Diag 3, No 2-142, T211 0623. Rooms with fan, private bathroom and TV. Recommended.

⊘ Eating

Manizales *p253, map p255*
Apart from the hotels, the best restaurants are on or near Cra 23 in El Cable and Barrio Milán the east part of the city.
♥♥♥ Chung Mi No. 2, Cra 23, No 30-10. Chinese foo in a good atmosphere opposite Parque Caldas.
♥ Las Vegas, C 23 no 22-15. Traditional Colombian fare served as a buffet. A large choice, from salad to yucca, rice, meats, soups and beans. Breakfast US$3.30, lunch US$4.40. Open 0600 until 2200 depending on custom.

♥ Pollo y Asado, C 23, Cra 22. Traditional Colombian *asadero* with the best rotisserie chicken in downtown. Also does burgers and steaks.

Barrio Milán
♥ Don Juaco Snaks, C 65A, No 23A-44. Sandwiches and burgers as well as typical dishes such as *ajiaco* and *mondongo*.
♥ Il Forno, Cra 23, No 73-86. Italian restaurant in pleasant surroundings serving pastas, pizzas and salads. Good vegetarian options.
♥ Juan Valdez, Cra 23, No 64-55. Part of the ubiquitous coffee chain, this one is in a good position next to the old cablecar line, has free Wi-Fi.
♥ Las Cuatro Estaciones, C 65, No 23A-32. Good selection of pastas and pizzas. Be sure to order big as helping can be a bit small.

Supía *p256*
There are several good places to eat on the Parque Principal.
♥ La Casona, Cra 6, No 33-36, good *bandejas* in pleasant surroundings.
La Cabaña de los Dulces, Cra 9, No 30-38. Sample some of the town's varieties of sweets such as *colación* and *blanqueados*.

Pereira *p262, map p262*
♥♥♥ Mediterráneo, Av Circunvalar, No 4-47. Steaks, seafood, fondus and crêpes in a relaxed atmosphere on an open terrace.
♥ Delicias de mi Tierra Pereirana, Cra 5, No 16-52. Cheap-as-chips canteen serving typical dishes for just over US$2.
♥ Delight, Cra 16, No 4B-35. Popular upmarket canteen serving *sancocho*, *sobrebarriga* and other typical dishes.
♥ Frisby, C19, No 7-65. The Colombian version of Kentucky Fried Chicken, only perhaps a little better.
♥ La Terracita Paisa, C 17, No 7-62. Typical regional food served on a 2nd-floor terrace decorated with antiques.
♥ La Tienda del Recuerdo, Cra 7, No 18-32. This typical *paisa* restaurant has live *mariachi* bands playing while you eat.

Salento p265

Like many small towns in Colombia, Salento's restaurants tend to close early and some only serve lunch. The local speciality is trout.

¶ La Fonda de los Arrieros, Cra 6, No 6-02. Restaurant on the plaza serving good trout and steaks, open until 2100.

Armenia p267, map p268

¶¶ Café Quindío, Cra 19, No 33N-41. Gourmet coffee shop and restaurant, serving recipes such as chicken or steak in coffee sauce as well as international dishes (Thai, French, Italian). This popular café next to Parque de la Vida also sells coffee products from its own farm and even has a school where you can learn about all aspects of coffee. The menu includes 29 varieties of coffee.

¶¶ El Rancho Argentino, Av Bolívar, No 13N-57. Another popular restaurant in the fashionable northern part of Armenia, this restaurant serves mainly *parrillas* but pastas too.

¶¶ Keizaki, Cra 13, No 8N-39. Relatively new restaurant serving sushi and other Asian dishes. There are several other good restaurants on the same block.

¶¶ La Fogata, Cra 13, No 14N-47. One of Armenia's most popular high-end restaurants, La Fogata serves all sorts of cuts of thick, juicy steaks as well as pork chops and typical dishes like *ajiaco*.

¶¶-¶ Anis, C 10N, No 13-94. This excellent little restaurant has a varied menu cooked to a high standard and with good presentation. The steaks are thick and cooked to perfection while it also offers salads, sandwiches, crêpes and other brunch options. It has a pleasant sunny patio with a wood-fired oven and even makes its own pasta. Recommended.

¶ Donde Nelson, Cra 13 with C 15. Family-run hole-in-the-wall, popular with locals, serving *almuerzo ejecutivo* for US$3.50.

¶ La Fonda Antioqueña, Cra 13, No 18-59. Pleasant *paisa* restaurant on a 2nd floor gallery festooned with antiques. Serves the usual dishes such as *bandeja paisa*, etc. Open till 1900.

¶ La Puerta Quindiana, C 17, No 15-40. This restaurant serves cheap *comida corriente* for US$3 with dishes such as *sancocho* a speciality, as well as good fruit juices.

¶ Natural Food Plaza, Cra 14, No 18N-40. Vegetarian restaurant with a varied menu that includes veggie burgers, crêpes, salads, Mexican, *tamales* and fruit juices. Also has a wholefood shop. A lunchtime *menú ejecutivo* is US$3.75.

Ibagué and around p269

¶¶ El Fogón Antioqueño, Cra 6, No 26-03. Good local dishes.

¶¶ La Vieja Enramada, Cra 8, No 15-03. Local and international dishes.

☉ Bars and clubs

Manizales p253, map p255

Most night clubs have a cover charge of between US$2.50 and US$5 per person, some include a few free drinks. Most clubs don't get going until 2300 or later. Manizales' Zona Rosa is in El Cable, which is centred around the old cable car station on Cra 23.

Bar Mediterráneo, plays mainly salsa and is very popular with locals and students.

Bar POP, a trendy nightclub/bar next to Cable Plaza shopping centre.

Buddha Bar, popular but expensive with a good atmosphere and friendly clientele.

Calle Ocho, is a fashionable club playing crossover Western/Colombian music.

VIP, probably the biggest nightclub in the area, plays all types of music.

Barrio Milán

The 2nd nightlife area, a little smaller and a taxi ride from Cable Plaza, is Barrio Milán. All bars are open until late.

Bar Babylon Cocktail, C 77, No 17-55, at the top end of Milán. Small, local video bar playing a mix of western

and Latin music, owner Adolfo speaks
a little English.
Bar Aguila, the biggest bar in Milán
and very popular with students. Open
Thu-Sat and plays mostly Latin music.
It's mostly outside, so bring a coat.
Son de Milan, a *salsateca*.

☻ Entertainment

Manizales *p253, map p255*
Cinema
**Centro Cultural y Convenciones los
Fundadores**, Cra 22 with C 33, has an
interesting carved-wood mural by Guillermo
Botero, who also has murals in the Club
Manizales, Hotel Las Colinas. Events held
here and at other locations during **Jazz and
Theatre Festival** in Sep/Oct.
Universidad Nacional, free films on
Tue and Thu.
Cable Plaza Cinema in El Cable has all the
latest releases but few films in English.

Pereira *p262, map p262*
Cinema
Several cinema complexes within
2 blocks of Plaza de Bolívar.

Theatre
Teatro Comfamiliar, Cra 5/C 22,
cultural activities.
Teatro Municipal Santiago Londoño,
Centro Comercial Fiducentro, Av 30 de
Agosto/C 19, T3357724, major
stage productions.

☻ Festivals and events

Manizales *p253, map p255*
Early Jan Feria de Manizales, includes
a coffee festival, bullfights, beauty parades
and folk dancing as well as general partying.

Pereira *p262, map p262*
Early Jul Feria del Libro (Book Fair)
Aug Fiestas de la Cosecha (Harvest Festival).
Late Oct Feria Gastronómica (Food Fair).

Ibagué and around *p269*
Jun The National Folklore Festival.
24 Jun San Juan; and
29 Jun San Pedro y San Pablo, both
commemorated by the separtments
of Tolima and Huila with bullfights,
fireworks, and music.
Dec Biannual choral festivals.

○ Shopping

Manizales *p253, map p255*
Cable Plaza in El Cable for more expensive
shops or **Centro Comercio de Parque Caldas**
for cheaper shopping.

▲ Activities and tours

Manizales *p253, map p255*
Colombia57, T3134015691/T0800 0789157
(UK freephone), www.colombia57.com.
British ex-pats Simon Locke and Russell
Coleman organize tailor-made trips around
the coffee zone and the rest of Colombia.
Well-organized and thoroughly researched.
Highly recommended.

Marmato *p257*
Marmato is not a village geared toward
tourism. There is little infrastructure and
it is a difficult place to reach. The locals,
however, are friendly and helpful.
Colombia57, see above, can arrange
tours to Marmato from Manizales,
providing transport, helmets and
boots, and knowledgeable local guides.

Parque Nacional Los Nevados *p260*
De Una, based in Bogotá, www.deuna
colombia.com, organize several treks,

including: a 3-day climb to the summit of Nevado del Tolima from Ibague, US$120; a 5-day trek from Valle de Cocora to Manizales passing by Laguna El Encanto, Laguna La Leona, Laguna del Otún and Laguna Verde Encantada, US$216; and a 5-day trek from Valle de Cocora to Ibague, including climbing Nevado del Tolima, US$195. Prices are per person with a minimum of 4 people per group, for a smaller group the price will increase. Price includes transport, park fees, camping fees, cooking equipment and a bilingual guide. A good level of physical fitness is required.

Pereira *p262, map p262*
D'p@seo, Cra 13, No 14-60, local 109, T3349883, www.dpaseo.com. Opposite Hotel Pereira. Arranges weekend trips to Los Nevados, trips on Río la Vieja. Mon-Sat 0800-1200, 1400-1900.

Armenia *p267, map p268*
Balsaje Los Remansos, Cra 7, No 15-08, Apto 201, Quimbaya, T7523937. Organizes *balsaje* excursions (punting down rivers on bamboo rafts) on the Río La Vieja.
Millenium Turs, C 19, No 32, N-11, Apto 402, T7496036, milleniumturs@hotmail.com. Does tours of the coffee region as well as walks into hills behind Armenia. Can arrange stays on coffee *fincas*. English, German, French, Italian and Japanese spoken. Recommended.
Territorio Avetura, Av Bolívar, No 14N-80, T7499568, www.territorioaventura.com.co. Organizes rafting, kayaking, parapenting, horse riding and zip wiring in local area.

⊕ Transport

Manizales *p253, map p255*
Air
Manizales has a small airport, **La Nubia**, 7 km east of the centre. To **Bogotá**, 50 mins, US$140, with **Avianca**, or **Aires**. To **Medellín**, 30 mins, US$130-150, with **Aires** or **ADA**.

Airline offices Avianca, Hotel Las Colinas, Cra 22, No 20-20, L1, T8832237. Aires Centre: Cra 23, No 60-26, local 3, T8812324, El Cable: Carrera 23, No 62-16, local 110, Torres de Panorama, Sancancio: Carrera 27A, No 66-30, local 760, T8873143.

Bus
The terminal with good restaurant is at C 19 between Cras 15 and 17, T8849183. To **Medellín**, 14 a day from 0430 to 2000, 6 hrs, US$17 with **Arauca**; by *kia* (7-seater mini van, faster) with **Flota Ospina**, 4½ hrs, US$18. To **Bogotá**, Expreso Bolivariano, US$20, 9 hrs, every hr 0630-2300. To **Honda**, US$14, Expreso Bolivariano. **Cali** with Ruana Azul, 6 hrs, US$17, every hr between 0400-2100; by *kia*, 4½ hrs, US$18, 10 a day 0630-1830 **Pereira**, with Expreso Palmira or Arauca, 2 hrs, US$4.40, half hourly, or in *kia* (Flota Ospina), every hr 0600-1800, 1½ hrs. **Armenia**, 3 hrs, US$8, with **Expreso Palmira**, hourly 0600-1800. To **Ibague**, 5 hrs, US$13, with Expreso Palmira. To **Buenaventura**, 7 hrs, US$15, with Ruana Azul at 0730 and 0930. To **Marmato**, 2 hrs, US$7, with **Flota Occidental** at 1200, 1500 and 1800. To **Supía**, 1½ hrs, US$5.50; in *colectivo*, US$7 with connections every 40 mins to Marmato. For Cartagena, Santa Marta and Turbo change at Medellín.

Car
To **Medellín**, see above. Manizales–Honda–Bogotá: all paved. The road climbs to 3700 m, with most superb scenery.
    Car hire Thrifty Rar Rental, in Hotel Carretero, Cra 23, No 35A-31, T8847047, www.thriftycolombia.com.

Marmato *p257*
Bus
From Manizales, 3 buses a day with **Flota Occidental** at 0615, 0830 and 1600, US$7, 2½ hrs. Return buses to Marmato leave at 1200, 1500 and 1600. To **Supía**, *chivas* and Willys jeeps take the high road over the mountain via San Juan. Alternatively, you can walk to Supía via the high road in 5 hrs.

Pereira p262, map p262
Air
Matecaña airport is 5 km to the west of the city with good services including 2 banks with ATMs and a Telecom office with long-distance facilities. To **Bogotá**, around 15 a day, Aces and Avianca. To **Medellín**, 4 most days, Aces. To **Cali**, 2 a day, Aires. To **Ibagué**, 2 a day, Aires, extended 3 days a week to **Neiva** and **Florencia**. Flights also to **Bucaramanga** and the **north coast**, Aires, local airlines to the **Chocó**.

Airline offices AeroRepública, Av Circunvalar, No 5-47, T3313232, Mon-Fri 0800-1800, Sat 0830-1200. Satena, Aeropuerto Matecaña Local 27, T3142774, satenapei@epm.net.co. Avianca, Cra 10, No 17-55, Edif Torre central, L 301 and at the airport.

Bus
The terminal is 1.5 km south of city centre, C 17, No 23-157; stores luggage. To **Armenia**, 1 hr, every 20 mins from 0600, US$3.30, a beautiful trip. To **Cali**, US$10.50, 4½-5 hrs, *colectivo* by day, bus by night with Expreso Trejos, same price. To **Medellín**, 6-8 hrs, every hr, US$17 with Bolivariano or Expreso Trejos. To/from **Bogotá**, US$10-12, 7 hrs (route is via Girardot, Ibagué – both cities bypassed – and Armenia), every hr 0630-2330 with Bolivariano. To **Buenaventura**, 3 a day with Expreso Trejos at 0730, 0930, 1130, US$17. To **Quibdó**, US$18 at 0500 and 0600.

Car
Car rental Hertz, Muelle Nacional, Suite 8, 2nd N, Mataceña airport, T3142678, www.hertz.com; RentaCar, Av 30 de agosto, No.30-30, Local 25, Centro Comercial Los Puntos, T3291155, www.rentacarpereira.com.

Salento p265
Microbuses (Cootranscir) to **Armenia** hourly, US$1.40, 40 mins, taxi US$7; to **Pereira** hourly, US$2.50, 1 hr; to **Medellín** *colectivos* 0400, 0930 and 1100 daily, US$14, 5 hrs.

Armenia p267, map p268
Air
Airport El Edén, 13 km from city. Scheduled direct flights only to: **Bogotá**, 4 daily, Aces, and **Medellín**, 3 daily, Aces.

Airline offices Avianca, C 21, No 13-23, L 4, T7410730 and at the airport, T7479911.

Bus
Terminal 15 blocks from centre at Cra 19/C 35. To **Bogotá**, 7-9 hrs, US$20, hourly until 2300. To **Cali**, 3-4 hrs, more than hourly, US$8.50. To **Medellín**, 6-7 hrs, hourly, US$19.50. To **Popayán**, 5-6 hrs, 7 a day from 0800 to 1700, US$17. To **Ipiales**, 14 hrs, at 1530 and 1830 with Bolivariano, US$30. To **Pasto**, 12 hrs, at 1820 and 2320 with Flota Magdalena, US$25. To **Manizales**, 3-4 hrs, more than hourly, US$9. To **Neiva**, 6-7 hrs, 7 a day with Coomotor or Cootranshuila from 1000-2200, US$19.50. To **Pitalito/San Agustín**, 10 hrs, at 1900, 2030 and 2230 with Coomotor or Cootranshuila, US$27. To **Buenaventura**, 5-6 hrs, at 0640, 0840, 1040 and 1400 with Expreso Trejos, US$14.50. To **Cartagena**, 20-22 hrs, at 2130 with Copetran, US$72. To **Bucaramanga**, 12-13 hrs, at 1730 with Coomotor, US$40.

Ibagué and around p269
Air
Daily Aires flights to **Bogotá**, **Cali** and **Medellín** and **Pereira**.

Bus
Terminal is between Cras 1-2 and C 19-20. Tourist police at terminal helpful. Frequent services to **Bogotá**, US$8, 4 hrs. To **Neiva**, US$8-9, 3 hrs, and many other places.

Cartago p270
Air
easyfly has daily flights to **Bogotá**.

Bus
To **Cali**, US$7, 3½ hrs. To **Armenia**, US$2, 2½-3 hrs. To **Pereira**, US$1.50, 45 mins. To **Medellín**, US$12, 7 hrs.

● Directory

Manizales *p253, map p255*
Banks Davivienda, Cra 23, No 22-04, T8842217, Centro, or Cra 23, No 63-22, local 56, T8852038. **Bancolombia**, Cra 22, No 20-55, T8783660, or C 66, No 22-56, T8816065. **HSBC**, Cra 23, No 56-42, T8857054. **Embassies and consulates** Germany, via al Magdalena, No 74-71, 10th floor, T8872928. **Italy**, Edif 7 Banco de Bogotá, Of 501, T8831935. **Spain**, C 36, no 22-22, T8845960. **Immigration** DAS, C 53, No 25A-35, T8810600 ext 153. **Internet** El Cable, Cra 23, No 63-82. Skype, headphones, international calls, fax and photocopying services. **Post office** Barrio Milán: Cra 23, No 73-90, piso 1, T8868819; Centro: Cra 22, C 27 esquina T8826166; El Cable: Edificio Torres Panorama, local 15, T8856900.

Pereira *p262, map p262*
Banks Many banks in the centre. *Casas de cambio* change cash and some exchange TCs but check at what time of day: several around Cra 9/C 18. **Internet/telephone** Cybernet, C 19, No 7-49. Lots of computers, has Skype and headphones. Also does international calls. **Post office** For airmail, Avianca, C 19, No 6-28, T3355297. Adpostal, C 19, No 9-75, T3341239.

Salento *p265*
Internet/telephone Real.Net, Cra 6, No 4-24. Skype and headphones. International calls. **Language Marcia Pozos**, T3112410727, marciapozos@ yahoo.com, is a qualified Universidad Nacional Spanish teacher and has the ringing endorsement of having taught the staff of the British embassy in Bogotá.

Armenia *p267, map p268*
Internet/telephone Cabinas del Café, Cra 18, No 19-34. Internet Jota y Efe, Cra 18, N0 21 Esquina, Local 3. **Post office** Avianca, Cra 14, no 19-38.

Contents

284 The Cauca Valley
- 284 Cali
- 289 West of Cali
- 291 Buenaventura
- 292 Around Buenaventura
- 294 Listings

301 Popayán and Tierradentro
- 301 Popayán
- 304 Tierradentro
- 305 Neiva
- 306 Desierto de Tatacoa
- 307 Parque Nacional Puracé
- 309 Listings

314 San Agustín and around
- 314 Ins and outs
- 314 Parque Arqueológico
- 315 Archaeological sites
- 316 South of San Agustín
- 317 Listings

320 The far south
- 320 Pasto
- 323 Pasto to the coast
- 324 South to Ecuador
- 326 Listings

Footprint features

- 282 Don't miss ...
- 289 Salsa
- 291 The brujitas of San Cipriano
- 302 The photographer of Popayán
- 306 The Queen of the Desert
- 323 Las Lajas

Border crossings

Colombia–Ecuador
- 325 Tumaco–San Lorenzo
- 325 Ipiales–Rumichaca

At a glance

⊗ **Getting around** Taxi or bus in Cali; walking in town centres. Intercity buses around region.

◉ **Time required** 2-3 days in Cali; 2-3 weeks for the rest of the region.

☼ **Weather** Hot in Cali and surrounding area; warm but cooler at night in Popayán, San Agustín and Tierradentro; cooler still in mountainous regions approaching the Ecuadorian border.

⊗ **When not to go** Good all year round.

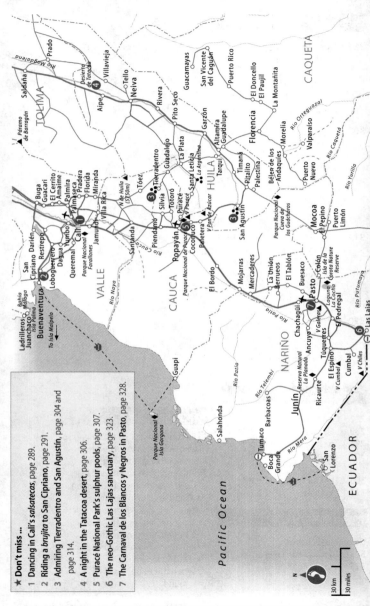

★ Don't miss ...

1 Dancing in Cali's *salsatecas*, page 289.

2 Riding a *brujita* to San Cipriano, page 291.

3 Admiring Tierradentro and San Agustín, page 304 and page 314.

4 A night in the Tatacoa desert, page 306.

5 Puracé National Park's sulphur pools, page 307.

6 The neo-Gothic Las Lajas sanctuary, page 323.

7 The Carnaval de los Blancos y Negros in Pasto, page 328.

Much of Southern Colombia is characterized by the three mountain ranges that eventually join up to form the high Andes, South America's spine. The people of this region have adapted to the physical obstacles these mountains present, while inaccessibility has kept at bay the cultural dilution that comes with modern advancements. The sensual city of Cali has branded itself as the capital of salsa music and sits in the tropical, sugar cane-rich plains of the Valle del Cauca. To the west lies the port of Buenaventura, gateway to the Pacific coast and its many isolated beaches and islands, most notable of which is Isla Gorgona. The Pan-American Highway continues south to the city of Popayán, known for its dazzling-white colonial buildings and its solemn Easter processions, second in size only to Sevilla in Spain . Hidden in the mountains east of Popayán are the mysterious archaeological sites of Tierradentro and San Agustín, while next to the Magdalena river lies the geographical anomaly that is the Tatacoa Desert.

From Popayán, the Cordillera Occidental reaches ever higher as it rises up to the highland towns of Pasto and Ipiales, ideal places to observe indigenous ways of life. Before crossing into Ecuador, the extraordinary Gothic cathedral that straddles a gorge at Las Lajas is worth a visit.

The Cauca Valley

South from Pereira and Armenia the Pan-American Highway drops to the hot, sugar-rich Valle del Cauca, a narrow strip of flat plains abundant in wheat, pineapple, livestock and sugar cane, flanked on either side by the slender fingers of two mountain ranges, the Cordillera Occidental and the Cordillera Central. The valley's capital is at Cali, a sweltering, sexy city known for the beautiful women and as the self-appointed capital of salsa music. The road continues south onto Popayán and eventually to Ecuador, while from Cali a cargo-only railway and a road run west high over mountains down to the port of Buenaventura, the largest settlement on the Pacific coast.
▶▶ For listings, see pages 294-300.

Cali ●②①①⊕⊕○▲●① ▶▶ *pp294-300. Colour map 3, A3.*

→ *Phone code: 2. Population: 1,850,000. Altitude: 1030 m.*

Cali may be second to Bogotá in terms of size, but this vibrant, prosperous city is very much número uno when it comes to partying. Cali calls itself the salsa capital of the world, and few could dispute that claim. The sensuous, tropical rhythms are ubiquitous, seeming to seep from every pore of the city. Cali's other major claim, and rather more contentious, is that it boasts the most beautiful women in the country.

Ins and outs

Alfonso Bonilla Aragón airport is 20 km to the northeast of Cali. The best way to the city is by minibus, which you will find at the far end of the pick-up road outside arrivals. They will take you to the bus terminal (ground floor), on the edge of the centre, every 10 minutes from 0500 to 2100. It takes approximately 30 minutes, US$2.50. From here taxis are relatively cheap to any destination in the city. Alternatively, take a taxi from the airport, US$25, 30 minutes. The minibuses to the airport, marked 'Aeropuerto', leave from the second floor of the bus terminal. There are direct flights to Cali from Mexico, Panama and several cities in the USA. The **bus terminal** ① *C 30N, No 2AN-29*, is a 25-minute walk from the centre following the river along Avenida 2N.

Getting around The centre of the city is comparatively small – most places of interest to the visitor are within comfortable walking distance. Transport by bus or taxi is tedious because of the density of the traffic. Cali's taxis have meters and can be flagged in the street, or ordered by telephone. Radio taxis include **Taxi Libre** ① *T4444444*, and **Taxis Valcali** ① *T4430000*. Local buses cost US$0.85.

Best time to visit There is little climate variation during the year, average temperatures stay around 25°C. It is hot and humid at midday but a strong breeze that blows up in the afternoon makes the evenings cool and pleasant. Rain can come at more or less any time but Cali is shielded from the heavy rainfalls of the Pacific coast by the Cordillera Occidental.

Orientation Cali is bounded on the west by the Cordillera and to the east by the marshy plains of the Río Cauca. Through the centre of the city runs the Río Cali, a tributary of the Cauca, with grass and exotic trees on its banks. North of the river, all streets have the suffix 'N', and Carreras become Avenidas. The city extends southwards 15 km from the Río Cali.

Near the southern end a new area is building up around Carrera 100 with the large Unicentro shopping mall and the residential community of Ciudad Jardín.

Safety In the early 1990s Cali achieved international notoriety through the success of its drug cartel. Known as the 'Gentlemen of Cali', thanks to their high society background, the Rodríguez Orejuela brothers and their associate José Santacruz Londoño profited from Pablo Escobar's war with the government, rising to supersede his Medellín organization. But in 1995, six of the seven heads were arrested and in 2006 the Rodríguez Orejuela brothers were extradited to the United States, effectively bringing and end to the era of the narco-trafficking cartel in Colombia. Although still associated with drug and anti-drug operations, the atmosphere in Cali is quite relaxed. Violent crime is still a problem in the city's barrios but less of a threat in more affluent areas. However, carry your passport (or photocopy) at all times and be prepared for police checks. At night, do not walk east or south of Calle 15 and Carrera 10. Do not change money on the street in any circumstances and avoid all people who approach, offering to sell. Take advice on where and where not to go.

Tourist offices **Secretaría de Cultura y Turismo** ① *Gobernación del Valle del Cauca building, p 2, T620 0063/64.* See also **www.caliescali.com** (news, chat, entertainment, music and tourist information on *La Guía*). For national parks, **MA** ① *Av 3G, No 37N-70, T6656124,* for information on Los Farallones de Cali and other parks, very helpful. Also **Fundación Farallones** ① *Cra 24B, No 2A-99,* on the same subject. For information on the many privately owned nature reserves in this part of Colombia, enquire at **Asociación Red Colombiana de Reservas Naturales de la Sociedad Civil** ① *C 2A, No 26-103, T5585046, www.resnatur.org.co.* Ask for maps of Cali at these tourist offices. None are very accurate. Try at **Instituto Geográfico Agustín Codazzi (IGAC)** ① *Cra 6, No 13-56, T8811351.* They have the best maps although they are probably out of date.

Background
After the collapse of the Incas in 1533, Sebastián Belalcázar left Pizarro's army in Peru and came north. He founded Quito in 1534 and established Popayán and Cali in 1536. He intended to continue northwards and establish other new settlements, but around Cali he encountered stiff resistance from the indigenous locals, which delayed him for several years so that others founded Antioquia and Bogotá. The first site of the city was beside the Río Lili near the present Ciudad Universitaria and Ciudad Jardín but it was moved north to the present location in 1539. Cali remained a dependency of Popayán and was dominated by Quito for 250 years, as north-south communications along the line of the cordillera are so much easier than across the mountain ranges. Indeed, until 1900, Cali was a leisurely colonial town. Then the railway came, and Cali became a rapidly expanding industrial complex serving the whole of southern Colombia. The railway has since been eclipsed by road and air links but today Cali is economically closely tied with the rest of Colombia.

The capital of Valle del Cauca Department is set in an exceptionally rich agricultural area producing sugar, cotton, rice, coffee and cattle, and acts as the southern capital of Colombia. It sits on the main route north from Ecuador along the Río Cauca and controls the passage to the only important port of Colombia's Pacific coast. Thanks to the port and the sugar industry, many Caribbeans and other groups of people came to the valley and now contribute to the city's wealth and entertainment. It was originally named Santiago de Cali, which name often officially used today. It has tropical climate, but with a freshness that makes for economic as well as cultural activity, producing 20% of the country's GNP.

Sights in the centre

Among the most interesting buildings in Cali are the church and monastery of **San Francisco** ① *Cra 6, C 9/10*. The brick church originates from 1757 and was structurally renovated inside in the 19th century and most recently in 1926. It has a fine ceiling and many 17th- and 18th-century images, carvings, and paintings. The altar came from Spain. A second church in the complex is the **Capilla de la Inmaculada**, with a long nave, well lit *reredos* and gold-headed columns. The adjoining 18th-century monastery has a splendidly proportioned domed bell tower in the mudejar style known as the *Torre Mudéjar*. On the opposite side of the square is the imposing 20-floor **Gobernación** building.

Cali

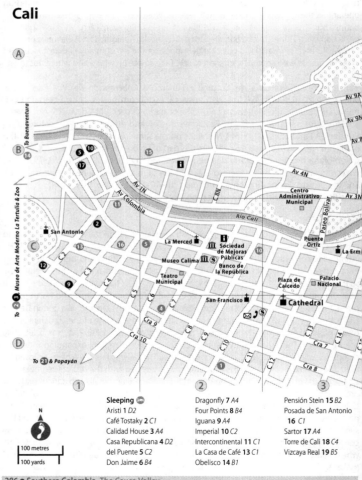

Sleeping 🛏
Aristi **1** *D2*
Café Tostaky **2** *C1*
Calidad House **3** *A4*
Casa Republicana **4** *D2*
del Puente **5** *C2*
Don Jaime **6** *B4*

Dragonfly **7** *A4*
Four Points **8** *B4*
Iguana **9** *A4*
Imperial **10** *C2*
Intercontinental **11** *C1*
La Casa de Café **13** *C1*
Obelisco **14** *B1*

Pensión Stein **15** *B2*
Posada de San Antonio
16 *C1*
Sartor **17** *A4*
Torre de Cali **18** *C4*
Vizcaya Real **19** *B5*

N

100 metres
100 yards

Cali's oldest church, **La Merced,** ① *Cra 4, No 6-117, T8804737*, dates from 1545 and was constructed on the symbolic site of the founding of the city nine years earlier. It is in the classical style with a fine altar. It has been well restored by the Banco Popular. The adjoining convent houses two museums: **Museo de Arte Colonial** (which includes the church), a collection of 16th- and 17th-century paintings, and the **Museo Arqueológico** ① *Cra 4, No 6-59, T8813229, Mon-Sat 1000-1300, 1400-1600, US$2,50*. This houses a good pre-Columbian pottery collection highlighting Calima and other Southwest Colombia cultures. By the well in the courtyard is a replica of a Tierradentro tomb.

Eating 🍴
Bahareque **2** *C1*
Café Tostaky **3** *C1*
D'Toluca **4** *B4*
El Balcón de Salo **5** *B1*
El Solar **6** *B3*
Granada Faro **7** *B4*

Kaoba **8** *A6*
La Colina **9** *C1*
La Tartine **10** *B1*
Ojo de Perro Azul **12** *C1*
Pampero **13** *A4*
Platillos Voladores **14** *B3*
Pizza al Paso **15** *A4*

Taisu **16** *B4*
Tortelli **17** *B1*

Bars & clubs 🍸
Blues Brothers **18** *A6*
Forum **19** *A6*
Kukara Makura **20** *A6*

Tin Tin Deo **21** *D1*
Zaperoco **22** *B4*

Opposite La Merced is the **Casa Arzobispal** ① *Cra 4, No 6-76*. This is one of the earliest buildings of Cali and the only surviving two-storied house of the period. Bolívar stayed here in 1822.

Nearby, in Banco de la República building, is the **Museo Calima (Museo de Oro)** ① *C 7, No 4-69, Tue-Sat, 1000-1700, free.* This is another of the national gold museums, of the usual high standard and well worth a visit. In addition to pre-Columbian gold work, well presented, with some exquisite tiny items magnified, it has an excellent pottery collection. There is a music room and library in the basement and exhibition halls.

Another church the visitor cannot fail to notice is **La Ermita** ① *by the river at Cra 1, C 12/13*. The original church was built here in 1602, but was totally destroyed by the 1925 earthquake. It was rebuilt between 1926 and 1942 with funds from public subscription, with Cologne cathedral in mind. There is a fine marble altar and the painting *El Señor de la Caña* reflecting the local importance of sugar cane, one of the few items that survived the earthquake. The neo-gothic blue and white exterior is striking. In the pleasant plaza in front of the church you can sit next to lifesize figures of notable *caleños* of the past, including Joaquin de Caycedo and Jorge Isaacs. Across the street is an example of the older architecture of the city, the ornate Colombia de Tabaco building.

The city's centre is the **Plaza de Caicedo**, with a statue of one of the independence leaders, Joaquín de Caycedo y Cuero. Facing the square is the **Catedral Metropolitana**, a large three-aisle church, with a clerestory, elaborate aisle niches and stained glass windows. The original church on the site dated from around 1539, the present building is mid-19th century. The **Palacio Nacional** is on the eastern side of the plaza, a French neo-classical style building (1933), now the city archive.

Cross the river by the delightful, pedestrianized **Puente Ortiz**, built in the 1840s, two blocks from the Plaza de Caicedo, to the **Paseo Bolívar**, alongside the Centro Administrativo Municipal (CAM) and the main post office. On the Paseo, are a bronze statue of *El Libertador* and a sculpture honouring Jorge Isaacs, the romantic 19th-century novelist, depicting the characters of his novel *María*.

A special feature of the centre of Cali is the ribbon of green along the river, lined with exotic and ancient trees that always give a freshness to the heat of the day. Several sculptures were commissioned in the late 1990s, now in position along the river: look out for the *María Mulatta* a black bird seen everywhere along the coasts of Colombia and the splendid bronze *El Gato del Río* by Hernando Tejada, inaugurated in 1996. Also notable are the tall palms of Plaza Caicedo and the trees of the San Antonio park overlooking the west of the city. Cali prides itself on its trees. Several are marked out for conservation, for example, the huge *ceiba* on Avenida 4N at Calle 10, by the viaduct.

Sights outside the centre

Along the river from the city centre is the **Museo de Arte Moderno La Tertulia** ① *Av Colombia, No 5-10 Oeste, Tue-Sun 1000-1800, US$2.50*, has exhibitions of South American including local art.

To the west of the city, a popular morning 'run' is up the hill to the 18th-century church of **San Antonio** on the Colina de San Antonio, built around 1747. It is a favourite place for weddings. There are some attractive colonial-style houses on the way and pleasant parkland on the top with fine views of the city, though partly obstructed by high-rise buildings.

Salsa

Salsa may have its roots in Cuba and have developed its sound in the Latin *barrios* of New York, but the people of Cali cheekily claim it's in their city that it has found its true home. It can be heard everywhere – on radios, in taxis, bars and nightclubs. So all-pervasive is its reach that it can be said that this horn-led music with its complex, syncopated beats has, literally, become part of the rhythm of everyday life.

Local groups such as Orquesta Guayacán, Grupo Niche and Jairo Varela have helped develop a distinctive sound, which is mirrored on the dancefloor by a style that is characterized by an upright upper body and intricate movements of the feet.

'No salsa, no dates', say the locals and at the weekend, sexual attraction is measured by moves on the dancefloors of Juanchito's enormous *salsatecas*. But salsa purists also head for traditional salsa bars nearer the centre such as Zaperoco where the dancing is the most important thing.

For a full view of the city, you can take a taxi to the **Monumento Las Tres Cruces**, at 1450 m, to the northwest of the city, a traditional pilgrimage site in Holy Week, or go to the huge statue of Christ **Monumento Cristo Rey**, at 1470 m above San Antonio to the west of the city. This statue can be seen for 50 km across the Río Cauca. It is also worthwhile going up the skyscraper Torre de Cali for a view of the city, but you may have to buy an expensive meal as well.

Zoológico De Cali ① *Cra 2A Oeste/C 14, entrance on the south bank of the Río Cali about 3 km upstream from the centre, T8927474, daily 0900-1800, US$4.50*, interesting and well organised collection of all types of South American animals, birds and reptiles. It makes very good use of the river as it enters the city. There is a small aquarium and an 'ant' auditorium.

The orchid garden, **Orchideorama** ① *Av 2N, No 48-10, T6643256, free, closed Sun*, is worth seeing. Major international show annually in mid-November.

A popular family park is **Acuaparque de la Caña** ① *Cra 8, No 39-01, El Troncal (about 4 km from the centre), T4384820, daily 0900-1700, adults US$6, children US$4.50*, with family entertainment including sports, swimming, riding and children's diversions.

From Cali it is 135 km south to Popayán. The road crosses the Río Cauca, then rejoins the main east bank route south at Villa Rica. About 17 km along the main road is **Santander**, an attractive town with a colonial chapel, Capilla de Dominguillo, worth a visit. Ceramics and *fique* handicrafts are sold here.

West of Cali ☺ ➤➤ *pp294-300.*

To the west of Cali is the northeast/southwest line of the Cordillera Occidental, which rises here to over 4000 m. A large section of this area and down to 200 m on the Pacific side is the Farallones de Cali National Park (see below). North of this are the road and rail links to Buenaventura. Along the main road (toll) there is much heavy traffic to Colombia's main Pacific port. There are however places to stop, eg San Cipriano and Córdoba, both near the railway, where you can rent small *cabañas* in the forest, swim in the rivers and visit the rainforest. Busy at weekends and holidays but quiet otherwise. The railway is being refurbished for freight transport.

Farallones National Park

① *Entrance to the park, US$1.50 per person.*

Both the toll and ordinary roads out of Cali and Buenaventura give beautiful views of mountains and jungle, and from the old road you can reach the Parque Nacional Farallones. Take the dirt road south from the plaza in El Queremal, at 1460 m, about an hour from Cali, 3½ hours from Buenaventura. At El Queremal, a pleasant local mountain village. Alternatively, take the road southwest out of Cali, or *colectivo* (one hour), to Pance. From Pance there is a path, about 30 minutes, to the environmental centre at the entrance to the park at El Topacio. There is good walking and bathing in the park and peaks to climb, one of

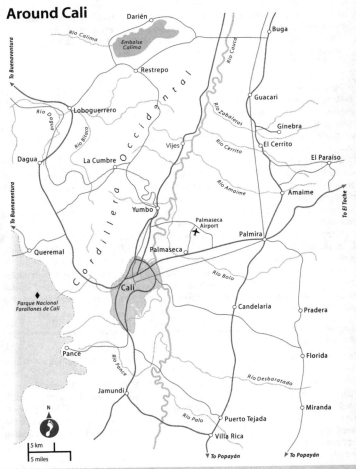

Around Cali

The brujitas of San Cipriano

What do you do when there's no road to your village and a cargo train trundles by just once a day? For the villagers of San Cipriano the answer was obvious: make your own train, or something vaguely resembling one. They came up with an innovative system consisting of carts mounted on the line that use large poles to punt them along. The whole effect resembles a witch riding a broomstick, hence the name. Lately, they have started using motorbikes strapped onto the trolleys. The back wheel sits on the line and powers the cart along like a motorbike with a sidecar.

There's little in terms of a braking system; the 10-minute descent through thick jungle to the village can be hairy and if the train comes along it's a desperate scramble to get the cart off the line, but there's no doubting that in the case of San Cipriano the journey is the destination.

which is the Pico de Loro, a steep slippery scramble for 2½ hours, but worth it for the views and the sound of the swooping birds. Busy at weekends, camping possible at US$6 for five people a night at El Topacio or at Quebrada Honda, near the Río Pance. You will need a permit from MA in Cali (see page 300 for more information). It is best to go with a guide.

San Cipriano

If the expression 'the journey is the destination' had been coined about one specific place then San Cipriano, 20 km before Buenaventura, would be it. Sat in steaming jungle next to a shallow river, San Cipriano is only accessible by the main railway line between Cali and Buenaventura, which only carries cargo. To compensate for the lack of roads to their village the locals have come up with an ingenious transport system to ferry people to and fro, see box, above. Passage on one of these improvised rail carts is US$2.20. Beware of young boys trying to charge you more.

On arrival at the village you will have to pay US$1 at the Fundación San Cipriano office to enter the reserve. Enquire here about guides for walks in the forest, including one to a waterfall, La Cascada Veinteadora. Most houses near the river hire out inflatable rubber rings for floating down the river, US$2.70.

The village and its environs were declared a national reserve in 1979, and Fundación San Cipriano has 8564 ha of protected forest, through which runs the San Cipriano river. It is noted for the rich variety of animal life which can be seen and heard, which includes spectacled bears, spider monkeys, toucans and several varieties of hummingbird.

San Cipriano was founded in the 18th century as a base for hunting, tree felling and gold panning. Today, most people live off tourism or work at the local water works.

Buenaventura ⬤🅵🅻🅴🅲 ›› pp294-300. Colour map 3, A2.

→ Phone code: 2. Population: 202,000.

Colombia's only important port on the Pacific is Buenaventura, 145 km by road from Cali over a pass in the Western Cordillera. The commercial centre is now entirely paved and has some impressive buildings, but the rest of the town is poor, with unpaved streets lined with wooden shacks. It is more expensive than Cali and it is difficult to eat cheaply or well. On a hill near the centre is the **cathedral** and a good view of the town can be seen from the nearby **El Mirador** Edificio del Café. There is a festive atmosphere every night. **Warning** This town is one of Colombia's main drug- and people-trafficking centres and has severe poverty; this has led to high levels of violent crime and homicide. You are advised to avoid walking about at night and to stick within a couple of blocks of the seafront.

Buenaventura was founded in 1540, but not on its present site. It now stands on the island of Cascajal, 16 km at the end of the Bay of Buenaventura. The port handles 80% of Colombia's coffee exports, and 60% of the nation's total exports, including sugar and frozen shrimp. South of the town a swampy coast stretches as far as Tumaco (see page 324). To the north lies the deeply jungled Chocó Department, with abundant wildlife and some good beaches.

Ins and outs

Getting there The **bus terminal** is at Carrera 5/Calle 7. It is 560 km by sea from Panama, 708 km by road from Bogotá. From Cali, the new road climbs 12 km to Saladito, a fresh 10°C cooler than the city. Many *caleños* enjoy the roadside restaurants, especially at weekends in this sector. The highest point is reached at Km 18 where the old road turns off left through El Queremal to Buenaventura. Dagua, 828m, 46 km from Cali, is in a semi-arid pineapple-growing zone, a good place for refreshments. Here the railway comes alongside the road, both following the Río Dagua to the coast. Further down, tropical forests are continuous with several places to stop and bathe on the way.

Climate Mean temperature, 27°C. It rains nearly every day, particularly at night; the average annual rainfall is 7400 mm (relative humidity 88%). There are some problems with malaria.

Tourist information Enquire at **Embarcaciones Asturias** ① *Muelle Turístico, T2404048*, about trips around Buenaventura. **Cámara de Comercio** nearby is also helpful.

Around Buenaventura ⊜▲ ▸▸ *pp294-300.*

North of Buenaventura is the beautiful coastline of the Bahía de Málaga, with rocky promontories sagging under the weight of thick tropical vegetation. Squadrons of pelicans patrol its glassy green waters and from a boat you will catch glimpses of some inviting golden sand beaches. These are all accessible from **Juanchaco**, one hour on a lancha from Buenaventura. Juanchaco has cheap accommodation and restaurants but its beach is polluted and its streets muddy. **Ladrilleros** is just around the headland and has much better beaches, albeit a bit grey, backed by picturesque cliffs and with many sea caves and freshwater falls to explore. The village itself is quiet and pretty with rickety clapboard houses and dirt tracks for streets.

Bahía Málaga → *Colour map 3, A2.*

With 265 species per hectare the inland bay of Bahía Málaga boasts the greatest plant biodiversity on the planet. Just as impressive is the number of animals: there are 60 species of amphibian, 114 reptiles, 148 types of fish and over 400 species of bird. Some 3500 people subsist primarily as fishing communities on its various islands. In its eastern corner is the waterfall **Las Sierpes**, which falls 65 m directly into the sea. The bay also has some fine beaches, including **Playa Dorada** (golden sand), **Juan de Dios** (white sand),

and **Chucheros**, which has a waterfall falling onto the beach, creating a freshwater pool. All these are accessible by lancha from Buenaventura or Juanchaco.

Partly because of the richness of the water in this region, this is the location of spectacular dolphin and humpback whale sightings, as the whales migrate south with their calves from July to early October each year. There are also all kinds of sea birds to see including pelicans, and frigate birds. A good place is near the Isla Palma, an island off Juanchaco owned by the Colombian Navy. A number of tours are on offer, see page 299.

Another worthwhile activity near Ladrilleros is a tour round the inland sea canals. This network of tidal mangrove rivers, consisting of 90% fresh water, winds its way through thick jungle with encroaching vines. A tour in canoe of motorboat (US$14) includes a visit to a swimming hole fed by a waterfall. Enquire at Eco-Guías, page 299, for more details.

Isla Gorgona → *Colour map 3, A1.*

① *Visits to the island are managed and run by Aviatur, Av 6 Norte, No 37B-94 (opposite CC Chipichape), T6645050 in Cali or C 4, No 8-69, T8208674 in Popayán, www.concesiones parquesnaturales.com. Accommodation per couple ranges from US$86 to US$311 depending on type. All visitors must have a permit before arriving at the island, obtainable from Aviatur. It is recommended to book accommodation and boat tickets well in advance during high season. Entrance fee US $14 for foreigners.*

Until 1984 the island of Gorgona was Colombia's high-security prison (a sort of Alcatraz). The prison is derelict but some parts can still be clearly seen. Convicts were dissuaded from escaping by the poisonous snakes on the island (after whom Francisco Pizarro named the island) and the sharks patrolling the 46 km to the mainland (both snakes and sharks are still there). The national park boasts many unspoilt, deserted sandy beaches. From the paths you can see monkeys, iguanas, and a wealth of flora and fauna.(Rubber boots are provided and recommended.) There is an abundance of birds (pelicans, cormorants, geese, herons) that use the island as a migration stop-over. Snorkelling and diving is rewarding, equipment can be hired (but take your own if possible), there are many exotic fish and turtles to be seen. Killer whales visit the area from July to September.

Currently there are two ways of getting to the island. One way is via the town of Guapi flying with Satena from Cali or Popayán, from which there are launches to the island, 1½ hours. Alternatively, launches can be contracted from Buenaventura, a journey of four hours to Gorgona, US$130.

Embarcaciones Asturias ① *offices at the Muelle Turistico in Buenaventura, T2404048, barcoasturias@hotmail.com,* offer a weekend package leaving Buenaventura on a Friday at 1900 and returning Monday, US$290 per person, including accommodation on boat, food, permit and snorkelling equipment.

Isla Malpelo

Declared a UNESCO site in 2006, Isla Mapelo is located 506 km from Buenaventura in the Pacific and is an acclaimed birdwatching haven with great diving opportunities. The island is considered to be one of the world's best places to observe hammerhead sharks in great numbers. Boats leave from Buenaventura, a 36-hour bumpy voyage. There are no places to stay on the island and camping is not allowed. Contact **MA office** ① *T2432009,* in Bogotá, for more information. **Embarcaciones Asturias** in Buenaventura offers an eight-day tour, including transport and accommodation for US$1650.

For Sleeping and Eating price codes and other relevant information, see pages 31-36.

● Sleeping

Cali *p284, map p286*

LL Intercontinental, Av Colombia, No 2-72, T6847000, www.intercontinental.com. The most expensive hotel in town, the Intercontinental has all the services you would expect with a half-size Olympic pool, sauna, Turkish bath, large rooms with plasma TVs and a 24-hr casino. Additionally, it is well placed on the edge of San Antonio. Prices drop at weekends.

A Aristi, Cra 9, No 10-04, T8822521, www.hotelaristi.com.co. Serving Cali's elite since 1952, this is another hotel that has seen better days. Nevertheless, it is situated just 2 blocks from Plaza Bolívar and has Wi-Fi, a rooftop pool and Turkish bath.

A Obelisco, Av Colombia, No 4 Oeste-49, T8933019, www.hotelobeliscocali.com. One of Cali's traditional upmarket hotels, the Obelisco is sorely in need of a facelift. It does, however, have a pool and sauna and Wi-Fi in its pizzeria.

B Casa Republicana, C 7, No 6-74, T8960949, www.hotelcasarepublicana.com. Gorgeous Republican-era building with a lovely courtyard full of large plants. Has good rooms with cable TV, Wi-Fi and a good restaurant serving lunch for US$4.

C Hotel del Puente, C 5, No 4-36, T8938484. A little noisy and lacking some basic things such as loo seats but it's well situated on the edge of San Antonio.

C Hotel Imperial, C 9, No 3-93, T8899571, www.hotelimperialdecali.com. This hotel feels a little dated but has good facilities such as a pool and restaurant on a terrace, internet, cable TV, parking, sauna and a/c.

C Posada de San Antonio, Cra 5, No 3-37, T8937413, www.posadadesanantonio.com. With rooms set around a couple of sunny, leafy patios and decorated with Calima indigenous artefacts, this *bahareque* building dating back to 1906 represents good value for money. Use of internet, Wi-Fi and breakfast included only add to that feeling.

E Café Tostaky, Cra 10, No 1-76, T8930651, www.cafetostaky.blogspot.com. Situated at the bottom of San Antonio park, this sweet little backpackers' hostel, run by a French-Colombian couple, has airy rooms above a café of the same name. Facilities include use of a kitchen, a TV room with DVDs and hot water in shared bathrooms. Recommended.

E La Casa Café, Cra 6, No 2-13, T8937011, www.lacasacafecali.blogspot.com. Brand new backpackers' hostel/internet café/house of coffee in San Antonio. The hostel has simple rooms with high ceilings and wooden floorboards while the café hosts storytelling and live music nights.

Barrio Granada and around

L Four Points, C 18 Norte, No 4N-08, T6859999, www.fourpoints.com. Slick new hotel with lots of steel, glass and brick in a pleasant suburb of Cali, with a swimming pool, gym, Wi-Fi and a la carte restaurant. Currently under refurbishment, there's a large disparity between new and old rooms.

AL Vizcaya Real, C 20 Norte, No 5N-30, T6831000, www.hotelvizcayareal.com. Located on a palm-lined avenue, with good facilities, including a small pool, gym, Turkish bath and an internet room, the beds are a bit short.

A Don Jaime, Av 6 Norte, No 15N-25, T6672828, www.hoteldonjaime.com. Large but dated hotel on the noisy Av 6 with a/c, cable TV, Wi-Fi and breakfast included.

A Pensión Stein, Av 4 Norte, No 3-33, T6614927, www.hotelstein.com.co. Owned by the Swiss consulate (and situated next to it), this fortress-like colonial house is popular with couples come to Cali to adopt orphans. The rooms are comfortable with writing desks and cable TV while it also has a swimming pool, gym and a restaurant serving Swiss food.

A Torre de Cali, Av de las Américas, No 18N-26, T6833535, www.glhhoteles.com. From its 41-floor tower, the Torre de Cali has one of the best views in town. The rooms are large with big TVs but the decor is a bit dated. There are significant discounts at weekends.
C Sartor, Av 8 Norte, No 20-50, T6686482, hotelsartor@yahoo.com. This hotel has an interesting entrance with 2 large pine trees in a tiny courtyard. The rooms are basic and have hot water en suite bathrooms but small beds. Has Wi-Fi, cable TV and laundry service.
E Dragonfly, Av 9 Norte, No 21N-30, T4004200. Located in a beautiful, slightly dilapidated art deco building, this English-run apartment/hotel has enormous basic rooms at very reasonable prices. With Wi-Fi, a TV room and a good salsa rooms but its greatest bonus is the swimming pool. A little hard to find: look for the brass statue of a cheetah. Medium- and long-term rents available.
E-F Calidad House, C 17 Norte, No 9AN-39, T6612338, www.calidadhouse.com. This backpacker's hostel is something of an anomaly: when the English owner is there it is an excellent choice, with a kitchen, BBQ, and cheap dorms and a sunny patio. When he's away the rude staff create an unpleasant atmosphere.
E-F Iguana, Av 9 Norte, No 22N-46, T3137686024, www.iguana.com.co. Spread over 2 pleasant suburban houses on the edge of the fashionable Barrio Granada, this has long been Cali's best-known backpacker's hostel. Several private rooms, some with en suite bathrooms, a kitchen, garden, TV room with DVDs, Spanish and salsa classes and great local information. Run by Urs from Switzerland, his Colombian wife runs yoga weekends.

San Cipriano *p291*
Accommodation in San Cipriano is about as basic as it gets, though there is running water and electricity.
E Cabañas Donato, T3117827421. Just beyond Hotel David, this has *cabañas* by the river with mosquito nets provided, good food and friendly service.

E Hotel David, towards the end of the village, which is run by the lovely Luz Mari and her family. She has basic rooms including a chalet above her restaurant with clean showers and fan provided. She also guarantees that if you get bitten by mosquitoes during the night she won't charge!

Buenaventura *p291*
AL Hotel Estelar Estación, C 2, No 1A-08, T2434070, www.hotelesestelar.com. With its white neo-classical façade, the 80-year-old Estación gleams in comparison to the rest of Buenaventura. Smartly dressed bellboys and sculpted gardens add to the old world charm. Also with a large swimming pool, sauna, cable TV and a restaurant serving *criollo* food. Be sure to ask for a room in the old part of the hotel, which has more character. There are healthy discounts available, especially at weekends. The hotel can also organize whale-watching trips to the nearby Bahía de Málaga.
D Los Delfines, C 1, No 5A-03, T2415450, hotellosdelfines@mibuenaventura.com. 4 blocks up the hill from the *muelle*, this hotel is good value with clean rooms, a/c, cable TV, private bathrooms and a breezy terrace.
D Titanic, C 1, No 2A-55, T2412046. Handily located about a block from the *muelle turistico*, this hotel has clean rooms with en suite bathrooms and beds with crisp, white sheets. Its 6th-floor restaurant has great sea views and serves *almuerzos* at US$3.80, as well as á la carte options. Cable TV, a safe in each room and an internet salon make it a good option if you get stuck in Buenaventura.

Around Buenaventura *p292*
Ladrilleros
B Cabañas Reserva Aguamarina, T3117283213, www.reservaaguamarina.com. Colourful wooden *cabañas* set amongst lush tropical gardens. Fan, cable TV and en suite bathrooms. 2 meals included in price. Owner John Janio also runs Eco-guías, which organizes whale-watching tours and other activities.

B Palma Real, T2460335, www.hotelpalma realcolombia.com. Up on a cliff, this hotel affords spectacular glimpses of the sea through a canopy of trees. It has a good pool and jacuzzi and private access down a jungle path to the beach below. The rooms, in a clapboard house, are a bit small and the walls a little flimsy, but there are 2 meals at its restaurant thrown into the price.
D Doña Francia, T2460373. This little place has a couple of good, clean rooms with fan and a shared bath. Ask at the restaurant of the same name around the corner.

● Eating

Cali p284, map p286
Cali has a good restaurant scene. In the centre, the area around Parque de Peñón, just north of San Antonio, has an excellent selection of restaurants serving all types of international food, while San Antonio itself has several cafés with very agreeable atmospheres. In the north, the sheer volume of eateries in Granada makes for some difficult dining dilemmas.
¶¶ La Tartine, C 3 Oeste, No 1-74, T8936617. Classic French-owned restaurant serving delicacies such as snails and *chateaubriand* in eccentric surroundings.
¶¶ Tortelli, C 3 Oeste, No 3-15, T8933227. Little Italian restaurant serving home-made pasta.
¶ Bahareque, C 2, No 4-23. This laid-back restaurant has a hint of a lounge feel about it. Open til 0400 on weekends there is frequently live music and the place often doesn't get going until late. Ultra friendly owners Marly and José are a wealth of information on the local music and dance scene. It serves typical Colombian food as well as salads.
¶ Café Tostaky, C 10, No 1-76. Café from the hostel of the same name, good atmosphere, serves croissants, crêpes, *croque-monsieurs* and French breakfasts on Sun.
¶ El Balcón de Salo, Cra 3 Oeste, No 2-65, T8933235. Arabic restaurant with a outdoor

patio serving *kofte*, kebabs and salads as well as steaks, etc.
¶ La Colina, C 3, No 10-35. This restaurant serves what according to one traveller are the best pizzas he had eaten in Central or South America. Also on the menu are crêpes and particularly good puddings – try the vanilla, chocolate and *arequipe* split.
¶ Ojo de Perro Azul, Cra 9, No 1-27. Bright bohemian hangout with cards, dominoes, chess and a wide selection of mixed drinks at reasonable prices (cuba libre is US$4.40). Serves mostly *picadas* and *tostadas* but has a few traditional Colombian mains on the menu. The funky animal-print furniture is mostly fake but at least one zebra died to decorate the floor.

Barrio Granada and around
¶¶¶ El Solar, C 15 Norte, No 9, N-62, T6534628. With a great atmosphere created by an open-air gravel patio shaded by trees, and a varied international menu of Asian, Italian and Mexican cuisines, a popular *caleño* choice.
¶¶¶ Granada Faro, Av 9 Norte, No 15AN-02, T6674625, www.granfaro.com. Another Cali culinary fixture, the Granada Faro serves Mediterranean-Peruvian fusion.
¶¶¶ Platillos Voladores, C 14 Norte, No 9N-32, T6687588, www.platillosvoladores.com. One of Cali's smartest restaurants, Platillos Voladores (it means 'flying saucers') serves excellent quality Asian-Colombian fusion food.
¶¶ Pampero, C 21N, No 9-17, T6613117. Pitch perfect Argentine steaks on pleasant terrace with good service. Recommended.
¶¶ Taisu, C 16N, No 8N-74, T6612281. Taisu serves a variety of Asian cuisines, including sushi, *teppanyaki* and various stir-fried dishes.
¶ D'Toluca, C 17N, No 8N-46, T6618390. Good little Mexican restaurant serving fajitas, tacos and burritos at reasonable prices.
¶ Kaoba, C 28N, No 4N-42, T6534902. Serves one of the best *almuerzos ejecutivos* in Cali.
¶ Pizza al Paso, C 18N, No 9N-29, T6836974. Pizzas, pastas and salads in very agreeable surroundings, this chain of restaurants also puts on art and music events.

Buenaventura p291
Most hotels have their own restaurant, otherwise there are several cheap joints along the promenade.

🎵 Bars and clubs

Cali p284, map p286

Cali is legendary for its nightlife and especially so for its *salsatecas* – salsa-playing discos. The most popular with *caleños* can be found on Av 6 Norte where there are dozens of venues to choose from, although the real salsa purists would direct you to **Zaperoco**, Av 5N, No 16-46, www.zape roco.com. An alternative is **Tin Tin Deo**, C 5, No 38-71, T5141537, which attracts a liberal crowd of students and teachers and is more forgiving on salsa beginners. But it's not just salsa, there's bars playing rock, jazz, blues and electronic music as well.
Blues Brothers, Av 6AN, No 21-40. Jazz and live rock bands.
Kukara Makura, C 28N, No 2bis-97. Was the in place in Cali at the time of writing, playing electronic music.
Forum, C 25N, No 5-68. Electronic music.
   Bars in town close by 0300, after which many people head to Barrio Juanchito, which has a range of salsa bars and discos, including huge, hi-tech *salsatecas* (eg the popular Don José). It is worth visiting just to watch couples dancing salsa and to join in, if you dare. Go with locals and couples; groups of foreign male tourists might have a hard time getting in. Most advisable to take a registered radio taxi there and back; 15-min ride out of Cali, across the bridge over the Río Cauca.

🎭 Entertainment

Cali p284, map p286
Cinema
Centro Colombo-Americano (see page 300 for contact details). Films are shown on Wed nights.

Alianza Colombo-Francesa, Av 6N, No 21-34, also shows films on Fri nights.
Museo La Tertulia, also shows good films.

Theatre
Teatro Aire Libre Los Cristales, Cra 14, No 6-00, T5582009. All kinds of musical and artistic presentations.
Teatro Experimental, C 7, No 8-63, T8843820. Theatre productions most weekends by resident company.
Teatro Jorge Isaacs, Cra 3, No 12-28, T8899322, www.teatrojorgeisaacs.com. Neo-classical 1930s building declared a National Monument in 1984. Puts on jazz and pop music events as well as comedy nights.
Teatro La Máscara, Cra 10, No 3-40, T8936640. Feminist theatre ensemble putting on alternative productions.
Teatro Municipal, Cra 5, No 6-64, T6843578, www.teatromunicipal.net. Opened in 1918, hosts major cultural activities including opera, ballet and weekly classical concerts and is also home to the Cali Symphony orchestra.

🎉 Festivals and events

Cali p284, map p286
25 Dec to 3 Jan Feria Internacional de Cali, centred at Plaza Canaveralejo on C 5 but engulfing the whole city, with bullfights, horse parades, masquerade balls, sporting contests and salsa competitions everywhere with groups coming from all over the world.
Jun Festival Internacional de Arte (painting, sculpture, theatre, music, etc).
Jun Feria Artesanal at Parque Panamericano, C 5, handicrafts and excellent leather goods.
Aug The Festival de Música del Pacífico Petronio Alvarez champions music from Colombia's Pacific coast. Recommended.
Sep The AjazzGo festival, www.ajazzgo festival.com, with international artists.

O Shopping

Cali *p284, map p286*
Artesanías Pacandé, Av.6N, No 17A-53.
Typical regional handicrafts.
Centro Artesanal La Loma de la Cruz,
C 5 entre Cra 15 y 16. Permanent handicraft
market, nice setting and pleasant
neighbourhood, safe, cafés around
the park. Open 1130-2030.
Ceramicas Palomar, Cra 12 with C 2.
Good pottery.
La Caleñita, Cra 24, No 8-53. Good selection
of typical handicrafts.
Librería Nacional, Cra 5, No 11-50, almost
next to the cathedral on Plaza de Caicedo.
Bookshop with a café, as do most branches
elsewhere in the city. Also at the airport and
in all major shopping centres. Bookstalls on
the sidewalk on Cra 10 near C 10.
Platería Ramírez, C 1A, No 4B-44 Oeste,
San Antonio. Good selection of jewellery,
lessons offered in jewellery making.

▲ Activites and tours

Cali *p284, map p286* .
Bullring
The new, bullring, the **Plaza de Toros
Cañaveralejo**, is 5 km from the city centre
along C 5. Bullfights take place at the end of
Dec, beginning of Jan.

Cycling
Bicicletas Todo Terreno, C 5, No 57-54,
T5521579, also at Av 8AN, No17-33,
T6612456, bltcolombia@emcali.net.co.
Cycle shop, hires mountain bikes and
organizes tours in the local area.

Dance classes
Academia El Manicero, C 5, No 39-71,
T3154550232. Classes for individuals or
groups. Prof Ximena Castillo, T3167078885
(mob) is also recommended for 1-on-1
classes. Also enquire at Hostal Iguana,
see page 295.

Diving
Contact **Rafael Lozano**, T3137676099 (mob),
for diving trips to Isla Gorgona and Malpelo.
Speaks English, lots of experience and very
responsible. Recommended.
Casco Antiguo Diving Centre, Cra 34,
No 3-89 (Parque del Perro), cascoantiguo@
telesat.com.co. PADI certified. Organize
all-inclusive expensive weekend diving tours
to Gorgona Island, US$600per person and
8-day advanced diving tours to Isla Malpelo
(36-hr boat ride from Buenaventura US$2500).

Football
Cali's 2 major football teams, América de Cali
and Deportivo Cali both play at the **Pascual
Guerrero Stadium**, which holds 50,000 people.

Kitesurfing
Harold Granados, T3147110481, can organize
equipment and lessons on Lago Calima.

Parapenting
Speak to **Rob Ottomani**, T3146787972.
German and English spoken.

Tour operators
Aviatur, Cra 5, No. 8-12, T889 3121,
www.aviatur.com. For tours to Isla
Gorgona, and other services.
Ecocolombia Tours, Cra 37A, No 6-18,
T5140829. Trips to Gorgona, Juanchaco,
diving, tours in and around Cali.
Recommended.
Kaffe Erde, Av 4N, No 4N-79, T6615475,
kaffeeerde@hosteltrail.com. From the
backpackers' hostel of the same name,
organizes tours in the local area.
Panturismo, C 18N, No 8-27, T668 2255, and
other branches, including at airport, T6663021.
Organizes all-inclusive trips to Gorgona.
Vela, Cra 4, No 8-64, local 104, T889 0760.
Student travel agency, cheap tickets.
Recommended.

Yoga
Hostal Iguana (see Sleeping) organizes
yoga weekends.

Around Buenaventura *p292*
Eco-Guías, T3137506430 (mob), www.reservaaguamarina.com, can organize whale watching and boat trips, as well as diving, snorkelling and kayaking excursions. **Hotel Estación**, Buenaventura, run tours mid/late Jul to end Sep, hopefully for whale sighting: 3 nights/4 days, including all meals and boat trip, US$264 per person.

⊖ Transport

Cali *p284, map p286*
Air
Alfonso Bonilla Aragón airport, 20 km from city, T4422624, has banks, including Banco Popular, and ATMs near domestic departures/ arrivals. The **Telecom** office with international telephone facilities, is near international departures, as is the tax-exemption office. Internet is available. Frequent services to **Bogotá**, **Medellín**, **Cartagena**, **Ipiales** and other Colombian cities with **Satena** and **Avianca**. International flights to **Miami**, **New York**, **Ecuador** and **Panama**.

Airline offices AeroRepública, C 26N, No 6N-16, Aires, Av 6N, No 20-73, T6604777. **American**, Hotel Intercontinental, Av Colombia, No 2-72. COPA, Centro Comercial Chipichape L 210, T6652399. **Avianca**, Av 8N, No 24AN-07, T6882900 or Cra 6, No 11-42, T8816408. **Iberia**, Av 5CN, No 23DN-37, T6602250. **Satena**, C 8, No 5-19, T8857709. **TAME**, Cra 4, No 12-41. For Cali–Quito flights. **Varig**, Av 6N, No 17-92, T6672610.

Bus
The bus terminal is at C 30N, No 2AN-29, 25 mins' walk from the centre following the river along Av 2N and about 10 mins from Barrio Granada Bus information at www.terminalcali.com. Hotel information available, left luggage US$1.20 per item for 12 hrs, good food at terminal. *Casa de cambio* (cash only), banks and ATMs. Showers on 2nd level (US$0.40). There are

plenty of local buses between the bus station and the centre, which charge US$0.40. Taxi from centre to bus station, US$1.50.

Busetas (**Velotax** and others) charge 50% more than buses but save time; *taxi-colectivos* are about 2½ times bus prices and even quicker. To **Popayán**, US$9, 2½-3 hrs, also *colectivos*, US$9. To **Pasto**, US$11, 8-9 hrs. To **Ipiales** (direct), US$22, 12 hrs; to **San Agustín**, 9 hrs, US$14-16. To **Cartago**, 3½ hrs, US$4. To **Armenia**, US$9. To **Ibagué**, US$8, 6-7 hrs. To **Manizales**, US$15, 7 hrs. To **Medellín**, US$22, 8-10 hrs. To **Bogotá**, 10-15 hrs, by Magdalena, T6687504 (recommended), US$31 (sit on the left of the bus). To **Buenaventura**, 3 hrs with Expreso Palmira, US$8.

Car
Car rental Hertz, Av Colombia No 2-72 (Hotel Intercontinental), T8920437, also office at airport, T6663283. **Colombia Rent a Car**, Av 8, No 16N-50, Of 1. **National**, C 5, No 39-36, T5244432, aiport, T6663016.

Taxi
Ensure that meters are used. Prices are posted in the window: minimum fare is US$2. On Sun and holidays and at night an extra charge is made.

Buenaventura *p291*
Air
Flights to **Cali** and **Bogotá**.

Bus
The toll road to Cali is fully paved; the toll is about US$1.30 for cars and US$0.30 for *moto* The ordinary road is not paved. To **Cali** there are plenty of buses, US$8.50, 4 hrs; *colectivos* also run at 30-min intervals to Cali.

Sea
Cargo boats to **Nuquí** and **Bahía Solano** are slow, intermittent and uncomfortable. They leave from the Puente del Piñal. 1 or 2 boats

leave a week, stopping at Nuquí, 18 hrs, and going on to Bahía Solano, 24 hrs from Buenaventura, US$55 1 way.

⊙ Directory

Cali *p284, map p286*
Banks Davivienda, C 11, No 8-03 (Centro) or Av 6N, No 22-08 (norte). Banco de Bogotá, Cra 4, No 11-55 (centro) or Av 8N, No 20N-67. Bancolombia, Cra 5, No 10-79 (centro) or C15N, No 6N-56. Citibank, Av 5N, No 23AN-49. HSBC, Av 6N, No 25N-11. Banco Agrario, C11, No 5-28. Many other banks and ATMs in main commercial areas. Casas de Cambio Cambiamos, Av 5N, No 23DN-40. Giros y Financias (Western Union), Av 6N, No 30N-67. Casa de Cambios Titán, C 11, No 4-42. **Cultural centres** Alianza Colombo Francesa, Av 6N, No 21-34, T6613431. Centro Cultural Colombo-Americano, C 13N, No 8-45, T687 58 00. All give language classes, show films and have other events, enquire for programme. Centro Cultural de Cali, Cra 5, No 6-05, T8858851. Centro Cultural Comfandi, C 8, No 6-45, T3340000. **Embassies and consulates** France, Av 3N, No 18N-24, Of 405, T883 5904. Germany, C 1B, No 66B-29, Barrio El Refugio, T323 8402. Switzerland, Av 4N, No 3-33, T661 4927 (same building as Pensión Stein).

UK, C 22N, No 6-42, Of 401, Edif Centro Granada, T667 7725, britishcali@ uniweb.net.co. **Immigration** DAS office Av 3AN, No 50-20, T 6643809/10.
Internet Unimegas, Av 6, No 17A-57, T6603853. Has Skype and head- phones. Cosmonet, Av 6N, No 17N-65, T6535228. Skype and headphones, scanning and photocopying, as well as international calls.
Laundry Lavaprisa, Av 8N, No 12-08.
Media 2 local daily newspapers are *La Nación* and *El País*. **Medical services** Cíinica del Occidente, C 18N, No 5-34. Centro Médico Imbanaco, Cra 38A, No 5A-100. Clínica Fundación Valle de Lili, Cra 98, No 18-49. Clínica Oftalmológica de Cali, C 26N, No 6N-46. Optician Optica Alemana, Av 6N, No 21N-51. **Post office** Adpostal, for national service, C 10, No 6-25; Deprisa, for international service, C 9, No 4-45.**Telecom** C 10, No 6-25.

Buenaventura *p291*
Banks Banco Popular, Cra 2, No 2-37, changes US$ cash TCs. Bancolombia, C 1A, No 3-55, cash against Visa. Banco del Occidente, Cra 2, No 2-39, cash against Mastercard. Western Union, C 1, No 3-97, Of 205, T2422766. **Immigration** DAS near Avianca post office, T2419592. **Internet** Ciber P@cifico, C 1, No 2-11. Internet and local calls. **Post office** Avianca, C 8, No 26-05. **Telecom** C 3/Cra 3.

Popayán and Tierradentro

South of Cali is Popayán, one of the country's oldest Spanish settlements, which gleams like a beacon in the crisp sunshine of the Cordillera Central's mountain air. Its colonial centre may have suffered severe damage after a March 1983 earthquake hit the region, but an extensive restoration program has left little sign of the tragedy and the city's dazzling white buildings appear much as they would have to the Spanish sugar plantation owners who first came here to escape the heat of the Cauca Valley. Popayán has a cultured air about it, no doubt aided by its large student population. But there must be something in the water because it has produced more Colombian presidents than any other city, while down the years it has been a home to many notable painters, writers and composers and its famously austere Semana Santa celebrations are second in size only to those of Seville in Spain.

To the Spanish, Popayán was a strategic link between Lima and Quito and Bogotá and Cartagena. For today's traveller, the city makes a convenient jumping-off point for visiting the remote archaeological sites of Tierradentro and San Agustín, the indigenous market at Silvia, or a break from the heat and partying in Cali. ▸▸ *For listings, see pages 309-313.*

Popayán ⊙⊙⊙⊙⊙⊙▲⊙⊙ ▸▸ *pp309-313. Colour map 3, B3.*

→ *Phone code: 2. Population: 258,000. Altitude: 1760 m.*

The city of Popayán has managed to retain its colonial character, which is remarkable given that it was partially destroyed by the March 1983 earthquake and extensively restored. Many of the streets are cobbled and the two-storey buildings are in rococo Andalucían style, with beautiful old monasteries and cloisters of pure Spanish classic architecture.

Ins and outs

Getting there The **airport** is 20 minutes' walk from the centre. Popayán's **bus terminal** is near the airport, 15 minutes' walk from the centre (Ruta 2-Centro bus, terminal to centre, US$0.30, or taxi, US$1.65). Luggage can be stored safely (receipt given); there is a charge to use the toilets. From the bus station, walk up Carrera 11 and take a left at Calle 4 to reach the centre. Take care if you cross any of the bridges over the river going north, especially at night.

Tourist office There is a recently established office on the Parque Principal with a reasonable selection of maps and brochures. **Cámara de Comercio de Cauca, Cultura y Turismo** ① *Cra 7, No 4-36, T8243625, www.cccauca.org.co.*

Background

Popayán was founded by Sebastián de Belalcázar, Francisco Pizarro's lieutenant, in 1536, in the valley of the Pubenza, a peaceful landscape of palm, bamboo, and the sharp-leaved agave. The early settlers after setting up their sugar estates in the hot, damp Cauca valley, retreated to Popayán to live, for the city is high enough to give it a delightful climate. After the conquest of the indigenous Pijao, Popayán became the regional seat of government, subject until 1717 to the Audiencia of Quito, and later to the Audiencia of Bogotá. Popayán has given no fewer than eleven presidents to the Republic. The scientist Francisco José de Caldas was born here in 1771. It was he who discovered how to determine altitude by variation in the boiling point of water, and it was to him that Mutis

The photographer of Popayán

Gilberto Hernández has been taking portraits of the people of Popayán for almost 40 years. The all-singing, all-dancing box camera he uses is older than him. A Swiss army knife of a camera, it acts both as image taker and darkroom. For just a few dollars he will take a picture, develop it inside the box and even embellish it with hand paints. You can find him every day by the statue in the Plaza Mayor.

(of the famous *Expedición Botánica*) entrusted the directorship of the newly founded Observatory at Bogotá. He was a passionate partisan of independence, and was executed in 1815 during Morillo's 'Reign of Terror'.

Today, Popayán is the capital of the Department of Cauca. To north, south, and east the broken green plain is bounded by mountains. To the southeast rises the cone of the volcano Puracé (4646 m). The Río Molino runs through the town, a tributary, of the Río Cauca, which rises near Puracé and flows past Popayán a few kilometres to the north.

Sights
① *Museums not open on Mon.*

The **cathedral** ① *C 5/Cra 6*, was built around 1900, is the third on the site and was beautifully restored after the 1983 earthquake. It has a fine marble Madonna sculpture behind the altar by Buenaventura Malagón.

San Agustín ① *C 7/Cra 6*, is notable for the gilt altar piece and the unusual statue of Christ kneeling on the globe. **Santo Domingo** ① *C 4/Cra 5*, has some fine wood carvings, now used by the Universidad del Cauca whose building next door on Carrera 5, and is worth a visit. **La Ermita** ① *C 5/Cra 2*, on the site of the first chapel established by Sebastián de Belalcázar, dates from the 16th century. **La Encarnación** ① *C 5/Cra 5*, dates from 1764 and has a fine retable, is also used for religious music festivals. **San Francisco** ① *C 4/Cra 9*, dating from about 1775, has been frequently damaged by earthquakes and is now partly restored, note the fascinating figures on the pulpit stairs. **El Carmen** ① *C 4/Cra 3*, is a monastery church constructed about 1730 with *mudéjar* influences.

Museo de Historia Natural ① *Cra 2, No 1A-25*, has good displays of archaeological and geological items with sections on insects (particularly good on butterflies), reptiles, mammals and birds. Other museums are **Museo Negret** ① *C 5, No 10-23*, with works, photographs and furniture of Negret, **Museo Guillermo Valencia** ① *Cra 6, No 2-69*, birthplace of the poet, and **Museo Casa Mosquera** ① *C 3, No 5-14*, where General Tomás Cipriano de Mosquera lived, four times President of Colombia. A small collection of indigenous artefacts is held in **Banco de la República** ① *Cra 6, No 2-28*.

Walk to **Belén chapel** ① *C 4/Cra 0*, with a fine view of the city, seeing the statues en route, and then continue to **El Cerro de las Tres Cruces** if you have the energy, and on to the equestrian statue of Belalcázar on the **Morro de Tulcán**, which overlooks the city. This hill is the site of a pre-Columbian pyramid. Next to El Morro is Rincón Payanés, also known as El Pueblito Patojo, which has scale models of the town's landmarks and a number of handicraft stalls and cafes.

A fine arched bridge built in 1868, **Puente del Humilladero** crosses the Río Molino at Carrera 6. Public presentations and concerts are given in the gardens below. It is said that Bolívar marched over the nearby **Puente Chiquito**, built in 1713.

Excursions

The little town of **Silvia** lies in a high valley northeast of Popayán. The local Guambianos wear their typical blue and fuchsia costumes, and are very gregarious and friendly. You can watch them spinning and weaving their textiles. The Tuesday market seems to be full of indigenous Otavalo from Ecuador and their goods – more expensive than in Otavalo. The market is at its best between 0600 and 0830. There's not much to buy, but it's very colourful. There are several indigenous settlements in the hills around Silvia, a typical one to visit is **La Campana**, 45 minutes on the bus, 2½ hours' walk downhill back to Silvia. It is not safe to park cars in the street at night in Silvia. There is a small **Museo de Artsesanías** ① *Cra 2, No 14-19*, with exhibits of local crafts, past and present. Tourist information is 1½ blocks up from the plazuela on the right-hand side. There are beautiful places to walk and ride around Silvia.

About 25 km from Popayán, on the road to San Agustín, is **Coconuco**, a particularly beautiful spot, surrounded by green hills and cascading waterfalls. The village is famous for its hot springs. **Aguas Hirviendas** ① *entry US$1.65*, just outside the village, has several concrete pools, one of which has water hot enough to boil and egg in five minutes. Open 24 hours, this is a popular spot at weekends but quiet during the week. Further up the valley is **Aguas Tibias** ① *entry US$2.80*, whose waters are warm rather than hot. These pools, run by an indigenous family, have a rather more rustic feel to them and include a waterslide and therapeutic mud bath.

Popayán

Sleeping
Casa Familiar El Descanso 1
Casa Familiar Turística 2
Colonial 4
Hostel Trail Guesthouse 3
La Casona del Virrey 5
La Plazuela 6
Los Balcones 7
Los Portales 8
Monasterio 9

Pass Home 10

Eating
El Muro 1
Italiano 2
Jengibre 6
Juan Valdez 8
Kaldivia Café 9
La Cave 3
Madeira Café 10

Pan Tolima 5
Verde y Mostaza 7

Bars & clubs
El Sotareño 4
Iguana Afro-Club 11
Tijuana 12

You can reach Coconuco by bus from Popayán, one hour, US$2.20. From there you can walk to either of the springs or catch a jeep or mototaxi. Buses to San Agustín pass by both sites.

Tierradentro ⊖⊙⊖⊙ ⤝ pp309-313. Colour map 3, B4.

Tierradentro is one of Colombia's great pre-Columbian attractions. Scattered throughout the area are man-made burial caves painted with red, black and white geometric patterns. Some are shallow, others up to 8 m deep. The surrounding hills are spectacular, and there are many small indigenous villages to explore (get exact directions before setting out). For many years the unforgiving mountains of this region were a FARC stronghold, which stunted any kind of tourism development. Today, the guerrilla presence is no more but the area is still emerging from its isolation and the volume of visitors is only a trickle.

Try to go to Tierradentro for a week and just walk in the hills. The people are very friendly, and you can stop and ask at almost any house to buy *guarapo*, a local slightly fermented drink. It's great to sit and talk and enjoy the hospitality and at night enjoy the spectacular night skies. If you don't have that much time, do try to stay at least two days.

Indigenous Páez can be seen on market days at Inzá (Saturday), and Belalcázar (Saturday); both start at 0600. An excellent guide to the Páez and their culture is *Valores Culturales de Tierradentro* by Mauricio Puerta Restrepo, published by the Instituto Colombiano de Antropología (available at the Gold Museum in Bogotá).

Ins and outs
Getting there
The road from Popayán to Tierradentro is extremely rough, but this is compensated by the beautiful scenery; 67 km beyond Totoró is **Inzá**. There are several stone statues in the new plaza. About 9 km beyond Inzá is the Cruce de Pisimbalá, sometimes known as the Cruce de San Andrés or simply El Cruce, where a road turns off to **San Andrés de Pisimbalá** (4 km), the village at the far end of the Tierradentro Park.

Tourist information
The **Casa de Cultura**, in a building just as you enter the village, has good information. Helpful, they can organize guides to local indigenous villages.

Sights
Tierradentro museum ⓘ *0800-1600, but may close at lunchtime and the entry ticket is valid for the museum and all sites, US$3.80, valid for 3 days.* Before reaching Pisimbalá, you pass the Tierradentro Museum. The well-maintained museum is in two parts, an archaeological section including a model of the Tierradentro region with details of the sites and what has been found. The second floor is dedicated to an overview of the Páez and their culture, past and present. This is all very well worth visiting before going to the sites and the staff are very helpful also with local information.

Tierradentro

To Santa Rosa

El Duende (1700m)
Quebrada Los Gruesa
Segovia (1650m)
To La Pirámide
Quebrada La Virgen
El Tablón (1700m)
Quebrada Chapequis
San Andrés de Pisimbalá
Quebrada San Andrés
Alto de San Andrés (1750m)
Museum & Administration
To El Cruce, Inzá and La Plata
Quebrada El Escaño
El Aguacate (2000m)

N

500 metres
500 yards

At Pisimbalá, about 2 km beyond and up the hill from the museum, there is a unique and beautiful **colonial missionary church** with a thatched roof, dating back to the 17th century. This is a charming village, peaceful and friendly. Around the cobbled square, the locals lay their coffee to dry on the grass outside their chocolate box houses, while chickens wander in and out of the church and swallows dive between its eaves.

Tierradentro Archaeological Park

At the archway directly opposite the museum, or at Pisimbalá village, you can hire horses (US$2 an hour, make sure they are in good condition) – or you can walk – to the burial caves. There are four cave sites – Segovia, El Duende, Alto de San Andrés and El Aguacate. The main caves are lit, but a torch (your own or one borrowed from the park administration) is advisable.

At Segovia (15 minutes' walk up behind the museum across the river), the guard is very informative (Spanish only) and turns lights on in the main tombs. Segovia has around 30 tombs, five of which are lit: Nos 9, 10 and 12 are best decorated; Nos 8 and 28 are also impressive. Check if photography is permitted. Some 15 minutes up the hill beyond Segovia is El Duende (two of the four tombs are very good). From El Duende continue directly up to a rough road descending to Pisimbalá (40 minutes). El Tablón, with eight stone statues, is just off the road 20-30 minutes' walk down. El Alto de San Andrés is 20 minutes from Pisimbalá (Nos 1 and 5 tombs the best – the guard is very helpful). From the back of El Alto it's 1½ hours up and down hills, with a final long climb to El Aguacate. Only one tomb is maintained although there may be 30 more. The views from El Aguacate are superb. You can continue to the museum.

Some say it's better to do this section starting from the museum. Either way, it is a splendid walk. The whole area is good for birdwatching. For a longer hike, ask about the Páez reserve at Tumbichutzwe, a strenuous three- to four-day walk, or less on horseback. When walking between the sites, take a hat and plenty of water. It gets crowded at Easter. Women are advised not to wander around this area alone at night.

Neiva ●🅿🅰🅶 ▶ pp309-313. Colour map 3, A5.

→ *Phone code: 8. Population: 330,000.*

Capital of the Department of Huila, Neiva is a hot, modern city on the east bank of the Río Magdalena. Surrounded by arid cattle plains, the snow-capped Nevado del Huila looms large to the west. It has a series of pleasant plazas and hosts the Festival Nacional del Reinado del Bambuco in late June/early July, which incorporates the fiestas de San Juan and San Pedro. A raucous affair, it involves Bambuco dancing competitions and various parades in which bikini-clad beauty queens float downriver on boats and up to 5000 (often) drunken women ride horses through the streets. It culminates in the crowning of a Bambuco queen.

Neiva was founded in 1539 when Belalcázar came across from Popayán on his quest for El Dorado. By the riverside a monument has been erected to commemorate Rodrigo Arenas Betancur's struggles in the fight for independence from the Spanish. The cathedral was destroyed in an earthquake in 1967.

Around Neiva

A 30-minute drive south from Neiva is the pretty little town of Rivera, famous for its thermal springs. At the weekend it livens up with plenty of activity around its picturesque plaza and its a popular destination for locals wishing to escape the heat of Neiva.

The Queen of the Desert

Doña Rosita Martínez is 92 years old, she thinks. Born in the desert, she has spent her life using its meagre resources to scratch out a living. Her skin may be as leathery as a lizard's and her eyesight beginning to fade yet she has enough faculties intact to tend to her goats and enjoy the solitude of the night sky.

She has lost count of her offspring, though she does know she had 13 sons, each of whom has produced children and grandchildren. She was crowned 'The Queen of the Desert' by a group of American astronomers when they came down to witness the solar eclipse of 1991.

Today she lives with her niece on the goat farm she's tended for over 50 years.

The springs are 5 km north of the town. There are several options but the most popular, **Termales de Rivera** ① *Entry US$6.50, open until midnight at weekends*, are set around exuberant tropical gardens and have two restaurants, changing rooms and lockers, a cold swimming pool to cool down and an excellent waterslide. The complex has several (**A**) rooms onsight. A tuk-tuk or taxi from town is US$2.80. There are several hotels in town (**C-D**).

Desierto de Tatacoa ●●◐ ⇒ *pp309-313*.

Driving through the lush plains and mountains of Huila it might be difficult to imagine that a desert sits just around the corner. But just 50 km north of Neiva is the Tatacoa desert, a 370-sq-km area of scrub and surreal rock formations dotted with Candelabra and Prickly Pear cacti. Named after a snake that used to thrive in its unforgiving conditions, it is wedged between two mountain ranges that absorb the region's rainfall, starving it of moisture.

It presented a challenging obstacle to the Spanish conquistador Juan Alonso on his quest for El Dorado. He was following the Magdalena river and looking for a route to Popayán when he stumbled across the desert, which he subsequently named El Valle de las Tristezas (The Valley of Sorrow). In 1550 he founded a town on the site on the desert's edge and named it San Juan de Nepomuceno. It was later razed to the ground by the indigenous locals but was rebuilt by Diego de Ospina y Medinilla in 1562 and renamed **Villavieja**. The town played an important role in the 1000-Day War at the turn of the 20th century when a battle between the Liberals and Conservatives was fought nearby.

Villavieja has a particularly charming parque principal, surrounded on all sides by 18th-century colonial buildings and with a replica of a Megatherium, an elephant-sized sloth that existed here in the Pleistocene epoch, in the centre. The **Capilla de Santa Bárbara** was built by Jesuit priests in 1630, making it the oldest church in Hulia. It was recently restored, although the local priest keeps it under lock and key and it is difficult to gain access. Next to the church is the **Palaeontological Museum** ① *entry US$2.70*, with displays of fossils of armadillos, turtles and crocodiles found in the desert, mainly from the Miocene period. Also worth visiting is the railway station, decommissioned since 1975, a reminder of Villavieja's former role as an important staging post on the Bogotá–Neiva line.

The **desert** itself begins 10 km outside Villavieja. On top of a small incline some 15 minutes' drive from Villavieja is the **Observatorio Astronómico de la Tatacoa** ① *www.tatacoa-astronomia.com*, run by stellar enthusiast Javier Fernando Rua. Tatacoa's clear skies and almost non-existent light pollution make it perhaps the best place in

Colombia for star gazing and Javier gives an excellent talk every evening at 1830 on the observatory roof, with telescopes and a laser to point out individual constellations, US$2.70 per person. Camping is permitted next to the observatory. Javier hires tents, US$5.50 for a two-person tent.

Opposite the observatory is a viewpoint looking out over El Cuzco, a labyrinthine landscape of ochre red hillocks and plateaus that would not look out of place in a Star Trek episode, and where pop star Shakira filmed one of her early music videos. You can walk down into the miniature valley; it is particularly spectacular at sundown.

Some 8 km beyond El Cuzco, is Los Hoyos with similar topography only the earth is grey here. Enterprising locals have built a swimming pool amongst the rock formations, fed by water from a natural spring. Entry US$1.65 (pay at the *estadero*).

Parque Nacional Puracé ►► *Colour map 3, B3.*

① *Standard entrance fee to the park is US$0.60 (for the Termales at San Juan or climbing the volcanoes).*

The National Park contains Volcán Puracé (4646 m), Pan de Azúcar (4670 m) with its permanent snow summit, and the line of nine craters known as the Volcanes los Coconucos. A strenuous two-day hike can be made around the summits. The park also encompasses the sources of four of Colombia's greatest rivers: the Magdalena, Cauca, Caquetá and Patía. Virtually all the park is over 3000 m and covers an area of 86,600 ha. The Andean Condor is being reintroduced to the wild here from Californian zoos, and there are many other birds to be seen. The park's fauna include the spectacled bear and mountain tapir. Pilimbalá is a good base from which to explore the northern end of the park, where there are Páez settlements. Although much of the park is *páramo*, there are also many species of orchids to be found. For those who do not wish to make the strenuous climb up Volcán Puracé there are many waterfalls, lakes and some technicolour sulphur pools to visit.

Ins and outs

All these places beyond Puracé village can be reached by any bus from Popayán to La Plata or Garzón. The last bus returning to Popayán in daylight leaves the visitor centre at about 1700. The bus service can be erratic so be prepared to spend a cold night at 3000 m. The Park is open all week, but reduced service on Monday. From Popayán a road crosses the Central Cordillera to Garzón on the paved highway south of Neiva. At Km 18 from Popayán, the road turning up to the right (south) leads to Coconuco (see page 303) and San Agustín (see page 314).

Around the park

The valley road climbs to the small town of **Puracé**, at Km 12 (30 km from Popayán), which has several old buildings. Behind the school a path leads for 500 m to Chorrera de las Monjas waterfalls on the Río Vinagre, notable for the milky white water due to concentrations of sulphur and other minerals. At Km 22, look for the spectacular San Francisco waterfall on the opposite side of the valley. At Km 23 is the turning right to Puracé sulphur mines (6 km) which can be visited by applying to Industrias Puracé SA ① *C 4, No 7-32 Popayán*, or, better still, through the Popayán tourist office. About 1 km along this road is a turning left leading in 1.5 km to **Pilimbalá** in the Puracé National Park. There are several buses daily to Puracé from Popayán, the last returning about 1730.

At Pilimbalá saloon cars will struggle up the last stretch to the centre, but it is an easy 2.5 km walk from Km 23.

The walk to the **Cascada de San Nicolás** from Pilimbalá is recommended, turn right when you see the abandoned cabin and continue steadily uphill through very muddy terrain, rubber boots advisable. The waterfall is spectacular, take care on the slippery overhanging rocks. At Km 37, the visitor centre has a good geology/ethnology museum. The rangers are very helpful and will allow you to stay there. The centre has picnic shelters, a good restaurant (rainbow trout a speciality) and three *cabañas* that hold eight, US$11-15, depending on season. There is a shared (cold water) bathroom and a small fireplace. Camping costs US$2.20 per person. Sleeping bags or warm clothing is recommended to supplement bedding provided. There's also a good scale model of the Park.

Half an hour's walk past the visitor centre on the road to La Plata are the Termales de San Juan. The toxic, sulphurous gases released by these hot pools means that swimming is not advisable but a walkway allows for a tour through the colourful mosses and algae surrounding the bubbling, multi-coloured pools and along the milky-white streams that run off them. There's a basic place to eat where the bus stops and a cabin with information about the National Park. Buses are not regular but up until 1700 there should be something every hour or so. Hitching a lift for around US$1 should also be possible.

Climbing Volcán Puracé

The hike to the summit is demanding; loose ash makes footholds difficult. Avoid getting down wind of the fumaroles, and do not be tempted to climb down into the crater. Although the best weather is reported to be December to March and July to August, this massif makes its own climate, and high winds, rain and sub-zero temperatures can come in quickly at any time. A marked trail goes from behind the park office and eventually joins the road leading to a set of telecommunications antennae. These installations are no longer guarded by the military **but the area around them is mined; don't take shortcuts**. The summit is about one hour beyond the military buildings. Start early; the total time from Pilimbalá is at least four hours up and 2½ down, and you may need to take shelter if there is a sudden storm. Rangers will not allow you to start after 1200. An alternative route is from the sulphur mine (at 3000 m), or driving, with permission, to the military base. It is also possible to walk round the crater (30 minutes). Rope and crampons are useful above the snowline if you want to continue to Pan de Azúcar and the Coconucos. For this trek, high-altitude camping and mountaineering equipment are required and a guide is strongly recommended. A descent over the *páramo* to Paletará on the Popayán–San Agustín road is also possible.

Continuing on the main road to La Plata, at Km 31 there is a viewpoint for Laguna Rafael, at Km 35 the Cascada de Bedón (also chemically charged water) and at Km 37 the entrance to the most northerly part of the Puracé National Park where there is another park centre (see above).

For Sleeping and Eating price codes and other relevant information, see pages 31-36.

● Sleeping

Popayán *p301, map p303*
Hotel prices include taxes, but are subject to a 100% or more increase in some cases for Holy Week and festivals, eg 5-6 Jan.

L Monasterio, C 4, No 10-14, T2-8242191, hdannmo@tvoconectado.com. Run by the ubiquitous Dann group, this 17th-century Franciscan monastery, with its cobbled courtyards and fountains, emanates tranquillity. The rooms are comfortable and it has a swimming pool and sauna.

A La Plazuela, C 5, No 8-13, T2-8241084, hotellaplazuela@hotmail.com. Located opposite the Iglesia San José, this beautiful colonial building has good-sized rooms with antique furniture set around a colonnaded, cobbled courtyard. There is Wi-Fi throughout the building, cable TV and breakfast included.

A Los Balcones, Cra 7, No 2-75, T2-8242030, hotellosbalcones@emtel.net.co. Los Balcones is a mixed bag. It has some enormous rooms, including one in the attic with stained glass skylights, while others are small. Ancient TVs and antique furniture give it a certain charm while Wi-Fi and a free internet room are the hotel's concession to modernity.

B La Casona del Virrey, C 4, No 5-78, T2-8240836, hotellacasonadelvirrey@ hotmail.com. Most hotels in Popayán are beautiful colonial buildings but la Casona del Virrey is a cut above the rest. It has a gorgeous spiral staircase leading up to rooms that look down on a cobbled courtyard. Many of the rooms have wooden floorboards and original wainscot panelling. Modern services include Wi-Fi. Recommended.

C Los Portales, C 5, No 10-125, T2-8210139, losportaleshotel@yahoo.com. This sweet little hotel has rooms set around 3 leafy, sunny courtyards with water features. It also has cable TV and an internet room.

D Hotel Colonial, C 5, No 10-94, T2-8317848, hotelcolonial@hotmail.es. This hotel has clean – if a little dark – rooms with comfortable beds. It has a restaurant serving home-cooked food, cable TV, hot water and free local calls.

D Pass Home, C 5, No 10-114, T3164489513 (mob). This hotel is a bit of a rabbit warren with basic rooms opening onto narrow corridors, but they have private bathrooms with hot water and cable TV.

E Casa Familiar El Descanso, Cra 5, No 2-41, T2-8240029. This family house has been a popular backpackers' choice for many years. With lots of plants and antiques , it is a peaceful place of just 5 rooms and 3 shared bathrooms. The owners speak German and English and will happily share their local knowledge.

E Casa Familiar Turística, Cra 5, No 2-07, T2-8244853. Another popular backpackers' choice, this little place has simple rooms with incredibly high ceilings. It has good notice boards with information and messages from other travellers.

E-F HostelTrail Guesthouse, Cra 11, No 4-16, T3146960805 (mob), www.hosteltrail.com. This excellent, efficiently run backpackers' hostel is run by Scottish couple Tony and Kim. The rooms are comfortable and clean (most with shared bathroom) and have Wi-Fi access, while there are cheap dorms with bunks, good communal areas, a kitchen, DVD room, and lock-up. Tony and Kim have extensive knowledge of the local area.

Tierradentro *p304, map p304*
E Residencias Pisimbalá, near the museum, T3116124645 (mob). The Pisimbalá has rooms with private bathrooms and hot water as well as the cheaper option of shared cold-water bathrooms. It has a good little restaurant, while camping costs US$1.20 per person.

E-F Hospedaje Ricabet, near the museum, T3127954636 (mob). This little *hospedaje* has a bright courtyard bursting with colourful flowers and clean rooms and en suite bathrooms with hot water. Rooms with a shared bath are a little cheaper.

F El Cauchito, in the village, this family home has 3 basic rooms and friendly service. The bathrooms are shared and there is no hot water.

F El Viajero, in the village, another family home with a friendly owner, the rooms are basic but clean and the shower is *al clima*. Food available on request.

F Los Llanos, 100 m past the church. Pleasant colonial building with clean, basic rooms and a colourful courtyard.

F Hospedaje Luzerna, next to the museum. Run by a lovely old couple, this little place has clean, basic rooms and very good hot showers (with 30 mins' forewarning).

Neiva *p305*

A Hotel Neiva Plaza, C 7, No 4-62, T8-8710806. Neiva's traditional smart hotel for more than 50 years, the Plaza has good, comfortable rooms, a restaurant and a swimming pool.

D Andino, C 9, No 5-82, T8710184. This centrally located hotel's rooms are a little small and dark but nonetheless clean and with cable TV.

E Tayronas, C 8, No 3-46, T8713038. You'll be greeted by the smell of incense and a reception covered in pre-Columbian artefacts as you enter this hotel, which has dark, small rooms with en suite bathrooms.

Desierto de Tatacoa *p306*
Villavieja

E La Casona, C 3, No 3-60, T8-8797636, hotellacasonavillavieja@yahoo.es. This gorgeous old building on the parque principal once had Simon Bolívar stay the night and has a shady backyard full of well-presented tables. Its monasterial rooms are crammed with beds but the owner won't fill them up if you ask for privacy. Recommended.

E La Portada al Sol, T3132172983 (mob). This posada, built on the site of a Jesuit *finca* on the edge of town, has simple rooms with

fan and private bathroom. Food can be prepared on request.

F Residencia Geraldo Calderón. This little place has a couple of very basic rooms with shared bathrooms in the backyard of a colonial house.

The desert

Camping at the observatory is US$5.50 for a 2-person tent, less if you bring your own. There are showers and good food prepared with forewarning.

There are also several *posadas nativas*, run by local families. Enquire at the **Asociación de Operadores Turísticos** on the Parque Principal, T3143152067 (mob). You can also call the *posadas* direct. Try: **Elvira Cleves**, T312 5598576 (mob), who can also arrange stays with her mother Doña Rosalia, 'The Queen of the Desert' (see box, page 306). At Los Hoyos, Señora Ofanda Sott, T3115365027 (mob).

🍴 Eating

Popayán *p301, map p303*

Popayán has a tradition of good food. In 2005 the city was named a UNESCO City of Gastronomy. Local specialities include *tamales de pipián*.

🍴 El Muro, Cra 8, No 4-11, T2-8240539. This little place serves vegetarian US$2.50 *almuerzos* with daily menus ranging from quinoa salad to pizzas and veggie burgers. At night it converts into a dimly lit bar.

🍴 Jengibre, Cra 7, No 2-71, T2-8205456. Good lunchtime venue serving *almuerzos* for US$4.20 as well as á la carte options.

🍴 La Cave, C 4, No 2-07, T3167537670 (mob). This French-owned bistro is famous for its salad dressing, which is available to take home. Atmospheric French music will make francophiles feel right at home, as will the selection of pastries and tartes. Try the chicken breast in nut, mustard and honey sauce, a house speciality.

🍴 La Viña, C 4, No 7-07, T2-8240602. Open 24 hrs a day, this *parrillada* restaurant has an enormous selection of juicy, Argentine-style steaks accompanied by good salads.

Pan Tolima, C 4, No 5-84. On the corner of the parque, try this bakery for a good selection of breads and other breakfast snacks.

Restaurante Italiano, C 4, No 8-83, T2-8240607. This Swiss-run restaurant has been serving an excellent selection of pastas, pizzas, crêpes and fondues since 1995 with much love and attention. Recommended.

Verde y Mostaza, Cra 4 con C 4 esquina. Popular with students, this little restaurant serves up cheap fast food such as crêpes, pizzas and burgers.

Cafés

Popayán has a thriving café culture, with many of them located in gorgeous colonial buildings.

Juan Valdez, Cra 7, No 4-40. Part of the ubiquitous chain, this one is housed in a beautiful courtyard with 4 enormous palm trees. Large selection of coffees and merchandise on sale. Has Wi-Fi.

Kaldivia, C 5, No 5-63. Popular with the locals, this café has excellent frappes as well as brownies and ice creams.

Madeira Café, C 3 esq con Cra 4. Good selection of coffees, milkshakes, brownies, fruit juices and cheesecakes.

Tierradentro *p304, map p304*
La Portada, on the edge of the village, does *almuerzos* for US$2.50.
Pisimbalá, near the museum, has good, cheap food. Recommended.

Neiva *p305*
Carbonara, C 9, No 6-41. Cheap *almuerzos* served on a pleasant terrace. Next door is an internet café.
Confucio, Cra 6, No 9-34. Popular Chinese restaurant.
Frutería y Heladería Alaska, Cra 6, No 8-40. This little fruit and ice cream spot does delicious fruit salads, though be sure to inform them if you don't want ice cream with your breakfast fruit salad.

La Casona, Cra 4, No 12-37, T8-8721454. This restaurant serves up cheap *almuerzos* in the smart courtyard of an old house. A la carte dishes include baby beef and catfish.

Yoga Inbound, C 9, No 5-74, T9-8717895. Indian-influenced vegetarian restaurant serving lunchtime buffets, US$2.70, consisting of soups, salads and soya products.

Bars and clubs

Popayán *p301, map p303*
El Sotareño, C 6, No 8-05. Run by an old couple from San Agustín this eccentric bar plays old tango LPs from the 1940s and 50s as well as *bolero* and *ranchero* music.
Iguana Afro-Club, C 4, No 9-67. Good music, jazz, salsa, friendly owner.
Tijuana, Cra 9, No 4-68. Mix of music, popular.

Festivals and events

Popayán *p301, map p303*
5 Jan Día de los Negros; and
6 Jan Día de los Blancos; both are like those at Pasto, but a lot less wet.
Easter Semana Santa (Holy Week). The processions, every night until Good Friday, are spectacular; the city is very crowded. The children's processions in the following week are easier to see. The children assume all the roles of the official processions to the delight of parents and onlookers. During Holy Week the Museo de Arte Religioso opens up its vaults and displays several large emeralds, including one the size of an avocado. Also during Semana Santa there is an international sacred music festival, founded in 1964. Orchestras and groups from many countries have participated in the past. At the same time there are presentations at Santander de Quilichoa on the main road halfway between Popayán and Cali.

O Shopping

Popayán *p301, map p303*
During the week, the open markets are interesting. For handicrafts, there are lots of stands at Rincón Payanés, next to El Morro.
Bolívar market, C 1N, Cra 5. Best in the early morning – local foods such as *pipián*, *tamales* and *empanadas*.
The Mercado Esmeralda, on C 5, west of the centre. A little bigger and also worth a visit.

▲ Activities and tours

Popayán *p301, map p303*
Tour operators
Luna Paz Tours, C 8, No 7-61, T3155139593 (mob). Organizes tours to Tierradentro as well as further afield destinations in Colombia.
Aviatur, C 4, No 8-69, T2-8208674. For Isla Gorgona and Malpelo.

Tierradentro *p304, map p304*
Cayo Oidos Galindo, T3102292971 (mob), based in La Plata, spent 15 years working with archaeologists from Banco de la República unearthing many of Tierradentro's tombs. Organizes tours of Tierradentro and surrounding villages with accommodation and food provided. Can arrange English-speaking guides. Recommended.

Desierto de Tatacoa *p306*
The Asociación de Operadores Turísticos de La Tatacoa, T3143152067/T3114992512 (mob), found on the Parque Principal, can arrange guides, transport and accommodation in the desert. Alternatively, contact astronomer and manager of the observatory Javier Fernando Rua, T8797585/T3104656765 (mob), who can make arrangements with local guides and transport.

⊙ Transport

Popayán *p301, map p303*
Air To **Bogotá** with **Avianca** (Cra 7, No 5-77) and **Satena** (Cra 9, No 4-14), daily. To **Guapi**, 3 times a week with **Satena**.

Bus To **Bogotá**, Expreso Bolivariano, US$36, 12-16 hrs. To **Cali**, US$5.50, 2½-3 hrs, or **Velotax** microbus, US$9, *colectivos* leave from the main plaza. To **Pasto**, US$15, 4-6 hrs, spectacular scenery (sit on right). To **Ipiales**, Expreso Bolivariano, US$16, 6-7 hrs, runs every hour but many buses arrive full from Cali, book in advance. To **San Agustín** via La Plata, **Coomotor**, 13 hrs, US$13, once a day. **Via Isnos**, Cootranshuila or Estelar, several a day mainly midmorning to afternoon, US$15.50, 6-8 hrs. Sit on the left for the best views. To **Tierradentro** (Cruce de Pisimbalá, also known as Cruce de San Andrés or San Andrés de Pisimbalá), 5 daily 0500-1500, US$8, 4-6 hrs continues to La Plata. To **La Plata**, US$9, 5 hrs, with **Cootranshuila** also Sotracauca. To **Puracé**, Cootranshuila US$1.20, 2 hrs.

Taxi No meters; normal price within city is US$1.65.

Warning Avoid travelling by night between Popayán and San Agustín, the roads have been reported dangerous in the past. Additionally, they are in very bad condition. Also we have received many reports of theft on the buses between these towns; do not trust 'helpfuls' and do not put bags on the luggage rack.

Silvia
Bus From **Popayán**, daily **Coomotorista** and **Belalcázar**, several *busetas* in the morning (US$2.50).

Tierradentro *p304, map p304*

Bus To **La Plata**, buses leave from San Andrés, passing by the museum at 0500, 0600 and 0800. Otherwise, you must go to El Cruce. From La Plata, *colectivos* leave when full for **Tierradentro**, US$4.40 per person, with Cootransplateño and others. From Popayán daily 1030, US$8, 4-6 hrs to **Cruce Pisimbalá**. Best to take early buses, as afternoon buses will leave you at the Cruce in the dark. Walk uphill (about 2 km, 30 mins) to the museum and on, 20 mins, to the village. If you want to go to Silvia, take this bus route and change to a *colectivo* (US$1.50) at Totoró. Buses and *camionetas* from the Cruce to **La Plata** (en route to San Agustín, see below) US$4.50, 4-5 hrs or more frequent *colectivo* jeeps, US$6. If you cannot get a direct Cruce–La Plata bus, take one going to **Páez** (Belalcázar) (US$1.50), alight at Guadualejo, 17 km east of Inzá, from where there is a more frequent service to La Plata.

Neiva *p305*

Air Several flights daily with **Avianca** or **Aires**, 1 hr.

Bus To **Bogotá**, 5½ hrs, US$15, with Bolivariano or Coomotor. To **Rivera**, *colectivo*, US$1.50, 25 mins. To **Villavieja**, *colectivo*, 30 mins, To **La Plata**, 2 hrs, US$5.50, *colectivo*.

Desierto de Tatacoa *p306*

To **Neiva**, US$4, 1 hr, from the Parque Principal in Villavieja or from the terminal in Neiva.

To the **desert** transport is expensive, US$11 per person as far as El Cuzco, 15 mins. The walk takes 1 hr but bear in mind that temperatures can reach up to 49°C so be sure to take lots of water, a hat, and sun cream. To **Bogotá**, take a *colectivo* to Neiva and transfer there. Alternatively, it's possible to cross the Río Magdalena in a motorized canoe, US$1.10. Walk past the cemetery down to the river and shout if there is no-one there as they might be waiting on the other side. From the far side of the river

it's a 1.5-km walk to the town of Aipe from where it is possible to hail down buses, US$11, on the main Neiva–Bogotá highway, about 250 m from the parque principal. From the river, follow the path until you reach the edge of town and walk up C 5 past the parque. A taxi from the centre of Aipe to the main road, US$2 (recommended).

● Directory

Popayán *p301, map p303*

Language classes The HostelTrail Guesthouse organizes Spanish lessons with graduates from the Universidad del Cauca, US$6.50 per hr for up to 10 hrs, US$5.50 per hr for courses longer than 10 hrs. Also language exchanges with students of English.

Silvia

Banks Banco Cooperativo, Cra 6, Banco del Estado, and others will change TCs. Some, eg Banco Popular, C 4, No 5-48, will give cash advances against Visa cards or **Banco del Occidente** against MasterCard. **Banco de Bogotá**, C 4, No 6-44. **Davivienda**, Cra 9, No 00, gives largest withdrawals. **Bancolombia**, Cra 6, No 4-49. **Titan**, good rates offered, Cra 7, No 6-40, T2-824 4659, inside CC Luis Martínez, Mon-Fri 0800-1200, 1400-1700, Sat 0830-1200. They also offer an international money transfer service. There are other *cambios*, but their rates are poor. **Internet** Cafeto Internet, Cr 9, No 5-42, T2-824 3400. Good value, open late. **Post office** Correos de Colombia/Adpostal, C 14, No 2-56, T2-8244564. **Security** DAS, C 4, No 10B-66, T2-8231889 ext 108. **Telephone** Telecom, Cra 4 y C 3; closes 2000. You can make international calls for less than 3 mins.

Tierradentro *p304, map p304*

Telephone There are no landlines in Tierradentro at present but mobile phones work and locals will sell you *minutos*.

San Agustín and around

▶▶ Phone code: 8. Colour map 3, B3. Population: 7000. Altitude: 1700 m.

Famed for its mysterious pre-Columbian stone figures of men, animals and gods, the little town of San Agustín is also an opportunity to enjoy the rural landscape of Colombia at its finest. The largest collection of religious monuments and megalithic sculptures in South America, the statues uncovered in this wild, spectacular countryside were hewn from stone between 3300 BC and the arrival of the Spanish. Little is known about the culture that produced them, further adding to their fascination. Many of the figures have been moved to an archaeological park just outside the town but you can also visit some which remain at their original spots, ensconced in rolling green hills rich in colourful, sub-tropical flowers and tumbling brooks. Here, the Río Magdalena is at its angriest, kicking and screaming into life as it begins its journey through the heart of Colombia towards the Atlantic coast. ▶▶ *For listings, see pages 317-319.*

Ins and outs

Tourist offices
There are four tour agencies masquerading as 'tourist offices'. While they may well give out useful advice, much of this will be clouded by contracts they hold with various hotels and other operators around town. For impartial advice visit the **Oficina Municipal de Turismo** on the plaza cívica or the tourist police at the police station just nearby, **Oficina de Policía de Turismo** ① *C 3, No 11-86.* For cultural information there is a **Casa de Cultura** ① *Cra 3, No 3-61.*

Climate
The rainy season is April to June/July, but since the weather often comes up from the Amazon basin to the southeast, it rains somewhat during most of the year, hence the beautiful green landscape; the driest months are November to March. The days are warm but sweaters are needed in the evenings; average temperature 18°C.

Recommended reading
The best books on the subject are *Exploraciones Arqueológicas en San Agustín*, by Luis Duque Gómez (Bogotá, 1966, 500 pages) or *San Agustín, Reseña Arqueológica*, by the same author (1963, 112 pages); a leaflet in English is obtainable from tourist offices. The Colombian Institute of Archaeology has published a booklet (English/Spanish) on San Agustín and Tierradentro; it may be available at museums in San Agustín and San Andrés.

Warning Beware of 'guides' and touts who approach you in the street. Have nothing to do with anyone offering drugs, pre-Columbian objects, gold, emeralds or other precious minerals for sale. Enquire about safety before walking to the more distant monuments.

Parque Arqueológico

① *Entrance to the park and museum is US$4, entrance to Alto de los Idolos is US$2.70.*
The nearest archaeological sites are in the Parque Arqueológico, which includes the **Bosque de las Estatuas**. The park, which was declared a World Heritage Site by UNESCO

in 1995, is about 2.5 km from San Agustín, less than 1 km from the **Hotel Osoguaico**. The statues in the park are in situ, though some have been set up on end and fenced in. Those in the Bosque de las Estatuas have been moved and rearranged, and linked by gravel footpaths.

Apart from the distinctive statues, the most notable features of the San Agustín site are the **Mesitas** (barrows) consisting of large vertical stone slabs, standing in circular enclosures about 25 m in diameter. These were probably originally roofed over with statues set inside and out. There is some doubt if they were primarily in places of ceremony or tombs. There are four Mesitas, Mesita D is beside the museum area near the entrance to the park, you will visit B, A and C following the trail. Beyond Mesita C are the carved rocks in and around the stream at the **Fuente de Lavapatas** in the park, where the water runs through carved channels. The park authorities have reduced the water flow to the Fuente as there was considerable damage being caused by too much water. It is however now easier to see the engravings on the rocks. The **Alto de Lavapatas**, above the Fuente, has an extensive view. It closes at 1600. There are refreshment stands at 'Fuente' and on the way up to Lavapatas.

Within the park children sell various things including *guama* fruit, which comes in a large pea-like pod. They have a refreshing moist flavour, but do not eat the black seeds!

There is also a **museum** ① *0800-1800 daily*, in the park, which contains pottery and artefacts and a good scale model of the local sites giving an excellent idea of the topography of the area.

You can get a very good idea of the park, the Bosque and the museum in the course of three hours' walking, or add in El Tablón and La Chaquira (see below) for a full day. The whole site leaves an unforgettable impression, from the strength and strangeness of the statues, and the great beauty of the rolling green landscape.

In the town is the **Museo Arqueológico Julio César Cubillos** ① *Cra 11, No 3-61, open Mon-Sat until 2300*, with a good library, videos in Spanish and English, and light refreshments.

Archaeological sites

El Tablón (five sculptures brought together under a bamboo roof) is reached up Carrera 14, over the brow of the hill and 250 m to a marked track to the right, then down to the left. Continue down the path, muddy in wet weather, ford a stream and follow signs to the Río Magdalena canyon. **La Chaquira** (figures carved on rocks) is dramatically set half way down to the river. Walking time round trip from San Agustín is two hours. Plenty of houses offer refreshments as far as El Tablón. There are many pleasant paths to follow in this area, ask locally for ideas.

Continue along the road from San Agustín for the site of **La Pelota**, where two painted statues were found in 1984. It's a three-hour return trip, six hours if you include El Tablón and La Chaquira, 15 km in all. Archaeological discoveries in 1984/1986 include some unique polychromed sculptures at **El Purutal** near La Pelota and a series of at least 30 stones carved with animals and other designs in high relief. These are known as **Los Petroglifos** and can be found on the right bank of the Río Magdalena, near the **Estrecho** (narrows) to which jeeps run.

Also part of the UNESCO site is **Alto de los Idolos**, about 10 km by horse or on foot (US$2.70). It's a lovely, if strenuous, walk, steep in places, via **Puente de la Chaquira**. Here on a hill overlooking San Agustín are more and different statues known as *vigilantes*, each guarding a burial mound (one is an unusual rat totem). The few excavated have disclosed large stone sarcophagi, some covered by stone slabs bearing a sculpted likeness of the inmate (the site is open until 1600).

Alto de los Idolos can also be reached from **San José de Isnos** (5 km northeast) 27 km by road from San Agustín. The road passes the **Salto del Mortiño**, a 170 m fall about 7 km before Isnos, 500 m off the road. Isnos' market day is Saturday.

About 6 km north of Isnos is **Alto de las Piedras**, which has a few interesting tombs and monoliths, including the famous 'Doble Yo'. Only slightly less remarkable than the statues are the orchids growing nearby. Bordones is 8 km further on. Turn left at end of the village and there is (500 m) parking for the **Salto de Bordones** falls.

Tours around San Agustín

Horse hire You are strongly advised to hire horses for trips around San Agustín through hotels The centre for horses (**Asociación de Acompañantes y Alquiladores de Caballos** ① *along C 5 on the road to the park*, costs about US$11.65 per hour, per rider. If you require a guide, you must add the hire cost of his horse. Pacho, T3118277972 (mob) and Abuy, T3114533959 (mob) come highly recommended as guides and are contactable through El Maco or La Casa de Nelly. There are fixed tariffs for 20 or so standard trips.

Vehicle tours Jeeps may be hired for between four to five people. Prices vary according to the number of sites to be visited, but the daily rate is about US$16.50 per person with a minimum of four people. Try bargaining for a lower price.

Guides There are countless guides in town offering tours of the various sites. Some give a better service than others. Enquire at your hotel or at the tourist office for advice. Some recommended names are Marino Bravo, T3132214006 (speaks good English), Gloria, T3124402010 and Carlos Bolaños, T3114595753.

South of San Agustín

Southeast of San Agustín is the little town of **Pitalito**. It has little to offer the tourist except that it is here that the brightly painted, imaginative ceramics are made that are often used in tourist advertisements for southern Colombia. Most notable are the extravagantly decorated *chivas*, the ubiquitous country buses of the region. Many other items are produced, a delightful art form expressing a popular culture.

South of Pitalito is the **Cueva de los Guácharos National Park**. Between December and June swarms of oilbirds (*guácharos*) may be seen; they are nocturnal, with a unique radar-location system. The reserve also contains many of the unusual and spectacular cock-of-the-rock (a type of bird). The rangers are particularly friendly, providing tours and basic accommodation; permission to visit the park must be obtained from the **MA offices in Pitalito** ① *Cra 4, No 4-21*. Take a bus to Palestina, US$1.20, one hour, and then walk for six hours along an eroded, muddy path to reach the park. The 9000-ha park extends to the crest of the Cordillera Oriental, here rising to over 3000 m. It is mostly rain and cloudforest with an abundance of wildlife, but inaccessible. The main interest centres on the valley of the Río Suárez, a tributary of the Magdalena, which here flows through limestone caves and gorges. There are three caves to visit, Cueva Chiquita near the entrance, Cueva del Indio, 740 m long with interesting calcium formations, and further upstream, the Cueva de los Guácharos with a natural bridge over the river. Entry to the park US$3.20. Accommodation (when available), US$5 per night per person. Another unpaved road from Pitalito goes southwest to Mocoa through remote jungle, crossing the Río Caquetá 25 km before Mocoa. This is a faster way to get to Ecuador. Up until recently security was poor on this route due to strong guerrilla and narco trafficker presence but lately it has improved, though the road still suffers from many landslides and accidents.

◉ San Agustín and around listings → Phone code: 8.

For Sleeping and Eating price codes and other relevant information, see pages 31-36.

◉ Sleeping

San Agustín *p314*
B Yalconia, Vía al Parque Arqueológico, T8373013, hyalconia@gmail.com. The only mid-range hotel in town, the Yalconia is a modern building with cleanish rooms, although some of the paintwork is starting to deteriorate a little.
D El Jardín, Cra 11, No 4-10, T8373455, www.hosteltrail.com/eljardin. In town, this colonial house has a colourful patio decorated with hanging baskets, snake skins and animal pelts as well as a couple of chirpy songbirds. The rooms are simple but clean and it has a restaurant serving fixed-menu lunches at US$3.30. There are also dorms, which cost US$10 per person.
D Hacienda Anacaona, Vía al Estrecho, T8379390, www.anacaona-colombia.com. This traditional *finca* has comfortable, spacious rooms and a colourful garden with fine views into the hills as well as a restaurant serving typical regional food such as trout and *sancocho*.
E Casa de Nelly, Km 2 Vía Parque Archeológico, T3115350412 (mob), hotelrestaurantebarcasadenelly@yahoo.com. On top of the hill on the road to the archeological park, this lovely old house has colourful rooms and *cabañas* set in a gorgeous garden bursting with subtropical flowers and bushes. There's a kitchen serving home cooked pastas and pizzas as well as a thatched kiosk with hammocks for taking in the atmosphere.

E Casa del Sol Naciente, T3115876464, www.refugioecologicocasadelsol naciente.com. Located 1 km from town, this rustic retreat has a several *cabañas*, including 2 that must have one of the most spectacular views in Colombia, looking down into a gorge through with the the torrid Magdalena river racing along the bottom. With a vegetable and herb garden and an open air bath, this is a place for nature lovers, though it's best not to opt for a room in the main house, which is a little dark.
E El Maco, T8373437, www.elmaco.ch. This Swiss-run *finca*, 1 km outside town, has several comfortable *cabañas* and a teepee in colourful gardens full of animals as well as one of the best restaurants in town serving up delicious Thai curries and organic products. There's internet, board games, a ping-pong table and a book exchange but best of all René is one of the most knowledgeable sources of information on the local area and can arrange horse riding and other activities.
E La Casa de François, T3143582930 (mob), 200 m via El Tablón, www.lacasade francois.com. Just outside town, this French-run hostel has private rooms with bathrooms as well as dorms set in 2 ha of gardens blooming with orchids and other flowers. There's a kitchen that's free to use while François and his Colombian girlfriend cook up a varied menu of home-made food for US$2.70, as well as crêpes and home-baked bread. Other pluses include bike and horse hire and Wi-Fi.
    Camping Next to Yalconia is Camping San Agustín, US$1.60 per person with own

tent, US$5.50 to hire tent, clean, pleasant, safe (guards), showers, toilets, lights, laundry service, horse hire.

● Eating

San Agustín *p314*
Tap water in San Agustín is not safe to drink.
♥ Brahama, C 5, No 15-11, T3014171077 (mob). This small restaurant serves up the usual Colombian fare as well as some good vegetarian options.
♥ Donde Richard, C 5, No 23-45, T3124326399. On the outskirts of town, this is considered one of the better restaurants in San Agustín, with excellent quality steak, chicken and fish dishes cooked in agreeable surroundings and accompanied by soups and salads.
♥ El Fogón, C 5, No 14-30, T8373431. Festooned with local trinkets and antiques, El Fogón does á la carte and *comidas corrientes*, including fish, steaks, and *patacón*.
♥ El Maco, T8373437. It's a healthy 1-km walk from town but El Maco serves some of the best food in San Agustín, including excellent Thai curries and pastas as well as organic options. Recommended.
♥ La Rana Verde, Cra 11, No 2-26, T3142678123 (mob). Good little lunchtime venue serving fixed-menu meals for US$2.20.
♥ Surabhi, C 5, No 14-09, T3133457519 (mob). Surabhi serves up tasty regional specialities. *Almuerzos* cost US$2.20.

● Festivals and events

San Agustín *p314*
Mid-Jul (not a fixed date) The fiesta of Santa María del Carmen is held in San Agustín.
24 Jun Festival in San Juan, with horse races and dances.
29 Jun Festival in San Pedro, with horse races, dances, fancy dress, competitions and other events.

1st week of Oct La Semana Cultural Integrada is celebrated in the Casa de Cultura, with many folklore events from all parts of the country.
End Oct/beginning Nov The Feria de San Agustín is held, with livestock shows and horse displays.

● Shopping

San Agustín *p314*
Film is available in several shops.
Leather goods are beautiful and priced reasonably. Many local shops make boots to your own design (double-check the price beforehand).
No name, C 5, No 14-25. Local artisan Angélica hasn't got round to naming her shop yet but its worth visiting just for the smell of her home-made leather goods.

▲ Activities and tours

San Agustín *p314*
Chaska Tours, T8373437, www.chaska tours.net. Run by Swissman René Suter (who also owns the hostel **El Maco**), this agency organizes tours around San Agustín as well as to Tierradentro, Puracé and the Tatacoa desert. English and German spoken. Recommended.
Magdalena Rafting, T3112714788, www.magdalenarafting.com. French-run adventure sports company specializing in white water rafting (full day, Grade IV rapids, US$40 pp), as well as kayaking and caving.
Pacho, T311827797, is a very good horse-riding guide. As well as to the various archaelogical sites he also does tours to Lago Magdalena, the source of the Río Magdalena, US$27 for guidance plus US$20 per person.
Piscina Municipal, behind the **Yalconia**. A clean swimming pool, with water fed from a natural spring, busy at weekends, US$1 per day.

☺ Transport

San Agustín *p314*
Bus

To **Bogotá** by *buseta* (Taxis Verdes, C 3, No 11-02, T8373068, 0500, 0700 and 1900 direct, US$23, 9 hrs or by bus **Coomotor**, C 3, No 10-71), 4 a day, day buses, US$29. From Bogotá, **Taxis Verdes**, 0300, 9 hrs, US$21.50. **Coomotor**, 3 a day at 0730, 0900 and 2100, 10-12 hrs, US$21.50-29 (depending on type of bus). More frequent services to **Pitalito** with **Coomotor** or **Cootranshuila**, 8 hrs, US$24 from which *colectivos* leave for San Agustín, US$2.70, 45 mins. To **Neiva**, 6 buses a day, including **Coomotor** and **Cootranshuila**, 6 hrs, US$6. To **Pitalito** 1½ hrs, US$2.70 by *colectivo*, or any bus to Neiva. To **Popayán**, services at 0600, 0900, 1100, 1400, and 1630 with **Cootranshuila**, US$15, or with **Estelar** (smaller bus, faster). You may have to take a *colectivo* to Km 5 on Popayán–Pitalito road and catch a bus from there. From Popayán, with **Estelar**, 7 a day 0800-2130, and **Cootranshuila**, 6 a day 0600-2100, US$15. Sometimes buses will only stop at San Agustín if there are enough passengers with that destination. Otherwise they drop off at turning and continue to Pitalito. They arrange for *colectivos* to pick up (no extra charge). To **Tierradentro**, take early transport to Pitalito (US$2.70), 1 direct bus with **Cootransmayo** at 0630 otherwise *colectivo* or taxi. From Pitalito there are direct buses at 1000 and 1400 to **La Plata** (US$8.30), finally *colectivo* to **Tierradentro** (US$4.40). If you miss the connection to La Plata at Pitalito do the same route but go via Garzón (this road is in much better condition) and take a *colectivo* from La Plata. To **Pasto via Mocoa**, 11 hrs, take a bus or *colectivo* to Pitalito, where there are buses or Kia's (**Pony Express**) to Mocoa, US$11. From Mocoa to Pasto, US$19. There is also transport from here to Laguna Cocha. This is a far quicker route to Pasto than going via Popayán and relatively safe from guerrilla activity but take advice before going. Do not travel at night and bear in mind that this road is prone to landslides and traffic accidents.

Note Bus times change constantly. Enquire at bus station or hotel before setting out.

❶ Directory

San Agustín *p314*
Banks Travellers are advised to change TCs before arriving in San Agustín; enquire at the travel office and the small shop opposite the police station who may exchange cash. **Caja Agraria**, C 4/Cra 13, and **Ultrahuilca Redeban**, Cra 3, No 12-7, will give cash advances against Visa card. **Almacén de Todo**, opposite the town hall, will cash TCs but at a bad rate. **Internet** Connections are slow in San Agustín. **Weblive.com**, Cra 12, No 4-14.

The far south

From Popayán to Ecuador, the Pan-American highway travels through arguably the most spectacular scenery in Colombia, at first dipping into humid agricultural land before rising again as it nears the highland city of Pasto. It is a forever engaging ride as the landscape becomes increasingly dramatic; at times the road follows in the shadow of the Western Cordillera, as waves of small hills roll out towards its edges like crumpled sheets on an unmade bed. Beyond Pasto it is even more impressive as the road snakes its way ever upward, clinging to the edges of steep escarpments painstakingly planted with maize, peas and wheat, over deep gorges that plunge down to torrid rivers. The area is dominated by volcanos, some of them active, especially those that look over the border town of Ipiales. Near Pasto is Laguna La Cocha, which has a national park well worth visiting on the Isla de Corota. Just outside Ipiales is the extraordinary Gothic church of Las Lajas that straddles a deep gorge and is a magnet for miracle-seekers and pilgrims. To the west its a long ride down to the Pacific coast at Tumaco where salt marshes and mangroves have created a distinct eco system. On the way the private nature reserve of La Planada has a unique population of native birds and a conservation programme of special interest to ecologists. ›› For listings, see pages 326-329.

Pasto ●●●●●○▲●● ›› *pp326-329. Colour map 3, B2.*

→ *Phone code: 2. Population: 399,000. Altitude: 2534 m.*

The capital of the Department of Nariño stands upon a high plateau in the southwest, 88 km from Ecuador. Pasto (full name San Juan de Pasto), is overlooked from the west by Galeras Volcano (when not in cloud) and to the east by green hills not yet suburbanized by the city, and enjoys a very attractive setting. Surrounded by hills and swirling clouds, it still retains some of its colonial character, but has not been helped by several serious earthquakes in the meantime. A little unfairly, the people of Pasto have a reputation throughout the rest of Colombia as being very stupid and are the butt of many jokes. What is fair to say is that they are extremely friendly.

Ins and outs

The **airport** is at Cano, 40 km north of Pasto; by *colectivo* (beautiful drive), 45 minutes. US$2.40 or US$13.50 by taxi. There are no currency-exchange facilities, but the shop will change US$ bills at a poor rate. All interurban buses leave from the new **terminal** ① *Cra 6, C 16, 4 km from the centre.* To get there by taxi, US$2 or take city bus No 4 from the centre.

The **tourist office** ① *Just off the main plaza, C 18, No 25-25, T234962, friendly and helpful, open 0800-1200 and 1400-1800 Mon-Fri, closed Sat-Sun*, will advise on money changing.

Background

The city was founded in 1539 by Lorenzo de Aldana, who came up from Quito, and is therefore one of the oldest cities of Colombia. During the wars of independence, it was a stronghold of the Royalists and the last town to fall into the hands of the patriots. Simón Bolívar directed the bloodiest battle of the independence war against the forces of Basilio García on 7 April 1822. His headquarters was nearby in Bomboná. Then the people of Nariño Department wanted to join Ecuador when that country split off from Gran Colombia in 1830, but were prevented by Colombian troops. Today Pasto is a centre for the agricultural and cattle industries of the region. Pasto varnish (*barniz*) is mixed locally, to embellish the strikingly colourful local wooden bowls.

Sights

A legacy of colonial times is the considerable number of churches. The **cathedral** is a large but not distinguished building, sombre in its appearance and austere inside. **San Juan Bautista** church (St John the Baptist) is the oldest in Pasto, though the finely decorated building dates from 1669, a replacement for the original of 1539 after damage by earthquakes. The church of **Cristo Rey** ⓘ *C 20, No 24-64, near the centre*, has a striking

Pasto

Sleeping
Canchalá 1
Casa Madrigal 2
Chambú 3
Don Saúl 4
Fernando Plaza 5
Galerías 6
Koala Inn 7
Loft 8
María Belén 9
Metropol 10
Morasurco 11

Eating
El Gastronom' 1
Guadalquivir Café 2
Inca Cuy 3
Loto Verde 4
Parrilla Chipichape 5
Picantería Ipiales 6

yellow stone west front with octagonal angelic turrets. **La Merced** ① *C 18 y Cra 22*, has rich decoration and gold ornamentation.

The **Museo de Oro del Banco de la República** ① *C 19, No 21-27, T215777, Tue-Sat 1000-1700, free*, has a small well-displayed collection of pre-Columbian pieces from the cultures of South Colombia, a library and auditorium. Another museum in the city centre is the **Museo Alfonso Zambrano** ① *C 20, No 29-78*, which houses a private collection of indigenous and colonial, especially *quiteño* (from Quito), and period arts. Alfonso Zambrano was a renowned local woodcarver. The **Museo Maridíaz** ① *C 18, No 32A-39*, is mainly concerned with religious art and relics from the region.

From the church of **Santiago Apóstol** ① *Cra 23 y C 13*, there is a good view of the green mountains beyond the city. Four blocks to the north are the green tiled domes of the **San Felipe** church ① *C 12 y Cra 27*, opposite the monastery of the **Inmaculada Concepción**. The interior courtyard of the **municipal building** ① *corner of C 19 y Cra 24, on the main plaza*, has two tiers of colonnaded balconies.

Volcán Galeras

The volcano Galeras (4276 m), quiescent since 1934, began erupting again in 1989 and again in 2005. Check at the tourist office whether it is possible to climb on the mountain – it has been officially closed since 1995. A road climbs up the mountain to a ranger station and police post at 3700 m where you will be stopped. From there, a rough road goes to the summit near which there is a TV relay station. It is reported that this area is now mined to discourage unauthorised visitors, at least one of whom has died as a result. The volcano itself has claimed several victims including a British geologist, Geoffrey Brown, who died in 1993 when the volcano erupted just as he was setting up equipment to measure gravity changes which, it is hoped, will help eventually to predict volcanic activity.

On the north side of the volcano lies the village of **Sandoná** where Panama hats are made. They can be seen lying in the streets in the process of being finished. Sandoná market day is Saturday. There are frequently buses daily, 1½ hours, US$2. There are good walks on the lower slopes through Catambuco and Jongovito (where bricks are made).

Laguna La Cocha

About 25 km east of Pasto, on the road to Mocoa is **Laguna La Cocha**, 2760 m, the largest lake in South Colombia (sometimes called Lago Guamuez). It is 14 km long and 4.5 km wide. Near the north end of the lake is the Santuario de Fauna y Flora **Isla de la Corota** nature reserve (10 minutes by boat from the **Hotel Sindanamoy**). This is the smallest protected area administered by the Colombian National Parks service and can be visited in a day. The island was the ritual centre for Quillacinga and Mocoa cultures for several centuries. There is now a small chapel near where you land on the island. There is a research unit and an interesting information centre and a marked path to see the many varieties of trees, small mammals and birds of the island. There are good viewing points of the lake, which is also surrounded by forested mountains. A (free) pass to visit the island is needed.

Around the lake are 15 or 20 private nature reserves run by a local association to protect prime forest areas and the páramo of the Guamuez river, part of the Putumayo river system. Several of these reserves have trails for visitors. Take *botas pantomeras* (rubber boots) and wet-weather clothing if you plan to hike. Average temperature at the lake is 12°C. For information on reserves around Laguna La Cocha, contact **Asociación para el Desarrollo Campesino** ① *C 10, No 36-28, Pasto, T231022*.

Las Lajas

In 1754 María Mueces de Quiñonez was traveling from the village of Potosí to Ipiales with her deaf-mute daughter Rosa when she stopped to rest by a cave next to the Guaitara river. Rosa escaped her clutches and ran into the cave. Some moments later she emerged and spoke for the first time in her life, saying: "Mother, look at the *mestiza* over there holding a boy in her arms". María did not look in the cave but grabbed Rosa and continued on her way. When in Ipiales, she recounted what had happened, though no one took what she said seriously.

A few days later, Rosa disappeared from home. María guessed that her daughter must have gone to the cave. Rosa had often said that the Lady was calling her. María ran to Las Lajas and found her daughter in front of a lady and playing with a child. María fell to her knees before the Virgin Mary and Baby Jesus.

From that day, she and Rosa often went to the cave to place wild flowers and candles in the cracks in the rocks.

One day Rosa fell gravely ill and died. A distraught María decided to take her daughter's body to Las Lajas to ask the Lady to restore Rosa to life.

The Virgin resurrected Rosa and María returned home brimming with joy. Crowds began to visit the cave, curious about what had happened. They discovered a picture of the mysterious Lady on the wall of the grotto that is still there to this day.

That same year Fray Gabriel Villa Fuerte returned to the spot and built a straw church, and as more pilgrims visited the miraculous spot, a new cathedral was planned on the other side of the river. The first stone was laid in 1899 and the extraordinary Gothic Revival structure was finally finished in 1949.

Today it is a popular destination for religious believers from all parts of Latin America and is commonly described as 'topographically the most beautiful in the world, in religious terms the most visited in the Americas and architecturally the most audacious and original in Colombia'.

By the lake, 3 km from the main road, is the **C Chalet Guamuez**, T7219306, recommended, with chalets, boats and jeep trips. Try also **C Sindamanoy**, T236433, chalet style, government-run, good views, and tent camping allowed with manager's permission. There are also cheap and friendly places to stay in and near **El Encano** (sometimes shown on maps as 'El Encanto'), with many restaurants serving trout.

Beyond El Encano there is a steep climb over the Sierra, where a large statue of the Virgin marks the entry into the Putumayo. The road then descends steeply to Sibundoy, Mocoa and Puerto Asís. For many years this has been guerrilla territory and a drug growing and processing area. It is also the centre of the government-led coca eradication programme. While security has improved markedly in this area in the past two years we advise anybody to err on the side of caution and refrain from visiting this part of Colombia.

Pasto to the coast

The 250 km road west from Pasto to Tumaco is paved, but is subject to landslides – check in Pasto. It leaves the Pan-Americana 40 km south of Pasto at El Pedregal, passing the brick factories of the high plains of the Cordillera Occidental. At **Túquerres** (3050 m), the Thursday market is good for ponchos. A short distance beyond Túquerres is a track to the right which leads in 2½ hours up to the Corponariño cabin where you can stay the night and then a further 1½ hours to the spectacular **Laguna Verde** fed by sulphur springs. The lake is in the large crater of Volcán Azufral (4070 m), still intermittantly active – beware of fumeroles. For information on walking and climbing in this area, enquire in Túquerres.

The road continues to El Espino (no hotels) where it divides, left 36 km to Ipiales, and right to Tumaco. About 90 km from Túquerres, before the town of Ricaurte, is the village of **Chucunez**.

Reserva Natural La Planada → *Colour map 3, B1.*

A dirt road branches south here, and after crossing the river climbs for 7 km to **Reserva Natural La Planada**, a private 3200-ha nature reserve created in 1982 by Fundación FES La Planada, This patch of dense cloudforest on a unique flat-topped mountain is home to a wide variety of flora and fauna and believed to have one of the highest concentrations of native bird species in South America.

The foundation has initiated a programme reintroducing the spectacled bear to the reserve. There are also many orchids and bromeliads to be seen from the nature trails. Day visitors are welcome but camping is prohibited. Check at the tourist office on whether it is safe to climb on the mountain and whether you need a permit. The visitor centre has maps and details of nature trails. There is accommodation on site, comfortable cabins, hot water, with three meals US$12.50 per day. For further information contact **Reserva Natural La Planada** ① *T927753396/97, fesplan@col2.tele com.com.co.* Fundación FES has published a fine illustrated book on the reserve, US$25, proceeds help conservation.

Tumaco → *Colour map 3, B1. Phone code: 2. Population: 169,000.*

Tumaco isn't exactly the most appealing of places. It suffers from high unemployment, poor living conditions, poor roads and has problems with water and electricity supplies. To make matters worse, it is in one of the world's rainiest areas, and the yearly average temperature is about 30°C. The movement of the tides governs most of the activities in the area, especially transport. The northern part of the town is built on stilts out over the sea (safe to visit only in daylight). A natural arch on the main beach, north of the town and port, is reputed to be the hiding place of Henry Morgan's treasure. Swimming is not recommended from the town's beaches, which are polluted; stalls provide refreshment on the beach. Swimming is safe, however, at El Morro beach, north of the town, only on the incoming tide (the outgoing tide uncovers poisonous rays).

The area is noted for the archaeological finds associated with the Tumaco culture. Ask for Pacho Cantin at El Morro Beach who will guide you through the caves. The coastal area around Tumaco is mangrove swamp, with many rivers and inlets on which lie hundreds of villages and settlements; negotiate with boatmen for a visit to the swamps or the beautiful island tourist resort of **Boca Grande**. There are several places to stay in the F category. There are water taxis north up the coast, across the bay to Salahonda and beyond. **Warning** This area is known for its coca plantations. Take advice before visiting.

South to Ecuador ⊜❼⊜❶ » *pp326-329.*

Passing through deep valleys and a spectacular gorge, buses on the paved Pan-American Highway cover the 84 km from Pasto to Ipiales in 1½ to two hours. The road crosses the spectacular gorge of the Río Guáitara at 1750 m, near El Pedregal, where *choclo* (corn) is cooked in many forms by the roadside.

Border essentials: Colombia–Ecuador

Tumaco–San Lorenzo

It is possible to travel to Ecuador by boat. Part of the trip is by river, which is very beautiful, and part on the open sea, which can be very rough; a plastic sheet to cover your belongings is essential. Take suncream.

Colombian immigration DAS C23, Manzana 10, Casa16, Barrio Pradomar, T7272010; obtain a stamp for leaving Colombia here; office open weekdays only. Visas for Ecuador (if required) should be obtained in Cali or Pasto. Entry stamps for Ecuador must be obtained in the coastal towns.

Entering Colombia from Tumaco You will have to go to Ipiales to obtain the entry stamp. Apparently the 24/48 hours 'unofficial' entry is not a problem, but do not obtain any Colombian stamps in your passport before presentation to DAS in Ipiales. DAS in Pasto is not authorized to give entry stamps for overland or sea crossings, and the DAS office in Tumaco seems to be only semi-official.

Ipiales–Rumichaca

Ipiales is 2 km from the Rumichaca bridge across the Río Carchi into Ecuador. The frontier post stands beside a natural bridge, on a concrete bridge, where customs and passport examinations take place from 0600 to 2100.

Colombian immigration and customs All Colombian offices are in one complex: DAS (immigration, exit stamp given here), customs, INTRA (Deptartment of Transportation, car papers stamped here; if leaving Colombia you must show your vehicle entry permit) and ICA (Dept of Agriculture for plant and animal quarantine). There is also a restaurant, Telecom for long-distance phone calls, clean bathrooms (ask for key, US$0.10) and ample parking.

Ecuadorean immigration and customs The Ecuadorean side is older and more chaotic than the modern Colombian complex, but is adequate. There is a modern Andinatel office for phone calls. Ask for 90 days on entering Ecuador if you need it, otherwise you will be given 30 days. You are not allowed to cross to Ipiales for the day without having your passport stamped. Both Ecuadorean exit stamp and Colombian entry stamp are required. Although no one will stop you at the border, you risk serious consequences in Colombia if you are caught with your documents 'out of order'.

Crossing by private vehicle The vehicle is supposed to be fumigated against diseases that affect coffee trees, at the ICA office; the certificate must be presented in El Pedregal, 40 km beyond Ipiales on the road to Pasto. (This fumigation process is not always carried out.) You can buy insurance for your car in Colombia at Banco Agrario, in the plaza. In addition, car owners must present title deeds to the vehicle with a photocopy, and the vehicle's chassis and engine number.

Ecuadorean consulate In the DAS complex (above); weekdays 0900-1230, 1430-1700.

Exchange There are many moneychangers near the bridge on both sides. Travellers report better rates on the Colombian side, but check all calculations.

Transport From Ipiales to the border, *colectivo* from Calle 14/Carrera 11, wait till all seats are full, US$0.80. From border to Tulcán (Parque Ayora near the cemetery six blocks from the centre) US$0.75, to Tulcán bus station, US$1. Taxi to or from border, US$3.50. From Ipiales airport to the border by taxi, about US$6.50.

Ipiales → *Colour map 3, C2. Phone code: 2. Population: 109,000. Altitude: 2898 m.*

Ipiales, 'the city of the three volcanoes', stands close to Colombia's main border crossing with Ecuador and is famous for its colourful Friday morning indigenous market. The **Catedral Bodas de Plata** is worth visiting. There is a small museum, set up by Banco de la República. San Luis airport is 6.5 km out of town. Buses to most destinations leave from a new terminal at Carrera 3 with Calle 6, It has good facilities with a 24-hour left-luggage facility, US$1.10 per item and toilets, US$0.27. Most buses leave from here but **Bolivariano** and **Transipiales** have kiosks at the border and will collect passengers from here for main destinations further into Colombia.

The city's main attraction, 7 km east on a paved road, is the Sanctuary of the Virgin of **Las Lajas** ① *US$0.55, mass at the church Mon-Fri 0600, 0700, 0900, 1100, 1500 and 1700, Sun, every hour 0600-1200, 1500-1700,* which was declared a National Monument in 1984. Seen from the approach road, looking down into the canyon, the Sanctuary is a magnificent architectural conception, set on a bridge over the Río Guáitara. it is very heavily ornamented in the Gothic style. The altar is set into the rock face of the canyon where the Virgin Mary appeared around 1750. This forms one end of the sanctuary with the façade facing a wide plaza that completes the bridge over the canyon. There are walks to nearby shrines in dramatic scenery. It is a 10 to 15-minute walk down to the sanctuary from the village along a path lined with plaques giving thanks for miracles rendered by the virgin as well as a statue of Manuel de Rivera, a blind man cured by the virgin who walked through Ecuador begging for alms as thanks. He raised 388 pesos and 7 reales. Pilgrims come from all over Colombia and Ecuador (very crowded at Easter) and the Sanctuary must be second only to Lourdes in the number of miracles claimed for it, although the church only recognizes one. In the vaults of the church is an interesting museum telling the history of the construction of the church as well as religious artefacts and some interesting taxidermy – a 'two-headed' and an 'eight-legged' sheep, presumably examples of further miracles but clumsily stitched together from many animals.

There are several basic hotels and a small number of restaurants at Las Lajas. You may also stay at the convent, simple but cheerful. Try local guinea pig and boiled potatoes for lunch (or guinea-pig betting in the central plaza may be more to your taste).

Getting there Ipiales town buses going 'near the Sanctuary' leave you 2.5 km short. Take a *colectivo* from outside the bus station, US$1 per person, taxi, US$6 return (it's about a 1½ hours' walk, 7 km).

◉ **The far south listings** → *Phone code: 2.*

For Sleeping and Eating price codes and other relevant information, see pages 31-36.

● **Sleeping**

Pasto *p320, map p321*
AL Morasurco, Av de los Estudiantes, T7313250, www.hotelmorasurco.com. Located on the northern outskirts of town, Pasto's most expensive hotel has rooms with large beds, cable TV, Wi-Fi, parking and a Turkish bath.

A Don Saul, C 17, N0 23-52, T7224480, hoteldonsaul@computronix.com.co. This hotel stays close to its Jordanian owners' roots with murals depicting Arabic scenes and a restaurant serving Middle Eastern food. Recently refurbished, it has very large beds, a sauna, Turkish bath, cable TV and Wi-Fi, while breakfast is included in the price.
A Hotel Galerías, Cra 26, No 18-71, p 3, T7237390, www.hotel-galerias.com. Situated in the town's main shopping centre, the

Galerías has good-sized rooms as well as Wi-Fi, parking and a good restaurant with a typical Colombian menu.

A Loft Hotel, C 18, N0 22-33, T7226733, www.lofthotelpasto.com. Comfortable hotel with minimalist decor and extras such as Wi-Fi, an internnet room, and a spa. There's a 20% discount if you show a copy of Footprint Colombia.

B Casa Madrigal, Cra 26, No 15-37, T7234592, hotelcasamadrigal@hotmail.com. This hotel has spacious rooms with good beds and cable TV, parking, a restaurant, Wi-Fi and breakfast included.

B Fernando Plaza, C 20, No 21B-16, T7291432, www.hotelfernandoplaza.com. Smart, newish hotel with lots of good details such as beds with orthopaedic mattresses and stereos and Wi-Fi in every room. It also has a restaurant serving steak and seafood.

D Chambu, Cra 20, No 17 esquina, T7213129. This hotel has clean, basic rooms and good extras, such as Wi-Fi, an internet room, parking and a restaurant serving *comida corriente* at US$3.30, as well as friendly staff.

E Canchalá, C 17, No 20A-38, T7213965. This hotel has clean but small rooms with private bathrooms and but its position on a busy street makes it a little noisy.

E Koala Inn, C 18, No 22-27, T7221101. This creaky hostel is the best backpackers' option in town. It has an enormous central atrium, large, antiquated rooms, some with private bathrooms, and good information on the local area. There is a small café serving decent breakfasts.

E Metropol, C 15, No 21-41, T7212498. Decent hotel with small but clean rooms with cable TV and en suite bathrooms.

G María Belén, C 13, No 19-15, T7230277. Very basic but passable hotel with cable TV, en suite bathrooms with hot water and grumpy staff.

Ipiales *p326*

C Angasmayo, C 16, No 6-38, T7732140, hotelangasmayo@hotmail.com. The slick, minimalist lobby of this hotel is misleading as it appears to be the only part of the building that has seen a lick of paint in the last 10 years. However, the rooms will do and it also has internet access, parking, a restaurant with breakfast included, and a discotheque.

C Los Andes, Cra 5, No 14-44, T7734338, www.hotellosandes.com. Just a block from the Parque Principal, this hotel has large, spotless rooms, plus parking, Wi-Fi and breakfast included. A gym and sauna were under refurbishment at time of writing.

D Santa Isabel 2, Cra 7, No 14-27, T7734172. Smart, centrally placed hotel with good services such as Wi-Fi in reception, an internet room, parking and a restaurant.

E Emperador, Cra 5, No 14-43, T7252413. With good clean rooms with cable TV and private bathrooms with hot water, this hotel is the pick of the bunch of the budget options. Also has parking and is well placed 1 block from the Parque Principal.

E Metropol, Cra 2, No 6-10, T7737976. Opposite the bus station, this basic hotel has passable rooms with cable TV and en suite bathrooms with hot water as well as a small café in reception, As with all hotels near bus stations, take care walking around at night.

E Señorial, C 14, No 4-36, T7734610. Basic hotel with clean rooms, en suite bathrooms with hot water and cable TV.

F Belmonte, Cra 4, No 12-11, T7732771. Basic but clean hotel offering rooms with cable TV and shared bathrooms.

Eating

Pasto *p320, map p321*

† **El Gastronom'**, Av los Estudiantes, No 32A-68, T7313477. Located in the northern part of town near the Hotel Morasurco, this French-run restaurant serves a la carte Gallic dishes as well as *almuerzo* for US$5. Home delivery is also available.

† **Guadalquivir Café**, C 19, No 24-84, T7239504. Another Pasto stalwart with more than 35 years of existence, this atmospheric café serves up good home-made snacks such

as *tamales*, *empanadas de añejo* and *envueltos de choclo*.

Inca Cuy, C 29, No 13-65, T7238050. Tucked down a narrow corridor behind the Plaza de Bombona, a large statue of a guinea pig ought to tell you what this restaurant specializes in. Be warned that fried *cuy*, as it is known, takes an hour to prepare, so it's best to phone ahead.

Loto Verde, Cra 24, No 13-79. Formerly known as Govinda's, this Hare Krishna-run café serves up vegetarian lunches for US$2.

Parrilla Chipichape, C 18, No 27-88, T7291684. This is one of Pasto's most popular restaurants, renowned for its barbecued steaks and pork steamed in aluminium foil. On Sun it serves *ajiaco santafereño* and *sancocho de pollo*.

Picantería Ipiales, C 19, No 23-37, T7230393. Despite its modern decor this restaurant specializes in typical food from Nariño, specifically pork-based dishes such as *lapigancho*. *Almuerzos* cost US$2.80.

Ipiales *p326*

Mi Casita, C 9, No 6-12, T7732754. A local favourite, this canteen-style restaurant serves up typical Colombian specialities such as *mondongo* and several variations of *bandeja*.

Rancho Grande, Cra 7, No 14-51, T7732665. With an interior built primarily in bamboo, Rancho Grande is an agreeable place to enjoy steaks, chicken, seafood and fast food.

Entertainment

Pasto *p320, map p321*
Teatro Agustín Aqualongo, C 16/Cra 16.

Festivals and events

Pasto *p320, map p321*
Christmas to 6 Jan New Year fiesta, with parades and general festivities.
4 Jan Parades commemorate the **Llegada de la Familia Castañeda**. Apparently this

peasant family, full of characters, came from El Encanio to Pasto in 1928. They are recreated in the parades.
5 Jan Día de los Negros. People dump their hands in black grease and smear each other's faces (nice!)
6 Jan Día de los Blancos. People throw talc or flour at each other. Local people wear their oldest clothes.
28 Dec and **5 Feb** Fiesta de las Aguas, when anything that moves gets drenched with water from balconies and even from fire engines' hoses. All towns in the region are involved in this legalized water war.
31 Dec Concurso de Años Viejos, in Pasto and also in Ipiales, when huge dolls are burnt. They represent the old year and sometimes lampoon local people – which must be especially insulting here!

Shopping

Pasto *p320, map p321*
Leather goods shops are on C 17 and 18. Try the municipal market for handicrafts.
Artesanía-Mercado Bomboná, C 14 y Cra 27.
Artesanías Mopa-Mopa, Cra 25, No 13-14, for *barniz*.
Artesanías Nariño, C 26, No 18-91.
Casa del Barniz de Pasto, C 13, No 24-9.
Instituto Geográfico Agustín Codazzi, in the Banco de la República building, C 18A, No 21A-18. Maps of Colombia and cities, limited selection.
Ley on C 18, next to **Avianca** postal office. On the main plaza (C 19 y Cra 25) is a shopping centre with many shops and restaurants.
Los Dos Puentes, Cra 24 with C 21. A campesino market selling fruit, vegetables and flowers.

Activities and tours

Pasto *p320, map p321*
Every Sun a game of paddle ball is played across the border on the edge of the town

(bus marked San Lorenzo) similar to that played across the border in Ibarra, Ecuador. **Emproturn**, C 19, No 31B-44, T7310975, emproturn@gmail.com. Organizes tours in and around Pasto. Can arrange private transport from Cali.

⊖ Transport

Pasto p320, map p321
Air
To **Bogotá**, 3 flights daily, 1 hr 55 mins, with Avianca and Satena. To **Cali**, 2 flights daily, 50 mins, Avianca.
   Airline offices Avianca, CC Galerías, local 214, T7232320 or at the airport. Satena, Cosmocentro 2000, C 19, No 27-05, local 208, T7290442.

Bus
To Bogotá, 18 hrs, US$43 (Bolivariano Pullman), 10 a day. To **Ipiales**, Cooperativo Supertaxis del Sur US$3, 2 hrs, frequent; by bus, US$2.70, sit on left hand side for the views. To **Popayán**, ordinary buses take 10-12 hrs, US$8; expresses take 5-8 hrs, cost US$13. To **Cali**, US$16, expresses, 8½-10 hrs. To **Bucaramanga**, 27 hrs, US$65, To **Medellín**, 18 hrs, US$42. To **Mocoa**, 8 hrs, US$7.25.

Ipiales p326
Air
To **Bogotá**, **Medellín** and **Puerto Asis** with Satena. San Luis airport is 6.5 km out of town. Taxi to centre US$4.

Bus
To **Popayán**, Expreso Bolivariano, Transipiales or Cootranar, US$15.50, 7½ hrs, hourly departures, 0430-2030, sit in the right-hand side for best views. Bus to **Cali**, US$19.50, 10-12 hrs. To **Pasto**, every hr, US$2.70, 1½ hrs. Buses to **Bogotá** leave every hr from 0500, 24 hrs, US$47 To **Medellín**, Expreso Bolivariano, 22 hrs, US$43.

ⓘ Directory

Pasto p320, map p321
Banks For changing TCs, BanColombia, C 19, No 24-52. Banco de Bogotá, C 19, No 24-68 will change TCs 0930-1130. If going to Tumaco, this is the last place where TCs can be cashed. Davivienda, CC el Liceo, C 17, No 25-12, gives largest advances on Visa. Casas de cambio, at Cra 25, No 18-97, and C 19, No 24-86, by the main plaza, changes US dollars into local currency. Western Union, CC El Liceo, Cra 26, No 17-12, Local 128.
Immigration DAS: C 17, No 29-70, will give exit stamps if you are going on to Ecuador.
Internet Pc-Rent, Pasaje Corazón de Jesús, C 18, No 25-36. **Medical services** Cruz Roja (Red Cross), Cra 25, no 13-26. **Post office** Correos de Colombia, C 15 betw. Cra 23 and Cra 24. **Telecom** Long-distance calls, C 17 y Cra 23.

Ipiales p326
Banks It is not possible to cash Tcs, but cash is no problem; Bancolombia, cash against Visa. Casa de Cambio at Cra 6, No 14-09, other *cambios* on the plaza. There are money changers in the street, in the plaza and on the border, but they may take advantage of you if the banks are closed. Coming from Ecuador, peso rates compare well in Ipiales with elsewhere in Colombia. **Telephone** International calls from Cra 6 between C 6/7, opposite Banco de Occidente.

Contents

334 Los Llanos
    334 Villavicencio
    335 Around Villavicencio
    336 Listings

338 Amazonia
    338 Leticia and around
    341 Amacayacú National
         Park
    341 Puerto Nariño
    342 Up the Río Yavarí
    343 Listings

Footprint features

332 Don't miss ...
335 Cowboy culture
340 Amazon forest
342 Kapax – tarzan of the Amazon

Border crossings

Colombia–Brazil and Peru
339 Leticia–Tabatinga and
      Santa Rosa

Los Llanos & Amazonia

At a glance

⊖ **Getting around** Walking or taxi in Leticia; river taxi to destinations on the Amazon. Buses or private car to explore Los Llanos.
⊛ **Time required** 1-2 weeks.
☼ **Weather** Very hot all year round; driest between Jun and Aug in Amazonas.
⊗ **When not to go** Good all year.

VENEZUELA

Cúcuta
Villa Rosario
Pamplona
Puerto
Wilches
Bucaramanga
Chitaga
Rio Arauca
Arauca
Barrancabermeja
San Gil
Parque Nacional Tamá
Sierra Nevada
del Cocuy
ARAUCA
Rio Casanare
SANTANDER
Tame
Barbosa
BOYACA
Dultama
Sogamoso
Rio Meta
Puerto
Carreño
Chiquinquirá
Pore
El Pretexto
Casuarito
Tunja
Yopal
CASANARE
Trinidad
La Primavera
Rio Tomo
Nemocón
Orocué
Santa Rita
BOGOTA
Parque Nacional Chingaza
San Pedro
de Arimena
VICHADA
Rio Tuparro
Rio Vichada
Restrepp
Cumaral
San Miguel
1 Puerto Gaitán
Villavicencio
Acacias
Puerto
López
Guamal
2
Parque Nacional Sumapaz
META
Rio Guaviare
Puerto
Inírida
3 Granada
Mesetas
San Juan
de Arama
Rio Infreda
Vista Hermosa
GUAINIA
Parque Nacional
Natural Serranía
de la Macarena
San José del
Guaviare
Rio Guainia
La Macarena
Calamar
Rio Vaupes
VAUPES
Bocas de
Casiquiare
GUAVIARE
Rio Apaporis
Mitú
CAQUETA
Rio Mesay
Rio Caquetá
Araracuara
Puerto
Santander
Rio
Caquetá
AMAZONAS
La Chorrera
Rio Igara Parana
Rio Cahuinari
San Rafael
El Encanto
Bocas de
Cahuinari
BRAZIL
Rio Putumayo
PERU
Tarapaca
Parque
Nacional
Amacayacú
Puerto Nariño **4**
6 5
Rio Amazonas
Leticia
7
Rio Yavari

★ **Don't miss ...**

1 Sunset over the savannah plains, page 334.
2 Learning about *llanero* life on a *hacienda*, page 335.
3 Whitewater rafting down the Río Ariari, page 337.
4 Seeing the world's smallest monkey, page 339.
5 Caiman and pink river-dolphin spotting, page 341.
6 Visiting the Tikuna tribe, page 341.
7 Río Yavarí's private nature reserves, pages 342 and 343.

N

100 km
100 miles

A look at a map of Colombia reveals that an immense area east of Bogotá, with barely a town or road to be seen, makes up more than a quarter of the country's land mass. This is the Llanos, vast tracts of fertile cattle plains that stretch from the edge of the Department of Boyacá almost as far as the Amazon river and from the mountains of Bogotá as far as Venezuela (and beyond). Yet this region contains just a fraction of Colombia's population and much of the area is inaccessible by road. The Llanos' isolation has provided effective and convenient cover for guerrillas and cocaine-production factories and it is here that the war with armed groups such as the FARC continues. But impressive gains by the government in the last few years have made some of this cowboy country safe to visit again, particularly Villavicencio and its immediate surroundings.

Further south, the grassy pastures make way for seemingly infinite hectares of pristine jungle, accessible only by boat or plane. The city of Leticia sits on the Amazon river and forms a three-pronged frontier with Brazil and Peru. This is the gateway to the Colombian Amazon and national parks such as Amacayacú and the impressively neat village of Puerto Nariño will give travellers the opportunity to observe some of this majestic river's wildlife at close range. Even better is a quick excursion to the Yavarí river in Brazil, whose private nature reserves provide excellent facilities for birdwatching, sports fishing and dolphin and caiman spotting.

Los Llanos

The vast plains that unfurl eastwards towards Venezuela like a green carpet from the mountainous folds of central Colombia make up almost a quarter of the country. These are the Llanos, comprising the departments of Arauca, Casanare, Vichada, Guainia, Meta, Vaupes and Guaviare – a land of cattle ranches, cowboys, música llanera, and spectacular sunsets. For many years this area has been at the heart of the guerrilla war and a centre of drug production. Much of it still is, but certain parts are beginning to open up thanks to increased security. In particular, Villavicencio and its immediate surroundings are safe and many Colombians take their holidays on the numerous cattle fincas that have been converted into very comfortable rental homes. With the construction of a new tunnel down the mountain from Bogotá, 'Villavo', as the locals call it, is a convenient 1½-hour drive from the capital.

The people are warm and hospitable, great horsemen with a touch of the Wild West. Once you hear the music of the llaneros, you will never forget it. ▸▸ *For listings, see pages 336-337.*

Ins and outs

If driving, plenty of reserve gasoline should be carried as there are few service stations. Also take food and plenty of water. Fishing tackle could be useful. Everybody lets you hang up your hammock or pitch your tent, but mosquito nets are a must. Roads are only tracks left by previous vehicles but are easy from late December till early April and the very devil during the rest of the year. More information on the *llanos* can be obtained from the office of the **Gobernación del Departamento de Meta** ① *C 34/Cra 14, Bogotá*. We recommend you take good advice from reliable sources before driving around the Llanos independently.

Villavicencio ●●❷❀❂▲❸❸ ▸▸ *pp336-337. Colour map 4, A1.*

→ *Phone code: 8. Population: 384,000 Altitude: 498 m.*

Locally shortened to Villavo (Vee-a-bo), Villavicencio is the capital of Meta Department. This is where *llaneros* come to stock up on provisions and blow off a little steam in the city's bars and clubs. Founded in 1840 by Esteban Aguirre, it was originally a staging post and market for the ranching activities of the Llanos, conveniently on the way to Bogotá. Villavicencio is a good centre for visiting the *llanos* stretching 800 km east as far as Puerto Carreño and Puerto Inírida on the Orinoco. Cattle raising is the great industry on the plains, sparsely inhabited mostly by *mestizos*.

Ins and outs

A spectacular 110-km road runs south east from Bogotá to Villavicencio, at the foot of the eastern slopes of the Eastern Cordillera. A tunnel has reduced the journey by road from Bogotá to 1½ hours. The airport, **La Vanguardia**, is 4 km northwest of the town. The **bus station** is outside town on the ring road to the east, on Avenida del Llano. A taxi costs US$2.

Tourist information

Instituto de Turismo del Meta ① *Cra 33, No 40-24, Edif Comité de Ganaderos, T6716666, www.turismometa.gov.co.* Contact **William Restrepo** ① *T3107663637*, who can organize guides and activities in the immediate vicinity of Villavicencio.

Cowboy culture

Llaneros have a distinct culture, worlds apart from the rest of Colombia. In fact, they share far more in common with their fellow ranchers across the border in the Venezuelan Llanos.

The first cowboys in the Americas – they preceded the gauchos of the Argentine *pampas* and the cattle herders of North America – they are predominantly a mixture of indigenous and Spanish heritage. They are known for their hardiness, appearing impervious to heat and cold and often riding their horses barefoot. They live an isolated life on these vast savannahs, tending their cows and returning to the few cities only for provisions and a spot of drinking.

They played an important part in the South American war of independence, initially siding with the Spanish, who exploited their distrust of the aristocratic *criollos*, until Simón Bolívar, recognizing their value as skilled horsemen, went to live among them and won them over.

They nicknamed him *culo de hierro*, or 'iron buttocks' for his feats of endurance in the saddle.

Today *llanero* culture is known for its distinctive music whose main instruments are the harp, maracas and a small guitar called a *cuatro*. The *joropo*, a *llanero* dance, has become the national dance of Venezuela, and of the Llanos of Colombia, and is celebrated during festivals such as the Torneo Internacional del Joropo in Villavicencio in late June/July.

Most important are the cattle. There are an estimated 12 million cows on the Llanos of Colombia and Venezuela, spread out over an area of 451,474 sq km. *Llaneros* are proud of their cattle-herding skills and there are annual tournaments that test their prowess at *coleo*, a kind of rodeo in which cowboys on horseback attempt to fell cattle by grabbing their tails and twisting them until they tumble. Villavicencio hosts the Encuentro Mundial de Coleo each October.

Sights

There is an attractive central plaza, **Parque de Los Libertadores** (also called Parque Santander), with many ancient *ceibas* and busts of Francisco Santander and Simón Bolívar. The cathedral of **Nuestra Señora del Carmen**, built in the middle of the 19th century, overlooks the plaza. A good place to see the city is from the **Monumento a Cristo Rey**, off Calle 40 to the southwest of the city. In the same direction, on the road to Acacias, is the **Monumento a Los Fundadores**, a sculpture by Rodrigo Arenas Betancur. There is a **botanical garden** 2 km from the centre.

Around Villavicencio

From Villavicencio, three roads run further into the Llanos. To the north is a popular route known as the Ruta del Piedemonte Llanero and on the road there are parks, indigenous communities and hot springs to visit.

Around 3 km northeast Villavicencio on the road to Restrepo is the **Bioparque Los Ocarros** ① *Km 3 via Restrepo, T6648490, www.bioparquelosocarros.com, US$4.70, children US$3.70*, a 5.5-ha thematic park set around lakes and forests with nearly 200 species endemic to the Llanos. The park runs educational talks and workshops.

Two kilometres beyond the park is the **Centro Cultural Etno Turístico El Maguare** ① *Km 5 vía Restrepo, Vereda La Poyata, T6648464, www.etniasvivas.org, US$2.20*, a community project set up and managed by the Uitoto. The community puts on ancestral dances in a traditional *maloca* as well as talks about the state of Colombia's indigenous people and workshops in how to use some of their traditional tools and weapons. Some of the proceeds go towards supporting displaced and marginalized indigenous groups.

Further along the road is the pleasant town of **Restrepo**, famous for its salt mines and its pretty church. Beyond is **Cumaral** which has palm tree plantations and is known as the best place to eat meat in the Llanos. A few kilometres north of Cumaral, near Barranca de Upía, is the **Reserva Natural Aguas Calientes**, which has a natural pool set in exuberant forest.

Running south from Villavicencio, the Ruta del Embrujo Llanero passes through **Acacías, Guamal** and **San Martín**, a cattle town. To the west of Guamal is the **Río Ariari** and **Cubarral**, which are inside the Parque Nacional Natural Sumapaz and where adventure sports such as whitewater rafting, paragliding and abseiling can be practised, as well as *balsaje* (floating downriver on bamboo rafts). The road eventually leads to **San Juan de Arama**, gateway to the Parque Nacional Natural Serranía de la Macarena, an enormous rock similar to the *tepuis* of Venezuela. The Caño Cristales river runs through the park, which depending on the time of year and the amount of algae found in its waters, gives the river an incredible technicolour sheen. **Note** Currently the park should be considered strictly off limits as it is still under FARC control. Take careful advice before going there.

The road east from Villavicencio, known as the Amanecer Llanero, passes through the Apiay oil field before reaching **Puerto López** on the Río Meta. A few kilometres beyond Puerto López is the 21-m-high El Obelisco at Alto Menegua, built to mark the geographic centre of Colombia. This colourful monument, built in 1993, displays elements of local prehistory, cultural heritage and a relief map of Colombia. From here there are wonderful views of the Llanos. A further 150 km east is **Puerto Gaitán**, where there are good views and excellent sunsets to be seen from the bridge across the Río Manacacías. Nearby it joins the Río Meta where there are some beautiful white-sand beaches.

◉ Los Llanos listings → Phone code: 8.

For Sleeping and Eating price codes and other relevant information, see pages 31-36.

● Sleeping

Villavicencio *p334*
AL Don Lolo, Cra 39, No 20-32, T6706020, www.donlolohotel.com. Like the **Gloria**, this hotel is no beauty. Rooms have cable TV, Wi-Fi, a/c, minibar and room service but are a little frayed round the edges. Restaurant and pool.
AL Hotel del Llano, Cra 30, No 49-77, T6717000, hotellan@etell.net.co. Tucked under the forested hills of the Cordillera Oriental, this is Villavo's smartest option with good rooms and a host of extras such as a spa, sauna, pool, restaurant, tour agency and Wi-Fi throughout.

AL María Gloria, Cra 38, No 20-26, T6720197. In an ugly building, with a good pool area with sauna and Turkish bath. Rooms feel a bit antiquated but have services such as a/c, flat-screen TV and Wi-Fi. Includes breakfast.
B Savoy, C 41, No 31-02, T6625007. Clean, simple rooms with a/c, cable TV and en suite bathrooms. Vegetarian restaurant downstairs.
C San Jorge Llanos, C 38, No 31-21, T6621682, hotelsanjorgellanollano@telecom.com.co. Good, with clean rooms, a/c and cable TV.
C Hotel de Oriente, C 38A, No 29A-43, T6626391. Good, large rooms, minibar, room service and en suite bathrooms, with fan instead of a/c is cheaper. Good security.
D Delfín Rosado, C 35, No 23-15, T6626896. The rooms may open up off dark corridors but

they are comfortable with fan, cable TV and a restaurant serving decent breakfasts.

E El Caporal, C 39, No 33-35, T6624011. Clean, simple rooms in a small hotel 1 block from the Parque Principal.

E Granja Los Girasoles, Barrio Chapinerito, T6642712. Youth hostel, 160 beds, 3 km from bus station.

E Turista del Llano, C 38, No 30A-42, T6626207. Rooms are a bit musty but it's in the centre of town, with cable TV, private bathrooms and towels and soap provided.

One of the best ways to get to know the Llanos is to stay on one of the cattle ranches available for hire. **Fincas y Eventos**, C 47 Bis, No 28-09, T3102856641 (mob), www.fincasy eventos.com, has over 90 homesteads.

🍴 Eating

Villavicencio *p334*

🍴 **Chop Suey**, C 38, No 30A-44, T6626852. Popular Chinese restaurant.

🍴 **Asadero La Llanerita**, C 35, No 27-16, T6623001. Slow-roasted meats cooked on a open barbecue, including *falda de Costilla*.

🍴 **Fonda Quindiana**, Cra 32, No 40-40, T662 6857. One of Villavo's oldest restaurants, with a great atmosphere. Typical dishes such as *frijoles* and *lengua en salsa* as well as *parrillas*.

🍴 **La Posada del Arriero**, C 41, No 30-08, T6641319. This restaurant serves typical dishes such as *mondongo* and *frijolada* as well as fish, chicken and steak, on a pleasant terrace painted orange and green.

🍴 **Toy-Wan**, C 40A, No 28-69, T6641758. Smart oriental restaurant, does spring rolls and stir fries.

🎉 Festivals and events

Villavicencio *p334*

Jun-Jul Torneo Internacional del Joropo, involving parades, singers and over 3000 couples dancing the *joropo* in the street.
Mid-Oct Encuentro Mundial de Coleo. *Coleo* is a sport similar to rodeo in which cowboys

tumble young calves by grabbing their tails and twisting them until they lose their balance.

🛍 Shopping

Villavicencio *p334*
Almacenes Ley, C 37, No 29-83 is a good place to stock up with provisions.

🎯 Activities and tours

Villavicencio *p334*
Tour operators
Vergel Tours, Cra 30, No 49-77 (in Hotel del Llano), T6825353, www.vergelaventura.com. Runs adventure-sport activities, including whitewater rafting, paragliding, horse riding and visits to hot springs. Recommended.

🚌 Transport

Villavicencio *p334*
Air
To **Bogotá**, Aires 2 a day, Satena 1-2 a day. To **Puerto Carreño**, Satena 5 a week. To **Medellín**, Satena 2 a week. Satena also flies to a number of other destinations in Los Llanos.

Bus
To Bogotá, *colectivos* and mini vans leave 20 times a day from 0400-2000, US$12, 1½ hrs.

🛈 Directory

Villavicencio *p334*
Banks Bancolombia and other banks near the Plaza. Most have ATMs. **Internet/phone** CS&S Consultores, C 38, No 33-13. Internet and international calls. Ibérica, Cra 32, No 39-40. Skype, headphones and stationery. **Media** Llanos 7 Días, a good weekly source of local information. **Police** T112 or T6625000. **Post office** Adpostal, C 39/Cra 32.

Amazonia

The Colombian Amazon forms part of the largest ecosystem on the planet. More than one third of all the species in the world live in the Amazon rainforest, a giant tropical forest and river basin with an area that stretches more than 5,400,000 sq km. Its lifeline is the Amazon river, the largest river in the world that begins its journey in the Andes of Peru and Ecuador and flows for over 6000 km across almost the entire width of the continent before reaching the Atlantic in Brazil. By the time it passes Leticia, capital of Colombian Amazonas, it is already well into its stride, and this section of the Amazon provides plenty of opportunities for nature lovers to observe its flora and fauna up close. From Leticia, vast swathes of forest run northwards with little human activity to interrupt their quiet splendour. There are no roads and indigenous communities live off the fishing and transport provided by tributaries that feed into the Amazon. ▸▸ *For listings, see pages 343-346.*

Leticia and around ⊜❼❻▲⊕❶ ▸▸ *pp343-346. Colour map 4, C2.*

→ *Phone code: 8. Population: 35,000.*

Leticia is a port town on the Amazon that shares a border with both Brazil and Peru. The city is clean, modern and safe, though rundown near the river. It is rapidly merging into one town with neighbouring **Tabatinga** in Brazil (for day visits to Tabatinga there's no need to pass through immigration). The best time to visit the area is from June to August, the early months of the dry season. The river is at its highest level in May, lowest in September. At weekends, accommodation may be difficult to find. Leticia is a good place to buy typical indigenous Amazonian products, and tourist services are better than in Tabatinga or Benjamin Constant.

Ins and outs

The airport is 1.5 km from town, taxi US$2; small terminal, few facilities. Expect to be searched before leaving Leticia airport, and on arrival in Bogotá from Leticia.

There is an obligatory US$7 environment tax payable on arrival in Leticia. You may also be asked for a yellow fever certificate. If you do not have one, you may have an inoculation administered on the spot (not recommended). ▸▸ *For border crossings, see box, page 339.*

Leticia

To Airport & Tarapaca
Stadium
To Iquitos (Peru)
Rio Amazonas
MA
Brazilian Consulate
Parque Santander
Banco de la República Museum
DAS
C 12
C 11
C 10
C 9
Almacen Uirapuru
To Manaos (Brazil)
Peruvian Consulate
Productos Naturales del Trapecio Amazonico
C 8
C 6
Cra 11
Cra 10
Cra 9
Cra 8
Cra 7
Cra 6
Cra 5

BRAZIL
To Marco & Tabatinga

N

200 metres
200 yards

Sleeping ⊜
Amira 1
Decalodge Ticuna 2
Fernando Real 3
La Frontera 4
Los Delfines 5
Mahuta Guesthouse 6
Mochileros 7
Yurupary 8

Eating ❼
Amazon Sazón 9
El Sabor 10
Tierras Amazónicas 11
Tierras Antioqueñas 12

Border essentials: Colombia–Brazil and Peru

Leticia–Tabatinga (Brazil) and Santa Rosa (Peru)

Colombian immigration DAS, Calle 9, No 8-32, T27189, Leticia, and at the airport. Exit stamps to leave Colombia by air or overland are given only at the airport. If flying into Leticia prior to leaving for Brazil or Peru, get an exit stamp while at the airport.

To enter Colombia you must have a tourist card to obtain an entry stamp, even if you are passing through Leticia en route between Brazil and Peru (the Colombian consul in **Manaus** may tell you otherwise; try to get a tourist card elsewhere). The Colombian consular office in Tabatinga issues tourist cards. Transit stamps can be obtained 24 hours at the DAS office. If visiting Leticia without intending to go anywhere else in Colombia, you may be allowed to enter without immigration or customs formalities (but TCs cannot be changed without an entry stamp). There are no customs formalities for everyday travel between Leticia and Tabatinga.

Brazilian immigration If visiting Brazil beyond Tabatinga you should pass through immigration. Exiting Colombia, get your passport stamped at the airport. Brazilian immigration is in Tabatinga on the main throroughfare from Leticia, open 0800-1200, 1400-1700.

Entry and exit stamps are given at the **Polícia Federal,** 10 minutes' walk from the Tabatinga docks, opposite **Café dos Navegantes** (walk through docks and follow road to its end, turn right at this T-junction for one block to the white building). If coming from Leticia, it is one block from the hospital on the road to Leticia. The office is open Mon-Fri 0800-1200, 1400-1800; also at airport, open Wed and Sat only. Proof of US$500 or onward ticket may be asked for. There are no facilities in Benjamin Constant although it is possible to buy supplies for boat journeys. One-week transit in Tabatinga is permitted.

In this frontier area, carry your passport at all times. If coming from Peru, you must have a Peruvian exit stamp and a yellow fever certificate.

Peruvian immigration Entry/exit formalities take place at Santa Rosa. Every boat leaving Peru stops here. There is also an immigration office in **Iquitos** (Malecón Tarapacá 382) where procedures for leaving can be checked.

For information, contact the **tourist office** ① *C 10, No 9-86. The World View of the Tukano Amazonian Indians* (Gerardo Reichel Dolmatoff, UK 1996) is a good account of local ecology and cultures of the northwest Amazon.

Sights

There's precious little in the way of sights around town, but the **Banco de la República** ① *Cra 11 y C 9,* has a museum that covers local ethnography and archaeology, housed in a beautiful building with various workshops and talks as well as a library and a terrace overlooking the Amazon.

Around Leticia

On **Monkey Island (La Isla de los Micos)** visits can be made to indigenous Yagua and Ticuna. There are not many monkeys on the island now, those left are semi-tame.

Amazon forest

It may all look the same from above as you fly into Leticia but the Amazon has three types of tropical forest, each with distinct ecosystems.

Terra firme, which is dry all year round and characterized by an abundance of tropical hardwoods, is where you are most likely to see large mammals. **Varzea** is flooded for half the year and contains less mammals but an abundance of birds. **Igapo** is always flooded and grows to a height of 3 m. This is where you are likely to see reptiles such as anacondas, caimans, boa constrictors and large fish. The area immediately around Leticia is characterized by varzea and igapo, while for terra firme you will have to venture inland from the river or into Brazil or Peru.

Agencies run overnight tours with full board. The price depends on the number of people in the group. If you choose to go on an organized tour, do not accept the first price and check that the equipment and supplies are sufficient for the length of the tour.

On night excursions to look for caiman, the boat should have powerful halogen lamps. You can swim in the Amazon and its tributaries, but do not dive; this disturbs the fish. Do not swim at sunrise or sunset when the fish are more active, nor when the water is shallow in dry season, nor if you have a wound that may open up and bleed. Take water-purification tablets since almost all the water here is taken from the river.

Around Leticia

Amacayacú National Park ◉ ►► pp343-346. Colour map 4, C2.

Some 60 km up the Amazon, at the mouth of the Matamatá Creek, is the entrance to the Parque Nacional Natural Amacayacú, which is 100 km from north to south and a total of nearly 300,000 ha. It is bounded by several rivers flowing into the Putumayo and Amazon systems. At one point it touches the border with Peru. It is claimed that there are over 500 species of bird to be seen in the park, and 150 or so species of mammal, including pink dolphin, *danta* and *manatí*. The smallest monkey in the world, *titi leoncito* (*Cebuella pygmaea*) may also be seen.

Ins and outs

Boat from Leticia is US$10.50 one way, 1½-two hours; with **Tres Fronteras** (if you buy a return check that your operator runs the day you wish to return). Buy your ticket early to secure a seat. Boats leave at 1000 and 1400 and go on to Puerto Nariño.

The park entrance is 60 km upstream, at the mouth of the Matamata Creek, two hours from Leticia. It is open 0700-1700; day visits cost US$10 for foreigners.

Sights

There is a jungle walk to a lookout (guides will point out plants, including those to avoid) and a rope bridge over the forest canopy, with wonderful views over the surrounding jungle (US$25). There are various other guided day treks through the jungle. Boats go to a nearby island to see Victoria Regia water lilies. The park's main problem is that for much of the year it is flooded, thus restricting the mount of activities that can be done.

Puerto Nariño ◉◉▲◉◉ ►► pp343-346. Colour map 4, C2.

→ *Phone code: 8.*

The Colombian Amazon's second largest settlement after Leticia, this little riverside village has banned all motorized traffic. As a result, it's a tranquil place, its streets no more than pathways, immaculately swept and lined with flowers and herbaceous borders, while most of its houses are brightly painted with carefully tended gardens. There's also an emphasis on good environmental practice; Puerto Nariño has plans to become Colombia's first environmentally sustainable town.

Sights

Just beyond the village is **Lago de Tarapoto**, a popular place for seeing pink river dolphins and caimans. Excursions in a *peque peque* (motorized canoe) cost about US$27-44 per person. Another, less well-known excursion is to Lago San Juan del Socó, a smaller lake but with a better chance of seeing wildlife than to Tarapoto's increasing popularity. Enquire at Malocas Napü; Ask for Lorena, T3134831958.

There are also guided walks to various indigenous communities such as **San Martín de Amacayacú**, home to the Tikuna tribe who will talk about their customs. The Tikuna have also built a fine viewing tower in the village for wildlife spotting, US$2.70.

In Puerto Nariño, be sure to visit **Fundación Natutama** ① *www.natutama.org, Mon-Fri (except Tues) 0800-1200, 1400-1700, free but contributions appreciated*. Natutama works to preserve the marine life of this part of the Amazon by organizing educational programs with local communities. At their visitor centre by the river there's an informative display of underwater life on the Amazon with life-size models of the various fish and reptiles,

Kapax – tarzan of the Amazon

In 1976, Alberto Lesmes Rojas, also known as Kapax, swam almost the entire length of the mighty Magdalean river. He swam from Neiva to Barranquilla, a distance of 1270 km. It took him one month and seven days and astonished his fellow Colombians and the rest of the world. His aim was to bring to the world's attention the fragility of this incredible ecosystem.

Kapax, born of a German father and indigenous mother in the town of Puerto Leguízamo in Putumayo, who has lived in Leticia for more than 30 years, has always felt an affinity with nature and his feats of endurance and knowledge of the tropical forest have earned him the nickname 'Tarzan of the Amazon'.

He now works as a guide for the Government of the Amazon, and he can often be seen at the Decalodge Ticuna hotel with his pet anaconda Cantalicia wrapped around his neck.

He hasn't given up on campaigning though. In 2001 he swam 120 km up the Amazon to Leticia from the Peruvian border and in 2004 he made the journey from Puerto Nariño to Leticia. Now over 60 years old, he plans to repeat the feat if he can find a patron to sponsor him.

---

as well as videos. This is a good way to inform yourself about the Amazon's ecosystems before venturing out to see it in person.

Up the Río Yavarí

West of Benjamin Constant, one of the Amazon's main tributaries, the Río Yavarí, forms the border between Peru and Brazil. This is one of the best places to observe wildlife on this section of the Amazon. There are several privately owned reserves here, with comfortable accommodation and excellent facilities for birdwatching, and dolphin and caiman spotting.

Ins and outs

There are no public river transport services up the Yavarí. **Palmarí** can organize private transport from Leticia, including transfer from the airport and stops at immigration to get your passport stamped. Alternatively, it is possible to make your own way there by catching a river taxi from Tabatinga to Benjamin Constant, 15 minutes, US$8, followed by a *colectivo* on the road to Atalaia do Norte, 40 minutes, US$5.50, where the reserve will arrange a pick-up for the final hour's journey by boat, US$25. This is quicker and cheaper than making the whole journey by boat, but less scenic.

Reserva Natural Palmarí

ⓘ *T4827148 (Bogotá), www.palmari.org, US$70 per person, includes all food and alcohol, activities (except jungle walks greater than 24 hrs, sport fishing and canopy), and Wi-Fi and internet access. Transport from Leticia not included.*

On a raised bank looking out over the Javarí river, this jungle lodge has been designed to maximize the visitor's chances of seeing as many types of flora and fauna as possible, thanks to the reserve's access to all three types of Amazon forest within a 10-minute walk.

Accommodation is in simple cabins or a large communal *maloca*, connected by wooden gangways, while there's a viewing platform for observing river dolphins and the many birds and monkeys that inhabit the primary forest immediately behind. The reserve has over 20 guides, employed from local communities, and equipment for bird watching, fishing (over 20 species of gamefish, including peacock bass and *arawana*) and kayaking. Within its 40 ha there are canopy platforms and natural pools for swimming and fishing.

With jungle walks ranging from one to 72 hours, this is one of the best places in the area to observe the Amazon's wildlife up close.

Colombian-German owner Axel Antoine-Feill has set up an organisation, the **Instituto de Desenvolvimiento Socioambiental do Vale do Javarí** ① *www.idsavj.org*, to work with local indigenous communities. All employees of the reserve come from five settlements close by and some of Palmari's profits are invested back into these communities. The reserve takes a strong stance on responsible environmental practice, with non-eco-friendly shampoos and soaps banned during the visitor's stay (the reserve provides its own approved brands).

Reserva Natural Heliconia

① *T5925773 (Leticia), www.amazonheliconia.com, US$280 per person (based on 2 people), including transport from Leticia and all food and activities (except canopy and massage treatments).*

Up a small tributary of the Yavarí, about an hour by *peque peque* from Palmari, this jungle lodge is about as isolated as you can get. It has several very comfortable *cabañas* (with bathrooms open to the forest behind) set around a jungle garden abounding in heliconia plants. The reserve organizes night-time caiman-spotting excursions as well as trips to visit local indigenous communities such as Santa Rita in nearby Peru. The forest behind provides opportunities for excellent walks, including a visit to an enormous ceiba tree, while there are special birdwatching and fishing tours.

◉ Amazonia listings

For Sleeping and Eating price codes and other relevant information, see pages 31-36.

● Sleeping

Leticia *p338, map p338*
LL Decalodge Ticuna, Cra 11, No 6-11, T5926600, www.decameron.com. Leticia's smartest hotel, run by the hotel chain Decameron, has comfortable rooms. with a/c and cable TV and a large swimming pool but there have been reports of poor service. Can arrange stays in Amacayacu National Park and trips to Monkey Island, to which they hold concessions.
A Amira, C 9, No 9-69, T5927767. This modern hotel has clean, comfortable rooms with a/c (almost half-price with fan), cable TV and private bathrooms with hot water.
B Fernando Real, Cra 9, No 8-80, T5927362. This hotel has an intimate atmosphere

with rooms opening up onto a patio bursting with heliconias. The bathrooms are a little small.
B La Frontera, Cra 11, No 6-106, T5925111, paraisoecologico@hotmail.com. As the name suggests, it's right on the border, so while it could be a bit noisy it's convenient if you are heading to Brazil. The rooms are clean with crisp, white sheets.
B Yurupary, C 8, No 7-26, T5924743, www.hotelyurupary.com. A good mid-range option, the Yurupary has large rooms with private bathrooms and hot water as well as a lovely pool fringed with tropical plants. Also arranges tours into the Amazon.
D Los Delfines, Cra 11, No 12-85, T5927488, losdelfinesleticia@hotmail.com. This hotel has a lovely patio bursting with tropical plants and rooms with private bath, fan and Wi-Fi.
E Mahatu Guesthouse, Cra 7, No 9-69, T3115391265 (mob), www.mahatu.com.

Another backpackers' hostel, this one is more comfortable and better organized. It has one private room in a *maloca* in an overgrown garden out back and a couple of dorms with bunks, as well as a kitchen and bike hire. Owner Gustavo René Alvarado speaks English, Flemish, French and Portuguese and organizes alternative tours of the Amazon. At the time of writing he was thinking of moving to another address, so check his website before pitching up.

E Mochileros, Cra 5, No 9-117, T5925991. Basic hostel designed specifically for backpackers with bunks-only rooms and shared bathrooms. Organizes economical tours.

Tabatinga (Brazil)

Reais or pesos accepted. In Nov 2008 1 real = 982 pesos.

B Takana, Rua Osvaldo Cruz, 970, T974123557, takanahotel@hotmail.com. The lobby of this hotel is festooned with wooden figurines of Amazonian animals while the rooms are comfortable and clean with private bathrooms with hot water and a/c. Recommended.

C Vitoria Regia, Rua da Patria, 820, T9734122668. Basic rooms with cable TV and private bathrooms. Prices negotiable.

E Hotel Santiago, Rua Pedro Teixeira, 49, T9734124680. Very basic but large rooms with private bathrooms.

F Hotel Pajé, Rua Pedro Teixeira, No 367, T9734122774. Next to the Santiago, this hostel is a little cheaper and a little cleaner.

Amacayacú National Park *p341*

Accommodation is managed by **Aviatur**, C 7, No 10-78, T592 6814 in Leticia (helpful), for the park direct T592 5600. There's a choice of private (**AL**) *malocas* or (**A**) dormitories. The Leticia office will also give information and arrange transport to the park.

Puerto Nariño *p341*

B Casa Selva, Cra 6, No 6-78, T3115219297, www.casaselvahotel.com. Very comfortable hotel with a fresh, airy feel about it. Rooms are spotless and it has a fine viewing platform on the roof. Can organize trips to nearby Lago de Tarapoto.

D Lomas del Paiyü, T3132370840. Small but clean rooms opening up off a long corridor. Ventilation could be a problem.

D Malocas Napü, C 4, No 5-72, T3104880998, olgabeco@yahoo.com. This *maloca* has a couple of comfortable private rooms with fans as well as the cheaper option of hammocks. Staff are very helpful. Recommended.

E El Alto del Aguila, 20 mins' walk from the village or 5 mins by boat, Héctor, local school teacher/missionary has cabins, will arrange trips to indigenous communities and to see dolphins at Lago Tarapoto. He has pet monkeys, parrots, *gavilanes* and a pair of young caiman.

E Hospedaje Manguaré, C 4, No 5-52, T3112764873 (mob). This small hotel has comfortable cabin-style rooms with fans and shared bathrooms. Bunks in dorms are US$8 pp. It also doubles up as the town chemist.

🍴 Eating

Leticia *p338, map p338*

🍴 **Amazón Sazón**, Cra 9, No 7-56. Great little restaurant serving *comida corriente* as well as good-sized sandwiches, pizzas and hearty breakfasts.

🍴 **El Sabor**, C 8, No 9-25, T5924774. *Comidas corrientes* in several price brackets. *Bandeja paisa*, pork and chicken on offer.

🍴 **Tierras Amazónicas**, C 8, No 7-50, T5924748. This restaurant has a good atmosphere, artisan decor and a varied menu of fish, chicken and steak dishes.

🍴 **Tierras Antioqueñas**, C 8, No 9-19. Good *almuerzos* of steak, chicken and *piracucu* fish (the largest freshwater fish in South America). *Bandeja paisa* is a speciality of the house.

Tabatinga (Brazil)

♦ **Tres Fronteras Do Amzonas**, Rua Rui Barbosa, Barrio San Francixe, T974122858. Excellent restaurant with dining in a series of *malocas*. The menu is a mix of Brazilian, Peruvian and Colombian.

♦ **Te Contei?**, Av da Amzide, 1813, Centro. Pay-by-the-kilo barbecued meats and salads from a buffet. By night they cook up excellent pizzas.

Puerto Nariño *p341*

There are 2 or 3 cheap restaurants near the waterfront, opposite the mini football pitch.

O Shopping

Leticia *p338, map p338*

Almacen Uirapuru, C 8, No 10-35, T5927056. Enormous shop selling handicrafts from the Amazon region. It also has a small museum at the back with free entry if you buy *artesanía*.

Productos Naturales del Trapecio Amazónico, C 8, No 9-87, CC Shopping Center, T5924796. This natural chemists is packed with powders and herbs gathered from the forest. Ethno-botanist José Raúl Cuéllar has been making treatments from the Amazon's plants for more than 30 years and sells them all over the world.

▲ Activities and tours

Leticia *p338, map p338*
Tour operators

SelvAventura, T3112871307 (mob), selvaventura@gmail.com. This small operator does something a little different from the norm, with tailor-made trips to the Río Tacana to meet indigenous communities, sleeping in *posadas* and opportunities for kayaking, caiman spotting and observation of the forest from canopy platforms. Prices start from US$80 per person. English, Portuguese and Spanish spoken.

Steve McAlear, T3133131106, stevemcalear@hotmail.com. Englishman Steve McAlear runs personalized tours to some of the area's more remote locations.

Puerto Nariño *p341*
Tour guides

Ever Sinarahua, **Clarindo López** and **Milciades Peña** are recommended for their local knowledge of flora and fauna and indigenous customs – enquire through Casa Selva. Also, **Pedro Nel Cuello** – enquire through **Fundación Natutama**, also recommended.

● Transport

Leticia *p338, map p338*

Air Satena (C 11, No 5-73, T5924845) and AeroRepública (C 7, No 10-36, T5927838) each fly to/from **Bogotá** (Tabatinga airport if Leticia's is closed) 1 a day. For good deals on Bogotá–Leticia flights we recommend the following agencies: Doble Vía, Cra 11, No 77-20, T2112754, good for AeroRepública; Vivir Volando, Cra 16, No 96-64, T6014676, www.vivirvolando.com, best for **Satena**.

Tabatinga (Brazil)

Taxi Between Leticia and Tabatinga costs US$5.50 (more if you want to stop at immigration offices or exchange houses). Beware of drivers who want to rush you (expensively) over the border before it 'closes'.

Colectivo US$0.80 (more after 1800). If you ask for the port, you will be dropped where there is transport to **Benjamin Constant** (for Brazil and upstream boats to Peru).

Manaus (Brazil)

Boat From Manaus to **Benjamin Constant**, boats normally go on to **Tabatinga**, and start from there when going to Manaus. Boats usually wait 1-2 days in both Tabatinga and Benjamin Constant before returning to

Manaus; you can stay on board. Tabatinga and Leticia are 15 mins from Benjamin Constant by river taxi, US$8.

From Tabatinga and Benjamin Constant boats take around 3 days to Manaus, and up to 8 days on the return trip up river.

Iquitos (Peru)
Boat Boats sail from Iquitos to a mud bank called **Islandia**, on the Peruvian side of a creek a short distance from **Benjamin Constant**. The journey time is a minimum of 2 days upstream, 8-36 hrs downstream, depending on the speed of the boat. Passengers leaving or entering Peru must visit immigration at Santa Rosa when the boat stops there. For entry into Brazil, formalities are done in Tabatinga; for Colombia, in Leticia. **Amazon Cruises and Adventures**, www.amazoncruise online.com, operates a service between Iquitos and **Tabatinga/Leticia**, US$795 per person, based on 2 people sharing, 3 nights in a 110-year-old Scottish-built river cruiser.

Puerto Nariño *p341*
Boat from **Leticia**, daily at 1000 and 1400 (check times as they often change), 2 hrs, US$14, with **Tres Fronteras**.

❻ Directory

Leticia *p338, map p338*
Banks Banco de Bogotá, will cash Tcs, has ATM on Cirrus network, good rates for Brazilian *reais*. There are street money changers, plenty of *cambios*, and banks for exchange. Shop around. **Internet Centel.net**, C 9, No 9-09. Skype and headphones as well as local and international calls. **Aloha.ne**t, C 11, No 7-22. Skype and headphones. **Post office** Adpostal, C8, No9-65, T5927977. **Telephone** Cra 11/C 9, near Parque Santander.

Puerto Nariño *p341*
Internet/telephone Internet and international calls (expensive) next to the school.

Contents

348 History

353 Modern Colombia
353 Recent history
355 The narcotics trade

356 Economy

358 Government

358 Education

359 Culture
359 Arts and crafts
361 Fine art and sculpture
365 Literature
368 Music and dance

370 People
371 Religion

371 Land and environment
371 Geology and landscape
375 Climate
376 Wildlife and vegetation
380 National parks

Footprint features

357 Colombian entrepreneurism
377 Flowers

Background

History

Pre-Columbian

Colombia was inhabited by various indigenous groups before the Spanish conquest. The most highly developed were the **Tayronas**, who had settlements along the Atlantic coast and on the slopes of the Sierra Nevada de Santa Marta. The Tayronas had a complex social organization, with an economy based on fishing, agriculture and commerce. They built paved roads, aqueducts, stone stairways and public plazas for ceremonies.

Another major group were the **Muisca**, a Chibcha-speaking people who dominated the central highlands of Colombia at the time of the conquest. Muisca and Chibcha can be considered the same language. Philologists identify the 'Chibchan' language to refer to a series of dialects extending from Nicaragua in Central America to Ecuador, almost all of which have now disappeared. Carbon dating places their earliest settlements at around BC 545. Their village confederation was ruled by the **Zipa** at Bogotá, and the **Zaque** at Hunza (now Tunja). The Zipas believed that they were descended from the Moon, and the Zaques from the Sun. Their livelihood came from trading at markets in corn, potatoes and beans. They were also accomplished goldsmiths, and traded emeralds, ceramics and textiles with other societies.

The **Sinú** had their chiefdoms in the present-day Department of Córdoba and parts of Antioquia and Sucre. They farmed yucca and maize on artificial mounds in the local marshlands with complex drainage systems to make the best use of high and low water levels. They also cultivated reeds used for textiles and basket-weaving, as well as working with gold. Much wealth was plundered from their tombs, known as 'guacas', by the Spaniards during the conquest.

The **Quimbayas** inhabited parts of the Valle del Cauca. They had a class system, and a society similar to that of the Muisca and Tayronas, except that some evidence suggests they practised ritual cannibalism.

'**Calima**' is a term used to classify the other indigenous groups living in the department of Valle del Cauca. They include the **Liles** (based near present-day Cali) and the **Gorrones** (based in the Cordillera Occidental). They were organized into small chiefdoms with economies based on fishing, hunting, beans, yucca and corn. They traded in gold, salt, textiles and slaves. Two other significant groups prospered in San Agustín and Tierradentro, in what is now the south of Colombia. Both left fascinating monuments but they had disappeared well before the conquest.

Spanish colonization

The first permanent settlement in Colombia was established in 1500-1507 by **Rodrigo de Bastidas** (1460-1526). He reached the country by sailing south along the Caribbean coast. After his return to Spain to face trial for insubordination, he was given permission to establish a colony. In 1525 he founded Santa Marta and named the river Magdalena. Cartagena was founded in 1533 by **Pedro de Heredia** and used as a central stockpile for the growing Spanish collection of treasure. Massive fortifications were built to protect it from pirate attacks. Santa Fe de Bogotá was founded by **Gonzalo Jiménez de Quesada** (1499-1579) in 1538. He arrived in Santa Marta in 1535 and continued up to the Sabana de Bogotá with his men: 200 made the trip by boat, 670 by land. **Sebastián de Belalcázar** (1495-1551), the lieutenant of Francisco Pizarro, was given instructions to explore southern Colombia and the Cauca Valley in 1535. He founded Cali and Popayán in 1536, and was made governor of Popayán in 1540. **Nicolás Federmann** (1506-1541), acting on behalf of the Welser financiers of Germany, led an expedition east to Coro and Cape Vela, then back to Barquisimeto and Meta. He arrived in the Sabana de Bogotá in 1538, where he met Belalcázar and Jiménez de Quesada.

Jiménez de Quesada named the territory he had conquered Nuevo Reino de Granada, because it reminded him of Granada in Spain. Santa Fe de Bogotá was named after the city of Santa Fe in Granada. The first secular government to be established after the conquest was the Audencia de Santa Fe de Bogotá, in 1550. After 1594, it shared ruling authority with the president of the New Kingdom of New Granada, the name given to the whole conquered area, which included Panama. The presidency was replaced in 1718 by a viceroyalty at Bogotá, which also controlled the provinces now known as Venezuela; it was independent of the viceroyalty of Peru, to which this vast area had previously been subject.

Independence from Spain

In 1793, a translation of the Rights of Man was published in Colombia by **Antonio Nariño** (1765-1823), an administrator and journalist, known as 'el Precursor' for his important role in the independence movement. He was imprisoned in Spain in 1794, but escaped and returned to Nueva Granada (as Colombia was then called) in 1797. He joined the patriot forces in 1810 and became president of Cundinamarca in 1812. He led a military campaign in the south in 1813, and was again imprisoned by the Spanish. Meanwhile **Simón Bolívar** (1783-1830) was leading a campaign for Venezuelan independence. Following the collapse of the First Republic of Venezuela in 1812, he joined the independence movement in Cartagena and had early successes in his 1812 Magdalena Campaign, which ended in Caracas, where the Second Republic was proclaimed. Again, the patriots lost control and Bolívar returned to Colombia, but was forced to flee to the West Indies when **General Pablo Morillo** launched the Spanish re-conquest.

Changes in Europe were also to affect the situation in Colombia. In 1808, Napoleon replaced Ferdinand VII of Spain with his own brother Joseph. The New World refused to recognize this, and several revolts erupted in Nueva Granada, culminating in a revolt at Bogotá and the establishment of a junta on 20 July 1810. Cartagena also bound itself to a junta set up at Tunja.

Simón Bolívar returned to the Llanos in 1816 and formed a new army. Their campaign for liberation involved a forced march over the Andes, in the face of incredible difficulties. After joining forces with **Francisco de Paulo Santander**'s Nueva Granada army, he defeated the royalists at the Battle of the Pantano de Vargas in July, winning the decisive victory at the Battle of Boyacá on 7 August. From 1819 to 1828 Bolívar was president of Gran Colombia, the new name for the union of Colombia, Venezuela, Panama and Ecuador, which lasted until the 1830s.

After the fall of Napoleon in 1815, the Spanish set about trying to reconquer the independent territories. The main Spanish general behind the task was Pablo Morillo (1778-1837), known as 'the Pacifier'. During his reign of terror (1816-1819), more than 300 patriot supporters were executed. Morillo set up the 'Consejo de Guerra Permanente' and the 'Consejo de Purificación'. The latter's aim was to punish crimes of treason. There was also a board of confiscations known as the 'Junta de Secuestros'. Morillo was linked to the re-establishment of the Inquisition, which saw many priests tried in military courts in South America.

The Spaniards left behind a considerable legacy in Colombia. Their main objective was to amass riches, notably gold, and ship them back to Spain. Protecting what they had collected from their English, French and Dutch rivals led to the massive fortifications of their main port, Cartagena. Most of what they built is still intact and has to be seen to be appreciated. However, they also brought with them culture and lifestyle, and some of their best colonial public and domestic architecture can be found in Colombia. They left their language and their religion and many institutions, including universities, continue to thrive today. The towns they planned and built are now being preserved. What they did not leave, however, were political institutions, and the search for a durable formula continues, 200 years after the Spaniards left.

Gran Colombia

La República de Gran Colombia was established by the revolutionary congress at present-day Ciudad Bolívar (Venezuela) on 17 December 1819. A general congress was held at Cúcuta on 1 January 1821, and it was here that the two opposing views that later sowed such dissent in Colombia first became apparent. Bolívar and Nariño were in favour of centralization; Santander, a realist, wanted a federation of sovereign states. Bolívar succeeded in enforcing his view and the 1821 constitution was drawn up, dividing Gran Colombia into 12 departments and 26 provinces. New laws were introduced to abolish the slave trade and allow free birth for the children of slaves born in Colombia, to redistribute indigenous lands and to abolish the Inquisition. This constitution lasted until 1830 when, following the breakaway of Venezuela and Ecuador, a new constitution was drawn up.

The next president after Bolívar was Francisco de Santander, from 1832 to 1837. Formerly the vice-president, he led a campaign of dissent against the alleged dictatorship of Bolívar, culminating in an assassination attempt on Bolívar on 25 September 1828. Santander went into exile but was later recalled for the presidency. His played an important role in establishing the administrative structure of the new republic of Colombia, and went on to become leader of congressional opposition from 1837 to 1840.

Colombia's civil wars

The new country was the scene of much dissent between the centralizing pro-clerical Conservatives and the federalizing anti-clerical Liberals. The Liberals were dominant from 1849, and the next 30 years saw countless insurrections and civil wars. In 1885 the Conservatives imposed a highly centralized constitution that was not modified over 100 years. Civil war had a disastrous effect on the economy, leading to the Paper Money Crisis of 1885, when Colombian currency suffered a dramatic fall in value and circulation had to be reduced to 12 million pesos in notes. Gold was not established as the standard for currency until 1903.

A Liberal revolt of 1899 against the rigidly partisan government of the Conservatives turned into the 'War of the Thousand Days', also known as 'La Rebelión'. It lasted from 17 October 1899 to 1 June 1903. The first Liberal victory was at Norte de Santander in December 1899, when government forces were defeated by rebel leader General Benjamín Herrera. The Battle of Palonegro, 11-26 May 1900, was won by the government forces, led by General Prospero Pinzón. This proved to be the decisive victory of the 'War of a Thousand Days'. 100,000 people had died before the Liberals were finally defeated.

During the independence wars, Panama remained loyal to Spain. Although it had been a state in Nueva Granada since 1855, it was practically self-governing until 1886, when the new Colombian constitution reduced it to a mere department. A bid for independence in

1903 was supported by the USA. The revolution lasted only four days (3-6 November), and by 18 November, the USA had signed a treaty allowing them to build the Panama Canal.

The authoritarian government of General **Rafael Reyes** (1850-1921), from 1904 to 1909, was known as the Quinquenio dictatorship. He created his own extra-legal national assembly in 1904. His territorial reorganization and his negotiations with the USA over Panama increased his unpopularity, leading to an assassination attempt in 1906. The new president from 1910 to 1914, **Carlos Eugenio Restrepo** (1867-1937), restored a legal form of government and began negotiations with the USA for the Urrutia-Thomson Treaty of 1914. This resulted in a US$25 million indemnity payment to Colombia over US involvement in the Panamanian revolution.

Colombia was also engaged in a dispute with its southern neigherbour, Peru, over Leticia, capital of the Comissariat of Amazonas. Peru had repudiated the Lozano-Salomon Treaty of 1922 by occupying Leticia, a part of Colombia according to the treaty. The dispute was submitted to the League of Nations in 1933, who took over the Leticia area and handed it back to Colombia in 1934.

La Violencia

The late 1940s to mid-1960s were dominated by a period known as 'La Violencia', incited by the assassination of the socialist mayor of Bogotá, **Jorge Eliécer Gaitán**, on 9 April 1948. The riots that ensued were known as the 'Bogotazo'. La Violencia was characterized by terrorism, murder and destruction of property. Simultaneous, though un-coordinated, outbursts persisted throughout the 1950s. Among the many victims were Protestants, who were persecuted 1948-1959. Some 115 Protestants were murdered and 42 of their buildings destroyed. Other contributing factors to La Violencia were anti-communist sentiments, economic deprivation and the prevailing partisan political system. In 1957 a unique political truce was formed, putting an end to the violence. The Liberal and Conservative parties became the Frente Nacional, a coalition under which the two parties supported a single presidential candidate and divided all political offices equally between them. Political stability was maintained for 16 years. Ultimately the Conservatives gained more from this accord, and unforeseen opposition was provoked in parties not involved in the agreement.

One of the biggest guerrilla organizations active after La Violencia was the Movimiento 19 de Abri1, known as M19. Their political wing was the Alianza Nacional Popular (ANAPO), founded by followers of the dictator **General Rojas Pinilla** (1900-1975). His Peronist tactics during his 1953-1957 presidency had resulted in his trial by national tribunal and he was overthrown on 10 May 1957. ANAPO opposed both Liberals and Conservatives. They became a major protest force during the late 1960s and 1970s, believing that the 1970 presidential elections, in which Rojas Pinillo was a candidate, had been rigged, and that fraudulent results had placed **Misael Pastrana Borrero** in power. MI9 took their name from the date of the election, 19 April 1970.

M19's agenda was to achieve a democratic socialist society. Their first public act was the theft of Bolívar's sword from Quinta de Bolívar in Bogotá. They sought to identify themselves with the legacy of the leader of the 19th-century independence movement. They also kidnapped José Rafael Mercado, president of the Confederation of Workers, in 1976, accusing him of fraud and misconduct in office, for which they tried and executed him. They then kidnapped Alvaro Gómez Hurtado, Communist Party leader and son of earlier president Gómez, to publicize demands for renewed talks with the government.

It was not until the late 1980s that negotiations got under way. A peace accord was reached in late 1989. The following year, M19 members surrendered their weapons and formed themselves into a bona fide political party, named Alianza Democrática, or M19-AD, with which they gained a significant percentage of the vote in the 1990 elections.

The other main terrorist organization after La Violencia was Fuerzas Armadas Revolucionarias de Colombia (FARC). Formed in 1964 under leader **Pedro Antonio Marín**, known as 'Tirofijo', they were aligned with the Communist Party. After 20 years of guerrilla activity they signed a truce with the government on 24 May 1984. FARC joined forces with the legitimate Unión Patriótica and went on to win 10 seats in the 1986 election, while the Liberals took the majority.

In 1985 many of Colombia's guerrilla movements merged into the 'Coordinadora Guerrillera Simón Bolívar' (CGSB), together with all organizations that had refused to sign the government amnesty offered by **President Belisario Betancur** in 1985. Their aim was to co-ordinate their actions against the government and the armed forces. Most of their actions were based along the upper Río Cauca and the department of Antioquia. Peace talks with the government in the early 1990s collapsed, followed in 1992-1993 by several indecisive but destructive offences on the part of both the guerrillas and the armed forces.

The 1994 presidential elections were won by another Liberal, **Ernesto Samper**. The main thrust of his programme was that Colombia's current economic strength should provide resources to tackle the social deprivation that was causing drug use and insurgency. He placed emphasis on bringing the FARC and the Ejército de Liberación Nacional (ELN) guerrillas to the negotiating table, and increasing public spending on social welfare. Revelations during 1995-1997 that Samper's election campaign had been financed partly by a US$6 million donation from the Cali Cartel saw the government's popularity decline. In 1996 further charges were brought against the president for links with the drugs mafia, although he was acquitted. The charges led to political instability and the attempted killing of Samper's lawyer. When the opposition leader Alvaro Gómez was assassinated, Samper declared a state of emergency.

When it was revealed that other ministers had links with the drugs mafia, suspicion arose that Samper's acquittal had only been to protect their own positions. International confidence was lost. The USA decided, in March 1996, to remove (decertify) Colombia from its list of countries making progress against drug trafficking. This made Colombia ineligible for US aid.

Colombia was decertified for the second time in March 1997 partly because the Cali leaders were continuing their business from prison, having been given light sentences. Whatever progress was being made to eradicate drugs plantations and stocks, the denial of US aid permitted little scope for the establishment of alternative crops. Many rural communities were therefore left without a means of support.

In May 1997 the government admitted for the first time to the escalating problem of paramilitary groups and their links with members of the armed forces. The most infamous of these is 'Autodefensas Campesinas de Córdoba y Urabá' (ACCU), who receive financial support from drugs cartels. The state department admitted that 48% of violent episodes in 1997 were carried out by paramilitaries. This was confirmed by the annual report of the Inter-American Human Rights Commission in June 1997. In March 1998, congressional elections were relatively peaceful; and the US withdrawal of decertification restrictions the same month, were a welcome boost of confidence. Two rounds of presidential elections in May and June 1998 also passed without excessive guerrilla disruption. The new president, **Andrés Pastrana**, voted in on a promise to find a formula for peace, immediately devoted his efforts to bringing the guerilla groups to the negotiating table. After a long, tortuous process with FARC, a large *zona de despeje* (demilitarized zone), was conceded, centred on San Vicente del Caguán in Caquetá. Not everyone was in favour of Pastrana's initiative, not least because FARC violence and extortion did not cease. In April 2000, the government proposed the ceding of a similar but smaller demilitarised zone to the ELN, situated on the west side of the Río Magdalena in the department of Bolívar and a small section of Antioquia, a *zona de encuentro*. Local communities of this agricultural area were dismayed and peacefully demonstrated by closing roads and causing disruption – another vitally interested group in the complicated political equation.

After a series of high-profile guerrilla terrorist actions, including the hijacking of a plane, attacks on several small towns and cities, and the kidnapping of several political figures, Pastrana ended the peace talks on 21 February 2002 and ordered the armed forces to start retaking the FARC-controlled zone.

Modern Colombia

Recent history

Alvaro Uribe succeeded Andrés Pastrana as president in May 2002. A Harvard- and Oxford-educated lawyer, he came to power promising to eradicate left-wing guerrillas' and right-wing paramilitaries' hold on the country.

To a large extent he has succeeded. Using US funding from Plan Colombia (see below), he boosted spending on the military and armed peasants in vulnerable regions. He has held formal peace talks with far-right paramilitaries and has managed to bring security to most of the urban areas of the country within the mountainous centre. In so doing he has pushed the guerrillas, who at one point held territory within an hour of Bogotá, to the margins of the country – to the dense jungles around the borders with Venezuela, Ecuador and Panama.

In terms of the state's fight against the FARC, which has been going on for more than 40 years, 2008 was Colombia's *annus mirabilis*. Three major successes – each of which would have been considered a major, standalone coup in their own right – have shifted the balance of the conflict overwhelmingly in favour of the government.

In March, the Colombian army executed a raid just over the border into Ecuador in which Luis Edgar Devia Silva (normally known by his nom de guerre, Raúl Reyes), the FARC's spokesperson and a member of the Secretariat, was killed.

In May, it was revealed that the FARC's founder and leader, Pedro Antonio Marín Marín, also known as Manuel Marulanda or Tirofijo ('Sureshot'), had died of a heart attack.

Then in July came the biggest blow of all – the dramatic rescue of Senator Ingrid Betancourt, who had been kidnapped six years previously while campaigning for the presidency. In many ways, Betancourt's imprisonment had come to symbolize the potency the FARC held over Colombia and her rescue severely dented the rebels' bargaining power.

These three strikes have led many analysts to sound the death knell of the FARC. They have been severely weakened, as has been evidenced by a number of high profile desertions during 2008. However, suggesting that the FARC have been neutralized may be premature. Alfonso Cano took over command after Marulanda's death and a number of bombings in late 2008 suggests they will continue to disrupt civilian life for years to come, while their bargaining power will remain intact while they still hold what is believed to be over 700 hostages.

Uribe enjoyed an 80% approval rating after the rescue of Betancourt and he is believed to be contemplating running for a third term after he persuaded the Colombian House of Representatives to change the constitution so that he could run for office again in 2006. He was re-elected with 60% of the vote and all the signs are that, if he succeeds in modifying the constitution, he would win again in 2010.

But he is not without his critics. Since 2006, 32 of Uribe's staunchest supporters in congress, including his cousin Mario Uribe, have been charged by the Colombian Supreme Court for alleged links to paramilitary groups, while his family has been accused by a high-ranking senator of hosting meetings in the 1980s, at one of their ranches in Antioquia, with death squads during which murders were plotted.

A Human Rights Watch report released in October 2008 concluded that President Uribe's government has been putting obstacles in the way of the Supreme Court's efforts to investigate the paramilitaries' mafia-like networks.

In spite of these scandals, Uribe's popularity is likely to remain undented while current security levels persist and the FARC remain on the run.

Relations with neighbours
In the last few years, diplomatic relations between Colombia and her neighbours have been at best frosty, at worst volatile. While much of Latin America has experienced a swing toward socialism and anti-American sentiment, Colombia has strengthened its ties with the USA and pursued a neo-liberal economical model. Uribe and the charismatic president of Venezuela, Hugo Chávez, the most outspoken critic of US 'imperialism', have displayed a barely disguised disdain for each other and their diametrically opposed ideologies. This nearly translated into war between the two nations after Colombia incurred into Ecuadorian territory in the pursuit of FARC commander Raúl Reyes in March 2008. President Rafael Correa accused Colombia of violating Ecuadorian sovereignty and Chávez responded to his ally's accusation by deploying troops and tanks to Venezuela's border with Colombia.

The crisis dissolved as quickly as it flared up and relations were improved after the rescue of Ingrid Betancourt and Chávez, who had previously called for the FARC to be treated as insurgents rather than terrorists, called for the guerrillas to lay down their arms.

Plan Colombia
Plan Colombia is a US-Colombian initiative designed to reduce the flow of cocaine into the USA. Conceived during the presidency of Andrés Pastrana, the original Plan Colombia asked for US aid to address the problem of social exclusion that has plagued Colombia since independence from the Spanish and that has forced peasant farmers to cultivate coca and gave birth to guerrilla movements like the FARC in the first place.

A second draft, presided over by US President Bill Clinton's advisers, had an entirely more militaristic slant and aimed to reduce the drug supply by providing extra firepower to the Colombian army in its pursuit of narco-traffickers and supplying equipment and civilian agents for the destruction of coca plantations.

The plan has come under heavy criticism for its fumigation policy, which has seen farmers' legal crops destroyed alongside illegal ones. NGOs also claim that the money provided by the US government, which tallies up to several billion dollars, has funded Colombian army units involved in extra judicial killings and other human rights abuses.

Despite the billions of dollars ploughed into the project, the plan has failed in its primary objective. A UN analysis has found that the eradication of coca plantations has been on a smaller scale than anticipated. What's more, the market price of cocaine has not increased significantly, something that would be expected if there were a shortage of the drug on the streets of the USA. Critics of the plan also argue that any eradication of coca production in Colombia would simply push cultivation back to countries such as Bolivia and Peru.

But the initiative has had a huge tangential success in that the money provided by the US government has helped the Colombian army in its victories over the FARC and for that has gained much approval in the eyes of many Colombians.

The narcotics trade

In Medellín and Cali, two cartels transformed Colombia's drugs trade into a major force in worldwide business and crime. Their methods were very different; Medellín's was violent and ostentatious, while Cali's was much more low-key. The Medellín Cartel processed and distributed 60-70% of cocaine exported to the USA during the 1980s. It was headed by **Pablo Escobar Gaviria** and **Jorge Luis Ochoa Vásquez**. Many members of Ochoa's family were also working for the cartel. In the late 1980s he was listed as a billionaire by *Forbes Magazine*.

In 1981, **Marta Nieves Ochoa Vásquez**, Jorge's sister, was kidnapped. MI9 were believed responsible. In response to the kidnapping, 'Muerte a Secuestradores' was formed by leaders of the drugs trade. Their strong anti-Communist beliefs led to alleged support from factions of the military. In 1984 Muerte a Secuestradores assassinated Carlos Toledo Plata, an ANAPO congressman who had later joined M19.

President César Gaviria Trujillo, the Liberal candidate who had won the 1990 presidential election, put into motion a pacification plan to end the drugs cartels' offensive and establish a peace agreement with the guerrillas. In a further display of reformist government, he appointed **Antonio Navarro Wolff**, former guerrilla leader now of the M19-AD, to the post of health minister.

As a result of the reform of the constitution in 1991, a further general election was held in October 1991 (although not due until 1994) and the Liberals retained a majority in the Senate and the House of Representatives. By 1991 the government had secured the surrender, under secret terms, of senior members of the Medellín cartel, namely Pablo Escobar and Jorge Luis Ochoa. One of the publicized conditions for their surrender was immunity from extradition and reduced sentences. Some of the senior traffickers and murderers got only five to eight years. President Gaviria received international support, including from the USA, for his stance against the drugs problem, which contrasted with previous president Barco's tougher, and unsuccessful stand.

In the National Constituent Assembly elections of 1991 the M19-AD won 19 of the 70 contested seats; the Liberals won 24; combined Conservative factions won 20. These results were followed by attempts to legitimize and modernize the political system, in an effort to deny remaining guerrilla groups any cause for protest and therefore lead to peace. The judicial system was strengthened and extradition was banned. However, the early 1990s saw high abstention rates in elections: 60-70% of the electorate didn't vote. This was blamed on loss of confidence in the political system and disruption of voting by guerrillas in some rural areas.

During the Gaviria term, it was reported the Pablo Escobar was continuing to direct the Medellín Cartel from inside his purpose-built prison at Envigado. The Cali Cartel's trade was growing in the wake of reduced activity by the Medellín Cartel. In July 1992, Escobar escaped during a transfer to army barracks. Drug-related violence in Bogotá increased in 1993, thought to be Escobar's way of persuading the government to offer better surrender conditions for him. A paramilitary vigilante group was formed, called 'Perseguidos Por Pablo Escobar' (PEPE). This was allegedly made up of relatives of Escobar's murder victims and members of the Cali Cartel, and it targeted Escobar's family. Escobar was finally shot by the armed forces on 2 December 1993 in Medellín, giving a temporary boost to the government's popularity. The Cali cartel capitalized on the death of Escobar and the dismantling of his empire. By the mid 1990s they controlled 70% of the world market in cocaine. But in June and July 1995, six of the seven heads of the cartel were arrested. In 2006, the Rodríguez brothers, Gilberto and Miguel, were extradited to the USA and pleaded guilty in Miami, Florida, to charges of conspiracy to import cocaine. This put an end to cartel control over the Colombian drug trade and it has now splintered into many individual groups, including paramilitary and guerrilla forces, although this has not stopped production in any significant way.

Economy

Structure of production

Colombia has varied natural resources and an economic structure which is no longer dependent on any one commodity. **Agriculture** is the major employer, providing about 15% of GDP and over half of total legal exports. The traditional crops are coffee, flowers, sugar cane, bananas, rice, maize and cotton. Colombia is the leading producer of mild Arabica **coffee** and second to Brazil in world production. Diversification since 1984, drought and disease have reduced output, but exports of coffee still amount to 15-20% of total exports, depending on world prices. About 900,000 ha are planted to coffee in the central Andes and production is around 10-11 million bags a year. **Sugar** production, at over 2 million metric tons, is second only to Brazil in South America. **Flowers**, mostly grown near Bogotá because of ease of access to the airport, are exported mainly to the USA. Expansion has been so successful that Colombia is the second largest exporter of cut flowers in the world after the Netherlands. The USA accounts for 73% of total sales of over US$500 million a year. **Bananas** are grown on the tropical lowlands, about 56 million boxes from around Urabá and 30 million south of Santa Marta, while sugar cane is grown in the Cauca Valley. **Manufacturing** contributes 19% of GDP, with farming activities such as food processing, drink and tobacco accounting for about a third of the sector's value added. Textiles and clothing are also important and provide an outlet for home-grown cotton.

The most dynamic sector of the economy in the 1980s was **mining**, with average annual growth rates of 18%, although rates in the 1990s have declined. Mining (coal, nickel, emeralds, gold and platinum) now accounts for about a fifth of total exports. **Coal** reserves are the largest in Latin America, which partial surveys have put at 16.5 billion tonnes. The largest deposits are in the Cerrejón region, where a huge project mines and exports steam coal from a purpose built port at Bahía de Portete. Production was 30 million tonnes in 1996 but was forecast to rise to 40 million tonnes by 2000 and 55-70 million tonnes by 2005. Coal is now the third largest export item by value. A mine at La Loma (César Department) and deposits in the Chocó are also being developed with railways and ports for export markets. With the exception of a few major projects, mining of precious metals is concentrated in the hands of small-scale producers with little technology or organization. Much of their output remains outside the formal economy. Colombia is a major producer of **gold**, **platinum** and **emeralds**, which have traditionally dominated the sector. Mining of precious metals, including silver, is primarily in the Department of Antioquia and El Chocó. Gold deposits

Colombian entrepreneurism

Colombia is a nation of small businesses. Millions make their living by hawking their wares on the street. Street artists, photographers, people hiring out their mobile phones by the minute, and countless street stalls selling everything from fruit juices to iguana eggs – they're an enterprising bunch.

Step onto one of the colourful buses and you'll want for nothing. Fizzy drinks and snacks will keep you nourished, while travelling salesmen have perfected the art of the five-minute pitch. They usually wait outside bus stations to flag down a passing vehicle. You're handed the product to examine while they execute a carefully prepared speech. By the time the bus reaches the outskirts of town they've collected any unwanted merchandise and usually leave with a few thousand pesos in their back pocket. But don't switch off from the sales talk – sometimes what they have to offer is quite useful!

have also been discovered on the borders of the Departments of Cauca and Valle, while others have been found in the Guainía, Vaupés and Guaviare regions near the Brazilian border.

Since the mid-1990s **oil** has held the position of top export earner contributing over a quarter of total exports. Traditionally, oil production came from the Magdalena Basin, but these are older fields which are running down. The discovery of the Caño Limón field near Arauca raised output to around 450,000 b/d. The Cusiana and Cupiagua fields, in the Llanos, came into full production in 1995; average output in 1996 was about 580,000 b/d but has not been significantly expanded because of guerrilla attacks and operational problems. Cusiana also has substantial reserves of **gas**. Investment is taking place to raise oil output, build refineries, petrochemical plants and pipelines, although guerrilla attacks and high taxes make operating in Colombia costly for foreign oil companies and investment has dropped.

Despite abundant hydrocarbons, some 78% of installed generating capacity is **hydroelectric**. Three quarters of the nation's hydroelectric potential is in the central zone, where 80% of the population live, giving hydroelectricity a natural advantage over thermal power, but after a severe drought in 1992 the government encouraged the construction of several thermal plants, due to come on stream in 1998-1999. Further problems have been encountered by deforestation and the effects of El Niño, causing drought in 1997-1998. Installed capacity was 13,400 by the end of 2005.

Recent trends

Current account surpluses in the late 1970s during a coffee price boom were turned into large deficits in the first half of the 1980s because of lower export receipts and rapidly rising imports. However, Colombia was able to avoid having to reschedule its foreign debt and took steps to adjust its external accounts. The devaluation of the peso was speeded up, reinforced by import restrictions and export incentives. The fiscal accounts were also turned around and the public sector deficit was reduced while economic growth remained positive throughout and per capita income increased. The World Bank and the IMF endorsed the Colombian economic strategy and commercial banks continued to lend to the country to refinance loans falling due. The Gaviria government accelerated the economic opening of the country and liberalized financial, investment, foreign exchange and tax legislation. High real interest rates encouraged capital inflows and economic stability encouraged foreign investors.

President Samper's 1995-1998 development plan emphasized spending on the social sector and productive infrastructure (with private sector involvement) to help combat poverty. However, the transfer of responsibilities to the regions has been accompanied by mismanagement and the combination of uncertainty surrounding the government's links with drugs, guerrilla activity and strikes. In February 1997, Samper yielded to demands for 20% pay rises for public sector workers, putting more pressure on the inflation rate. The trade deficit was also cause for concern as the coffee and banana markets slumped and the peso became over-valued as interest rates were kept high to compensate for the fiscal deficit. However, in September 1997 the peso fell, helped by lower interest rates, and the government turned to the domestic market for financing rather than raise capital abroad.

However, by the time Pastrama took office, unemployment had reached 15.8%, the fiscal deficit was rising, inflation was over 18% and gap growth falling. Pastrama instituted budget cuts but progress was hampered by the 1998 global financial crisis and the prolonged effects of El Niño. High domestic interest rates fuelled the recession which persisted until early 2000 when unemployment reached almost 21%. The construction industry was particularly hard hit as was the banking sector in which some major changes have taken place, including takeovers by foreign banking groups.

After the recession of the late 1990s, the Colombian economy recovered, thanks in part to improved security but also to austere government budgets, focussed efforts to reduce public debt levels, an export-oriented growth strategy and high commodity prices. Ongoing economic problems facing President Uribe include reforming the pension system, reducing high unemployment, and funding new exploration to offset declining oil production. The government's economic reforms and democratic security strategy, coupled with increased investment, have engendered a growing sense of confidence in the economy. In 2007, Colombia experienced one of its best years ever with an estimated GDP growth of 8.2%, unemployment fell to 11.2%, an inflation to 5.5%. However, with its emphasis on exportation, the global financial crisis looks set to affect Colombia. The peso plummeted against the dollar from a high of 1650 in July to 2350 in late October 2008.

Government

Senators and Representatives are elected by popular vote. The Senate has 102 members, and the Chamber of Representatives has 161. The president, who appoints his 13 ministers, is elected by direct vote for a term of four years, but cannot succeed himself in the next term. Every citizen over 18 can vote. Reform of the 1886 Constitution was undertaken by a Constituent Assembly in 1991 (see History, above). Administratively, the country is divided into 32 departments and the Special Capital District of Bogotá. Liberty of speech and the freedom of the press are in theory absolute but in practice more limited. The official language of Colombia is Spanish. Its religion is Roman Catholicism. There is complete freedom for all other creeds not contravening Christian morals or the law.

Education

Education is free, and since 1927 theoretically compulsory, but many children, especially in rural areas, do not attend. There are high standards of secondary and university education, when it is available. The literacy rate is about 91% of those over 15 years of age.

Culture

Arts and crafts

With the wide variety of climate, topography and geology, it is not surprising that Colombia has virtually all the materials, fibres, minerals and incentives to create useful and artistic products. Many of the techniques practised today have been inherited from the indigenous peoples who lived here before the conquest, some indeed have not changed in the intervening centuries and are as appropriate now as they were then.

Gold

Gold is very much associated with Colombia. It was gold that brought the Europeans to the New World, and where they found it first. The indigenous peoples had been using it for many centuries though not as a simple 'store of value'. Only when it had been made into jewellery, body ornaments or items for sacrificial rites for their gods did gold have value for them. It must have been incomprehensible to them, as well as a tragedy for posterity, when the Spaniards melted down the gold they obtained in order to ship it back to Europe.

Many of the *sierras* in the west of the country have traces of gold in the strata. Through erosion in the rainy climates of the region, panning for gold in the rivers was productive and probably has been practised here since around 800 BC. Even some deep shaft mines have been found in west Colombia.

The Quimbaya of the Cauca Valley produced 24 carat gold containers, helmets and pendants in their ascendancy from 1000-1500 AD and also worked with *tumbaga*, a gold-copper alloy. The Tolima of the Magdalena Valley made artefacts of pure gold and the Wayúu of the Guajira string beads, sometimes covered with gold, a tradition that continues today. When the Spaniards arrived, the Muisca of the Boyacá/Bogotá area were modelling figures in wax and covering them with clay. They then fired them, removed the melted wax and filled the mould with gold. By carefully prizing open the mould, they were able to make many replicas, thus inventing mass production.

Virtually all of today's techniques of the goldsmith were known to the early peoples of Colombia and there is a fine presentation on this subject at the museum in the Parque Arqueológico in Sogamoso, Boyacá, see page 106.

There are some good bargains to be had in Colombia for gold items, notably in Bogotá and Cartagena. Perhaps the most interesting place, however, is Mompós, Bolívar, where there is a tradition of fine gold filigree work.

No-one visiting Colombia should miss the Banco de la República's wonderful gold museums. The central collection of gold artefacts is in Bogotá but there are other smaller presentations in the main cities around the country, always worth a visit.

Textiles

Although Colombian textiles cannot rival those of Guatemala or Peru in terms of design and spectacular colour, some areas of the country have some fine traditions. For the Wayúu, *'ser mujer es saber tejer'* (to be a woman is to know how to weave). Cotton was available in north Colombia and textiles were traded for wool from the Santa Marta *sierra* nearby, also used as a raw material. The Cuna of northwest Colombia still make the decorative panels for garments known as *molas*. A speciality is the *mola* made of many layers of coloured cloth sewn together, then cut out using the different colours to create a pattern or a motif.

One striking costume is found in the south near Silvia, Cauca, where the indigenous Guambiano weave their own blue and fuchsia costumes as well as many other wool garments and blankets.

Basketry

By its nature, articles made of vegetable fibres do not survive for very long, but we know that the Spaniards found many examples of indigenous work in Colombia. The basket-weaving techniques of the Muisca have continued in Tenza, Boyacá, where people still use *caña de castilla* (Arundo donax), which is easier to work with than bamboo. The whole local village works in this cottage industry.

Another similar community enterprise is in Sandoná, Nariño, where, in addition to basket weaving, Panama hats are a speciality. Panama hats are so named for where they were initially sold, rather than where made. The workers on the canal in the early part of the 20th century were the first customers, followed by those passing through. They were made in Ecuador and in Sandoná where the local *iraca* palm fibre is used. Hats are also made in Sampués, Sucre, from 'arrowcane' which grows in the river lowlands nearby and good basket weaving using palma iraca can be found at Usiacurí, south of Barranquilla.

The finest quality basket weaving in the country is to be found along the northwest Pacific coast of Chocó where the indigenous Cholo use *werregue* palm to weave a texture so fine that the finished product can look like clay and be used to carry water. They have a flourishing trade nowadays in coarser but more colourful palm weaving products.

Wood

The Cholo also make interesting 'healing sticks', which have magical as well as healing powers. These are about 50 cm long with a pointed end and carved figures above. Held against the stomach of the patient, they drive away the evil spirits and cure the illness. Carved wooden masks are a feature of indigenous crafts in the Sierra Nevada de Santa Marta in the north and the Sibundoy people of Putumayo in the extreme south of the country, used for festivities and rituals. Interesting wood carvings are made by the Puinave people near Puerto Inírida. Wooden masks appear in the carnival in Barranquilla.

Perhaps the most important wood *artesanía* is found in Chiquinquirá (Boyacá). Carved musical instruments are a speciality and many other items including all sorts of items made of *tagua* nuts gathered in the forests of the Chocó and Amazonas. Guitars are also found in Marinilla near Medellín.

Leather

Leather and woodwork often go together, and the arrival of cattle brought the necessary raw material. Now, finely engraved leather covering carved wooden chairs and other furniture is made in Pasto (Nariño), an important centre.

Barniz

An added craft is that of the resin locally called *barniz*. This comes from seed pods of *Eleagia Utilis*, which grows at altitudes of over 2000 m in Putumayo. Nowadays, the resin is extracted by passing through a mill or by hammering. Previously this was done by chewing the seeds, commonly known as *mopa-mopa*, supposedly because of the strange sound made by the chewers attempting to speak as well as chew at the same time. After extraction, the resin is dyed and expertly stretched to paper thin sheets into which designs are cut to decorate wooden objects including masks, each colour produced individually, finally covered with a protective lacquer. Pasto is the most important centre for *barniz*.

Pottery

The best known pottery centre in Colombia is Ráquira, Boyacá. A large selection of products is made for household and ornamental use including many small items and are sold here and in towns round about. The large earthenware pots made here today are identical to those made by the Chibcha centuries ago. A similar pottery centre across the country, Carmen de Viboral, Antioquia, also produces ceramics that are known throughout Colombia.

Imaginative and amusing ceramics are made in Pitalito, Huila. This form of popular art, pottery adorned with scenes of everyday life, is typified by representations of the *chiva*, the omnipresent brightly coloured bus seen in many parts of Colombia.

A more unusual line of production is the 'blackware' made at La Chamba, Tolima. This small village is beside the Río Magdalena near Guamo, not generally marked on maps. The process involves using closed kilns, thus cutting down the use of oxygen which thereby causes the iron in the clay to turn from red to black. La Chamba is now a household name in Colombia and is finding acceptance abroad.

Fine art and sculpture

The colonial art of Colombia is rich and diverse, perhaps reflecting its geographical position between the Caribbean and the Pacific, but also because of the early rivalry between the two first important colonial settlements of Bogotá and Tunja. Both cities boast numerous museums and religious foundations with good collections of painting, sculpture and decorative arts. Throughout the colonial period works of art were imported from Europe and elsewhere in the Spanish territories, particularly from Quito to the south. Artists came from far afield to work in the wealthy Colombian centres. In contrast to colonial practice in Mexico and Ecuador there seems to have been little attempt to train native craftsmen in the dominant European artistic modes of painting and sculpture, perhaps because indigenous expertise lay in pottery and metalwork rather than carving or painting.

Early art from Spain

The conquerors brought the Christian religion and Christian art. The cathedral sacristy in Bogotá preserves what must be one of the first European imports: a fragile silk standard traditionally believed to have been carried by Jiménez de Quesada's troops at the foundation of Bogotá in 1538, and known as the **Cristo de la Conquista**. The emaciated, blood-spattered figure of Christ is in a mixture of paint and appliqué, with a swirling length of loin cloth around his hips. This seems to billow in the breeze, an impression that would have been all the stronger in its original context. It is hard to imagine anything more alien to native beliefs or native forms of art. Other early Christian images, especially pictures of the Virgin, must have tapped into local beliefs because they soon became the focus of popular cults: the **Virgen de Monguí**, for example, is a 16th-century Spanish painting, which tradition holds was sent over by Philip II, while the **Virgen de Chiquinquirá**, the patron of Colombia, was painted by the Andalucían **Alonso de Narváez** who settled in Tunja in the 1550s. Neither is outstanding as a work of art but both have been attributed with miraculous powers and versions can be found all over Colombia.

Although religious commissions dominated artistic production throughout the colonial period some remarkable secular wall paintings survive in Tunja that show another side to colonial society. In the late 16th and 17th centuries the houses of the city's founder, Gonzalo Suárez Rendón, of poet Juan de Castellanos and of city notary Juan de Vargas were decorated with colourful murals based on a wide range of printed sources. Those in the **Casa Vargas** are the most sophisticated, the combination of mythological figures, exotic animals, grotesques, heraldic cartouches and occasional Christian monogram resulting in a complex humanistic programme, probably devised by Castellanos. The diversity of style reflects the diversity of sources, which can be traced to French, Flemish, German and Spanish originals. The rhinoceros, for example, is derived from Dürer's famous woodcut of 1515 but reached Tunja via a Spanish architectural treatise by Juan de Arfe, published in Seville in 1587. The murals in the **Casa Suárez Rendón** derive in part from those in the Casa Vargas, but are less philosophical, more straightforwardly decorative. Nevertheless, these paintings imply that a highly cultured society imported the most-up-to-date books and prints from Europe.

Woodcarvings and sculpture

The new religious foundations in the Americas created a huge market for paintings and sculptures with which to adorn their altarpieces, and workshops in Andalucía flourished as a result. An outstanding example of imported polychrome sculpture is the dignified Crucifixion group of 1583 on the high altar of the chapel of the wealthy Mancipe family in the cathedral in Tunja, sent by **Juan Bautista Vázquez** (died 1589) from his workshop in Seville. Sculpture workshops were soon established in the Americas, however, and Colombian churches preserve a wealth of carved and polychrome wooden altarpieces, choir stalls, confessionals and pulpits, as well as decorative wooden ceilings, screens and wall panels. An early example is the ambitious high altar of the church of San Francisco in Bogotá. The central bays were redesigned in the late 18th century but the wings date from about 1620. The tightly ordered Renaissance structure frames panels of relief carving in two distinctive styles: in the upper storey each has a single, clearly defined saint, while in the lower storey the panels contain crowded narrative scenes, overflowing with energy (the torso of the figure of St Jerome leans right out towards the high altar) and lush vegetation. The unknown artist was probably trained in Andalucía.

Such altarpieces usually involved several different craftsmen. The carvings for that in the Jesuit church of San Ignacio in Bogotá (1635-1640), for example, were by an Italian, **Gian Battista Loessing**. Another important sculptor working in Colombia in the 17th century was **Pedro de Lugo Albarracín**, whose devotional images of the suffering Christ appealed to popular piety, and several, such as the powerful figure of the fallen Christ known as **El Señor de Monserrate** (1656) in the eponymous shrine on the hill above Bogotá have become pilgrimage destinations. Records of other sculptors with the same surname working in Bogotá and Tunja in the 17th century suggest that Pedro de Lugo was the father of a dynasty of craftsmen. **Lorenzo de Lugo**, for example, executed the eight large reliefs for the high altar of the chapel of Rosary in Santo Domingo, Tunja (c 1686). The architectural frame of this outstanding altarpiece includes numerous anthropomorphic supporting figures, *atlantes*, a common feature of colonial church furnishings in Colombia, and a change for craftsmen to indulge in fanciful invention constrained by Christian orthodoxy. A famous example is the androgynous figure on the pulpit stairs in San Francisco, Popayán, a basket of exotic fruit on its head, and a pineapple in its hand, but grotesque figures, sometimes semi-angelic, sometimes semi-demonic, can be spotted amongst the fronds of tropical foliage on almost any baroque altarpiece. In 18th century, figure sculptor **Pedro Laboria** from Andalucía introduced a new lightness of touch with his sinuous, almost dancing saints and angels (examples in Tunja cathedral and Santo Domingo, Bogotá).

Early paintings

As with sculpture, the demand for painting was met from a variety of sources. Works were imported from Europe, particularly from Andalucía and from the Netherlands. In the 17th century, enterprising sea captains would find room in their holds for a roll or two of canvases from the workshops of Zurbarán or Rubens to sell in the colonial ports. Itinerant artists worked their way round the viceregal centres in pursuit of lucrative commissions such as **Angelino Medoro** (c 1567-1631) from Rome who also worked in Quito and Lima before returning to Europe (see the two large canvases in the Mancipe chapel in Tunja cathedral, 1598). Quito was an important source both of artists and of works of art. Born in Quito, the Dominican **Pedro Bedón** (c 1556-1621) worked in Tunja in the late 16th century and his influence can be seen in the *bogotano* miniaturist **Francisco de Páramo** (active in the early 17th century), while **Miguel de Santiago** (c 1625-1706) sent numerous works to Colombia, including his esoteric 'Articles of the Faith' paintings now in Bogotá cathedral museum.

Santiago was an important influence on Colombia's best 17th-century artist, **Gregorio Vázquez de Arce y Cevallos** (1638-1711) who trained in the workshop of the extensive Figueroa family of painters but who was working independently by the time he was 20. A prolific and eclectic artist, Vázquez drew on a variety of sources: sometimes his stiff, hieratic figures reveal his debt to popular prints, sometimes his soft landscapes and sweet-faced Virgins demonstrate his familiarity with the work of Zurbarán and Murillo (good examples in the Museo de Arte Colonial, Bogotá). 18th century painting in Colombia follows the well-trodden paths of earlier generations of artists, with none of the confident exuberance found in sculpture. You will find his work in many of Bogotá's churches.

After independence

Independence from Spain did not bring independence from the traditions of colonial art. A survey of the galleries of ponderous churchmen and other civic dignitaries in the various museums suggests a more or less seamless production from the 17th to the 19th centuries: some appear sophisticated, some brutish, and the artist is not necessarily to blame. But artistic style changed little the struggle for independence did provide some new subject matter. Bolívar is endlessly celebrated in painting. An inventive example is that of 1819 in the Quinta de Bolívar in Bogotá, by **Pedro José Figueroa** where he stands with a protective arm around the shoulders of a diminutive female figure personifying the new and newly tamed republic, dressed in a silk gown, but still with bow, arrows and feather headdress, and seated on a caiman. The events of the wars of independence are recorded by **José María Espinosa** (1796-1883) in a series of paintings of the 1813-1816 campaigns (examples in the Quinta de Bolívar and the Academia de Historia, Bogotá). The painting of the death of General Santander of 1840 by **Luis García Hevia** in the Museo Nacional is sincere in its naivete, whereas **Alberto Urdaneta** (1845-1887) who studied in Paris with Meissonier and is a much more versatile artist, sometimes makes his subjects from recent history seem artificial and melodramatic (*Caldas marchando al patíbulo*, Museo Nacional). But Urdaneta is also remembered as an uncompromising caricaturist, so much so that on one occasion he was expelled from the country. The Museo Nacional in Bogotá has two contrasting portraits of the heroine Policarpa Salvatierra, executed by the Spanish in 1817, one a popular anecdotal version shows her *en route* to the scaffold, the other attributed to **Epifanio Garay** (1849-1903) nicely contrasts the formal society portrait with the drama of the event: she sits poised and beautiful while the ominously shadowy figure of a soldier appears in a doorway behind.

Interest in Colombia's natural resources produced scientific missions that, although organized by foreigners (the first by the Spanish botanist **Celestino Mutis** in the 18th century and the next by the Italian geographer **Agustín Codazzi** in the 19th), nevertheless helped to awaken an appreciation of the landscape, peoples and cultures of Colombia, past and present. The Venezuelan **Carmelo Fernández** (1811-1877) worked for Codazzi in 1851, producing carefully observed watercolours of the peoples and traditions of different provinces (examples in the Biblioteca Nacional). **Manuel María Paz** (1820-1902) held the same position in 1853 and his drawings of the pre-Columbian culture of San Agustín are the first of their kind. **Ramón Torres Méndez** (1809-1895) was not a member of the mission, but like them he travelled extensively in the countryside and his scenes from everyday life helped to make *costumbrista* subjects respectable.

20th century

During the first decades of the 20th century Colombian artists preferred to ignore the upheavals of the European art scene and hold on to the established traditions of academic figure and landscape painting. Almost the only interesting figure, **Andrés de Santamaría** (1860-1945), spent most of his life in Europe and developed a style that owed something to Cezanne and something to 17th-century Spanish art, but with an over-riding concern for a thickly textured painted surface that is entirely personal (*Self-portrait*, 1923, Museo Nacional, Bogotá). During the 1930s the more liberal political climate in Colombia encouraged the younger generation of Colombian artists to look for a more socially and politically relevant form of art which, conveniently, they found in the Mexican muralists. Instead of having to embrace the violent rupture with the past represented by modern European movements such as Cubism and Futurism, the muralists offered a way of continuing in a figurative tradition but now with a social conscience expressed in images of workers and peasants struggling against the forces of oppression. **Pedro Nel Gómez** (1899-1984) was the first to paint murals in public buildings, particularly in his native Medellín, and was followed by others such as **Alipio Jaramillo** (born 1913) and **Carlos Correa** (1912-1985). The sculptor **Rómulo Rozo** (1899-1964) was also influenced by the rhetoric of the Mexican muralists but also by the forms of Aztec and Mayan sculpture, and strove to achieve a comparable combination of simplicity and monumentality.

Only in the 1950s did Abstraction have any impact in Colombia. **Guillermo Wiederman** (1905-1968) arrived from Germany in 1939 and after a spell painting tropical landscapes began to experiment with an expressionist form of abstraction, full of light and space and colour. **Eduardo Ramírez Villamizar** (born 1923) also began painting in a figurative mode but moved into abstraction in the 1950s and subsequently into sculpture, to create, alongside his contemporary **Edgar Negret** (born 1920), some of the most interesting Constructivist work in Latin America. Both work in metal and have produced large, often brightly painted pieces for public spaces. Another important artist of this generation, **Alejandro Obregón** (1920-1992), avoided pure abstraction, preferring to include colourful figurative references with nationalistic overtones: carnations, guitars, condors. The slightly younger and internationally famous **Fernando Botero** (born 1932) has also tended to favour national themes.

Working both as a painter and a sculptor he takes figures from Colombian society – dictators, drug barons, smug priests, autocratic matrons, prostitutes, spoilt children – and inflates them to ludicrous proportions. His gigantic bronze figures and the angular, two-dimensional sheets of metal of Negret and Ramírez Villamizar represent the two poles of 20th-century artistic expression.

For the subsequent generation of artists Colombia's turbulent political history remains a recurrent preoccupation. **Luis Caballero** (1943-1995) was a masterful draughtsman who expressed his sympathy for the victims of officially sanctioned violence by the tender attention he devotes to their tortured, naked bodies. **Beatriz González** (born 1938) uses a pop idiom to present military and political leaders as big and bold but essentially empty. **Juan Camillo Uribe** (born 1945) manipulates the paraphernalia of popular religion – prayer cards, plastic angels, metallic trinkets – to construct wittily disturbing collages. Younger artists are exploring the tensions between the national and international demands of art, and are experimenting with a tremendous diversity of styles and media. There is certainly no shortage of talent. Many cities in Colombia now boast a lively art scene with regular public exhibitions of contemporary art and a good range of commercial galleries.

Rodrigo Arenas Betancur (born 1921) followed in Rozo's footsteps to become Colombia's best known sculptor of nationalistic public monuments. His gigantic and often rather melodramatic bronzes can be found in towns and cities throughout the country, as, for example his heroically naked *Bolívar* in Pereira, *Monumento a la Vida* in the Centro Suramericano in Medellín and the complex *Lanceros del Pantano de Vargas* near Paipa which must have been quite a challenge to the foundrymen. His sculptures are eminently worth seeking out.

Literature

The indigenous Colombian written language was discovered to be at its earliest stages at the time of the Spanish conquest in the 16th century. Consequently there are practically no records of pre-conquest literature. The poetic tradition was oral; one of the few transcribed examples of spoken poetry is 'El Yurupapy', an oral epic gathered from *indígena* in the Vaupés region in the 16th century, though not published until 1890.

The literature produced during the colonial period (1500-1816) was mainly by an ecclesiastical elite, written for the benefit of an upper-class minority. The predominant themes were the conquest itself, Catholicism and observations of the New World. The two major writers of this period had themselves been major conquistadores. **Gonzalo Jiménez de Quesada** (1499-1579), the founder of Bogotá in 1538, wrote *Antijovio* in 1567. The main purpose of this book was to defend Spain's reputation against accusations made by the Italian Paulo Jovii in his *Historiarum sui temporis libri XLV* (1552). Quesada sought to put the record straight on matters concerning the behaviour of his nation during the conquest of the New World.

Juan de Castellanos (1522-1607) wrote a lengthy chronicle of the conquest called *Elegías de varones ilustres de Indias* (*Elegy of Illustrious Men of the Indies*, 1589). It was written in the Italian verse style popular at the time, and has been called one of the longest poems ever written. The most important piece of narrative prose written during this period was *El carnero* (*The Butcher*, 1638) by **Juan Rodríguez Freile** (1566-1642). This is a picaresque account of a year in the life of Santa Fe de Bogotá, using a blend of historical fact and scandalous invention to create a deliciously amoral book for its time. Mystic writing was also popular during the middle years of the conquest. **Sor Francisca**

Josefa de Castillo y Guevara (1671-1742) was a nun who wrote baroque poetry, but was best known for her intimate spiritual diary *Afectos espirituales* (date unknown). Another Baroque poet of renown was **Hernando Domínguez Camargo** (1606-1659), who chronicled the life of Saint Ignatius in his epic *Poema heróica de San Ignacio de Loyola* (*Heroic Poem of St Ignatius of Loyola*, 1666).

The first major Colombian writer after the declaration of independence in 1824 was **Juan José Nieto** (1804-1866). His *Ingermina, o la hija de Calamar* (*Ingermina, or the Child of Calamar*, 1844) is a historical novel about the conquest of the Calamar Indians in the 16th century. The mid-19th century saw the publication in Bogotá of *El Mosaico*, a review centred around a literary group of the same name, founded by **José María Vergara y Vergara** (1831-1872). The prevailing style in the capital was *costumbrismo*, the depiction of local life and customs in realistic detail. Major *costumbrista* novels were *Manuela* (1858) by **Eugenio Díaz** (1804-1865) and *María* (1867), by **Jorge Isaacs** (1837-1895). Romantic poetry also defined the early years of independence, reflecting the strong influence Europe still had over Colombia. One of the exceptions was a poet from Mompós, **Candelario Obeso** (1849-1884), the first Colombian poet to use Afro-American colloquialisms in poetry. His *Cantos populares de mi tierrra* (*Popular Songs of my Land*, 1877) marked a progressive shift from the Romantic style, into a poetic language which reflected the true variety of Colombia's indigenous population.

Another important region in the development of Colombian literature was Antioquia, whose main city is Medellín. This region spawned the first crop of writers who were not of the upper-class elite which had dominated Colombian letters until the late 19th century. **Tomás Carrasquilla** (1858-1940) produced three major novels which reflected his humble middle-class background, and used a casual, spoken style to portray local customs and speech, and above all a love of the land. Another Antioquian of renown was **Samuel Velásquez** (1865-1941), whose novel *Madre* (*Mother*, 1897) gives a strong sense of the simple life of the countryside coupled with the religious passion of its inhabitants.

The beginning of the avant-garde in Colombia is marked by the publication of *Tergiversaciones* (*Distortions*) in 1925 by **León de Greiff** (1895-1976), in which he experimented with new techniques to create a completely original poetic idiom. Another important Modernist poet was **Porfirio Barba Jacob** (the pseudonym of Miguel Angel Osorio, 1883-1942), who was influenced by the French Parnassian poets and published melancholic verse, typified by *Rosas negras* (*Black Roses*, 1935).

Other novelists of the same era were pursuing a much more social realist style than their avant-garde counterparts. *La voragine* (*The Vortex*, 1924) by **José Eustacio Rivera** (1888-1928) deals with the narrator's own struggle for literary expression against a backdrop of the Amazonian rubber workers' struggle for survival. **César Uribe Piedrahita** (1897-1951) also chronicled the plight of rubber workers, and in *Mancha de aceite* (*Oil Stain*, 1935) he looks at the effects of the oil industry on the land and people of his country. The problems facing indigenous people began to get more attention from these socially aware writers; **Bernardo Arías Trujillo** (1903-1928) examined the lives of Afro-Americans in Colombia in *Risaralda*.

The late 1940s to the mid-1960s in Colombian society were dominated by La Violencia (see History, page 348). Literary output during this intensely violent period reflected the political concerns which had led to the violence; among the novels to stand out from the many personal tales of anger and disbelief was *El jardín de las Hartmann* (*The Garden of the Hartmanns*, 1978) by **Jorge Eliécer Prado** (born 1945), which charts the history of

La Violencia in Tolima, one of the most severely affected regions. What makes this book readable is the lack of historical facts and figures, typical of books set during La Violencia, and a more generalized view of the troubles.

Two important poetry movements to come out of La Violencia were the 'Mito' group and the 'Nadaistas'. *Mito* was a poetry magazine founded in 1955 by **Jorge Gaitán Durán** (1924-1962). It included **Eduardo Cote Lemus** (1928-1964), **Carlos Obregón** (1929-1965) and **Dora Castellanos** (born 1925). Their influences were contemporary French writers such as Genet and Sartre, and the Argentinean José Luis Borges. *Mito* came out during the dictatorship of Rojas Pinilla, and was one of the few outlets for free literary expression in the country. The Nadaista group were concerned with changing the elitist role of literature in the face of the violent conflict which affected everyone, and they felt should be addressed directly; they used avant-garde styles and techniques to achieve this.

By far the biggest influence on Colombian fiction was the publication, in 1967, of *Cien años de soledad* (*A Hundred Years of Solitude*) by **Gabriel García Márquez** (born 1927). He had published many short stories and novels in the 1950s and early 1960s. Among the most significant were *La hojarasca* (*Leaf Storm* in 1955) and *El coronel no tiene quien le escriba* (*No-one Writes to the Colonel*, 1958), a portrayal of a colonel and his wife struggling to cope with the tropical heat, political oppression and economic deprivation in their final years. But it was with *Cien años de soledad* that he became recognized as the major exponent of a new style generic to Latin American writers. Events were chronicled in a deadpan style; historical facts were blended with pure fantasy, the latter written matter-of-factly as if it were the truth; characters were vividly portrayed through their actions and brief dialogues rather than internal monologues. The style came to be known as Magic Realism in English, a translation of the Spanish 'Lo real maravilloso'. In 1975 Márquez published *El otoño del patriarca* (*The Autumn of the Patriarch*), which was a return to a favourite theme of his, the loneliness that power can bring. *Crónica de una muerte anunciada* (*Chronicle of a Death Foretold*, 1981) was set in an unnamed coastal city, but no doubt not far from Márquez's birthplace of Aracataca. It captures the docility and traditional stubbornness of the people of Colombia's Caribbean seaboard, an area in which Márquez had worked as a journalist in the 1950s. *El amor en los tiempos de cólera* (*Love in the Time of Cholera*, 1985) is set at the turn of the century, and concerns the affair between a couple of septuagenarians against the backdrop of another fictional city; Márquez skillfully blends Cartagena, Barranquilla and Santa Marta into one coastal town. Márquez has published nine novels in total, as well as articles and essays

Other important writers in the 1970s and 1980s include **Fanny Buitrago** and **Manuel Zapata Olivella**. In novels such as *Los Panamanes* (1979) and *Los amores de Afrodita* (*The Loves of Aphorodite*, 1983), Buitrago contrasts the legends and culture of the Caribbean coast with the needs of young people to move on, at the risk of being swallowed up by modern North American culture. Zapata Olivella has published a monumental novel, *El fusilamiento del diablo* (*The Shooting of the Devil*, 1986) covering the six centuries of African and Afro-American history.

Colombian postmodern literature has followed European theoretical trends, with many of Colombia's more avant-garde writers living and working in Europe. While retaining the Magic Realist tradition of dispensing with a subjective, authoritative narrator, the postmoderns have greatly distanced themselves from the Colombian tradition of orally based colloquial storytelling. But it is García Márquez who has done the most to capture the public imagination. By borrowing from Colombian traditions with a modernist approach, he has created a style that has made him an internationally renowned literary figure.

Music and dance

No South American country has a greater variety of music than Colombia, strategically placed where the Andes meet the Caribbean. The four major musical areas are: the mountain heartland; the Pacific coast; the Caribbean coast; and the Llanos or eastern plains. See also page 37.

Mountain heartland

The heartland covers the Andean highlands and intervening valleys of the Cauca and Magdalena and includes the country's three largest cities, Bogotá, Cali and Medellín. It is relatively gentle and sentimental music, accompanied largely by string instruments, with an occasional flute and a *chucho* or *carángano* shaker to lay down the rhythm. The preferred instrument of the highlands and by extension Colombia's national instrument, is the *tiple*, a small 12-stringed guitar, most of which are manufactured at Chiquinquirá in Boyacá. The national dance is the **bambuco**, whose lilting sounds are said to have inspired Colombian troops at the Battle of Ayacucho in 1824. It is to be found throughout the country's heartland for dancing, singing and instrumentalizing and has long transcended its folk origins. The choreography is complex, including many figures, such as Los Ochos, La Invitación, Los Codos, Los Coqueteos, La Perseguida and La Arrodilla. Other related dances are the **torbellino**, where the woman whirls like a top, the more stately Guabina, the Pasillo, Bunde, Sanjuanero and the picaresque **rajaleña**. Particularly celebrated melodies are the *Guabina Chiquinquireña* and the *Bunde Tolimense*. The following fiestas, among others, provide a good opportunity of seeing the music and dance: La Fiesta del Campesino on the first Sunday in June, the **Fiesta del Bambuco** in Neiva and **Festival Folklórico Colombiano** in Ibagué later in the month, the **Fiesta Nacional de la Guabina y el Tiple**, held in Velez in early August, the **Desfile de Silleteros** in Medellín in the same month and **Las Fiestas de Pubenza** in Popayán just after the New Year, where the Conjuntos de Chirimía process through the streets.

Pacific coast

On Colombia's tropical Pacific coast (and extending down into Esmeraldas in Ecuador) is to be found some of the most African sounding black music in all South America. The **currulao** and its variants, the **berejú** and **patacoré**, are extremely energetic recreational dances and the vocals are typically African-style call-and-response. This is the home of the *marimba* and the music is very percussion driven, including the upright *cununo* drum plus *bombos* and *redoblantes*. Wakes are important in this region and at these the **bundes**, **arrullos** and **alabaos** are sung. Best known is the 'Bunde de San Antonio'. The **jota chocoana** is a fine example of a Spanish dance taken by black people and turned into a satirical weapon against their masters. The regional fiestas are the **Festival Folklórico del Litoral** at Buenaventura in July and **San Francisco de Asís** at Quibdó on 4 August. Quibdó also features a **Fiesta de los Indios** at Easter.

Caribbean coast

The music of Colombia's Caribbean lowlands became popular for dancing throughout Latin America more than 30 years ago under the name of **Música Tropical** and has much more recently become an integral part of the Salsa repertory. It can be very roughly divided into cumbia and vallenato. The **cumbia** is a heavily black influenced dance form for several couples, the men forming an outer circle and the women an inner one. The men hold aloft a bottle of rum and the women a bundle of slim candles called *espermas*. The dance probably originated in what is now Panama, moved east into Cartagena, where it is now centred and quite recently further east to Barranquilla and Santa Marta. The most celebrated cumbias are those of Ciénaga, Mompós, Sampués, San Jacinto and Sincelejo. The instrumental accompaniment consists of *gaitas* or *flautas de caña de millo*, backed by drums. The *gaitas* ('male' and 'female') are vertical cactus flutes with beeswax heads, while the *cañas de millo* are smaller transverse flutes. The most famous conjuntos are the Gaiteros de San Jacinto, the Cumbia Soledeña and the Indios Selectos. Variants of the cumbia are the **porro**, **gaita**, **puya**, **bullerengue** and **mapalé**, these last two being much faster and more energetic. Lately cumbia has also become very much part of the vallenato repertoire and is therefore often played on the accordion. Cumbia has been superseded by vallenato in Colombia and today is probably heard more outside the country than in it, with Colombian migrants taking it with them to cities like Buenos Aires, Mexico City, Los Angeles – even London. While it has travelled, it has picked up influences to create new sub-genres such as **techno-cumbia** and **cumbia villera**, both popular in Peru and Argentina. **Vallenato** music comes from Valledupar in the department of César and is of relatively recent origin. It is built around one instrument, the accordion, albeit backed by *guacharaca* rasps and *caja* drums. The most popular rhythms are the paseo and the merengue, the latter having arrived from the Dominican Republic, where it is the national dance. Perhaps the first virtuoso accordionist was the legendary 'Francisco El Hombre', playing around the turn of the century. Today's best known names are those of Rafael Escalona, Alejandro Durán and Calixto Ochoa. In April the **Festival de la Leyenda Vallenata** is held in Valledupar and attended by thousands.

Barranquilla is the scene of South America's second most celebrated **carnival**, after that of Rio de Janeiro, with innumerable traditional masked groups, such as the *congos*, *toros*, *diablos* and *caimanes*. The **garabato** is a dance in which death is defeated. Barranquilla's carnival is less commercialized and more traditional than that of Rio and should be a 'must' for anyone with the opportunity to attend. Other important festivals in the region are the **Corralejas de Sincelejo** with its bullfights in January, **La Candelaria** in Cartagena on 2 February, the **Festival de la Cumbia** in El Banco in June, **Fiesta del Caimán** in Ciénaga in January and **Festival del Porro** in San Pelayo (Córdoba). To complete the music of the Caribbean region, the Colombian islands of San Andrés and Providencia, off the coast of Nicaragua, have a fascinating mix of mainland Colombian and Jamaican island music, with the calypso naturally a prominent feature. More recently two other genres have gained increasing popularity. **Champeta** originates in Cartagena and has roots in soukous, compas and reggae. It is characterized by very provocative dancing. **Reggaeton** has become a phenomenon throughout Latin America. Believed to have originated in Panama, it blends a merengue beat with rapping and influences from reggae and ragga.

Llanos

The fourth musical region is that of the great eastern plains, the so-called Llanos Orientales between the Ríos Arauca and Guaviare, a region where there is really no musical frontier between the two republics of Colombia and Venezuela. Here the **Joropo** reigns supreme as a dance, with its close relatives the **galerón**, the slower and more romantic **pasaje** and the breathlessly fast **corrido** and **zumba que zumba**. These are dances for couples, with a lot of heel tapping, the arms hanging down loosely to the sides. Arnulfo Briceño and Pentagrama Llanera are the big names and the harp is the only instrument that matters, although normally backed by *cuatro*, guitar, *tiple* and *maracas*. Where to see and hear it all is at the Festival Nacional del Joropo at Villavicencio in December.

People

The regions vary greatly in their racial make-up. Antioquia and Caldas are largely of European descent; Nariño has more indigenous roots; while people from the Cauca Valley are more African, descending form those brought to the area when sugar was introduced. Afro-Caribbeans are also prominent in the rural area near the Caribbean and the northwest Pacific coastline. No colour bar is legally recognized but is not entirely absent in certain centres. Population figures of cities and towns in the text are the best we can find but should not be relied upon. They will, however, give the traveller an idea of the size of the place and therefore the level of facilities that may be expected.

The birth and death rates vary greatly from one area of the country to another, but in general are similar to those of neighbouring countries. Likewise infant mortality rates, although these are only half those of Brazil. Hospitals and clinics are few in relation to the population. About 66% of the doctors are in the departmental capitals, which contain about half of the population, though all doctors have to spend a year in the country before they can get their final diploma. The best hospitals, notably in Bogotá and Medellín, are well equipped and have fine reputations attracting patients from other countries of Latin America.

An estimated 400,000 tribal peoples, from 60 ethnic groups, live in Colombia. Groups include the Wayúu (in the Guajira), the Kogi and Arhauco (Sierra Nevada de Santa Marta), indigenous Amazonians such as the Huitoto, the nomadic Nukak and the Ticuna, indigenous Andean and groups of the Llanos and in the Pacific coast rainforest.

Although the national and official language of Colombia is overwhelmingly Spanish, many indigenous groups still use only their own languages. The largest ethno-linguistic group are the 150,000 Chibchas. On the Caribbean coast, especially the islands, English or Creole are widely spoken. The diversity and importance of indigenous peoples was recognized in the 1991 constitutional reforms when Indians were granted the right to two senate seats; the National Colombian Indian Organization (ONIC) won a third seat in the October 1991 ballot. State recognition and the right to bilingual education has not, however, solved major problems of land rights, training and education, and justice.

Indigenous cultures

Santa Marta (*Wayúu*) Guajira
Barranquilla O Tayrona
Cartagena O (Kogi) (Arhuaco)
PANAMA
(Cuna) Sinú VENEZUELA
(Embera-Wunan) O Turbo Cúcuta O
(Chola) Sinú O Bucaramanga
(Cholo) Muisca
Medellín O Chibcha (U'wa)
Quimbaya O Tunja
Pereira O Maypure
Calima Tolima □ BOGOTÁ (Puihave)
Cali O (Páez)
Tierradentro
(Guambiano) O Neiva
Tumaco O Popayán
Tumaco San Agustín
O Pasto
ECUADOR
BRAZIL
(Huitoto)
N
PERU
(Tikuna)
Leticia
Not to scale
Guajira...... Pre-Columbian
(Wayúu)..... Present day

Religion

The vast majority of Colombians (93%) are nominal Roman Catholics, and though observance is not particularly high, daily Masses in most town churches makes it possible for visitors to see the interior of many churches. As elsewhere in Latin America, Protestant Evangelical Churches have made some progress in Colombia in recent years.

Land and environment

Geology and landscape

Colombia is the fourth largest in size of the 10 principal countries of South America, at 1,142,000 sq km slightly smaller than Peru and slightly larger than Bolivia. In terms of Europe, that is the size of France and Spain combined. The latest estimate of population is 42.2 million, marginally more than Argentina and second only to Brazil in the continent. The people are concentrated in the western third of the country: nevertheless the population density of 31.2 per sq km is only greater in Ecuador within South America. To the east, it is bounded by Venezuela and Brazil, to the south, by Peru and Ecuador and in the northwest by Panama. It is the only South American country with a coastline on the Pacific (1306 km) and the Caribbean (1600 km), with two small offshore islands in the Pacific. In the Caribbean, there are various coastal islands including the Rosario and San Bernardo groups and the more substantial San Andrés/Providencia archipelago off the coast of Nicaragua, plus several cays towards Jamaica.

Its greatest width east-west is 1200 km and it stretches 1800 km north-south, from 12°N to 4°S of the equator, with virtually all of one of its departments, Amazonas, south of the equator. The borders of Colombia have been stable since 1903 when Panama seceded, though Nicaragua occasionally revives a claim for the San Andrés group of islands and there are three minute uninhabited reefs claimed by Colombia and by the USA: Quita Sueño Bank, Roncador Cay and Serrana Bank.

Structure

As with other countries on the west side of the continent, Colombia is on the line of collision between the west moving South American Plate, and the Nasca Plate, moving east and sinking beneath it thus creating the Andes. Almost 55% of the country to the east is alluvial plains on top of ancient rocks of the Guiana Shield dating from the Pre-Cambrian era over 500 million years ago. This was at one time part of the land mass called 'Pangea' which geologists believe broke up between 150 and 125 million years ago and the Americas floated away from what became Africa and Europe. It is presumed that prior to this, what is now the Caribbean Sea was an extension of the Mediterranean Sea and in the course of time this expanded to separate the two halves of the Americas. During the Cretaceous period, around 100 million years ago, the Atlantic was undoubtedly connected to the Pacific Ocean, at least from time to time, but by the end of the Cretaceous, the Tertiary mountain building had begun and the emergence of Central America and eventually the Isthmus of Panama, sealed off the connection.

All the rest of Colombia to the west, apart from the islands, is the product of the Andean mountain building activity, which continues today. This began earlier in the Jurassic and Cretaceous eras with intense volcanic activity, but the maximum was in the late Tertiary (around 25 million years ago). Large areas of molten material were formed beneath the surface and were pushed up to form the large high plateaux with peaks formed from later volcanic activity. Some areas were folded and contorted and the original rocks metamorphosed to lose their former identity. In general, it is the mountain ranges to the west that were most affected in this way. Continuous weathering, especially during the ice ages of which the most recent was in the Pleistocene up to 10,000 years ago, has been responsible for deep deposits in the valleys and the plains of north Colombia and in the inland slopes of the Andes towards the Orinoco and Amazon.

Other than the coral islands just off the north coast, the Colombian islands of the Caribbean are all on a submarine ridge, which extends from Honduras and Nicaragua to Haiti, known as the Jamaica Ridge, which separates the Cayman Trench from the Colombia Basin, two of the deepest areas of the Caribbean Sea. Providencia is probably volcanic in origin but San Andrés has a less certain past, perhaps being an undersea mount which has been colonized by coral for millions of years, evidenced by the white sands and the limestone features. Little is known about the other reefs, banks and cays that belong to Colombia. The two Colombian island groups in the Pacific are quite different. Gorgona is one of the few islands off the South American Pacific coast which is on the continental shelf and no more than 30 km from the mainland. There is evidence of past volcanic activity on the island and it may represent a point on an otherwise submerged ridge parallel to the coast. By contrast, the Isla de Malpelo is on one of the structural lines of the east Pacific which runs due south from west Panama along the line of longitude 81°W which peters out off the coast of Ecuador. There is a deep trench between this line and the coast with depths down to 5000 m and clear signs of tectonic activity along the ridge including Malpelo which is the top of a volcanic structure. Further to the west there is another ridge running south from Central America, the Cocos Ridge, which leads to the Galápagos Islands.

Andes

To the south of Colombia, the Andes of Ecuador are a single high range with volcanic peaks up to nearly 5000 m, but north of the border they quickly split into three distinct Cordilleras named Occidental, Central and Oriental. The first two are close together for 400 km but separated by a fault line occupied by the Río Patía in the south and the Cauca in the north. The Cordillera Oriental gradually pulls eastwards creating a valley basin for Colombia's most important river, the Magdalena. This range crosses the northeast border into Venezuela and continues as the Cordillera de Mérida. A subsidiary range, called the Sierra de Perijá, continues north within Colombia to reach the Caribbean at Punta Gallinas on the Península de Guajira, the northernmost point of the South American mainland. Near this point is the Santa Marta massif, one of the biggest volcanic structures in the world with the highest mountain peak in Colombia at 5775 m.

All three of the Cordilleras have peaks, mostly volcanic, over 4000 m, the Central and Oriental over 5000 m, with permanent snow on the highest. Many are active and have caused great destruction in the past, both with gas and ash explosions and by creating ice and mud slides. The whole of the western half of the country is subject to earthquakes, demonstrating the unstable nature of the underlying geology, and the significant situation of the country at the point where the Andes make a dramatic turn to the east. Also, in the northwest, another range to the west of the Cordillera Occidental appears, the Serranía de Baudó, which becomes the spine of the Darién isthmus of Panama, eventually continuing westwards. Thus north Colombia is at the tectonic crossroads of the Americas.

Valleys

A glance at the map of Colombia will show the physical dominance of the cordilleras and the human dependence on the valleys between them. The fact that they run more or less north-south was a great advantage to the earlier explorers interested in finding gold and silver and the later settlers looking for good cultivable land. Even the earliest inhabitants were interested in the protection that the rugged land offered them but also in ways to migrate further south. As a consequence, the eastern half of the country has, until very recently, been ignored and still remains largely unexplored.

The valleys are structural basins between the *cordilleras* and not simply products of river erosion. In some places they are many kilometres broad, as for example between Cali and Popayán, yet the Patía and Cauca rivers flow in opposite directions. Elsewhere, the rivers go through narrow passages, eg near Honda on the Magdalena where rapids interrupt river navigation. However, the basins have been filled many metres thick with volcanic ash and dust which has produced very fertile terrain. This, together with the height above sea level has made for an agreeable environment, one of the most productive zones of the tropics worldwide.

By contrast, the cordilleras create formidable obstacles to lateral movements. The main routes from Bogotá to Cali and Manizales must cross the Cordillera Central by passes at 3250 m and 3700 m respectively, and virtually all the passes over the Cordillera Oriental exceed 3000 m. Many of the volcanic peaks in these ranges are over 5000 m and are capped with snow, hence the name *nevados*. Such is the nature of the terrain, no railway was ever built to cross the cordillerasexcept from Cali to Buenaventura.

The rivers themselves do not provide the most attractive human corridors as can be seen by the frequent diversions from the rivers by the main trunk roads. Fortunately, the surrounding countryside is frequently dominated by plateaux. These make good level sites for towns and cities (Bogotá itself is the best example). They also give long stretches of easy surface travel but are interrupted by spectacular descents and climbs where there are natural rifts or subsidiary river gorges. This makes for dramatic scenic trips by road throughout this area of Colombia.

Caribbean lowlands

From the Sierra de Perijá and the Sierra Nevada de Santa Marta westwards are the great plains of the lower Magdalena, which collects most of the water flowing north in Colombia to the Caribbean. The Cordilleras Central and Occidental finish at about 4°N, 350 km from the mouth of the river at Barranquilla. About 200 km from the sea, both the Magdalena and the Cauca flow into an area of swamps and lagoons which becomes a vast lake when water levels are high. This lowland is the result of the huge quantities of alluvium that has been brought down over the years from the mountains in the south of Colombia. While not comparable in length with the major rivers of the world, the average discharge at the mouth of the Magdalena is 7500 cu m per second similar to that of the Danube or about one third that of the Orinoco. To the north, the land slopes gently to the sandy beaches of the Caribbean and a string of inshore islands of considerable tourist attraction.

Beyond Barranquilla to the east, a sandbar encloses a salt lake that was formerly part of the Magdalena delta, now abandoned by the river which flows to the sea further west. On the far side of the lake, the Santa Marta massif comes down to the sea creating a interesting stretch of rocky bays and headlands. Further east again, the flatter land returns extending finally to the low hills of the Guajira peninsula at the north tip of the continent. This is a sandy, arid region, and is the modest northern end of the Cordillera Oriental.

At the west end of this section is the Gulf of Urabá and the border with Panama. The Río Atrato, which drains most of the area between the Cordillera Oriental and the Serranía de Baudó, reaches the sea here via another large swampy area where no land transport is possible. It is probable that this was formerly linked to the Gulf of Urabá which is itself now being filled up with material brought down by the Atrato and many other small streams. This was also probably an area where, in the much more distant past, the Atlantic was joined to the Pacific, a point not lost on the Colombians who periodically quote this as the site of a future rival to the Panama canal. There is little seismic activity in this region though there are occasional earthquakes and the mud lakes near Arboletes, Galerazamba and elsewhere near the coast are volcanic in origin.

Pacific coast

The Serranía de Baudó runs from Panama south to 4°N just north of Buenaventura. The basin between it and the Cordillera Occidental is drained by the Río Atrato to the north and the San Juan to the south with another river, the Baudó assisting the centre. This is an area of very high rainfall and access by any means is difficult. This coastline is very different from the north coast. Most of it is heavily forested but with very attractive small beaches interspersed with rocky stretches and affected with a wide tidal range, absent from the Caribbean. It has only recently been 'discovered' by the tourist industry and remains quiet owing to the difficulties and cost of getting there.

South of Buenaventura, there is another 300 km of coastline to Ecuador, but reasonable access is only possible at Buenaventura, and Tumaco in the extreme south. Rainfall here is still copious with many short rivers coming down from the Cordillera Occidental and creating alluvial plains along the coast typically with mangrove swamps, which continue into Ecuador. This part of the Colombian coast is also remote and unspoilt with a few fishing communities though tourism is beginning to take hold at the end of the two access roads. Further inland there are a few mineral deposits and gold mines which have attracted interest. There is no range of Tertiary hills here between the Andes and the coastline as in Ecuador.

Eastern plains

This section, representing more than half of Colombia, is in two parts. In the north are the grasslands known as *los llanos*, which stretch from the Cordillera Oriental across into Venezuela and on to the mouth of the Orinoco. Around 40% of the *llanos*, which means 'plains', are in Colombia. They are noted in both countries for the quality of the land for cattle raising which has been going on since the 16th century and are second only to the *Pampas* in Argentina for ranching in South America. Several important rivers, eg the Meta, flow from the mountains through this region to the Orinoco and act as transport routes. Slowly roads are being made into the interior but all-weather surfaces are virtually non-existent and land transport in the wet season is impossible. All important towns and villages and many *fincas* have their airstrips. In the extreme north of the area, near the border with Venezuela, oil was found some years ago and new finds are still being made.

The southern part of the section is tropical forest associated with the Amazon Basin. As far as the vegetation is concerned, the transition is, of course, gradual. However, the Río Guaviare is the most southerly tributary of the Orinoco and, with headwaters (here called the Guayabero) rising near Neiva in the Cordillera Oriental, has its source some 350 km further from the sea than those of the official source of the Orinoco in the Sierra Parima on the Brazil/Venezuela border. Two important rivers join to form the Guaviare near the town of San José, the Guayabero and the Ariari. Between them is an extraordinary geological anomaly, the Serranía de Macarena. It is a huge dissected block of crystalline rocks partly covered with stratified later formations, 140 km long and 30 km wide, that stands isolated 2000 m above the surrounding undulating forest and has been identified as a chunk of the Guiana Shield, the rest of which is hundreds of kilometres to the east, forming the border area between The Guianas, Venezuela and Brazil. Although there are some other low formations in this area of the country which are founded on the ancient basal rocks, as a remnant of 'Pangea', Macarena displays by far the oldest exposed rocks of Colombia.

South of the Guaviare Basin, all the waters of the region flow into the Amazon system. However, in the extreme east of the country, the Río Guainía drains the south part of the department of the same name which connects with another geographical curiosity, discovered by the great explorer Alexander von Humboldt. Some 250 km before joining the Guaviare, the Orinoco divides, with part of its flow going southwest as the 'Brazo Casiquiare', which eventually joins the Guianía to form the Negro and thence the Amazon. Other Colombian rivers feed the Negro, in particular the Vaupés, the longest tributary. Colombia therefore has the distinction of providing the true sources of the Orinoco and the Negro.

In the southern area, the climate becomes progressively wetter. Thick jungle covers much it though Colombia is no exception to the gradual destruction of the environment. The rivers Caquetá and Putumayo are important water routes to the Amazon proper but there is virtually no tourist traffic.

The extreme south of Colombia is Leticia, on the Amazon itself, a reminder of the original drawing of the maps which allowed all the western countries of South America except Chile to have access to the river and an exit to the South Atlantic.

Climate

Temperatures in Colombia are mainly affected by altitude and distance from the north and west coasts. The highest average temperatures in South America are in the Maracaibo lowlands of which Colombia has the southwest corner and the northwest extension into the Guajira Peninsula. Average annual temperatures in the Caribbean Lowlands are typically in excess of 25°C, modified downwards on the coast, yet, within sight of the coast are the permanent snows of Sierra Nevada de Santa Marta due to its altitude of over 5500 m. The temperature becomes oppressive where there is also high humidity.

Rainfall depends on the migrating northwest and southeast trade wind systems, the effect of the Andes acting as a weather barrier and some local situations along the coasts. There is high rainfall in the southeast where the southeast trade winds bring moisture all year into the Amazon Basin that is continually recycled to produce heavy daily precipitation all along the east edge of the Andes. This however tails off northwards into the *llanos* especially November to March when the wind systems move south and the southeast Trades are replaced by the northeast system. This is less effective in bringing moisture into the area because of the protection of the Venezuelan Andes. The rainfall in the lower reaches of the Magdalena Basin is also high, aided by the large swampy area which keeps the air saturated. The highest rainfall in the country is in the northwest near the border with Panama, brought about by the convergence of the trade wind systems interacting with warm, saturated air coming in from the Pacific. Here it rains daily most of the year with some respite from January to March but with a total on average of 8000 mm per year. This is one of the highest in the world. This heavy rain belt extends down the coast tailing off as Ecuador is approached. Unlike further south, the ocean here is warm and air over it readily condenses when it moves on to the land. However, this is a generalized pattern only.

Aberrations in the weather systems between November and March, when less rain normally falls, now labelled the *El Niño* phenomenon, also affect the western part of Colombia at least as far east as Bogotá. So far, the consequences have been much less dramatic than in Peru and Ecuador. However, be warned that the words of the tour operator or travel book writer 'the best time to visit' will sometimes be totally misleading!

Inland local features often determine the level of precipitation. To the east of Nevado de Huila (5750 m), for example, there is a small area of near desert caused by the effect of rain shadow. Near desert conditions also can be found on the tip of the continent, between Riohacha and Punta Gallina which is probably caused by descending air collecting rather than expelling moisture. Although there are occasional storms here (Colombia was marginally affected by the heavy rains that brought disaster to the Venezuelan coast in 1999), the normal Caribbean hurricane track fortunately passes well to the north of the Colombian coast.

Wildlife and vegetation

This neotropical zone is a land of superlatives, it contains the most extensive tropical rainforest in the world; the Amazon has by far the largest volume of any of the world's rivers and the Andes are the longest uninterrupted mountain chain. The fauna and flora are to a large extent determined by the influence of those mountains and the great rivers, particularly the Amazon and the Orinoco. There are also huge expanses of open terrain, tree-covered savannahs and arid regions. It is this immense range of habitats which makes Colombia one of the world's regions of high biological diversity.

This diversity arises not only from the wide range of habitats available, but also from the history of the continent. South America has essentially been an island for much of its geological past, joined only by a narrow isthmus to Central and North America at various times between 50 million and 25 million years ago. The present connection has been stable only for a few million years. Land passage played a significant role in the gradual colonization of South America by both flora and fauna from the north. When the land-link was broken these colonists evolved to a wide variety of forms free from the competitive pressures that prevailed elsewhere. When the land-bridge was re-established a new invasion of species took place from North America, adding to the diversity but also leading to numerous extinctions. Comparative stability has now ensued and has guaranteed the survival of many primitive groups like the opossums.

There are three Cordilleras of the Andes dominating the western part of Colombia. The rivers draining the area are referred to as white water (although more frequently brown because they contain a lot of sediment). This is in contrast to the rivers that drain the Guiana shield in neighbouring Venezuela, which are referred to as black or clear waters. The forests of the latter are of considerably lower productivity than those of the Andean countries.

Llanos

Northeast of the Andes and extending almost to the Caribbean coast, the lowland habitat characterized by open grasslands and small islands of trees is called the *llanos*. Poor drainage leads to the alternation between standing water and extreme desiccation, leading to large areas being devoid of trees except for some species of palm. Fire has also been responsible for maintaining this habitat type. Above 100 m this gives way to predominantly dry forest with seasonal rainfall and a pronounced drought. Gallery forest persists only in the regions surrounding rivers and streams. In contrast, arid conditions are also found in the vicinity of the northern Caribbean coast.

Flowers

An overabundance of floral species has helped make Colombia the world's second largest exporter of flowers, with over US$1 billion in sales annually. You name it, Colombia has it – everything from garden-variety roses and carnations to more exotic species like the bird of paradise and the heliconia. However, this country's undisputed crown jewel is the orchid. Over 3000 species of orchid are known to exist in Colombia, including the national flower, the majestic *Flor de Mayo*. A passion for these flowers led botanist Tom Hart Dyke into the treacherous Darién Gap in 2000,

a harrowing journey, including kidnap by guerrillas, that he recounts in his bestselling book, *The Cloud Garden*. For those who do not wish to risk life and limb to experience the best of Colombia's flora, check out the José Celestino Mutis **Botanical Gardens** in Bogota or the **Joaquín Antonio Uribe Botanical Gardens** in Medellín. The latter is particularly spectacular and contains a newly built 'orquideorama' that is not to be missed by orchid lovers. If you are lucky enough to be in Medellín during August, make sure to check out the flower festival that the city hosts every year.

Pacific West

The wet forests of the Pacific slopes of the western Andes provide an interesting contrast with the Amazon region by virtue of their high degree of endemism – species unique to an area. The region is often referred to as the Chocó and extends from the Darién Gap in Panama to northern Ecuador. The natural vegetation is tropical wet forest. Clouds that hang over the forest provide condensation, and this almost constant drenching by mist, fog and rain leads to a profusion of plants with intense competition for space, such that the trees and shrubs are all covered with a great variety of epiphytes – orchids, mosses, lichens and bromeliads. The area has been referred to by birders as the 'tanager coast' owing to the large mixed flocks of these colourful birds. There are many other species of endemic birds here apart from the tanagers. At La Planada, between Pasto and Tumaco, there is one of the highest concentrations of native birds in the continent and the forest reserve contains an immense diversity of orchids.

Overall, the fauna shows some interesting biogeographic patterns. Some species found here are those more common to Central and North America than to South America. The westernmost range defines a coastal strip with a fauna similar to Panama. Meanwhile, to the southeast, the fauna south of the river Guaviare is more typical of upper Amazon Basin of Brazil and Peru.

High Andes

From about 3600 m to 4400 m, the high Andes are covered by *páramo* typified by the grass (*Stipa-ichu*) or *pajonal* which grows here. *Páramo* is a distinct type of high-altitude moorland vegetation comprised of tall grasses and *frailejones (Espeletia)* a member of the Compositae family, which are only found in the Colombian *cordilleras* and the Sierra Nevada de Mérida in Venezuela. These extraordinary plants that grow to as much as 12 m, also frequently attract hummingbirds such as the black-tailed trainbearer and the great sapphirewing. Lakes and marshes are also a common feature since the ground is generally level. Interspersed among the grasses are clumps of club-moss and chuquiraguas. In the zone of the high *páramo* there are many lakes. Birds frequently seen in this area include the

Andean teal, Andean coot and a variety of hummingbird species. **Andean condor** (*Vultur gryphus*) the largest land bird, weighing 12 kg and with a wingspan of 3 m, may be seen effortlessly gliding on the updraft from the warmer valleys below.

Some protection from the severe climate and the icy winds that can blast this harsh environment may be provided in the deeply incised gorges. Here there may be a lush growth of shrubs, orchids, reeds and dwarf trees providing a marked visual contrast to the superficially drier *páramo*. In the favourable sheltered micro-climatic conditions provided in the gaps between the tall clumps of grass there nestle compact colonies of gentians, lupins and prostrate mosses. There is little evidence of mammal life here save for the occasional paw print of the Andean fox. **White-tailed deer**, once common here have been over-hunted.

Under 3600 m, the condensation of the moisture-laden upwelling air from the warm humid jungles to the east creates cloudforest. With a similar wide variety of epiphytes as found near the west coast. Both giant and dwarf tree ferns are characteristic. These are highly resistant to fire, the traditional manner of maintaining grazing lands. Pollination is effected by a variety of agents. Fragrant odours and bright colours are used by some orchids to attract nectivorous birds including some species of humming birds and insects. Others exude putrid smells to attract flies to carry out the same process. Tangled stands of bamboo intermingled with the *polylepis* forest are the dominant vegetation feature.

At high altitude *polylepis* forest clothes the deeply incised canyons and sides of the valleys. This is a tangled, lichen and fern be-decked world, dripping water from the moisture-laden air on to a mid-storey of tangled bamboo and lush tree ferns. A plentiful supply of bromeliads provide food for **spectacled bears**, now an endangered species. The steep slopes of the gullies are clothed in a dense blanket of giant cabbage-like paraguillas or umbrella plant. Tracks of mountain tapir are commonly found along river beaches, and the prints of the diminutive **pudu**, a small **Andean deer**, are also occasionally found. Mammals are rarely seen on the *páramo* during the day since most seek refuge in the fringing cloudforest, only venturing on to the open moors at night or under the protection of the swirling mists. But their presence is demonstrated by the tracks of **Andean fox** and marauding puma. Birds of the *páramo* include the mountain **caracara** and a variety of other raptors such as the **red-backed hawk**. Andean swifts, tapaculos, hummingbirds, fringillids and thrushes are common.

Masked **trogons** are also common in the *aliso* (birch) forests, evidence of recent colonization of areas devastated by the frequent landslides. Colourful tanagers and tiny hummingbirds are frequently encountered flitting between the myriad of flowers. At night the hills reverberate with the incessant croak of frogs and toads.

Eastern slopes of the Andes

The cloudforests of South America are found in a narrow strip that runs along the spine of the Andes from Colombia, through Ecuador and into Peru. On the western side of the Central Cordillera between 2000 m and 3000 m are the remaining stands of the **wax palm** (*Ceroxylon alpinum*), the tallest variety of palm tree that grow dramatically above the surrounding forest and often appear above the cloud blanket. On the eastern side of the Cordillera Oriental the dense, often impenetrable, forests clothing the steep slopes protect the headwaters of the streams and rivers that cascade from the Andes to form the mighty Amazon as it begins its slow 8000 km journey to the sea. A verdant kingdom of dripping epiphytic mosses, lichens, ferns and orchids grow in profusion despite the plummeting overnight temperatures. The high humidity resulting from the 2 m of rain that can fall in a year is responsible for the maintenance of the forest and it accumulates and leaks from the ground in a constant trickle that combines to form myriad icy, crystal-clear tumbling streams that cascade over precipitous waterfalls. In secluded areas flame-red Andean **cock-of-the-rock** give their spectacular display to females in the early morning mists. **Woolly monkeys** are also occasionally sighted as they descend the wooded slopes. Mixed flocks of colourful tanagers are commonly encountered, and the golden-headed **quetzal** and Amazon umbrella bird are occasionally seen.

At about 1500 m there is a gradual transition to the vast lowland forests of the Amazon Basin; surprisingly less jungle-like but warmer and more equable than the cloudforests clothing the mountains above. The daily temperature varies little during the year with a high of 23-32°C falling slightly to 20-26°C overnight. This lowland region also receives some 2 m of rainfall per year, most of it falling from November to April. The rest of the year is sufficiently dry, at least in the lowland areas, to inhibit the growth of epiphytes and orchids which were so characteristic of the highland areas. For a week or two in the rainy season the rivers flood the forest. The zone immediately surrounding this seasonally flooded forest is referred to as *terra firme* forest.

Colombian Amazonas

The lowland Amazon region can be seen at its best as the river passes the Amacayacu National Park. Flood waters from the Peruvian catchment area inundate the forest for a short period starting in January in its upper reaches to create a unique habitat called *várzea*. *Várzea* is a highly productive seasonally inundated forest found along the banks of the whitewater rivers; it is very rich as a consequence of the huge amount of silt and nutrients washed out of the mountains and trapped by the massive buttress-rooted trees. One of the commonest trees of the *várzea*, the Pará rubber tree, is the source of latex. The Brazilian rubber industry foundered in the 19th century when seeds of this tree were illegally taken to Asia to form the basis of huge rubber plantations and flourished in the absence of pest species. In the still-flowing reaches of the *várzea* permanently flooded areas are frequently found where vast carpets of floating water lilies, water lettuce and water hyacinth are home to the Amazonian manatee, a large herbivorous aquatic mammal which is the fresh-water relative of the dugong of the Caribbean. Vast numbers of spectacled caiman populate the lakes feeding on the highly productive fish community.

In the lowland forests, many of the trees are buttress rooted, with flanges extending 3-4 m up the trunk of the tree. Among the smaller trees stilt-like prop roots are also common. Frequently flowers are not well developed, and some emerge directly from the branches and even the trunk. This is possibly an adaptation for pollination by the profusion of bats, giving easier access than if they were obscured by leaves.

The vast river basin of the Amazon is home to an immense variety of species. The environment has largely dictated the lifestyle. Life in or around rivers, lakes, swamps and forest depend on the ability to swim and climb; amphibious and tree-dwelling animals are common. Once the entire Amazon Basin was a great inland sea and the river still contains mammals more typical of the coast, eg manatees and dolphins.

National parks

Colombia established its first national park in 1969 (Tayrona on the Caribbean coast) and now has 53 reserves comprising 40 National Nature Parks (PNN), 10 Flora and Fauna Sanctuaries (SFF), two National Nature Reserves and one Unique Natural Area (ANU), spread throughout the country and in virtually every department. They vary in size from the tiny island of Corota in the Laguna de la Cocha near the border with Ecuador to large areas of forest in the eastern lowlands. All the significant mountain areas are National Parks including the Sierra Nevada de Santa Marta, El Cocuy, El Nevado de Huila, Los Nevados (Tolima and Ruiz) and Puracé. There are 14 on or near the Caribbean and Pacific coasts including the off-shore islands.

National parks & reserves

All except the smallest parks normally have one or more centres staffed with rangers (*guardaparques*) who offer information and guidance for visitors. Most, however, are remote with difficult access and few facilities. Unlike some Latin American countries, most national parks in Colombia are virtually free of 'tourism' and are thus of particular interest to those looking for unspoilt natural surroundings.

For various reasons, unlike many countries where the main problem for national parks is visitor overcrowding, many of the parks in Colombia are difficult to visit. Unfortunately, because of their remoteness, some have been sanctuary to guerrilla groups or drug traffickers, some are sensitive indigenous territories and many are of difficult access and have few or no facilities. Lovers of wilderness, however, will enjoy the richness of the natural attractions and the freedom from oppressive tourism.

Apart from the national parks, there are a considerable number of private nature reserves, some exclusively for research, others open to the general public. Many of these are worth visiting: details are given in the text.

200 km
200 miles

ational parks
reserves ♦
to Fragua-Indiwasi PNN 46
macayacu PNN 45
ahuinarí PNN 44
atatumbo Barí PNN 10
hingaza PNN 24
iénaga Grande de Santa
Marta SFF 7
orales del Rosario &
San Bernardo PNN 8
ordillera de los
Picachos PNN 31
ueva de los
Guácharos PNN 39
Cocuy PNN 16
Corchal-El Mono
Hernández SFF 47
Tuparro PNN 23
arallones de Cali PNN 28
aleras SFF 41
orgona PNN 30
uanentá-Alto Río
Fonce SFF 17
uaque SFF 19
la de La Corota SFF 42
a Paya PNN 43
as Hermosas PNN 27
as Orquídeas PNN 15
os Colorados SFF 9
os Estoraques ANU 11
os Flamencos SFF 3

Nevado de Huila PNN 29
Nukak RNN 37
Old Providence McBean
   Lagoon PNN 1
Otún-Quimbaya SFF 48
Paramillo PNN 13
Picachos PNN 31
Pisba PNN 18
Puinawai RNN 38
Puracé PNN 36
Río Puré PNN 49
Sanquianga PNN 35
Selva de Florencia PNN 50
Serranía de
   Chiribiquete PNN 40
Serranía de los
   Yariguíes PNN 51
Sierra de la
   Macarena PNN 32
Sierra Nevada de Santa
   Marta PNN 4
Sumapaz PNN 26
Tamá PNN 14
Tatamá PNN 21
Tayrona PNN 5
Tinigua PNN 33
Utría PNN 20
Vía Parque Isla de
   Salamanca PNN 6

PNN Parque Nacional
        Natural

Contents

384	Basic Spanish for travellers
389	Index
395	Advertisers' index
396	Complete title listing
398	About the author
399	Acknowledgements
408	Credits

Footnotes

Basic Spanish for travellers

Learning Spanish is a useful part of the preparation for a trip to Latin America and no volumes of dictionaries, phrase books or word lists will provide the same enjoyment as being able to communicate directly with the people of the country you are visiting. It is a good idea to make an effort to grasp the basics before you go. As you travel you will pick up more of the language and the more you know, the more you will benefit from your stay.

General pronunciation

Whether you have been taught the 'Castilian' pronounciation (z and c followed by i or e are pronounced as the th in think) or the 'American' pronounciation (they are pronounced as s), you will encounter little difficulty in understanding either. Regional accents and usages vary, but the basic language is essentially the same everywhere.

Vowels

a	as in English cat
e	as in English best
i	as the ee in English feet
o	as in English shop
u	as the oo in English food
ai	as the i in English ride
ei	as ey in English they
oi	as oy in English toy

Consonants

Most consonants can be pronounced more or less as they are in English. The exceptions are:

g	before e or i is the same as j
h	is always silent (except in ch as in chair)
j	as the ch in Scottish loch
ll	as the y in yellow
ñ	as the ni in English onion
rr	trilled much more than in English
x	depending on its location, pronounced x, s, sh or j

Spanish words and phrases

Greetings, courtesies

hello	hola	thank you (very much)	(muchas) gracias
good morning	buenos días	I speak Spanish	hablo español
good afternoon/ evening/night	buenas tardes/noches	I don't speak Spanish	no hablo español
		do you speak English?	¿habla inglés?
goodbye	adiós/chao	I don't understand	no entiendo/ no comprendo
pleased to meet you	mucho gusto		
see you later	hasta luego	please speak slowly	hable despacio por favor
how are you?	¿cómo está? ¿cómo estás?	I am very sorry	lo siento mucho/ disculpe
I'm fine, thanks	estoy muy bien, gracias	what do you want?	¿qué quiere? ¿qué quieres?
I'm called...	me llamo...		
what is your name?	¿cómo se llama? ¿cómo te llamas?	I want	quiero
		I don't want it	no lo quiero
yes/no	sí/no	leave me alone	déjeme en paz/ no me moleste
please	por favor		
		good/bad	bueno/malo

Questions and requests

Have you got a room for two people?	Is tax included?
¿Tiene una habitación para dos personas?	*¿Están incluidos los impuestos?*
How do I get to_?	When does the bus leave (arrive)?
¿Cómo llego a_?	*¿A qué hora sale (llega) el autobús?*
How much does it cost?	When? *¿cuándo?*
¿Cuánto cuesta? ¿cuánto es?	Where is_? *¿dónde está_?*
I'd like to make a long-distance phone call	Where can I buy tickets?
Quisiera hacer una llamada de larga distancia	*¿Dónde puedo comprar boletos?*
Is service included?	Where is the nearest petrol station?
¿Está incluido el servicio?	*¿Dónde está la gasolinera más cercana?*
	Why? *¿por qué?*

Basics

bank	*el banco*	market	*el mercado*
bathroom/toilet	*el baño*	note/coin	*le billete/la moneda*
bill	*la factura/la cuenta*	police (policeman)	*la policía (el policía)*
cash	*el efectivo*	post office	*el correo*
cheap	*barato/a*	public telephone	*el teléfono público*
credit card	*la tarjeta de crédito*	supermarket	*el supermercado*
exchange house	*la casa de cambio*	ticket office	*la taquilla*
exchange rate	*el tipo de cambio*	traveller's cheques	*los cheques de viajero/*
expensive	*caro/a*		*los travelers*

Getting around

aeroplane	*el avión*	insured person	*el/la asegurado/a*
airport	*el aeropuerto*	to insure yourself against	*asegurarse contra*
arrival/departure	*la llegada/salida*	luggage	*el equipaje*
avenue	*la avenida*	motorway, freeway	*el autopista/la*
block	*la cuadra*		*carretera*
border	*la frontera*	north, south, west, east	*norte, sur, oeste*
bus station	*la terminal de*		*(occidente), este*
	autobuses/camiones		*(oriente)*
bus	*el bus/el autobús/*	Oil	*el aceite*
	el camión	to park	*estacionarse*
collective/		passport	*el pasaporte*
fixed-route taxi	*el colectivo*	petrol/gasoline	*la gasolina*
corner	*la esquina*	puncture	*el pinchazo/*
customs	*la aduana*		*la ponchadura*
first/second class	*primera/segunda clase*	street	*la calle*
left/right	*izquierda/derecha*	that way	*por allí/por allá*
ticket	*el boleto*	this way	*por aquí/por acá*
empty/full	*vacío/lleno*	tourist card/visa	*la tarjeta de turista*
highway, main road	*la carretera*	tyre	*la llanta*
immigration	*la inmigración*	unleaded	*sin plomo*
insurance	*el seguro*	to walk	*caminar/andar*

Accommodation

air conditioning	*el aire acondicionado*	power cut	*el apagón/corte*
all-inclusive	*todo incluido*	restaurant	*el restaurante*
bathroom, private	*el baño privado*	room/bedroom	*el cuarto/la habitación*
bed, double/single	*la cama matrimonial/ sencilla*	sheets	*las sábanas*
		shower	*la ducha/regadera*
blankets	*las cobijas/mantas*	soap	*el jabón*
to clean	*limpiar*	toilet	*el sanitario/excusado*
dining room	*el comedor*	toilet paper	*el papel higiénico*
guesthouse	*la casa de huéspedes*	towels, clean/dirty	*las toallas limpias/ sucias*
hotel	*el hotel*		
noisy	*ruidoso*	water, hot/cold	*el agua caliente/fría*
pillows	*las almohadas*		

Health

aspirin	*la aspirina*	diarrhoea	*la diarrea*
blood	*la sangre*	doctor	*el médico*
chemist	*la farmacia*	fever/sweat	*la fiebre/el sudor*
condoms	*los preservativos, los condones*	pain	*el dolor*
		head	*la cabeza*
contact lenses	*los lentes de contacto*	period/sanitary towels	*la regla/ las toallas femeninas*
contraceptives	*los anticonceptivos*		
contraceptive pill	*la píldora anti- conceptiva*	stomach	*el estómago*
		altitude sickness	*el soroche*

Family

family	*la familia*	boyfriend/girlfriend	*el novio/la novia*
brother/sister	*el hermano/la hermana*	friend	*el amigo/la amiga*
daughter/son	*la hija/el hijo*	married	*casado/a*
father/mother	*el padre/la madre*	single/unmarried	*soltero/a*
husband/wife	*el esposo (marido)/ la esposa*		

Months, days and time

January	*enero*	Monday	*lunes*
February	*febrero*	Tuesday	*martes*
March	*marzo*	Wednesday	*miércoles*
April	*abril*	Thursday	*jueves*
May	*mayo*	Friday	*viernes*
June	*junio*	Saturday	*sábado*
July	*julio*	Sunday	*domingo*
August	*agosto*		
September	*septiembre*	at one o'clock	*a la una*
October	*octubre*	at half past two	*a las dos y media*
November	*noviembre*	at a quarter to three	*a cuarto para las tres/ a las tres menos quince*
December	*diciembre*		
		it's one o'clock	*es la una*

it's seven o'clock	son las siete	in ten minutes	en diez minutos
it's six twenty	son las seis y veinte	five hours	cinco horas
it's five to nine	son las nueve menos cinco	does it take long?	¿tarda mucho?

Numbers

one	uno/una	sixteen	dieciséis
two	dos	seventeen	diecisiete
three	tres	eighteen	dieciocho
four	cuatro	nineteen	diecinueve
five	cinco	twenty	veinte
six	seis	twenty-one	veintiuno
seven	siete	thirty	treinta
eight	ocho	forty	cuarenta
nine	nueve	fifty	cincuenta
ten	diez	sixty	sesenta
eleven	once	seventy	setenta
twelve	doce	eighty	ochenta
thirteen	trece	ninety	noventa
fourteen	catorce	hundred	cien/ciento
fifteen	quince	thousand	mil

Food

avocado	el aguacate	goat	el chivo
baked	al horno	grapefruit	la toronja/el pomelo
bakery	la panadería	grill	la parrilla
banana	el plátano	grilled/griddled	a la plancha
beans	los frijoles/ las habichuelas	guava	la guayaba
beef	la carne de res	ham	el jamón
beef steak or pork fillet	el bistec	hamburger	la hamburguesa
boiled rice	el arroz blanco	hot, spicy	picante
bread	el pan	ice cream	el helado
breakfast	el desayuno	jam	la mermelada
butter	la mantequilla	knife	el cuchillo
cake	el pastel	lime	el limón
chewing gum	el chicle	lobster	la langosta
chicken	el pollo	lunch	el almuerzo/la comida
chilli or green pepper	el ají/pimiento	meal	la comida
clear soup, stock	el caldo	meat	la carne
cooked	cocido	minced meat	el picadillo
dining room	el comedor	onion	la cebolla
egg	el huevo	orange	la naranja
fish	el pescado	pepper	el pimiento
fork	el tenedor	pasty, turnover	la empanada/ el pastelito
fried	frito	pork	el cerdo
garlic	el ajo	potato	la papa

prawns	los camarones	spoon	la cuchara
raw	crudo	squash	la calabaza
restaurant	el restaurante	squid	los calamares
salad	la ensalada	supper	la cena
salt	la sal	sweet	dulce
sandwich	el bocadillo	to eat	comer
sauce	la salsa	toasted	tostado
sausage	la longaniza/el chorizo	turkey	el pavo
scrambled eggs	los huevos revueltos	vegetables	los legumbres/vegetales
seafood	los mariscos	without meat	sin carne
soup	la sopa	yam	el camote

Drink

beer	la cerveza	ice/without ice	el hielo/sin hielo
boiled	hervido/a	juice	el jugo
bottled	en botella	lemonade	la limonada
camomile tea	la manzanilla	milk	la leche
canned	en lata	mint	la menta
coffee	el café	rum	el ron
coffee, white	el café con leche	soft drink	el refresco
cold	frío	sugar	el azúcar
cup	la taza	tea	el té
drink	la bebida	to drink	beber/tomar
drunk	borracho/a	water	el agua
firewater	el aguardiente	water, carbonated	el agua mineral con gas
fruit milkshake	el batido/licuado	water, still mineral	el agua mineral sin gas
glass	el vaso	wine, red	el vino tinto
hot	caliente	wine, white	el vino blanco

Key verbs

to go	**ir**
I go	voy
you go (familiar)	vas
he, she, it goes, you (formal) go	va
we go	vamos
they, you (plural) go	van

to have (possess)	**tener**
I have	tengo
you (familiar) have	tienes
he, she, it, you (formal) have	tiene
we have	tenemos
they, you (plural) have	tienen
there is/are	hay

there isn't/aren't   no hay

to be	**ser** (permanent state)	**estar**
	(positional or temporary state)	
I am	soy	estoy
you are	eres	estás
he, she, it is, you (formal) are	es	está
we are	somos	estamos
they, you (plural) are	son	están

This section has been assembled on the basis of glossaries compiled by André de Mendonça and David Gilmour of South American Experience, London, and the Latin American Travel Advisor, No 9, March 1996

Index → Entries in bold refer to maps

A

Acacias 336
Acaime Nature Reserve 266
Acandí 166
accident and emergency 40
Albarracín, Pedro de Lugo
362
Almacén de Pólvora
(Gunpowder store) 144
Alto de Idolos 315
Alto de las Piedras 316
Amacayacú National Park
341
Amazonia 338
Andean condor 378
Andes 243, 372
Andrés de Santamaría 364
Aracataca 184
Aratoca 121
Arboletes 165
listings 169
Arías Trujillo, Bernado 366
Armenia 267, **268**
ins and outs 267
listings 276
sights 268
arts and crafts 359

B

Bahía Agua Dulce 208
Bahía de Cartagena 144
Bahía del Suroeste 208
Bahía Malaga 292
Bahía Manzanillo 208
Bahía Solano 251
listings 251
Baluarte de San Francisco
Javier 148, 150
Barichara 119, **119**
listings 125
Barniz 360
Barranquilla 174, **174, 175**
activities and tours 178
bars and clubs 177

directory 178
eating 177
entertainment 177
excursions 176
festivals and events 177
ins and outs 174
shopping 178
sights 175
sleeping 176
transport 178
basketry 360
bears, spectacled 378
Bedón, Pedro 363
Belalcázar, Sebastián de 301
Berlín 124
Betancur, Belisario 352
Betancur, Rodrigo Arenas
365
Biblioteca Bartolomé Calvo
150
Bioparque Los Ocarros 335
Boca Grande 144
Bocachica 151
Bocagrande 144, 145, 151,
324
Bogotá 53, 56, **58, 64, 72,
75**
bars and clubs 81
directory 87
eating 79
entertainment 81
festivals 82
getting around 56
getting there 56
La Candelaria 62
Museo de Oro 70
orientation 57
safety 60
shopping 82
sights 62
sleeping 76
tour operators 85
transport 85
Bolívar, Simón 164, 349

books 24
border crossings
Ecuador
  Ipiales–Rumichaca 325
  Tumaco–San Lorenzo
  325
Venezuela
  Cúcuta–Can Antonio 133
  Maicao 199
Borrero, Misael Pastrana 351
Botero, Fernando 364
Boyacá Department 98
Boyacá, Battle of 100
Bucaramanga 121, **122**
ins and outs 122
listings 126
sights 122
Buenaventura 291
listings 295
Buenaventura
ins and outs 292
Buitrago, Fanny 367
bus 29
business hours 46

C

Cabellero, Luis 365
Cabo de la Vela 197
caja vallenata 198
Cajamarca 270
Caldas, Francisco José
de 301
Cali 284, **290**
activities and tours 298
background 285
bars and clubs 297
directory 300
eating 296
eating 296
entertainment 297
festivals and events 297
ins and outs 284
shopping 298
sights 286

sleeping 294
transport 299
Camargo, Hernando
Domínguez 366
camping 32
Cañaveral 186
Capurganá 166
listings 170
Carmen de Viboral 238
Carrasquilla, Tomás 366
Cartagena 142, **146**
activities and tours 157
around the old city 144
background 143
bars and clubs 156
beaches 151
Bocachica beach 151
Bocagrande 151
directory 160
eating 155
entertainment 156
festivals 157
fortifications 144
getting around 142
inner city 148
ins and outs 142
listings 152
Marbella beach 151
outer city 145
ramparts 150
security 143
shopping 157
sights 144
transport 159
Cartago 270
Casa Bolivariana 164
Casa de Gabriel García
Márquez 150
Casa de la Aduana, Santa
Marta 181
Casa de Núñez 150
Casa de Santander 134
Casa del Marqués de
Valdehoyos 149
Casa del Virrey 270
Castellanos, Dora 367

Castellanos, Juan de 365
Cathedral, Cartagena 149
Cathedral, Santa Marta 182
Cauca Valley 284
Centro Internacional de
Convenciones 145
Cevallos, Gregorio Vázquez
de Arce y 363
Chapinero 74
Chicó 75
children 40
Chinchiná 262
Chipre 255
Chiquinquirá 104
Chocó 249
Chucunez 324
Ciénaga de Santa Marta 184
civil wars 350
climate 19, 375
coal 356
Cock-of-the-Rock 379
Coconuco 303
Codazzi, Agustín 364
coffee 356
Cojines del Zaque 100
Convento de Santo
Domingo 182
Corcora 266
Correa, Carlos 364
Cole Lemus, Eduardo 367
Cote, Eduardo Lemus 367
Coveñas 165
Cristo de la Conquista 361
Cubarral 336
Cúcuta 132, **132**
listings 135
Cueva de los Guácharos
National Park 316
Cueva de Morgan 205
Cuidad Perdida 187
trekking 188
culture 359
Cumaral 336
Curití 121
customs 40

D

Darién Gap 165
de Bastidas, Rodrigo 348
de Belalcázar, Sebastian 348
de Heredia, Pedro 348
de Lugo, Lorenzo 362
de Paulo Santander,
Francisco 349
de Quesada, Gonzalo
Jiménez 348, 365
de Santiago, Miguel 363
Desierto de Tatacoa 306
listings 310
Díaz, Eugenio 366
disabled travellers 40
diving 166, 184, 206
Doradal 242
listings 246
Dosquebrados 263
drugs 41, 47
Duitama 106
Durán, Jorge Gaitán 367

E

eating and drinking 33
economy 356
education 358
El Apóstol de los Negros 148
El Bodegón de la Candelaria
148
El Centro 145
El Cocuy 108
El Cove 205
El Encanto 323
El Esclavo de los Esclavos
148
El Fosíl 103
El Infiernito 103
El Peñol 239
El Poblado 227, **226**
listings 229
El Retiro 238
listings 245
El Tablón 315
El Valle 250
listings 251

electricity 41
Eliécer Gaitán, Jorge 351
embassies and consulates 41
emergency services 40
Entrerríos 243
Escobar Gaviria, Pablo 355
Espinosa, José María 363

F

Facatativá 90
Federmann, Nicolás 349
Fernández, Carmelo 364
festivals and events 16, 37
Figueroa, Pedro José 363
Filandia 265
fine art and sculpture 361
flights
    domestic 27
    international 26
Floridablanca 123
flowers 356
Francisco de Páramo 363
Freile, Juan Rodríguez 365
Fuerte Castillo Grande 144
Fuerte San José 144

G

Galerazamba 161
Garay, Epifanio 364
García Márquez, Gabriel 164, 184, 367
Gaviria Trujillo, César 355
gay and lesbian travellers 41
geology 371
Getsemaní 144
getting there
    foot 27
    river 27
    road 27
    sea 27
Girón 123, 124
    listings 126
gold 359
Gómez, Pedro Nel 364
González, Beatriz 365
Gorrones 348

government 358
Gran Colombia 350
Greiff, León de 366
guacharaca 198
Guaduas 91
Guajira Peninsula 197
Guamal 336
Guane 120
    listings 125
Guatapé 239
    listings 246
Guatavita Nueva 91
guerrillas 47
Guevara, Sor Francisca Josefa de Castillo y 366
Güicán 108

H

Hacienda Nápoles 242
hammocks 201
health 41
Hevia, Luis García 363
history 348
homestays 33
Hoyo Soplador 205

I

Ibagué 269
Iglesia de la Tercera Orden 145
Iguaque National Sanctuary 104
immigration 50
independence 349
India Catalina 150
insurance 42
internet 43
Inzá 304
Ipiales 326
    listings 327
Iquitos 339
Isaacs, Jorge 366
Isla de la Aguja 182, 184
Isla de la Corota 322
Isla Fuerte 165
Isla Gorgona 293
Isla Grande 161

Isla Malpelo 293
Islas de San Bernardo 164
Islas del Rosario 161
    listings 168
Ituango 243
Iza 106

J

Jacob, Porfirio Barba 366
Jaramillo, Alipio 364
Jardín 243
Jericó 243
Juanchaco 292

L

La Boquilla 152
Laboria, Pedro 363
La Chaquira 315
La Fe 239
La Gorda 149
Laguna, La 205
La Miel, Panama 167
La Pelota 315
La Popa hill 151
Ladrilleros 292
Lago de Tota 107
Laguna de Guatavita 91
Laguna La Cocha 322
landscape 371
language 43
Las Lajas 326
Lebrija 123
Legado de Piratas 205
Leticia 338, **338**
    listings 343
Liles 348
literature 365
Loessing, Gian Battista 362
Los Angeles 187
Los Llanos 334
    ins and outs 334

M

Macondo 184
Macuira National Park 198
Maicao 199
    listings 200

Makui 198
Manaure 197
  listings 200
Manaus 339
Manizales 253, **255**
  ins and outs 253
  listings 270
  sights 254
maps 31
Marbella 151
Marín, Pedro Antonio 352
Marmato 257
  listings 271
  sights 259
Marsella 264
Medellín 216, **218, 236, 240**
  bars and clubs 231
  directory 237
  eating 230
  entertainment 232
  festivals 233
  history 217
  ins and outs 216
  safety 217
  shopping 233
  sights 219
  sleeping 228
  transport 234
media 44
Medoro, Angelino 363
Méndez, Ramón Torres 364
Minca 188
  listings 191
Mirador Escalona 206
Mompós 163, **163**
  listings 168
money 45
Monguí 107
Monserrate 71
Montenegro 268
Morgan, Henry 324
Morillo, General Pablo 349
Múcura island 164
mud volcano 165
mudéjar 150
Muisca 348
music and dance 368
música tropical 198

Musichi 197
Mutis, Celestino 364

N
narcotics trade, the 355
Nariño, Antonio 102, 349
Narváez, Alonso de 361
national parks 14, 380, **380**
Navarro Wolff, Antonio 355
Nazareth 199
Negret, Edgar 364
Neiva 305
  listings 310
Nevado del Tolima 267
Nieto, Juan José 366
Norte de Santander
  Department 130
Nuquí 249
  listings 251

O
Obeso, Candelario 366
Obregón, Alejandro 364
Obregón, Carlos 367
Ochoa Vázquez, Jorge Luis
  355
Ochoa Vázquez, Marta
  Nieves 355
Old Providence 206
Olivella, Manuel Zapata 367
One Hundred Years of
  Solitude 184

P
Páez 304
Paipa 105
  listings 112
Pamplona 130
  listings 134
  sights 130
Paraguaipoa 199
Parque Arqueológico 314
Parque del Centenario 145
Parque Ecológico Río Blanco
  256
Parque Nacional del Café
  268

Parque Nacional Ensenada
  de Utria 250
Parque Nacional Farallones
  290
Parque Nacional Los
  Nevados 260, **261**
  sights 260
  sleeping 271
Parque Nacional Natural Old
  Providence 207
Parque Nacional Puracé 307
Parque Natural Nacional
  Macuira 199
Parque Ucumari 265
Paseo de los Mártires 145
Pasto 320
  background 320
  ins and outs 320
  listings 326
  sights 321
Pastrana, Andrés 352
Paz, Manuel María 364
Pedro Laboria 363
people 370
Pereira 262, **262**
  sights 264
Piedecuesta 123
Piedrahita, César Uribe 366
Pilimbalá 307
Pitalito 316
Planning your trip 7
Popayán 301
  background 301
  eating 310
  ins and outs 301
  listings 309
  sights 302
post 46
pottery 361
Pozo de Donato 100
Prado, Jorge Elicécer 366
Providencia 206, **207**
  beaches 208
  excursions 207
  ins and outs 206
  listings 210
public holidays 39
Puente de Occidente 245

Puente Heredia 145, 151
Puente Román 145, 150
Puerto Colombia 176
Puerto Gaitán 336
Puerto López 336
Puerto Nariño 341
Punta Gallinas 199
Punto Cero 224
Puracé 307

Q

Quibdó 249
   listings 251
Quimbaya 269
Quimbayas 348
Quinta de San Pedro
   Alejandrino 182

R

rail 28
rainfall and climate charts
   19
Ráquira 105
religion 371
Reserva Natural Cañón del
   Río Claro 241
   listings 246
Reserva Natural Heliconia
   343
Reserva Natural la Planada
   324
Reserva Natural Palmarí 342
restaurants 35
Restrepo 336
Restrepo, Carlos Eugenio
   351
Reyes, Rafael 351
Ricaurte, Antonio 102
Río Ariari 336
Río Chicamocha 121
Río Yavari 342
Riohacha 195, **196**
   listings 200
Rionegro 123, 238
Riosucio 243
Rivera, José Eustacio 366
Rodadero 183
   listings 189

Rojas Pinillo, General 351
Rozo, Rómulo 364
Rumichaca 325

S

safety 47
Salento 265
Salto de Bordones falls 316
Salto del Mortiño 316
Samper, Ernesto 352
San Agustín 314
   Bosque de las Estatuas
   314
   eating 318
   Fuente de Lavapatas 315
   ins and outs 314
   Parque Arqueológico 314
   sleeping 317
   transport 319
San Andrés 204, **203**, **204**
   diving 206
   excursions 206
   ins and outs 204
   listings 209
   sights 205
San Andrés de Pisimbalá
   304
San Blas archipelago 166
San Cipriano 291
   listings 295
San Diego 145
San Gil 117
   activities 117
   listings 124
San José de Isnos 316
San José de la Montaña 243
San Juan de Arama 336
San Lorenzo 188, 325
San Martín 336
San Pedro Claver 148
Sandoná 322
Santa Bárbara 242
Santa Fe de Antioquia 244,
   244
   sights 244
Santa Marta 179, **181**, **183**
   activities and tours 192
   background 180

   bars and clubs 192
   beaches 182
   directory 194
   eating 191
   festivals 192
   ins and outs 179
   orientation 180
   shopping 192
   sights 181
   sleeping 189
   transport 193
Santa Rosa de Cabal 262
   listings 271
Santa Rosa de Osos 243
Santander 289
Santander Department 117
Santuario Los Flamencos
   195
Sapzurro 167
   listings 170
sculpture 361
Seaflower, the 203
Señor de Monserrate 362
Sierra Nevada de Santa
   Marta 188
Sierra Nevada del Cocuy
   108, **109**
Silvia 303
Sinú 348
sleeping 31
snorkelling 166, 167, 184
Sogamoso 106
Soledad 176
spectacled bears 378
sport and activities 20
student travellers 48
Supía 256

T

Taganga 183
   listings 190
Tamá National Park 131
Tayrona National Park 185
   ins and outs 185
   listings 190
Tayronas 348
telephone 48
textiles 359

Tierradentro 304, **304**
  Archaeological Park 305
  ins and outs 304
  listings 309
  sights 304
time 48
tipping 48
Titipán 164
Tolú 164
  listings 169
tour operators 49
tourist information 49
Tumaco 324
Tunja 98, **99**
  sleeping 110
Túquerres 323
Turbo 165
  listings 169

U

Urdaneta, Alberto 363
Uribe, Alvaro 353
Uribe, Juan Camillo 365
Uribia 197
Usaquén 76

V

vaccinations 41
Valdivia 243
Valle de Cocora 266
Valledupar 196
  listings 200
vallenato 198
Vázquez, Juan Bautista 362
vegetation 376
Velásquez, Samuel 366
Vergara y Vergara, Jose
  María 366
Villa Concha 182
Villa de Leiva 101, **102**
  listings 110
Villa del Rosario 134
Villamizar, Eduardo Ramírez
  364
Villanueva 223
Villavicencio 334, 337
  listings 336
  sights 335
Villavieja 306
  listings 310
Villeta 90

Violencia, La 351
Visa 50
Volcán de Lodo 165
Volcán del Totumo 161
Volcán Galeras 322
Volcán Puracé 308
volunteering 52

W

Wiederman, Guillermo 364
wildlife 376
women travellers 48
woodcarvings 362

Y

Yarumal 243
youth hostels 33

Z

Zaque 348
Zipa 348
Zipaquirá 92
Zona Cafetera 253

Advertisers' index

Amerispan, USA 43
Aventure Colombia, Colombia 158
Black Sheep Hostel, Colombia 229
Casa Viena, Colombia 153
Colombia Quest, Colombia 85
Colombia Tourist Board – Proexport, Colombia inside back cover, 61
Colombia57 Tours, Travel & Logistics, Colombia 28
Colombian Highlands & Hostal Renancer, Colombia 111
Colombian Hostel Association, Colombia 32
DE UNA Colombia Tours, Colombia 29
Hostel Trail Latin America, Colombia 77
Surtrek, Ecuador 49

Complete title listing

Footprint publishes travel guides to more than 150 destinations worldwide. Each guide is packed with practical, concise and colourful information for everybody from first-time travellers to travel aficionados. The list is growing fast and current titles are noted below.
Available from all good bookshops and online
www.footprintbooks.com

(P) Denotes pocket guide

Latin America and Caribbean
Antigua & Leeward Islands (P)
Argentina
Belize, Guatemala &
    Southern Mexico
Bolivia
Brazil
Caribbean Islands
Dominican Republic (P)
Chile
Colombia
Costa Rica
Costa Rica, Nicaragua & Panama
Cuba
Cuzco & the Inca Heartland
Ecuador & Galápagos
Mexico & Central America
Nicaragua
Patagonia
Peru
Peru, Bolivia & Ecuador
South American Handbook

North America
Vancouver (P)
Western Canada

Africa
Cape Town (P)
Egypt
Kenya
Morocco
Namibia
South Africa Handbook

Middle East
Dubai (P)

Australasia
East Coast Australia
New Zealand
Sydney (P)
West Coast Australia

Asia
Borneo
Cambodia
India
Laos
Malaysia & Singapore
Northeast India
Rajasthan
South India
Sri Lanka
Southeast Asia Handbook
Tibet
Thailand
Vietnam
Vietnam, Cambodia & Laos

Europe
Andalucía
Antwerp & Ghent (P)
Barcelona (P)

Bologna (P)
Cardiff (P)
Costa de la Luz (P)
Croatia
Madrid (P)
Naples (P)
Northern Spain
Scotland Highlands & Islands
Seville (P)
Siena (P)
Tallinn (P)
Valencia (P)
Verona (P)

Activity guides
Diving the World
Mountain Biking the World
Skiing Europe
Snowboarding the World
Surfing Britain & Ireland
Surfing Europe
Surfing the World

Lifestyle guides
Body & Soul Escapes
Body & Soul Escapes:
  Britain & Ireland
European City Breaks
Travel Photography
Travel with Kids
Wine Travel Guide to the World

Also available: Traveller's Handbook
(WEXAS)

About the author

Charlie Devereux was born and lived in Panama until he was nine. Worried their son was developing too much of a taste for beach life, his British parents forcibly removed him from the country in 1984 (though there was also the matter of General Noriega and an impending US invasion). In the UK he worked variously as a photographer, photographer's agent and in publishing before deciding that journalism was his true calling. His Latin roots have drawn him back to the continent on several occasions and in 2008 he swapped the traffic fumes of London for the traffic fumes of Caracas, where he makes a living as a freelance journalist.

Acknowledgements

Thanks are due to many people without whose advice and support this book would not have been possible.

Thanks to Tiffany Fairey, David Ansell and Clare Stephens for accompanying me on sections of the journey and of the many travellers I met along the way, special mention must go to Teryk Morris, Matt and Courtney and Michael.

Many people imparted invaluable information along the way. Apologies if they have been mistakenly excluded from this list. Thanks to Germán Escobar, Tony Lloyd Wilkinson, Nadia Diamond and Alvaro Castañeda, Bogotá; Mathieu Perrot-Bohringer, Marco de la Ossa and Karina Cuello Taboada and Joan Mathieu Oyola at Corporación Turismo Cartagena. A special thanks to Loli Acuña and her beautiful family in Mompós; Hugo Arrieta, Santa Marta; Shaun Clohesy, San Gil; Kelvin Leeming, Paul Thoreson and Marion Finkelstein, Mariella Zapata and Julio Casadiego at Destino Colombia, Medellín; Simon Locke and Russell Coleman, Manizales; Tim Harbour, Salento; Yisel at Millenium Tours and Santiago Montoya, Armenia; Urs Diethelm, Cali; Tony Clark and Kim Macphee, Popayán; René Suter, San Agustín; Javier Fernando Rua, Tatacoa desert; Esmeralda Marín Avila, Villavicencio, Oscar Gilède, Villa de Leiva; Axel Antoine-Feill, Leticia; Robert Samet, Caracas.

Thanks to Richard McColl for writing the El Chocó section and to Erik Rupert for the Los Nevados and Sierra Nevada del Cocuy sections. Thanks to Craig Weigand for his contribution; and to Andrea Daza, Juliana Gómez and Alejandro Echverri at Proexport for their extremely professional support. A very special thanks to the Daza family for exemplifying Colombian hospitality.

Finally, thanks to everyone at Footprint: in particular, Ria Gane and Alan Murphy.

Notes

Notes

Notes

Notes

Notes

Notes

Notes

Notes

Credits

Footprint credits
Editor: Ria Gane
Map editor: Sarah Sorensen
Colour section: Kassia Gawronski

Managing Director: Andy Riddle
Publisher: Patrick Dawson
Editorial: Sara Chare, Nicola Gibbs, Jen
Haddington, Alice Jell, Felicity Laughton,
Alan Murphy
Cartography: Robert Lunn, Kevin Feeney,
Emma Bryers
Cover design: Robert Lunn
Design: Mytton Williams
Sales and marketing: Liz Harper,
Zoë Jackson, Hannah Bonnell
Advertising sales manager: Renu Sibal
Finance and administration: Elizabeth
Taylor

Photography credits
Front cover: Flower of *Curuba amarga*
Roberto Orrú/Alamy
Back cover: Lane in Cartagena
Hemis.fr/SuperStock

Contributing authors
Richard McColl: El Chocó section.
Erik Rupert: Sierra Nevada del Cocuy
and Los Nevados sections.

Manufactured in Italy by LegoPrint
Pulp from sustainable forests

Footprint feedback
We try as hard as we can to make each
Footprint guide as up to date as possible
but, of course, things always change. If you
want to let us know about your experiences –
good, bad or ugly – then don't delay, go to
www.footprintbooks.com and send in
your comments.

Publishing information
Footprint Colombia
3rd edition
© Footprint Handbooks Ltd
January 2009

ISBN: 978 1 906098 22 3
CIP DATA: A catalogue record for this book
is available from the British Library

® Footprint Handbooks and the Footprint
mark are a registered trademark of Footprint
Handbooks Ltd

Published by Footprint
6 Riverside Court
Lower Bristol Road
Bath BA2 3DZ, UK
T +44 (0)1225 469141
F +44 (0)1225 469461
discover@footprintbooks.com
www.footprintbooks.com

Distributed in the USA by Globe Pequot Press,
Guilford, Connecticut

Every effort has been made to ensure that
the facts in this guidebook are accurate.
However, travellers should still obtain
advice from consulates, airlines etc about
travel and visa requirements before travelling.
The authors and publishers cannot accept
responsibility for any loss, injury or
inconvenience however caused.

Colombia,
the only risk
is wanting
to stay.

Santa Marta
Tayrona Park Eco-habs

Colombia
is passion!
www.visitcolombia.com

Colombia,
the only risk
is wanting
to stay.

Cartagena de Indias
San Pedro Claver Church

Colombia
is passion!
www.visitcolombia.com